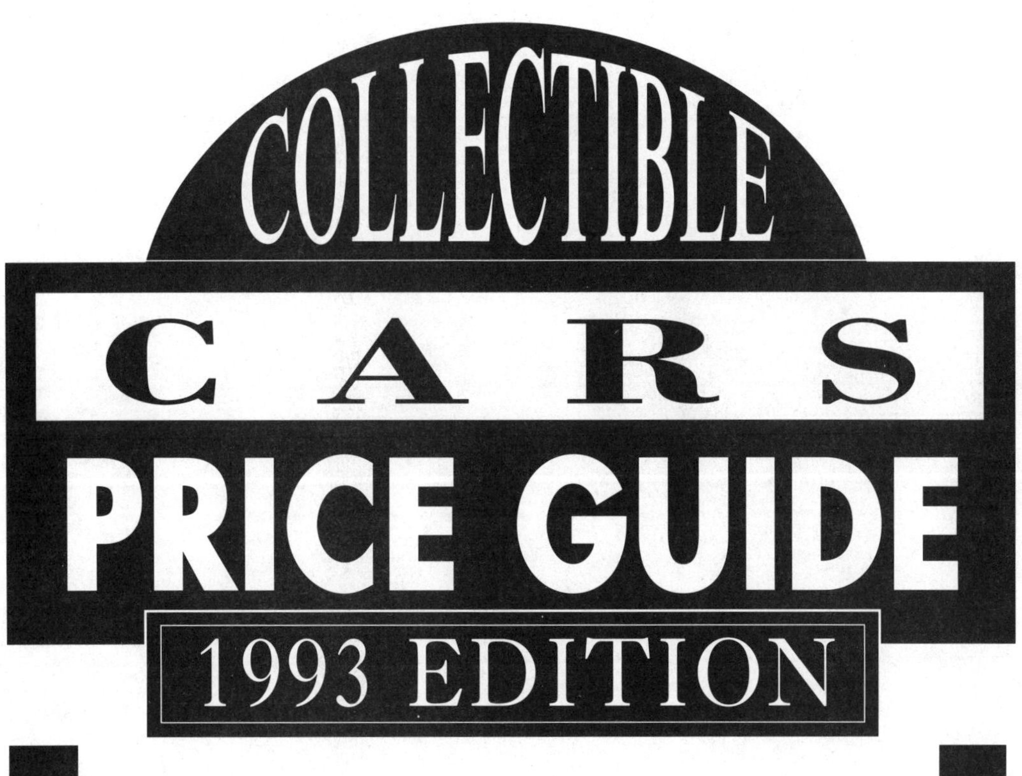

PUBLICATIONS
INTERNATIONAL, LTD.

CONTENTS

CONTENTS

CONTENTS

INTRODUCTION

Welcome to *the Collectible Cars Price Guide,* a book that not only prices collectible American cars from 1930-90, but also provides brief year-by-year historical sketches and pictures approximately 1700 separate models to aid in the instant recall of their styling. In addition, the text is liberally sprinkled with production figures for the most collectible models to give readers an idea of how common or rare they were when they rolled off the production line.

Prices and Condition

Here you may be in for a surprise. Unlike various "old-car price guides," we do not attempt to make hairline distinctions between individual models, body styles, or equipment, except where the market makes them or the gulf is obviously wide. Nor have we set up a complicated system of grading values based on a vehicle's condition or equipment. Instead, you'll find a more common-sense approach that covers three states of condition:

Restorable: This is what buffs mean by a car that's "all there." It has a body, chassis, engine, even an interior (or at least part of one). However, it may not be running and, at the very least, needs considerable work. This definition does not refer to "basket cases" or total rust-outs that are clearly unsalvageable. To be restorable, a car must have enough of its original "self" left so an owner can bring it back to life.

Good: This is either a "stock" original or an older restoration that is completely driveable and serviceable in its present state, but need obvious mechanical and/or cosmetic work. It's not a show winner by any means. It may need paint, new chrome, interior work, and some mechanical ministerings—but not a whole new interior or engine. This description also applies to a combination of, say, amateur mechanical work and a professional body rebuild.

Excellent: Here we mean a car in fine original or restored condition, capable of scoring at least 85 out of 100 points in typical show judging. Everything on it works as intended and nothing major has to be done, though there may be a small thing or two that isn't completely perfect, as it seems there always is. Prices for absolutely perfect "show cars" (right off the showroom floor!) will generally be higher.

The prices shown for each of these conditions are ranges that are sometimes wide. There are also some gaps and/or overlaps between conditions, so that a particular specimen you might be interested in buying could fall between them. The rationale for this pricing system is that it's simply impossible to peg collector cars as close to the mark as "used cars." There, values are usually quoted down to $25- and $50-increments based on whether or not a given unit has air conditioning, radio, automatic, or other equipment and how old it is or how many miles it's done.

Another element that influences the collector market, but not used car prices, is "interest value." For example, with a few notable exceptions, cars of the Seventies just aren't terribly collectible at present, and most may never be no matter how scarce they might become through attrition. Enthusiasts tend to regard most Detroit products in these years as more boring and thus less desirable than corresponding Sixties models.

But the main reason we cannot draw razor-sharp price distinctions is that they just don't exist. Compared to ordinary used cars, even those that are 10 or more years old, collector cars change hands far less often. Used-car value books track hundreds of thousands of sales made in the course of a few months, and can thus average prices with a fair degree of accuracy. Collector-car guides cover far fewer transactions that may take place over a year or more, and thus can't be anywhere near as precise.

1980-90 Pricing

In this section we have eliminated most of the "restorable" categories, except where a car is particularly desirable even in rough condition. The reason is that it would be economically impractical, given the complexity of modern cars, to buy one in "restorable" condition, because the cost of bringing it up to reasonable condition far outweighs the value of the car after the work is done.

What Is a Collectible Car?

In determining the cars to include here, the editors follow the preferences of the contemporary car collector movement. Essentially, that means you will find the Thirties covered in large chunks with virtually all models and body styles cited; the Forties through Sixties are covered year by year with all or almost all models cited; and the Seventies through 1990 are covered year by year with specific collectible—or potentially collectible—models cited.

The reasons for these distinctions should be of interest to the reader. As an era, the period of the Thirties has now moved from an age of nostalgia to one of history. While certain 1930s cars are still avidly sought after, they are being pursued now largely by people who understand and appreciate them in the intellectual or aesthetic sense, rather than by people for whom they are reminders of a lost youth. Cars of the 1930s change hands far less frequently than later models, leaving less distinct footprints as to prices and values.

The Forties through Sixties are clearly the years of greatest activity today, although interest in '40s models is already being driven more by historical or aesthetic factors than nostalgia. We recognize the prevailing collector interest in this 30-year period by covering virtually every model with price ranges, although again, it isn't possible in many cases to establish absolute values since the cars change hands in small quantities, and often very quietly.

Although certain cars of the Seventies are already very collectible, the vast majority are not, and cars of the Eighties are still too young to establish themselves in the collector field. Accordingly, we have dealt with these years mainly on the basis of what is either presently being collected, or what is likely to be collected within the next 20 years.

1952 Allstate Four two-door fastback sedan

Allstate

A rare make, but equally short in the number of collectors who care about it, the Allstate has fallen through the collector cracks. Club support fair, body parts scarce, mechanical parts reasonable; cheaper overall to buy restored than to restore. Future investment potential: modest.

1952-53

"The only all-new car for 1952," Allstate was born out of Sears Roebuck's desire to sell its own automobile again after a 40-year hiatus, and Kaiser-Frazer's wish to find an additional outlet for its Henry J—which, save for special trim and Allstate-built accessories like tires, batteries, and spark plugs, the Allstate was. The typical Allstate is worth about $1000 more than a corresponding Henry J, mainly through its rarity; remember, though, that it's not authentic unless tricked out with all the Sears Roebuck bits and pieces. Engine type, four or six, tends not to affect values much, but there's no doubt that the six is far more driveable and lively. This is not a substitute annuity account, but if true rarity (just 2363 built) appeals, you might be on the lookout.

	Restorable	Good	Excellent
sedan, 2d	$2,000-3,500	$3,500-6,000	$6,000-9,000

1930 American Austin 2-passenger coupe

American Austin

Now very scarce, though it enjoyed larger production numbers than its successor, the American Bantam, the American Austin is most often encountered at jumbo antique car meets like Hershey. Open bodies are quite collectible but rarely seen. Club support is fair, all parts scarce; best to buy restored. Future investment potential: good for open models, low for closed models.

1930-34

Produced in Butler, Pennsylvania, by Sir Herbert Austin and based entirely on the British Austin Seven with its two-main-bearing L-head four. Offered in roadster, runabout, cabriolet, and coupe models. Although over 8500 were built in the first year, sales dropped off rapidly—ironically, the better the economy got, the fewer people wanted Austins. After just under 20,000 had been built from 1930-34, it was replaced by the American Bantam (see following entry).

	Restorable	Good	Excellent
Open models	$2,500-6,000	$6,000-10,000	$10,000-15,000
Closed models	2,000-5,000	5,000-7,500	7,500-10,000

American Bantam

Though lower in production than the American Austin, the American Bantam seems to be seen almost as often, perhaps because of its many interesting body styles. Club support is fair, all parts scarce; best to buy restored. Future investment potential: good for open models, moderate for closed models.

1939 American Bantam Series 62 DeLuxe roadster

1938-41

A more Americanized Austin styled by Count Alexis de Sakhnoffsky, the Bantam was built at the old Austin works in Butler, Pennsylvania, under the management of Roy S. Evans. Engineered in part by racing wizard Harry Miller, the Bantam's L-head four had full pressure lubrication, and the cars also featured new three-speed gearboxes and cam-and-lever steering. After 1939, Bantams had three-main-bearing engines, much improved brakes, Monroe shock absorbers, Goodyear "air-form" seat cushions on deluxe models, and fender-mounted headlamps. None of this helped as only about 6700 were built from 1938-41, but they are all desirable points if you are in the market.

1939 American Bantam 60 two-door coupe

	Restorable	Good	Excellent
Speedster	$4,000-8,000	$8,000-13,000	$13,000-20,000
Other open mdls	3,000-7,000	7,000-11,000	11,000-16,000
Closed models	2,000-5,000	5,000-8,000	8,000-11,000

Auburn

One of the fabled trio of Auburn-Cord-Duesenberg, though it carries the least important cachet among the three thanks to its numerous lower-priced models. The car named for its home of Auburn, Indiana, has long been a favorite among collectors. Most models are still good value for money. Club support is excellent, body parts rare, mechanical parts fair; good restoration projects. Future investment potential: excellent for open models, moderate for closed.

1932 Auburn Custom Eight four-door sedan

1930-36

Auburn built sixes in 1930 and 1935-36, but its stock in trade was the straight eight, along with a handful of Twelves. The famous company was wiped out by the Depression by 1936, but has remained widely admired by the cognoscenti. Most desirable among the Eights are the Supercharged 851/852 models of 1935-36, followed by the luxurious Salon line of 1933 and 1935-36, when it was part of the non-supercharged 851/852 range. For 1933, Auburn also built some 2002 Twelves, plus 305 Salon Twelves. At only $975, the coupe was the

1932 Auburn Custom Eight cabriolet

1936 Auburn Supercharged Eight four-door sedan

least expensive twelve-cylinder car ever built, and even the luxurious top-line Custom Speedster Twelve cost only $1275. All Auburn engines were built by Lycoming, a subsidiary of the Cord empire. The magnificent boattail Speedsters, both Twelves and Eights, are among the finest expressions of Classic-era styling. It astonishes us that these cars, of which approximately 83,000 were built during the '30s, are still so relatively affordable on the 1993 market.

Sixes	Restorable	Good	Excellent
Open	$6,000-15,000	$15,000-28,000	$28,000-45,000
Closed	2,500-7,500	7,500-15,000	15,000-22,500
Twelves			
Speedster	20,000-50,000	50,000-100,000	100,000-135,000
Other open mdls	15,000-40,000	40,000-90,000	90,000-120,000
Closed models	7,500-18,000	18,000-27,500	27,500-40,000
Eights			
Speedster	18,000-45,000	45,000-95,000	95,000-125,000
Other open mdls	15,000-38,000	38,000-80,000	80,000-115,000
Clsd, non-s'chrgd	3,000-10,000	10,000-20,000	20,000-30,000
Clsd, s'chrgd	5,000-15,000	15,000-30,000	30,000-45,000

1970's Avanti II coupe

Avanti

A marque in its own right, the post-Studebaker Avanti has a relatively small but enthusiastic following. Prices are not outrageous, and a wide variety of examples exists. Club support is excellent, body and mechanical parts in reasonably good supply, although some hardware bits are impossible. Investment potential: moderate.

1965-82

Former South Bend Studebaker dealers Nathan Altman and Leo Newman rescued Studebaker's sport coupe and built it as a specialty limited edition into the early Eighties, using Corvette engines and an increasingly diverse range of interiors and colors. Differences from the original included reduced-radius wheel openings, less forward rake, and a higher hood line to accommodate the Corvette engine. Low production—an average of about 115 units per year during the 1965-82 period—guarantees that every Avanti is collectible, but quality control was variable throughout the car's history.

	Restorable	Good	Excellent
'65 Avanti II	$6,000-10,000	$10,000-18,000	$18,000-25,000
'66-'82 Avanti II	4,000-8,000	8,000-15,000	15,000-22,500

1983-85

These were years of radical change for the Avanti, which, under the new ownership of real estate developer and car enthusiast Steve Blake, was shorn of its roman numeral "II" designation and gradually altered along more modern lines. Blake aimed to improve quality control both inside and out, with new painting techniques, upgraded interiors, and less chrome—he soon dumped the chrome bumpers, fake dashboard wood, and mysterious toggle switches, adding body-colored, five-mph Kevlar bumpers, modern instruments, Recaro bucket seats, a leather wheel, and what he called a "zowie" stereo system. He planned and announced a convertible. But all this cost money and Blake was caught by cash flow problems, declaring bankruptcy in June 1985. He resigned the following February. Special Avantis to look for include the limited 20th Anniversary Edition (1983) and the sporty GT model (1984, production 50). For Avanti spotters, 1983 was the last year for parking lights in the front fenders; they moved to beneath the bumper in 1984, when 287 cars were built. GTs can be told by their Cibie driving lights.

	Restorable	Good	Excellent
'83-'85 Avanti	$8,000-12,500	$12,500-17,500	$17,500-20,000

1989 Avanti convertible coupe

1986-90

Bankrupt Avanti was bought in April 1986 by a South Bend businessman, Michael Kelly, who named it "The New Avanti Motor Corp." and began producing '87 models late in the year (no 1986 models were built), but soon the firm was taken over by the Cafaro Company and moved to Youngstown, Ohio. The convertible version Blake had planned was produced and the four-door was announced in early 1989, but the reorganized company again expired as the recession took hold in 1990.

1990 Avanti four-door sedan

	Restorable	Good	Excellent
'87-88 cpe	$10,000-14,000	$14,000-18,000	$18,000-23,000
'89-90 cpe	12,000-16,000	16,000-20,000	20,000-25,000
Convertible	15,000-20,000	20,000-22,500	22,500-28,000

Buick

One of the mainstays of the special-interest movement, Buick attracts a broad range of collectors evenly spread over all years of production but increasingly concentrated around 1950s and '60s models. Club support is excellent, with mechanical parts in reasonably good supply for most items, body parts less so. General investment potential: very good.

1930 Buick Series 60 7-passenger sedan

1930-39

By 1930, Buick had been firmly installed in the General Motors hierarchy as the car just one step down from Cadillac—the automobile bought by the Establishment, including those who could afford Cadillacs but preferred the less conspicuous, but almost equally luxurious, Buicks. The overhead-valve engine design for which Buick had long been known was confined to straight eights starting in 1931, and

1932 Buick Series 90 7-passenger limousine

1933 Buick Series 60 5-passenger Victoria coupe

1936 Buick Series 80 Roadmaster four-door sedan

1939 Buick Series 40 Special 4-passenger convertible

1940 Buick Series 40 Special convertible coupe

Buick lines of the early '30s comprised a wide variety of body styles from roadsters to limousines. "Silent Second Synchromesh" debuted in 1932, streamlined bodies and "Knee Action" independent front suspension in 1934, all-steel "Turret-Top" construction in 1936. By that year, which also saw the advent of the popular Buick Special, the Division's fortunes had returned to their pre-Depression levels. All-coil-spring suspension was another Buick innovation, announced for 1938. During the latter part of the decade Buick also built exceptional luxury models in the top-line Limited series, including formal sedans and limousines; bare Limited chassis were furnished to custom body builders, mainly for hearse, ambulance, and flower car applications. During the '30s, Buick production ranged from 46,924 cars for the 1933 model year to 220,346 in 1937. Generally, Buick's top-line open models were produced in very small numbers, often under 100 or even 50 units.

	Restorable	Good	Excellent
1930-33 Series 50-80			
Open	$4,000-10,000	$10,000-22,500	$22,500-32,500
Closed	2,000-6,000	6,000-12,000	12,000-20,000
1930-33 Series 90			
Open	6,000-15,000	15,000-30,000	30,000-50,000
Closed	3,000-9,000	9,000-15,000	15,000-25,000
1934-35 Series 40-60			
Open	3,000-7,500	7,500-15,000	15,000-25,000
Closed	1,500-4,000	4,000-8,000	8,000-13,000
1934-35 Series 90			
Open	4,500-10,000	10,000-20,000	20,000-30,000
Closed	3,000-8,000	8,000-12,000	12,000-20,000
1936-39 Special, Century			
Open	5,000-15,000	15,000-25,000	25,000-37,500
Closed	2,500-5,000	5,000-10,000	10,000-15,000
1936-39 Roadmaster, Limited			
Open, Rdmstr	7,500-18,000	18,000-28,000	28,000-42,000
Closed	3,000-8,000	8,000-12,000	12,000-20,000

1940

The Buick lineup was divided into five series bearing names as well as numbers. Series 40 Specials ranged from simple sedans to spectacular open bodies; Series 50 Supers comprised fewer models, including a woody wagon; both rode a shorter wheelbase and used the smaller 248-cubic-inch straight eight. Series 60 Centuries, 70 Roadmasters, and 80 and 90 Limiteds were powered by the 320-cid straight eight and had longer wheelbases, up to 140 inches. Many interesting body styles were built, including the Streamlined models, which lacked the conventional trunkback body of other Buicks. The Limited Convertible Phaeton (250 built) and Steamlined Convertible Phaeton (seven produced) are greatly sought after, as are custom bodies like the Town Cars by Brunn (one built) and Brewster. They're extremely rare, too, though total Buick output surged to 283,204 units for the model run.

	Restorable	Good	Excellent
Ser 40/50 open	$5,000-12,000	$12,000-20,000	$20,000-35,000
Ser 40/50 clsd	2,500-6,000	6,000-9,000	9,000-15,000
Ser 60/90 open	7,500-15,000	15,000-25,000	25,000-40,000
Ser 60/70 clsd	3,500-7,500	7,500-12,500	12,500-20,000
Ser 80/90 clsd	4,000-10,000	10,000-17,500	17,500-25,000

1941

A beautiful series of Limited open customs by Brunn, including a phaeton, Town Car, Landau, and Landau Brougham, marked Buick's banner year of 1941, when 377,428 cars were produced for the model year. The Roadmaster line was unchanged, the Century trimmed of open models and Club Coupe, and the woody wagon shifted from Super to Special series. Specials comprised the 118-inch-wheelbase Series 40 and the 121-inch-wheelbase Series 40A. The latter was offered with "Compound Carburetion," two carburetors with progressive linkage and, as a result, higher horsepower. Styling was evolutionary, marked by a bolder grille. Fastback body styling was offered on the Special and Century closed models, which did away with the old trunk-back look and was very popular.

Open bodies	Restorable	Good	Excellent
Special	$4,000-12,000	$12,000-18,000	$18,000-30,000
Super	5,000-15,000	15,000-25,000	25,000-35,000
Roadmaster	7,500-17,500	17,500-30,000	30,000-40,000
Limited (phtn)	15,000-25,000	25,000-37,500	37,500-50,000
Closed bodies			
Limited	5,000-10,000	10,000-17,500	17,500-25,000
Other mdls	2,500-8,000	8,000-14,000	14,000-20,000

1942

Car production at Buick ended in February 1942, which was unfortunate, since the line had been completely restyled along sleeker lines prefigured by the "Y-Job" show car created in 1938 by design chief Harley Earl's Art and Colour Studio. A wide, low, vertical-bar grille arrived, a theme that would last through 1954. Most '42s featured "Airfoil" front fenders that swept back through the entire length of the car to meet the leading edge of the rear fenders. Limiteds and Specials lacked the full sweep treatment, but their fenders extended well back into the doors. Cars built during calendar 1942 had painted metal instead of plated parts; cast iron pistons replaced aluminum on Specials and Supers, and base horsepower dropped to 110, or 118 with Compound Carburetion. Despite the short model year, 94,442 '42 Buicks rolled off the line, only 700 of them Limiteds.

1941 Buick Series 40 Special station wagon

1941 Buick Series 70 Roadmaster Convertible Phaeton

1941 Buick Series 70 Roadmaster convertible coupe

1942 Buick Series 40 Special Sedanet

1942 Buick Series 40 Special station wagon

1946 Buick Super four-door sedan

1946 Buick Roadmaster Sedanet

1947 Buick Special Sedanet

1948 Buick Roadmaster four-door sedan

	Restorable	Good	Excellent
Convertibles	$3,500-10,000	$10,000-22,500	$22,500-30,000
Special wagon	5,000-12,000	12,000-20,000	20,000-28,000
Closed bodies	2,000-5,000	5,000-10,000	10,000-15,000
Limited limo	2,500-7,500	7,500-12,500	12,500-17,500

1946

Custom-bodied models and the Limited and Century series were not revived when production resumed in late 1945, and Buick Division built only 2482 cars through December 31. But the assembly lines picked up speed in January, and 158,728 '46s were built. The early postwar Buicks were warmed over '42s, but available in a few new body styles: sedans and Sedanets (fastback coupes) in Special, Super, and Roadmaster guise; Super and Roadmaster convertibles; a Super Estate Wagon. Styling was cleaned up a bit as most models bore single instead of double side moldings, a simpler grille, and the first of Buick's distinctive "gunsight" hood ornaments. Wheelbase choices were 121 inches for the Special, 124 for the Super, 129 for the Roadmaster. Compound Carburetion was dropped. This lineup of models, wheelbases, and engines would continue through 1948 with only minor changes in horsepower.

	Restorable	Good	Excellent
Super cvt	$4,000-12,000	$12,000-20,000	$20,000-30,000
Rdmstr cvt	6,000-15,000	15,000-25,000	25,000-35,000
Station wagons	6,000-15,000	15,000-22,500	22,500-32,000
Sedans	1,000-3,000	3,000-6,000	6,000-9,000
Sedanets	2,000-4,000	4,000-7,500	7,500-11,000

1947

The 1947 Buicks can be distinguished by a new wing-top grille that gave them a lower look than the 1946 models. A new, more elaborate crest was mounted above the grille, with a base that blended it into the grillework. Drivetrains, including horsepower, and chassis were identical to 1946-48 with only minor changes in horsepower. Production shot up to 277,134 units, which included an amazing 38,371 Super and Roadmaster convertibles, highest in the industry.

	Restorable	Good	Excellent
Super cvt	$4,000-12,000	$12,000-20,000	$20,000-30,000
Rdmstr cvt	6,000-15,000	15,000-25,000	25,000-35,000
Station wagons	6,000-15,000	15,000-22,500	22,500-32,000
Sedans	1,000-3,000	3,000-6,000	6,000-9,000
Sedanets	2,000-4,000	4,000-7,500	7,500-11,000

1948

The most important news this year was Dynaflow Drive, Buick's new automatic transmission, a $244 option on the Roadmaster only. Demand for this torque convertor automatic was so high that the Division was forced to double its planned production. By 1950, Dynaflow was being fitted to 85 percent of all Buicks sold. Styling-wise, Specials received a full-length chrome belt molding, while Supers and Roadmasters adopted front fender nameplates. Instrument panel gauges were gold colored and steering wheels were three-spoke sprung designs with semicircular horn rings. Output slipped to 219,718 units as Buick readied all-new 1949 models.

	Restorable	Good	Excellent
Super cvt	$4,000-12,000	$12,000-20,000	$20,000-30,000
Rdmstr cvt	6,000-15,000	15,000-25,000	25,000-35,000
Station wagons	6,000-15,000	15,000-22,500	22,500-32,000
Sedans	1,000-3,000	3,000-6,000	6,000-9,000
Sedanets	2,000-4,000	4,000-7,500	7,500-11,000

1948 Buick Super four-door station wagon

1949

Soaring in popularity with its brand-new styling for 1949, Buick Division surged to nearly 325,000 units for the model year, placing it right behind the "Low-Priced Three" of Chevrolet, Ford, and Plymouth. Harley Earl's styling was aircraft inspired, very trim and graceful; bodies featured the first of Buick's now famous portholes, an idea inspired by Ned Nickles of Harley Earl's design staff. An important new body style was the Riviera hardtop, on the Roadmaster chassis, one of the first mass-production hardtops that ushered in a poplar trend. Rivieras came with either straight side moldings or "sweep-spear" trim; the latter quickly became another Buick hallmark. Mechanically, however, the '49s were little changed, except for slightly higher compression and horsepower. Body styles were also largely unchanged from 1948.

1949 Buick Roadmaster four-door sedan

	Restorable	Good	Excellent
Super cvt	$4,000-12,000	$12,000-20,000	$20,000-30,000
Rdmstr cvt	6,000-15,000	15,000-25,000	25,000-35,000
Rdmstr Riviera	2,500-6,000	6,000-12,000	12,000-20,000
Rdmstr, closed	2,500-5,000	5,000-10,000	10,000-17,50[illegible]
Other sedans	1,000-3,000	3,000-6,000	6,000-9,00
Other sedanets	2,000-4,000	4,000-7,500	7,500-11,000
Station wagons	6,000-15,000	15,000-22,500	22,500-32,000

1949 Buick Super Sedanet

1949 Buick Roadmaster Riviera hardtop coupe

1950

Swoopy styling was all the rage as Buick followed 1949, "Year of the VentiPort," with 1950, "Year of the Sweepspear": the attractive curved side moldings that had appeared on late '49 Rivieras and a few Roadmaster convertibles, and were now applied to most DeLuxe Supers and Roadmasters. Buick continued to rely on a trio of straight-eight, valve-in-head engines, but horsepower was up slightly across the board, ranging from 115-152 bhp. There was also a choice between conventional notchback sedans and a Jetback design (a fastback also called Sedanet), and the Riviera hardtop body style was extended to the Super. Roadmasters increased their model range with an up-market Riviera DeLuxe hardtop at $220 more than the base Riviera, a Jetback sedanet, and a DeLuxe four-door also bearing the Riviera name. The 1950 models can be instantly identified by their unique "bucktooth" grille, containing teeth reaching down past the front bumper. Model year output shot up sharply to 670,256 units, including 66,762 total Riviera hardtops and 15,223 convertibles.

1950 Buick Special four-door sedan

1950 Buick Super Riviera hardtop coupe

	Restorable	Good	Excellent
Rdmstr cvt	$5,000-12,000	$12,000-20,000	$20,000-27,500
Rdmstr Riviera	2,500-5,000	5,000-10,000	10,000-17,500
Rdmstr Sedanet	2,000-4,000	4,000-8,000	8,000-12,500
Super cvt	5,000-10,000	10,000-17,500	17,500-25,000
Super Riviera	2,000-4,000	4,000-8,000	8,000-12,500
Station wagons	5,000-10,000	10,000-17,500	17,500-25,000
Other clsd bodies	1,000-4,000	4,000-7,500	7,500-10,000

1951

A year of minor, evolutionary changes, 1951 saw production drop to 404,657—good, though a far cry from 1950. The postwar seller's market was easing and the effects of the Korean War were beginning to be felt. Narrower grille teeth now resided between a bumper lowered in the center and the grille surround, and the hood badge was set into an oval. As before, Roadmasters sported four portholes, other models three, but they migrated from the hood back onto the fenders. The Jetback models were dropped, save for the Super, which saw just 1500 units before it, too, disappeared. Jetbacks were replaced in the Special line by notchback two-door sedans; 57,011 were built. Estate Wagons were quite rare: 2212 Supers, 679 Roadmasters.

1951 Buick Roadmaster Estate station wagon

1951 Buick Super Deluxe Jetback sedan

	Restorable	Good	Excellent
Rdmstr cvt	$5,000-12,000	$12,000-20,000	$20,000-27,000
Rdmstr Riviera	2,500-5,000	5,000-10,000	10,000-17,500
Super cvt	5,000-10,000	10,000-17,500	17,500-25,000
Super Jetback	2,000-3,500	3,500-6,500	6,500-10,000
Special cvt	4,000-8,000	8,000-12,500	12,500-18,000
Super/Special Riv	2,000-4,000	4,000-8,000	8,000-12,500
Station wagons	5,000-10,000	10,000-17,500	17,500-25,000
Other clsd bodies	1,000-4,000	4,000-7,500	7,500-10,000

1951 Buick Roadmaster Riviera four-door sedan

1952

Only minor detail changes were made to the line this year, the most obvious being hubcaps with smaller central dishes bearing the Buick crest and rear fenders that sprouted chrome fins on all but the baseline Specials. New sweepspear moldings were noted, as were higher, squared-off trunk decks. The model lineup was little altered save for the dropping of the Special business coupe and the Super Jetback. Output tumbled to 303,745 units, due largely to Korean War production cutbacks ordered by the government. Estate Wagon production was just 1641 Supers and 359 Roadmasters.

1952 Buick Roadmaster convertible coupe

	Restorable	Good	Excellent
Rdmstr cvt	$5,000-12,000	$12,000-20,000	$20,000-27,500
Rdmstr Riviera	2,500-5,000	5,000-10,000	10,000-17,500
Super cvt	5,000-10,000	10,000-17,500	17,500-25,000
Special cvt	4,000-8,000	8,000-12,500	12,500-18,000
Super/Special Riv	2,000-4,000	4,000-8,000	8,000-12,500
Station wagons	5,000-10,000	10,000-17,500	17,500-25,000
Other clsd bodies	1,000-4,000	4,000-7,500	7,500-10,000

1952 Buick Roadmaster Riviera hardtop coupe

1953

Buick celebrated its Golden Anniversary this year by placing special badges on the cars. A heavier facelift featured revised front-end styling and squared-off rear fenders. Supers and Roadmasters got a new 322-cid overhead-valve V-8 with

164/170/188 bhp; Specials continued with the 263.3-cid straight eight, now with 120/125 bhp. This was the last year for the woody wagons: 1830 Supers, 670 Roadmasters. A notable new model was the Skylark convertible, part of the Roadmaster series in 1953, with a special low-cut body, unique side trim, standard chrome wire wheels, and other deluxe features. Skylarks are scarce (only 1690 built) and the few sales often take place quietly between Buick specialists. The '53 Skylark is more in demand than the '54, though both ought to be into six figures by the turn of the century, making both of them good buys today. Top values for the '53 have increased by $20,000 in the last two years, the recession notwithstanding. Overall, model year output jumped to 488,805 units.

	Restorable	Good	Excellent
Skylark cvt	$9,000-20,000	$20,000-40,000	$40,000-55,000
Rdmstr cvt	5,000-12,500	12,500-20,000	20,000-30,000
Other cvts	5,000-10,000	10,000-17,500	17,500-25,000
Station wagons	5,000-10,000	10,000-17,500	17,500-25,000
Rdmstr Riviera	2,500-7,500	7,500-13,000	13,000-20,000
Other Rivieras	2,000-5,000	5,000-9,000	9,000-12,500
Sedans	1,000-3,500	3,500-6,000	6,000-10,000

1954

For 1954, all Buicks had V-8s (the Special's straight eight was dropped) and the division built 444,609 cars for the model run. However, 531,463 calendar-year units knocked Plymouth out of third place, elevating Buick into a position it hadn't held since 1930. Much of the success was owed to the Special with its small and potent V-8. Also for '54, Buick reintroduced its luxury hot-rod, the Century, now packing the Roadmaster's 195/200 horsepower V-8 in the Special's lighter body. The '54 Skylark—with its curious concave fender cutouts behind the wheel arches and gaudy taillights—was less impressive than the '53, and only 836 were sold before the model was discontinued. An all-steel wagon was offered in the Special and Century series, with output totalling 3213 units.

	Restorable	Good	Excellent
Skylark	$7,500-18,000	$18,000-32,500	$32,500-47,500
Convertibles	6,000-12,500	12,500-20,000	20,000-35,000
Rdmstr Riviera	2,500-7,500	7,500-13,000	13,000-20,000
Other Rivieras	2,000-5,000	5,000-9,000	9,000-12,500
Sedans & wagons	1,000-3,500	3,500-6,000	6,000-10,000

1955

Buick model year production skyrocketed to 738,814, a record that would stand until 1973. The success was again based on the Special, now one of the industry's most popular models. Four-door hardtops, also called Rivieras, joined the Special and Century series, and with 121,497 built the rest of the industry scrambled to play catch-up. In 1955, Buick finally departed from the toothy look it had used since before the war, adopting a blunt, mesh-type grille and prominent "Dagmar" bumper guards. Also seen were thinner sweepspears and a flared tail with heavily chromed taillight units.

1953 Buick Roadmaster Riviera hardtop coupe

1953 Buick Roadmaster Skylark convertible coupe

1954 Buick Roadmaster convertible coupe

1954 Buick Roadmaster Riviera four-door sedan

1955 Buick Century Riviera hardtop sedan

1956 Buick Roadmaster Riviera hardtop sedan

1957 Buick Century Riviera hardtop coupe

1957 Buick Super Riviera hardtop sedan

	Restorable	Good	Excellent
Rdmstr/Century cvts	$7,500-16,000	$16,000-24,000	$24,000-38,000
Special/Super cvts	6,000-13,000	13,000-20,000	20,000-32,000
Riviera coupes	3,000-8,000	8,000-13,000	13,000-20,000
Riviera sdns & wgns	1,500-4,000	4,000-7,500	7,500-10,000
Sedans	500-3,000	3,000-6,000	6,000-10,000

1956

A mild 1956 facelift (with new front sheetmetal) left the Buick line relatively unchanged, and industry sales were off this year, too. Thus Buicks didn't sell in the vast quantities of 1955, though 572,024 units for the model run was hardly bad. A curiosity was the appearance of the model year on exterior nameplates, a practice soon abandoned when customers complained that it made their cars look dated after a year or so. With the horsepower race in full swing, the '56s were the most powerful yet: Special, 220 horses; other models, 255. A '56 Century could do 0-60 in 10.5 seconds and topped out at 110 mph, and every Buick could do at least 100. All four series listed convertibles; production totaled 21,276, down from 23,863 in 1955.

	Restorable	Good	Excellent
Convertibles	$7,500-15,000	$15,000-25,000	$25,000-38,000
Riviera cpes	3,000-8,000	8,000-13,000	13,000-20,000
Riviera sdns & wgns	1,500-4,000	4,000-7,500	7,500-10,000
Sedans	500-3,000	3,000-6,000	6,000-9,000

1957

The '57 Buicks were clean, well-styled automobiles, stretched out in appearance from 1955-56, with shallower sweepspears and streamlined, teardrop-shaped portholes. Model additions were few but interesting: four-door hardtop Caballero Century and Special wagons, plus a Series 75 Roadmaster based on the Series 70. Offered as a two- or four-door Riviera (2404 and 12,250 built), 75s came with every possible accessory except air standard: Dynaflow, power steering, power brakes, flexible-spoke steering wheel, dual exhausts, automatic windshield washers and wide-angle wipers, back-up lights, clock, special interior with deep-pile carpeting, and more. Many—but not all—hardtop and sedan models sported three-piece rear windows with ridges running the length of the roof to the bottom of the rear deck, and through the rear window dividers. Despite new styling, production nosedived 29.2 percent to 405,098, allowing high-flying Plymouth to retake third place.

	Restorable	Good	Excellent
Rdmstr cvt	$7,500-15,000	$15,000-25,000	$25,000-37,500
Super/Century cvt	6,500-12,000	12,000-20,000	20,000-28,000
Special cvt	5,000-10,000	10,000-17,500	17,500-25,000
Riviera cpes, wgns	2,500-5,000	5,000-12,500	12,500-18,000
Riviera sedans	1,500-4,000	4,000-7,500	7,500-10,000
Sedans	500-2,500	2,500-5,000	5,000-8,000

1958

Long widely criticized for its chrome-laden styling led by no fewer than 160 chrome squares in a huge "Fashion-Aire Dynastar" grille, the 1958 Buick was a better car than it looked and good value for money. Considerable collector attention has been focused on the '58 Limited, an old series name that returned this year. Total output tumbled 40 percent to 241,908 units and a dismal fifth place in sales, but the economic recession was more to blame than the styling, which was basically in line with concurrent tastes. Limited production was extremely limited: 5571 four-door Rivieras, 1026 two-door Rivieras, 839 convertibles.

	Restorable	Good	Excellent
Limited cvt	$12,000-20,000	$20,000-35,000	$35,000-52,000
Limited htp cpe	5,000-9,000	9,000-15,000	15,000-23,000
Limited htp sdn	3,500-7,500	7,500-10,000	10,000-15,000
Rdmstr cvt	7,500-15,000	15,000-25,000	25,000-37,500
Super/Century cvt	6,500-12,000	12,000-20,000	20,000-28,000
Special cvt	5,000-10,000	10,000-17,500	17,500-25,000
Riviera cpes, wgns	2,500-5,000	5,000-12,500	12,500-18,000
Riviera sedans	1,500-4,000	4,000-7,500	7,500-10,000
Sedans	500-2,500	2,500-5,000	5,000-8,000

1958 Buick Century convertible coupe

1958 Buick Century Caballero hardtop station wagon

1959

Buick styling made a powerful comeback for 1959 with a fresh, sleek design dominated by the now almost mandatory tailfins—among the broadest in the industry and probably the most deeply flared. Because they were tapered into a sleek body with a minimum of chrome, however, they came off well. The new look was emphasized via new series names: LeSabre, Century, Invicta, Electra, Electra 225. Collector prices generally reflect the model hierarchy, though the LeSabre should be considered, because it was the best handling of the four (along with the Invicta), and a LeSabre convertible (10,489 built) is an excellent buy at around $4000-$5000 less than an Invicta or Electra 225. A new 401-cid, 325-bhp V-8 powered all models save the LeSabre, which made do with 364 cubes and 250 bhp. Production this year jumped 18 percent to 285,089 units, but Buick fell to seventh place on the sales charts. Electra 225s are fairly rare with just 22,428 built, 5493 of them ragtops.

	Restorable	Good	Excellent
LeSabre cvt	$6,000-10,000	$10,000-15,000	$15,000-20,000
Other cvts	7,000-12,500	12,500-17,500	17,500-24,000
Electra htp cpe	2,500-5,000	5,000-7,500	7,500-10,000
Other models	1,500-3,000	3,000-5,000	5,000-7,500

1959 Buick Electra hardtop coupe

1960 Buick Invicta hardtop coupe

1960

The 1960 Buicks lacked the styling flair of the sharp-edged '59s, but in some ways were better cars. Body styles and drivetrains were little altered, aside from the option of two- or three-seat station wagons and the choice of a 235-bhp LeSabre 364 V-8 that drank regular gas or a 300-bhp high-performance 364 (250 bhp was still standard). Buyer interest flagged, so model year production fell 11 percent

1960 Buick Electra 225 hardtop sedan

1961 Buick Invicta hardtop coupe

1962 Buick Special Skylark hardtop coupe

1962 Buick Electra 225 hardtop coupe

1962 Buick Invicta Wildcat Sport Coupe hardtop

to 253,999 units, but total convertible output rose 19.3 percent to 25,570 units. Though 1960 styling was rounded and more confused, this hasn't seemed to affect collector values, which are more or less on par with the '59s. Given a choice, however, we would stick to the '59 as the purer design, expecting that fact to count for something as time passes. Though Buick fell to ninth place in industry output, the division built its 10-millionth car in January 1960.

	Restorable	Good	Excellent
LeSabre cvt	$6,000-10,000	$10,000-15,000	$15,000-20,000
Other cvts	7,000-12,500	12,500-17,500	17,500-24,000
Electra htp cpe	2,500-5,000	5,000-7,500	7,500-10,000
Other models	1,500-3,000	3,000-5,000	5,000-7,500

1961

Buick's major news for 1961 was the new compact Special with a 112.1-inch wheelbase, 188.4-inch overall length, and a smooth new 215-cid, 155-bhp aluminum-block V-8. Topping the Special line from mid-year was a familiar name, Skylark: a luxurious $2621 pillared coupe with bucket seats, vinyl roof, special trim and grille, and a 185-bhp version of the 215 V-8. The 1961 full-size Buicks were handsomely restyled and shorn of tailfins, and though they retained nearly identical wheelbases of 123/126 inches, they weighed 100-300 pounds less than their 1960 counterparts and were slightly trimmer. Convertibles, especially the $3382 LeSabre, have been overlooked, and tend to be bargains compared with open versions of other marques from the era. Full-size output plummeted to 189,982, but the 87,444 Specials (including 12,683 Skylarks) helped boost overall production to 277,426 units.

	Restorable	Good	Excellent
LeSabre cvt	$2,500-5,000	$5,000-9,000	$9,000-13,000
Invicta cvt	3,000-6,000	6,000-10,000	10,000-15,000
Electra 225 cvt	3,500-7,000	7,000-11,000	11,000-17,000
Skylark	1,500-3,000	3,000-5,000	5,000-7,000
Hardtop bodies	1,000-3,000	3,000-4,500	4,500-6,000
Other models	500-2,500	2,500-4,000	4,000-5,000

1962

Responding to the demand for bucket-seat sporty cars, Buick at mid-year introduced the $3927 Wildcat, an Invicta-based luxury hardtop equipped with buckets, vinyl top, and distinctive interior trim. Some 2000 were produced. Simultaneously, the baseline Electra series was dropped, leaving the Electra 225, albeit with one of the largest engines in the industry, the 325-bhp 401 V-8. Another deletion was the LeSabre convertible, but Invicta ragtop output more than tripled to 13,471 units. Important additions to the Special range were a convertible (base, DeLuxe, and Skylark—7918, 8332, and 8913 built), a Skylark hardtop (34,060 sold), and an optional four-speed manual gearbox. The Buick Special debuted an excellent new V-6 (198 cid, 135 bhp), but DeLuxe Specials and Skylarks retained the V-8. The latter, in 190-bhp guise, provided real performance: 0-60 in about 10 seconds and 110 mph tops. Total output soared to 400,150 units: 154,467 Specials and 245,683 big Buicks.

	Restorable	Good	Excellent
Invicta cvt	$3,000-6,000	$6,000-10,000	$10,000-15,000
Electra 225 cvt	3,500-7,000	7,000-11,000	11,000-17,000
Skylark hardtop	1,500-3,000	3,000-5,000	5,000-7,000
Skylark cvt	3,000-6,000	6,000-9,000	9,000-15,000
Wildcat hardtop	2,000-4,000	4,000-7,000	7,000-10,000
Other hardtops	1,000-3,000	3,000-4,500	4,500-6,000
Other models	500-2,500	2,500-4,000	4,000-5,000

1962 Buick Invicta four-door station wagon

1963

A Buick bombshell, the new $4333 Riviera "personal-luxury" coupe, took aim squarely at Ford's high-flying Thunderbird. A styling and engineering masterpiece, it rode a 117-inch wheelbase, measured more than a foot shorter than full-size Buicks, and handled as well as it performed. First year output was 40,000 units. The bucket-seat Wildcat became a three-model series with the addition of a four-door hardtop and convertible; 12,185, 17,519, and 6021 were built. Meanwhile, Buick reduced the Invicta series to a single station wagon (3491 produced) and bolstered the LeSabre line by returning a wagon and convertible (5556 and 9975 built). Among Skylarks, the V-6 was now standard, the V-8 optional, and styling had become bulkier and more conventional. As a result, the '63 Skylark soft top (10,212 built) is generally considered less desirable than the '62. Of the 458,606 Buicks produced, 149,538 were compacts.

1963 Buick LeSabre convertible coupe

1963 Buick Riviera hardtop coupe

	Restorable	Good	Excellent
Riviera	$2,000-5,000	$5,000-8,000	$8,000-12,000
LeSabre cvt	3,000-6,000	6,000-10,000	10,000-15,000
Electra/Wildcat cvt	3,500-7,000	7,000-12,000	12,000-18,000
Skylark hardtop	1,500-3,000	3,000-5,000	5,000-7,000
Skylark cvt	2,000-4,000	4,000-7,000	7,000-10,000
Hardtop coupes	2,000-4,000	4,000-7,500	7,500-11,000
Hardtop sedan	1,000-3,000	3,000-4,500	4,500-6,000
Other models	500-2,500	2,500-4,000	4,000-5,000

1964 Buick Special Skylark convertible coupe

1964

After a five-year run, the Invicta disappeared. Meanwhile, the Special was redesigned along more conventional—and larger—lines (now on a 115-inch wheelbase) and gained two 120-inch-wheelbase Sportwagons boasting a "Vista-Dome" step-up roof and all-vinyl interior. Standard-size Buicks were longer, up to 224 inches overall, but their chiseled styling complemented their dimensions. Wildcats continued their hot-rod image with the Electra engine in the LeSabre bodyshell, and the Riviera continued with little change. But Buick's new Twin Turbine Hydra-Matic was smoother and less troublesome than its 1963 Turbine Drive, which in turn had been an improvement on Dynaflow. With total output of 511,666 units, Buick was now back up to fifth place on the sales charts.

1965 Buick LeSabre Custom hardtop coupe

1965 Buick Riviera Gran Sport hardtop coupe

1966 Buick Riviera hardtop coupe

1966 Buick Wildcat Gran Sport convertible coupe

	Restorable	Good	Excellent
Riviera	$2,000-5,000	$5,000-8,000	$8,000-12,000
Full-size cvts	3,000-6,000	6,000-10,000	10,000-15,000
Special cvt	3,000-4,000	4,000-8,000	8,000-11,000
Skylark cvt	4,000-6,000	6,000-10,000	10,000-14,000
Hardtop coupes	2,000-4,000	4,000-7,500	7,500-10,000
Other models	1,000-3,000	3,000-4,500	4,500-6,000

1965

Buick Division attempted to bracket every possible market sector in this banner sales year by offering standard and Custom trim levels for the full-size cars (and even a third DeLuxe level for Wildcats). An important addition to the Special line was the Skylark Gran Sport, a $200 option package built around the potent 401-cid V-8 (Buick called it a 400), three-speed all-synchromesh transmission (four-speed optional), "handling" suspension, oversize tires, special trim, and required-option bucket seats. As Buick's initial muscle car, the Gran Sport did well in 1965, scoring 15,000 sales. Most were Sport Coupe hardtops; convertibles and pillared coupes each saw fewer than 2500 copies. Aside from hidden headlamps, the Riviera was little different, but a new package, the Riviera Gran Sport, offered two four-barrel carbs and 360 bhp, beefed-up Turbine Drive, dual exhausts, Positraction, and special trim. Only 3335 (of 34,586 total Rivieras) were built, and they are highly collectible. The big Buicks were restyled along still more chiseled lines than 1964. Total Buick production jumped to 600,148 units.

	Restorable	Good	Excellent
Riviera	$2,000-5,000	$5,000-8,000	$8,000-12,000
Riviera GS	4,000-7,000	7,000-10,000	10,000-15,000
Full-size cvts	3,000-6,000	6,000-10,000	10,000-15,000
Special cvt	3,000-4,000	4,000-8,000	8,000-11,000
Skylark cvt	4,000-6,000	6,000-9,000	9,000-12,000
Gran Sport cvt	5,000-7,500	7,500-10,000	10,000-14,000
Gran Sport htp/cpe	3,500-5,000	5,000-7,500	7,500-11,000
Hardtop coupes	2,000-4,000	4,000-7,500	7,500-10,000
Other models	1,000-3,000	3,000-4,500	4,500-6,000

1966

An all-new and striking Riviera led the Buick line. Riding now on a 119-inch wheelbase, it was powered by the 340-bhp 425 V-8 that had been optional in 1965. Rarely has one classic design followed another, but the second-generation Riviera was an exception, and it still looks sensational nearly 30 years later. Of 45,348 Rivieras, 5718 received Gran Sport equipment, but that doesn't affect prices as significantly as on the '65 model. Among the full-size cars, the Wildcat grew longer, the Electra shorter, while LeSabres shared a new 220-bhp 340 V-8 with the Sportwagons, of which 21,610 found customers. The hot Skylark Gran Sport became a separate series, with 9934 Sport Coupes, 2047 ragtops, and 1835 pillared coupes built. Gran Sport equipment, highlighted by a 340-bhp Wildcat 465 V-8 (401 cid), was also listed for the Wildcat for $254.71. Overall, Buick output dropped seven percent to 558,870 units, good only for seventh place in industry standings.

	Restorable	Good	Excellent
Riviera	$2,000-4,000	$4,000-7,000	$7,000-9,500
Full-size cvts	3,000-6,000	6,000-10,000	10,000-15,000
Skylark cvt	4,000-6,000	6,000-9,000	9,000-12,000
Gran Sport cvt	5,000-7,500	7,500-10,000	10,000-14,000
Gran Sport htp/cpe	3,500-5,000	5,000-7,500	7,500-11,000
Other models	1,000-3,000	3,000-4,500	4,500-7,000

1967 Buick Electra 225 hardtop coupe

1967

A vast, 430-cubic-inch V-8 was new this year, and standard equipment in every big Buick except the LeSabre. The muscle car Gran Sport was called GS-340 or GS-400 according to engine displacement (260 or 340 bhp), but the GS-340 came as a hardtop only (3692 built). With the exception of the Riviera, all models were facelifted, and the Special and Sportwagon series were thinned out. Buick built 562,507 cars, and moved up to fifth in model year production. Series output was Special, 193,333 (including 13,813 GS); LeSabre, 155,190; Wildcat, 70,881; Electra, 100,304; Riviera, 42,799 (including 4837 GS).

	Restorable	Good	Excellent
Riviera	$2,000-4,000	$4,000-7,000	$7,000-9,500
Full-size cvts	3,000-6,000	6,000-10,000	10,000-15,000
Skylark cvt	4,000-6,000	6,000-9,000	9,000-13,000
Gran Sport cvt	5,000-7,500	7,500-10,000	10,000-14,000
Gran Sport htp/cpe	2,500-4,000	4,000-6,500	6,500-9,000
Other models	1,000-3,000	3,000-4,500	4,500-7,000

1968 Buick GS-400 hardtop coupe

1968 Buick Sportwagon four-door

1968

The Gran Sport muscle car now used GM's all-new B-body with the two-door 112-inch wheelbase, offering a choice of engines: GS-350 or GS-400 hardtop (8317 and 10,473 built) or GS-400 convertible (2454 built). The usual identifying grille, scoops, stripes, and badgework adorned the bodies. The GS-350 V-8, which cranked out 280 bhp, was new. Rivieras used the previous shell, but looked heavier thanks to a new combination bumper-grille and bumper-taillights. Of the 49,284 Rivs produced, 5337 were GS models. All Buicks responded to federal safety mandates with padded dashboards, roller switches instead of knobs, side marker lights, headrests, etc., which had come into play following recent legislation. Model year production spurted to 651,823.

1968 Buick Wildcat convertible coupe

	Restorable	Good	Excellent
Riviera	$1,500-3,000	$3,000-5,000	$5,000-7,000
Full-size cvts	3,000-6,000	6,000-10,000	10,000-15,000
Skylark cvt	3,500-5,000	5,000-9,000	9,000-12,000
Gran Sport cvt	5,000-7,500	7,500-10,000	10,000-14,000
Gran Sport htp/cpe	2,500-4,000	4,000-6,500	6,500-9,000
Other models	1,000-3,000	3,000-4,500	4,500-7,000

1969 Buick Riviera hardtop coupe

1969

Buick Division built 665,422 '69s, once again placing fifth in industry production. This was a year of facelifts, with head-and-tail changes for Specials,

1969 Buick Wildcat Custom hardtop coupe

1969 Buick GS-400 hardtop coupe

1970 Buick GS-455 Stage 1 hardtop coupe

1970 Buick Riviera hardtop coupe

1970 Buick Wildcat hardtop coupe

Skylarks, and Rivieras, a reskin for the standard-size LeSabre, Electra 225, and Wildcat, the last downsized to LeSabre's 123-inch wheelbase. Except to meet federal mandates, the Riv showed few obvious changes. Under its skin, however, was a new front suspension and a special electric fuel pump, inside a new center console. Among mid-size Gran Sports was a ringer: the "California GS," with Gran Sport trim but the baseline Special 250 V-8. This, obviously, was not a traditional GS, and should be considered only a glorified Special. GS output came to 4933 GS-350 hardtops, 6356 GS-400 hardtops, and 1776 GS-400 ragtops. Riviera output rose to 52,872 (including 5272 Gran Sports)—and for the first and only time edged out Ford's T-Bird. Among the full-size ragtops were 3620 LeSabres, 2374 Wildcats, and 8294 Electra 225s.

	Restorable	Good	Excellent
Riviera	$1,500-3,000	$3,000-5,000	$5,000-7,000
Full-size cvts	3,000-6,000	6,000-10,000	10,000-15,000
Skylark cvt	3,500-5,000	5,000-9,000	9,000-12,000
Gran Sport cvt	5,000-7,500	7,500-10,000	10,000-15,000
Gran Sport htp	3,000-4,500	4,500-7,500	7,500-11,000
California GS	2,000-3,500	3,500-6,500	6,500-8,500
Other models	1,000-2,500	2,500-4,000	4,000-6,000

1970

This was the last year for the truly enormous Electra Custom 225 convertible, which means that each of the 6045 examples produced demands a premium because of last-of-the-line distinction. LeSabre and Wildcat convertibles continued, however, with 2487 and 1244 built. New in the muscle car field was the GS-455, a true factory hot rod. It was the only Buick intermediate with the new 455-cubic-inch V-8, replacing the 430 as Buick's largest. Derived from the GS-455, the GS-X had a "Stage I" performance package, including a high-lift cam and 360 horses (or even 370). GS-Xs sported fiberglass spoilers at both ends, matte-black hood, and full-length racing stripes; production was just 678 units. The Riviera featured a new vertical-bar grille, intriguing "French-look" side trim, and the 370-bhp 455. Output dipped to 37,336 units, 3505 of them GS-equipped. More notably, the Special nameplate was eliminated after a 35-year run (save for a 1959-60 hiatus); the baseline Skylark was now the bottom-rung model. Total output held steady at 666,501, and the 15-millionth Buick was built in October 1969.

	Restorable	Good	Excellent
Skylark cvt	$3,500-5,000	$5,000-9,000	$9,000-12,000
GS-455 cvt	5,000-7,500	7,500-10,000	10,000-15,000
GS/GS-455 htp	3,000-4,500	4,500-7,500	7,500-12,000
GS-455 Stage 1, cvt	6,000-9,000	9,000-15,000	15,000-20,000
GS-455 Stage 1, htp	4,500-6,000	6,000-9,000	9,000-14,000
GS-X	6,000-10,000	10,000-17,000	17,000-25,000
Riviera	1,500-3,000	3,000-5,000	5,000-7,000
LeS/W'cat cvt	3,000-6,000	6,000-10,000	10,000-14,000
Electra 225 cvt	4,000-7,500	7,500-12,000	12,000-17,500
Other models	1,000-2,500	2,500-4,000	4,000-6,000

1971

Clearly the most interesting '71 Buick was the all-new Riviera with its "boattail" rear end, designed by Jerry Hirshberg under Bill Mitchell at GM styling. Hirshberg called the car "slightly eccentric," but its unique looks guaranteed a collector following years later. When new, however, it wasn't so popular—output fell to 33,810 units, 3175 of them Gran Sports. The muscle car Gran Sport continued to offer GS Stage 1 and GS-455 options, and the GS-X package; the 455 offered 315, 330, or 345 gross horsepower (on lower compression). Total GS output was 8268 hardtops, 902 ragtops. The mid-range Wildcat was gone, replaced by the Centurion, offered in two- and four-door hardtop and drop-top guise. Output increased from 23,615 '70 Wildcats to 29,398 '71 Centurians (including 2161 ragtops). Total Buick production tumbled to 551,188 units.

	Restorable	Good	Excellent
Skylark cvt	$2,500-4,000	$4,000-7,500	$7,500-10,000
GS-350 cvt	3,000-5,000	5,000-7,500	7,500-12,000
GS-350 htp	1,500-3,500	3,500-5,500	5,500-8,000
GS-455 cvt	5,000-7,500	7,500-10,000	10,000-15,000
GS-455 htp	3,000-4,500	4,500-7,500	7,500-12,000
GS-455 Stage 1, cvt	6,000-9,000	9,000-15,000	15,000-20,000
GS-455 Stage 1, htp	4,500-6,000	6,000-9,000	9,000-13,000
GS-X	5,000-10,000	10,000-15,000	15,000-20,000
Riviera	2,000-3,500	3,500-5,000	5,000-6,500
LeS/Century (cvt)	2,500-4,500	4,500-7,500	7,500-10,000
Other models	1,000-2,500	2,500-4,000	4,000-6,000

1972

Muscle car mania had peaked and tapered off almost as quickly as it had arrived, and federal mandates were making it harder to produce high-performance engines. High insurance rates were also a problem. For 1972, Buick produced only 7723 mid-size GS hardtops and 852 ragtops, plus 2171 GS Rivieras. New for Skylarks was the "Sun Coupe," a sunroof option sporting a fold-back vinyl panel rather than a solid piece of glass or metal. All models were facelifted and the Riviera continued with its distinctive boattail rear end. Ragtop sales were quite low at this point: 3608 Skylark Customs, 2037 LeSabre Customs, 2396 Centurians. Total Buick production soared to 679,921 cars, though this was only good for a sixth place standing.

	Restorable	Good	Excellent
Skylark cvt	$2,500-4,000	$4,000-7,500	$7,500-10,000
GS-350 cvt	3,000-5,000	5,000-7,500	7,500-12,000
GS-350 htp	1,500-3,500	3,500-5,500	5,500-8,000
GS-455 cvt	5,000-7,500	7,500-10,000	10,000-15,000
GS-455 htp	3,000-4,500	4,500-7,500	7,500-12,000
Riviera	2,000-3,500	3,500-5,000	5,000-6,500
LeS/Century cvt	2,500-4,500	4,500-7,500	7,500-10,000
Other models	1,000-2,500	2,500-4,000	4,000-6,000

1973

For 1973, Buick introduced its new compact Apollo, a Chevy Nova clone; its 111-inch wheelbase

1971 Buick LeSabre hardtop sedan

1971 Buick Riviera hardtop coupe

1971 Buick GS-455 hardtop coupe

1972 Buick Riviera hardtop coupe

1973 Buick Riviera GS hardtop coupe

1974 Buick Century hardtop coupe

was the shortest Buick had used since 1924. It also replaced the Skylark and Gran Sport series with the Century, using GM's newly designed A-body platform, with so-called "Colonnade" styling that eliminated the traditional hardtop. Since there were no compact or intermediate convertibles, no collectible cars have issued from these '73s. Gran Sport, GS-455, and Stage 1 equipment were available for the Century, but that matters only if the car is a coupe, preferably a Century Regal. Happily for those who still wanted top-down motoring, Centurion ragtops were still available, though just 5739 were built. Riviera styling changed markedly up back, where a conventional federally required crash bumper replaced the contoured 1971-72 bumper that had better set off the unique boattail. This design compromise makes the 1973 Riviera less desirable than the 1971-72 models. The '73 was the last boattail, which during its three-year run saw production of 101,618 units, 9279 of them GS-equipped. Total Buick production took another big jump for '73, to 821,165, finally topping the old record set in 1955.

	Restorable	Good	Excellent
Century GS cpe	$1,000-2,500	$2,500-4,000	$4,000-6,000
Century GS-455	1,500-3,000	3,000-4,500	4,500-6,500
Century GS Stage 1	2,500-4,000	4,000-5,500	5,500-7,000
Century cvt	2,500-4,500	4,500-7,000	7,000-9,500
Riviera	2,000-3,500	3,500-5,000	5,000-6,000

1974

The Centurion series was eliminated due to slow sales (44,976 in 1973), so the LeSabre line expanded to fill the gap, including a convertible. Emission controls continued to exact a toll, and the optional 270-bhp Riviera 455 was eliminated, leaving 210- and 245-bhp versions. An upmarket Electra 225 with a "Limited" badge was produced, and sold well (46,137 units). The Century's performance options put in their final year. Now just a conventional luxury coupe with thick "B" pillars, the Riviera showed little of the distinction it had previously enjoyed. What had once been "big, flashy, fast and unique," as *Road Test* put it, was now simply big. Output skidded to 20,129, including 4119 with the GS option. Still, if you want a plush four-seater, a mint '74 Riv doesn't cost a king's ransom. Due in large part to the first oil embargo, total Buick production plummeted to 495,063 units.

	Restorable	Good	Excellent
Century GS cpe	$1,000-2,5000	$2,500-4,000	$4,000-6,000
Century GS-455	1,500-3,000	3,000-4,500	4,500-6,500
Century Stage 1	2,500-4,000	4,000-5,500	5,500-7,000
LeSabre cvt	2,500-4,500	4,500-7,000	7,000-9,500
Riviera	1,500-2,500	2,500-3,500	3,500-4,500

1975

With its 97-inch wheelbase, the Skyhawk hatchback coupe was the smallest Buick since 1911. Cloned from the Chevrolet Vega/Monza, it gave Buick a subcompact to blunt sharply higher fuel prices. Production ended up at 29,448 units. The

Skylark name, meanwhile, was revived for a deluxe version of the compact Apollo. Though heavy for its size, it offered decent performance and economy. High-performance packages were eliminated, and the LeSabre had the honor of being Buick's last full-size convertible; 5300 were built. The little-changed Riviera sported thinner vertical grille bars and smooth-finished wheel covers. Output totaled just 17,306 units, 3101 of them with the GS option. Still reeling from the oil crisis, Buick watched production drop to 481,768.

	Restorable	Good	Excellent
LeSabre cvt	$2,500-4,500	$4,500-7,000	$7,000-9,500
Riviera	1,500-2,500	2,500-3,500	3,500-4,500

1975 Buick LeSabre convertible coupe

1976

By collector standards, this was a pretty dull year for Buick. The last convertible was gone, Apollo was renamed Skylark, which was often confused with the smaller, lackluster Skyhawk. Emphasis was on trick accessories, like the Astroroof, with sliding shade and tinted roof band. The 231 V-6, which Buick had bought back after selling the rights, was the staple powerplant, standard on all models except Electras, Rivieras, and wagons, which continued to use the 455, now down to 205 net horsepower. The only obvious change to the Riviera was its turbine-style wheel covers. Output rebounded slightly to 20,082, while total Buick production saw a healthy increase to 737,466 units as America forgot about the 1973-74 oil embargo.

	Restorable	Good	Excellent
Riviera	$1,500-2,500	$2,500-3,500	$3,500-4,500

1977

General Motors "downsized" with a vengeance this year, spurred on by the recent Arab oil embargo and government fuel economy mandates set to begin in 1978. Buick shrank the LeSabre and Electra almost to Century size, losing 600-800 pounds in the process. This allowed smaller engines, yet the big Buicks retained most of their interior space. The Riviera became a high-spec version of the B-body LeSabre, losing half a foot in length, though it would return to the corporate E-body platform two years later. The 455 V-8 was replaced this year by a 185-bhp 403 designed to meet prescribed emissions levels. Though still low, Riviera production increased to 26,138 units, and total Buick output jumped to a record 845,234, topping the mark recently set in 1973. Also, in May 1977, Buick built its 20-millionth car.

	Restorable	Good	Excellent
Riviera	$500-1,500	$1,500-2,500	$2,500-3,500

1978

Buick created the modern overhead-valve V-6 in 1962, dropped it in 1967, and bought it back in

1978 Buick Regal Sport Coupe

1979 Buick Riviera S hardtop coupe

1980 Buick Regal Sport Coupe

1974, but it wasn't until 1978 that engineers decided to give it serious performance with a turbocharger. This raised horsepower of the 231-cid mill from 105 to 150 and torque from 185 to 245 lbs/ft with a two-barrel carb. The four-barrel option gave 165 bhp and 265 lbs/ft. The Regal was downsized this year and sharply restyled to do battle with personal coupes like the Mercury Cougar and Chrysler Cordoba. It lost 560 pounds and a foot of length. The Turbo coupe was a peripheral product, a tiny percentage of the 200,000-300,000 Regals built each year through 1981. Its rarity and technical interest place it among the collectible. The Riviera remained a glorified two-door sedan for this model year, with a less ornate, vertical-bar grille and oblong instead of square cornering/marker lights on the front fenders. Output eased to 20,535, while total Buick production fell to 803,187, third best on record.

	Restorable	Good	Excellent
Riviera	$500-1,500	$1,500-2,500	$2,500-3,500
Regal Turbo cpe	500-1,500	1,500-3,000	3,000-4,000

1979

The second-year Turbo coupes could be identified by large oblong cornering lamps on the front fenders and multi-spoke wheels. A new Riviera debuted, using a redesigned GM E-body and front-wheel drive for the first time in its history. With its elegant squared-off lines and full wheel cutouts, it looked more like the personal-luxury car it had been before 1974. The downsized body also made it a foot shorter and two inches shorter in wheelbase (114 inches) than the '78 Riv. The most collectible model was the $10,960 S Type, with a four-barrel turbocharged V-6 like that of the Regal Turbo coupe (but with 185 horsepower), bucket seats (leather optional), firm suspension, black trim around windows, and sport wheel covers. At $10,684, the standard Riviera got a 350-cid, 160-bhp V-8 rather than the blown V-6. Regal Turbo horsepower came in at 170 this year. Riviera output skyrocketed 250 percent to 52,181, though Buick as a whole dropped back to 727,275 units.

	Restorable	Good	Excellent
Riviera	$1,000-2,000	$2,000-3,000	$3,000-4,500
Riviera S Type	1,500-2,500	2,500-4,000	4,000-5,500
Regal Turbo cpe	500-1,500	1,500-3,000	3,000-4,500

1980

Detail improvements were made to both collectible Buicks this year. The Riviera was refined with match-mounted tires and wheels, retuned shock absorbers, and new body mounts. Halogen high-beam headlamps were standard on Regal Turbo coupes and the Riviera S Type. Regals could be distinguished by new headlamps and coarser, vertical-bar grille texture. Although Buick production set a new record of 854,011 units, Riviera output eased a bit to 48,621.

	Restorable	Good	Excellent
Riviera	$1,000-2,000	$2,000-3,000	$3,000-4,500
Riviera S Type	1,500-2,500	2,500-4,000	4,000-5,500
Regal Turbo cpe	500-1,500	1,500-3,000	3,000-4,500

1981

The Regal was handsomely restyled along more aerodynamic lines, featuring a raked front end and spoiler-type, squared-off rear; its drag coefficient was reduced 18 percent compared to the previous model. Turbo coupes were identified by a hood bulge carrying "Turbo 3.8 Litre" lettering. Rivieras were facelifted via a more prominent, finer-mesh grille and gray rub strips on bumpers; there were also some useful suspension refinements. Collectors should avoid both the optional 350-cid diesel and the new standard engine, a 125-bhp 252 V-6. The Riviera to look for is the T-Type, successor to the S Type. Although diesels and V-8s could also be had on the T-Type, the 231 V-6 was standard. Other T-Type features included GR70-15 tires, black trim accents and rearview mirrors, the Grand Touring performance package (firm suspension, quick steering), woodgrained dash, and optional "Concert Sound" six-speaker stereo. Production this year was 52,007 Rivieras, 856,996 total Buicks, another record.

	Restorable	Good	Excellent
Riviera	$1,000-2,000	$2,000-3,500	$3,500-5,000
Riviera T-Type	1,500-2,500	2,500-4,000	4,000-6,000
Regal Turbo cpe	1,000-2,000	2,000-3,500	3,500-5,000

1981 Buick Riviera hardtop coupe

1981 Buick Regal Sport Coupe

1982

New to the line at mid-year—at a cool $25,000—was a Buick destined to be collectible: the Riviera convertible, Buick's first soft top since 1975. Built by American Sun Roof in Lansing, Michigan, these cars were converted from semi-finished Riviera coupes assembled in Linden, New Jersey, painted white or Firemist red, and fitted with four-speed overdrive automatic, full independent suspension, four-wheel disc brakes, power everything, and red leather upholstery. Production was only 1248, most of them V-8s, which they needed because performance with the V-6 was sluggish. Coupe output was 42,823. Buick also took advantage of its stock car racing success with the Regal Grand National, painted silver-gray and charcoal with red striping, T-top, cloth-and-leather bucket seats, and sharp alloy wheels. But it was a toothless wonder with its 4.1-liter V-6, which was good for only 125 horsepower. After only 215 were built, the Grand National was temporarily scrubbed for 1983. Meanwhile, Buick also produced 2022 Regal Sport Coupe turbos with a more satisfying 170 horses. Total Buick production dipped to 739,984 units.

1982 Buick Riviera T-Type hardtop coupe

1982 Buick Regal Grand National hardtop coupe

	Restorable	Good	Excellent
Riviera cvt	*	$6,500-9,500	$9,500-12,000
Riviera cpe	*	2,500-4,000	4,000-6,000
Regal T-Type cpe	*	2,500-3,500	3,500-4,500
Regal Grand Nat'l	*	3,000-4,500	4,500-5,500

* Purchase only in good or excellent condition

1984 Buick Regal Grand National hardtop coupe

1983

The second-year Riviera ragtop was virtually identical to the '82; identification can only be made by vehicle identification number (VIN). Output was again tiny: 1850 units, 128 of them V-6s. As in 1982, the droptop was available only in white and red; two-thirds were white in both years. Meanwhile, Buick built 47,153 Riviera coupes plus 1331 T-Type Turbo coupes. The Regal T-Type coupe (3732 built) carried its usual identifying hood bulge with special nameplate, and underneath lurked the familiar turbocharged 3.8-liter V-6. Crisp handling, quick power steering, and extra dashboard gauges were included. A T-Type Decor Package offered black exterior accents, special paint jobs, and a sport steering wheel. There was even an optional "Turbo 3.8 Litre" stand-up hood ornament.

	Restorable	Good	Excellent
Riviera cvt	*	$6,500-9,500	$9,500-13,000
Riviera cpe	*	2,500-4,000	4,000-6,000
Rgl T-Type Turbo	*	3,000-4,000	4,000-5,000

* Purchase only in good or excellent condition

1984

At $10,000 more than the coupe, the Riviera ragtop was a dud on the market. Only 500 were built this year: 47 with the 4.1 V-6, only 11 with the Turbo V-6, the rest V-8s. White cars outnumbered red 280 to 220. The eggcrate grille was replaced by a fine vertical-bar affair that looked beautiful, but Buick's claim that the ragtop Riv was "an American Rolls-Royce" sounded a bit optimistic. The Regal Grand National returned with a bang, packing a 200-bhp Turbo Port Injection V-6, all-black paint, and minimal body ornamentation. Inside were Lear-Siegler bucket seats and lots of needle instruments. Grand National production was included in the 5401 T-Type Turbos produced for the model run. Buick Division enjoyed another record year with output reaching 987,980 cars.

	Restorable	Good	Excellent
Riviera cvt	*	$7,500-10,000	$10,000-14,000
Riviera cpe	*	2,500-4,000	4,000-6,000
Regal Grand Nat'l	*	5,000-7,000	7,000-9,000
Rgl T-Type Turbo	*	3,500-4,500	4,500-5,500

* Purchase only in good or excellent condition

1985

In this the final year for the Riviera convertible, only 400 were built. Essentially identical to the '84s, most came with V-8s, and 250 of them were red. At this writing, soft top prices have stabilized, and a very nice example can be had for just over five figures; as time goes on, and the economy improves, prices will begin to gradually rise. The last of the first-generation front-drive Rivs went out with a bang: 63,836 coupes plus 1069 T-Type Turbos. The '85 Grand National, though nearly identical to the '84, can be identified by six bright grille accents; GNX models carried the special features mentioned under 1984 and a GNX badge above the Buick name on the grille. *Car and Driver* reported an astonishing acceleration figure for the GNX: 0-60 in 4.7 seconds. Production: 2102 Grand Nationals, 2067 T-Type Turbo Regals.

	Restorable	Good	Excellent
Riviera cvt	*	$7,500-10,000	$10,000-14,000
Riviera cpe	*	2,500-4,000	4,000-6,000
Regal Grand Nat'l	*	5,000-7,000	7,000-9,000
Rgl T-Type Turbo	*	3,500-4,500	4,500-5,500

* Purchase only in good or excellent condition

1986

Two famous Buick models were notable in 1986: the LeSabre Grand National and the Century Gran Sport. The LeSabre GN was created specially for stock car racing, and thus saw production of only 117. Most were painted solid black, equipped with leather steering wheel and closed rear quarters, taut suspension, Eagle GT tires on 15-inch alloy wheels, and powered by the SFI 3.8-liter V-6. The Century Gran Sport was based around a T-Type coupe in solid black, and with 15-inch aluminum wheels, rear spoiler, 231 SFI V-6, and sport suspension. Though it had special decals, these could be omitted by the purchaser—and if they were the Buick name did not appear anywhere on the exterior. Output was 1029, and the GS was withdrawn for 1987. Riding a 108-inch wheelbase, the all-new downsized Riviera debuted an Electronic Control Center video screen, a touch-sensitive dash panel replacing conventional switches and gauges for the climate system, stereo, and other functions. This confusing device was dropped in 1990. The public wasn't enamored of the smaller Riviera, so output nosedived to 20,096 coupes and 2042 T-Types.

	Restorable	Good	Excellent
Riviera	*	$3,000-5,000	$5,000-6,500
Regal Grand Nat'l	*	6,500-8,500	8,500-15,000
Rgl T-Type Turbo	*	3,500-4,500	4,500-5,500
LeS Grand Nat'l	*	10,000-20,000	20,000-30,000
Century Gran Sport	*	4,500-6,000	6,000-8,000

* Purchase only in good or excellent condition

1987

The ultimate Regal-based Buick was the GNX, of which just 547 were built. It boasted engine, body, and suspension modifications by McLaren Engines: intercooler, transmission oil cooler, ceramic turbine, and computer engine monitoring system. GNX drivetrains featured a modified rear suspension with Panhard rod and longitudinal torque bar, 16-inch aluminum wheels, Eagle GT tires, and flared fenders. Other Regals of interest were the Grand National (20,193 built) and the T-Type (8541 produced). Riviera continued its downward sales spiral: 12,636 coupes, 2587 T-Types.

	Restorable	Good	Excellent
Riviera	*	$4,000-6,000	$6,000-7,500

1986 Buick Riviera T-Type coupe

1987 Buick Riviera coupe

1988 Buick Reatta 2-passenger coupe

1988 Buick Regal Gran Sport hardtop coupe

1989 Buick Riviera hardtop coupe

1989 Buick Reatta 2-passenger coupe

	Restorable	Good	Excellent
Regal Grand Nat'l	*	8,000-11,000	11,000-16,000
Regal GNX	*	6,500-8,000	8,000-10,000
Rgl T-Type Turbo	*	4,500-5,500	5,500-7,000

* Purchase only in good or excellent condition

1988

A sensational new Buick was introduced this year: Reatta, a luxury two-seater selling for about half the price of the Cadillac Allanté. It was built at the Reatta Craft Centre, a section of the Lansing works set aside for the purpose. A new departure for Buick, Reatta used the front-wheel-drive Riviera pan as a base for its smooth, purposeful two-seater coupe styling. Although the V-6 was familiar, it had a new, counter-rotating balance shaft, and its left and right banks were realigned. It came with antilock brakes, air conditioning, full power accessories, climate control, central locking, cruise control, leather seats and steering wheel, and theft alarm. First year output was 4708 units. Also new was the handsome Regal coupe, first of the front-drive GM intermediates, with smooth aero styling and a claimed 0.31 drag coefficient. The familiar 2.8 liter V-6 and four-speed overdrive automatic comprised the Regal's powertrain. Regals had full independent suspension, four-wheel power disc brakes, power steering, and a stainless steel exhaust system. The Limited model was more deluxe than the Custom. Production: 64,773 Customs, 65,224 Limiteds. Riviera carried on (barely) with 6560 coupes and 2065 T-Types.

	Restorable	Good	Excellent
Reatta	*	$7,000-10,000	$10,000-13,000
Riviera	*	5,000-7,000	7,000-9,000
Riviera T-Type	*	6,000-8,500	8,500-10,000
Regal coupe	*	4,000-5,500	5,500-7,000

* Purchase only in good or excellent condition

1989

Buick tried to rekindle interest in its slow-selling Riviera by adding 11 inches to its length (longer than the Electra) and recapturing the look of previous models. A 165-bhp V-6 was the only available engine. Look for the Grand Touring package with stiffer suspension, 2.97:1 axle ratio, wider tires on alloy wheels, leather-wrapped steering wheel and shifter, quick-ratio power steering. Aside from a remote keyless entry system as standard equipment, the Reatta coupe was unchanged. The Regal coupe received a much livelier 3.1-liter V-6 at mid-year, and new options including anti-lock brakes and power sunroof. The 3.1 version of the '89 Regal is definitely worth looking for. Out of the model year production of 506,787 U.S. units (plus about 75,000 Canadian-assembled Regals), 21,189 were Rivieras, 7009 Reattas.

	Restorable	Good	Excellent
Reatta	*	$9,000-11,000	$11,000-14,000
Riviera	*	8,000-10,000	10,000-12,000
Regal 3.1 coupe	*	5,000-7,000	7,000-8,500

* Purchase only in good or excellent condition

1990

In mid-year, a Reatta convertible bowed, sharing the coupe's 3.8-liter V-6 and long list of standard equipment. To the delight of everyone, Reatta dashboards now came with conventional switches and gauges for the climate system, stereo, and other features, replacing the electronic-control video screen. Output this year was 6383 coupes and 2132 ragtops, but after a run of 1313 coupes and 305 soft tops for 1991, the Reatta would become history. Total 1988-91 production: 19,413 coupes, 2437 convertibles. Though Regal added a new four-door sedan, the pretty Regal coupe was little changed. Calendar year output was 105,360 units. The Riviera boasted a new interior, which, like Reatta's, dumped the video screen. The GT suspension remained available and the powertrain was unchanged. Output edged upward to 22,526 for the model run.

	Restorable	Good	Excellent
Reatta cvt	*	$15,000-18,000	$18,000-22,000
Reatta cpe	*	12,000-14,000	14,000-17,000
Riviera	*	10,000-12,500	12,500-15,000
Regal coupe	*	7,000-9,000	9,000-11,000

* Purchase only in good or excellent condition

1990 Buick Reatta convertible coupe

1990 Buick Reatta coupe

Cadillac

Cadillac

Although Cadillacs began being collected later than such rivals as Packards and Lincolns (mainly Continentals), the make is now established as a prime interest among North American enthusiasts. From the multi-cylinder true Classics of the '30s through the early overhead-valve V-8s to the contemporary Eldorados and Sevilles, Cadillacs enjoy wide appeal and are almost always good investments. Club support is excellent, body and mechanical parts supplies good, and future investment potential excellent.

1930-39

Through 1933, Cadillac built some of the finest luxury cars in the American industry. A noticeable change occurred in 1934, however, as the division responded to the Depression by trimming costs, dropping many custom bodies, and resorting increasingly to production line methods in the construction of its product. Styling moved away from upright forms and toward pontoon fenders, sloped radiators, and rakish rear decks. Cadillac designed and built most of its bodies in-house via Fisher and Fleetwood, rather than sending many bare chassis to independent body builders, thus preserving a consistent Cadillac "look" over the years.

The very best Cadillacs of the '30s are the custom-built, open-bodied V-12s and V-16s, originally with overhead-valve engines (which was changed to an L-head V-16 for 1938, at which time the V-12 dis-

1930 Cadillac Eight five-passenger sedan

1930 Cadillac Eight Fleetwood roadster

1931 Cadillac Eight 2-passenger coupe

1932 Cadillac Eight 5-passenger coupe

1932 Cadillac Series 355-B Eight four-door sedan

1934 Cadillac Eight Fleetwood Aero-Dynamic coupe

1934 Cadillac Eight Convertible Sedan

1935 Cadillac Eight 5-passenger sedan

appeared). Singular among V-16 four-door sedans were the early "Madam X" limited editions, with their thin, slightly raked windshield pillars, tapered belt moldings, and thin chrome edgings around side windows. Flat Madam X-type windshields were also found on other body styles. But Cadillac built far more V-8s than multi-cylinder cars, and there are many examples to choose from that will provide satisfying ownership as well as good return on investment. Cadillac V-8s were 353-cid L-heads through 1935, followed by a redesigned 346 in 1936 that would continue through 1948. The smaller 121-inch-wheelbase '36 Series Sixty had a 322, then adopted the 346 for '37. The '30s were years of technological progress: helical-cut synchromesh three-speed gears in 1932, "No-Draft Ventilation" and vacuum-assisted brakes in 1933, independent front suspension in 1934, all-steel bodies in 1935, hydraulic brakes (except on Sixteens) in 1936, the first Cadillac eggcrate grille in 1937, column gearshift and optional turn signals in 1938. Production ranged from a low of 3173 total units in 1933 to 14,255 in 1930 and 14,147 in 1937. Given the wide range generally offered, many models were extremely rare even when new, particularly the open multi-cylinder cars. And, of course, all 1925-35 Cadillacs and all V-12s and V-16s are CCCA-recognized Classics, plus all 1936-39 models (including the 1938-39 Sixty Special) save for the Series Sixty and Sixty-One models.

Sixteens

	Restorable	Good	Excellent
'30-32 open	$60,000-200,000	$200,000-350,000	$350,000-500,000
'30-32 closed	20,000-60,000	60,000-90,000	90,000-150,000
'30-31 Madam X	30,000-90,000	90,000-125,000	125,000-250,000
'30-33 lwb	40,000-90,000	90,000-180,000	180,000-350,000
'33 open	40,000-90,000	90,000-180,000	180,000-350,000
'33 closed	30,000-80,000	80,000-150,000	150,000-250,000
'34 sedans	20,000-50,000	50,000-85,000	85,000-150,000
'34 other bodies	35,000-90,000	90,000-175,000	175,000-275,000
'35 open	40,000-90,000	90,000-175,000	175,000-250,000
'35 452D clsd	25,000-60,000	60,000-100,000	100,000-175,000
'35 452E clsd	20,000-40,000	40,000-75,000	75,000-100,000
'36-37 open	20,000-50,000	50,000-95,000	95,000-170,000
'36-37 closed	10,000-30,000	30,000-60,000	60,000-100,000
'38-39 open	15,000-35,000	35,000-75,000	75,000-115,000
'38-39 closed	8,000-25,000	25,000-50,000	50,000-75,000

Twelves

'30-32 open	40,000-150,000	150,000-225,000	225,000-300,000
'30-32 closed	20,000-50,000	50,000-80,000	80,000-140,000
'33 open	25,000-60,000	60,000-100,000	100,000-160,000
'33 closed	7,500-25,000	25,000-50,000	50,000-75,000
'34-35 open	15,000-40,000	40,000-85,000	85,000-115,000
'34-37 closed	5,000-20,000	20,000-35,000	35,000-60,000
'37 open	10,000-30,000	30,000-55,000	55,000-75,000

Open V-8s

'30-33 Fisher	10,000-40,000	40,000-80,000	80,000-120,000
'34-35 Fisher	10,000-30,000	30,000-60,000	60,000-90,000
'30-33 Fleetwood	20,000-60,000	60,000-90,000	90,000-150,000
'34-35 Fleetwood	10,000-30,000	30,000-70,000	70,000-100,000
'36-38	10,000-25,000	25,000-50,000	50,000-70,000

Closed V-8s

'30-33 Fisher	5,000-15,000	15,000-30,000	30,000-45,000
'34-35 Fisher	5,000-15,000	15,000-25,000	25,000-40,000
'30-35 Fleetwood	7,500-20,000	20,000-35,000	35,000-50,000

	Restorable	Good	Excellent
'36	6,000-15,000	15,000-30,000	30,000-50,000
'37-38 Fisher	3,000-10,000	10,000-17,500	17,500-25,000
'37-38 Fleetwood	7,500-20,000	20,000-35,000	35,000-55,000

1940

With only 61 produced, the Series Ninety Sixteen made its final appearance, sharing its 141.3-inch chassis with the Series Seventy-Five V-8 as since 1938. Major emphasis was on the V-8s, led by the crisp 127-inch-wheelbase Sixty Special with its thin door and window pillars and squared-off roofline. Introduced in 1938, this model was the first direct styling effort of future GM design chief Bill Mitchell. It came as a Town Sedan and Imperial division-window sedan with or without a sunroof; a Town Car was available with either a painted metal or leather-covered rear roof. Only 15 Town Cars were built, compared to 4482 sedans (3703 and 5506 had been sold for 1938 and '39). A step down from the Series Ninety Sixteens and Seventy-Five V-8s was the Seventy-Two, utilizing a 138-inch-wheelbase chassis for a line of sedans and Town Cars. The least expensive 1940 Caddy was the 129-inch-chassis Series Sixty-Two, priced from $1685 to $2195. Including both a glamorous convertible coupe and sedan, the Sixty-Twos would—as time passed—account for the lion's share of Cadillac sales. Total output for 1940 was 13,043 units.

	Restorable	Good	Excellent
62 open	$10,000-20,000	$20,000-40,000	$40,000-60,000
62 closed	3,000-12,000	12,000-18,000	18,000-30,000
60 Special	7,500-15,000	15,000-35,000	35,000-50,000
60 Special Town Car	12,000-20,000	20,000-40,000	40,000-60,000
72 sedans	4,000-15,000	15,000-30,000	30,000-45,000
75 open	15,000-30,000	30,000-55,000	55,000-80,000
75 closed	10,000-20,000	20,000-45,000	45,000-65,000
Sixteen open	15,000-35,000	35,000-75,000	75,000-120,000
Sixteen closed	8,000-25,000	25,000-50,000	50,000-75,000

1941

The '41 Cadillacs wore a fresh face, a complex redesign featuring an eggcrate grille with the center section highest; this would remain a Cadillac styling tradition into the '70s. Taillights were made more prominent, and the one on the left concealed the gas filler cap—another hallmark. All '41s used the tried-and-true 346-cid L-head V-8 rated at 150 bhp, and beginning this year it could be mated to a four-speed Hydra-Matic transmission. There were several new series—a price-leader Sixty-One, a single-body Sixty-Three sedan, and four varieties of long-wheelbase Sixty-Sevens—but the Sixteen and Seventy-Two had departed. The number of chassis was reduced to three. Cadillac's marketing plan now was to offer a broad price span in the upper end of the market, and this paid off with record production of 66,130 units for '41, aided in part by the LaSalle's demise. Only 400 Sixty-Two convertible sedans were built in this its last year.

1939 Cadillac Sixty Special four-door sedan

1940 Cadillac Fleetwood Series Seventy-Five Coupe

1940 Cadillac Sixty Special four-door sedan

1941 Cadillac Series Sixty-Two convertible sedan

1941 Cadillac Series Sixty-Two convertible coupe

1942 Cadillac Series Sixty-Three four-door sedan

1946 Cadillac Sixty Special four-door sedan

1946 Cadillac Series Sixty-One Touring Sedan

1947 Cadillac Series Sixty-Two Touring Sedan

1946 Cadillac Series Sixty-Two coupe

	Restorable	Good	Excellent
62 open	$10,000-20,000	$20,000-40,000	$40,000-50,000
62 & 63 closed	3,000-12,000	12,000-18,000	18,000-30,000
60 Special	7,500-15,000	15,000-32,500	32,500-45,000
67 & 75	3,000-9,000	9,000-17,500	17,500-25,000

1942

This model year, Cadillac's Fortieth Anniversary, was cut short by America's entry into World War II, causing the end of car production. Style-wise this was unfortunate, because Cadillac had brought in a new body with long pontoon fenders running back into the front doors, matching rear fenders, and fastback styling on the Sixty-One and Sixty-Two "Sedanets." The Sixty Special, meanwhile, rode a longer 133-inch wheelbase and looked more like other Cadillacs. In early February, Cadillac shut down production and converted to war work, making tanks, aircraft engines, and munitions until the defeat of Japan. The '42s are sought after for their status as the last prewar Cadillacs, as well as their scarcity—16,511 built, including 2150 "blackout" models with painted bumpers, grille, and trim.

	Restorable	Good	Excellent
62 convertible	$5,000-15,000	$15,000-25,000	$25,000-40,000
60 Special & 75	4,000-12,000	12,000-20,000	20,000-27,500
61, 62, 63, 67 clsd	2,500-8,000	8,000-14,000	14,000-22,000

1946

Though Cadillac resumed car production in late 1945, it managed to build only about 1000 Series Sixty-Two sedans before the end of the year, and just 29,214 cars for the model year. The '46s were slightly revised '42s, sporting the famous Cadillac "V" and crest on the hood for the first time. Model offerings were greatly reduced with the demise of the Series Sixty-Three and Sixty-Seven, and the division-window Sixty Special didn't return either. What remained were the fastback coupe and notchback sedan Series Sixty-One and Sixty-Two, Fleetwood Sixty Special sedan, and the long-wheelbase Seventy-Fives. Hydra-Matic remained an option. A sole convertible was offered in the Sixty-Two series; this is the most prized body style, but unfortunately only 1342 were built. Sixty Specials weren't that common either, with just 5700 rolling off the assembly line. Sedanet output settled in at 800 Sixty-Ones and 2323 Sixty-Twos.

	Restorable	Good	Excellent
61 & 62 sedans	$2,000-4,000	$4,000-8,000	$8,000-13,000
61 & 62 coupes	3,000-5,000	5,000-11,000	11,000-17,000
62 convertible	8,000-17,500	17,500-27,500	27,500-40,000
60 Special	2,500-4,500	4,500-9,000	9,000-15,000
75 sdns/limos	3,500-7,500	7,500-14,000	14,000-22,500

1947

For one more year Cadillac relied on its prewar styling, making the '47s almost identical to the '46s. Round rather than rectangular parking lights and script instead of block-letter fender nameplates were the main visual differences. The Sixty Special lost the vertical chrome ribs on the roof's rear quarters, which had marked the '46 model; the Seventy-Five omitted its stainless steel-trimmed running boards. Prices were $150 to $200 higher in 1947 and production regained its prewar stride: 61,926 Cadillacs were produced for the model run, most of them Sixty-Twos: 25,834 sedans, 7245 Sedanet fastbacks, and 6755 convertibles.

	Restorable	Good	Excellent
61 & 62 sedans	$2,000-4,000	$4,000-8,000	$8,000-13,000
61 & 62 coupes	3,000-5,000	5,000-11,000	11,000-17,000
62 convertible	8,000-17,500	17,500-27,500	27,500-40,000
60 Special	2,500-4,500	4,500-9,000	9,000-15,000
75 sdns/limos	3,500-7,500	7,500-14,000	14,000-22,500

1948 Cadillac Series Sixty-One coupe

1948 Cadillac Series Sixty-Two Touring Sedan

1948 Cadillac Series Sixty-One Touring Sedan

1949 Cadillac Series Sixty-Two Coupe de Ville hardtop

1948

Cadillac announced its first all-new postwar design on all models except the Seventy-Five: a slim, elegantly rounded body designed by Bill Mitchell, Harley Earl, Frank Hershey, and Art Ross. Its tailfinned and rounded rear fenders, cockpit-like curved windshield, and the Sixty Special's bodyside simulated air scoops had been inspired before the war by the then-secret Lockheed P-38 Lightning pursuit fighter. The tailfin, Mitchell said, "gave definition" to the rear for the first time; it quickly became a favorite Cadillac hallmark. Up front, Cadillac retained its traditional grille shape in a larger pattern. The '48 "drum" style dashboard was unique this year; expensive to manufacture, it was replaced with a simpler arrangement in 1949. Despite a late model launch in March, output came to 52,706 units, including 5450 Sixty-Two ragtops and 6561 Sixty Special sedans.

	Restorable	Good	Excellent
61 & 62 sedans	$2,000-4,000	$4,000-8,000	$8,000-13,000
61 & 62 coupes	3,000-5,000	5,000-11,000	11,000-17,000
62 convertible	8,000-17,500	17,500-27,500	27,500-40,000
60 Special	2,500-4,500	4,500-9,000	9,000-15,000
75 sdns/limos	3,500-7,500	7,500-14,000	14,000-22,500

1949

Two more bold steps into the future came in 1949: Cadillac's new, powerful 331-cid overhead-valve V-8, replacing the long-running L-head 346; and the Coupe de Ville, Cadillac's first hardtop, designed to offer the look and airiness of a convertible with a solid steel roof. Priced at $3497 base, the de Ville found just 2150 customers, mainly because it was introduced late in the model run. In subsequent years it caught on fast and accounted for a large percentage of production. The new engine, designed by Ed Cole, Jack Gordon, and Harry Barr, was lighter and capable of much higher compression to take advantage of higher octane fuels; it also featured "oversquare" dimensions, wedge-shaped combustion chambers, and "slipper" pistons, which traveled low between crankshaft counterweights, allowing for short connecting rods and low reciprocating weight. The Series Seventy-Five continued with

1949 Cadillac Series Sixty-Two convertible coupe

1950 Cadillac Series Sixty-One four-door sedan

1950 Cadillac Sixty Special four-door sedan

1951 Cadillac Series Sixty-Two convertible coupe

its prewar body one last time, though with the new engine. With so much going for it, Cadillac set a new production record: 92,554 cars. Only 1502 were Seventy-Fives, not counting 1861 commercial chassis produced on an extended 163-inch wheelbase. In this the last year for the Sedanet fastback coupes, 6409 were built as Sixty-Ones, 7515 as Sixty-Twos.

	Restorable	Good	Excellent
61 & 62 sedans	$2,000-4,000	$4,000-8,000	$8,000-13,000
61 & 62 coupes	3,000-5,000	5,000-11,000	11,000-17,000
62 convertible	8,000-17,500	17,500-27,500	27,500-40,000
62 Cpe de Ville	4,000-7,500	7,500-15,000	15,000-22,500
60 Special	2,500-4,500	4,500-9,000	9,000-15,000
75 sdns/limos	3,500-8,000	8,000-14,000	14,000-24,500

1950

Having established its new look, Cadillac strove for year-to-year consistency in appearance, a practice that had stood Packard well in the prewar luxury field and was equally sound business for Cadillac. All 1950 models looked bulkier, sported a new, one-piece curved windshield, and the Series Seventy-Five was finally redesigned along the same lines as the mainstream models. The Sixty Special's wheelbase lost three inches, to 130. In these years, the Sixty-One and Sixty-Two were still relatively light; the latter could do 0-60 in 13 seconds and top 100 mph. The Sixty-One, this year on a 122-inch-wheelbase, was lighter and thus a bit faster than the 126-inch Sixty-Two. In fact, a nearly stock version finished tenth overall at the Le Mans 24-hour endurance race, averaging 81.5 mph. The updated styling and Korean War panic buying spurred output to 103,857 units, another record. Surprisingly, just 6986 were convertibles, 4507 Coupe de Villes—plus 6434 similar-looking Sixty-Two coupes, which had fixed window pillars. An additional 11,839 Sixty-One coupes were produced.

	Restorable	Good	Excellent
61 & 62 sedans	$2,000-4,000	$4,000-8,000	$8,000-12,000
61 & 62 coupes	3,000-5,000	5,000-11,000	11,000-15,000
62 convertible	8,000-15,000	15,000-25,000	25,000-35,000
62 Cpe de Ville	4,000-7,500	7,500-15,000	15,000-20,000
60 Special	2,500-4,500	4,500-9,000	9,000-15,000
75 7/9P sedans	3,500-8,000	8,000-14,000	14,000-22,500

1951

Small auxiliary grilles under the headlamps distinguished the '51 Cadillacs, which comprised a model lineup identical to 1950. The bottom-line Sixty-One, with its shorter wheelbase and stick shift as standard, put in its final appearance this year: postwar prosperity and the huge demand for new cars meant that Cadillac no longer needed a model bracketed at the bottom of the luxury field. Only 4700 were built in this final year (2400 of them coupes)—the last Cadillacs base-priced at under $3000. Series Sixty-Two Coupe de Villes numbered 10,241, convertibles 6117.

	Restorable	Good	Excellent
61/62 sedans	$2,000-4,000	$4,000-8,000	$8,000-12,000
61/62 coupes	3,000-5,000	5,000-11,000	11,000-15,000
62 convertible	8,000-15,000	15,000-25,000	25,000-35,000
62 Cpe de Ville	4,000-7,500	7,500-15,000	15,000-20,000
60 Special	2,500-4,500	4,500-9,000	9,000-15,000
75 8/9P sedans	3,500-8,000	8,000-14,000	14,000-22,500

1952

Lacking the Series Sixty-One, Cadillac fielded one of its smallest lineups in recent history, comprising the usual quartet of standard-bearing Sixty-Twos (sedan, coupe, convertible, Coupe de Ville), the Fleetwood Sixty Special, and the Seventy-Five sedan and Imperial Sedan. As usual, a large number of Seventy-Fives (1694 this year) were supplied in bare chassis form to commercial body builders, mainly for hearse production. Model year recognition was found under the headlamps, where small winged badges replaced the previous year's auxiliary grilles. Hydra-Matic was now standard across the line. After a record 110,713 cars in 1951, Korean War cutbacks forced model year production down to 90,259 units for '52.

	Restorable	Good	Excellent
62 sedan	$2,000-4,000	$4,000-8,000	$8,000-12,000
62 coupe	3,000-5,000	5,000-11,000	11,000-15,000
62 convertible	8,000-15,000	15,000-25,000	25,000-35,000
62 Cpe de Ville	4,000-7,500	7,500-15,000	15,000-20,000
60 Special	2,500-4,500	4,500-9,000	9,000-15,000
75 sedan/limo	3,500-8,000	8,000-14,000	14,000-22,500

1953

Cadillac made history in 1953 with the limited edition, ultra-expensive $7750 Eldorado, a convertible with a custom leather interior and special cut-down panoramic windshield. A metal lid covered the top when lowered, and wire wheels were standard. Though a striking car, only 532 were sold. Styling features this year included one-piece rear windows and massive "Dagmar" bumper guards, named for the bosom of a concurrent starlet: large conical center sections were spring-loaded, to "give" during minor collisions. Output of the 331 V-8 jumped from 190 to 210 bhp this year. Production increased to 109,651 units, including a record 20,000 Sixty Specials.

	Restorable	Good	Excellent
62 sedan	$2,000-4,000	$4,000-8,000	$8,000-12,000
62 coupe	3,000-5,000	5,000-11,000	11,000-15,000
62 convertible	8,000-15,000	15,000-25,000	25,000-35,000
62 Cpe de Ville	4,000-7,500	7,500-15,000	15,000-20,000
62 Eldo cvt	15,000-35,000	35,000-65,000	65,000-95,000
60 Special	2,500-4,500	4,500-9,000	9,000-15,000
75 sedan/limo	3,500-8,000	8,000-14,000	14,000-22,500

1954

A major restyle brought longer, lower, wider Cadillacs, and horsepower went up again, to 230. Wheelbases were lengthened throughout the line: 129 inches for Sixty-Twos, 133 for Sixty Specials, 149.8 for Seventy-Fives. The club coupe body style

1951 Cadillac Series Sixty-Two Coupe de Ville hardtop

1952 Cadillac Sixty Special four-door sedan

1953 Cadillac Series Sixty-Two Coupe de Ville hardtop

1953 Cadillac Fleetwood Seventy-Five sedan

1953 Cadillac Series Sixty-Two convertible coupe

1954 Cadillac Series Sixty-Two convertible coupe

1954 Cadillac Fleetwood Sixty Special four-door sedan

1954 Cadillac Series Sixty-Two hardtop coupe

1956 Cadillac Series Sixty-Two Coupe de Ville hardtop

was eliminated, replaced by a $3838 Sixty-Two hardtop, priced $423 under the Coupe de Ville. To encourage Eldorado sales, Cadillac fielded a less customized '54 on the Sixty-Two body but strutting more trim, including a broad ribbed stainless steel panel on the lower rear quarters. Now priced at $5738 (down $2012), the Eldo ragtop sold better: 2150 copies. The '54 Caddy looked much like the '55; the differences for '54 were large, round parking lights within the grille (instead of oblong units outside it on the '55), finer grille texture, and '53-like side trim. Although output for '54 fell to 96,680 units, hardtop production was up: 17,460 Sixty-Twos, 17,170 Sixty-Two Coupe de Villes.

	Restorable	Good	Excellent
62 sedan	$2,000-4,000	$4,000-9,000	$9,000-14,000
62 convertible	10,000-18,000	18,000-30,000	30,000-40,000
62 Cpe de Ville	4,000-7,500	7,500-15,000	15,000-20,000
62 Eldo cvt	9,000-20,000	20,000-35,000	35,000-50,000
60 Special	2,500-4,500	4,500-9,000	9,000-15,000
75 sedan/limo	3,500-8,000	8,000-14,000	14,000-22,500

1955

With the horsepower race in full swing, Cadillac kept up by raising horsepower to 250 in the 331 V-8's final year, and to 270 for the Eldorado via twin four-barrel carbs. Styling was very similar to 1954, though the new L-shaped side trim was a dead giveaway, except on Seventy-Fives, which retained the '54 look. Beginning in 1955, Eldorados were distinctively styled at the rear, boasting sharply pointed "shark fin" rear fenders above twin "jet-tube" taillights. In banner '55, Cadillac production surged to 140,777 units, a new record. Some highlights: Coupe de Ville, 33,300; Sixty-Two convertible, 8150; Eldorado, 3950; Sixty Special, 18,300.

	Restorable	Good	Excellent
62 sedan	$2,000-4,000	$4,000-9,000	$9,000-14,000
62 convertible	10,000-18,000	18,000-30,000	30,000-40,000
62 hardtop	4,000-7,500	7,500-15,000	15,000-20,000
62 Eldo cvt	9,000-20,000	20,000-35,000	35,000-50,000
60 Special	2,500-4,500	4,500-9,000	9,000-15,000
75 sedan/limo	3,500-8,000	8,000-14,000	14,000-22,500

1956

This year, Cadillac debuted its first four-door hardtop, the Sedan de Ville, and expanded the Eldorado line with a two-door hardtop, the Seville. The ragtop was now called Biarritz. A new 365-cid V-8 bowed, delivering 305 bhp for Eldorados (still with twin quads), 285 bhp elsewhere. Eldorados retained the distinctive shark-fin rear fenders as well as the sumptuous interiors. Both Seville and Biarritz are avidly sought after today, especially because, with their unique sheetmetal, they cannot be "faked" by adding Eldorado trim to a Sixty-Two soft top or hardtop. Fleetwood sedans continued to comprise the Sixty Special four-door and Seventy-Five long-wheelbase bodies. The latter retained the '54 side trim, but adopted the new rear bumpers, finer-mesh grille, and oblong parking lights moved into the bumpers. In a down year for the industry, Cadillac production increased to 154,577 units, led by 41,732 Sedan de Villes, which ousted the Sixty-Two four-door sedan as the most popular model.

	Restorable	Good	Excellent
Eldo Biarritz cvt	$12,000-20,000	$20,000-35,000	$35,000-50,000
Eldo Seville htp	7,500-12,500	12,500-20,000	20,000-30,000
62 sedan	3,500-6,500	6,500-10,000	10,000-14,000
62 hardtops	5,000-9,000	9,000-14,000	14,000-20,000
62 convertible	9,000-17,500	17,500-27,500	27,500-42,500
Fleetwood sdns	3,500-8,500	8,500-15,000	15,000-20,000

1957

The Cadillac line was completely restyled, inspired by the Eldorado Brougham and Park Avenue show cars of 1955. A production Eldorado Brougham was brought out at a princely $13,074, eclipsing the $10,000 price tag of the rival two-door Continental Mark II. This interesting pillarless sedan had center-opening doors, brushed stainless steel roof, complicated (and troublesome) air suspension, and a host of standard special accessories, including perfume atomizer, cigarette and tissue dispensers, magnetized silver tumblers, etc. There were 45 choices of interior colors and trim, including Karakul or lambskin carpeting. The Brougham, which saw just 400 copies, also had standard quad headlamps, a "first" shared with the '57 Nash. All Caddys, save for the Seventy-Fives, were now either hardtops or convertibles—pillared sedans had been eliminated. The Eldorado became a separate series from the Sixty-Two. Total output eased to 146,841 units. Eldorados lost ground—1800 for the Biarritz, 2100 for the Seville—but the Sixty Special spurted 42 percent to 24,000 units.

	Restorable	Good	Excellent
Eldo Brougham	$10,000-15,000	$15,000-22,500	$22,500-30,000
Eldo Biarritz cvt	12,000-20,000	20,000-30,000	30,000-42,500
Eldo Seville htp	7,500-12,500	12,500-17,500	17,500-25,000
62 hardtop cpe	3,000-5,000	5,000-8,000	8,000-12,000
62 hardtop sdn	5,000-9,000	9,000-12,000	12,000-18,000
62 convertible	9,000-17,500	17,500-27,500	27,500-38,000
Fleetwood sdns	3,500-8,500	8,500-15,000	15,000-20,000

1958

GM styling regressed generally in 1958, and Cadillac was no exception. The cars were big, laden with chrome, and far less memorable than usual. Production fell to 121,778 units, though this can be laid at the door of the recession rather than styling. The de Ville became a Sixty-Two sub-series, and that line was expanded by a special extended-deck four-door sedan that found 20,952 takers. Horsepower was 310 for all models, and all were available with cruise control, high-pressure cooling system, two-speaker signal-seeking radio, and automatic parking brake release. The Brougham continued with little change; 304 were built. Eldorado output plummeted to 815 Biarritzes and 855 Sevilles, while the Sedan de Ville was the year's best seller with 23,989 built.

1957 Cadillac Fleetwood Sixty Special hardtop sedan

1957 Cadillac Series 75 Limousine

1957 Cadillac Series Sixty-Two hardtop coupe

1957 Cadillac Eldorado Seville hardtop coupe

1957 Cadillac Eldorado Brougham hardtop sedan

1958 Cadillac Series Sixty-Two Coupe de Ville hardtop

1959 Cadillac Coupe de Ville hardtop

1960 Cadillac Fleetwood Sixty Special hardtop sedan

	Restorable	Good	Excellent
Eldo Brougham	$10,000-15,000	$15,000-22,500	$22,500-30,000
Eldo Biarritz cvt	12,000-18,000	18,000-28,000	28,000-38,000
Eldo Seville htp	6,500-10,000	10,000-15,000	15,000-23,000
62 hardtop cpe	3,000-5,000	5,000-8,000	8,000-11,000
62 hardtop sdn	5,000-9,000	9,000-12,000	12,000-17,000
62 convertible	9,000-17,500	17,500-27,500	27,500-36,000
Fleetwood sdns	3,500-8,500	8,500-15,000	15,000-20,000

1959

Cadillac's total restyle for 1959 produced the tallest tailfins of the tailfin era. Engineering updates created an improved suspension and power steering, plus a new 390-cid V-8 with 325 horses (345 with triple two-barrel carbs for Eldorados). The '59 lineup included convertibles, two-door hardtops, and four- and six-window hardtop sedans. The Series Seventy-Five nine-passenger sedan and limo received the new styling, as well as a new greenhouse with door openings wrapped into the roof. Cadillac built 142,272 cars for 1959, a marked improvement over 1958. The Eldorado Brougham was now a semi-import, its bodies sent to Pinin Farina in Italy for final assembly and trim. Though only 99 were built, it was less individualized than in 1957-58. Collectors today lust over the Eldorado Biarritz, but since only 1320 were built they often have to settle for the slightly less flashy Sixty-Two ragtop, which enjoyed a production run of 11,130.

	Restorable	Good	Excellent
Eldo Brougham	$10,000-15,000	$15,000-22,500	$22,500-30,000
Eldo Biarritz cvt	15,000-35,000	35,000-50,000	50,000-85,000
Eldo Seville htp	9,000-15,000	15,000-25,000	25,000-35,000
62 hardtop sdn	4,000-7,000	7,000-12,000	12,000-16,000
62 hardtop cpe	7,000-11,000	11,000-15,000	15,000-22,000
62 convertible	12,000-27,500	27,500-37,500	37,500-50,000
Fleetwood sdns	3,500-8,500	8,500-15,000	15,000-20,000

1960

A serious facelift reduced the tailfins and restrained chrome on the 1960 Cadillacs. A carryover feature was a choice of rooflines on hardtop sedans in the Sixty-Two and de Ville series. Prices were unchanged, and so were the basic mechanical specs. Standard horsepower remained 325, Eldorado 345. The Pinin Farina-built Eldorado Brougham, in its final appearance, saw 101 examples built. Total output held steady at 142,184 units, but Sixty-Two ragtops increased to 14,000 while the Eldorado Biarritz declined to 1285. With 26,824 built, the Sixty-Two six-window hardtop sedan was the year's best seller; only 9984 buyers selected the four-window Sixty-Two.

	Restorable	Good	Excellent
Eldo Brougham	$10,000-15,000	$15,000-22,500	$22,500-30,000
Eldo Biarritz cvt	12,000-25,000	25,000-40,000	40,000-70,000
Eldo Seville htp	9,000-15,000	15,000-25,000	25,000-35,000
62 hardtop sdn	3,000-6,000	6,000-10,000	10,000-13,000
62 hardtop cpe	6,000-10,000	10,000-14,000	14,000-19,000
62 convertible	12,000-27,500	27,500-37,500	37,500-50,000
Fleetwood sdns	3,500-8,500	8,500-15,000	15,000-20,000

1961

Styling this year began to show the influence of Bill Mitchell, who had taken over from Harley Earl in 1958. The '61s were cleaner than any Cadillac in years, the grille a modest grid, the windshield large but no longer wrapped at the sides. The Eldorado Seville and Brougham were dropped, leaving the Biarritz the sole Eldorado for the first time since 1955. Biarritz also lost its hotted up 390 V-8—all Cadillacs were now rated at 325 bhp. All 15,500 Sixty Specials sported a formal-look greenhouse with a crease above the rear window and a roof covered with simulated leather. Model year output reached 138,379 units, and six-window hardtops outsold the four-window models 5-to-1. The Sixty-Two ragtop set a new record, 15,500 units, and the Biarritz edged up to 1450.

	Restorable	Good	Excellent
Eldo Biarritz cvt	$7,000-15,000	$15,000-25,000	$25,000-37,500
62 hardtop sdn	2,500-5,000	5,000-7,500	7,500-11,000
62 hardtop cpe	6,000-10,000	10,000-14,000	14,000-18,000
62 convertible	6,000-12,500	12,500-20,500	20,500-27,500
Fleetwood sdns	2,500-5,000	5,000-8,000	8,000-15,000

1961 Cadillac Coupe de Ville hardtop

1962 Cadillac Series Sixty-Two Sedan de Ville hardtop

1962 Cadillac Series Sixty-Two convertible coupe

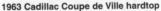

1962

With Cadillac having achieved the desired, more conservative look, few changes were made for 1962. However, tailfins were lowered some more and cornering lights were added to front fenders. Detail trim changes included a crosshatch grille with a horizontal divider bar and taillight ensembles placed within a vertical recess at each end of the rear bumper. New models were the Sixty-Two Town Sedan and de Ville Park Avenue, short-deck four-door hardtops that sold 2600 examples apiece. A dual braking system appeared; engines remained the same. Production climbed to a new record, 160,840, though Biarritz output was identical to 1961.

	Restorable	Good	Excellent
Eldo Biarritz cvt	$7,000-15,000	$15,000-25,000	$25,000-37,500
62 hardtop sdn	2,500-5,000	5,000-7,500	7,500-11,000
62 hardtop cpe	6,000-10,000	10,000-14,000	14,000-18,000
62 convertible	6,000-12,500	12,500-20,500	20,500-27,500
Fleetwood sdns	2,500-5,000	5,000-8,000	8,000-15,000

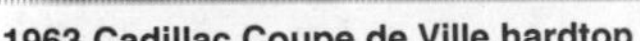

1963 Cadillac Coupe de Ville hardtop

1963 Cadillac Sedan de Ville 4-window hardtop

1963

A new stiffer, lighter V-8 was introduced, dimensionally the same but more durable and smoother. Styling was yet more conservative, with mini-tailfins, a massive grille encompassing parking lights, and new body panels and side moldings with a less sculptured look. Elongated vertical taillights were introduced at the rear. Standard equipment included Hydra-Matic, power steering and brakes, heater, remote-control outside mirror, and back-up lights. A six-way power seat was standard on Eldorados, power windows standard on all but Sixty-Twos. Even power vent windows were offered. Self-adjusting brakes, cornering lights, and turn signal re-

1964 Cadillac Sedan de Ville 4-window hardtop

1964 Cadillac Coupe de Ville hardtop

1965 Cadillac Sedan de Ville hardtop

1965 Cadillac Fleetwood Eldorado convertible

peaters on front fenders were also standard. The public liked what it saw, sending production to yet another record: 163,174 units, including 1825 Biarritz convertibles.

	Restorable	Good	Excellent
Eldo Biarritz cvt	$7,000-12,000	$12,000-20,000	$20,000-30,000
62 hardtop sdn	2,000-4,000	4,000-6,000	6,000-8,000
62 hardtop cpe	3,000-5,000	5,000-8,000	8,000-12,000
62 convertible	5,000-10,000	10,000-17,500	17,500-25,000
Fleetwood sdns	2,500-5,000	5,000-8,000	8,000-15,000

1964

This model year was an extension of 1963. New, even lower tailfins (the last time they would appear) created an unbroken beltline, accentuating length. A body-color horizontal grille divider bar and new taillamp housings provided model year recognition at a glance. New Comfort-Control heating-air conditioning maintained a set temperature regardless of outside conditions—it has been on the Cadillac spec sheet ever since. Output edged up once again, this time to 165,909. With 39,674 built, the four-window Sedan de Ville was the most popular '64 Caddy, followed by the Coupe de Ville with 38,195 units. The collectors' favorite Biarritz (now labeled Fleetwood) chipped in with 1870 units, and the Sixty Special contributed 14,550.

	Restorable	Good	Excellent
Eldo Fltwd cvt	$7,000-12,000	$12,000-20,000	$20,000-30,000
62 hardtop sdn	2,000-4,000	4,000-6,000	6,000-8,000
62 hardtop cpe	3,000-5,000	5,000-8,000	8,000-12,000
62 convertible	5,000-10,000	10,000-17,500	17,500-25,000
Fleetwood sdns	2,500-5,000	5,000-8,000	8,000-15,000

1965

The Sixty-Two was dropped after a quarter-century, replaced by the Calais. Both it, plus the de Ville and Eldorado, rode the 129.5-inch wheelbase adopted in 1961. Other models were retained, although a new $194 Fleetwood Brougham option with padded vinyl roof, special trim, and C-pillar identification was offered for the Sixty Special. Cadillac enjoyed still another a banner year, producing 182,435 vehicles. The major styling change was a longer, lower silhouette and the complete absence of tailfins (though the squared-off styling still hinted at them). The Sixty Special regained its customary 133-inch wheelbase for the first time since 1958. A flush-top contour on rear quarter panels, curved glass side windows, stacked quad headlights, and 340 horsepower were features of the '65s. Turbo Hydra-Matic dual-range automatic transmission and a perimeter type frame were featured on all models except the Seventy-Five. The de Ville hardtop sedan and coupe were again the sales leaders, 45,535 and 43,345 units, but the Fleetwood Eldorado ragtop and Sixty Special saw increases to 2125 and 18,100, respectively.

	Restorable	Good	Excellent
Eldo Fltwd cvt	$5,000-10,000	$10,000-15,000	$15,000-20,000

	Restorable	Good	Excellent
Calais/de Ville 4d	2,000-4,000	4,000-6,000	6,000-8,000
Calais/de Ville 2d htp	3,000-5,000	5,000-8,000	8,000-12,000
de Ville cvt	4,000-8,000	8,000-12,500	12,500-17,500
Fleetwood sdns	2,500-5,000	5,000-8,000	8,000-15,000

1966

Cadillac knocked on the 200,000-car threshold this year as it cranked out 196,685 vehicles. The lineup featured a mild facelift with a new front bumper and grille and integrated vertical taillight housings. The Seventy-Five now shared the perimeter frame, and was fully restyled for the occasion. Variable-ratio power steering was introduced on all models; a new option was carbon cloth seat heating pads. The Fleetwood Brougham moved up one step by becoming a separate Sixty Special model, and it outsold the base model 13,630 to 5455. Convertibles did well again this year: 19,200 de Villes (same as in 1965) and 2250 Eldorados (up 125 units).

	Restorable	Good	Excellent
Eldo Fltwd cvt	$5,000-10,000	$10,000-15,000	$15,000-20,000
Calais/de Ville 4d	2,000-4,000	4,000-6,000	6,000-8,000
Calais/de Ville 2d htp	3,000-5,000	5,000-8,000	8,000-12,000
de Ville cvt	4,000-8,000	8,000-12,500	12,500-17,500
Brougham & 60 Special	2,500-5,000	5,000-7,000	7,000-10,000
75 sedan/limo	2,500-5,000	5,000-8,000	8,000-15,000

1966 Cadillac Fleetwood Brougham four-door sedan

1966 Cadillac Coupe de Ville hardtop

1967 Cadillac Coupe de Ville hardtop

1967

The new '67 front-wheel-drive Eldorado (properly Fleetwood Eldorado) was the most significant single Cadillac model of the decade. Based on Oldsmobile's Toronado personal-luxury coupe, it offered luxury combined with outstanding roadability and brilliant styling. Six years in the planning, this lineal successor to the 1957-58 Eldorado Brougham rode a compact (for Cadillac) 120-inch wheelbase and was base priced at $6277. The rest of the line was broken into the usual Calais, de Ville and Fleetwood series, with restyled front ends containing forward-raked grilles and a stronger hint of fins up back. All models were powered by the 340-horsepower 429 V-8, as since 1964. And this was the year that Cadillac produced 200,000 cars, and just exactly that. The new Eldorado found 17,930 buyers, just slightly below the 18,202 that chose the de Ville convertible, now the only soft top in the Cadillac lineup.

	Restorable	Good	Excellent
Eldo hardtop	$2,500-5,000	$5,000-7,000	$7,000-10,000
Calais/de Ville 4d	2,000-4,000	4,000-6,000	6,000-8,000
Calais/de Ville 2d htp	3,000-5,000	5,000-8,000	8,000-10,000
de Ville cvt	4,000-8,000	8,000-11,000	11,000-15,000
Brougham & 60 Special	2,500-5,000	5,000-7,000	7,000-10,000
75 sedan/limo	2,500-5,000	5,000-8,000	8,000-12,000

1968 Cadillac de Ville convertible

1968 Cadillac Fleetwood Brougham four-door sedan

1969 Cadillac Fleetwood Eldorado hardtop coupe

1969 Cadillac Sedan de Ville hardtop

1969 Cadillac Coupe de Ville hardtop

1968

An all-new 472-cid V-8 with 375 horsepower was introduced, designed to meet government emission control requirements. Other new features included hidden windshield wipers and many safety devices mandated by the government. The Eldorado sported a new grille, longer hood, side marker lights, and larger taillights. Other models received longer hoods, a revised grille, and a trunklid shaped to hold more luggage. Less economical than its predecessor, the 472 packed high performance: a Coupe de Ville could do 0-60 in 7.8 seconds. Production soared to another record, 230,003 units. Eldorado increased to 24,528, de Ville ragtops numbered 18,025, while the Seventy-Fives saw 805 nine-passenger sedans and 995 limos (plus 2413 commercial chassis).

	Restorable	Good	Excellent
Eldo hardtop	$2,500-5,000	$5,000-7,000	$7,000-10,000
Calais/de Ville 4d	2,000-4,000	4,000-6,000	6,000-8,000
Calais/de Ville 2d htp	3,000-5,000	5,000-8,000	8,000-10,000
de Ville cvt	4,000-8,000	8,000-11,000	11,000-15,000
Brougham & 60 Special	2,500-5,000	5,000-7,000	7,000-10,000
75 sedan/limo	2,500-5,000	5,000-8,000	8,000-12,000

1969

For 1969, Cadillac production dipped slightly to 223,237 vehicles. The revised Eldo front end deleted the hidden headlights of 1967-68, and adopted a taller fine-mesh grille split by a horizontal front bumper bar. Other models were restyled with a new front end featuring a more formal-looking grille, horizontally mounted quad headlights, and wraparound parking lights set into blunter fenders. Wraparound vertical taillights rode atop the rear bumper, and the roofline was squarer. An unpopular change was the elimination of front vent windows. Eldorado and de Ville ragtop output dropped slightly to 23,333 and 16,445, while Fleetwood Brougham production climbed a bit to 17,300 (plus 2545 base Sixty Specials).

	Restorable	Good	Excellent
Eldo hardtop	$2,500-5,000	$5,000-7,000	$7,000-10,000
Calais/de Ville 4d	1,000-3,000	3,000-4,500	4,500-6,000
Calais/de Ville 2d htp	2,000-4,000	4,000-6,000	6,000-8,000
de Ville cvt	4,000-8,000	8,000-11,000	11,000-15,000
Fleetwood sdns	1,500-3,000	3,000-6,000	6,000-9,000

1970

The Eldorado boasted a new 400-bhp, 8.2-liter engine and a badge to prove it—at 500 cubic inches it was the largest production car engine in the world. Other models retained the 472 with 375 bhp. New were integral steering knuckles, bias-ply fiberglass-belted tires, a radio antenna imbedded in the windshield, and more safety features, among them an energy-absorbing steering column. Cadillac offered an anti-theft ignition key warning buzzer and a steering column/transmission lock which disengaged with the starter switch. A new grille with bright vertical accents and the first Cadillac "winged crest" were main styling changes. The result was yet another production record: 238,744. By series, this came to 5187 Calais, 181,719 de Villes (including 15,172 soft tops), 28,842 Eldorados, 18,651 Sixty Specials (including 16,913 Fleetwood Broughams), and 4622 Seventy-Fives (2506 of them commercial chassis).

	Restorable	Good	Excellent
Eldo hardtop	$2,500-5,000	$5,000-7,000	$7,000-10,000
Calais/de Ville 4d	1,000-3,000	3,000-4,500	4,500-6,000
Calais/de Ville 2d htp	2,000-4,000	4,000-6,000	6,000-8,000
de Ville cvt	4,000-8,000	8,000-11,000	11,000-15,000
Fleetwood sdns	1,500-3,000	3,000-6,000	6,000-9,000

1970 Cadillac de Ville convertible

1970 Cadillac Coupe de Ville hardtop

1971

Calais remained the least expensive model, and perhaps because it wasn't much cheaper than the de Ville, it was taking a smaller share of overall output each year. The Eldorado, adopting a longer 126.3-inch wheelbase, became heavier and bulkier, and would continue as such through 1978, with few changes apart from those mandated by government safety and emissions standards. The "hardtop" retained frameless door glass, but there was a B-pillar between front and rear side windows. Cadillac's big cars on the GM C-body continued to dominate sales but, since the Eldorado now gained a convertible body style, the de Ville ragtop was dropped. The two family-size Fleetwoods, the Fleetwood Brougham and Sixty Special, were merged into a single Sixty Special Brougham beginning this year. Output declined to 188,537 vehicles, with the restyled Eldorado scoring 20,568 hardtops and 6800 convertibles. The Sixty Special Brougham found 15,200 takers, while Calais managed 6929 units.

1971 Cadillac Fleetwood Eldorado two-door hardtop

1971 Cadillac Fleetwood Sixty Special Brougham sedan

	Restorable	Good	Excellent
Eldo convertible	$4,000-8,000	$8,000-11,000	$11,000-15,000
Eldo hardtop	2,500-5,000	5,000-7,000	7,000-10,000
Calais/de Ville 4d htp	1,000-3,000	3,000-4,500	4,500-6,000
Calais/de Ville 2d htp	2,000-4,000	4,000-6,000	6,000-8,000
Fleetwood sdns	1,500-3,000	3,000-6,000	6,000-8,000

1972 Cadillac Coupe de Ville hardtop

1972

The Calais was almost superfluous now, accounting for 7775 sales, while the de Ville hardtops, coupe and sedan, continued as Cadillac's breadwinners, selling 194,811 between them. The Sixty Special Brougham had achieved definite popularity, and sold 20,750 copies. Changes were restricted to detail styling modifications, but horsepower was now expressed in net rather than gross figures: 235 for the 500-cubic-inch Eldorado, 220 for the 472 V-8 engine on other models. Total production of 267,787 cars set another Cadillac record.

1972 Cadillac Fleetwood Eldorado convertible

1973 Cadillac Coupe de Ville hardtop

1973 Cadillac Fleetwood Eldorado coupe

1973 Cadillac Fleetwood Eldorado convertible

1974 Cadillac Fleetwood Eldorado coupe

	Restorable	Good	Excellent
Eldo convertible	$4,000-8,000	$8,000-11,000	$11,000-15,000
Eldorado hardtop	2,500-5,000	5,000-7,000	7,000-10,000
Calais/de Ville 4d htp	1,000-3,000	3,000-4,500	4,500-6,000
Calais/de Ville 2d htp	2,000-4,000	4,000-6,000	6,000-8,000
Fleetwood sdns	1,500-3,000	3,000-6,000	6,000-8,000

1973

Another great Cadillac year produced yet another record: 304,839 vehicles—the first time the lofty 300,000 mark had been topped. The cars were given a facelift, but were chiefly recognizable by their enormous, clumsy looking energy-absorbing bumpers (a problem industry-wide), to which the vertical-accent grilles were now directly attached. A grille section was also built into the bottom of the bumper for a more "classic" look. The Eldorado featured an aggressive eggcrate grille and chiseled hood, plus large rectangular parking/turn signal lights under the headlamps. Notable by their absence were the Fifties-style vertical bodyside simulated air intakes of 1971-72. The long-running Sixty Special didn't appear this year as such—the "owner-driver" Fleetwood on its special 133-inch wheelbase was called Fleetwood Brougham, a name still in use. It was available optionally with a Brougham d'Elegance trim option, consisting of an ultra-posh interior with reading lamps and other niceties. The Eldorado saw production increase to 51,451 (including 9315 soft tops), while the Fleetwood Brougham accounted for 24,800 units.

	Restorable	Good	Excellent
Eldo convertible	$4,000-8,000	$8,000-11,000	$11,000-15,000
Eldo hardtop	2,000-4,000	4,000-6,000	6,000-8,000
Calais/de Ville 4d htp	1,000-2,500	2,500-3,500	3,500-5,000
Calais/de Ville 2d htp	1,500-3,000	3,000-4,500	4,500-7,000
Fleetwood sdns	1,500-3,000	3,000-4,500	4,500-7,000

1974

Massive eggcrate grilles, new lighting designs, fixed rectangular quarter windows for coupes (ending the true two-door hardtops), lower profiles, and rear chrome bumper ends with built-in taillights comprised styling changes this year. New, too, were optional trim packages, which are things to look for: the de Ville d'Elegance (velour upholstery, both models), Cabriolet (landau type rear roof treatment), and the Coupe de Ville (a Cabriolet with power sun roof). Held over from 1973 was the "Brougham d'Elegance" package; one step up was the "Talisman" with velour upholstered armchair seating for four, separated by upholstered consoles containing writing sets and vanities. Production declined to 242,330, with Eldorado down to 40,412 (7600 convertibles), Fleetwood Brougham to 18,250. Among the Seventy-Fives were 895 sedans, 1005 nine-passenger limos, and 2265 commercial chassis.

	Restorable	Good	Excellent
Eldo convertible	$4,000-8,000	$8,000-11,000	$11,000-15,000
Eldo hardtop	2,000-4,000	4,000-6,000	6,000-8,000
Calais/de Ville 4d htp	1,000-2,500	2,500-3,500	3,500-5,000
Calais/de Ville 2d	1,500-3,000	3,000-4,500	4,500-7,000
Fleetwood sdns	1,500-3,000	3,000-4,500	4,500-7,000
Fleetwood Talisman	2,500-3,500	3,500-5,500	5,500-8,500

1975

Cadillac broke with its big car tradition with the new Seville, a loaded and luxurious special version of the GM X-body compact Chevy Nova, powered by an efficient 350-cid, 180-bhp V-8 with electronic fuel injection and delivering sparkling performance. The "international-size" Seville (114.3-inch wheelbase) was 1000 pounds lighter and 27 inches shorter than a de Ville, but rode just as well according to testers. Because this car was right for the times, buyers responded enthusiastically—16,355 were built despite a mid-year debut and $12,479 price, higher than any Cadillac save for Series Seventy-Five models. Other Caddys all had the 500-cid V-8 now, but it was down 20 bhp to 190. Also new for '75 were quad rectangular headlamps, seen on all models, while big Cadillacs sported finer crosshatched grilles, and Calais/de Ville models got triangular rear quarter windows. Though production headed upward to 264,732, Calais continued to languish as only 8300 were called for—not even enough to match the 8950 Eldorado convertibles sold.

	Restorable	Good	Excellent
Eldo convertible	$4,000-8,000	$8,000-12,000	$12,000-16,000
Eldorado hardtop	2,000-4,000	4,000-6,000	6,000-8,000
Seville	2,000-4,000	4,000-6,500	6,500-9,000
Calais/de Ville 4d	1,000-2,500	2,500-3,500	3,500-5,000
Calais/de Ville 2d	1,500-3,000	3,000-4,500	4,500-7,000
Fleetwood sdns	1,500-3,000	3,000-4,500	4,500-7,000

1976

Cadillac produced its alleged "last" convertible this year, though this body style would be revived by the division eight years later. The last 200 of the 14,000 '76 Eldorado ragtops, which sported a special badge and were finished in white inside and out, were eagerly snapped up by collectors, but over the years values haven't gone significantly higher than earlier Eldo soft tops. (Asking prices are sometimes far higher than earlier models, but this is no guarantee that actual sales reach those levels.) Styling was mildly changed on the last of the "big" Cadillacs, with new cross-hatched grilles, revised vinyl roof trim, new interiors, and an optional 215-bhp, 500-cid V-8. The Seville scored 43,772 sales in its first full model year, the Eldorado coupe found 35,184 buyers, and 24,500 Fleetwood Broughams were called for, but the Calais—now in its last year—withered to 6200. As usual, de Ville was the sales champ, accounting for 182,159 of Cadillac's record production run of 309,139 cars. Though little noticed, this was the last year for the four-door hardtop; 1700 Calais models and 67,677 de Villes were produced.

1974 Cadillac Fleetwood Sixty Special Brougham sedan

1975 Cadillac Coupe de Ville

1975 Cadillac Seville four-door sedan

1975 Cadillac Fleetwood Eldorado coupe

1976 Cadillac Coupe de Ville

1976 Cadillac Calais hardtop sedan

1977 Cadillac Seville four-door sedan

1977 Cadillac Fleetwood Brougham four-door sedan

1978 Cadillac Seville four-door sedan

1978 Cadillac Eldorado Custom Biarritz Classic Coupe

	Restorable	Good	Excellent
Eldo convertible	$4,000-8,000	$8,000-12,000	$12,000-20,000
Eldo hardtop	2,000-4,000	4,000-6,000	6,000-8,000
Seville	2,000-4,000	4,000-6,500	6,500-9,000
Calais/de Ville 4d htp	1,000-2,500	2,500-3,500	3,500-5,000
Calais/de Ville 2d cpe	1,500-3,000	3,000-4,500	4,500-7,000
Fleetwood sdns	1,500-3,000	3,000-4,500	4,500-7,000

1977

De Villes and Fleetwood Broughams, downsized to a 121.5-inch wheelbase, were new from the ground up: 8-12 inches shorter and nearly 1000 pounds lighter on average. They also had a cleaner, more efficient engine for all models save Seville: a new fuel-injected 425-cid V-8 rated at 180 horsepower, with 195 optional. De Villes from 1977 and beyond are not being actively collected. However, the Biarritz version of the Eldorado hardtop is worth looking for, since it already commands distinctly higher prices than the standard Eldo. Buyers liked the new smaller Caddys, as total output soared to another record: 358,488 units. Of that number, 234,171 were de Villes, followed by 47,344 Eldorados, 45,060 Sevilles, and 28,000 Fleetwood Broughams. In addition, Cadillac built 2614 Fleetwood limos (144.5-inch wheelbase) and 1299 commercial chassis (157.5-inch chassis).

	Restorable	Good	Excellent
Eldorado	$1,500-3,000	$3,000-4,500	$4,500-6,500
Eldo Biarritz	$2,000-4,000	$4,000-6,000	$6,000-8,000
Seville	$2,000-3,500	$3,500-5,000	$5,000-6,000
Fleetwood sdns	$1,500-3,000	$3,000-4,500	$4,500-7,000

1978

Cadillac continued to enjoy good sales with its downsized de Villes and Seville, which added a premium Eleganté model with deluxe interior and special exterior trim, like engraved taillight emblems and accent striping. Mechanically, Cadillac introduced a diesel engine option for the Seville—a 350-cid, 120-bhp V-8—but this is not recommended for collectors. The model lineup was essentially unchanged from 1977, as was total production of 349,684 units. In its last year before downsizing, the two-and-a-half-ton Eldorado found favor with 46,816 buyers, and the Seville continued its winning ways by finding 56,985 customers.

	Restorable	Good	Excellent
Eldorado	$1,500-3,000	$3,000-4,500	$4,500-6,500
Eldo Biarritz	2,000-4,000	4,000-6,000	6,000-8,000
Seville (gasoline)	2,000-3,500	3,500-5,000	5,000-6,000
Fleetwood sedans	1,500-3,000	3,000-4,500	4,500-7,000

1979

Downsizing was applied to the Fleetwood Eldorado, which lost more than 1100 pounds (to 3792), 20 inches in length (to 204), and 12.4 inches in wheelbase (to 113.9)—and gained handsome new styling. An unusual touch for an upmarket domestic was independent rear suspension, more compact than the previous beam axle, which made the wheelbase reduction possible with little sacrifice in passenger room. Options for all Cadillacs included dual electric remote-control door mirrors, automatic retractable radio antenna, a choice of eight-track or cassette stereo tape players, 40-channel CB radio, and "Tripmaster" on-board travel computer. The latter gave digital readouts for average mpg and speed, miles to destination, and estimated arrival time, plus engine rpm, coolant temperature, and electrical system voltage. Diesel power was now available across the line except for limos. Among Sevilles, look for the interesting San Remo convertible, an aftermarket conversion that looked like Cadillac had built it. Eldorado ragtop conversions were also done by several firms. Cadillac production hit still another record—383,138 units—and the new Eldorado shared the bounty as 67,436 were quickly snapped up.

	Restorable	Good	Excellent
Eldorado	$1,500-3,000	$3,000-4,500	$4,500-6,500
Eldo Biarritz	2,000-4,000	4,000-6,000	6,000-8,000
Seville & Fleetwood	2,000-3,500	3,500-5,000	5,000-6,000
Seville San Remo	3,500-5,000	5,000-7,500	7,500-9,000

1980

Leading the line was a completely overhauled Seville with a daring and controversial "trunkback" rear end, conceived by designer Wayne Cady in the tradition of razor-edge English coachwork by Hooper and Vanden Plas during the '50s. Although not everyone approved, this was the most distinctive new Cadillac since the tailfinned '48. Seville also acquired the Eldorado's front-wheel-drive chassis and fully independent suspension with automatic self-leveling, thus setting a new standard for engineering sophistication among American cars. The finest mint, low-mileage "humpback" Seville we've seen was advertised recently for $10,000, and that's well above the average—half as much will buy a good one. So this interesting Caddy looks like a very reasonable investment at the moment. The biggest V-8 offered was now a 145/150-bhp 368, and at mid-year a 252-cid V-6 was made optional in de Villes and Fleetwood Broughams. These models featured new front and rear styling and rooflines; also new was a Fleetwood Brougham coupe. No matter, the shock wave of the second energy crisis pushed production way down, to 230,028 units, including 39,344 Sevilles and 52,685 Eldorados.

	Restorable	Good	Excellent
Eldorado	$1,500-3,000	$3,000-4,500	$4,500-6,500
Eldo Biarritz	2,000-4,000	$4,000-6,000	$6,000-8,000
Seville (gasoline)	2,000-3,500	$3,500-5,000	$5,000-7,500
Fleetwood Brougham	1,500-2,500	$2,500-4,000	$4,000-5,000

1981

The humpback Seville returned little changed, identifiable via its new, vertical textured grille; cast

1979 Cadillac Eldorado coupe

1979 Cadillac Eldorado coupe

1979 Cadillac Seville Eleganté four-door sedan

1980 Cadillac Seville Eleganté four-door sedan

1980 Cadillac Eldorado Biarritz coupe

1981 Cadillac Eldorado coupe

1981 Cadillac Seville four-door sedan

1982 Cadillac Eldorado Touring Coupe

1982 Cadillac Fleetwood Brougham Coupe d'Elegance

1982 Cadillac Eldorado Biarritz coupe

aluminum wheels were standard, chrome wires optional. A controversial engine option this year was the "variable displacement" fuel-injected 368 V-8-6-4, standard on Eldorados. Designed to operate through a microprocessor on four, six, or eight cylinders as the situation demanded, this engine was fraught with problems, though collectors remind us that the system can easily be disabled to allow eight-cylinder operation only. Eldorados featured an on-board Computer Diagnostic System, larger red medallions in the new wheel covers, finer grillework, and an optional stiffer Touring Suspension. Total production edged up to 240,189, but Seville output plummeted to 28,631, while Eldorado increased to 60,643 units.

	Restorable	Good	Excellent
Eldorado	$1,500-3,000	$3,000-4,500	$4,500-6,500
Eldo Biarritz	2,000-4,000	$4,000-6,000	$6,000-8,000
Seville (gasoline)	2,000-3,500	$3,500-5,000	$5,000-7,500
Fleetwood Brgm	1,500-2,500	$2,500-4,000	$4,000-5,000
Fleetwood Limo	3,000-5,000	$5,000-7,000	$7,000-9,000

1982

Cadillac this year introduced what is generally considered a turkey: the Cimarron, its version of the GM front-drive J-body cars. With its 112-cid, 88-bhp four, it didn't sell very well (25,968 the first year)—and a lot of history-minded enthusiasts predicted as much. It is certainly not among the collectible Cadillacs. A new aluminum 4.1-liter (249-cid) V-8, the 125-bhp "HT-4100 DFI Power System," featured digital electronic fuel injection; it was coupled to a new four-speed overdrive automatic transmission and standard in all de Villes, Fleetwood Broughams, Eldorados, and Sevilles. The Seville diesel option was dropped, but a 252-cid, 125-bhp Buick V-6 was optional. The arrival of the HT-4100 makes the '82 Seville particularly desirable. A full cabriolet roof option was new to the Eldorado, but the limited-edition Touring Coupe was of far more interest to collectors. It featured the Touring Suspension, upgraded tires on aluminum wheels, cloisonné hood ornament, leather wrapped steering wheel, and Sterling Silver paint with red-over-black accent striping. Of the 235,584 cars built for '82, 19,998 were Sevilles, 52,018 Eldorados (including 1700 Touring Coupes), and 1000 Fleetwood limos (plus 450 commercial chassis).

	Restorable	Good	Excellent
Eldorado	$1,500-3,000	$3,000-4,500	$4,500-6,500
Eldo Biarritz	2,000-4,000	4,000-6,000	6,000-8,000
Eldo Touring Coupe	2,500-4,500	4,500-6,500	6,500-9,000
Seville	2,000-3,500	3,500-5,000	5,000-7,500
Fleetwood Brgm	1,500-2,500	2,500-4,000	4,000-5,000
Fleetwood Limo	3,000-5,000	5,000-7,500	7,500-9,500

1983

Cadillac production took an upturn to 292,814 units, due mainly to an improving economy. A new sound system, minor exterior trim changes, and a bit more horsepower (135) were changes for the Eldorado, which saw output jump to 67,416 units, 1197 of them Touring Coupes. The sound system, developed by GM Delco and Bose, was tuned to interior acoustics and had four integrated speaker/amp units. Similar changes attended the Seville, which featured a minor front-end facelift with Cadillac script on the grille, clear lenses for parking and turn signal lamps, and new optional aluminum wheels. Buyers drove 30,430 examples home.

	Restorable	Good	Excellent
Eldorado	$1,500-3,000	$3,000-4,500	$4,500-6,500
Eldo Biarritz	2,000-4,000	4,000-6,000	6,000-8,000
Eldo Touring Cpe	2,500-4,500	4,500-6,500	6,500-9,000
Seville	2,000-3,500	3,500-5,000	5,000-7,500
Fleetwood Brgm	1,500-2,500	2,500-4,000	4,000-5,000
Fleetwood Limo	3,500-5,500	5,500-8,000	8,000-10,000

1984

Cadillac offered its first convertible since 1976, the Eldorado Biarritz with power top, glass rear window, and rear side windows that raised or lowered automatically with the top. It was available in white, blue, or metallic red, all with a white top. Frame rails and crossmembers were reinforced, and the body structure bolstered for necessary rigidity. The top included a color-coordinated cloth headliner that improved sound insulation. The Seville received minor exterior changes and new upholstery options: knit cloth or optional leather and vinyl, both in a tufted pillow design. New aluminum alloy wheels were optional. Cadillac production picked up to 300,300 units, 39,997 being Sevilles. For Eldorado, output was 74,506 coupes, 3300 convertibles, and 815 Touring Coupes. The Fleetwood Brougham breakout was 39,650 sedans and 4500 coupes.

	Restorable	Good	Excellent
Eldorado	$1,500-3,000	$3,000-4,500	$4,500-6,500
Eldo Touring Cpe	2,500-4,500	4,500-6,500	6,500-9,000
Eldo Biarritz cvt	5,000-8,000	8,000-11,000	11,000-15,000
Seville	2,000-3,500	3,500-5,000	5,000-8,000
Fleetwood Brgm	1,500-2,500	2,500-4,000	4,000-6,000
Fleetwood Limo	3,500-5,500	5,500-8,000	8,000-11,000

1985

The front-drive Eldorado and Seville, sharing the same front-drive platform with the Buick Riviera and Olds Toronado, were putting in their last year before the next downsizing. This called for a specially trimmed Commemorative Edition Eldorado, which was limited to 2463 units. It's valued now in the neighborhood of the Touring Coupe. Optional for the Biarritz convertible, of which just 2300 were built, was an electric defogger for the glass rear window. It would not return for '86. A new spoked alloy wheel was available on both Eldo and Seville, while base Sevilles had an optional finned alloy wheel with gray color accents. Seville Eleganté models featured a new windshield designed to eliminate cuts from broken glass in accidents—this was not available on any other '85 Cadillac model. Total production in-

1984 Cadillac Fleetwood Brougham Sedan d'Elegance

1984 Cadillac Eldorado Biarritz convertible coupe

1984 Cadillac Seville four-door sedan

1985 Cadillac Eldorado coupe

1985 Cadillac Seville Eleganté four-door sedan

1986 Cadillac Eldorado coupe

1987 Cadillac Seville four-door sedan

creased to 332,767 units, though Seville held steady at 39,755. Of 55,450 Fleetwood Broughams, only 3000 were coupes, so the two-door was dropped at the end of the model run. Eldorado Touring Coupe orders fell to just 585, so it too disappeared (temporarily) after 1985. With only 405 built, Fleetwood limos were extremely rare this year. The all-new front-drive de Villes have thus far been of little interest to collectors.

	Restorable	Good	Excellent
Eldorado	$1,500-3,000	$3,000-4,500	$4,500-6,500
Eldo Touring Cpe	2,500-4,500	4,500-6,500	6,500-9,000
Eldo Biarritz cvt	5,000-8,000	8,000-11,000	11,000-15,000
Seville	2,500-4,000	4,000-6,000	6,000-9,000
Fleetwood Limo	4,500-6,500	6,500-9,500	9,500-13,000

1986

Cadillac redesigned the Eldorado and Seville, trimming length by over 16 inches and curb weight by more than 350 pounds. The humpback Seville thus departed, and models from this year forward generally have not achieved collectibility. Seville and Eldorado were built on the same front-drive chassis as the Riviera and Toronado, but Cadillac retained its unique 4.1-liter V-8, mounted transversely. Both cars were functionally the same under the skin. Exterior body panels used galvanized metal, which should strongly resist corrosion. Standard features included a floor-mount shift lever, digital instruments, and tilt steering wheel; real walnut veneer was standard on Seville and the top-line Eldorado Biarritz. The America II, a spring model commemorating America's Cup in yachting, sported white paint, metallic blue lower bodysides, turbine-spoke alloy wheels trimmed in blue, and leather interior. It was limited to 1500 copies, while the regular models saw 21,342 built. Seville faired even more poorly: 19,098. The Fleetwood Seventy-Five, meanwhile, found exactly 1000 buyers (plus 350 chassis).

	Restorable	Good	Excellent
Eldo Biarritz/ America II	$3,000-4,500	$4,500-6,000	$6,000-8,500
Fleetwood 75 limo	5,500-8,000	8,000-11,000	11,000-15,000

1987

A new and exciting "international" Cadillac, the Allanté, bowed as an intended rival to the Mercedes 560SL and Chrysler-Maserati Q-coupe, among others. Built on a shortened Eldorado platform with modified mechanicals, it listed for around $50,000. Interior and exterior design was by Pininfarina, who supplied bodies from a new facility near Turin, Italy. Up to 125 mph and a 0-60-mph time of 9.5 seconds were available from a tuned version of the aluminum 4.1 V-8, which boasted multi-point fuel injection, roller valve lifters, high-flow cylinder heads, and tuned intake manifold. The Allanté was an excellent effort, and low production—3363 the first year—suggests that it will eventually be highly collectible, but time must pass before that happens, and the cars are still depreciating at this writing. Cadillac production faltered to 283,183 units, which included 17,775

Eldorados and 302 Fleetwood Seventy-Five limos (plus 577 chassis).

	Restorable	Good	Excellent
Allanté	$10,000-12,000	$12,000-15,000	$15,000-17,000
Eldo Biarritz	3,500-5,000	5,000-8,000	8,000-10,000
Fleetwood 75 limo	8,000-9,500	9,500-12,500	12,500-15,000

1988

Two interior colors, a standard decklid power pull-down feature, and optional analog instruments were added to the Allanté, which could now be had in red and black as well as the original white, silver, gold, and maroon. The Eldorado was powered by a new 155-bhp 4.5-liter V-8, had new rear sheetmetal, and anti-lock brakes (ABS) as an option. The rear fenders stretched three inches longer, the back end was squared off with new vertical taillamps, the rear roof pillars were reshaped, and a new grille and hood rode up front. Worth looking for are Eldos with the optional Touring Suspension, which improved handling considerably. Eldorado production came to 22,968, while Allanté slid to 2569 units.

	Restorable	Good	Excellent
Allanté	$15,000-20,000	$20,000-22,500	$22,500-25,000
Eldo Biarritz	7,000-9,000	9,000-11,000	11,000-12,500
Fleetwood limo	10,000-13,000	$13,000-16,000	$16,000-18,000

1989

The Allanté now came with a larger, more powerful 200-bhp engine, so the 0-60-mph romp now took just 8.3 seconds, and top speed came in at about 135 mph. Also featured were variable-assist power steering, automatically adjusting shock absorbers, and bigger tires. The new 4.5-liter (273-cid) V-8 used the same aluminum block of other fwd Cadillacs, but came with a low-restriction exhaust. A plus was the manual soft top, which was much improved. The Eldorado still ran with a 155-bhp version of the 4.5 V-8, shared with the de Ville/Fleetwood line. Allanté output increased to 3296 units, and of the 27,807 Eldorados produced, 7174 had the Biarritz option.

	Restorable	Good	Excellent
Allanté	$20,000-24,000	$24,000-26,000	$26,000-29,000
Eldo Biarritz	9,000-10,500	10,500-12,500	12,500-14,000

1990

Allanté became the first front-drive car with traction control, a new standard feature using the anti-lock brake sensors to detect wheel slip during acceleration or steady cruising. Other improvements included a driver's-side airbag and retuned electronic shock absorbers. A compact disc player was added to the sound system. Revised exterior styling marked the '90 Eldo, which shared the Seville platform and 4.5-liter V-8, this year with multi-point fuel injection. Horsepower was up to 180. The body fea-

1988 Cadillac Allanté convertible coupe

1990 Cadillac Eldorado Touring Coupe

tured new bumper moldings, taillamps, and other minor design changes. Anti-lock brakes were optional. Reinstated this year was the Touring Coupe, which featured a leather and wood interior, Touring Suspension, special forged aluminum wheels, distinctive trim, and faster final gearing. Cadillac produced 23,036 Eldorados for the model year, but look instead for one of the 1507 Touring Coupes built. Allanté, meanwhile, accounted for 3101 sales.

	Restorable	Good	Excellent
Allanté	$23,000-27,000	$27,000-30,000	$30,000-34,000
Eldo Biarritz/ Touring Cpe	10,000-12,000	12,000-14,500	14,500-17,500

1963 Checker Marathon four-door sedan

1964 Checker Marathon four-door station wagon

1979 Checker Marathon four-door sedan

Checker

Kalamazoo's famous taxicab, produced in limited quantities as a passenger car, has a minor collector following, but the most interesting examples seem to be those Checkers decked out in commercial guise as taxis. Club support is good, and the mechanical parts supply is also good, but the body parts supply is poor. A Checker requires only a modest investment—but has much to be modest about.

1960-82

The Superba and passenger car version of the Checker taxi began production in 1960; a more deluxe Marathon model was added in 1962 and the Superba was dropped after 1963. All models had the familiar, upright, tank-like styling that was Checker's hallmark. (Checker president Morris Markin once turned down a request to take on the production of the defunct Studebaker Avanti because he "didn't want to build something so ugly.") Four-door sedans and wagons were offered through 1974, sedans only from 1975 to 1982. Between 1962 and '74, Checker also offered a limousine on a 129-inch wheelbase. Checker engines were initially Continental L-head sixes, later converted to overhead valves; Chevrolet sixes and V-8s were used after 1965. Sales usually ran 6000-7000 per year, Checker's best year being 1962 when 8173 cars were built. Still, about five-sixths of production comprised taxis. With the addition of girder-like five-mph "Federal" bumpers in 1974, a car that already looked dated now also became ugly. Though a handsome new Checker was designed by Ghia in 1970, it never entered production, and as Checker's cab business continued to decline, the company ceased car production in mid-1982.

	Restorable	Good	Excellent
Sedans & wagons	$500-2,000	$2,000-4,000	$4,000-6,500
Limousines	1,000-2,500	2,500-5,000	5,000-7,500

Chevrolet

Once an also-ran to such marques as Ford—and even Packard—in the early days of the car collecting avocation, Chevrolet during the Seventies became King of the Hill, with a vast following of enthusiasts and a score or more of active clubs producing professional publications and phenomenal national and local events. A strong parts and services industry exists, producing many excellent replicas of hard-to-find original parts. While Chevys of the '30s and early '40s have been as flat as comparable Fords recently, models of the '50s through early '70s are at their zenith as collectibles today, and cost a premium compared to similar models from Chevrolet's erstwhile rivals, or even its General Motors relatives. A Chevy Nomad wagon, for instance, costs considerably more than a Pontiac Safari in like condition. Club support and parts availability: excellent. Investment value: mixed, strongest between 1955 and 1970 model years, especially for Corvettes, Camaros, and muscle-car versions of Chevrolet and Chevelle.

1930-39

The Chevy Six, designed by Ormond Hunt to one-up Ford's four-cylinder Model A, produced 50 horsepower in 1930. With improvements over time, this solid, overhead-valve engine remained Chevy's standard powerplant for nearly three decades. For the 1933 Eagle and '34 Master, it got a new combustion chamber and longer stroke, and was known as the "Blue-Flame Six." In 1937, it was redesigned with "square" dimensions. Chevrolet began the Thirties with elegant little cars taking their styling cues from such GM bluebloods as Cadillac and LaSalle. By 1933, Chevys had Cadillac-type "No-Draft" ventilation, airplane-style instruments, and safety glass. "Knee-Action" independent front suspension arrived in 1934, streamlined styling in 1936, the new engine with 85 horsepower in 1937. A big plus in the sales battle with Ford was hydraulic brakes, which Chevy adopted for 1936. The most collectible Chevys from this period are the open models: roadsters, cabriolets, landaus, and phaetons in the early part of the decade, convertible coupes later. Wood-bodied station wagons, introduced as regular production models in 1939, are also highly desirable. Production during the '30s ranged from 313,404 cars in 1932 to a high of 918,278 in 1936, but despite the high numbers open Chevys were always relatively rare. For example, in 1936 Chevy built only 3629 2/4-passenger cabriolets.

	Restorable	Good	Excellent
1930-32 open	$5,000-12,500	$12,500-20,000	$20,000-32,500
1933-39 open	3,500-10,000	10,000-17,500	17,500-27,500
1930-32 coupes	2,500-6,000	6,000-12,000	12,000-17,500
1933-39 coupes	1,000-4,000	4,000-7,500	7,500-10,000

1930 Chevrolet Series AD Universal Coach two-door

1932 Chevrolet Series BA Confederate DeLuxe roadster

1934 Chevrolet Master Six coupe

1936 Chevrolet Master DeLuxe Sport Coupe

1937 Chevrolet Master Town Sedan

1939 Chevrolet Master 85 Town Sedan

1940 Chevrolet Master DeLuxe Sport Sedan

1940 Chevrolet Special DeLuxe four-door station wagon

1941 Chevrolet Master DeLuxe coupe

1941 Chevrolet Special DeLuxe four-door station wagon

1942 Chevrolet Special DeLuxe Fleetline Aerosedan

	Restorable	Good	Excellent
1930-32 sedans	1,500-4,500	4,500-9,500	9,500-14,000
1933-39 sedans	500-2,500	2,500-5,000	5,000-9,000
Station wagons	4,000-10,000	10,000-15,000	15,00-20,000

1940

Chevy listed three series for 1940: Master, Master DeLuxe, and Special DeLuxe.

After its absence in 1939, a convertible returned to the nicely facelifted line as a $898 Special DeLuxe, with leather upholstery and Chevy's first power-operated top, making it—and the handsome woody wagon—prime collectibles of almost equal value. The restyle, marked by a horizontal-bar grille, alligator-opening hood, and semi-integrated headlights, benefitted from a slightly longer 113-inch wheelbase, and sealed beam headlamps were provided for the first time. After building 577,278 cars for 1939, production climbed to 764,616 for 1940, but only 11,829 were ragtops. Still, that was more than any open Chevy model had sold in some years. The eight-passenger wagons came in two flavors, $903 Master and $934 Special DeLuxe, but output was only 411 and 2493 units, respectively. Most often called for was the $761 Town (two-door) Sedan, of which 205,910 were produced. Coupes were surprisingly popular: 125,989 in all three series, well over half Special DeLuxes.

	Restorable	Good	Excellent
Convertible	$4,000-10,000	$10,000-17,000	$17,000-25,000
Wagons	4,000-10,000	10,000-16,000	16,000-24,000
Coupes	1,500-4,500	4,500-8,500	8,500-13,000
Sedans	1,000-3,500	3,500-7,000	7,000-10,000

1941

A major facelift resulted in one of the best styled Chevrolets in history, producing huge sales: 1,008,976. The elegant $949 Special DeLuxe convertible (15,296 built) and $995 Special DeLuxe woody wagon (2045 built) head the most wanted list, but the $877 Special DeLuxe Fleetline sedan (34,162 built) with its formal blind quarters also attracts attention. Performance was up five bhp to 90, but still didn't rank with that of Ford's V-8. For this year, the Master series was dropped, so only 11 models were offered instead of 14. Optional vacuum shift allowed fingertip gear changes.

	Restorable	Good	Excellent
Convertible	$4,000-10,000	$10,000-17,000	$17,000-27,000
Wagon	4,000-10,000	10,000-16,000	16,000-28,000
Coupes	1,500-4,000	4,000-7,500	7,500-11,500
Sedans	1,000-3,500	3,500-7,000	7,000-9,500

1942

General Motors restyled heavily for 1942, with Chevrolets gaining new "fadeaway" fenders that extended into the front doors. The grille was also heavier and more "important" looking. Two interesting models in the new, luxurious Fleetline series were the two-door fastback Aerosedan and the four-door notchback Sportmaster sedan, identifiable by their three chrome speedlines decorating front and rear fenders. Production ceased in early February 1942 after just 254,885 cars had been built, and the last of them were almost devoid of chrome, with grilles and hubcaps painted. This year, only 1182 convertibles and 1057 wagons were produced. The Aerosedan and Sportmaster were more numerous with 61,885 and 14,530 built.

	Restorable	Good	Excellent
Convertible	$4,000-10,000	$10,000-17,000	$17,000-27,000
Wagon	4,000-10,000	10,000-16,000	16,000-28,000
Coupes	1,500-3,500	3,500-7,000	7,000-10,000
Sedans	1,000-3,000	3,000-6,000	6,000-8,500
Fleetlines	1,500-4,500	4,500-7,000	7,000-10,000

1946

The first postwar Chevrolets were close copies of the 1942 models, identifiable by their new grille with a smooth curved chrome surround and four (rather than six) horizontal bars. The old Master and Master Deluxe series were now called Stylemaster and Fleetmaster, respectively. The Fleetmaster convertible and wagon rank as the most desirable collectibles, although the Fleetline series continued with the Aerosedan two-door fastback and Sportmaster four-door sedan. Output reached 398,028 units, including 4508 ragtops, 804 wagons, 57,932 Aerosedans, and 7501 Sportmasters.

	Restorable	Good	Excellent
Convertible	$4,000-10,000	$10,000-14,000	$14,000-23,000
Wagon	4,000-10,000	10,000-15,000	15,000-25,000
Coupes	1,500-3,500	3,500-7,000	7,000-9,500
Sedans	1,000-3,000	3,000-6,000	6,000-8,500
Fleetlines	1,500-4,500	4,500-7,000	7,000-10,000

1947

A full-width four-bar grille distinguished the 1947 models. Fleetlines were becoming extremely popular despite their slightly higher cost, about $30, and these cars remain sought after by modern collectors. The $1371 Sportmaster four-door's blind-quarter sedan body wasn't quite as dashing as the $1313 Aerosedan's two-door fastback, so even though more common the Aerosedans are worth a fraction more than Sportmasters in comparable condition—production was 159,407 and 54,531. The Stylemaster and Fleetmaster sport coupes, of which 94,174 were built in total, are bargain collectibles which make for pleasant ownership on a low budget. Convertible output spurted this year to 28,443 units, while the wagon increased to 4912.

	Restorable	Good	Excellent
Convertible	$4,000-10,000	$10,000-14,000	$14,000-23,000
Wagon	4,000-10,000	10,000-15,000	15,000-25,000
Coupe	1,500-3,500	3,500-7,000	7,000-9,500
Sedans	1,000-3,000	3,000-6,000	6,000-8,500
Fleetlines	1,500-4,500	4,500-7,000	7,000-10,000

1942 Chevrolet Special DeLuxe Fleetline Sportmaster

1946 Chevrolet Fleetline Aerosedan

1946 Chevrolet Fleetmaster convertible coupe

1947 Chevrolet Fleetmaster four-door station wagon

1948 Chevrolet Fleetline Sportmaster Sedan

1948 Chevrolet Fleetmaster four-door sedan

1949 Chevrolet Styleline DeLuxe "woody" wagon

1949 Chevrolet Styleline DeLuxe four-door sedan

1948

A revised grille sporting a bold vertical center bar was the final refinement of Chevrolet's prewar styling, due for replacement in 1949. Coupes and the $1434 Aerosedan, which look great and are nice to drive, were built in large numbers: 111,695 and 211,861, respectively. The $2013 wagon was Chevy's last to make liberal use of genuine wood. This was also the final year for Chevrolet's vacuum gearshift and foot-operated starter. Also, engines acquired interchangeable main bearings, which can make a difference during overhauls. Production edged upward to 696,449 units, of which 20,471 were ragtops, 10,171 wagons.

	Restorable	Good	Excellent
Convertible	$4,000-10,000	$10,000-14,000	$14,000-24,000
Wagon	4,000-10,000	10,000-15,000	15,000-26,000
Coupes	1,500-3,500	3,500-7,000	7,000-9,500
Sedans	1,000-3,000	3,000-6,000	6,000-8,500
Fleetlines	1,500-4,500	4,500-7,000	7,000-10,500

1949

An all-new postwar design featuring smooth, rounded lines looked rather larger, but concealed a powertrain that hadn't changed much. Both wood- and steel-paneled Styleline DeLuxe station wagons were offered at $2267. Though it used less timber, the woody was the last of its type, and is worth more. It was also rarer: 3342, compared to 6006 all-steel models, which offered simulated wood trim. The handsome Styleline DeLuxe convertible appealed to 32,392 buyers. Unlike Ford and Plymouth, Chevy hedged its bets by offering not only Styleline notchback sedans, but Fleetline two- and four-door fastbacks. Though less popular than the notchbacks when new, the fastbacks are sought out now, especially in the chromier DeLuxe—as opposed to plainer Special—trim. Also popular, with 108,432 built, was the Styleline Sport Coupe (and business coupe) with a sportier-looking long rear deck. The '49s haven't caught on to the degree of the earlier postwar Chevys, but nevertheless appeal to a legion of fans.

	Restorable	Good	Excellent
Convertible	$4,000-9,000	$9,000-16,000	$16,000-23,000
Wagon (wood)	3,000-7,500	7,500-12,500	12,500-17,500
Wagon (steel)	1,500-4,000	4,000-7,000	7,000-10,000
Styleline Sport Cpe	1,250-3,000	3,000-6,000	6,000-9,000
Other models	1,000-2,500	2,500-5,000	5,000-7,500

1950

Introduced less than a year after the Cadillac, Oldsmobile, and Buick hardtops, the pretty new $1741 Styleline DeLuxe Bel Air offered the virtues of a convertible without the wind-in-the-hair and rain-in-the-face drawbacks. Extremely well trimmed, it outsold the ragtop 76,662 to 32,810. On today's market, it costs less than half the price of a comparable ragtop. The woody wagon was dropped, and production of the all-steel wagon, reduced to $1994, soared to 166,995 units. Powerglide two-speed automatic was new—and popular—and came with a larger 235.5-cid, 105-bhp six. At the low end of the price scale, the two-door Fleetline fastback is a better investment than the notchback: more distinctive, just a few dollars more. Despite an extremely modest facelift that included minor grille and taillight changes, 1950 was a banner year for Chevy as production increased from 1,118,308 in 1949 to 1,498,590.

	Restorable	Good	Excellent
Convertible	$4,500-9,000	$9,000-16,000	$16,000-24,000
Wagon	1,500-4,000	4,000-7,000	7,000-10,000
Styleline Sport Cpe	1,250-3,000	3,000-6,000	6,000-9,000
Styleline Bel Air	1,500-4,000	4,000-7,500	7,500-10,500
Other models	1,000-2,500	2,500-5,000	5,000-7,500

1950 Chevrolet Styleline DeLuxe four-door sedan

1951 Chevrolet Styleline DeLuxe convertible coupe

1951 Chevrolet Styleline DeLuxe Bel Air hardtop coupe

1951

This year was a virtual repeat of 1950 as to model offerings, but a slightly more ambitious restyle—featuring new grille, side trim, and taillights mounted on squared-off rear fenders—kept the cars looking fresh. The Bel Air hardtop, which found 103,356 buyers, remains a good buy; convertibles, down to 20,172 units for '51, are expensive, but cheaper than comparable '51 Fords. Two-door Fleetline fastbacks were still available, along with a four-door that didn't wear the angled body quite as handsomely. Model year production retreated to 1,229,986 units, while wagon output plummeted to 23,586. Sport Coupes, including the business coupe, attracted 100,977 shoppers.

	Restorable	Good	Excellent
Convertible	$4,500-9,000	$9,000-16,000	$16,000-24,000
Wagon	1,500-4,000	4,000-7,000	7,000-10,000
Styleline Sport Cpe	1,250-3,000	3,000-6,000	6,000-9,000
Styleline Bel Air	1,500-4,000	4,000-7,500	7,500-11,000
Other models	1,000-2,500	2,500-5,000	5,000-7,500

1952 Chevrolet Styleline DeLuxe four-door sedan

1952 Chevrolet Styleline DeLuxe convertible coupe

1952

Little more than a toothier grille, wider parking lights, and revised side trim differentiated the final examples of the first postwar restyle. Fastbacks were now waning in popularity, so only the Fleetline DeLuxe two-door sedan remained—a distinctive, even rakish body that appealed to just 37,164 buyers in 1952—and is often overlooked by today's collectors. Styleline Specials had less chrome than DeLuxe models, and are valued a few hundred dollars lower, so the DeLuxe is a better investment. The $2006 Bel Air, with its wrapped backlight and convertible-style interior remains a bargain on today's market; output was down to 74,634 examples. The $2128 convertible slipped further to 11,975 units, while the $2,297 wagon dropped to 12,756.

	Restorable	Good	Excellent
Convertible	$4,500-9,000	$9,000-16,000	$16,000-25,000
Wagon	1,500-4,000	4,000-7,000	7,000-10,500
Styleline Sport Cpe	1,250-3,000	3,000-6,000	6,000-9,000

1953 Chevrolet Bel Air hardtop coupe

1953 Chevrolet Two-Ten DeLuxe Handyman wagon

1953 Chevrolet Bel Air four-door sedan

1954 Chevrolet Bel Air four-door sedan

	Restorable	Good	Excellent
Styleline Bel Air	1,500-4,000	4,000-7,500	7,500-11,500
Other models	1,000-2,500	2,500-5,000	5,000-7,500

1953

Chevrolet was reskinned for 1953, with a boxier, shorter, taller design highlighted by colorful trim and clean lines. Except for the convertible—24,047 Bel Airs and 5617 Two-Tens were produced—all remain low-budget collectibles, overshadowed by the 1955-57 models. Two-tone paint jobs applied the roof color to rear fender sweep panels on Bel Airs, now a four-model series. Engines had more power: 105 and 115 bhp. The top-line Bel Airs are far more desirable than the cheaper trimmed One-Fiftys or mid-line Two-Tens. The Corvette sports car made its debut at mid-year, all being white with a 150-bhp six-cylinder engine and Powerglide automatic. With only 300 built, they rank today among the cream of '50s collector cars. Following a government dictated production cutback to 818,142 cars for '52 (because of the Korean War), output bounced back to 1,346,475 for '53. Of that, 99,028 were Bel Air hardtops and 14,045 were Two-Ten hardtops. Station wagons, now in three models, nailed down 48,654 sales.

	Restorable	Good	Excellent
Corvette	$10,000-20,000	$20,000-35,000	$35,000-55,000
Bel Air cvt	6,000-12,000	12,000-20,000	20,000-30,000
Bel Air htp	2,500-5,000	5,000-8,000	8,000-13,000
Bel Air sdn & cpe	1,250-3,500	3,500-5,500	5,500-8,500
Two-Ten cvt	4,000-10,000	10,000-18,000	18,000-26,000
Wagons	1,500-3,000	3,000-6,500	6,500-9,500
Other models	1,000-2,500	2,500-5,000	5,000-7,500

1954

A modest facelift gave the second year of this styling sequence a cleaner look, especially at the front and rear. The "floating" grille was flanked by oblong parking lights, while the smoother taillights/back-up lights were integrated vertically. Engine power rose to 115, 125 with Powerglide. Lacking the funds for a Bel Air ragtop or hardtop (19,383 and 66,378 built), collectors should consider a Two-Ten Delray two-door. Sporting an attractive vinyl interior, it accounted for 66,403 sales. Bel Air sedans, also nicely trimmed, were popular: 143,573 two-doors and 248,750 four-doors. The '54 Corvette, though hardly bargain-priced, is less costly than the '53 because 3640 were produced for the model year. Total model year car production dipped to 1,143,561 units.

	Restorable	Good	Excellent
Corvette	$10,000-20,000	$20,000-30,000	$30,000-45,000
Bel Air cvt	6,000-12,000	12,000-20,000	20,000-31,000
Bel Air htp	2,500-5,000	5,000-8,000	8,000-13,000
Bel Air sdn & cpe	1,250-3500	3,500-5,500	5,500-8,500
Two-Ten Delray cpe	1,250-4,000	4,000-6,000	6,000-8,000
Wagons	1,500-3,000	3,000-6,500	6,500-9,000
Other models	1,000-2,500	2,500-5,000	5,000-7,500

1955

It was an all-new Chevrolet in its time, but today it's a modern classic: the memorable '55, packing a 265-cid V-8 with 162 and 180 bhp as an option to the traditional six. Its boxy profile, colorful paint and trim, and famous eggcrate grille add up to a package that costs plenty, relative to other Chevys. The low-end One-Fifty two-door (66,416 built) would be a budget choice, especially with the V-8 and stick shift. Highly collectible: the hardtop-like Nomad wagon, its styling derived from a 1954 GM Motorama show car. Just 8386 were called for. Factory air conditioning or the presence of Power-Pack V-8s sends values skyward, whereas six-cylinder examples are worth considerably less. Production totaled 1,704,667 cars, with the highly desirable Bel Air convertible and Sport Coupe scoring 41,292 and 185,562 units. The Two-Ten Sport Coupe was plainer and rarer; 11,675 were sold. Nearly all of the 674 '55 Corvettes built carried a V-8, and some had manual shift.

	Restorable	Good	Excellent
Corvette	$9,000-20,000	$20,000-35,000	$35,000-60,000
Bel air cvt	5,500-12,000	12,000-24,000	24,000-36,000
Bel Air Nomad wgn	4,000-9,000	9,000-16,000	16,000-25,000
Bel Air htp	4,500-10,000	10,000-18,000	18,000-28,000
Bel Air Beauville wgn	1,500-4,000	4,000-8,000	8,000-12,500
Bel Air sedans	1,500-4,000	4,000-8,000	8,000-12,000
Two-Ten htp	3,500-8,000	8,000-14,000	14,000-21,000
Two-Ten Delray cpe	1,500-5,000	5,000-8,000	8,000-12,500
Two-Ten, other	1,000-3,000	3,000-5,500	5,500-9,500
Handyman wgn	1,000-3,000	3,000-5,500	5,500-8,500
One-Fifty, other	1,000-3,000	3,000-5,000	5,000-7,500

1955 Chevrolet Bel Air Sport Coupe hardtop

1955 Chevrolet Bel Air Beauville four-door wagon

1956 Chevrolet Two-Ten Townsman four-door wagon

1956 Chevrolet Corvette convertible coupe

1956

Although appearance was brighter and brasher than in 1955, the facelifted '56 Chevy—with its massive grille, revised side trim, and chromier taillights—never caught on to the same degree, then or now. Production dropped to 1,567,117 cars. A handsome Bel Air four-door hardtop Sport Sedan joined the line, attracting 103,602 buyers, but isn't a prime collectible. Two-door Sport Coupes (128,382 built) are better bets, and cost more, while the convertible (41,268 built) is still the most desirable. Nomad fell back to just 7886 units. With twin four-barrel carbs, the 265 V-8 developed up to 225 bhp, but lots of sixes were sold. Corvette's second-generation model rebounded to 3467 sales, helped by rakish styling with concave body sculptures, a neater front end, smoother rear end, and a 225 bhp V-8. Look for 'Vettes with the optional hardtop.

	Restorable	Good	Excellent
Corvette	$10,000-20,000	$20,000-40,000	$40,000-65,000
Bel air cvt	5,000-11,000	11,000-22,000	22,000-33,000
Bel Air Nomad wgn	3,500-8,000	8,000-14,000	14,000-22,000
Bel Air 2d htp	4,000-10,000	10,000-17,000	17,000-26,000
Bel Air 4d htp	1,500-4,000	4,000-8,000	8,000-12,000
Bel Air Beauville wgn	1,500-4,000	4,000-7,500	7,500-11,500

1957 Chevrolet Bel Air convertible coupe

1957 Chevrolet Bel Air Sport Coupe hardtop

1958 Chevrolet Bel Air Impala convertible coupe

1958 Chevrolet Bel Air Impala Sport Coupe hardtop

1958 Chevrolet Corvette convertible coupe

	Restorable	Good	Excellent
Bel Air sedans	1,250-4,000	4,000-7,000	7,000-10,000
Two-Ten 2d htp	3,000-7,000	7,000-13,000	13,000-19,000
Two-Ten Delray cpe	1,500-4,500	4,500-7,500	7,500-12,000
Two-Ten, other	1,000-3,500	3,500-5,500	5,500-9,000
Handyman wgn	1,000-3,000	3,000-5,000	5,000-8,000
One-Fifty, other	1,000-3,000	3,000-5,000	5,000-7,000

1957

Probably the most popular Chevrolet of all, the '57 wasn't viewed as notable by Chevy at the time—merely a rehash of the 1955 body to keep it competitive with all-new Fords and Plymouths. But the facelift, marked by sharp tailfins and a combination bumper-grille, was a good one. With it came a larger, 283-cid V-8 packing up to 270 bhp with standard carburetion, 283 with Ramjet fuel injection. Among collectors of the "classic" 1955-57 Chevys, the '57s are considered by many to be the most desirable of the three years. They weren't the most numerous, however, as production eased off to 1,505,910 units. Included among the Bel Airs were 166,426 Sport Coupes, 137,672 Sport Sedans, 47,562 convertibles, and 6103 Nomads. Two-Tens accounted for 22,631 Sport Coupes and 16,178 Sport Sedans. The Corvette, slightly facelifted, also benefitted from the new 283 V-8, and "fuelie" 'Vettes developed a phenomenal 250 and 283 horsepower. No wonder production nearly doubled to 6339.

	Restorable	Good	Excellent
Corvette	$10,000-20,000	$20,000-45,000	$45,000-65,000
Bel Air cvt	7,500-15,000	15,000-27,500	27,500-39,000
Bel Air Nomad wgn	4,500-10,000	10,000-16,000	16,000-25,000
Bel Air 2d htp	4,000-10,000	10,000-17,000	17,000-26,000
Bel Air 4d htp	1,500-4,000	4,000-8,000	8,000-12,000
Bel Air Beauville wgn	1,500-4,000	4,000-7,500	7,500-11,500
Bel Air sedans	1,250-4,000	4,000-7,000	7,000-12,000
Two-Ten 2d htp	4,000-8,000	8,000-14000	14,000-20,000
Two-Ten, other	1,000-3,500	3,500-6,500	6,500-10,000
One-Ten, all	500-2,500	2,500-5,000	5,000-8,000

1958

Not until recently did the '58 Chevrolets hit their peak value, having long been eclipsed by their 1955-57 predecessors. The new longer, lower, heavier bodyshell lasted only one year, trading the former angles for rounded corners and shedding tailfins. Six engine choices were available, led by a 348-cid V-8 with up to 315 horsepower. Best buy: the Impala two-door hardtop and convertible, part of the Bel Air series. They sold well—55,989 ragtops and an estimated 43,000 Sport Coupes in a recession year that knocked Chevy production to 1,142,460 cars. Bel Airs (not including Impala) nudged a half-million units. The Nomad, though it commands a premium compared to other wagons, adopted a conventional wagon style. Corvette was restyled again with quad headlamps in a more ornate, bulkier body with better handling and outstanding performance, and was rewarded with a 47-percent increase in output to 9168 units.

	Restorable	Good	Excellent
Corvette	$7,000-15,000	$15,000-30,000	$30,000-55,000
Bel Air Impala cvt	8,000-15,000	15,000-30,000	30,000-45,000
Bel Air Impala htp	5,000-12,000	12,000-20,000	20,000-30,000
Bel Air 2d htp	2,000-5,000	5,000-9,000	9,000-15,000
Bel Air, other	1,000-3,000	3,000-5,500	5,500-8,000
Nomad 4d wagon	1,250-3,500	3,500-6,000	6,000-9,500
Other models	750-2,500	2,500-4,500	4,500-7,000

1959

Swoopy horizontal "bat-wing" tailfins above huge "cats-eye" taillights and a decklid "large enough to land a Piper Cub" (according to *Mechanix Illustrated*'s Tom McCahill) gave the '59 Chevy's back end a massive look. Derided by some, cheered by others, it was Chevy's version of '50s excess. A dozen horsepower ratings were offered with the six and 283 and 348 V-8s. As a result of its 1958 popularity, Impala became a separate top-line series listing four body styles. Of the approximately 473,000 built, 65,800 were convertibles. With 1,462,140 total cars produced, Chevy just barely edged out the conservatively styled '59 Ford in model year production, but lost the calendar year race. Corvettes, listing at $3875, tossed aside their simulated hood louvers, but added trailing radius rods to halt rear axle windup under hard acceleration. Production moved up to 9670 units.

	Restorable	Good	Excellent
Corvette	$7,000-14,000	$14,000-28,000	$28,000-50,000
Impala cvt	5,000-12,000	12,000-22,000	22,000-33,000
Impala 2d htp	3,000-8,000	8,000-13,000	13,000-20,000
Impala, other	1,500-3,000	3,000-5,000	5,000-8,000
Other models	1,000-2,000	2,000-4,000	4,000-7,000

1960

Chevrolet launched its Volkswagen-killer, the air-cooled, rear-engine Corvair—the most sophisticated of the Big Three's new compacts designed to stem the import invasion. The mid-year Monza began the craze for bucket-seat, stick-shift compact coupes with luxurious interiors. Engineered by a talented team led by Ed Cole, the Corvair was a technical marvel—but early models were troublesome, tending to leak oil, throw fanbelts, and oversteer with gay abandon. The nearly identical Corvette got a rear anti-sway bar to improve handling, and saw sales improve to just over 10,000 units for the first time. After the wild '59s, the big Chevys looked tamer, and perhaps less interesting to collectors. Smaller, round taillights, two or three per side, rode below clipped-back tailfins. Total Chevy production this year came to 1,653,168 cars. The new Corvair accounted for 250,007 units, but only 11,926 were the more desirable Monza coupes.

	Restorable	Good	Excellent
Corvette	$7,500-15,000	$15,000-30,000	$30,000-50,000

1959 Chevrolet Impala convertible coupe

1959 Chevrolet Parkwood four-door station wagon

1959 Chevrolet El Camino pickup truck

1960 Chevrolet Impala convertible coupe

1960 Chevrolet Corvair 500 four-door sedan

1961 Chevrolet Impala Sport Coupe hardtop

1961 Chevrolet Bel Air Sport Coupe hardtop

1961 Chevrolet Corvair 700 Lakewood four-door wagon

1961 Chevrolet Corvette convertible coupe

1962 Chevrolet Bel Air Sport Coupe hardtop

	Restorable	Good	Excellent
Impala cvt	5,000-10,000	10,000-20,000	20,000-30,000
Impala 2d htp	2,000-6,000	6,000-10,000	10,000-16,000
Impala, other	1,250-3,000	3,000-5,000	5,000-7,500
Bel Air 2d htp	1,250-3,000	3,000-5,000	5,000-8,000
Corvair Monza	1,250-3,000	3,000-5,000	5,000-8,000
Corvair, other	1,000-2,500	2,500-4,000	4,000-6,000
Other models	1,000-2,000	2,000-4,000	4,000-6,500

1961

Corvair added a pair of appealing Lakewood station wagons, unique low-production cars much prized by Corvair collectors today, plus an optional four-speed stick shift, now equally desirable. Output rose to 282,075, but only 25,042 were wagons. Monza, meanwhile, enjoyed a good year: 109,945 coupes and 33,745 four-door sedans. Sport Coupe versions of the restyled full-size body boasted a long, airy "bubbletop" roofline with massive quarter windows, an excellent basis for the new Super Sport package with bucket seats. Only 453 examples of the prized SS convertible were built, and just 142 had the mighty 409-cid V-8 instead of the usual 348. Impalas accounted for about 426,400 sales, with ragtops still strong at 64,600. Corvette sported a new "duck-tail" rear-end design prefiguring the shape of the forthcoming '63 Sting Ray; up front rode a new mesh grille. Sales increased to 10,939 units.

	Restorable	Good	Excellent
Corvette	$6,500-12,000	$12,000-24,000	$24,000-42,000
Impala cvt	4,000-10,000	10,000-16,000	16,000-23,000
Impala SS cvt	5,000-12,000	12,000-18,000	18,000-30,000
Impala 2d htp	2,000-5,000	5,000-9,000	9,000-14,000
Impala SS 2d htp	3,000-7,000	7,000-12,000	12,000-20,000
Impala, other	1,250-3,000	3,000-5,000	5,000-7,500
Bel Air 2d htp	2,000-5,000	5,000-8,000	8,000-13,000
Corvair Monza cpe	1,250-3,000	3,000-5,000	5,000-8,000
Corvair, other	1,000-2,500	2,500-4,000	4,000-6,000
Other models	1,000-2,000	2,000-4,000	4,000-7,000

1962

A more conventional compact, Chevy II, arrived to do battle with Ford's Falcon, which the Corvair hadn't accomplished. Chevy IIs were powered by fours or sixes; top-line Novas—59,586 hardtops and 23,741 convertibles—are low-budget collector cars. Super Sport trim was now available on most Impalas, but the hardtop and ragtop are most prized, especially with the 409 V-8, which adds plenty to their value. How many of the 704,900 Impalas built were SS models isn't known. Corvair's new Monza Spyder convertible and coupe (2574 and 6894 built) had a 150-bhp turbocharged engine and a load of sporty extras. The 2362 Monza wagons produced are scarcer than Spyders, and nearly as costly. A 327-cid V-8 with 250-360 horsepower boosted Corvette performance, and its bodyside "cove" molding was de-emphasized, its grille blacked out, and anodized aluminum trim graced the rocker panels. Looking a lot like the classic '63, it attracted 14,531 buyers, making it a hot item today.

	Restorable	Good	Excellent
Corvette	$7,000-15,000	$15,000-30,000	$30,000-48,000

	Restorable	Good	Excellent
Impala cvt	4,000-10,000	10,000-16,000	16,000-25,000
Impala SS cvt	5,000-12,000	12,000-19,000	19,000-30,000
Impala 2d htp	2,500-6,000	6,000-10,000	10,000-16,000
Impala SS 2d htp	3,000-7,000	7,000-12,000	12,000-20,000
Impala, other	1,000-3,000	3,000-5,000	5,000-8,000
Bel Air 2d htp	2,000-5,000	5,000-8,000	8,000-13,000
Other full-size	750-2,000	2,000-4,000	4,000-5,500
Corvair			
Monza cvt	2,000-3,500	3,500-6,000	6,000-9,000
Monza wgn	2,000-4,000	4,000-6,000	6,000-8,500
Monza Spyder cvt	2,000-5,000	5,000-7,500	7,500-12,000
Monza Spyder cpe	1,500-4,000	4,000-6,500	6,500-10,000
Other models	1,000-2,500	2,500-4,500	4,500-6,500
Chevy II			
Convertible	1,500-3,000	3,000-6,000	6,000-10,000
Other models	500-1,500	1,500-3,000	3,000-5,000

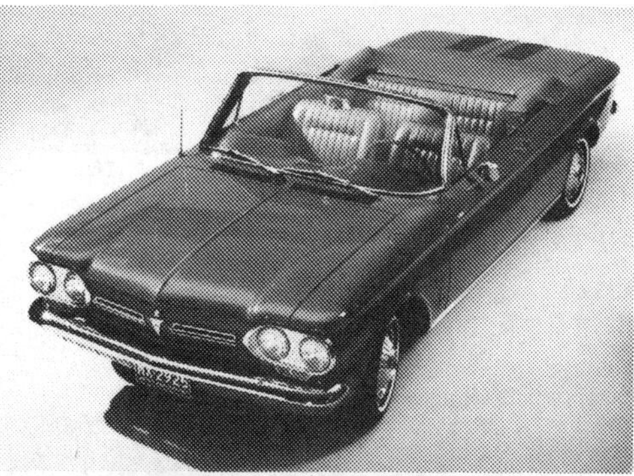

1962 Chevrolet Corvair Monza convertible coupe

1963

The new Corvette Sting Ray, with brilliant styling derived from the "Mako Shark" and other 'Vette show cars, was the sensation of the year for Chevrolet. Sporting hidden headlights, split backlight, and a "twin-cockpit" interior, it was the best 'Vette yet. Though expensive today, it remains loaded with investment potential; note that the coupe's split rear window was only offered this year—a factor making it as valuable as the convertible, which is rare for any closed body style. Though other Chevy series received only facelifts, production increased from about 2,072,000 cars to 2,148,000. Of interest: 87,415 and 24,823 Chevy II Nova hardtops and ragtops; 832,600 Impalas, including SS models; 117,917 and 36,693 Corvair Monza coupes and soft tops, plus 11,627 and 7472 Monza Spyder coupes and ragtops; 10,594 and 10,919 Corvette coupes and soft tops.

1963 Chevrolet Impala SS convertible coupe

1963 Chevrolet Corvette Sting Ray coupe

	Restorable	Good	Excellent
Corvette	$8,000-15,000	$15,000-30,000	$30,000-45,000
	(add $3,000 for 360 bhp, $2,000 for 340 bhp)		
Impala cvt	4,000-9,000	9,000-15,000	15,000-24,000
Impala SS cvt	5,000-11,000	11,000-18,000	18,000-28,000
Impala 2d htp	2,500-6,000	6,000-10,000	10,000-15,000
Impala SS 2d htp	3,000-7,000	7,000-12,000	12,000-18,000
Impala, other	1,000-3,000	3,000-5,000	5,000-7,500
Other full-size	750-2,000	2,000-4,000	4,000-5,500
Corvair			
Monza cvt	2,000-3,500	3,500-6,000	6,000-9,000
Monza Spyder cvt	2,000-5,000	5,000-7,500	7,500-12,000
Monza Spyder cpe	1,500-4,000	4,000-6,500	6,500-10,000
Other models	1,000-2,500	2,500-4,500	4,500-6,500
Chevy II			
Convertible	2,000-3,500	3,500-7,000	7,000-11,500
Other models	500-1,500	1,500-3,000	3,000-5,000

1964

With the addition of the mid-size Chevelle, another Chevy was eligible for SS equipment. Among workaday Chevelles, the Malibu line costs less than a big Impala, and is slower to draw collectors. A Malibu hardtop or soft top with V-8 is the best in-

1964 Chevrolet Impala convertible coupe

1964 Chevrolet Chevelle Malibu SS Sport Coupe

1964 Chevrolet Corvair Monza Spyder convertible

1965 Chevrolet Caprice hardtop sedan

vestment—78,800 of both body styles were built with all engine combinations. The Nova lost its ragtop, leaving only bucket-seat SS and bench-seat Sport Coupe hardtops (10,576 and 20,251 built), but they could have the 283 or 327 V-8, making them stormers. Chassis changes improved Corvair's handling dramatically, and a larger 164-cid flat six with 95-150 horses was available. Spyder output was 6480 coupes and 4761 ragtops. Big Chevy Impalas and SS models, sporting revised sheetmetal, reached nearly 900,000 units, but only a few got the 425-bhp 409 V-8. The Corvette coupe lost its distinctive split window, and both coupe and roadster (8304 and 13,925 produced) sported cleaner styling details.

	Restorable	Good	Excellent
Corvette cvt	$8,000-14,000	$14,000-27,000	$27,000-43,000
Corvette cpe	6,000-12,000	12,000-24,000	24,000-39,00
(add $6,000 for 375 bhp, $3,000 for 365 bhp)			
Impala cvt	4,000-9,000	9,000-15,000	15,000-23,000
Impala SS cvt	5,000-10,000	10,000-17,000	17,000-27,000
Impala 2d htp	2,500-6,000	6,000-10,000	10,000-15,000
Impala SS 2d htp	3,000-7,000	7,000-12,000	12,000-19,000
Impala, other	1,000-3,000	3,000-5,000	5,000-7,500
Other full-size	750-2,000	2,000-4,000	4,000-5,500
Corvair			
Monza cvt	2,000-3,500	3,500-6,000	6,000-9,000
Monza Spyder cvt	2,000-5,000	5,000-7,500	7,500-12,000
Monza Spyder cpe	1,500-4,000	4,000-6,500	6,500-10,000
Other models	1,000-2,500	2,500-4,500	4,500-6,500
Chevy II			
Nova SS cpe	1,500-3,500	3,500-7,000	7,000-12,000
Other models	500-1,500	1,500-3,000	3,000-5,000
Chevelle			
Malibu cvt	4,000-8,000	8,000-12,000	12,000-20,000
Malibu SS cvt	5,000-9,000	9,000-14,000	14,000-24,000
Malibu 2d htp	2,000-5,000	5,000-8,000	8,000-14,000
Malibu SS 2d htp	3,000-6,000	6,000-10,000	10,000-17,000
Other models	500-2,000	2000-3,500	3,500-5,500

1965

After four years of subtle "grille" changes, a dramatic restyling produced a magnificent new Corvair hailed as one of the classic pieces of '60s industrial design. Topping the line was the Corsa, available with a 140-bhp or optional 180-bhp turbocharged flat six. Some 20,291 coupes and 8353 convertibles were sold; Monzas were four times as numerous. Full-size Chevys were also completely new, gaining a bulkier appearance. Collector interest from this point on is modest, even for the Super Sport models, of which nearly a quarter of a million were built (27,842 of them ragtops). A Chevelle Malibu SS with the 327 V-8 is worth a look—much more so any of the 201 SS 396s produced. Only 9100 little-changed Nova Super Sports were requested, but about half of them were pleasingly quick because they got 283 or 327 V-8s. Corvettes sported functional triple front fender louvers, and a few got the first Mark IV 396 V-8 with a whopping 425 horsepower. 'Vettes numbered 8186 coupes and 15,376 soft tops.

	Restorable	Good	Excellent
Corvette cvt	$8,000-14,000	$14,000-28,000	$28,000-45,000
Corvette cpe	6,000-12,000	12,000-24,000	24,000-39,00
(add $10,000 for Mark IV, $3,000 for 365 bhp)			
Impala cvt	3,000-7,000	7,000-12,000	12,000-19,000
Impala SS cvt	4,000-8,000	8,000-13,000	13,000-22,000
Impala 2d htp	1,500-4,500	4,500-7,000	7,000-11,000
Impala SS 2d htp	3,000-7,000	7,000-12,000	12,000-19,000
Impala, other	1,000-3,000	3,000-5,000	5,000-7,000
Other full-size	750-2,000	2,000-4,000	4,000-5,500
Corvair			
Corsa cvt	2,000-4,000	4,000-7,000	7,000-12,000
Corsa cpe	2,000-3,000	3,000-6,000	6,000-9,000
Monza cvt	2,000-3,500	3,500-6,000	6,000-9,500
Other models	1,000-2,500	2,500-4,500	4,500-6,500
Chevy II			
Nova SS cpe	1,500-3,500	3,500-7,000	7,000-12,000
Other models	500-1,500	1,500-3,000	3,000-5,000
Chevelle			
Malibu cvt	3,000-6,000	6,000-10,000	10,000-18,000
Malibu SS cvt	5,000-10,000	10,000-16,000	16,000-27,500
Malibu 2d htp	2,000-4,500	4,500-7,000	7,000-11,000
Malibu SS 2d htp	3,000-7,000	7,000-11,000	11,000-20,000
Other models	500-2,000	2000-3,500	3,500-5,500

1966

Performance and luxury were emphasized this year in the big Chevys. Impalas gained the 427 V-8 option and Caprice, a luxury package in 1965, became a separate series. Of the 119,300 SS hardtops and convertibles, 15,872 were the latter. Chevy II Novas wore attractive new sheetmetal; the Nova SS hardtop numbered about 16,300 V-8s and 6700 sixes. Top pick was a 350-bhp hop-up of the 327. Only the 396 V-8 went into the mildly facelifted Chevelle Super Sport hardtop and soft top, swift gas guzzlers that nonetheless attracted 72,300 hotfoots. The unchanged Corvair watched sales plummet; Corsa's final season saw 7330 hardtops and 3142 ragtops. Corvette dropped the 396 in favor of a torquier 390/425-bhp 427 V-8 and was rewarded with orders for 9958 coupes and 17,762 roadsters.

	Restorable	Good	Excellent
Corvette cvt	$8,000-14,000	$14,000-28,000	$28,000-50,000
Corvette cpe	6,000-12,000	12,000-24,000	24,000-44,000
(add $10,000 for 427/425 bhp)			
Caprice 2d htp	2,000-5,000	5,000-8,000	8,000-14,000
Caprice, 4d	1,250-3,000	3,000-5,000	5,000-7,500
Impala cvt	3,500-7,500	7,500-12,000	12,000-19,000
Impala SS cvt	4,000-9,000	9,000-14,000	14,000-24,000
Impala 2d htp	1,500-4,500	4,500-7,500	7,500-12,000
Impala SS 2d htp	2,000-6,000	6,000-10,000	10,000-15,000
Impala, other	1,000-3,000	3,000-5,000	5,000-6,500
Other full-size	750-2,000	2,000-4,000	4,000-5,500
Corvair			
Corsa cvt	2,000-4,000	4,000-7,000	7,000-12,000
Corsa cpe	2,000-3,000	3,000-6,000	6,000-9,000
Monza cvt	2,000-3,500	3,500-6,000	6,000-9,500
Other models	1,000-2,500	2,500-4,500	4,500-6,500
Chevy II			
Nova SS cpe	1,250-2,750	2,750-5,000	5,000-10,000
Other models	500-1,500	1,500-3,000	3,000-6,000

1965 Chevrolet Chevelle Malibu SS convertible coupe

1965 Chevrolet Corvair Corsa Sport Coupe hardtop

1966 Chevrolet Caprice hardtop sedan

1966 Chevrolet Corvair Monza hardtop sedan

1966 Chevrolet Chevelle SS 396 Sport Coupe hardtop

1967 Chevrolet Camaro hardtop coupe

1967 Chevrolet Camaro SS 350 hardtop coupe

1967 Chevrolet Impala 427 Sport Coupe hardtop

1967 Chevrolet Chevelle SS 396 Sport Coupe hardtop

	Restorable	Good	Excellent
Chevelle			
Malibu cvt	3,500-7,000	7,000-11,500	11,500-20,000
Malibu SS 396 cvt	5,000-12,000	12,000-18,000	18,000-29,000
Malibu 2d htp	2,000-5,000	5,000-7,500	7,500-12,000
Malibu SS 396 htp	3,500-7,500	7,500-12,500	12,500-22,000
Other models	500-2,000	2,000-3,500	3,500-5,000

1967

Camaro, a rival to Ford's hot-selling Mustang, was announced this year—a car blending sporty ponycar styling and good performance, especially with a 350 or 396 V-8. Of the 220,917 Camaros built, the top collector choice is the Z/28 with its special trim and Trans-Am racing-inspired 302 V-8. Only 602 were built. Super Sport and Rally Sport Camaros are also popular, and much cheaper. Even "ordinary" models draw attention and offer investment potential, whether convertible or coupe. Rare, specially built Yenko Camaros bring far more dollars, Indy Pace Car replicas only a few thousand extra. The Corvette Sting Ray was in the final year of its styling cycle, and though this edition was the cleanest looking of the five years output eased to 14,436 roadsters and 8504 coupes. Facelifts were seen elsewhere in the Chevy lineup, and SS models were still popular: 10,100 Novas, 63,000 Malibus, and 74,000 Impalas. At 27,253 units, Corvair was fading fast. Total production came to roughly 2,193,100 units, and would remain above two million until 1975.

	Restorable	Good	Excellent
Corvette cvt	$9,000-17,000	$17,000-33,000	$33,000-58,000
Corvette coupe	8,000-15,000	15,000-30,000	30,000-55,000
(add $10,000 for 390 bhp, $12,000 for 400 bhp, $15,000 for 425 bhp)			
Caprice 2d htp	1,750-4,000	4,000-7,000	7,000-12,500
Caprice, other	1,250-3,000	3,000-5,000	5,000-7,500
Impala cvt	3,000-7,000	7,000-12,000	12,000-18,000
Impala SS cvt	4,000-8,000	8,000-14,000	14,000-22,000
Impala 2d htp	1,500-4,000	4,000-7,000	7,000-12,000
Impala SS 2d htp	2,000-4,500	4,500-8,000	8,000-14,000
Impala, other	1,000-3,000	3,000-4,500	4,500-6,000
Other full-size	750-2,000	2,000-4,000	4,000-5,500
Corvair			
Monza cvt	2,000-5,000	5,000-7,000	7,000-10,000
Other models	1,000-3,000	3,000-5,000	5,000-7,000
Chevy II			
Nova SS cpe	1,500-3,500	3,500-6,000	6,000-9,500
Nova 2d htp	1,500-3,000	3,000-5,000	5,000-8,000
Other models	500-1,500	1,500-2,500	2,500-4,500
Chevelle			
Malibu cvt	2,500-6,000	6,000-10,000	10,000-15,000
Malibu SS 396 cvt	5,000-10,000	10,000-15,000	15,000-25,000
Malibu 2d htp	1,000-2,000	2,000-3,500	3,500-5,500
Malibu SS 396 htp	3,500-7,500	7,500-12,500	12,500-22,000
Other models	500-2,000	2,000-3,500	3,500-5,000
Camaro			
Convertible	3,000-7,500	7,500-15,000	15,000-22,000
Z/28 cpe	3,500-8,000	8,000-18,000	18,000-24,000
Yenko cpe	10,000-25,000	25,000-40,000	40,000-65,000
Hardtop cpe	2,000-6,000	6,000-11,000	11,000-18,000

1968

The advent of government emissions and safety regulations caused numerous driveability and styling problems which Chevrolet took time to surmount, and a distinct watershed exists starting this model year, with fewer collectible models. Chevelles and Novas ("Chevy II" was being phased out) were restyled, more rounded and closer in appearance. Both still listed Super Sport editions, but Nova's was an option package rather than a separate series. Ditto the Impala Super Sport. Nova SS pillared coupes are modestly priced hot performers with the big V-8s, partly due to lack of hardtops and ragtops, but only 2858 were built. Chevelle's SS 396, with 60,499 hardtops and 2286 ragtops produced, commands more dollars. Camaro Z/28s became more plentiful to the tune of 7199 units. The Corvette was fully redesigned, based on the Mako Shark II show car: bulkier, less roomy, and slower to rise in value now than prior Sting Rays. No matter, demand increased to 18,630 roadsters and 9936 coupes. Corvair continued to lose ground to 15,399 cars, including 1386 Monza soft tops, while the full-size models continued to impress with 710,900 Impalas and 115,500 Caprices rolling off the line.

	Restorable	Good	Excellent
Corvette cvt	$5,500-12,000	$12,000-22,000	$22,000-35,000
Corvette cpe	4,500-10,000	10,000-19,000	19,000-30,000
(add $5,000 for 390/400 bhp, $7,500 for LT-1, 435 bhp)			
Caprice 2d htp	1,500-3,000	3,000-5,000	5,000-8,500
Impala cvt	3,000-7,000	7,000-12,000	12,000-18,000
Impala 2d htp	1,250-2,500	2,500-4,500	4,500-8,000
Nova SS cpe	1,500-2,500	2,500-4,000	4,000-7,000
(add $1,000-1,500 for Impala SS package)			
Corvair			
Monza cvt	2,000-5,000	5,000-7,000	7,000-10,000
Monza 2d htp	1,000-3,000	3,000-5,000	5,000-7,000
Chevelle			
Malibu cvt	2,000-5,000	5,000-8,000	8,000-14,000
Malibu SS 396 cvt	5,000-9,000	9,000-14,000	14,000-23,000
Malibu 2d htp	1,000-2,500	2,500-4,500	4,500-7,500
Malibu SS 396 htp	3,500-7,500	7,500-12,500	12,500-22,000
Camaro			
Convertible	3,000-7,500	7,500-15,000	15,000-19,000
Z/28 cpe	3,500-8,000	8,000-18,000	18,000-20,000
Yenko cpe	10,000-25,000	25,000-40,000	40,000-60,000
Hardtop cpe	2,000-6,000	6,000-11,000	11,000-18,000

1969

After a pitiful 6000 cars (521 soft tops), Corvair was axed, and these last models often suffered driveability problems caused by an air pump used to meet emissions rules. Full-size Chevys, which garnered nearly 1.2 million sales, were restyled with a new plastic grille, sculptured bodysides, and oblong taillamps. On one hand, all of the 166,900 Caprices built could be ordered with hidden headlamps, but on the other only 2455 Impala Super Sports emerged with the 427 V-8. Just a handful of the reskinned '69 Camaros boasted the mighty ZL-1 rac-

1968 Chevrolet Caprice hardtop coupe

1968 Chevrolet Chevelle SS 396 Sport Coupe hardtop

1968 Chevrolet Chevy II Nova coupe

1968 Chevrolet Corvette Sting Ray convertible coupe

1968 Chevrolet Corvette Sting Ray coupe

1969 Chevrolet Caprice Custom Coupe

1969 Chevrolet Camaro Z/28 hardtop coupe

1969 Chevrolet Chevelle SS 396 Sport Coupe hardtop

1969 Chevrolet Corvair Monza convertible coupe

1970 Chevrolet Impala Custom Coupe

1970 Chevrolet Chevelle SS 396 Sport Coupe hardtop

ing engine, but demand dictated 19,014 Z/28s and 17,573 ragtops. The latter would not return in 1970. The little-changed Corvette added a "Stingray" (one word) nameplate, but sales spurted to 16,632 roadsters and 22,130 coupes. This marked the first time the closed model outsold the open 'Vette—and the change would be permanent. An SS 396 option was offered on Chevelle 300 and Malibu two-door models, and 86,307 buyers brought one home.

	Restorable	Good	Excellent
Corvette cvt	$5,500-11,000	$11,000-21,000	$21,000-32,000
Corvette cpe	4,500-9,000	9,000-18,000	18,000-27,000
(add $5,000 for 390/400 bhp, $7,500 for LT-1, 435 bhp)			
Caprice 2d htp	1,500-3,000	3,000-5,000	5,000-8,500
Impala cvt	2,000-5,000	5,000-9,000	9,000-15,000
Impala 2d htp	1,250-2,500	2,500-4,500	4,500-8,000
Nova SS cpe	1,500-2,500	2,500-4,000	4,000-7,000
(add $1,000-1,500 for Impala SS package)			
Corvair			
Monza cvt	$2,000-5,000	$5,000-7,000	$7,000-11,000
Monza 2d htp	1,000-3,000	3,000-5,000	5,000-8,000
Chevelle			
Malibu cvt	2,000-5,000	5,000-8,000	8,000-14,000
SS 396 cvt	4,500-9,000	9,000-14,000	14,000-22,000
Malibu 2d htp	1,500-3,500	3,500-6,000	6,000-10,000
SS 396 2d htp	3,500-7,000	7,000-11,000	11,000-19,000
Camaro			
Convertible	3,000-6,000	6,000-11,000	11,000-18,000
Z/28 cpe	3,000-7,000	7,000-13,000	13,000-19,000
ZL-1 cpe	8,000-15,000	15,000-30,000	30,000-50,000
Indy Pace Car replica	3,000-6,500	6,500-12,000	12,000-18,000
Hardtop cpe	1,750-4,500	4,500-9,000	9,000-15,000

1970

A stunning restyle gave Camaro a curvy fastback shape that would last through 1981, but the convertible was gone. Though engine choices included a new 350 V-8 (as well as 350- and 375-bhp 396 V-8s), performance slipped. Yet, these second-generation 1970½ Camaros have risen steadily in value, especially the 8733 Z/28s produced. All 27,136 Rally Sport models wore a distinctive protruding, split-bumper nose. Also for 1970, Chevrolet introduced its personal-luxury coupe, the Monte Carlo, with handsome long-hood/short-deck proportions and good performance—and 130,657 sales. Most carried the 350 V-8, but the sizzling SS 454 with a V-8 of that many cubes packed 360 horses. The 454 was also available on the Malibu SS hardtop or soft top, and after mid-year a 450-bhp 454 was listed. Just 3733 Chevelles came with the monster engine. Corvettes, too, could be had with the 454, with 390 and 460 horses. Even so, 'Vette production fell to 6648 ragtops and 10,668 coupes. Nova SS models were still around with 350- and 396-cid engines with up to 375 bhp. Full-size Chevys dropped below one million units this year, and there were no more SS models. Collectors, however, give thanks for the 9562 Impala convertibles that were produced.

	Restorable	Good	Excellent
Corvette cvt	$5,000-10,000	$10,000-18,000	$18,000-28,000
Corvette cpe	4,000-8,000	8,000-15,000	15,000-25,000
(add $5,000 for 454/390 bhp, $8,500 for LT-1, 370 bhp)			
Impala cvt	2,000-5,000	5,000-9,000	9,000-15,000
Nova SS V-8	1,500-2,500	2,500-4,000	4,000-7,000
Monte Carlo	1,500-4,500	4,500-9,000	9,000-12,000
Monte Carlo SS 454	2,500-6,000	6,000-10,000	10,000-15,000
Chevelle			
Malibu cvt	2,000-5,000	5,000-8,500	8,500-15,000
SS 396 cvt	4,000-9,000	9,000-16,000	16,000-25,000
SS 454 cvt	6,000-11,000	11,000-20,000	20,000-32,000
Malibu 2d htp	1,500-3,500	3,500-6,500	6,500-11,000
SS 396 2d htp	2,000-6,000	6,000-9,500	9,500-16,000
SS 454 2d htp	4,000-9,000	9,000-16,000	16,000-25,000
Camaro			
Coupe	1,750-4,500	4,500-8,500	8,500-14,000
Rally/SS cpe	2,000-5,000	5,000-10,000	10,000-17,000
Z/28 cpe	3,000-7,000	7,000-13,000	13,000-19,000

1971

Chevrolet brought out its all-new Vega subcompact, a car which, in retrospect, would have better been left on the drawing board. Collectors shun it. Chevelle was mildly restyled with single headlights, and its SS edition now embraced the 350 V-8 with 245/270 horses or the big-block 454 with 365/425. Output approximated 60,700 and 19,292, respectively. There was also a lower-priced "Heavy Chevy" hardtop with specific go-fast trim and a base 307 V-8. Again, Z/28 was the hot Camaro, and remains so today, though its performance was declining. And so were sales, to 4862 units. Nova still offered an SS coupe (7015 produced), now with a 270-horse 350 V-8, though the mid-year Rally Nova boasted a 330-bhp 350 with unique boy-racer trim. The bolder-looking Impala held firm with a convertible, though it struggled to find 4576 buyers. Impala and Caprice hardtops from the late-Sixties/early Seventies are plentiful, and well-equipped versions are worthy of consideration by big-car fanciers. Corvette, meanwhile, sailed along looking as before. With 7121 ragtops and 14,680 coupes requested, the latter now outsold the former by more than 2-to-1 because of the semi-convertible T-top, air conditioning, and better security from thieves.

	Restorable	Good	Excellent
Corvette cvt	$5,000-8,500	$8,500-16,000	$16,000-26,000
Corvette cpe	4,000-7,000	7,000-14,000	14,000-23,000
(add $3,000 for 454/365 bhp, $6,000 for LT-1, 330 bhp)			
Impala cvt	2,000-5,000	5,000-8,000	8,000-12,000
Caprice 2d htp	1,500-3,000	3,000-4,500	4,500-6,500
Nova SS cpe	1,500-2,500	2,500-4,000	4,000-7,500
Monte Carlo 2d htp	1,500-4,500	4,500-9,000	9,000-12,000
Monte Carlo SS 454	2,500-6,000	6,000-10,000	10,000-15,000
Chevelle			
Malibu cvt	2,500-6,000	6,000-10,000	10,000-17,000
SS 350 cvt	4,000-8,000	8,000-13,000	13,000-22,500
SS 454 cvt	5,000-10,000	10,000-17,000	17,000-26,000
Malibu 2d htp	1,500-4,500	4,500-8,500	8,500-13,000
SS 350 2d htp	2,500-6,000	6,000-10,000	10,000-17,500
SS 454 2d htp	4,000-8,000	8,000-13,000	13,000-20,000

1970 Chevrolet Camaro Rally Sport coupe

1970 Chevrolet Monte Carlo hardtop coupe

1971 Chevrolet Caprice hardtop coupe

1971 Chevrolet Camaro SS coupe

1971 Chevrolet Chevelle SS 454 Sport Coupe hardtop

1972 Chevrolet Impala Custom Coupe

1972 Chevrolet Chevelle Malibu Sport Sedan hardtop

1972 Chevrolet Monte Carlo hardtop coupe

1973 Chevrolet Monte Carlo coupe

1973 Chevrolet Chevelle Malibu coupe

1972

A "Heavy Chevy" sport coupe with black-out grille, essentially an economy Chevelle SS, had appeared during the 1971 model year and returned for all of 1972. A double horizontal-bar grille and one-piece parking lights identified the '72 Chevelles and Malibus. SS packages were still offered; the SS 454 went to about 3000 buyers, while the SS-350, with the 175-bhp 350 V-8, was more popular: 21,950 customers drove one home. The SS 350 could also be had with the 130-bhp 307 V-8 and the 240-bhp 402 V-8. This was the last year for the Malibu convertible, which found only 4853 buyers; with 212,388 produced, two-door hardtops were far more common. Full-size models, Chevelles, Monte Carlos, and Corvettes could all still have a 270-horsepower 454 V-8. Chevy's Impalas and Caprices were even bigger, now riding a 122-inch wheelbase (wagons 125) and measuring 220 inches overall (wagons 226). Just over one million full-size models were sold, including 65,513 Caprice two-door hardtops, 52,692 Impala hardtops, and 6456 Impala ragtops. Only 2575 Z28 Camaros were built, partly due to a strike, which enhanced their rarity. RS and SS Camaro options continued. A total of 68,656 Camaros were built for '72, nearly all of them V-8s. The Monte Carlo faced the model year with a coarser-pattern eggcrate grille flanked by vertical parking lights, and was rewarded with a production increase to 180,819 units. A handful of '72 Corvettes, which looked just like the '71s, carried a ZR-1 racing package that included the 255-bhp, 350-cid LT-1 engine. Convertibles slipped in popularity to 6508 units, while the coupe enjoyed a 40-percent increase to 20,486. All in all, Chevy racked up a production run of 2,420,564 cars this year.

	Restorable	Good	Excellent
Corvette cvt	$4,500-8,500	$8,500-16,000	$16,000-26,000
Corvette cpe	3,500-7,000	7,000-14,000	14,000-23,000
(add $3,000 for 454/270 bhp, $6,000 for LT-1, 255 bhp)			
Impala cvt	2,000-4,500	4,500-8,000	8,000-12,000
Nova SS	1,500-2,500	2,500-4,000	4,000-7,500
Monte Carlo	2,000-4,500	4,500-9,000	9,000-12,000
Monte Carlo SS 454	3,000-6,000	6,000-10,000	10,000-16,000
Chevelle			
Malibu cvt	2,500-6,000	6,000-10,000	10,000-16,000
SS 350 cvt	4,000-8,000	8,000-13,000	13,000-22,500
SS 454 cvt	5,000-10,000	10,000-17,000	17,000-26,000
Malibu 2d htp	1,500-4,500	4,500-8,500	8,500-12,000
SS 350 2d htp	2,500-6,000	6,000-10,000	10,000-17,500
SS 454 2d htp	4,000-8,000	8,000-14,000	14,000-20,000
Camaro			
Z28 coupe	2,500-5,500	5,500-11,000	11,000-17,500
Other models	1,750-4,500	4,500-8,500	8,500-14,000

1973

A new name this year was Laguna, a top trim level for the all-new Chevelle, which no longer came as a traditional pillarless hardtop or convertible—now only in pillared "Colonnade" style. Top-line Lagunas had integral urethane front ends and a special grille incorporating the parking lights. By Chevy standards they were relatively exclusive, as only 13,095 four-door and 42,941 two-door Colonnades were requested. As before, two wheelbases were used, 112 and 116 inches. Malibus still came with the SS package, either 350 or 454, and of the 28,647 SS Malibus produced less than 3000 were 454s. Monte Carlo was restyled on the Malibu's longer 116-inch wheelbase, appearing now with narrow opera windows and swoopy bodyside sculpturing. Base, S, and Landau versions were offered, and together they accounted for 290,693 sales, 177,963 of them the S with tightened suspension and radial-ply tires. Camaro added an LT (Luxury Touring) coupe with a standard 145-bhp 350 V-8; it enjoyed a run of 32,327 units. Air conditioning was available for the first time on Z28s, which were now powered by a 245-bhp 350 V-8. Output rose to 11,574. The '73 Corvette, 30,465 strong this year, wore a new domed hood and "soft" integrated front bumper. Chevrolet's only convertible, aside from the Corvette, was the Caprice Classic, which replaced Impala; 7339 were built. Novas, sporting a new grille, could be had with an optional sunroof, as well as an SS appearance package and extra-cost V-8s up to a 175-bhp 350. The SS package adorned 35,542 Novas for '73. The market was up this year, and so was Chevy, to 2,579,509 cars.

	Restorable	Good	Excellent
Corvette cvt	$4,500-8,500	$8,500-16,000	$16,000-26,000
Corvette cpe	3,500-7,000	7,000-14,000	14,000-23,000
	(add $3,000 for 454/275 bhp)		
Caprice cvt	1,500-3,000	3,000-6,000	6,000-10,000
Nova SS	1,500-2,500	2,500-4,000	4,000-6,500
Monte Carlo	1,000-2,000	2,000-4,000	4,000-6,000
Monte Carlo SS	1,000-3,000	3,000-5,000	5,000-7,000
Chevelle Laguna cpe	1,000-2,500	2,500-4,000	4,000-6,000
Camaro Z28	2,000-5,000	5,000-9,500	9,500-15,000
Camaro LT	1,500-4,500	4,500-8,000	8,000-13,000
Camaro	1,500-4,000	4,000-7,500	7,500-12,000

1974

Camaro received a soft-nose facelift with an angled urethane front end, eggcrate grille, and heavy five-mph crash bumpers. This would be the last year for the Z28 until 1977, even though 13,802 were sold. Total output surged to 151,008, which included 48,963 Type LTs. This year, the Laguna name was used only on a sporty Type S-3 Colonnade Chevelle coupe with swivel bucket seats, Rally wheels, and special exterior graphics. It makes for an attractive low-budget collectible if you can find one of the remaining 15,792 examples Chevy produced. All full-size Chevrolets now had V-8s (starting with a 145-bhp 350 and ending with a 235-bhp 454) mated to Turbo Hydra-Matic. Sadly, there were no more two-door hardtops, though Chevy did its best to make the two-doors—now with extra wide B-pillars—attractive. It succeeded in selling 207,582 of them in Impala and Caprice guise. The Caprice Classic convertible was still available, but attracted only 4670 customers. Monte Carlos sported a revised eggcrate

1974 Chevrolet Caprice coupe

1974 Chevrolet Caprice convertible coupe

1974 Chevrolet Camaro coupe

1974 Chevrolet Corvette Stingray coupe

1975 Corvette Stingray coupe

1975 Chevrolet Monza 2+2 fastback coupe

grille and smoother taillights, and saw output climb to 184,873 S models and 127,344 Landaus. Novas could still be optioned with the appearance-only SS package, and 21,419 were for '74. For $140, it provided a black-out grille, black or red striping, Sport mirrors, and prominent SS badges. Top engine option was a 185-bhp 350 V-8, but this had to be purchased separately. Vega, strutting a new laid-back louvered grille, offered a GT package for all models; it came with an 85-bhp version of the aluminum/silicon four (a 10-bhp increase), sporty wheels, fat tires, full-instrumentation dash, and special graphics. Corvettes, sporting a sloping rear-end restyle matching the previous year's front-end update, offered the 454 V-8, now rated at 270 horsepower, for the last time. Production increased to 32,028 coupes and 5474 roadsters. Despite the Arab oil embargo, total production—2,333,839 units—held up fairly well, though 20 percent of all Chevys built this year were Vegas.

	Restorable	Good	Excellent
Corvette cvt	$4,500-8,500	$8,500-15,000	$15,000-25,000
Corvette cpe	3,500-7,000	7,000-13,000	13,000-22,000
	(add $3,000 for 454/275 bhp)		
Caprice cvt	1,500-3,000	3,000-6,000	6,000-11,000
Nova SS	1,500-2,500	2,500-4,000	4,000-5,000
Monte Carlo	1,000-2,000	2,000-4,000	4,000-6,000
Laguna S-3	1,000-3,000	3,000-5,000	5,000-7,500
Camaro Z28	2,000-5,000	5,000-8,000	8,000-13,000
Camaro LT	1,500-4,000	4,000-7,000	7,000-11,000
Camaro	1,500-3,500	3,500-7,500	7,500-10,000

1975

The first Vega with collector interest, the Cosworth coupe, appeared this year. Its twin-cam, 16-valve cylinder head was designed in England, and with Bendix fuel injection it delivered 111 bhp, power the Vega truly needed. This year, all Cosworths were black with gold striping. Few of the 2061 produced still exist, fewer in passable shape, though there is an active club to help owners. A new Vega-based subcompact, the Monza, debuted this year. Available with an 87-bhp four or 110-bhp V-8, the fastback 2+2 has modest collector interest. Interestingly, its styling was taken from a Ferrari, though the resemblance ended there. Also offered was a notchback Monza Towne coupe, though this is of less interest. Output came to 69,238 coupes and 66,965 fastbacks. Caprice and Corvette convertibles made their final appearance this year with production runs of 8349 and 4629 units. Corvette lost its 454 option, leaving two 350 V-8s rated at 165 and 205 bhp. Coupe production edged up to 33,836. The Laguna S-3 received a unique sloping urethane front end and louvered opera windows; how many were built is unknown. Monte Carlo wore a fussier grille and taillights, and demand fell 17 percent to 258,909 units. Nova received a handsome restyle this year, taking on a European look. A hatchback coupe joined the lineup, but the SS package lost favor as only 9067 were ordered. The full effect of the Arab oil embargo was felt this year as total Chevy production tumbled to 1,755,773 cars.

	Restorable	Good	Excellent
Corvette cvt	$4,500-8,500	$8,500-15,000	$15,000-25,000
Corvette cpe	3,500-7,000	7,000-13,000	13,000-22,000
Caprice cvt	2,000-4,000	4,000-8,000	8,000-14,000
Nova SS	1,500-2,500	2,500-3,500	3,500-5,000
Monte Carlo	1,000-2,000	2,000-4,000	4,000-6,000
Laguna S-3	1,000-3,000	3,000-5,000	5,000-7,500
Monza 2+2	500-2,000	2,000-3,000	3,000-4,000
Cosworth Vega	1,000-3,000	3,000-5,000	5,000-8,000
Camaro LT	1,000-3,000	3,000-6,000	6,000-9,000
Camaro	1,000-3,000	3,000-5,000	5,000-8,000

1976

Even fewer Cosworth Vegas—just 1447—were built for the second and final year. They were now available in a variety of colors and with an optional five-speed gearbox. Sales of the Monza dropped to 80,905, 34,170 being the fastback. Those with a more "baroque" taste might want to consider the notchback coupe with the Cabriolet package, a $256 option with a padded half vinyl roof and opera windows. This year marked the last appearance of the big Chevy four-door hardtop, a body style that had been a fixture for 20 years. For 1975-76 it was a six-window design called Sport Sedan. Production for the final edition was 18,265 Impala S and 55,308 Caprice Classic models. Gone was the Bel Air nameplate that had been around for a quarter century, and making their final appearances were the 400 and 454 V-8s, the latter downgraded slightly to 225 horsepower. Monte Carlos were now powered by two versions of the 305 V-8, 140 or 145 horsepower, and stylists grafted on a three-slot grille flanked by stacked rectangular quad headlamps. Buyers liked the new, more formal look—they drove 353,272 S and Landau models home. An interesting aftermarket offshoot was a Custom Cloud kit that made the Monte look a lot like a Rolls-Royce. Rolls put an end to the imitation after less than 200 kits had been delivered. Though down to only one model, a coupe, Corvette output set a new record: 46,558 units. Removable roof panels were still standard, as since 1968. Of absolutely no interest to collectors was the debut of the subcompact Chevette, a "T-car" based on GM of Germany's Opel Kadett.

1976 Chevrolet Monte Carlo Landau coupe

1977 Chevrolet Monte Carlo Landau coupe

1977 Chevrolet Monza Spyder fastback coupe

	Restorable	Good	Excellent
Corvette	$3,500-7,000	$7,000-12,500	$12,500-21,000
Caprice cvt	2,000-4,000	4,000-8,000	8,000-14,000
Nova SS	1,500-2,500	2,500-3,500	3,500-5,000
Monte Carlo	1,000-2,000	2,000-4,000	4,000-6,000
Laguna S-3	750-2,000	2,000-3,500	3,500-5,000
Monza 2+2	500-2,000	2,000-3,000	3,000-4,000
Cosworth Vega	1,000-3,000	3,000-5,000	5,000-8,000
Camaro LT	1,000-3,000	3,000-4,500	4,500-7,000
Camaro	1,000-2,500	2,500-4,000	4,000-6,000

1977

Camaro's Z28 returned after a two-year absence. Not so quick as before, it was powered by a detuned 170-bhp 350 V-8 (Chevy's largest engine this year), but it handled extremely well and had bold graphics and bright colors. Valuation is modest, partly because so many were built, 14,349 in all. Full-size Chevys were downsized this year, a risky venture by

1978 Chevrolet Corvette coupe

1978 Chevrolet Monte Carlo coupe

1978 Chevrolet Camaro Z28 coupe

1978 Chevrolet Monza fastback coupe

GM that paid off with an exceptionally good product, but nothing collectible has developed in this area, though the 1977-79 Impala/Caprice coupes with the severely bent rear windows have a modest following. Impala coupes numbered 55,347, Caprices 62,366. The Nova SS finally disappeared, replaced by a Rally coupe package with unique grille, body striping, and Rally wheels. It is just barely collectible. Monte Carols featured a modest facelift, and went on to attract 411,038 customers. Corvette Stingrays continued much as before. Despite a base price of $8648, production increased to 49,213 units. Total Chevy production jumped to 2,543,153, more than 700,000 ahead of Ford.

	Restorable	Good	Excellent
Corvette	$3,500-7,000	$7,000-12,500	$12,500-21,000
Nova Rallye cpe	500-1,500	1,500-2,500	2,500-3,500
Monte Carlo	1,000-2,000	2,000-4,000	4,000-5,500
Monza 2+2	500-2,000	2,000-3,000	3,000-4,000
Camaro Z28	1,000-3,000	3,000-5,500	5,500-8,000
Camaro, other	1,000-3,000	3,000-4,500	4,500-7,000

1978

Malibu dropped its Chevelle designation and was downsized, but even though 358,636 were built, the result produced no cars for today's collectors. Camaros were available with glass panels in a T-bar roof and had a new integrated bumperless molded nose. Z28s, of which 54,907 were built, could be quickly identified by slanted front fender air slots. They were powered this year by a 185-horse 350 V-8. Monte Carlo was also downsized and restyled, with a 105-bhp 231 V-6 or 145-bhp 305 V-8. Monzas came with four, six, or eight cylinders and four horsepower ratings: 85, 90, 105, and 145 bhp. Two station wagons, rebadged Vegas, were offered this year. Corvettes added a fastback roofline with a large wraparound backlight. Two special models were the Pace Car Replica and Silver Anniversary Edition; 6200 and 2500 were produced. (Note: many Pace Cars have been "created" from conventional models; be sure of the car's documentation before purchasing one.) Total Chevy production eased a bit this year to 2,375,436 units.

	Restorable	Good	Excellent
Corvette	$3,500-7,000	$7,000-13,000	$13,000-22,500
Corvette Pace Car	4,500-8,500	8,500-16,000	16,000-27,000
Corvette Silver Ann.	4,500-8,500	8,500-15,000	15,000-26,000
Nova Rallye cpe	500-1,500	1,500-2,500	2,500-3,500
Monte Carlo	750-1,500	1,500-3,250	3,250-5,250
Monza 2+2	500-2,000	2,000-3,000	3,000-4,000
Camaro Z28	1,000-3,000	3,000-5,000	5,000-7,000

1979

A Camaro Berlinetta debuted wearing a bright grille, black rocker panels, and dual pinstriping. It found 67,236 buyers. The Z28 ran with black-out moldings, scooped hood, large Z28 decals on the doors, and a 175-bhp 350 V-8. It was more popular than ever—84,877 were built. The uniquely trimmed Rally Sport was far rarer as only 19,101 were produced. Monzas were lightly facelifted, with the 2+2 Sport fastback still carrying a unique grille and quad rectangular headlights. As before, Spyder performance and appearance options were optional. A total of 30,662 Sports were sold. Malibus could be ordered with a 125-bhp 267 V-8 or optional 160-bhp 350. Coupes numbered 225,073, Landaus 92,850. This was the Nova's final season because it was replaced late in the year by the all-new front-wheel-drive Citation, which was officially listed as a 1980 model. The $12,313 Corvette received a minor trim reshuffling, and was rewarded with a record 53,807 sales. Horsepower from the 350 V-8 edged up to 195 standard, 225 optional.

	Restorable	Good	Excellent
Corvette	$3,500-7,000	$7,000-13,000	$13,000-22,000
Nova Rallye cpe	500-1,500	1,500-2,500	2,500-3,500
Monte Carlo	750-1,500	1,500-3,250	3,250-5,500
Monza 2+2	500-2,000	2,000-3,000	3,000-4,000
Camaro Z28	1,000-2,500	2,500-5,000	5,000-7,000
Camaro, other	1,000-3,000	3,000-4,500	4,500-6,000

1980

Chevy's first front-drive venture, the Citation, achieved notoriety as one of the infamous X-cars, which were unfortunately plagued by numerous first-year recalls. The X-11, a $500 package for all body styles included a 115-bhp V-6 plus appearance, tire, wheel, and suspension upgrades, is at least mildly collectible—but the 170-horsepower turbocharged V-6 that became available in Monte Carlos makes for a better investment. After a two-year lapse, Monte Carlos again featured quad rectangular headlamps. Output sagged to 116,580 coupes and 32,262 Landaus. New engines went into Camaros: a 229 V-6 and 267 V-8 (115 and 120 bhp), with the 305 and 350 V-8s still available (155 and 190 bhp). Production this year was 68,174 sport coupes, 12,015 RS models, 26,679 Berlinettas, and 45,137 Z28s. Corvettes shed nearly 200 pounds and wore a mildly changed front end with air dam and low hood, and could be ordered with a smaller, 180-bhp 305 V-8. The 350 came with 190 and 230 bhp. Output this year fell to 40,614 units. Total Chevy production held steady at 2,288,745.

	Restorable	Good	Excellent
Corvette	*	$7,000-13,000	$13,000-22,000
Citation X-11	*	500-1,000	1,000-2,500
Monte Carlo	*	1,500-3,500	3500-6,000
Monza 2+2	*	2,000-3,000	3,000-3,500
Camaro Z28	*	2,500-5,000	5,000-7,000
Camaro, other	*	3,000-4,500	4,500-6,000

*Purchase only in good or excellent condition

1981

The subcompact Chevette got a diesel engine option this year, but only 13,152 out of 433,600 buyers chose it. Citation's X-11 included a power bulge hood with more power beneath it—135 horses from a high output 173-cid V-6. This made it a better car

1979 Chevrolet Monza fastback coupe

1980 Chevrolet Monza Spyder fastback coupe

1980 Chevrolet Citation X-11 Club Coupe

1980 Chevrolet Camaro Z28 coupe

1981 Chevrolet Monte Carlo coupe

1982 Chevrolet Camaro Z28 coupe

than before, and is the only example worth noting here. Total Citation production was an amazing 811,540 units. Camaro Z28s had a 175-bhp 350 V-8 and four-speed manual shift, though a 165-bhp 305 was also listed. Camaros with the T-top are particularly collectible. Z28s numbered 43,272, Berlinettas 20,253. Monte Carlos were a bit more aerodynamic this year, though output fell to 149,659 coupes and 38,191 Landaus. Corvettes with automatic were available with a fiberglass-reinforced plastic single-leaf spring at the rear to save weight. Even though priced at a hefty $15,248, 40,606 Corvettes were purchased. Total production in this recession year was down to 1,659,286 units.

	Restorable	Good	Excellent
Corvette	*	$7,000-13,000	$13,000-21,000
Citation X-11	*	500-1,000	1,000-2,000
Monte Carlo	*	1,500-3,500	3,500-6,000
Camaro Z28	*	2,500-5,000	5,000-7,500
Camaro, other	*	3,000-4,500	4,500-6,500

*Purchase only in good or excellent condition

1982

The compact J-car Cavalier and mid-size A-car Celebrity were the next front-drive models for Chevrolet. Though offered in a range of body styles (including station wagons for the Cavalier), there wasn't much for enthusiasts to cheer about concerning these two bread-and-butter cars from Chevy. An 88-horsepower 1.8-liter four powered the Cavalier, while the Celebrity had a 90-bhp four or 112-bhp V-6. Camaro finally entered its third generation this year, with a slick new body featuring a glass hatchback, no-grille nose, recessed headlights, and a shorter 101-inch wheelbase. A 145-bhp 305 V-8 was standard in the Z28; a 170-bhp Cross-Fire 305 was optional. Z28s were attractive enough to entice 63,563 buyers, while 39,744 customers chose the Berlinetta. Other Camaros had either a four or V-6, and for $790 one could have a T-bar roof with removable glass panels. No more turbos were installed in Monte Carlos, leaving a 150-bhp 350 V-8 as the top engine option. Production fell to 92,392 units. Corvettes all had automatic transmission, which helped trigger a sales plunge to 25,407. A throttle-body injection system boosted horsepower to 200. A $22,537 Collector Edition model sported silver-gold metallic paint and many standard features; 6759 were built. All Corvettes were assembled in Bowling Green, Kentucky, this year.

	Restorable	Good	Excellent
Corvette	*	$7,000-13,000	$13,000-21,000
Corvette Coll Ed	*	8,000-15,000	15,000-26,000
Citation X-11	*	500-1,000	1,000-2,000
Monte Carlo	*	2,500-4,250	3,250-6,500
Camaro Z28	*	2,500-5,000	5,000-7,500
Camaro, other	*	3,000-4,500	4,500-6,000

*Purchase only in good or excellent condition

1983

There was no Corvette at all for this model year; an all-new '84 was planned for an early introduction.

Late in the year a Cavalier convertible arrived, Chevy's first ragtop since 1975. Most were white with single headlamps—clearly they are the first possibly collectible Cavaliers, though only 627 were produced. Perhaps more tempting was a Camaro with an optional five-speed gearbox mated to the 175-bhp 305 V-8. Little changed otherwise, Camaro saw output fall back to 153,831 units. A sporty-looking "S" package was available on Chevettes, while Celebrities, Malibus, and Monte Carlos could be had with an 85-bhp diesel V-6. Avoid it, as well as the 105-bhp diesel V-8 offered in some models beginning in 1980. Malibu lost its coupe for '83. Monte Carlo sported a revised grille, but the car of interest to collectors was the new Monte Carlo SS with the 175-bhp 305 V-8, Turbo Hydra-Matic, stiffer F41 suspension, upgraded wheels and tires, and SS graphics. Of the 96,319 Monte Carlos sold 1983, just 4714 were SS models. Total Chevy car production slipped from 1,290,023 in model year 1982 to 1,208,536 in 1983.

	Restorable	Good	Excellent
Cavalier cvt	*	$2,000-3,000	$3,000-4,000
Citation X-11	*	500-1,000	1,000-2,000
Camaro Z28	*	2,500-4,000	4,000-6,000
Camaro, other	*	2,000-3,000	3,000-5,000
Monte Carlo SS	*	2,500-5,000	5,000-7,000

* Purchase only in good or excellent condition

1983 Chevrolet Monte Carlo SS coupe

1984 Chevrolet Corvette coupe

1984

Except for its basic engine, the '84 Corvette was all-new, with a standard, removable roof panel and fuel-injected 205-bhp 350 V-8. Both a computer-controlled four-speed manual and automatic transmission were available. Base price was up sharply to $21,800, but production came in at a satisfying 51,547 units. Citation became Citation II for '84, though actual changes were few. The X/11 package was still available. Cavalier's facelift highlighted quad headlamps and an eggcrate grille, and a sportier Type 10 edition became available. The convertible was a Type 10, and 5486 were delivered. The Malibu series was dropped, but the Monte Carlo soldiered on, led by the SS coupe. It found 24,050 customers this year, accounting for about 18 percent of production. Its 305 V-8 was good for 180 horses. Camaros saw little change, though an electronic dash and roof console were featured in Berlinettas. The Z28 got a boost to 190 bhp. Output was 127,292 sport coupes, 33,400 Berlinettas, and 100,416 Z28s. The Celebrity line received a station wagon body style and an optional Eurosport package that included black-out trim, Rally wheels, and Sport suspension. How many were installed isn't known, but only 29,191 out of 309,288 Celebritys built were coupes. An improving economy helped push Chevrolet production to 1,828,934 units.

	Restorable	Good	Excellent
Corvette	*	$7,500-10,000	$10,000-12,000
Cavalier Type 10 cvt	*	2,000-3,000	3,000-4,000
Citation X-11	*	500-1,000	1,000-2,000

1985 Chevrolet Camaro IROC-Z coupe

1986 Chevrolet Monte Carlo SS coupe

1986 Chevrolet Monte Carlo SS Aerocoupe

	Restorable	Good	Excellent
Camaro Z28	*	2,500-4,000	4,000-5,000
Camaro, other	*	2,000-3,000	3,000-4,000
Monte Carlo SS	*	3,000-4,000	4,000-5,000

* Purchase only in good or excellent condition

1985

Camaros entered in the International Race of Champions inspired the IROC-Z coupe, which had a special suspension with 16-inch wheels. Either a fuel injected or carbureted 305 V-8 could be ordered. Base Camaros still had fours or V-6s. Production this year was 97,966 sport coupes, 13,649 Berlinettas, 47,022 Z28s, and 21,177 IROC-Zs. Cavaliers continued with a three-model Type 10 lineup: coupe, hatchback coupe, and convertible. The last found only 4108 buyers. Citation II finished out its final year still offering the X-11 option. A larger 262-cid V-6 became standard in the Monte Carlo, with the 305 V-8 optional; a 180-bhp high-output 305 went into the Monte SS, which enjoyed a production run of 35,484 units. Corvette added multi-port fuel injection, boosting horsepower to 230, but production tumbled to 39,729. This would be the last year for the Impala nameplate—all future big Chevys would be badged Caprice.

	Restorable	Good	Excellent
Corvette	*	$8,000-10,000	$10,000-12,000
Cavalier cvt	*	2,000-3,000	3,000-4,000
Citation X-11	*	500-1,000	1,000-2,000
Camaro IROC-Z	*	3,000-4,500	4,500-6,000
Camaro Z28	*	3,000-4,000	4,000-5,000
Camaro, other	*	2,000-3,000	3,000-4,000
Monte Carlo SS	*	3,000-4,000	4,000-5,000

* Purchase only in good or excellent condition

1986

Corvette came in convertible form for the first time in a decade, with Bosch anti-lock braking. Of the 35,109 'Vettes produced, 7315 were ragtops. Cavalier added a performance-oriented Z24 model with a 135-horsepower fuel-injected V-6 as well as a semi-sporty RS series. Of interest are the 36,365 Z24 coupes and 10,226 three-door hatchbacks produced, plus 5785 RS convertibles. Base Camaros, of which 99,517 were built, gained a sport suspension and tuned exhaust. The Berlinetta garnered only 4479 sales, so it would be gone at the end of the year. Meanwhile, the Z28 attracted 38,547 customers, the IROC-Z 49,585. Though only 200 were built, the Monte Carlo's seldom-seen Aerocoupe with the "bubble-back" rear window and short rear deck ranks as a top collectible, but a less costly LS with aero nose and flush headlights is worth a look. It accounted for 27,428 sales. At 41,164 units, the SS coupe was more successful. Bolstered by sales of 167,749 subcompact Novas built for Chevy by Toyota in California, total Chevrolet production increased to 1,699,436 units.

	Restorable	Good	Excellent
Corvette cvt	*	$11,000-13,000	$13,000-17,000
Corvette cpe	*	9,000-11,500	11,500-13,000

	Restorable	Good	Excellent
Corvette Pace Car cvt	*	11,000-13,000	13,000-20,000
Cavalier RS cvt	*	3,000-4,000	4,000-5,000
Cavalier Z24 cpe	*	2,500-3,500	3,500-4,500
Camaro IROC-Z	*	4,000-5,000	5,000-6,500
Camaro Z28	*	4,000-5,000	5,000-6,000
Camaro, other	*	2,000-3,500	3,500-5,000
Monte Carlo SS	*	2,000-3,000	3,000-4,000
Monte Carlo SS Aerocoupe	*	4,000-5,000	5,000-7,000

* Purchase only in good or excellent condition

1987 Chevrolet Cavalier Z24 Club Coupe

1987

Corvette's 350 V-8, rated at 225 horsepower, became available in the IROC-Z Camaro, while four-cylinder engines left the lineup. In addition, a convertible rejoined the roster, the first since 1969. Production totaled 137,760, including 52,863 Z28/IROC-Z coupes and 263 base ragtops and 744 Z28/IROC-Z convertibles. Later in the year, the Corsica sedan and Beretta coupe, both on a 103.4-inch wheelbase, took up the role of the abandoned front-drive Citation. The 8072 coupes and 8973 sedans produced went mainly into rental fleets. A new "Generation II" V-6 was optional in Cavaliers, which saw output of 5826 RS convertibles, 42,890 Z24 coupes, and 4517 Z24 hatchback coupes. The fastback Monte Carlo Aerocoupe again leads in collectibility among non-Corvettes; 6052 were built this year. In addition, 72,993 LS and SS Monte Carlo coupes were built. After 46,208 Chevettes were produced, the nameplate was retired. Only 3110 Caprice Classic coupes were ordered, so the model was withdrawn at the end of the model run. The Eurosport option remained available on the Celebrity. Total Chevy production fell to 1,344,718 units, including 150,006 Novas.

1987 Chevrolet Corvette coupe

1987 Chevrolet Camaro IROC-Z convertible coupe

	Restorable	Good	Excellent
Corvette cvt	*	$12,000-15,000	$15,000-18,000
Corvette cpe	*	10,000-13,000	13,000-15,000
Cavalier RS cvt	*	4,000-5,500	5,500-6,500
Cavalier Z24 cpe	*	3,000-4,750	4,750-5,500
Camaro IROC-Z	*	5,000-6,500	6,500-7,500
Camaro Z28 cpe	*	4,500-5,500	5,500-6,500
Camaro cpe	*	3,000-4,000	4,000-5,000
Monte Carlo SS	*	4,000-6,000	6,000-7,000
Monte Carlo SS Aerocoupe	*	6,000-8,000	8,000-10,000

* Purchase only in good or excellent condition

1988 Chevrolet Cavalier Z24 Club Coupe

1988

Though no Z28 Camaro was available, the IROC-Z offered enough excitement for performance fans. Some Z28 equipment wound up on base Camaros, too. Output was 66,605 sport coupes, 24,050 IROC-Z coupes, 1859 base convertibles, and 3761 IROC-Z ragtops. Fresh sheetmetal gave the Cavalier a new, aerodynamic look, including composite headlamps and a smoother coupe roofline. Cavalier's hot Z24 now came in convertible form, making it a definite one to watch in future years. It found 8745 buyers, compared to 55,658 for the Z24 coupe. This was the final season for the rear-drive Monte Carlos, which saw 13,970 LS and 16,204 SS coupes built.

1988 Chevrolet Corvette coupe

1988 Chevrolet Camaro IROC-Z coupe

1989 Chevrolet Cavalier Z24 convertible coupe

1989 Chevrolet Camaro IROC-Z coupe with T-top

In their first full year on the market, Corsica and Beretta attracted 291,163 sedan and 275,098 coupe customers. A GT package was available for Beretta; it included V-6 power, sport suspension, high-performance tires, 15-inch aluminum wheels, and decklid luggage rack. Late in the model year, a Beretta GTU appeared. It was the basic GT with a "ducktail" rear spoiler, bigger 16-inch wheels and tires, and GTU badging. Only 3814 were built. Corvette received new standard 16-inch wheels and tires, with 17-inch rubber optional. Base prices for the coupe and convertible were now $29,480 and $34,820, which may partly explain a sales slide to 15,382 coupes and 7407 ragtops. Total car production for the year came to 1,557,072.

	Restorable	Good	Excellent
Corvette cvt	*	$13,000-18,000	$18,000-21,000
Corvette cpe	*	12,000-15,000	15,000-18,000
Cavalier Z24 cvt	*	6,000-7,500	7,500-9,000
Cavalier Z24 cpe	*	4,000-5,000	5,000-6,500
Camaro IROC-Z cvt	*	8,500-10,000	10,000-13,000
Camaro IROC-Z cpe	*	6,000-7,500	7,500-9,000
Camaro cvt	*	7,000-8,500	8,500-10,000
Camaro cpe	*	4,000-5,000	5,000-6,500
Monte Carlo SS	*	6,500-8,000	8,000-9,000

* Purchase only in good or excellent condition

1989

Camaro gained a "pass-key" theft deterrent system and the base model was now the RS. V-8s available this year were the 305-cid unit with 170 and 220 horsepower and a 230-bhp 350. Cavalier RS models were dropped, replaced by an RS option package offering Sport suspension, 14-inch tires, Rally wheels, and a gauge package with tachometer. The Celebrity dropped its coupe model, leaving just a four-door sedan and wagon, but it retained the Eurosport option with Sport suspension, quick-ratio steering, black-out exterior trim, 195/75R14 all-season tires on Rally wheels. The Beretta GT, now with 15 x 7-inch aluminum wheels standard, became a model in its own right. The GTU was still around, finding 8913 buyers, and a sporty Corsica GTZ four-door joined the lineup. All three got the 2.8-liter, 130-bhp V-6. A six-speed ZF manual gearbox became available on Corvettes, along with optional Selective Ride Control, which many thought useful; even the new-generation Corvettes still rode like sleds, and that wasn't necessary on performance cars by the late 1980s. Total calendar year Chevy sales (with Geo) came to 1,232,761 units, which included 23,928 Corvettes, 95,469 Camaros, 295,715 Cavaliers, and 326,006 Berettas/Corsicas.

	Restorable	Good	Excellent
Corvette cvt	*	$16,000-20,000	$20,000-24,000
Corvette cpe	*	13,000-17,000	17,000-20,000
Cavalier Z24 cvt	*	8,000-9,500	9,500-11,000
Cavalier Z24 cpe	*	6,000-7,000	7,000-8,000
Camaro IROC-Z cvt	*	10,000-13,000	13,000-15,000
Camaro IROC-Z cpe	*	7,500-9,000	9,000-10,000

	Restorable	Good	Excellent
Camaro cvt	*	8,000-10,000	10,000-12,000
Camaro cpe	*	4,500-6,000	6,000-7,500

* Purchase only in good or excellent condition

1990 Chevrolet Corvette convertible (with hardtop)

1990

No question about the prime future collectible this year: it was the long-awaited, much-rumored, ultra-hot, 380-horsepower ZR-1 Corvette. Designed by Lotus and built by Mercury Marine, the ZR-1's LT-5 engine was created to deliver sizzling acceleration. Styling differed from standard Corvettes, with convex rear end and square taillamps plus fat fenders and extra-wide tires. Chevy announced it would build about 3000 the first year, but sales stumbled after the initial enthusiasm and only about 400 were planned for 1993. Total 'Vette sales for calendar 1990 were 22,690 units. No convertible Cavalier was offered because a soft top Beretta was expected, but it never went into production, so the Cavalier ragtop was reinstated a bit later. This year, the Beretta GT got a 135-bhp 3.1 V-6, and a sportier GTZ (replacing the GTU) ran with Oldsmobile's 180-bhp 2.3-liter High Output Quad Four. It featured a unique grille and rocker-panel extensions and 16-inch alloy wheels. The Camaro IROC-Z got standard limited-slip differential and added standard equipment, while the Cavalier Z24 adopted the 3.1-liter V-6. Celebrity was down now to just a wagon, replaced otherwise by the 107.5-inch-wheelbase Lumina coupe and sedan. Either could be had as a Euro model with the 3.1-liter V-6, black-out exterior trim, decklid spoiler, sport suspension, and 15- or 16-inch wheels. Total Chevy calendar year sales held steady at 1,235,351, 22,690 of them Corvettes, 77,599 Camaros.

1990 Chevrolet Corvette ZR-1 coupe

1990 Chevrolet Camaro RS coupe

	Restorable	Good	Excellent
Corvette ZR-1 cpe	*	$25,000-40,000	$40,000-55,000
Corvette cvt	*	17,000-22,000	22,000-27,000
Corvette cpe	*	14,000-18,000	18,000-23,000
Cavalier Z24 cpe	*	6,000-7,500	7,500-9,000
Camaro IROC-Z cvt	*	11,000-15,000	15,000-18,800
Camaro IROC Z cpe	*	9,000-10,000	10,000-13,000
Camaro cvt	*	9,000-12,000	12,000-13,000
Camaro cpe	*	7,000-9,000	9,000-10,000

* Purchase only in good or excellent condition

Chrysler

1931 Chrysler with special body

As collector cars, Chryslers are spotty. The status of the big, CCCA-recognized classic Custom Imperials of the early '30s is established, and there is a minor boomlet for the ugly but interesting Airflow. Among postwar models, the early Town and Country is one of the most expensive collectibles you can buy, and the "Letter Series" 300 has always been in strong demand. But run-of-the-mill Chryslers haven't attracted a wide collector following; con-

1931 Chrysler Series CG Imperial Laundalet by LeBaron

1932 Chrysler Series CH Imperial Town Car by LeBaron

1933 Chrysler Series CL Imperial Custom limousine

1934 Chrysler Series CU Airflow Eight four-door sedan

1937 Chrysler Series C16 Royal Six rumble-seat coupe

versely, some of them are underrated, and excellent buys at today's prices. Club support is excellent, body and mechanical parts supply generally good, and investment potential is excellent for the models mentioned above, modest for others.

1930-39

Chrysler's 1930 lineup consisted of five series riding five wheelbases, 109-136 inches, and powered by four sixes ranging from 195.6 to 309.3 cubic inches and developing 62-100 horsepower. The make's first eight—a nine-main-bearing, 384.8-cid, 125-bhp L-head—appeared for 1931, simultaneously with the rakish and graceful new 145-inch-wheelbase Custom Imperial Model CG, some of which boasted coachwork by Locke, Derham, Murphy, Waterhouse, and LeBaron. They are the most beautiful Chryslers ever built. As the Model CL, these fine cars continued through 1933, after which Airflow styling was adopted across the board. The streamlined Airflow was indeed aerodynamic, and provided fine performance, but its unconventional styling never caught on with the public and by 1937 Chrysler had switched back almost entirely to conventional, potato-shaped designs with barrel grilles and pod headlamps. A new 1938 model was the New York Special, with one of the first color-keyed interiors. The Chrysler line was fully redesigned for 1939 with headlamps set into the fenders, a lower grille, and elongated fenders.

Chrysler did produce a line of conventional square-rigged models during the Airflow years, but in the beginning these were at the bottom of the line. With the exception of convertibles, CG/CL Imperials, and the largest Airflows, Chryslers from the '30s are undervalued. Sedans, and even the more rakish coupes, show no signs of changing in this respect, but are good buys if you're on a budget—especially the trim-looking club coupes. Among the Ray Dietrich-styled '39s, the big New Yorker is attractive and a good buy for the money if it's in good shape; extensive restorations of such peripheral collectibles should be avoided. Chrysler production during the '30s ranged from a low of 25,699 in 1932 to 106,120 in 1937, but open models can be hard to come by.

	Restorable	Good	Excellent
1930-34 Sixes, open	$5,000-10,000	$10,000-20,000	$20,000-30,000
1930-34 Sixes, closed	1,500-5,000	5,000-8,000	8,000-12,000
1931-33 Eights, open	5,000-12,000	12,000-25,000	25,000-42,500
1931-33 Eights, closed	3,000-7,500	7,500-11,000	11,000-15,000

1931-33 Imperial

Standard, open	7,500-15,000	15,000-25,000	25,000-40,000
Standard, closed	2,500-7,000	7,000-10,000	10,000-15,000
Custom, open	40,000-100,000	100,000-200,000	200,000-325,000
Custom, closed	10,000-30,000	30,000-75,000	75,000-100,000

Airflows

1934 Imperial Custom	8,000-20,000	20,000-50,000	50,000-80,000

	Restorable	Good	Excellent
1934 other models	3,500-12,000	12,000-18,000	18,000-25,000
1935 Imperial CW	7,000-17,500	17,500-40,000	40,000-60,000
1935 Imperial C3 limo	5,000-15,000	15,000-25,000	25,000-35,000
1935 Imperial C3	4,000-12,000	12,000-20,000	20,000-27,500
1935 other models	3,000-8,000	8,000-14,000	14,000-22,500
1936 Imperial limo	10,000-20,000	20,000-35,000	35,000-45,000
1936 Imperial	3,000-10,000	10,000-17,500	17,500-27,500
1937	2,500-7,500	7,500-15,000	15,000-22,500

Non-Airflows

	Restorable	Good	Excellent
1937 Imperial	3,000-8,000	8,000-17,000	17,000-25,000
1937 Imperial, lwb	6,000-12,000	12,000-25,000	25,000-35,000
1937 Derham, open	15,000-30,000	30,000-60,000	60,000-90,000
1938 New York Special	2,500-5,000	5,000-10,000	10,000-15,000
1938 Derham, open	10,000-25,000	25,000-50,000	50,000-80,000
1938-39 Derham, closed	4,000-8,000	8,000-14,000	14,000-22,500
1939 Derham, open	8,000-20,000	20,000-40,000	40,000-60,000
1935-38, other open	3,500-10,000	10,000-20,000	20,000-30,000
1935-39, other closed	2,000-5,000	5,000-8,000	8,000-12,000

1940

The Dietrich-styled '40 models were attractive and spanned a broad range, including Series C-25 sixes—Royal, Windsor—and C-26 eights—Traveler, New Yorker, Saratoga—on longish and very long chassis. A 145.5-inch wheelbase carried all C-27 Crown Imperial sedans and limos; 850 were produced. All C-25s ran with a 241.5-cid six good for 108/112 bhp, and rode a 122.5-inch wheelbase, save for eight passenger models, which were stretched an extra 11 inches. C-26s and C27s boasted a 323.5-cid L-head straight eight developing 132/135/143 bhp, and the C-26s rode a 128.5-inch chassis. Fluid Drive semi-automatic transmission was standard on the Imperial, optional on Saratoga and New Yorker. Of interest were the Windsor and New Yorker Highlander coupes and convertibles trimmed with a special plaid material. Adding class were two semi-show cars from LeBaron, the Newport phaeton and Thunderbolt convertible; six of each were built. Ralph Roberts designed the LeBaron, a dual-cowl job on an Imperial chassis; Alex Tremulis of Briggs did the Thunderbolt, which had a rounded body, hidden wheels, and a retractable hardtop with a single bench seat mounted on the New Yorker chassis. Because 83 percent of the 92,419-car production run was two- and four-door sedans, coupes and convertibles are not plentiful.

	Restorable	Good	Excellent
Convertibles	$4,000-10,000	$10,000-15,000	$15,000-25,000
Crown Imperial	2,500-7,500	7,500-12,500	12,500-20,000
Newport	50,000-125,000	125,000-250,000	250,000-350,000
Thunderbolt	50,000-125,000	125,000-225,000	225,000-300,000
Other models	1,500-5,000	5,000-8,000	8,000-13,000

1938 Chrysler Series C19 New Yorker four-door sedan

1939 Chrysler Series C23 New Yorker Club Coupe

1939 Chrysler Series C24 Imperial four-door sedan

1940 Chrysler Series C25 Royal coupe

1940 Chrysler Series C26 Saratoga four-door sedan

1941 Chrysler Series C30 New Yorker convertible coupe

1941 Chrysler Series C33 Crown Imperial sedan

1942 Chrysler Series C34W Windsor convertible coupe

1942 Chrysler New Yorker with black-out trim

1941

The Town and Country made its first appearance—a station wagon with a basic steel shell trimmed with wood and unique "clamshell" rear doors hinged at the sides. Built on the six-cylinder Windsor chassis, the T&C seated six or nine passengers. Buyers chose 997 T&Cs, all but 200 seating nine. Styling changes this year were confined to a simpler grille and more ornate taillamps, and the Traveler models disappeared from the New Yorker roster. Upholstery options included Highlander Plaid (woven plastic and leatherette in tartan pattern) and Navajo (resembling blankets of Southwest Indians). Fluid Drive was standard on all eight-cylinder models, and a new more sophisticated four-speed Vacamatic semi-automatic was optional. Production spurted to 161,704, but convertibles numbered just 4432 Windsors and 1295 New Yorkers. Saratoga and New Yorker club and business coupes combined totaled 2916, while only 1595 Crown Imperial sedans and limos were purchased, and 894 of those were "special" Town Sedans on the shorter New Yorker wheelbase, but badged as Imperials.

	Restorable	Good	Excellent
Convertibles	$5,000-10,000	$10,000-17,000	$17,000-28,000
Crown Imperial	2,500-7,500	7,500-12,500	12,500-20,000
Town & Country wgn	5,000-12,000	12,000-18,000	18,000-27,500
Other models	1,500-5,000	5,000-8,000	8,000-13,000

(add $1,000-3,000 for Highlander, $2,000-4,000 for Navajo interiors)

1942

Significantly facelifted, the '42s looked smoother with a wraparound grille sweeping to the front wheelwells and the hood was sleeker, opening from the front instead of the sides. Running boards were hidden under flares at the door bottoms. Highlander Plaid remained optional, and a new "Thunderbird" upholstery pattern was also offered, again in Indian style. Engines, six and eight, were slightly more powerful at 120 and 140 bhp, and the Town and Country continued as a wagon model. Per government mandate, Chryslers built after January 1, 1942, carried painted rather than chrome-plated trim. Production shut down for the duration of the war in early February, which is why only 36,586 '42 Chryslers left the assembly lines. Town and Country output hit 999, but there was only time to build 574 Windsor ragtops and 401 like New Yorkers and 450 Crown Imperials. Derham Custom Body Company of Rosemont, Pennsylvania, built a few custom Town Cars (open over the driver's compartment) and convertible sedans based on the Crown Imperial limo—they're particularly desirable.

	Restorable	Good	Excellent
Convertibles	$5,000-8,000	$8,000-15,000	$15,000-24,000
Derham Customs, closed	5,000-10,000	10,000-15,000	15,000-20,000
Derham Customs, open	7,500-15,000	15,000-22,500	22,500-35,000
Town & Country wgn	5,000-12,000	12,000-18,000	18,000-27,500

	Restorable	Good	Excellent
Other models	1,500-5,000	5,000-8,000	8,000-13,000

(add $1,000-3,000 for Highlander, $2,000-4,000 for Thunderbird interiors)

1946

Chrysler followed industry practice by introducing a restyled version of its 1942 model postwar. More changed than most of its competition, it featured fenders that flowed smoothly into the front doors and cleaner sides with less bright trim. The grille was a cacophony of chrome and stainless steel, one of the most elaborate in the industry, with almost as much shiny stuff as the grille of a Rolls-Royce. The '46 Town and Country comprised two sedans: Six and Eight (4124 and 100 built). There was also an eight-cylinder convertible that found 1935 buyers, plus one six-cylinder convertible. Seven true hardtops were also constructed, but these are considered prototypes; their value would be double that of a convertible. Prices, which had almost reached $90,000 for convertibles a few years ago, have lately been coming down, though T&Cs have been expensive for a long time. Restoration costs of these wood-trimmed land yachts can be stupendous, so buyers should take this into account when shopping. Car for car, a T&C convertible is worth more than twice as much as a New Yorker convertible.

1946-48 Chrysler New Yorker convertible coupe

1946-48 Chrysler Saratoga four-door sedan

	Restorable	Good	Excellent
Town & Country cvt	$10,000-20,000	$20,000-40,000	$40,000-60,000
T&C 6-cyl sdn	5,000-15,000	15,000-25,000	25,000-35,000
T&C 8-cyl sdn	10,000-18,000	18,000-30,000	30,000-40,000
New Yorker cvt	5,000-12,000	12,000-20,000	20,000-27,500
Windsor cvt	4,000-10,000	10,000-15,000	15,000-22,500
Crown Imperial	2,500-5,000	5,000-10,000	10,000-15,000
Other models	1,500-4,000	4,000-7,000	7,000-10,000

1947

Only detail changes occurred this year, with minor alterations to fender trim, hubcaps, colors, carburetion, and instruments. Goodyear low-pressure Super Cushion tires were phased in. The Traveler name reappeared in the Windsor series, returning as a luxury utility car with special paint and interior and an attractive wooden luggage rack. Unlike the comparable DeSoto Suburban, the Traveler did not have fold-down triple-seats or wooden floorboards in the rear; instead it had a conventional trunk compartment. Eight-cylinder models were unchanged except for a new eight-passenger sedan in the Crown Imperial series. Town and Country production this year was 2651 six-cylinder sedans and 3136 eight-cylinder convertibles.

	Restorable	Good	Excellent
Town & Country cvt	$10,000-20,000	$20,000-40,000	$40,000-60,000
Town & Country sdn	5,000-15,000	15,000-25,000	25,000-35,000
New Yorker cvt	5,000-12,000	12,000-20,000	20,000-27,500
Windsor cvt	4,000-10,000	10,000-15,000	15,000-22,500
Crown Imperial	2,500-5,000	5,000-10,000	10,000-15,000
Other models	1,500-4,000	4,000-7,000	7,000-10,000

1946-48 Chrysler Town and Country convertible coupe

1949 Chrysler New Yorker convertible coupe

1949 Chrysler New Yorker four-door sedan

1949 Chrysler Crown Imperial 8-passenger limousine

1948 (and early 1949)

These cars were continuations of the 1947 model run. After 1175 copies, the Town & Country sedan was discontinued at mid-year, leaving the convertible, which finished with 3309 units, as the only T&C body style. In the end, 12,526 T&Cs were built from 1946-early '49. Because the all-new '49s weren't ready at the usual fall introduction time, a number of '48s were reserialed as '49s through spring 1949. From 1946 through early 1949, Chrysler produced 3000 New Yorker convertibles, 11,200 Windsor ragtops, 10,735 New Yorker Club Coupes (plus 31,565 club coupes in other series), and 701 New Yorker business coupes (and another 3275 in other series). Meanwhile, 242,065 four-door sedans had been built, not counting 4182 Travelers. Crown Imperials during these three years numbered only 750 eight-passenger sedans and 650 limousines, while the six-cylinder Royal and Windsor limos totaled 1665 units.

	Restorable	Good	Excellent
Town & Country cvt	$10,000-20,000	$20,000-40,000	$40,000-60,000
Town & Country sdn	5,000-15,000	15,000-25,000	25,000-35,000
New Yorker cvt	5,000-12,000	2,000-20,000	20,000-27,500
Windsor cvt	4,000-10,000	10,000-15,000	15,000-22,500
Crown Imperial	12,500-5,000	5,000-10,000	10,000-15,000
Other models	1,500-4,000	4,000-7,000	7,000-10,000

1949

The 1949 Chrysler was boxy and ornate, with a massive grille, lots of chrome on the sides, and curious tacked-on vertical taillights ending in a little hump (only the Crown Imperial was spared those gaudy devices). A new Imperial sedan on the New Yorker wheelbase and a pretty Royal woody were introduced, and the Town and Country convertible returned. Though the six- and eight-cylinder limos retained their 139.5- and 145.5-inch wheelbases, they were longer on the regular models: Royal and Windsor, 125.5 inches; Saratoga and New Yorker, 131.5. A host of gimmick names for certain Chrysler features—Safety-Level Ride, Hydra-Lizer shocks, Safety-Rim wheels, Full-Flow oil filter, Cycle-Bonded brake linings—disguised the fact that there were few mechanical changes, for the line was still trundling along with its two underpowered L-head engines. Some production figures: Royal wagon, 1035; Windsor convertible, 3234; Windsor limo, 73; New Yorker soft top, 1137; Town and Country convertible, 1000; Imperial sedan, 50; Crown Imperial, 85.

	Restorable	Good	Excellent
Town & Country cvt	$10,000-20,000	$20,000-40,000	$40,000-60,000
Other cvt	2,500-7,500	7,500-15,000	15,000-22,000
Royal woody wagon	5,000-10,000	10,000-18,000	18,000-22,000
Crown Imperial	2,500-5,000	5,000-10,000	10,000-15,000
Imperial sdn	2,000-4,500	4,500-9,000	9,000-13,000
Other models	1,500-4,000	4,000-7,000	7,000-10,000

1950

The boxy look was carried over, but several traditional models were on their way out. The bottom-line six-cylinder Royals, which sold for less than $2200, were dropped after this year. The exotic wood-decorated Town and Country was retained as a single model—a Newport hardtop this time—with no convertible counterpart; from 1951 the Town and Country name would be applied to wagons. Chrysler's first mass-production hardtop, the Newport, debuted in three different series: Windsor, New Yorker, T&C (9925, 2800, and 700 sold). The '50 was cleaner than the '49 due to a less fussy but still broad chromium smile and squarish taillights that were neatly faired into the rear fenders. Notably, this would be the last year that Chrysler would rely solely on its aged L-head engines. Output soared to 179,299 cars, but convertibles sold poorly: 2201 Windsors and 899 New Yorkers. Ditto the Royal wagons: 599 woodies, 100 all-steel units. Likewise Crown Imperials: 209 sedans, 205 limos. The shorter-wheelbase Imperial sedans, however, totaled 10,650.

	Restorable	Good	Excellent
Town & Country htp	$7,500-15,000	$15,000-28,000	$28,000-40,000
Other hardtops	3,000-6,000	6,000-9,000	9,000-13,000
Convertibles	5,000-10,000	10,000-15,000	15,000-21,000
Royal woody wagon	5,000-10,000	10,000-18,000	18,000-22,000
Crown Imperial	2,500-5,000	5,000-10,000	10,000-15,000
Imperial sdn	2,000-4,500	4,500-9,000	9,000-13,000
Other models	1,500-4,000	4,000-7,000	7,000-10,000

1951

Chryslers remained boxy and, though cleaner (especially the grille), duller than ever. History was made this year, however, with Chrysler's new 331-cid hemi-head V-8, whose 180 horsepower came standard on Saratogas, New Yorkers, and Imperials (Windsors retained the L-head six). The Hemi offered exceptional volumetric efficiency and truly outstanding performance. Also, with a lower compression ratio it could burn lower-octane fuel than competitive overhead-valve V-8s, yet it was capable of producing at least as much power per cubic inch. A stock Saratoga would run from 0-60 in as little as 10 seconds and achieve close to 110 mph flat out. Bill Sterling drove one to win the Mexican Road Race stock-car class, and came in third overall behind two Ferraris. Chrysler listed three convertibles this year—Windsor, New Yorker, and Imperial (2646, 1386, and 650 built)—though curiously, values are about the same. Newport hardtops were more numerous: Windsor, 6426; New Yorker, 3654; Imperial, 749. Wagon and limo production was as tiny as ever.

	Restorable	Good	Excellent
Convertibles	$5,000-10,000	$10,000-15,000	$15,000-21,000
Hardtops	2,500-5,000	5,000-9,000	9,000-15,000
Crown Imperial	2,500-5,000	5,000-10,000	10,000-15,000

1950 Chrysler New Yorker Newport hardtop coupe

1951 Chrysler New Yorker Newport hardtop coupe

1951 Chrysler New Yorker four-door sedan

1952 Chrysler Saratoga four-door sedan

1953 Chrysler New Yorker DeLuxe Newport hardtop

1954 Chrysler Custom Imperial Newport hardtop coupe

1954 Chrysler New Yorker DeLuxe convertible coupe

	Restorable	Good	Excellent
Station wagons	2,500-5,000	5,000-12,000	12,000-18,000
Other models	1,500-4,000	4,000-7,000	7,000-10,000

1952

Because of Korean War commitments by most motor vehicle manufacturers, it was doubtful for awhile that '52 models would appear at all. But appear they did, though production was restricted industry-wide by the government. Instant identification of the little-altered Chrysler can be made at the rear, where the back-up lights were incorporated into the taillights. Windsors still ran with the 264.5-cid L-head six, increased by three bhp to 119. Production dipped from 163,613 in 1951 to 87,470 for 1952. As usual, the bulk of output was four-door sedans: 70,029 units.

	Restorable	Good	Excellent
Convertibles	$5,000-10,000	$10,000-15,000	$15,000-21,000
Newport hardtops	2,500-5,000	5,000-9,000	9,000-15,000
Crown Imperial	2,500-5,000	5,000-10,000	10,000-15,000
Station wagons	2,500-5,000	5,000-12,000	12,000-18,000
Other models	1,500-4,000	4,000-7,000	7,000-10,000

1953

A modest but effective facelift gave Chrysler more up-to-date, smoother lines, squared-up rear fenders, and reverse-slant C-pillars on sedans and coupes. Still, the boxy look prevailed. The Saratoga nameplate was dropped. This left a revised lineup of Windsor, Windsor DeLuxe, New Yorker, and New Yorker DeLuxe, all now on the 125.5-inch wheelbase. Imperials became Custom Imperials, on a longer 133.3-inch span. Crown Imperials, of which only 160 were built, retained the 145.5-inch stretch. The Hemi V-8 remained at its original 180 bhp, but Chrysler finally got its first fully automatic transmission in June 1953: two-speed PowerFlite. Understandably, six-cylinder Windsors were selling in decreasing quantities as the horsepower race intensified. Total production soared to 170,006, but convertibles were as rare as ever: 1250 Windsor DeLuxes, 950 New Yorker DeLuxes. Town and Country wagons did slightly better: 1242 Windsors, 1399 New Yorkers. So did the Newport hardtops: 5642 Windsor DeLuxes, 2525 New Yorkers, 3715 New Yorker DeLuxes, 823 Custom Imperials.

	Restorable	Good	Excellent
Windsor DeLuxe cvt	$5,000-10,000	$10,000-13,000	$13,000-19,000
New Yorker DeLuxe cvt	5,000-10,000	10,000-15,000	15,000-23,500
Newport hardtops	2,500-5,000	5,000-9,000	9,000-15,000
Imperial Town Limo	2,500-4,000	4,000-8,000	8,000-12,000
Crown Imperial	2,500-5,000	5,000-10,000	10,000-15,000
Station wagons	2,500-5,000	5,000-10,000	10,000-16,000
Other models	1,500-4,000	4,000-7,000	7,000-10,000

1954

Chrysler had a disastrous year, but had been planning its 1955 models for nearly 30 months and was playing a holding game. The Windsor's L-head six was built for the last time. Though virtual replicas of 1953, all but Imperials can be told apart by a small scoop in the grille centers and added chrome trim. The lineup was simplified as the base Windsor series disappeared. Windsor DeLuxes, New Yorkers, and Imperials each had a distinctive grille treatment. Hemi V-8 horsepower was up to 195 on the New Yorker, 235 for Imperial. Production plummeted 38 percent to 105,030. In this, the last year for club coupes, Chrysler produced 5659 Windsor DeLuxes, 2079 New Yorkers, and 1861 New Yorker DeLuxes. They're a bargain for collectors. Crown Imperials totaled just 100 units, and only 500 Windsor DeLuxe and 724 New Yorker DeLuxe ragtops saw the light of day.

	Restorable	Good	Excellent
Windsor DeLuxe cvt	$5,000-10,000	$10,000-13,000	$13,000-19,000
New Yorker DeLuxe cvt	5,000-10,000	10,000-15,000	15,000-23,500
Newport hardtops	2,500-5,000	5,000-9,000	9,000-15,000
Custom Imperial Twn Limo	2,500-4,000	4,000-8,000	8,000-12,000
Crown Imperial	2,500-5,000	5,000-10,000	10,000-15,000
Station wagons	2,500-5,000	5,000-10,000	10,000-16,000
Other models	1,500-4,000	4,000-7,000	7,000-10,000

1955

Imperial became a separate make for 1955. Chrysler, meanwhile, hyped "The New 100 Million Dollar Look," with a wraparound windshield, tall "Twin Tower" taillights, divided eggcrate grille (in two versions), and wild two- and three-tone paint combinations. There were only two series this year—Windsor DeLuxe and New Yorker DeLuxe—both on a 125-inch chassis. The model count dropped to 11 from 16 (not counting '54 Imperials), and long-wheelbase Chryslers were history. Windsors got a 188-bhp 301 V-8, New Yorkers a 250-bhp 331. A novelty was the "Range Selector" PowerFlite shift lever sticking out of the dashboard. Hardtops were the rage, so both series listed two trim levels: Windsor Nassau and Newport, New Yorker Newport and St. Regis. A special model destined to become legendary was the 300 (officially C-300), a mighty 300-horsepower hardtop that dominated stock-car racing in 1955-56. Only 1725 were built. Total output spurted to 152,777 units. Windsor DeLuxes accounted for 1395 ragtops, 1983 Town & Country wagons, 18,474 Nassaus, 13,126 Newports. New Yorkers were less common: 946 soft tops, 1036 wagons, 5777 Newports, 11,076 St Regis. The '55 Chryslers were well-built and solid, and hold up better than their successors, but it pays to buy the best example you can find.

	Restorable	Good	Excellent
C-300 hardtop	$8,000-15,000	$15,000-20,000	$20,000-27,500
Windsor convertible	5,000-10,000	10,000-13,000	13,000-18,000
New Yorker convertible	5,000-10,000	10,000-15,000	15,000-22,500

1955 Chrysler C-300 hardtop coupe

1955 Chrysler New Yorker DeLuxe Town & Country

1955 Chrysler New Yorker DeLuxe four-door sedan

1955 Chrysler Windsor DeLuxe four-door sedan

1956 Chrysler New Yorker convertible coupe

1956 Chrysler New Yorker four-door sedan

1957 Chrysler Saratoga four-door sedan

1957 Chrysler Saratoga hardtop sedan

Hardtops	2,500-6,000	6,000-10,000	10,000-17,000
Other models	1,500-4,000	4,000-7,000	7,000-10,000

1956

For this facelift year Chrysler grew tailfins: modest, and neatly housing tall three-way-visible taillights. The divided '55 grille gave way to a single, bolder unit housing strong horizontal bars on Windsors and a fine mesh on New Yorkers. A new four-door hardtop was added for both series, and the DeLuxe part of the name was dropped for both. One of the industry's best automatic transmissions, three-speed TorqueFlite, became a mid-year option; this was also the year Chrysler adopted pushbutton controls for the automatic. With larger engines (331 and 354 cid), horsepower jumped to 225 for Windsors, 260 for New Yorkers. In a down year industry-wide, production dropped to 128,322. The C-300 hardtop, now 300-B, retreated to 1102 units despite more horses: 340 or 355. Ragtops became even scarcer, 1011 Windsors and 921 New Yorkers, but Town & Country wagons actually increased to 2700 Windsors and 1070 New Yorkers.

	Restorable	Good	Excellent
300-B hardtop	$8,000-15,000	$15,000-20,000	$20,000-27,500
Windsor convertible	5,000-10,000	10,000-13,000	13,000-18,000
New Yorker convertible	5,000-10,000	10,000-15,000	15,000-22,500
Hardtops, 2d	2,500-6,000	6,000-10,000	10,000-17,000
Hardtops, 4d	2,000-5,000	5,000-8,500	8,500-12,000
Other models	1,500-4,000	4,000-7,000	7,000-10,000

1957

The Windsor ragtop vanished, but the Saratoga mid-range series reappeared with a sedan and two hardtops and a 295-bhp Hemi. Styling was all-new and superb, marked by high-flying fins and a daringly low beltline, but workmanship slipped badly. A new feature was Torsion-Aire front suspension, using torsion bars instead of coil springs and eliminating most of the upward force caused by road irregularities. Torsion bars were a Chrysler feature into the '80s, proving how well they worked. The 300-C, with 375 and 390 bhp, acquired a convertible—all 484 of which have recently soared near the early postwar Town and Country in collector esteem and market value. The hardtop added another 1918 sales. Of the 124,675 cars produced, hardtops were plentiful, but just 1049 New Yorker soft tops were called for. Town & Country wagons numbered 2035 Windsors and 1391 New Yorkers.

	Restorable	Good	Excellent
300-C convertible	$12,000-22,500	$22,500-35,000	$35,000-50,000
300-C hardtop	8,000-17,500	17,500-22,500	22,500-32,500
New Yorker convertible	6,000-12,000	12,000-18,000	18,000-25,000
Hardtops, 2d	3,500-7,500	7,500-13,000	13,000-18,000
Hardtops, 4d	2,000-5,000	5,000-8,500	8,500-12,000
Other models	1,500-4,000	4,000-7,000	7,000-10,000

1958

Partly as a result of buyer dissatisfaction with quality, partly because of a sharp recession, 1958 was a terrible year for Chrysler as output skidded to 63,683 units. Further, there were no major styling changes to enhance sales appeal—just an inept facelift, highlighted by smaller taillights that looked lost inside the '57's unchanged tailfins. Front bumpers, grille textures, and side trim were also shuffled about. Windsors were cut back to a 122-inch wheelbase (still 126 for other series). Chrysler's hopes were pinned now on chief stylist Virgil Exner's restyle for 1959. Though only 618 hardtops and 191 convertibles were built in the 300-D line, they kept the potent 392 Hemi with 380/390 bhp. Horsepower in other lines was 290 for Newports, 310 for Saratogas, and 345 for New Yorkers. Ragtops were particularly rare: 2 Newports (likely prototypes) and 666 New Yorkers. Town & Country wagons weren't exactly plentiful either, as only 2856 of all models were called for.

	Restorable	Good	Excellent
300-D convertible	$12,000-22,500	$22,500-35,000	$35,000-50,000
300-D hardtop	8,000-17,500	17,500-22,500	22,500-32,500
Other convertibles	6,000-12,000	12,000-18,000	18,00-25,000
Hardtops, 2d	3,500-7,500	7,500-13,000	13,000-18,000
Hardtops, 4d	2,000-5,000	5,000-8,500	8,500-11,000
Other models	1,500-4,000	4,000-7,000	7,000-10,000

1959

The '59 lineup featured a so-so facelift that kept the same fins and rooflines, but added new front and rear styling and revamped side trim. A Windsor convertible reappeared, but only 961 customers requested one. The Hemi was dropped favor of a new wedgehead V-8, and for that reason the 300-E has been criticized as a weakling. It wasn't—tests indicated 0-60 in 8.5 seconds and quarter-mile runs of 17 seconds at 90 mph. But production was low: 550 hardtops, 140 ragtops. Values for the '59 Chryslers depend more on condition than the individual type—New Yorker, Windsor, or Saratoga—except that the Windsor convertible is worth much less than the New Yorker, of which only 286 were built. Jacquard upholstery that looked great new doesn't hold up well; engines, though strong, are hellish to repair when they go wrong. Despite Chrysler's difficulties, output rose 10 percent to 69,970, just over half of them four-door sedans.

	Restorable	Good	Excellent
300-E convertible	$10,000-20,000	$20,000-30,000	$30,000-42,000
300-E hardtop	8,000-17,500	17,500-22,500	22,500-32,500
New Yorker convertible	4,000-8,000	8,000-15,000	15,000-22,000
Windsor convertible	3,000-6,000	6,000-12,000	12,000-17,000
Hardtops, 2d	2,500-5,000	5,000-8,000	8,000-13,000
Hardtops, 4d	2,000-4,000	4,000-7,000	7,000-11,000
Other models	1,500-3,500	3,500-6,000	6,000-9,000

1958 Chrysler New Yorker hardtop coupe

1959 Chrysler New Yorker hardtop sedan

1959 Chrysler Windsor hardtop coupe

1959 Chrysler New Yorker Town & Country wagon

1959 Chrysler 300-E hardtop coupe

1960 Chrysler 300-F hardtop coupe

1960 Chrysler New Yorker hardtop sedan

1961 Chrysler 300-G hardtop coupe

1961 Chrysler New Yorker hardtop sedan

1961 Chrysler Newport convertible coupe

1960

Though the heavily restyled '60s still wore tailfins, now slanted outwards, they were cleaner than the '59s, and the first Chryslers with unit body construction. This made them less prone to looseness or rattles, but more likely to rust. The most exciting '60 was the 300-F, combining racy styling with road-hugging suspension and an optional Pont-a-Mousson four-speed gearbox. Optional ram induction manifolding boosted output of its 413 V-8 from 375 to 400 bhp. The 300-F did the standing quarter mile in 16 seconds flat; it rode hard but cornered better than most anything its size. A half-dozen different axle ratios could be ordered, from stump pullers to long-legged cruisers—Andy Granatelli turned nearly 190 mph for the flying mile. Demand nearly doubled to 964 hardtops and 248 ragtops. The Saratoga series, never a big seller, put in its last year, offered as a two- or four-door hardtop or four-door sedan, as before. Despite the new styling, production improved only modestly to 77,285 units. Windsor tallied 1467 convertibles and 2146 Town & Country wagons; the New Yorker counted 556 soft tops and 1295 wagons.

	Restorable	Good	Excellent
300-F convertible	$15,000-25,000	$25,000-40,000	$40,000-55,000
300-F hardtop	8,000-17,500	17,500-22,500	22,500-32,500
New Yorker convertible	3,000-6,000	6,000-10,000	10,000-17,500
Windsor convertible	3,000-5,000	5,000-8,000	8,000-14,000
Other models	1,500-3,000	3,000-5,000	5,000-8,000

1961

The last of Virgil Exner's elaborately plumed models, the '61 Chryslers were the cleanest in years, with lots of glass and aggressive, inverted trapezoidal grillework flanked by slanted quad headlights. There were optional swivel seats (as since 1959), and four-way hazard flashers. A six-model 122-inch-wheelbase Newport series arrived at a cut-rate price ($2964-$3622) below the Windsor, and was so popular that it replaced Windsor in 1962. This all helped, for total output jumped to 96,454 units, 57,102 of which were Newports. The 300-G also enjoyed better times: 1280 hardtops and 337 ragtops. Convertibles numbered 2135 Newports and 576 New Yorkers.

	Restorable	Good	Excellent
300-G convertible	$17,500-27,500	$27,500-42,500	$42,500-52,500
300-G hardtop	8,000-17,500	17,500-22,500	22,500-30,000
New Yorker convertible	3,000-6,000	6,000-10,000	10,000-17,500
Newport convertible	3,000-5,000	5,000-9,000	9,000-14,000
Other models	1,500-3,000	3,000-5,000	5,000-7,000

1962

Stylist Virgil Exner designed the '62s, but was replaced by the time they were in production by

Elwood Engel, former Lincoln designer. For 1962, Exner offered what he called "plucked chickens": bodies almost identical to 1961 up front, but devoid of tailfins. The result was a clean, if perhaps less exciting, lineup. With the Windsor series gone, a new "non-letter" 300 series debuted, trading off the reputation of the "letter" 300s. These were sporty-looking cars with fashionable features such as bucket seats and center console. The desirable convertible models appeared in the Newport and 300 series this year, along with the soft top 300-H (2051, 1848, and 123 built). The pubic approved of the changes as demand rose to 128,921. By body style, output came to 68,670 four-door sedans, 23,686 hardtop coupes, 16,361 hardtop sedans, and 7155 wagons.

	Restorable	Good	Excellent
300-H cvt	$12,500-22,500	$22,500-35,000	$35,000-45,000
300-H hardtop	8,000-17,500	17,500-22,500	22,500-30,000
300 convertible	4,000-6,000	6,000-10,000	10,000-15,000
300 hardtop, 2d	2,000-3,500	3,500-6,500	6,500-9,000
Newport cvt	2,500-4,000	4,000-8,000	8,000-12,000
Other models	1,500-3,000	3,000-5,000	5,000-7,000

1963

The "crisp, clean custom look" was how Chrysler described the first shapes crafted largely by Elwood Engel: chunky cars, all on the short 122-inch wheelbase, making the New Yorker the same size as the Newport and 300s. Two limited-edition models to watch for: the 300 Pace Setter two-door hardtop and convertible and the New Yorker Salon. The Pace Setter commemorated Chrysler's selection to pace the Indy 500, and flaunted crossed-flag emblems and other special trim; 306 hardtops and 1861 ragtops were built. The ultra-luxurious Salon hardtop sedan came with standard air, AM/FM, Auto-Pilot, power brakes/steering/seats/windows, TorqueFlite, color-keyed wheel covers, and vinyl-covered roof. Just 593 were produced. In the letter series 300, "I" was skipped and the convertible was dropped, leaving the 300-J with just the hardtop, of which 400 rolled off the assembly line. Total production was nearly identical to 1962: 128,937 units.

	Restorable	Good	Excellent
300-J hardtop	$6,000-10,000	$10,000-15,000	$15,000-20,000
300 convertible	4,000-6,000	6,000-10,000	10,000-14,000
300 2d hardtop	2,000-3,500	3,500-6,000	6,000-8,000
300 Pace Setter cvt	6,000-7,500	7,500-12,000	12,000-16,000
300 Pace Setter htp	3,500-5,000	5,000-7,500	7,500-9,500
Newport convertible	2,500-4,000	4,000-8,000	8,000-12,000
Other models	1,500-3,000	3,000-5,000	5,000-7,000

1964

The 300-K reintroduced a convertible, and the general line was lightly facelifted. Identification points were revised grille patterns and six-sided (rather than round) taillights. These big, handsome Chryslers are among the few bargain barges of the Sixties—late in taking hold among collectors and outshone by their predecessors. As a result, one

1962 Chrysler New Yorker hardtop sedan

1962 Chrysler 300 hardtop coupe

1963 Chrysler 300 hardtop coupe

1963 Chrysler New Yorker Salon hardtop sedan

1966 Chrysler 300-L hardtop coupe

can still buy a Newport, or even a non-letter 300 convertible, for under $10,000, which means that these ragtops are definitely underpriced and stand to appreciate strongly in the 1990s. Although collectors think less of post-1962 letter-series 300s, their prices continue to rise, and figures far exceeding our ranges have been paid for exceptional examples at auction. The 300-K was more popular than ever with 3022 coupes and 625 ragtops sold. A mid-year model was called the Silver 300, a hardtop coupe painted that color and fitted with a special black leather-and-vinyl interior and a three-quarter-length black vinyl roof. Some 2152 were built as 300s, plus another 255 as 300-Ks. In total, 153,319 Chryslers were produced, the best year since 1953. Town & Countrys accounted for 9554 units, the New Yorker Salon tripled to 1621, while the Newport recorded 2176 soft tops, the 300, 1401.

	Restorable	Good	Excellent
300-K convertible	$10,000-18,000	$18,000-27,500	$27,500-35,000
300-K hardtop	6,000-10,000	10,000-15,000	15,000-20,000
300 convertible	4,000-6,000	6,000-10,000	10,000-14,000
300 2d hardtop	2,000-3,500	3,500-6,000	6,000-7,500
Newport convertible	2,000-3,500	3,500-7,000	7,000-10,000
Other models	1,000-2,500	2,500-4,000	4,000-6,000

1965

The first Chryslers entirely designed by Elwood Engel, the '65s were smaller on the outside but larger on the inside, benefitting from a longer 124-inch wheelbase. Fully restyled, they were handsome cars with much the same chiseled fuselage as Engel's earlier 1961 Lincoln Continental. The luxurious New Yorker Town & Country wagon was dropped after this year, after only 3065 were sold; the Newport T&C, which found 8421 buyers, was continued. The Chrysler 300-L was the last of the letter series cars, though very little different from the non-letter 300s this year; 2845 were built, including 440 ragtops. Overall, Chrysler built 206,089 cars, a record. Convertible production was 3192 Newports and 1418 non-letter 300s.

	Restorable	Good	Excellent
300-L convertible	$8,000-12,000	$12,000-17,500	$17,500-25,000
300-L hardtop	6,000-10,000	10,000-15,000	15,000-20,000
300 convertible	4,000-6,000	6,000-10,000	10,000-14,000
300 2d hardtop	2,000-3,500	3,500-6,000	6,000-7,500
Newport convertible	2,000-3,500	3,500-7,000	7,000-10,000
Other models	1,000-2,500	2,500-4,000	4,000-6,000

1966

From this year through 1968, all wagons carried the Newport name. All-vinyl upholstery was used instead of cloth-and-vinyl as in Newport sedans. Standard features included power steering and brakes and TorqueFlite automatic. Wagons also had a three-in-one front seat that looked like a conventional bench. Each half could be adjusted individually and there was a reclining seatback on the passenger's side. This was also the first year for the popular 440 V-8, standard on the New Yorker in 350-bhp guise; other Chryslers used the 383-inch engine: 270 bhp for Newports, 325 for 300s (optional for Newports). Otherwise, the '66s were basically the same save for grille textures and trim. No matter, production moved upward to another record: 264,848 units. Wagons more than doubled to 17,602, while convertibles held steady at 3085 Newports and 2500 300s.

	Restorable	Good	Excellent
300 convertible	$4,000-6,000	$6,000-10,000	$10,000-14,000
300 2d hardtop	2,000-3,500	3,500-6,000	6,000-9,000
Newport convertible	2,000-3,500	3,500-7,000	7,000-10,000
Other models	1,000-2,500	2,500-4,000	4,000-6,000

1967

A three-model Newport Custom series bowed, priced from $3347 to $3485, about $200 above the Newport: "a giant step in luxury, a tiny step in price." Customs had deluxe interiors done in jacquard or textured vinyl upholstery with pull-down center armrests. The dash of a fully equipped Newport Custom had eight toggle switches, three thumbwheels, 16 pushbuttons, three sliding levers, and 12 other controls to "put you in charge of almost every option in the book." It also took a book to understand. Vinyl-covered lift handles were used on the trunklid. Despite new lower-body sheetmetal and revised front and rear ends, the cars maintained their Chrysler "look." In a down year for the industry, Chrysler fell to 218,742 units. Newport and 300 convertibles came in at 2891 and 1594 units, while Newport wagons tallied 14,703. Hardtop coupes were popular: 26,583 Newports, 14,193 Newport Customs, 11,556 300s, and 6885 New Yorkers.

	Restorable	Good	Excellent
300 convertible	$4,000-6,000	$6,000-10,000	$10,000-14,000
300 2d hardtop	2,000-3,500	3,500-6,000	6,000-7,500
Newport convertible	2,000-3,500	3,500-7,000	7,000-10,000
Other models	1,000-2,500	2,500-4,000	4,000-6,000

1968

Mid-year specials were the focus of the 1968 spring selling season. Sportsgrain simulated wood paneling—like that on the wagons—was offered as a $126 option on Newport hardtops and convertibles, allowing nostalgia addicts to create a "sort-of" Town & Country. They're extremely rare: 965 hardtops, 175 ragtops. Newport Special two- and four-door hardtops were available with turquoise color schemes, which were later extended to the 300 series. Newports and New Yorkers received strongly vee'd grilles, while the 300 sported hidden headlights and quintuple hash marks on the front fend-

1967 Chrysler Newport hardtop coupe

1968 Chrysler Newport convertible coupe

1968 Chrysler 300 hardtop coupe

1968 Chrysler Newport Custom hardtop coupe

1969 Chrysler Newport Custom hardtop sedan

1970 Chrysler Newport Custom hardtop sedan

1970 Chrysler 300 convertible coupe

1970 Chrysler 300H (Hurst) hardtop coupe

ers. Production was at record levels, 264,853 units, although this vintage has not produced any memorable collector Chryslers. Convertibles this year numbered 2847 Newports and 2161 300s.

	Restorable	Good	Excellent
300 convertible	$4,000-6,000	$6,000-10,000	$10,000-14,000
300 2d hardtop	2,000-3,500	3,500-6,000	6,000-7,500
Newport convertible	2,000-3,500	3,500-7,000	7,000-10,000
Other models	1,000-2,500	2,500-4,000	4,000-6,000

1969

The "fuselage-styled" 1969 Chryslers—long, wide, clean, and aggressive—sold nearly as well as the record-breaking '68s, 260,773 units, but were better looking. Up front rode a combination bumper-grille, followed by smooth, uncluttered bodysides. In all, this was perhaps the most beautiful Chrysler of the decade, on par with the '65s. Wheelbase remained at 124 inches, but other dimensions kept growing: almost 225 inches overall and 80 inches wide, about as large as an American passenger car would ever get.

	Restorable	Good	Excellent
300 convertible	$3,000-5,000	$5,000-8,000	$8,000-11,000
Newport convertible	2,000-3,500	3,500-6,000	6,000-9,000
Other models	1,000-2,500	2,500-4,000	4,000-6,000

1970

Chrysler introduced the first Cordoba—not the luxury coupe of the mid-'70s, but a trim package for Newport hardtops: gold paint with special vinyl roof and bodyside moldings, gold wheels and grille, and "Aztec Eagle" upholstery. Production came to 1868 coupes and 1873 sedans. Newports were now offered with the 440-cid V-8. A special Newport 440 hardtop was listed, complete with TorqueFlite, vinyl roof, and special accessories. The '70 to look for, however, is the 300-H or 300-Hurst, named for its Hurst floorshift attached to an automatic gearbox. Performance wheels, H70x15 white-letter tires, the 440 V-8, and heavy duty suspension were standard, set off by a gold and white paint job, custom fiberglass hood with air scoop, rear deck spoiler, special grille paint, pinstriping, and a custom interior. Only 501 were built, one of them a ragtop. Industry output was way down this year, and so was Chrysler's, to 180,777. Convertibles plummeted nearly 50 percent to 1124 Newports and 1077 300s.

	Restorable	Good	Excellent
300 convertibles	$3,000-5,000	$5,000-8,000	$8,000-11,000
300-H convertible	6,500-12,000	12,000-15,000	15,000-18,000
300-H hardtop	4,000-6,000	6,000-8,000	8,000-10,000
Newport convertible	2,000-3,500	3,500-6,000	6,000-9,000
Other models	1,000-2,500	2,500-4,000	4,000-6,000

1971

This was the last year for what Chrysler called "fuselage styling," though the 1972-73 models were still based on the 1969 shell. Designs were clean, although easy-switch items like grilles, taillights, and side decoration were altered more than was necessary, and became tackier-looking in the process. More important from the collector standpoint is that Chrysler abandoned the convertible this year, and wouldn't revive it for over a decade. Thus, from the enthusiast standpoint, there is little to consider. The most desirable model is the 300 two-door hardtop, as this series was in its final year. Production slipped slightly to 175,188 cars, of which 7256 were 300 hardtop coupes. In that body style, there were also 13,549 Newports, 8,500 Newport Royals (slightly cut-rate Newports), 5527 Newport Customs, and 4485 New Yorkers.

	Restorable	Good	Excellent
300 2d hardtop	$2,000-3,000	$3,000-4,000	$4,000-5,000
New Yorker 2d htp	2,000-3,000	3,000-4,000	4,000-5,000

1972

A new engine, more adaptable to emissions tuning than the old 383, was introduced: the 400, with 190-bhp *net.* A smaller 360 was adopted for the Newport Royal series, which actually got its start in 1971. Brought in as the 300 departed, the Royal was priced below the now-discontinued Newport. Electronic ignition was also featured. New Yorkers retained the 440 big-block, but with added emission controls. Chrysler was down now to four body styles: two hardtops, a pillared sedan, and a wagon. Making the most of what it had, the company offered a new top-of-the-line New Yorker Brougham with high-grade interiors. Broughams have attracted a few collectors as examples of the last truly elephantine American passenger cars; priced at $5222-$5350, they came as two- and four-door hardtops and four-door sedans, with production runs of 4635, 20,328, and 5971 units. Total output this year rebounded to 204,704 units.

	Restorable	Good	Excellent
New Yorker Brougham, htp cpe	$1,500-3,000	$3,000-4,000	$4,000-5,000
New Yorker Brougham, 4d	1,000-2,500	2,500-3,000	3,000-4,000

1973

After fussing with the Newport Royal name in 1971-72, it was summarily axed for 1973. The model lineup now consisted of Newport, Newport Custom, Town & Country, New Yorker, and New Yorker Brougham. The '73s featured new sheetmetal and a more conventional front end, stylists having dropped the combination bumper-grille that had been around since 1969. Bumpers were bulkier, to deal with Federal crash regulations, pushing over-

1971 Chrysler Newport hardtop coupe

1972 Chrysler Newport Royal hardtop coupe

1973 Chrysler Newport Royal hardtop coupe

1973 Chrysler New Yorker four-door sedan

1974 Chrysler New Yorker hardtop sedan

1975 Chrysler Cordoba coupe

1975 Chrysler New Yorker Brougham hardtop sedan

all lengths to a gargantuan 230-231 inches. Having promised in the early Sixties that "there will never be a small Chrysler," the division was still plugging the full-size product—but even though production was up to 234,223 units, the pledge would soon be broken. The breakdown for New Yorker Broughams was 7980 hardtop coupes, 13,165 hardtop sedans, and 4533 four-door sedans.

	Restorable	Good	Excellent
New Yorker Brougham, htp cpe	$1,500-3,000	$3,000-4,000	$4,000-5,000
New Yorker Brougham, 4d models	1,000-2,500	2,500-3,000	3,000-4,000

1974

This year brought more of the same in a completely restyled package, but it wasn't enough in light of the Arab oil embargo and resulting gas lines. Production crashed 49 percent to 117,373 units. Though still riding a 124-inch wheelbase, the all-new, more formal-looking Chryslers were nearly a half-foot shorter, but also about 200 pounds heavier. The model lineup was unchanged, with New Yorker Broughams accounting for 7980 hardtop coupes, 13,165 hardtop sedans, and 4533 pillared sedans. Hardtop lovers looking for a big-car bargain might consider one of the 13,784 Newport or 7206 Newport Customs produced.

	Restorable	Good	Excellent
New Yorker Brougham, htp cpe	$1,500-3,000	$3,000-4,000	$4,000-5,000
NY Brougham, 4d models	1,000-2,500	2,500-3,000	3,000-4,000

1975

The new personal-luxury Cordoba, a badly needed star in the Chrysler firmament, was a departure for a company which a decade earlier had vowed there would "never be a small Chrysler." Though it broke new ground for Chrysler, it was in fact a clone to the revamped Dodge Charger that also went on sale this year, though its styling was more "classic." Some say it resembled a Jaguar XJ6, and that was all to the good; others say it was a copy of the very successful Chevy Monte Carlo. In point of fact, the Cordoba's 115-inch wheelbase was actually a half-inch shorter than the Chevy's, but it weighed 500 pounds more mainly because of its higher level of standard equipment. The Corinthian name was emphasized with an optional Spanish leather interior, advertised in the dulcet tones of actor Ricardo Montalban. Standard upholstery was crushed velour or brocade cloth and vinyl. With 150,105 first year sales, Cordoba handily outsold all of the '74 Chrysler models combined. Big Chryslers lost the New Yorker series and another 15 percent in sales, though the New Yorker Brougham held steady. Total production rebounded to 251,549, the best since 1969.

	Restorable	Good	Excellent
New Yorker Brougham 2d htp	$1,000-2,500	$2,500-3,500	$3,500-4,500
NY Brougham, 4d models	500-1,500	1,500-2,500	2,500-3,500
Cordoba	1,500-2,500	2,500-3,500	3,500-5,000

1976

For the first time in 22 years, there was no Imperial in Chrysler showrooms. That's because the Imperial—waterfall grille and all—became the New Yorker Brougham at the whim of a nameplate change and a lower price. The top-line New Yorker Brougham boasted standard leather, velour, or brocade upholstery, plus shag carpets, imitation walnut trim, filigree moldings, and much more. Economy, such as it was, was boosted with a lower final-drive ratio and an optional "Fuel Pacer" system tied to an intake manifold pressure sensor connected to a warning light that glowed when the gas pedal was hit too hard. Given hard times, the Chrysler/Imperial deception didn't work; Chrysler production dipped to 222,153. Cordoba, with its new fine-line grille, also slipped, to 120,462 units. Bargain hunters appreciate the Imperial look on a Chrysler (Imperial fans don't), and they're far more available and virtually identical: all 11,510 hardtop coupes and 28,327 hardtop sedans.

1976 Chrysler New Yorker Brougham hardtop sedan

1976 Chrysler Cordoba coupe

	Restorable	Good	Excellent
New Yorker Brougham, 2d htp	$1,000-2,500	$2,500-3,500	$3,500-4,500
New Yorker Brougham, 4d models	500-1,500	1,500-2,500	2,500-3,500
Cordoba	1,500-2,500	2,500-3,500	3,500-5,000

1977 Chrysler New Yorker Brougham hardtop sedan

1977

Chrysler downsized, not by dropping the big New Yorker, but by adding a new 3600-pound, four-model line with an old name: LeBaron. Cleanly styled in the upright Mercedes/Ford Granada idiom, it came as a coupe or sedan with the workhorse 318 V-8. Despite its humble Plymouth Volaré origins, it sold well—54,851 coupes and sedans in base and Medallion versions—even though it hasn't become collectible. The rest of the '77 line was little changed, though Cordobas could be optioned with a T-top roof—a useful thing to look for now. Buyers agreed then, too, as they drove home 183,146 Cordobas. Apparently Chrysler was doing something right, for total production soared to a record 399,297 cars. Surprisingly, perhaps, 76,342 were the big New Yorker Broughams. This was also the last year for the big Town & Country wagon, which ended its run by finding 8569 buyers.

1977 Chrysler Cordoba coupe with Crown Roof option

	Restorable	Good	Excellent
New Yorker Brougham, 2d htp	$1,000-2,500	$2,500-3,500	$3,500-4,500

1978 Chrysler New Yorker Brougham hardtop sedan

1978 Chrysler Cordoba coupe with Crown Roof option

1979 Chrysler Cordoba coupe

	Restorable	Good	Excellent
New Yorker Brougham, 4d models	500-1,500	1,500-2,500	2,500-3,500
Cordoba	1,500-2,500	2,500-3,500	3,500-4,500

1978

The Town & Country wagon, a fixture at Chrysler since 1950, moved down to the LeBaron chassis. Volaré-sized on a 112.7-inch wheelbase, production increased to 25,256, assisted by a $700 price cut. LeBarons proliferated from four models to seven (14 counting the newly available 90-bhp Slant Six engine variants), prodding sales upward to 145,690. As with the LeBaron, Cordoba listed lower-priced "S" versions, which got a 155-bhp, 360-cid V-8. Regular models ran with a 190-bhp Lean Burn 400, and even the old faithful 318 V-8, now also a Lean Burn, was listed with 140/155 bhp. More to the point was the squarer front-end styling highlighted by stacked rectangular headlamps—not everybody thought this an improvement, perhaps reflected by the fact that output sank to 124,825. The big 440 V-8 was still a big-car option, but few were ordered, most customers preferring the more economical 400. More telling, this was the last year for the big New Yorker Brougham, which managed to snare 44,559 customers. Chrysler's attempt to keep up with the difficult times netted 354,029 buyers.

	Restorable	Good	Excellent
New Yorker Brougham, 2d htp	$1,000-2,500	$2,500-3,500	$3,500-4,500
New Yorker Brougham, 4d models	500-1,500	1,500-2,500	2,500-3,500
Cordoba	1,500-2,500	2,500-3,500	3,500-4,500

1979

Tradition was served by the Cordoba 300, a trim package on Chrysler's personal-luxury coupe recalling the styling theme of the old letter series with black-out cross-bar grille, bucket seats, red-white-blue emblems, special trim, and standard big engine—though by this time the best Chrysler had was a 195-horse 360. The package sold for $2040, and 3811 Cordobas had it. Among Newports and New Yorkers, the downsized R-body was smaller (118.5-inch wheelbase) and lighter (by more than 1000 pounds) than the old mastodons, but still looked heavy. It sold better too, 132,936 units this year, but fizzled quickly as output went into a free fall to 28,574 for 1980. People's tastes were changing, and Chrysler—which had handed people the same old stuff for years—was in deep financial trouble. Help was on the way in Lee Iacocca, the recently fired Ford sales ace, who took Chrysler's helm and immediately applied for government loan guarantees to save the company and back its modernization effort. In spite of everything, Chrysler built 349,450 cars for the model year, 88,015 of them Cordobas.

	Restorable	Good	Excellent
Cordoba 300	$2,500-3,500	$3,500-5,000	$5,000-6,500
Cordoba	1,500-2,500	2,500-3,500	3,500-4,500

1980 Chrysler Cordoba Crown coupe

1981 Chrysler Cordoba coupe

1982 Chrysler Cordoba LS coupe

1980

The Cordoba, riding a 112.7-inch wheelbase, was all-new and smaller, now with the trusty Slant Six standard, though a 318 V-8 was optional. (It scarcely bears mentioning that V-8s are far more desirable from the collector standpoint.) Cordoba's upright, classic-style grille looked good, and its stand-up hood ornament was a special "Cordoba coin" minted by the Franklin Mint. A "Cabriolet" roof option comprised a fabric padded top, which provided a convertible look at the expense of visibility. The "consummate Cordoba" Crown Corinthian edition (2069 built) featured special paint jobs (black metallic or cream-on-beige) with matching interiors. Unfortunately, Chrysler's problems and the second energy crisis did nothing for sales: 164,510 units, less than half the previous year. Cordoba fared no better: 53,471.

	Restorable	Good	Excellent
Cordoba Crown	*	$3,500-5,000	$5,000-6,500
Cordoba	*	3,500-4,500	4,500-5,500

* Purchase only in good or excellent condition

1981

The base Cordoba was little changed, but a new variation was the LS, carrying a cross-bar 300-style grille and body-colored taillamp bezels. It also sported red, white, and blue accent stripes on bodysides and decklids, high-back vinyl bucket seats, and body-color rearview mirrors. Alas, the 318 V-8 was the largest engine offered. The up-market Corinthian Edition package was continued, with just 1957 built. Times were really tough now, with total Chrysler production crashing to 73,596 units. Cordobas numbered only 20,293—and just 7315 of them were the more desirable LS. Big Chryslers were nearly non-existent: 3622 Newports and 6548 New Yorkers.

	Restorable	Good	Excellent
Cordoba	*	$2,000-3,000	$3,000-4,000

* Purchase only in good or excellent condition

1982

Early fruits of the Iacocca leadership were the K-car-based front-wheel-drive LeBarons, not to mention the first Chrysler convertible since 1970. Introduced in mid-year, the new soft top was a conversion job by Cars & Concepts in Brighton, Michigan, which cut and reinforced LeBaron coupes and installed a nicely crafted power top with a tailored boot. Up-market was the Mark Cross option, with designer buckets, standard air, automatic, power windows, and power door locks. The 99.9-inch-wheelbase ragtop (which didn't have rear-quarter windows the first year) was an instant hit, with

1983 Chrysler Cordoba coupe

3045 base models and 9780 Medallions produced out of a total 90,319 LeBarons. The '82 Cordoba was very similar to the '81, and output declined further to 14,898, of which 3136 were the LS model. Though the Newport was dropped, the New Yorker recovered nicely to 50,509 sales, some of them equipped with the Slant Six.

	Restorable	Good	Excellent
Cordoba	*	$2,000-3,000	$3,000-4,000
LeBaron cvt	*	3,000-4,000	4,000-5,000
LeBaron Mark Cross cvt	*	3,500-4,500	4,500-6,000

* Purchase only in good or excellent condition

1983

The luxurious LeBaron version of the Chrysler K-car continued, along with its Mark Cross leather-seat variation. An interesting version of the ragtop, the Mark Cross Town & Country wore simulated wood trim. Of the 9891 convertibles built, 5441 got the Mark Cross package and 1520 teased woodpeckers. Though LeBaron production declined to 71,085, a new E Class four-door riding a 103.3-inch wheelbase added 39,258 sales. A more upmarket E Class-based New Yorker ($10,950) added a further 33,832 units. Harking back to the early Fifties, when Chrysler always offered a long-wheelbase model, the division introduced an $18,900 four-door Executive sedan on a 124-inch wheelbase and a $21,900 limousine on a 131-inch stretch. There was even a power-operated division window for the latter. Also new was an optional travel computer and a Mitsubishi 2.6-liter, 93-bhp four (standard on the limo) for the front-drive models. Standard features included halogen headlamps. For its final year, the little-changed Cordoba dropped the LS; only 13,471 were built. The big New Yorker was replaced by a Volaré-based New Yorker Fifth Avenue on a 112.7-inch wheelbase, and scored an encouraging 83,501 sales. The Slant Six was standard, though the 130-bhp 318 V-8 was more popular. Total production nudged the quarter-million mark.

	Restorable	Good	Excellent
Cordoba	*	$2,000-3,500	$3,000-5,000
LeBaron cvt	*	2,000-3,500	3,500-5,000
Mark Cross cvt	*	2,500-3,500	3,500-5,500
Town & Country cvt	*	3,000-4,500	4,500-6,500
LeBaron limousine	*	1,500-3,000	3,000-4,500

* Purchase only in good or excellent condition

1984

Laser, Chrysler's new sporty coupe, was a clone of the similar Dodge Daytona; both were built on a revised 97-inch-wheelbase K-car platform. Look for the XE, with its turbocharged 2.2, port fuel injection, and 142 bhp. XEs also got an electronic instrument cluster (nobody's perfect), firmer suspension, 15-

inch tires, bucket seats with adjustable lumbar bladders, and a 22-function message center giving visual and audible warnings of mechanical failures (which can be disconnected). Out of 59,858 Lasers, 25,882 were XEs. Hope and pray that all the goodies are still operating on yours. A new model, the five-door hatchback LeBaron GTS (Grand Touring Sedan), rode a 103.1-inch wheelbase, and did offer relatively grand touring in LS form. During its first year it attracted 60,783 buyers, 27,607 of whom chose the sportier LS. Though the New Yorker Fifth Avenue lost the first part of its name this year, it still recorded 79,441 sales. LeBaron convertibles had an excellent year: 6828 base models, 8275 Mark Cross editions, and 1105 Town & Countrys. Executives remained strictly limited editions—196 sedans and 594 limos. Chrysler enjoyed its best year ever: 333,240 units.

	Restorable	Good	Excellent
Laser XE	*	$1,000-2,000	$2,000-2,500
LeBaron cvt	*	2,500-3,500	3,500-4,500
Mark Cross cvt	*	3,000-4,000	4,000-5,000
Mark Cross Town & County cvt	*	3,500-4,500	4,500-5,500
LeBaron limousine	*	2,000-3,500	3,500-4,500

* Purchase only in good or excellent condition

1985

Lasers got an improved five-speed with upshift indicator light plus better seatback adjustments; XEs came with cast aluminum wheels as standard. A mid-year Laser option was the XT package, featuring a T-bar roof with removable panels. Output fell nonetheless to 32,673 base models and 18,193 XEs. Automatic was now standard on the LeBaron, which recorded 9196 base convertibles and 6684 Mark Cross editions, but only 595 Town & Countrys. The 2.6-liter limousine continued without the sedan, adding "Ultimate Sound" stereo with graphic equalizer and separate illumination front and rear. Just 759 were ordered. No matter, Chrysler saw another record-breaking year: 375,894 units.

	Restorable	Good	Excellent
Laser XE & XT	*	$1,500-2,500	$2,500-3,000
LeBaron cvt	*	3,000-4,000	4,000-4,500
Mark Cross cvt	*	3,500-4,500	4,500-5,500
Mark Cross Town & County cvt	*	4,000-5,000	5,000-6,000
LeBaron limousine	*	2,500-4,000	4,000-5,000

* Purchase only in good or excellent condition

1986

A new 2.5-liter, 97-bhp four with balancing shafts and throttle-body fuel injection was new in all Chrysler front-drive cars including the Laser, which was now in its last year. Sales were down to 21,123 base hatchbacks, 8560 XEs, and 6989 XTs. The XT, introduced in late 1985, was a performance

1984 Chrysler Laser Turbo coupe

1984 Chrysler LeBaron convertible coupe

1985 Chrysler Laser Turbo coupe

1986 Chrysler Laser XT Turbo coupe

1986 Chrysler LeBaron Town & Country convertible

1987 Chrysler LeBaron Turbo convertible

package featuring the 146-bhp 2.2 Turbo, firm suspension, and aerodynamic styling aids. The 2.5 precluded the Mitsubishi 2.6 which had been standard in the limousine; the Turbo 2.2 succeeded it in that application, though that amounted to only 138 cars. The limo would not be back for 1987. Chrysler's sporty trio of LeBaron convertibles continued; 12,578 base, 6905 Mark Cross, and 501 Town & Countrys found buyers. Though still very good, total sales eased off to 357,564 units.

	Restorable	Good	Excellent
Laser XE & XT	*	$2,000-3,000	$3,000-3,500
LeBaron cvt	*	3,000-4,000	4,000-4,500
Mark Cross cvt	*	3,500-4,500	4,500-5,500
Mark Cross Town & Country cvt	*	4,000-5,000	5,000-6,000
LeBaron limousine	*	2,500-4,000	4,000-5,000

* Purchase only in good or excellent condition

1987

One could say that the Laser was replaced by the Conquest, a rear-drive sports coupe built by Mitsubishi, but not a shred of collector interest seems destined ever to arise over this one. One could also argue that the Laser's real replacement was the new J-body LeBaron coupe and convertible. Though still based on the familiar K-car's 100.3-inch wheelbase, they sported more rounded, aerodynamic styling, and were instantly popular: 75,415 coupes and 8025 ragtops. A five-speed manual gearbox and 2.5-liter engine came standard, with the Turbo 2.2 optional. Elsewhere in the lineup, the LeBaron GTS hatchback was fading fast, as only 39,050 were called for—and that included 15,278 Premium sport sedans. Meanwhile, the Fifth Avenue slipped from 104,744 to 70,579 units. All told, Chrysler produced 321,906 cars for the model run.

	Restorable	Good	Excellent
LeBaron convertible	*	$4,000-5,000	$5,000-7,000

* Purchase only in good or excellent condition

1988

Two LeBaron convertibles were now available: base Highline and deluxe Premium. Both came with electric rear window defogger, 500-amp battery, and wider P195/70R-14 tires. These sharply priced and well-equipped models made Chrysler the world's largest purveyor of ragtops: 23,150 Highlines, 15,037 Premiums. Premiums were so well equipped that they're the ones to look for. The 2.5-liter four remained standard, the Turbo 2.2 optional; five-speed remained standard on base models. Mid-year saw the introduction of the more collectible LeBaron GTC, specially trimmed and equipped, and in monochromatic white. Output was only 2943 coupes and 2754 convertibles, but the GTC was successful enough that it was continued, though in a choice of colors. In addition, the New Yorker was new—sort of. It rode a 104.3-inch wheelbase and had V-6 power, but despite its new clothes it was still a K-car at heart. Total production took another hit, this time to 250,916, although this was still excellent by historical standards.

	Restorable	Good	Excellent
LeBaron cvt	*	$5,500-7,000	$7,000-8,000
LeBaron Premium cvt	*	6,000-7,500	7,500-8,500
LeBaron GTC cvt	*	7,000-8,500	8,500-10,000

* Purchase only in good or excellent condition

1988 Chrysler's TC by Maserati convertible coupe

1989 Chrysler LeBaron Turbo GTC convertible coupe

1990 Chrysler LeBaron Turbo GTC convertible coupe

1989

After a gestation period that would rival a brontosaurus, Chrysler finally introduced the $30,000 "The Chrysler TC by Maserati." The initials first stood for "Turbo Coupe," but the final product was a convertible, and it looked so much like a Chrysler LeBaron that people questioned its $10,000-$15,000 price premium. With the better of its two engines—a 200-bhp turbocharged, intercooled, dual-overhead-cam, 16-valve, 2.2-liter four designed by Maserati—it was quick, but this engine came only with a Getrag five-speed manual transmission. If you wanted automatic, you got the box-stock eight-valve version with 174 horsepower. TCs had Maserati-tuned suspension and anti-lock, four-wheel disk brakes, plus a removable hardtop with '55 Thunderbird-style opera windows. Chrysler contracted for 7500, and most were sold over the next couple of years at tremendous discounts. LeBaron convertibles received four-wheel disc brakes and a driver-side air bag. Model year sales fell to 214,720 units.

	Restorable	Good	Excellent
TC by Maserati	*	$14,000-18,000	$18,000-22,000
LeBaron cvt	*	6,000-7,500	7,500-9,000
LeBaron Premium cvt	*	7,000-8,500	8,500-10,000
LeBaron GTC cvt	*	8,000-9,500	9,500-11,000

* Purchase only in good or excellent condition

1990

A new woodgrain steering wheel and available V-6 engine marked the 1990 changes for the front-drive TC, now listing at $33,000. Again, one could opt at no extra cost for one of two drivetrains: the five-speed with the 200-bhp four, or the automatic, which now came with a smoother 3.0-liter Mitsubishi V-6. It's difficult to predict where the TC will go as a collectible, though the heft of opinion holds that it didn't compete in the Euro-sport-luxury field, being based overmuch on worthy but unrefined mass-production componentry. Still, it carried a famous name, and we know several people who have picked up pristine used examples at the lower end of the prices noted—which will continue to come down. The V-6 was also available on LeBaron convertibles. Total sales for 1990 slid to 186,000 units.

	Restorable	Good	Excellent
TC by Maserati	*	$16,000-20,000	$20,000-25,000
LeBaron 4-cyl cvt	*	8,500-10,000	10,000-12,000
LeBaron V-6 cvt	*	9,000-11,000	11,000-13,000
LeBaron V-6 Premium cvt	*	10,000-12,000	12,000-14,000

* Purchase only in good or excellent condition

1956 Continental Mark II hardtop coupe

1958 Continental Mark III Landau hardtop sedan

1958 Continental Mark III convertible coupe

Continental

Continental was registered as a separate make for only three years. For other Continentals, look under "Lincoln." The 1956-57 Mark II became collectible almost from new; the 1958 Mark III is also sought after for its overt Fifties styling. Club support is very good, mechanical parts supply moderately good, body parts difficult. Investment potential: very good.

1956-57

Eight years after the last first-generation Continental, its lineal successor appeared. The Mark II was beautifully styled by a crack team including Gordon Buehrig of Cord fame. Engineer Harley Copp's "cow belly" frame dipped low to permit high seating without a tall body. With Multi-Drive three-speed automatic and a balanced, individually tested 368-cid V-8, the Mark II was an image leader designed for prestige, not sales—and sell it didn't. Its price was $10,000, almost double a Cadillac Sixty-Two, and this limited the market considerably. There was virtually no change in the Mark II for 1957, though horsepower was raised from 285 to 300. A convertible had been contemplated, but only one prototype was actually constructed by the Derham coachworks. (Recently, more convertibles have been built by a specialty firm, to very exacting, high-quality standards.) Mark II production totaled 3012 for both 1956 and '57. Ford opted for a cheapened Continental in 1958.

	Restorable	Good	Excellent
Mark II htp	$4,000-10,000	$10,000-20,000	$20,000-30,000

1958

The 1958 Continental Mark III was essentially a high-line Lincoln in four flavors: sedan, Landau four-door hardtop, two-door hardtop, and convertible. Compared to the '58 Lincoln, it featured a finer eggcrate grille texture, which was repeated up back. Like the Lincoln, it sported liberal bright metal, prominent tailfins, and canted quad headlamps. List price of the coupe was cut 40 percent compared to the Mark II, an effort to make the Continental commercially valuable rather than simply an image maker. Lincoln's new 430-cid V-8 delivered 375 horsepower. Production came to 1283 sedans, 2328 hardtop coupes, 5891 Landaus, and 3048 ragtops.

After 1958, Continental was folded back into Lincoln-Mercury Division, and the 1959-60 Mark IV and Mark V were officially sold as Lincoln models.

	Restorable	Good	Excellent
Sedan, 4d	$2,500-5,000	$5,000-7,500	$7,500-10,000
Landau 4d htp	2,500-5,000	5,000-8,000	8,000-11,000
Hardtop, 2d	3,500-6,000	6,000-8,500	8,500-12,000
Convertible	5,000-10,000	10,000-20,000	20,000-30,000

Cord

One of the mainstays of the collector car movement since the founding of the Classic Car Club of America in 1953, the automobile named for Errett Lobban Cord remains highly desirable and—if you don't mind a sedan—not as expensive as most other Classics in the Auburn-Cord-Duesenberg field. Club support is excellent, mechanical parts supply good, thanks to considerable part replication by Cord specialists. Body parts are scarce except for smaller replicated items. (Cords were not produced during 1933-35.)

1930 Cord L-29 2/4-passenger cabriolet

1937 Cord 812 convertible coupe

1937 Cord 812 Supercharged four-door sedan

1930-32

Cord's low-slung L-29, a classic masterpiece designed by Harry Miller and Cornelius Van Ranst, broke new ground for American cars with its front-wheel drive, but it was underpowered with its adopted Auburn 125-bhp L-head straight eight. Mechanical components were Flash Gordon stuff: three speed sliding-pinion transmission sandwiched between clutch and differential; hydraulic brakes mounted inboard; Houdaille-Hershey shocks on all four wheels; Cardan constant-velocity joints on the front halfshafts. Bodywork was beautiful, as was the front end designed by Al Leamy. A high price and the Depression made the L-29 unsuccessful; total production, including some during 1929, was—depending on source—5010 or 4429.

	Restorable	Good	Excellent
Phaeton	$30,000-75,000	$75,000-120,000	$120,000-165,000
Cabriolet	25,000-65,000	65,000-100,000	100,000-135,000
Sdn & Brghm	10,000-25,000	25,000-50,000	50,000-75,000

1936-37

The Cord marque returned with the 810, an all-new design that has proved to be one of the most recognizable of Classic cars. Its innovative "coffin nose" styling and concealed headlamps were conceived by Gordon Buehrig, Dale Cosper, Dick Roberson, and Paul Laurenzen. Power came from a Lycoming V-8 connected to a four-speed electric pre-selector gearbox (set your gear, stab the clutch pedal to shift). A phaeton, Sportsman cabriolet, and two four-door sedans were offered: the fastback Beverly is preferred by connoisseurs to the bustle-back Westchester. For the 1937 Cord 812, a long-wheelbase Custom sedan was added, along with an optional supercharger that upped horsepower from 115 to 190. Sprouting from the left-hand side of the hood on blown cars were beautiful exposed exhaust pipes. This was the ultimate, and sadly the last, Cord automobile. And rare, too: just 1174 model 810s and 1146 model 812s were registered.

	Restorable	Good	Excellent
Sportsman cabrio	$15,000-35,000	$35,000-75,000	$75,000-110,000
Phaeton	15,000-35,000	35,000-70,000	70,000-100,000
Beverly sdn	10,000-20,000	20,000-40,000	40,000-60,000
Westchester sdn	8,000-15,000	15,000-35,000	35,000-55,000
1937 lwb Custom	10,000-20,000	20,000-40,00	40,000-60,000

1940 Crosley convertible coupe

1946 Crosley Four two-door sedan

1948 Crosley Four two-door station wagon

Crosley

People who sell refrigerators usually don't do well building cars. Powel Crosley, Jr., did better than most, conceiving of a small econo-car sold in hardware or appliance stores. Excepting open models, collectors have been slow to appreciate Crosleys. Club support is moderate, parts supply decidedly low, investment potential modest for open cars, low for others.

1939-42

Crosley began with an 80-inch wheelbase and a convertible body, and after some early engine disasters settled on an air-cooled Waukeshaw two-cylinder with two main bearings and 12 bhp. For 1940-42 there were five models priced as low as $299: a standard and DeLuxe sedan with convertible top, a wagon, a full convertible, and a "covered wagon" with canvas top. There were also a few commercial bodies, mainly pickups. Beginning in 1941, some Crosleys were sold by car dealers.

	Restorable	Good	Excellent
All models	$500-1,500	$1,500-2,500	$2,500-4,500

1946-52

Two-door sedans and convertibles and station wagons, along with a handful of commercial bodies, constituted Crosley production during 1946-48, when pent-up demand for cars saw production soar, hitting 29,084 in 1948, mostly wagons. As the big manufacturers got into gear, however, Crosley sales slid, and were only 2075 in the final year, 1952. The most interesting Crosleys were the 1949-52 Hotshot roadster (without doors) and the 1950-52 Super Sports (with conventional doors and better trim) on a longer, 85-inch wheelbase. These pocket rockets, of which 2498 were built in total, could do 90 mph, and one of them copped the Index of Performance at the Sebring Twelve Hours in 1951. Crosley was absorbed into General Tire in 1952, and car production was halted.

	Restorable	Good	Excellent
1949-52 rdstrs	$1,000-2,500	$2,500-5,000	$5,000-7,000
Other models	500-1,500	1,500-2,500	2,500-4,500

1950 Crosley Super Sports roadster

DeSoto

Eclipsed by the more luxurious Chrysler on one side, and the sportier Dodge on the other, DeSoto—conceived in 1928 (as a '29 model) to fill a market gap—was condemned to the life of an also-ran, and that has been its latterday status among collectors, too. Nevertheless, DeSoto produced many interesting and some very fast cars, and the marque appeals to those who like something different. Club support is very good, mechanical parts supply modest, body parts scarce. Investment potential is very good for convertibles, much lower for closed models.

1930 DeSoto Series CF Eight convertible coupe

1930-39

DeSotos through 1931 were formal, bolt-upright cars, the 1932-33s more rounded, and the post-1933s streamlined, particularly the 1934-36 DeSoto Airflows. From 1933-39, DeSotos all had sixes, with modest power. Unlike Chrysler, DeSoto offered only Airflow bodies in 1934, and took a beating; 1935 saw a hasty retreat to the more conventional Airstream, with a pretty, angled grille, slab sides, and rounded deck—sales shot up 116 percent. But DeSoto rode out the decade with larger and mundane cars. Airflows were dropped after 1936, when long sedans and limousines were added. Styling, by Raymond H. Dietrich, was very conservative. By 1938, DeSoto had settled into a consistent pattern: DeLuxe and Custom models priced around $900 and $1000, powered by the same six-cylinder engines and sharing the same chassis, with long-wheelbase models available in each series. Production during the decade ranged from a low of 13,940 in 1934 to a high of 81,775 in 1937. Open models were always very rare. From 1930-32 roadsters, phaetons, and convertibles were available: combined output for 1930 totaled 3639; for 1931, 2830; and for 1932, 2129. After this, convertibles were the only open models offered: 412 coupes and 132 sedans for 1933, none in 1934, 226 convertible coupes for 1935, 350 coupes and 215 sedans for 1936, 992 coupes and 426 sedans for 1937, 431 coupes and 88 sedans for 1938, and no ragtops for 1939 (though a sliding sunroof was offered).

1933 DeSoto Series SD 7-passenger sedan

1934 DeSoto Series SE Airflow four-door sedan

1938 DeSoto Six Touring Sedan

1939 DeSoto Custom Touring Sedan

1940 DeSoto DeLuxe coupe

1941 DeSoto Custom four-door sedan

1942 DeSoto Custom two-door sedan

1942 DeSoto Custom club coupe

	Restorable	Good	Excellent
1930-38 open	$4,000-10,000	$10,000-20,000	$20,000-30,000
1930-33 closed	1,500-4,000	4,000-7,000	7,000-10,000
1934-36 Airflow	2,500-5,000	5,000-8,000	8,000-10,000
1935-39 closed	2,000-4,000	4,000-6,000	6,000-8,000

1940

DeSoto lost some sales this year because with its new divided grille and almost identical contours it looked so much like a Plymouth, albeit on a longer 122.5-inch wheelbase. As before, there were two series, DeLuxe and Custom, though a convertible coupe was added to the Custom range. The engine remained a 228.1-cid L-head six developing 100 bhp, with 105 bhp optional. A total of 65,467 DeSotos were built for the model run, including 1085 soft tops, 9880 coupes and business coupes, and 382 long-wheelbase sedans/limos.

	Restorable	Good	Excellent
Custom cvt	$4,000-10,000	$10,000-17,500	$17,500-25,000
Cpe & lwb sdns	1,500-4,000	4,000-6,500	6,500-9,000
Other models	500-2,000	2,000-4,500	4,500-7,000

1941

The model lineup was unchanged and the wheelbase actually shrank an inch (but remained at 139.5 for long-wheelbase models), but DeSotos looked more like the $1000-$1200 cars they were thanks to a bolder front end, featuring the first of the vertical grille "teeth" that were to remain a DeSoto design hallmark through 1955. A single 105-bhp six was offered, and it could now be mated to a "Simplimatic" semi-automatic transmission, a four-speed variant of Chrysler's famed Fluid Drive. DeSoto built 97,497 cars this year, and 2937 were convertibles, so the odds of finding a '41 ragtop are better than for the '40 model.

	Restorable	Good	Excellent
Custom cvt	$4,000-10,000	$10,000-17,500	$17,500-25,000
Cpe & lwb sdns	1,500-4,000	4,000-6,500	6,500-9,000
Other models	500-2,000	2,000-4,500	4,500-7,000

1942

Production was cut short by America's entry into World War II, and DeSoto shut down car production in early February of that year. Production was only 24,015 of the '42s, which featured a much bolder grille, but the resultant scarcity does not seem to have affected today's market values very much at all. Neither, surprisingly, does the one really interesting design feature of the '42 DeSoto: hidden headlamps, the first on a production car since the 1936-37 Cord. This is a case where enthusiasts should prefer their judgement to what the market says: body style for body style, the '42 DeSoto is rarer and more desirable than the 1940 or '41. Besides that, styling was better, the illuminated "flying lady" hood mascot was a nice example of automotive art, and a larger 236.6-cid six cranked out 115 horses. Among sedans, look for the plush Fifth

Avenue version of the Custom Town Sedan, distinguished by an exterior nameplate and a luxurious leather and Bedford cloth interior. Convertibles numbered just 489 for '42, long-wheelbase sedans/limos 148.

	Restorable	Good	Excellent
Custom cvt	$5,000-12,000	$12,000-18,000	$18,000-27,500
Cpe & lwb sdns	1,500-4,000	4,000-7,500	7,500-10,000
Other models	500-2,000	2,000-5,500	5,500-8,000

1946 DeSoto Custom Suburban 8-passenger sedan

1947 DeSoto Custom four-door sedan

1946

The slightly "squarer" L-head six that had appeared in 1942 came back at 109 bhp for the first postwar DeSotos, which lacked hidden headlights but gained smoother bodysides via fenders neatly blended into the doors. The long-wheelbase DeLuxe sedan and Custom business coupe were dropped as repetitious. New on the long wheelbase was the Suburban, designed for hotel and livery work, featuring a fold-down rear seat without trunk partition, wood-garnished interior panels, and a beautiful metal-and-wood roof rack. This is a highly collectible DeSoto today; 7500 were built in the 1946-early '49 period. Despite a slow production start-up, about 66,900 DeSotos were built for 1946.

	Restorable	Good	Excellent
Custom cvt	$4,000-9,000	$9,000-17,000	$17,000-24,000
Suburban	2,000-4,000	4,000-7,000	7,000-11,000
Other models	500-2,000	2,000-5,500	5,500-8,000

1947

The 1947 DeSotos were "the same, only more so": an identical lineup, produced in greater quantity—production was up 35 percent to 87,000 units. DeSoto, incidentally, built close to 12,000 taxicabs during 1946-48, including New York City's famous "Skyview" with glass roof panel. Taxis were actually the fifth most popular DeSoto body style, but original examples are extremely scarce today.

	Restorable	Good	Excellent
Custom cvt	$4,000-9,000	$9,000-17,000	$17,000-24,000
Suburban	2,000-4,000	4,000-7,000	7,000-11,000
Other models	500-2,000	2,000-5,500	5,500-8,000

1948

Again, the DeSoto line went unchanged; serial numbers are the only way to identify a '48, though production was up another 10,000 units and this is the most common of the three identical model years. The '48 body, with its handsome flying lady mascot and thin vertical grille teeth, made a brief final appearance in the early part of the '49 model year, filling a void while the all-new '49 models were being readied. During the 1946-early 1949 period, DeSoto built 8100 Custom convertibles, 38,720 Club Coupes, 1950 business coupes, 14,351 two-door sedans, 3650 seven-passenger sedans/limos, and 158,439 four-door sedans.

1950 DeSoto Custom Sportsman hardtop coupe

	Restorable	Good	Excellent
Custom cvt	$4,000-9,000	$9,000-17,000	$17,000-24,000
Suburban	2,000-4,000	4,000-7,000	7,000-11,000
Other models	500-2,000	2,000-5,500	5,500-8,000

1949

In line with the rest of Chrysler Corporation, DeSoto restyled its "true" 1949 models, which were finally introduced in March of that year. Wheelbase of the standard-length bodies was stretched to 125.5 inches, but the cars looked as boxy as their Chrysler, Dodge, and Plymouth stablemates. The front end retained the trademark vertical grille teeth, but the female mascot was replaced by a rather nice bust of Hernando DeSoto, which glowed brightly in the dark. Interior panels were woodgrained. A wagon finally appeared, a DeLuxe series nine-passenger woody, while the Custom got a long-wheelbase Suburban fitted with jump seats, giving it nine-passenger capacity. The Carry-All, on the standard wheelbase, had a fold-down seat similar to the Suburban; cheaper than either the woody or the Suburban, it outsold them both: respective output was 2,690, 850, and 129. Given the short model run for the real '49s, a total of 94,371 was quite good. Collectors will want to consider the convertible, which found 3385 buyers, while the budget-minded might like a Club Coupe (actually a six-passenger two-door sedan). With forward-slanted B-pillars it looked more rakish than the more upright four-door sedans; 6807 DeLuxes and 18,431 Customs were produced.

	Restorable	Good	Excellent
Custom cvt	$3,000-7,500	$7,500-13,000	$13,000-20,000
DeLuxe woody wgn	2,500-5,000	5,000-9,000	9,000-15,000
Other models	500-2,000	2,000-5,500	5,500-8,000

1950

DeSoto's first "hardtop convertible," the Sportsman, debuted in the Custom line, along with its first all-steel station wagon, which would replace the woody wagon entirely in 1951. A front-end facelift gave the DeSoto a revised grille with more uniform teeth and round (rather than rectangular) parking lights, and taillights were now neatly blended into the rear fenders. Introduced back in 1942, the L-head six was rated at 112 bhp, as since 1949. In a banner year for the industry, DeSoto saw output jump to 133,854 units. Some highlights: 4600 Sportsmans, 600 woody wagons, 100 all-steel wagons, 2900 convertibles, 3900 Carry-Alls, 623 Suburbans, 969 long-wheelbase sedans.

	Restorable	Good	Excellent
Custom cvt	$3,000-7,500	$7,500-13,000	$13,000-20,000
Sportsman htp	2,500-4,000	4,000-8,000	8,000-11,000
DeLuxe woody wgn	2,500-5,000	5,000-9,000	9,000-15,000
Other models	500-2,000	2,000-5,500	5,500-8,000

1951

Responding to complaints that its cars were too upright and boxy, DeSoto lowered the '51 in appearance if not in fact by a slick front end facelift, which decreased the grille cavity and elongated the front of the hood. There were but nine grille teeth this year. Horsepower was raised to 116. The Sportsman, like other hardtops, combined the airiness and deluxe interior of a convertible with the snugness of a steel top, with wind-down side windows that allowed a complete sweep along the beltline. The discontinued woody wagon was totally replaced by the steel version.

	Restorable	Good	Excellent
Custom cvt	$3,000-7,500	$7,500-13,000	13,000-20,000
Sportsman htp	2,500-4,000	4,000-8,000	8,000-11,000
Other models	500-2,000	2,000-5,500	5,500-8,000

1951 DeSoto Custom four-door sedan

1953 DeSoto FireDome convertible coupe

1953 DeSoto FireDome 8-passenger sedan

1952

For 1952, DeSoto was the most recognizably changed among Chrysler's four makes, with a prominent hood scoop replacing the Hernando DeSoto hood ornament of 1951. Also new was a wider crest on the hood, but these changes didn't take place until February 1952. That's when the big news was announced: a 276.1-cid hemi-head V-8, based on the Chrysler Hemi, developing 160 bhp. A new series name for the engine, FireDome, was created, carrying a full ration of body styles. Also new to DeSoto for '52 were optional power steering, electric power windows, and tinted glass. DeLuxe and Custom production figures were combined for 1951-52, showing 3950 convertibles, 8750 Sportsman hardtops, and 1440 wagons. Although 45,800 FireDomes were sold during the remainder of 1952, only 850 were convertibles, 3000 Sportsmans, and 550 wagons. The total production run for 1951-52 was 190,449 cars.

	Restorable	Good	Excellent
Convertibles	$3,000-7,500	$7,500-13,000	$13,000-20,000
Sportsman htps	2,500-4,000	4,000-8,000	8,000-11,000
Other models	500-2,000	2,000-5,500	5,500-8,000

1953

With the FireDome V-8's tremendous popularity, DeSoto combined its six-cylinder models this year into a single series, the Powermaster. Customers continued to prefer power, however, and by the end of the model year FireDomes were outselling Powermasters two to one. There was no Powermaster convertible. Styling was flashier, with one-piece windshields for the first time, wall-to-wall grille teeth (11 of them), bright trim flashes along the bodysides, squared-up rear fenders, and reverse-slant C-pillars for sedans and coupes. FireDomes carried prominent "V" badges on their front fenders. Model year production spurted to 130,404 units, among them 1700 ragtops, 4700 FireDome Sportsman hardtops, 1470 Powermaster

1954 DeSoto FireDome four-door sedan

1955 DeSoto Fireflite Sportsman hardtop coupe

1955 DeSoto Fireflite convertible coupe

1956 DeSoto Firedome hardtop coupe

Sportsmans, 1600 total wagons, and 425 long-wheelbase models. The Club Coupe, meanwhile, found 8063 six-cylinder buyers and 14,591 V-8 takers. The bulk of sales was, as always, four-door sedans: 33,644 Powermasters, 64,211 FireDomes.

	Restorable	Good	Excellent
Firedome cvt	$3,000-7,500	$7,500-13,000	$13,000-20,000
Sportsman htps	2,500-4,000	4,000-8,000	8,000-11,000
Other models	500-2,000	2,000-5,500	5,500-8,000

1954

The DeSoto lineup was a repeat of 1953, with the FireDome raised to 170 bhp and the 116-bhp Powermaster selling fewer examples than ever. This was to be the last year for a DeSoto six, and some are extremely scarce—the Powermaster Sportsman, discontinued early, saw only 250 copies. Styling changes included round rather than oblong parking lights flanking nine grille teeth, elongated side trim, and a "cockpit" style dash grouping the instruments under a lip below the steering wheel. Optional was PowerFlite two-speed automatic, an advance on DeSoto's long-running semi-automatic Fluid Drive. A springtime model was the Coronado, a luxury four-door sedan in the FireDome series featuring a dressed-up interior, medallions on the C-pillars, extra chrome trim around the rain gutters, and Coronado script on the rear fenders. How many were built is unknown as they were counted in with the 45,095 FireDome four-doors sold. Total output plummeted to 76,580 units. Among FireDomes, 1025 soft tops, 4382 Sportsmans, 946 wagons, and 165 long-wheelbase sedans were produced. This was the final year for the Club Coupes, 8063 of which were Powermasters and 14,591 FireDomes.

	Restorable	Good	Excellent
Firedome cvt	$3,000-7,500	$7,500-14,000	$14,000-21,000
Sportsman htps	2,500-4,000	4,000-8,000	8,000-12,000
Other models	500-2,000	2,000-5,500	5,500-8,000

1955

A flashy restyle by Virgil Exner, the demise of the six, and a larger 291-cid V-8 in two stages of tune—185 or 200 bhp—marked the highly accepted '55 DeSoto line. The glitziest of Chrysler Corporation's '55 makes, all models featured a 126-inch wheelbase, wrap-around windshield, push-me/pull-you door handles, twin-cockpit gullwing-style dash, and lots of color inside and out. Firedomes (now with a small "d") included a cheaper Special hardtop at $110 less than the Sportsman. Leading the Fireflite line was the Coronado sedan with a three-tone (turquoise, black, and white) paint job and color-keyed interior. PowerFlite was found on 95 percent of the cars, controlled by a menacing shaft sprouting out of the dashboard. DeSoto output shot up to 114,765 units. Firedome Sportsmans and Special hardtops accounted for 28,944 units, while the convertible sold only 625, the station wagon 1803. Fireflite Sportsmans numbered 10,313, the convertible 775, and the four-door sedan 26,637 (including Coronado).

	Restorable	Good	Excellent
Convertibles	$4,000-8,000	$8,000-17,500	$17,500-25,000
Sportsman htp	2,500-5,000	5,000-12,000	12,000-15,000
Special htp	1,500-4,000	4,000-8,000	8,000-12,000
Fireflite Coronado	2,500-4,000	4,000-6,000	6,000-9,000
Other models	500-1,500	1,500-3,500	3,500-6,500

1956

Horsepower rose to 230/255 via a larger 330.4-cid V-8 for 1956. Also noted was an enthusiastic but not-so-successful facelift: the teeth were yanked from the grille in favor of a wire mesh, unreadable gold-on-white instruments appeared on the dash, and tailfins sprouted at the rear, encasing triple lollipop tail- and back-up lights. Highlight of the year was the limited-edition Adventurer, a gold-embellished two-door hardtop super DeSoto, powered by a 341.4-cid Hemi with 320 horsepower. Just 996 were built. There was also a Fireflite Pacesetter convertible, trimmed to match the DeSoto that paced the Indianapolis 500 this year. Only an estimated 100 were produced. Another introduction was the first DeSoto four-door hardtops: Fireflite Sportsman, Firedome Sportsman, and Firedome Seville. Output was 3350, 1645, and 4030, respectively. Cadillac, which had also begun using the Seville badge on its new '56 Eldorado hardtop, persuaded DeSoto to withdraw the name for 1957. Convertibles were again rare: 646 Firedomes and 1385 Fireflites. Overall production was down only slightly to 110,418 units.

	Restorable	Good	Excellent
Adventurer htp	$2,500-5,000	$5,000-10,000	$10,000-15,000
Fireflite cvt	3,000-8,000	8,000-15,000	15,000-23,000
Pacesetter cvt	5,000-9,000	9,000-15,000	15,000-25,000
Firedome cvt	3,000-7,000	7,000-14,000	14,000-20,000
Sportsman 2d htp	2,000-4,000	4,000-7,000	7,000-12,000
Sportsman 4d htp	1,000-2,000	2,000-4,000	4,000-7,000
Other models	500-1,500	1,500-3,500	3,500-5,500

1957

DeSoto saw a sales increase this year to 117,514 cars, coming as close as it ever did to passing Chrysler. The reason was its styling and performance, both of which were exactly in tune with the market. One of the cleanest of the "Forward Look" Chrysler products, it featured smooth lines, tall tailfins, an ultra-clean front end, and lots of glass. Helping sales was a low-cost Firesweep series based on the shorter 122-inch Dodge wheelbase, extending DeSoto's market territory down toward Dodge's. Ironically, this caused a marketing realignment that would soon squeeze DeSoto out of the Chrysler hierarchy entirely. The Adventurer was now available as a convertible—the most collectible DeSoto in history, though only 300 were built. With 1650 called for, the Adventurer hardtop was far more popular. Both boasted 345 horsepower from

1956 DeSoto Fireflite convertible coupe

1955 DeSoto Fireflite Coronado four-door sedan

1957 DeSoto Fireflite Shopper station wagon

1957 DeSoto Fireflite four-door sedan

1957 DeSoto Adventurer convertible coupe

1957 DeSoto Firedome four-door sedan

1958 Desoto Fireflite convertible coupe

345 cubic inches, the same magic "1 h.p. per cu. in." that Chevy was hyping in 1957. The two other soft tops, Firedome and Fireflite, accounted for 1297 and 1151 sales. Station wagons were found in the Firesweep and Fireflite series: six-passenger Shoppers and nine-seater Explorers. Between the four of them, they snagged 5239 shoppers. The tally among Sportsman two-door hardtops was 13,333 Firesweeps, 12,179 Firedomes, and 7217 Fireflites.

	Restorable	Good	Excellent
Adventurer cvt	$5,000-12,000	$12,000-18,000	$18,000-25,000
Adventurer htp	2,500-5,000	5,000-10,000	10,000-15,000
Fireflite cvt	3,000-8,000	8,000-15,000	15,000-23
Firedome cvt	3,000-7,000	7,000-14,000	14,000-20,000
Sportsman 2d htps	2,000-3,500	3,500-6,000	6,000-10,000
Sportsman 4d htps	1,000-2,000	2,000-5,000	5,000-8,000
Other models	500-1,500	1,500-3,500	3,500-6,000

1958

The '58s were basically the same as the '57s except for a mild facelift. The grille became busier (and less attractive), while side trim moved higher on the bodysides, looking more like a 1957 Plymouth Fury or Belvedere; all models now came with quad headlamps. One model was added, a Firesweep convertible, meaning there were now no fewer than four ragtops: Firesweep, Firedome, Fireflite, and Adventurer (production: 700, 519, 474, and 82). At $4,100 base, the last was the most expensive DeSoto in history, though still $1300 less than a Chrysler 300-D. Engines were new—wedgehead V-8s with 350 and 361 cubic inches, the former assigned to the Firesweep, the latter available in four states of tune from 295 to 355 bhp. Though a sharp recession hurt sales industry-wide, DeSoto nosedived 58 percent to 49,445 units, and was even outsold by Edsel. The four wagon models attracted 3357 buyers, but the two-door Sportsman hardtops were more plentiful: 13,244, plus 350 of the highly desirable Adventurers. In a telling move, DeSoto was pulled out of its exclusive Wyoming Avenue assembly plant in Detroit; all future DeSotos would be built alongside Chryslers in the Jefferson Avenue plant in Detroit, except for Firesweeps, which would continue to be built in Dodge facilities.

	Restorable	Good	Excellent
Adventurer cvt	$5,000-12,000	$12,000-18,000	$18,000-25,000
Adventurer htp	2,500-5,000	5,000-10,000	10,000-15,000
Fireflite cvt	3,000-8,000	8,000-15,000	15,000-23,000
Other cvts	3,000-7,000	7,000-14,000	14,000-20,000
Sportsman 2d htps	2,000-3,500	3,500-6,000	6,000-12,000
Sportsman 4d htps	1,000-2,000	2,000-5,000	5,000-8,000
Other models	500-1,500	1,500-3,500	3,500-6,000

1959

Production decreased a further 7.5 percent this year to 45,724, edging out Edsel by less than 1000 units. Rumors began to circulate that DeSoto would be discontinued. Sticking with the '57 bodyshell and 122-inch wheelbase, the cars received a heavy facelift, looking much busier up front where a massive "twin-nostril," two-tier bumper was topped by a thin cross-hatch grille. Full-length side trim swooped downward on the rear-quarter panels before shooting up to the tip of the fins, which continued to house the triple taillights familiar since 1956. A new engine, Chrysler's famous 383 V-8, came standard on the Firedome, Fireflite, and Adventurer with 305, 325, and 350 horsepower (the last with dual four-barrel carbs). Firesweeps got a 295-bhp 361 V-8. The complicated four-series, 18-model lineup with three or four types of every body style was continued, resulting in some very low convertible production figures: 596 Firesweeps, 299 Firedomes, 186 Fireflites, 97 Adventurers. The Shopper and Explorer wagons were down to 2937 units this year, Sportsman hardtop sedans to 7983, Sportsman hardtop coupes to 9736. In addition, 590 Adventurer two-door hardtops were built. Amidst the gloom of falling sales, DeSoto rolled out its two-millionth car during the model year. This was also DeSoto's 30th Anniversary, which was duly noted in the spring with a Seville trim variation for the Firesweep and Firedome two- and four-door hardtops. Exact figures aren't known, but production was limited.

	Restorable	Good	Excellent
Adventurer cvt	$5,000-10,000	$10,000-15,000	$15,000-22,500
Other cvts	4,000-8,000	8,000-12,000	12,000-18,000
Adventurer htp	2,500-5,000	5,000-8,000	8,000-12,000
Sportsman 2d htps	2,000-3,500	3,500-6,000	6,000-10,000
Sportsman 4d htps	1,000-2,000	2,000-5,000	5,000-8,000
Other models	500-1,500	1,500-3,500	3,500-6,000

1960

DeSoto's decline became even more obvious as it was merged into a combination DeSoto-Plymouth-Valiant Division. And in spite of being extensively and handsomely restyled, 1960 DeSoto output skidded to just 25,581 units. A compact luxury model had been planned for 1962, but after 1960's sales results, it was shelved. Partly to keep it from intruding on Chrysler, the DeSoto lineup was severely trimmed to six models. The Firesweep and Firedome series were dropped, while the Adventurer and Fireflite moved down a notch in market position. A big, aggressive grille and tall canted fins with neatly fared-in taillamps marked the '60s, as did Unibody construction. Convertibles and wagons, so numerous the year before, were eliminated. Fireflites, now with the 295-bhp 361 V-8, recorded output of 3494 hardtop coupes, 1958 hardtop sedans, and 9032 four-door sedans. The no-longer-unique Adventurer ran with the 305-bhp 383; 3092 hardtop coupes, 2759 hardtop sedans, and 5746 four-door sedans were built. Prices this year spanned $3017-$3727, a far narrower market niche than the $2904-$4749 range in 1959.

1959 DeSoto Fireflite Sportsman hardtop coupe

1960 DeSoto Adventurer four-door sedan

1960 DeSoto Adventurer Sportsman hardtop coupe

1961 DeSoto hardtop coupe

	Restorable	Good	Excellent
Adventurer 2d htp	$2,000-3,500	$3,500-7,000	$7,000-10,000
Fireflite 2d htp	2,000-3,000	3,000-5,500	5,500-8,500
Hardtops, 4d	1,000-2,000	2,000-5,000	5,000-8,000
Sedans, 4d	500-1,500	1,500-3,500	3,500-6,000

1961

DeSoto went out in a phase of gory: a gross facelift in which a blunt, screened grille was set above a crosshatch grille flanked by angled quad headlamps and garish parking lights. There was no model hierarchy, only a DeSoto hardtop coupe and hardtop sedan. Production was 911 and 2123, respectively. Both models were powered by the 361 V-8, detuned to a 9.1:1 compression ratio and 265 horsepower. Ironically, DeSoto's demise came almost exactly one year after Edsel's, and after almost exactly the same number of cars had been built in the last model year. Thus, after being announced on October 15, 1960, DeSoto was dead as of November 30. It was an ignoble end to an honorable life, and collectors tend to see it that way: despite their status as the last of the line, the '61 DeSotos are not much sought after and their values are no higher than 1958-60 counterparts.

	Restorable	Good	Excellent
Hardtop, 2d	$2,000-3,000	$3,000-6,000	$6,000-10,000
Hardtop, 4d	1,000-2,000	2,000-5,000	5,000-8,000

1930 Dodge Series DD New Six four-door sedan

1933 Dodge Eight 3-window coupe

Dodge

Generally speaking, Dodge isn't a widely collected make. None of its cars are recognized as "Classics" by the Classic Car Club of America, and until the mid-Fifties its postwar production was pretty dull stuff. But from 1955 through 1971, Dodge built many interesting and exciting cars that are now widely sought after, but since then the pickings have been relatively meager—despite Dodge's latterday reputation as the most sporting of Chrysler Corporation makes. Club support is fair, mechanical parts supply good, body parts supply uneven.

1930-39

Chrysler bought Dodge in 1928, but made no immediate change to the Dodge Brothers' philosophy of producing reliable, dull transportation. Early '30s models were powered by a wide range of inline L-head sixes and eights. The former came in sizes from 189.8 to 241.5 cubic inches with horsepower ratings of 61-79. Eights, which ended after 1933, displaced 220.7, 240.3 and 282.1 cid with 75-92 horses. For all engines, smoothness and low-end torque were emphasized over performance. Three- and four-speed transmissions were offered, and all

Dodges boasted hydraulic brakes. As the most conservatively styled Chrysler product, Dodge never got an Airflow—a blessing in hindsight. The famous ram hood ornament was first seen in 1932. Bodies stood upright and foursquare through 1934, the year a 217.8-cid, 87-bhp six was adopted. It would continue as Dodge's sole powerplant—and with the same horsepower rating—through 1940. A waterfall grille and rounded, skirted fenders were brought in for 1935 as part of the corporate-wide "Airstream" look. By 1939, Dodges had acquired extended pontoon-style fenders, elongated rear decks, and a sharp-edge frontal motif. Numerous Dodge body styles embraced most open types of the period, including roadsters and phaetons early in the decade and a convertible sedan during 1933-34 (the most valuable) and 1936-38, and convertible coupes throughout. A long-wheelbase chassis appeared in 1935 for a seven-passenger sedan and limousine; the 128-inch chassis was stretched to 132 for 1937. One of the more innovative designs came in 1937, introducing no-snag door handles, recessed dash knobs, flush-mounted gauges, ultra-low driveshaft tunnel, one-piece steel roof construction, and built-in defroster. The redesigned '39s—which Dodge dubbed "Luxury Liners"—celebrated both the World's Fair and Dodge's Silver Anniversary with two ranges: Special and DeLuxe, a two-series setup that would last for years. Curiously, there were no open models this year. Dodge production during the '30s ranged from 27,555 units in 1932 to 295,047 in 1937. As with other Chrysler makes, open models were never numerous in the '30s: just 1345 convertible coupes and 473 convertible sedans were produced in 1937, for example.

	Restorable	Good	Excellent
1933-34 cvt sdn	$5,000-12,000	$12,000-22,500	$22,500-32,500
Other open mdls	4,000-10,000	10,000-20,000	20,000-30,000
Closed models	1,500-4,000	4,000-7,000	7,000-10,000

1940

The first batch of Forties Dodges was grouped into Special and DeLuxe series, both mounted on a 119.5-inch wheelbase (up from 117 in 1939), and priced from $755 to $1170. Bodies were larger and smoother, highlighted by a neat horizontal-bar grille divided into upper and lower sections. The Special series comprised a coupe and two- and four-door sedans; the top-line DeLuxe offered those models plus a convertible, a larger coupe, plus a long-wheelbase sedan and limousine on a 139.5-inch chassis. Running boards, declining rapidly in popularity, were made a $10 option this year. Of the 195,505 '40 models built, 129,001 were top-line DeLuxes. Long-wheelbase seven-passenger models saw production of 932 sedans and 79 limos, and 298 chassis were ordered. Convertibles numbered 2100, business coupes 24,751, coupes (with folding "opera" seats in back) 8028. Sedans were easily the most popular with 47,538 two-doors and 111,779 four-doors built. A feature this year was optional

1936 Dodge Beauty Winner Six Touring Sedan

1937 Dodge Series D5 trunkback four-door sedan

1938 Dodge Series D8 trunkback four-door sedan

1939 Dodge Luxury Liner DeLuxe fastback four-door

1940 Dodge Luxury Liner DeLuxe two-door sedan

two-tone paint, with the fenders, hood and deck done in the contrasting shade. This pattern gave the cars a taxicab look that wasn't popular.

	Restorable	Good	Excellent
Convertible	$3,000-8,000	$8,000-15,000	$15,000-25,000
Other models	1,500-4,000	4,000-7,000	7,000-10,000

1941 Dodge Luxury Liner Custom convertible coupe

1941 Dodge Luxury Liner Custom four-door sedan

1941

This year Dodge strutted a clean facelift involving a bold, split horizontal grille that came up in a "V" to blend into the headlights. Parking lights were now mounted outboard of the headlights, and taillights sat in long housings atop the rear fenders. Similar front-fender housings were employed for cars equipped with extra-cost turn signals. All these changes greatly improved Dodge's appearance. DeLuxe moved down to designate the cheaper line, while the new top series became the Custom. The 2/4-passenger coupe was replaced by a $995 six-passenger Custom Club Coupe. Meanwhile, a $1062 four-door Town Sedan with blind rear roof quarters was added, and the $962 Custom two-door sedan was now called Brougham. Fluid Drive semi-automatic shift became optional, and after seven years the 217.8-cid six was boosted to 91 bhp via higher compression. Total production increased to 237,002, which included the following Customs: 3554 ragtops, 18,024 Club Coupes, 20,146 Broughams, 16,074 Town Sedans, 72,067 four-door sedans, 601 seven-passenger sedans, and 50 limos.

	Restorable	Good	Excellent
Convertible	$3,000-8,000	$8,000-15,000	$15,000-25,000
Other models	1,500-4,000	4,000-7,000	7,000-10,000

1942 Dodge Custom club coupe

1942 Dodge Custom business coupe

1942

In the abbreviated 1942 model year, by the time production halted in early February Dodge had built just 68,522 cars. They were good looking but not radical, with a full-width, horizontal-bar grille—heavier and wider-looking than 1941—featuring a prominent cross-hatched and vee'd center section. Nearly flush rectangular taillights rode up back. Optional fender skirts carried bright moldings to blend with front and rear fender trim on Customs, which made the cars look longer and lower. Performance was improved with a larger 230.2-cid six with 105 bhp. A Club Coupe was added to the DeLuxe line, though there was time to build only 3314 examples. Among standard-wheelbase body styles, the Custom convertible was the scarcest at only 1185 units. But actually, all '42s were relatively scarce, with just 4659 Custom Club Coupes, 4047 Town Sedans, 201 long-wheelbase sedans, and 9 limos produced.

	Restorable	Good	Excellent
Convertible	$3,000-8,000	$8,000-15,000	$15,000-25,000
Other models	1,500-4,000	4,000-7,000	7,000-10,000

1946

After the war Dodge got off to a fast start and built 163,490 cars to finish fourth in production behind the "Low-Priced Three," where it hadn't been since 1937. Series offerings remained DeLuxe and Custom, but three models were dropped: DeLuxe Club Coupe, Custom Brougham, and Custom limo. The mild but effective facelift by A. B. Grisinger, John Chika, and Herb Weissinger—all shortly to depart for Kaiser-Frazer—consisted of a new grille with wide horizontal and vertical bars forming a bold rectangle pattern. Large square parking lights flanked the grille, which was topped by the Dodge nameplate. Bodysides looked much smoother because the front fenders were now blended neatly into the front doors. Mechanical changes included an unexplained drop to 102 horsepower, relocation of the starter from a foot pedal to a button on the dash, and front brakes equipped with double wheel cylinders. The transmission was revised and in-line fuel and oil filters became standard. Postwar prices were up sharply, with a DeLuxe business coupe listing at $1299 at the bottom end and the Custom long-wheelbase sedan retailing for $1743 at the top.

	Restorable	Good	Excellent
Convertible	$3,000-7,000	$7,000-12,000	$12,000-22,500
Other models	1,500-3,500	3,500-5,500	5,500-8,000

1946 Dodge Custom convertible coupe

1946-48 Dodge DeLuxe two-door sedan

1947

Prices were up again this year, but at least Fluid Drive was standard for all Dodges. This was an important selling point in an age when people were tiring of manual shift. Fluid Drive combined a conventional clutch with a torque convertor and electrical shifting circuits. There were two forward gear positions: "Low" for first and second, and "High" for third and fourth. Low was used for fast starts or towing. Normally, the driver shifted directly into High and pressed on the accelerator until about 15 mph, let up on it, and then a slight "clunk" announced the shift from third to fourth. Though the clutch still had to be used to shift from Low to High or reverse, most normal driving was done in High and there was no need to shift. The penalty was extremely leisurely acceleration. Sharp eyes would catch a more detailed ram hood ornament, but there was no change in the model line-up; 1947 serial number spans were 30799738-31011765 (Detroit) and 45002146-45022452 (Los Angeles). Total estimated production this year was 243,160 units, good for fifth place in industry standings.

	Restorable	Good	Excellent
Convertible	$3,000-7,000	$7,000-12,000	$12,000-22,500
Other models	1,500-3,500	3,500-5,500	5,500-8,000

1948

Again, serial numbers are the only real way to tell this year's models from the previous two years. Number spans were 31011766-31201086 (Detroit)

1949 Dodge Coronet four-door sedan

and 45022453-45041545 (Los Angeles). After slipping slightly in 1947, Dodge returned to fourth place in industry production on the strength of 243,340 units. The '48s were extended into 1949—higher serial numbers denote these—between December 1948 and February 1949, when the "genuine" all-new '49s were announced. Production figures for specific models were all combined for 1946-48. They were, for DeLuxes: 27,600 business coupes, 81,399 two-door sedans, and 61,987 four-door sedans. For Customs: 103,800 Club Coupes, 9500 convertibles, 333,911 four-door sedans, 27,800 Town Sedans, 3698 long-wheelbase sedans, and two prototype limos. In addition, Dodge constructed 302 chassis.

	Restorable	Good	Excellent
Convertible	$3,000-7,000	$7,000-12,000	$12,000-22,500
Other bodies	1,500-3,500	3,500-5,500	5,500-8,000

1949

The new '49s were completely restyled, though still powered by the same 230.2-cid L-head six, which mysteriously gained one horsepower. There were two series, led by the 115-inch D-29 Wayfarer offered as a semi-fastback sedan, coupe, and roadster with side curtains. D-30 Dodges, riding a 123.5-inch chassis, came as a Meadowbrook four-door and four Coronets: four-door, Club Coupe, convertible, and woody wagon. The Coronet Town Sedan, a trim option, cost $85 more than the Coronet and offered luxurious Bedford cord upholstery. The squarish body styling, looking very conservative, was led off by a chromey grille that managed to maintain the rectangle theme of 1946-48 and look like a junior Chrysler at the same time. Like other Chrysler cars, most models received retrograde tacked-on taillights, and the center trunk-mounted brake light, a decade-long feature, was back for its last year. Collectors today are especially interested in the Wayfarer roadster, the last of a type, though the Wayfarer three-passenger coupe is also worth considering as a budget collectible. The scarce woody wagon is definitely worth a look. Those three models saw output of 5420, 9342, and 800 units, respectively. The Wayfarer two-door sedan, which looked less blocky than other Dodges, attracted 49,054 buyers. Meanwhile, among Coronets, the convertible found just 2411 customers, while the Club Coupe went to 45,435 new homes. Of the total production run of 256,857 cars, 144,390 were Meadowbrook and Coronet four-door sedans.

	Restorable	Good	Excellent
Wayfarer rdstr	$4,000-8,000	$8,000-14,000	$14,000-22,500
Coronet cvt	3,000-7,000	7,000-12,000	12,000-20,000
Coronet wgn	2,500-5,000	5,000-8,000	8,000-12,000
Other models	1,000-3,000	3,000-5,000	5,000-7,500

1950

The boxy '49 bodyshell was nicely facelifted for 1950 with a cleaner grille featuring two strong horizontal bars with round parking lights at each end and a Dodge crest in the center, topped by a curved grille-surround trim piece. Vertical taillights were neatly integrated into the revised rear fenders. In June 1950, a Diplomat "hardtop convertible" joined the Coronet line. Four-speed Gyro-Matic, an improvement on three-speed Fluid Drive, carried over from 1949, as did the standard Fluid Drive. All models continued to be powered by the sturdy L-head six, which would survive through the decade. Two basic model lines were fielded: the D33 Wayfarer, whose roadster had become a Sportabout with roll-up windows late in the 1949 model year; and the D34, comprising Meadowbrook and Coronet sedans, plus a Coronet wagon, coupe, convertible, and hardtop. Coronet was also offered as a long-wheelbase sedan, mainly for commercial purposes. Dodge, benefitting from a banner sales year for the industry, built 341,797 cars for 1950. A few highlights: 2903 Sportabouts, 7500 Wayfarer coupes, 65,000 Wayfarer two-door sedans, 1800 Coronet ragtops, 3600 Diplomats, 600 Coronet woody wagons, 100 Coronet Sierra all-steel wagons, and 1300 eight-passenger sedans.

	Restorable	Good	Excellent
Convertibles	$3,000-7,000	$7,000-12,000	$12,000-20,000
Diplomat htp	2,500-5,000	5,000-8,000	8,000-12,000
Coronet woody wgn	2,500-5,000	5,000-8,000	8,000-12,000
Other models	1,000-3,000	3,000-5,000	5,000-7,500

1951

With no change in wheelbase, styling became slightly smoother and sleeker for 1951 via a lower hood and grille opening. A single horizontal grille bar ran nearly the width of the car, curving downward at the extreme ends to enclose round parking lights. Five tiny vertical strips reached from the grille bar upward to the hood. More rounded front and rear bumpers and bumper guards also helped smooth out the styling. The model lineup remained as before. Starting at $1795 for the three-passenger business coupe, Wayfarers set the price pace. Coronets supplied the widest variety of body styles priced from $2132 to $2916, while the Meadowbrook filled the gap with a $2059 four-door sedan. The woody wagon was dropped. Production eased off to about 290,000 units.

	Restorable	Good	Excellent
Convertibles	$3,000-7,000	$7,000-12,000	$12,000-20,000
Diplomat htp	2,500-5,000	5,000-8,000	8,000-12,000
Other models	1,000-3,000	3,000-5,000	5,000-7,500

1952

Dodge fielded the same line of models for '52, save for the Wayfarer Sportabout convertible, which was dropped. Only 1002 had been built, all in 1951. The '52s were unchanged in appearance except that the trim bar just above the bumper was painted, taillights incorporated a little reflector, and there was

1950 Dodge Coronet four-door sedan

1950 Dodge Coronet Diplomat hardtop coupe

1952 Dodge Coronet four-door sedan

1953 Dodge Coronet Eight four-door sedan

a new decklid handle. Production dropped by a third, mainly because of Korean War defense priorities. Only 1150 long-wheelbase sedans were built throughout 1951-52. Other production figures for the two years were 6702 Wayfarer business coupes and 70,700 two-door sedans. Meadowbrook and Coronet four-door sedans numbered 329,202 units. Coronets accounted for 56,103 Club Coupes, 5550 convertibles, 21,600 Diplomats, and 4000 wagons.

	Restorable	Good	Excellent
Coronet cvt	$3,000-7,000	$7,000-12,000	$12,000-20,000
Diplomat htp	2,500-5,000	5,000-8,000	8,000-12,000
Other model	1,000-3,000	3,000-5,000	5,000-7,500

1953

The '53s were among the first production Chrysler products styled by Virgil Exner, who had come from Studebaker a few years earlier. All-new, they sported a revised version of the 1951-52 grille, lower hood/higher fenders, completely flat bodysides, higher squared-up rear fenders, one-piece windshield, and new greenhouses with more glass area. Surprisingly light, the '53 Dodges handled well and provided good economy. That's because they were smaller, riding a 119-inch wheelbase in four-door sedan and Club Coupe guise and a 114-inch Plymouth chassis for the two-door wagons, hardtop, and convertible. Dodge performance was up, thanks to a 200-pound weight reduction—and the new Red Ram V-8, a scaled-down 241.3-cid version of the Chrysler Hemi with 140 horsepower. Not only did V-8 Dodges break 196 AAA stock-car speed records, but one scored 23.4 miles per gallon in the Mobilgas Economy Run. Still available for Meadowbrooks and some Coronets was the 103-bhp six. The Wayfarer series was discontinued this year (as was the four-door wagon), while the Meadowbrook line was expanded to include a coupe and wagon. Production took a healthy leap to 320,008 units, of which a bit over 180,000 were V-8s. Coronet V-8 output was 124,059 four-door sedans, 32,439 Club Coupes, 17,334 Diplomat hardtops, 4100 convertibles, and 5400 Sierra wagons.

	Restorable	Good	Excellent
Coronet cvt	$3,000-7,000	$7,000-12,000	$12,000-20,000
Diplomat htp	2,500-5,000	5,000-8,000	8,000-12,000
Other models	1,000-3,000	3,000-5,000	5,000-7,500

1954

Only detail changes were made this year, including a handsome new grille and more attractive side trim. Overall length was up four to five inches, and four-door wagons returned to the lineup. Topping the Meadowbrooks and Coronets, all of which could be ordered with V-8s now—not to mention fully automatic PowerFlite transmission—was a new, luxurious Royal series. Announced at mid-year was the Royal 500 convertible, named for the famed Indianapolis race. Dodge paced the event this year, and Pace Car replicas with Kelsey-Hayes chrome wire wheels were produced. They came with outside spare tire, special trim, 500 badging, and a 150-bhp version of the Red Ram. Dealers could even specify a four-barrel Offenhauser manifold, which raised horsepower to nearer 200. Of the 2000 Royal convertibles built, only 701 were 500s. Dodge's reputation as a performance car was established—especially after Dodges finished 1-2-3-4-6-9 in the Medium Stock class at the punishing Mexican Road Race. Alas, all this didn't impress buyers, for production skidded to 154,648 units, 112,206 of which were four-door sedans. Some other sample figures: 100 Coronet hardtops, 50 Coronet ragtops, 3852 Royal hardtops, 8900 Royal Club Coupes, 9489 Coronet Sierra two-door wagons, 1300 four-door wagons. Collectors should note the rare hardtops and convertibles prepared for the spring selling season—they wore unique bodyside two-toning.

	Restorable	Good	Excellent
Royal cvt	$3,000-7,000	$7,000-12,000	$12,000-20,000
Royal 500 cvt	5,000-10,000	10,000-17,500	17,500-25,000
Royal htp	2,500-5,000	5,000-8,000	8,000-12,000
Other models	1,000-3,000	3,000-5,000	5,000-7,500

1955

A flashy, handsome restyle by designer Maury Baldwin made the '55 Dodge one of the most attractive ever. Up front, a split grille and sculpted bonnet announced the new wraparound windshield, which flowed smoothly toward a clean rear deck, set off on the upper-end Custom Royal by neat chrome tailfins above stacked twin taillights. The Meadowbrook series was eliminated, leaving Coronets, Royals, and Custom Royals in 20 models. The Dodge V-8 was punched out to 270.1 cid and 175 bhp. On Custom Royals it boasted 183 or 193 horses. There is some confusion over the word "Lancer" this year. It was applied to Coronet, Royal, and Custom Royal hardtops, as well as to Custom Royal convertibles and a luxury trim version of the Custom Royal four-door sedan. The Dodge "La Femme" was a mid-year Custom Royal Lancer lady's package, done up with a pink-and-white exterior, special upholstery, and fitted with a parasol and cosmetic kit behind the front seats. The '55 Dodges are avidly sought after, but prices now are well down from their 1989-90 peaks. Production this year recovered to 276,936. Custom Royals included 3302 Lancer convertibles, 30,499 Lancer hardtops, and 55,503 four-door sedans (how many had the Lancer trim package isn't known). In addition, 26,727 Coronet and 25,831 Royal Lancer hardtops were produced. La Femme output isn't known, but is assumed to have been under 1000 units.

	Restorable	Good	Excellent
Custom Royal cvt	$4,000-8,000	$8,000-16,000	$16,000-20,000
Custom Royal htp	2,500-5,000	5,000-8,000	8,000-12,000
La Femme htp	3,500-6,000	6,000-9,000	9,000-15,000
Other hardtops	2,000-4,000	4,000-7,000	7,000-10,000
Other models	1,000-3,000	3,000-5,000	5,000-7,500

1954 Dodge Royal Sport Coupe hardtop

1955 Dodge Coronet V-8 four-door sedan

1955 Dodge Royal Sierra four-door station wagon

1955 Dodge Coronet Six two-door sedan

1955 Dodge Royal V-8 four-door sedan

1956 Dodge Custom Royal Lancer hardtop sedan

1956 Dodge Custom Royal La Femme hardtop coupe

1957 Dodge Custom Royal Lancer hardtop sedan

1957 Dodge Custom Royal Lancer convertible coupe

1957 Dodge Custom Royal Lancer hardtop coupe

1956

All Chrysler products sported tailfins this year, relatively modest compared to what was coming for '57. PowerFlite two-speed automatic transmission, which had arrived with steering column-mounted control in 1954 and received a dashboard control lever in 1955, was now controlled via pushbuttons at the left side of the dash. Nicely facelifted styling and new interiors were enhanced by a new 315-cid V-8, good for 218 bhp on Royals and Custom Royals (Coronets got a 189-bhp 270 V-8 or 131-bhp six). An optional D-500 performance package available on any model developed 260 horsepower with a four-barrel carb, 295 with twin quads (D-500-1). Dodge also added a four-door Lancer hardtop in all three series—the Lancer designation was now applied to hardtops only. A Golden Lancer painted in the style of DeSoto's Adventurer, and a Western-style trim option called the "Texan," were offered. The La Femme was back for a final appearance, this time in two-tone lavender, and again with special interior and pouches behind the front seat for milady's umbrella, raincoat, and cosmetics. Output dropped to 240,686 units, 142,613 of them Coronets, 48,780 Royals, and 49,293 Custom Royals. Unfortunately, no breakdowns exist for the special models noted above, although the numbers were certainly small.

	Restorable	Good	Excellent
Custom Royal cvt	$4,000-8,000	$8,000-16,000	$16,000-20,000
Custom Royal htp	2,500-5,000	5,000-8,000	8,000-12,000
Golden Lancer/Texan	3,500-6,000	6,000-9,000	9,000-15,000
La Femme htp	3,500-6,000	6,000-9,000	9,000-15,000
D-500 cvt	5,000-10,000	10,000-18,000	18,000-22,500
D-500 htp	3,500-6,000	6,000-10,000	10,000-15,000
Other htps	2,000-4,000	4,000-7,000	7,000-10,000
Other models	1,000-3,000	3,000-5,000	5,000-7,500

(D-500 package: add 25%)

1957

With its massive bumper-grille and acres of glass, the smoothly restyled "Forward Look" Dodge looked both aggressive and modern. Though eyes may have focused on the tall fins, this was the finest handling Dodge ever, due mainly to its new Torsion-Aire (torsion-bar) front suspension. And Dodges were more powerful, too, with an array of Hemis from the mild 325-cid V-8 with 245 and 260 bhp to the D-500 with the same 325 tuned to 285 and 310 horsepower. There was even a mighty D-500 354 V-8 packing 340 horses. Not only that, the D-500 package was offered even on plebeian—and lighter—Coronet sedans, and wore a badge to prove it. Included were stiffer shocks, springs, and torsion bars. The old 230.2-cid six was still around, too, rated now at 138 horsepower, but it was available only on the low-line Coronet two- and four-door sedans. A Coronet convertible joined the lineup, but it's worth less than the Custom Royal, which can be told by its plusher interior and six "teeth" atop the front bumpers. Total production was 287,608.

	Restorable	Good	Excellent
Cust Royal cvt	$4,000-8,000	$8,000-16,000	$16,000-20,000
Coronet cvt	4,000-7,500	7,500-12,000	12,000-16,000
Cust Royal 2d htp	2,500-5,000	5,000-8,000	8,000-12,000
Other 2d htps	2,000-4,000	4,000-7,000	7,000-10,000
Other models	1,000-3,000	3,000-5,000	5,000-7,500

(D-500 package: add 25%)

1957 Dodge Coronet Club Sedan two-door

1958

Still riding a 122-inch wheelbase, the '58 Dodge continued with the same body and chassis, which saw a mild but attractive facelift featuring standard quad headlamps, a less massive-looking grille with a crosshatch background, notched taillight housings, and slightly different side trim. The model lineup was generally unchanged, though a six-cylinder Coronet Lancer two-door hardtop was added. In addition, an ultra-luxurious Custom Royal Regal Lancer with unique side trim bowed in February, and 1163 of these $3245 two-door hardtops were built. Other Custom Royals attracted 23,949 customers. The D-500 option now came with a new 361 wedgehead V-8 developing 305 horsepower. A Super D-500 with dual quad carbs claimed 320 bhp, and with Bendix electronic fuel injection the ante was upped to 333 horses—a staggering performance machine. Total production nosedived to 137,861 units, leaving Dodge in ninth place for the year, down from seventh the year before. Though partly due to a short but severe recession, all 1957 Chrysler Corporation cars had earned a bad reputation for shoddy assembly. They were also rust prone, and this would also hurt sales in future years.

1958 Dodge Custom Royal Lancer hardtop coupe

1958 Dodge Custom Royal Lancer hardtop sedan

	Restorable	Good	Excellent
Cust Royal cvt	$4,000-8,000	$8,000-16,000	$16,000-20,000
Coronet cvt	4,000-7,500	7,500-12,000	12,000-16,000
Regal Lanc 2d htp	3,000-5,500	5,500-9,000	9,000-13,000
Cust Royal 2d htp	2,500-5,000	5,000-8,000	8,000-12,000
Other 2d htps	2,000-4,000	4,000-7,000	7,000-10,000
Other models	1,000-3,000	3,000-5,000	5,000-7,500

(D-500 package: add 25%)

1959 Dodge Custom Royal four-door sedan

1959

During a dismal 1958, Dodge was planning its first "compact," but in 1959 the division had to carry on with a mainly unchanged lineup and a moderate facelift that offered the "*Newest* of everything great...." This consisted a more rounded grille with parking lights moved outboard and a finer mesh background, curiously eyebrowed headlights, lower bodyside trim, more deeply notched fins, and smoother taillights. As in recent years, Coronet represented the bottom of the line and had the only six-cylinder models—three of them. Notably, this would be the last year for the hoary L-head six, which ended its career at 138 bhp. There was also a five-model line of Coronet V-8s (326 cid, 255 bhp), including a convertible. Royals and Custom Royals ran with 295/305-bhp 361 V-8s, while the D-500 package debuted the new 383 V-8, packing 320

1960 Dodge Dart Phoenix convertible coupe

1960 Dodge Dart Pioneer hardtop coupe

1960 Dodge Dart Seneca four-door sedan

1960 Dodge Dart Seneca two-door sedan

1961 Dodge Dart Phoenix convertible coupe

horsepower with a four-barrel carb and 345 horses with dual four-barrel carbs. Look for Chrysler Corporation's famous swivel-seat option on upper-end models. The '59 restyle helped a bit as production rose to 156,385 units, enough to move Dodge back into eighth place.

	Restorable	Good	Excellent
Cust Royal cvt	$4,000-8,000	$8,000-16,000	$16,000-20,000
Coronet cvt	4,000-7,500	7,500-12,000	12,000-16,000
Regal Lanc 2d htp	3,000-5,500	5,500-9,000	9,000-13,000
Cust Royal 2d htp	2,500-5,000	5,000-8,000	8,000-12,000
Other 2d htps	2,000-4,000	4,000-7,000	7,000-10,000
Other models	1,000-3,000	3,000-5,000	5,000-7,500

(D-500 package: add 25%)

1960

Dodge recognized the growing demand for smaller cars by adding the new lower-priced Dart line of sixes and V-8s with a 118-inch wheelbase (122 for wagons). They consisted of Seneca, Pioneer, and Phoenix. The senior models, Matador and Polara, rode the usual 122-inch chassis and were offered with larger 361- and 383-cid V-8s only (295-330 bhp). Dart's base engine was the tough new overhead-valve Slant Six with 225 cubic inches and 145 horsepower. Dart V-8s came with another soon-to-be-famous engine, the 318, rated at 230 horses. Like the Slant Six, it was solid and reliable. Dart Phoenix models could be optioned with the big V-8s. D-500 power, 330 horsepower, came via ram induction. A leading feature was unit body/chassis construction; the '60 was also completely restyled. All cars had chrome-laden front ends, large blunt grilles (crosshatch pattern for Matador/Polara, fine vertical bars for Darts), and reworked tailfins (taller on Matador/Polara). Despite the heavy appearance, most Dodges were relatively light, with good performance. Buyers liked what they saw, snapping up 367,804 cars, enough to push Dodge into sixth place in the sales race. Of the total, 323,168 were Darts (73,175 top-line Phoenix models), 27,908 Matadors, and 16,728 Polaras. Convertibles came in Dart Phoenix and Polara guise, and 8817 of both types were built. Hardtops totaled 54,345 two-doors and 20,216 four-doors.

	Restorable	Good	Excellent
Convertibles	$3,000-7,000	$7,000-10,000	$10,000-15,000
2d hardtops	2,000-5,000	5,000-8,000	8,000-11,000
4d hardtops	1,500-4,000	4,000-6,500	6,500-8,500
Other models	1,000-2,500	2,500-5,000	5,000-7,000

(D-500 package: add 25%)

1961

Dodge was ready for the compact sales wars with its new Lancer, a Valiant clone on the same 106.5-inch-wheelbase unit body/chassis with the Slant Six engine. Lancer's appearance was different up front: where Valiant's grille was square, Lancer's comprised fine horizontal bars running wall-to-wall. The standard Slant Six had 170 or 225 cid (101 and 145 bhp). In its first year, Lancer attracted 74,876 buyers. The Dart was facelifted, with a full-width concave grille incorporating the headlamps, curious reverse-slant tailfins, and low-mounted horizontal taillights. The senior line, pared down to Polaras only, sprouted larger fins and flaunted unusual "jet-tube" taillights perched in the bodyside coves created as the reverse-slant fins reversed direction toward the front of the car. Though Polaras came standard with a 265-bhp 361 V-8, a D-500 version pumped out 305. In addition, the 383 D-500 variations were good for 305 and 330 horsepower (the latter with twin four-barrel carbs), while a 413-cid wedgehead called the Super D-500 developed 350 horses and a Super Ram Induction D-500 413 with dual quads cranked out 375. All this power couldn't overcome the unpopular styling, however, and total Dodge production fell to 269,367 units, including 74,776 Lancers—good only for ninth place in industry standings. Polaras, in five body styles, attracted but 14,032 buyers. Convertibles were predictably rare: 4361 Darts and Polaras combined.

	Restorable	Good	Excellent
Convertibles	$3,000-7,000	$7,000-10,000	$10,000-15,000
2d hardtops	2,000-5,000	5,000-8,000	8,000-11,000
Other models	1,000-2,500	2,500-5,000	5,000-7,000

(D-500 package: add 20%)

1962

Dart and Polara 500 received a brand new body on a shorter 116-inch wheelbase, shedding up to 400 pounds and six inches. It was the first across-the-board downsizing in Detroit history, but it was ahead of its time, and the '62s didn't sell well—240,484 in all. The styling was controversial as well, with two of the quad headlights within the grille, which didn't help matters. What did help Dodge this year was a separate six-model line of big, Chrysler-based cars with a Dodge front end: Custom 880. Bowing at mid-year, it came with a 265-bhp version of the 361 V-8. The Custom 880 found 17,505 willing buyers, including 684 who chose the convertible and 1761 who preferred the two-door hardtop. Performance was abetted this year by release of the Ramcharger 413 V-8, a wedgehead packing 410/415 bhp with 11.0:1 and 12.0:1 compression, respectively, and twin four-barrel carbs. The lightly facelifted Lancer responded to the bucket-seat craze with a sporty hardtop, the Lancer GT—a good car with the 225 engine option. Of the 64,351 Lancers sold, 13,683 were GTs. Dart/Polara 500 convertibles numbered 5340, two-door hardtops 19,738.

	Restorable	Good	Excellent
Convertibles	$2,500-5,000	$5,000-9,000	$9,000-13,000
2d hardtops	1,500-3,000	3,000-6,000	6,000-9,000
Lancer GT htp	1,500-3,000	3,000-6,000	6,000-8,000
Other models	1,000-2,500	2,500-5,000	5,000-7,000

(Ramcharger 413: add 25%)

1961 Dodge Dart Phoenix hardtop coupe

1961 Dodge Lancer 770 hardtop coupe

1961 Dodge Lancer 770 four-door station wagon

1962 Dodge Polara 500 convertible coupe

1962 Dodge Dart 440 hardtop sedan

1962 Dodge Lancer 770 four-door sedan

1963 Dodge Polara hardtop sedan (sans nameplate)

1963 Dodge Custom 880 hardtop sedan

1954 Dodge Polara hardtop coupe

1964 Dodge Polara 500 convertible coupe

1964 Dodge Dart GT hardtop coupe

1963

Dodge reversed course quickly with a three-inch longer wheelbase for its standard models, now called the 330, 440, Polara, and Polara 500. The last, which came only as a very luxurious convertible and hardtop, saw a combined production run of 12,268 units. The division emphasized performance this year by replacing the 361 (except as the base engine in 880/Custom 880) with no less than five horsepower ratings ranging from 305-360. The 360-bhp version was optional for 880 models. Also offered now was a 426 Ramcharger wedge in four horsepower ratings: 370, 375, 415, and 425. The last two, running dual quads, were "not a street machine," Dodge said frankly. Ramchargers were available in the lighter 330 and 440 models, a combination that dominated the 1962 National Hot Rod Association, winning the championship for Dodge. The Lancer was replaced by a larger, prettier 111-inch-wheelbase compact called Dart, which offered a full range of six-cylinder hardtops, sedans, wagons (106-inch wheelbase), and convertibles in 170, 270, and GT series. The GT hardtop and ragtop enjoyed a production run of 34,227 units. The big 880 saw 28,266 units produced, including 822 Custom convertibles and 2804 Custom two-door hardtops. Among the "standard-size" Dodges, 7256 Polara 500 hardtops and soft tops rolled off the assembly line. Overall, Dodge output was up sharply to 446,129 units, good for seventh place in the sales race.

	Restorable	Good	Excellent
Polara/500 cvts	$2,500-5,000	$5,000-8,000	$8,000-12,000
Polara/500 2d htps	1,500-3,000	3,000-5,000	5,000-7,500
Dart GT cvt	2,000-4,000	4,000-7,000	7,000-9,500
Dart GT 2d htp	1,500-3,500	3,500-5,500	5,500-8,000
Dart 270 cvt	1,500-3,000	3,000-5,000	5,000-7,000
Other models	500-2,000	2,000-4,000	4,000-6,000

(Ramcharger 413: add 25%)

1964

The '64 model year was substantially the same as 1963, distinguished by attractive facelifts. This year, however, Darts could be ordered with the new 273-cid, 180-bhp Valiant V-8. The GT hardtop and convertible were good looking and priced remarkably low—they still are on today's collector market, and are lively with the V-8. A total of 12,170 GT hardtop and convertible V-8s were produced, plus 37,660 six-cylinder GTs. The standard Dodges came with the usual six and an assortment of V-8s starting with the 318, while the big Chrysler-based 880 continued as before, ringing up 1058 convertible and 3798 two-door hardtop sales. The fabled Hemi made its return in February 1964, and Dodge's Hemi-powered intermediates—along with their Plymouth counterparts—made their mark loud and clear in stock car and drag racing. Hemis were rated at 415 and 425 horsepower, both with dual four-barrel carbs and 11.0:1 or 12.5:1 compression (the 426 wedge was still available in 365-bhp guise). In the late Eighties, Hemis enjoyed a tremendous boom in prices, which have since come back to earth. Total Dodge production jumped to a record 501,781 cars, which included 17,787 examples of the desirable Polara 500 V-8s.

	Restorable	Good	Excellent
Polara/500 cvts	$2,500-5,000	$5,000-8,000	$8,000-12,000
Polara/500 2d htps	1,500-3,000	3,000-5,000	5,000-7,500
Dart GT cvt	2,000-4,000	4,000-7,000	7,000-9,500
Dart GT htp	1,500-3,500	3,500-5,500	5,500-8,000
Dart 270 cvt	1,500-3,000	3,000-5,000	6,000-7,000
Other models	500-2,000	2,000-4,000	4,000-6,000

(For 415-bhp Hemi: add 25%; for 425-bhp Hemi: add 50%)

1964 Dodge Custom 880 convertible coupe

1965

The old Coronet name returned as a 117-inch-wheelbase intermediate with crisp styling and lots of performance. Included was a special 115-inch-wheelbase Coronet Hemi-Charger, a two-door sedan weighing just 3200 pounds and selling for the same number of dollars. That included heavy-duty suspension, four-speed transmission, and "police" brakes. This Dodge rocket could accelerate to 60 in seven seconds; in racing tune it developed up to 430 horses, mastering its stock-car competition. Only a few were built. The stock '65s included a glamorous Coronet 500 hardtop and convertible, with bucket seats and center console. Highlighting the Dodge lineup was a new line of completely restyled big Dodges consolidated into Polara and Custom 880 series, plus a single sports/luxury Monaco hardtop, all on a 121-inch chassis. Dodge engines began as before with the 101-bhp Slant Six and ended up with the mighty Hemis. Production dipped slightly to 489,065 units, of which about 18,000 were Dart GT V-8s and 13,096 were Monaco hardtops. Other breakouts are not available.

1965 Dodge Monaco hardtop coupe

1965 Dodge Coronet 500 hardtop coupe

	Restorable	Good	Excellent
Hemi-Charger	$10,000-20,000	$20,000-30,000	$30,000-45,000
Convertibles	2,500-5,000	5,000-8,000	8,000-12,000
2d hardtops	1,500-3,000	3,000-5,000	5,000-7,500
Other models	500-2,000	2,000-4,000	4,000-6,000

1966 Dodge Coronet 500 hardtop coupe

1966

The first Dodge Charger, a fastback with hidden headlamps, fold-down split-back rear seat, sporty interior, and standard V-8 was a new addition to the line; engine options included the 361, 383, and 426 Hemi. Manual transmission, "Rallye" suspension, and a long list of luxury items could also be had. All Chargers are collectible, Hemis in particular. More typical is a 383 with TorqueFlite automatic, which could easily do 110 mph. A total of 37,344 were produced. Other Dodge offerings continued with the usual facelifts: six-cylinder and V-8 Darts and Coronets, the latter in standard, DeLuxe, 440, and 500 trim stages. Dart GTs accounted for 30,041 hardtops and convertibles, probably about half of them V-8s. All variations of the Coronet 500 found 55,683 buyers. The Custom 880 name disappeared, blended now into a full-line Monaco series, of which

1966 Dodge Polara hardtop sedan

1966 Dodge Dart GT convertible coupe

1967 Dodge Monaco hardtop sedan

1967 Dodge Coronet R/T hardtop coupe

1967 Dodge Dart GT hardtop coupe

1967 Dodge Charger fastback hardtop coupe

the Monaco 500 hardtop is worth considering (10,840 produced). Though engine offerings were basically the same as in 1965, the Dart now ran with an optional 235-horsepower version of the 273 V-8 and a new extra-cost 440-cubic-inch mill rated at 350 bhp found its way to the big Dodges. The Division was on a roll now as it moved into fifth place in the production race with 632,658 cars built.

	Restorable	Good	Excellent
Hemi models	$10,000-20,000	$20,000-30,000	$30,000-45,000
Charger	2,500-4,000	4,000-7,000	7,000-11,000
Coronet R/T 2d htp	3,500-5,000	5,000-8,500	8,500-11,000
Coronet R/T cvt	5,000-8,500	8,500-13,000	13,000-18,500
Other cvts	3,000-6,000	6,000-9,000	9,000-12,000
Monaco 500 2d htp	2,000-4,000	4,000-6,000	6,000-8,000
Other models	500-2,000	2,000-4,000	4,000-6,000

1967

Most models were restyled, and the Dart received a bulk of the attention. Though it wasn't really any bigger, it looked it. Hardtops, sedans, and convertibles continued, but the wagons were dropped. Of the 38,225 Dart GTs produced, about three-fifths got V-8s. The heavily restyled Monaco and Polara adopted the Chrysler Newport's 122-inch-wheelbase and sported reverse-slant rear quarter windows on the two-door hardtops, giving them a lower profile. Output of the top-line Monaco 500 hardtop with its standard 325-bhp 383 dropped by half to 5237 units. A 375-bhp 440 V-8 was optional on Polaras, Monacos, and Chargers as well. The little-changed Charger (look for fender-mounted turn signals) was also still available with the Hemi, but it suffered as production plummeted to 15,788 units. Coronets sported a minor facelift featuring narrow vertical grille bars, and that theme was repeated at the rear on top-line models. The big news was the Coronet R/T muscle model, which came standard with the 375-bhp 440, TorqueFlite, stiff suspension, wide tires, oversize brakes, and R/T badging. Options included the Hemi V-8, four-speed stick shift, and front disc brakes. As a leader of the "Dodge Rebellion," the R/T captured 9553 hardtop and 628 convertible buyers. Overall Dodge output stumbled to 465,732 units, pushing the make back to seventh place.

	Restorable	Good	Excellent
Hemi models	$10,000-20,000	$20,000-30,000	$30,000-45,000
Charger	2,500-4,000	4,000-7,000	7,000-11,000
Coronet R/T htp	3,500-5,000	5,000-8,500	8,500-11,000
Coronet R/T cvt	5,000-8,500	8,500-13,000	13,000-18,500
Other cvts	3,000-6,000	6,000-9,000	9,000-12,000
Monaco 500 htp	2,000-4,000	4,000-6,000	6,000-8,000
Other models	500-2,000	2,000-4,000	4,000-6,000

1968

The Dart and Polara/Monaco lines were facelifted this year, but the Coronet and Charger emerged all-new—the best-looking Dodge intermediates of their era. This was partly due to a swoopier roofline with a tunnel-back rear window and "Coke-bottle" bodyside styling. Both the Charger, with its hidden headlights, and the sportiest Coronets are highly collectible as a result, especially those with the hottest V-8s. The Charger—hardtop only—was an immediate hit, scoring 96,108 sales. At $2934, base models came with the Slant Six (were any actually built?), so look for those with optional V-8s or the R/T variant that came with the 375-bhp 440 Magnum as standard. Coronet R/Ts, also with the 440, found 10,849 homes for the hardtop and ragtop combined. Also new this year was Dodge's budget muscle car, the Coronet Super Bee. It was a light, fast coupe equipped with a special 335-bhp 383, four-speed manual, requisite heavy-duty equipment, "Power Bulge" hood, vinyl interior, Super Bee badging, bumblebee stripes around the tail, and a low $3027 base price. Several variations appeared among compacts. The Dart GTS was a plush, grand touring hardtop or convertible ($3189 and $3383), powered by a new lightweight 340-cid, 275-bhp V-8 or optional 300-bhp 383. Production totaled 8745 units. In addition to the Super Bee, GTS and R/Ts comprised Dodge's "Scat Pack," each denoted by the bumblebee stripes. The ultimate R/T engine was of course the 425-bhp Hemi, still a star on the nation's dragstrips and high-speed ovals. Hemis, though still valued very highly, are bringing about half what they brought in the 1989 boom. All in all, 1968 was a Dodge year—the 627,533 cars produced moved the Division up a notch into sixth place in industry standings.

	Restorable	Good	Excellent
Hemi models	$10,000-20,000	$20,000-30,000	$30,000-45,000
Dart GT cvt	2,500-4,000	4,000-7,000	7,000-9,000
Dart GTS 340 cvt	3,500-5,000	5,000-9,000	9,000-12,000
Dart GTS 383 cvt	4,500-6,000	6,000-11,000	11,000-15,000
Dart GT htp	1,000-3,000	3,000-5,000	5,000-8,000
Dart GTS 340 htp	2,000-4,000	4,000-6,000	6,000-9,000
Dart GTS 383 htp	4,000-5,500	5,500-10,000	10,000-13,000
Charger	2,500-4,000	4,000-7,000	7,000-11,000
Charger R/T	3,500-5,000	5,000-7,500	7,500-14,000
Coronet Super Bee 383	2,500-4,000	4,000-6,500	6,500-10,000
Coronet R/T 2d htp	3,500-5,000	5,000-8,500	8,500-14,000
Coronet R/T cvt	5,000-9,500	9,500-14,000	14,000-20,000
Other cvt	3,000-6,000	6,000-9,000	9,000-12,000
Monaco 500 2d htp	2,000-4,000	4,000-6,000	6,000-8,000
Other models	500-2,000	2,000-4,000	4,000-6,000

1969

The Charger Daytona, built especially to provide a winner for the famed Daytona 500 race, flaunted a wind-cheating bullet nose with hidden headlamps, a front spoiler, aerodynamic fastback roof, and a towering rear-deck stabilizer. Compared with the Charger 500 (a special designed for track work with the Magnum 440 or Hemi 426), the Daytona was 20 percent more aerodynamic. Dodge built 505 to qualify for racing, but the Daytona was less successful

1968 Dodge Coronet R/T hardtop coupe

1968 Dodge Monaco 500 hardtop coupe

1968 Dodge Polara hardtop sedan

1968 Dodge Dart GTS hardtop coupe

1968 Dodge Charger hardtop coupe

1969 Dodge Polara 500 hardtop coupe

1969 Dodge Polara four-door station wagon

1969 Dodge Charger Hemi hardtop coupe

1969 Dodge Dart Swinger hardtop coupe

1969 Dodge Charger Daytona hardtop coupe

than was hoped. Like the Charger 500, Daytonas came with the Magnum 440 or Hemi 426. The Charger 500, incidentally, saw production of just 392 units, 52 of them Hemis. Darts this year included a low-cost, high-powered hardtop, the $2836 Swinger 340. Amazingly, you could even buy a little Dart converted to the Magnum 440 by Hurst-Campbell in Michigan—not a good combination, except for the dragstrips. Output of these specials was 48 for '68 and about 600 in 1969. The Coronet Super Bee, Dodge's version of the Plymouth Road Runner, was a separate series hardtop or coupe with 383, Hemi, and 440 V-8 available this year; the last could be ordered with triple two-barrel carbs as the 6-Pack engine (also sometimes spelled Six Pak). Production of all combinations was 27,846. Charger R/T, meanwhile, continued with the 440 and 426 Hemi, attracting 7238 customers this year. The regular Charger line enjoyed a production run of 89,704, among them 20,057 R/Ts. Despite the bewildering array of performance models, total Dodge production eased off to 611,645 units for the model year.

	Restorable	Good	Excellent
Daytona Hemi & 440	$15,000-25,000	$25,000-45,000	$45,000-60,000
Other Hemis	10,000-20,000	20,000-30,000	30,000-45,000
Dart GT cvt	2,500-4,000	4,000-7,000	7,000-9,000
Dart GT 340 cvt	3,500-5,000	5,000-9,000	9,000-12,000
Dart GT 383/440 cvt	4,500-6,000	6,000-12,000	12,000-17,000
Dart GT htp	1,000-3,000	3,000-5,000	5,000-8,000
Dart Swinger 340 htp	2,000-4,000	4,000-6,000	6,000-9,000
Dart GT 383/440 htp	4,000-5,500	5,500-10,000	10,000-14,000
Charger	2,500-4,000	4,000-7,000	7,000-11,000
Charger R/T	3,500-6,000	6,000-9,500	9,500-16,000
Charger 500 (440)	5,000-10,000	10,000-18,000	18,000-30,000
Super Bee 383/440	3,500-4,500	4,500-9,000	9,000-13,000
Super Bee 440 6-Pack	5,000-9,500	9,500-14,000	14,000-20,000
Coronet R/T 2d htp	3,500-5,000	5,000-8,500	8,500-14,000
Coronet R/T cvt	5,000-9,500	9,500-14,000	14,000-20,000
Other cvts	3,000-6,000	6,000-9,000	9,000-12,000
Other models	500-2,000	2,000-4,000	4,000-6,000

1970

Better late than never, Dodge's answer to the Mustang appeared: the Challenger, a close-coupled coupe or convertible with a wide variety of six-cylinder and V-8 engines. A vinyl-roofed coupe with a small backlight made it the Special Edition; 6584 were produced as base models, along with another 3979 T/As. The T/A (for Trans Am racing) was a Challenger that was specially decorated and came with a triple two-barrel-carb 340 V-8 rated at 290 bhp (true output about 350) and four-speed as standard. Just 2539 were built. Dart and Coronet received a new split grille, the Dart a longer hood and new rear-end styling. The Dart Swinger 340 hardtop was relatively popular with 13,785 produced. The Charger sported a full-width grille surrounded by a massive loop bumper and was again offered with a six—which models are not much sought after. One to look for: the 440 6-Pack with triple two-barrel carbs. The hot R/T hardtop found favor with 10,337 buyers. The Daytona was dropped, while the senior Polara and Monaco were restyled. Convertibles were pared down, available only in three basic models: Challenger (3173 base and 1070 R/Ts built), Coronet (924 500s and 296 R/Ts), and Polara (842). Performance cars had already passed their peak, so perhaps Dodge was beginning to suffer for it—total production for the model year was 543,019 units.

	Restorable	Good	Excellent
Hemi models	$10,000-20,000	$20,000-30,000	$30,000-45,000
Dart Swinger 340	2,000-4,000	4,000-6,000	6,000-8,000
Challenger cpe	2,500-5,000	5,000-7,500	7,500-10,000
Challenger R/T 440	3,500-7,000	7,000-10,000	10,000-15,000
Challenger T/A cpe	5,000-10,000	10,000-17,500	17,500-25,000
Challenger cvt	4,000-8,000	8,000-12,000	12,000-18,000
Chal R/T 440 cvt	7,000-12,000	12,000-18,000	18,000-25,000
Charger & Chgr 500	2,500-4,000	4,000-7,000	7,000-12,000
Charger R/T	5,000-8,000	8,000-13,000	13,000-20,000
Charger R/T 6-Pack	7,500-15,000	15,000-24,000	24,000-32,000
Super Bee 383/440	3,500-4,500	4,500-9,000	9,000-13,000
Super Bee 440 6-Pack	5,000-9,500	9,500-14,000	14,000-20,000
Coronet R/T 2d htp	3,500-5,000	5,000-8,500	8,500-14,000
Coronet R/T cvt	5,000-9,500	9,500-14,000	14,000-20,000
Other cvt	3,000-6,000	6,000-9,000	9,000-12,000
Other models	500-2,000	2,000-4,000	4,000-6,000

1971

The last great year for Dodge muscle cars, 1971 saw a broad line of models spanning a huge market bracket: compact Darts (including a newly named Demon coupe), sporty Challengers, intermediate Coronets, a restyled and more conventional Charger, and the big Polara and Monaco. The mighty Hemi with 425 horses powered the Hemi-Charger and Challengers; a detuned 335-bhp version was available for Polara and Monaco. Already, though, the effect of Federal regulations and a shortage of young men courtesy of the Viet Nam war were having their effect. The Coronet lost its handsome line of coupes and convertibles with their Super Bee and R/T options, and only one soft top, the Challenger, was left in the line. There was, however, a Super Bee in the Charger range, offering standard 383, three-speed stick, stiff suspension, Rallye gauges, and other appropriate components at low cost. Production increased slightly to 551,386. The results for some of the more interesting models follows: Dart Demon 340, 10,098; Challenger convertible, 2165; R/T coupe, 4630; Charger 500 hardtop, 11,948; Super Bee, 5054; SE, 15,811; R/T, 3118; Monaco hardtop coupe, 3195.

	Restorable	Good	Excellent
Dart Demon 340 cpe	$2,000-4,000	$4,000-6,000	$6,000-8,000
Challenger cpe	2,500-5,000	5,000-7,500	7,500-10,000

1970 Dodge Challenger hardtop coupe

1970 Dodge Dart Swinger 340 hardtop coupe

1971 Dodge Charger 500 hardtop coupe

1971 Dodge Charger 500 hardtop coupe

1971 Dodge Challenger R/T hardtop coupe

1972 Dodge Charger hardtop coupe

1972 Dodge Dart Swinger hardtop coupe

1973 Dodge Dart Swinger hardtop coupe

1972 Dodge Dart Demon fastback coupe

	Restorable	Good	Excellent
Chal R/T 440	3,500-7,000	7,000-10,000	10,000-15,000
Hemi-Chal htp	9,000-20,000	20,000-30,000	30,000-45,000
Challenger cvt	4,000-8,000	8,000-12,000	12,000-18,000
Chal R/T 440	7,000-12,000	12,000-18,000	18,000-25,000
Chal Hemi	20,000-30,000	30,000-40,000	40,000-60,000
Charger	2,500-4,000	4,000-7,000	7,000-11,000
Chgr Super Bee	4,000-7,000	7,000-10,000	10,000-15,000
Chgr R/T (440)	5,000-8,000	8,000-13,000	13,000-20,000
Chgr R/T 6-Pack	7,500-15,000	15,000-24,000	24,000-30,000
Hemi-Charger	12,000-22,000	22,000-35,000	35,000-48,000
Polara/Monaco Hemi	2,500-5,000	5,000-8,000	8,000-12,000
Other models	500-2,000	2,000-4,000	4,000-6,000

1972

More government regulations and high insurance premiums contributed to the rapid decline of Dodge (and other) muscle cars. Heavy chops of performance components were made this year. Gone were the Hemis, convertibles, Super Bees, and R/Ts. The Magnum 440 was still around, but with horsepower expressed in net rather than gross bhp (which was more accurate), though real output was down in any case due to lower compression ratios for unleaded gas. Charger's base V-8 was the 150-bhp 318, with a 190-bhp 400 optional and the 240-bhp 340 for the Charger Rallye. The 440 carried five horsepower ratings from 230-330 bhp, while the new 400 V-8 came in at 190, 250, and 255 bhp, and was widely used throughout the lineup. For the most part, styling changes were relatively minor, although the Polara and Monaco received a more extensive facelift, the latter now sporting hidden headlights. Despite the gloom and doom among performance fans, total production rose to 577,870 units, more than half of them Darts, including 8750 Demon 340s. Challenger output stalled at 26,658, and only 8123 of them were the sportier Rallye coupe. Of the 75,594 Chargers built, 22,430 were the more luxurious SE models. From this point on, the collectibility of Dodge products decreases substantially.

	Restorable	Good	Excellent
Challenger	$2,500-4,000	$4,000-6,500	$6,500-8,000
Chal 340/360	3,500-5,000	5,000-7,500	7,500-10,000
Charger cpe	1,500-3,000	3,000-4,500	4,500-7,000
Chgr Rallye 440	3,000-5,000	5,000-7,000	7,000-9,000
Other models	500-2,000	2,000-3,000	3,000-4,000

1973

Emphasis was on refinement, "extra care in engineering." This was the next-to-last year for the Challenger—born too late to do much in the ponycar market, which just wasn't broad enough anymore to support much more than Mustang and Camaro. This year, Challenger saw a production run of 32,596. The Polara models had a new front end which resembled, the pundits said, nothing more than an Oldsmobile. The Monaco was unchanged save for massive crash-bumpers that were added across the board. All Challengers were V-8s this year, starting with the 150-bhp 318. The 440 V-8 now numbered just two versions with 220 and 280 bhp. Still alive, though now in its last year, the 240-bhp 340 V-8 was standard in the Dart Sport 340 (there had been complaints about the Demon name), optional in Challenger, Coronet, and Charger. The '73 model year was excellent as 665,536 Dodges rolled off the assembly lines. This included 11,315 Dart 340 coupes, 119,318 Chargers, 6432 Polara hardtop coupes, and 6133 Monaco hardtop coupes.

	Restorable	Good	Excellent
Challenger	$2,500-4,000	$4,000-6,500	$6,500-8,000
Challenger 340/360	3,500-5,000	5,000-7,500	7,500-10,000
Charger cpe	1,500-3,000	3,000-4,500	4,500-7,000
Charger Rallye 440	3,000-5,000	5,000-7,000	7,000-9,000
Other models	500-2,000	2,000-3,000	3,000-4,000

1974

Dodge's Sixtieth Anniversary year was a grim one for the enthusiast. Full-size cars were redesigned, sharing sheetmetal with Chrysler models. The Challenger made its last appearance, unchanged from 1973, though output ended with a whimper: 16,437. Chargers continued on their special 115-inch wheelbase with reasonably sleek styling and semi-fastback rooflines. Top engine remained the 440, available with 275 bhp on the Coronet and Charger only. The Polara range was dropped, leaving Monaco the only full-size Dodge. A 180-bhp 360 was the base engine, with 400 and 440 V-8s with up to 250 bhp optional. The Arab oil embargo, which started in late 1973, caused production to wither to 477,728 units. Charger skidded to 74,376, and hardtop coupe production for the all-new Monacos was disappointing: 3347 base models, 6649 Customs, 4863 Broughams. A performance-oriented Dart 360 coupe with 245 horsepower replaced the 340, but only 3951 were sold.

	Restorable	Good	Excellent
Challenger	$2,500-4,000	$4,000-6,500	$6,500-8,000
Challenger 340/360	3,500-5,000	5,000-7,500	7,500-10,000
Charger cpe	1,500-3,000	3,000-4,500	4,500-7,000
Charger Rallye 440	3,000-5,000	5,000-7,000	7,000-9,000
Other models	500-2,000	2,000-3,000	3,000-4,000

1975

Unsold cars piled up at the factory and dealerships as Dodge faced one of the worst of its periodic sales crises—only 377,462 cars were built for the model run. The Charger, completely redesigned, was now a version of the new personal-luxury Chrysler Cordoba, offered as an "SE" (Special Edition) coupe and designed to compete with the Chevrolet Monte Carlo and the new Ford Elite. At 30,812 units, it managed only one-fifth Cordoba's output. The Coronet line was also restyled, while detail changes were made to the Monaco. With 210,039 built, Darts continued to shore up Dodge sales, with the Swinger hardtop attracting 45,495 buyers. An upmarket Special Edition Dart hardtop found only 5680 takers. The Dart 360 coupe, however, was rare with just 1043 built.

1974 Dodge Charger coupe

1974 Dodge Monaco Brougham hardtop sedan

1974 Dodge Challenger hardtop coupe

1975 Dodge Charger SE (Special Edition) coupe

1976 Dodge Charger Daytona coupe

1977 Dodge Aspen R/T coupe

	Restorable	Good	Excellent
Charger SE	$1,000-2,000	$2,000-3,000	$3,000-4,000

1976

The reliable and good looking Dart, which sold well even in the worst of times, made its final appearance in 1976. Alongside came its eventual replacement, the Aspen, a far less successful compact. Though the Aspen had more interior space and a wider list of luxury options, it won the dubious distinction of being the most recalled car in history (up until that time) because of poor quality control and widespread body rust-through. Despite the existence of an R/T coupe—with 318 or 360 V-8, blacked out grille, customized back end, decals, racing stripes, and Rallye wheels—it is hard to conceive of a collectible Aspen. The only Dodge worth serious thought as a collectible now was the Charger, some of which were decked out as "Daytonas," a tape/stripe package that had no significance as to powerplant. The only 440 V-8 left was a 205-bhp version, and that was for the little-changed Monaco only. A number of 400 V-8s was listed, however, a 240-bhp unit being the most powerful listed for the Charger. Dodge production rallied to 430,641 units, and the Charger did better too: 13,826 coupes with fixed rear quarter windows, 9906 hardtops, and 42,168 SEs. Among Monacos, buyers chose 2915 Royal and 4076 Royal Brougham hardtop coupes.

	Restorable	Good	Excellent
Charger SE	$1,000-2,000	$2,000-3,000	$3,000-4,000
Aspen R/T	500-1,000	1,000-2,000	2,000-3,000

1977

At mid-year, Dodge introduced the Diplomat, an old name dating back to 1950, based this time on Chrysler's 112.7-inch-wheelbase LeBaron intermediate—itself based on the Dodge Aspen four-door chassis. The Diplomat sold well, though, and Dodge needed sales desperately. Though offered as a four-door sedan and a coupe, the coupe was the better seller this year: 14,023 base models and 9215 Medallions. The Charger SE offered a T-bar roof option with removable glass panel. About 5000 of the 42,542 Chargers built bore the Daytona package: decals, stripes, customized back end, and a weird two-tone package with the second color plastered around the wheel wells. Dodge production continued to rally, this year to 526,254 units, 312,646 of them Aspens. How many of the Aspen coupes carried the R/T packages isn't known. Monaco—now officially called Royal Monaco—saw production of 3360 base and 8309 Brougham hardtop coupes.

	Restorable	Good	Excellent
Charger SE	$1,000-2,000	$2,000-3,000	$3,000-4,000
Aspen R/T	500-1,000	1,000-2,000	2,000-3,000

1978

Magnum XE, a Charger with a Cord-like front end (thanks to glass-covered headlamps and a horizontal louver grille) relieved the utter boredom this year. Louvers matching the grille style could be ordered for its opera windows. A T-bar roof option or power-sunroof were offered and the 318 V-8 was standard, though 360 and 400 V-8s were optional (the 440 was dropped this year). Later came the Magnum GT, with body-color fender flares, heavy duty shocks, and white letter tires on slotted wheels. A total of 55,431 Magnums were produced, along with just 2800 Charger SE coupes. Dodge's front-wheel-drive, four-cylinder subcompact Omni made its first appearance this year as a five-door hatchback riding a 99.2-inch wheelbase. Though of no interest to collectors, it found 81,611 buyers. Monaco—without Royal ahead of it—was downsized to a 117.4-inch wheelbase, 114.9 for coupes, of which 10,291 base models and 6842 Broughams were built. Total Dodge production fell back to 467,720 units for the model run. As before, it's not known how many of the Aspen 75,599 coupes wore R/T garb.

	Restorable	Good	Excellent
Charger SE	$1,000-2,000	$2,000-3,000	$3,000-4,000
Magnum XE/GT	1,000-2,500	2,500-3,500	3,500-5,000
Aspen R/T	500-1,000	1,000-2,000	2,000-3,000

1978 Dodge Magnum XE coupe

1979 Dodge Magnum XE coupe

1979 Dodge Omni 024 hatchback coupe

1979

After a sad four years as a Cordoba-copy, the Charger disappeared altogether, leaving the Magnum XE as Dodge's personal-luxury coupe. Production of the latter was down to 30,354 units. Aspen, which had been offered with "R/T" trim for the past few years, could now be had as a "Sunrise Coupe," adding flared wheel openings, bucket seats, aluminum wheels, and slotted rear side windows to the R/T package; with the 195-bhp 360 V-8 (the most powerful engine Dodge offered this year), this is as close to collectible as an Aspen will ever come. Total Aspen coupe output was down to 42,833. New to Omni was a slick-looking hatchback coupe, the 024, which made a pretense of sportiness with its vinyl bucket seats, optional Rallye instruments, and Sport package: black accents, sport steering wheel, body-color wheels, extra instruments. The 024 ran with a 70-horsepower, 104.7-cid four, and attracted 57,384 buyers. The full-size Monaco became the St. Regis this year as a four-door sedan only; 34,972 were built. Dodge production continued to drop, this year to 404,266 units.

	Restorable	Good	Excellent
Magnum XE	$1,000-2,500	$2,500-3,500	$3,500-5,000
Aspen Sunrise cpe	500-1,000	1,000-2,000	2,000-3,000
Omni 024 Spt cpe	500-1,000	1,000-2,000	2,000-3,000

1980

Dodge downsized, replacing the Magnum XE with the Mirada: six inches shorter, 400 pounds lighter,

1981 Dodge Mirada coupe with CMX package

1981 Dodge Aries two-door sedan

and powered by a Slant Six instead of a V-8 (though the 318 and 360 V-8s were optional). This paralleled and shared a body with the new Chrysler Cordoba. Miradas could be had with fabric-covered roofs to simulate a convertible; this has no effect on modern values. Sales, at 32,746 units, were a disappointment. Aspen's Sunrise coupe returned, with plaid bucket seats, special wheel covers, and identifying tape stripes. The Aspen was now in its last year, so the existence of 285 Aspen R/Ts (blacked-out grille and other exterior accents, tape-stripes and painted wheels) ought at least to be mentioned. Aspen coupe output plummeted to 25,061 during its last year. Diplomat coupes didn't fare very well, either: 5884 base models, 6849 Salons, 2131 Medallions. Among Omnis was a "De Tomaso" coupe, with bright red or yellow body, black accents, air dams, wheel flares, a sporty interior, a tight suspension—and 65 horsepower like any other 024. Coupe production this year totaled 61,650, while Dodge as a whole skidded to 308,638 units, partly because Chrysler's widely publicized precarious financial position scared away potential buyers.

	Restorable	Good	Excellent
Mirada cpe	$1,000-2,000	$2,000-3,000	$3,000-4,000
Aspen Sunrise & R/T	500-1,000	1,000-2,000	2,000-3,000
Omni 024 De Tomaso	500-1,000	1,000-2,000	2,000-3,000

1981

The big news was the company-saving K-car, Aries in Dodge's case. The fact that 1981 marks the first of these historically important cars may make the better examples somewhat collectible some day: our choice would be one of only 537 Aeries SE two-door sedans wearing a simulated convertible top. Total production of Aries two- and four-door sedans and wagons came to an encouraging 155,781 units. Omni performance was improved thanks to a new and long-lived 2.2-liter, 84-bhp four, which later replaced the original 1.7 and was a major step forward in performance. The 024 coupe, including a new Miser model, saw sales wither to 35,983, probably because it was too close price-wise to the new Aries. Even though the new front-drive Dodges were doing well, total production hit a low of 274,277 this year. The old rear-drive models were fading fast: 24,170 Diplomats in all three body styles, 11,899 Miradas (now down to an 85-bhp Slant Six or optional 130-bhp 318 V-8), and 5388 St. Regis sedans. Fortunately for Dodge, better times weren't too far away.

Restorable	Good	Excellent	
Mirada cpe	$1,000-2,000	$2,000-3,000	$3,000-4,000
Aries SE 2d/cvt top	500-1,000	1,000-2,000	2,000-3,000
Omni 024 De Tomaso	500-1,000	1,000-2,000	2,000-3,000

1982

The Charger name was resurrected on a performance Omni coupe with the 2.2 four, and 14,420 found buyers. But more important to enthusiasts was the mid-year revival of the Dodge convertible, a 400-series model riding what was called the "Super-K" platform (still on the 99.9-inch wheelbase) and built from coupes by Cars & Concepts in Brighton, Michigan. Like other Super-Ks, the soft top 400 was well equipped, featuring radio, carpets, door chimes, digital clock, center armrests. Standard on all ragtops was the larger Mitsubishi-built 2.6-liter four rated at 92 bhp. Four-speed manual shift was standard, TorqueFlite automatic optional. These first year convertibles, of which just 5541 were built, did not have rear-quarter windows. Despite three lines of front-wheel-drive cars—Omni, Aires, 400—Dodge's sales recovery was stalled by the early '80s recession, and so production took another dip to 241,385. St. Regis was gone, leaving the Diplomat and Mirada as the last of the rear-drivers; their output hardly counted: 26,591 Diplomats (four-door sedan only this year), 6818 Miradas. An interesting model this year was the five-door Omni Euro-Sedan with black-out trim and exterior stripes and upmarket sporty interior, but only 639 were built.

	Restorable	Good	Excellent
Mirada cpe	*	$2,000-3,000	$3,000-4,000
Charger 2.2	*	1,000-2,000	2,000-3,000
400 cvt	*	2,000-3,000	3,000-4,000

* Purchase only in good or excellent condition

1982 Dodge 400 convertible coupe

1982 Dodge Charger 2.2 hatchback coupe

1982 Dodge Mirada coupe with CMX package

1983

L-body coupes, formerly Omni 024s, were now all called Chargers, with the up-market Charger 2.2 boasting 10 more horsepower and optional five-speed manual gearbox. Mid-year brought the Shelby Charger 2.2, named for high performance legend Carroll Shelby, with front air dam, rear roof appliqués, special paint and tape treatment. Output was 22,535 base Chargers, 10,448 2.2s, and 8251 Shelbys. The five-speed was also optional on the 400 convertible, which attracted 4888 buyers and was now built in-house by Chrysler; equally useful, if you find it, is the road package with larger sway bars, stiffer shocks, faster-ratio power steering. The "Voice Alert" message center may be safely ignored, though some 400s carried a useful electronic travel computer. New this year was the 600, a two-model series with a base and ES (Euro-Sport) four-door sedan on a K-car chassis stretched to a 103.1-inch wheelbase; 33,488 were sold. Aside from new colors, the Mirada was unchanged, but only 5597 were built for this its last year. Diplomat limped along with 24,444 sales. Dodge's sales turnaround finally began this year with a production uptick to 285,808 units.

	Restorable	Good	Excellent
Mirada cpe	*	$2,000-3,000	$3,000-4,000
Charger 2.2	*	1,000-2,000	2,000-3,000

1983 Dodge Charger Shelby hatchback coupe

1983 Dodge Charger Shelby hatchback coupe

	Restorable	Good	Excellent
Shelby Charger	*	1,500-2,500	2,500-3,500
400 cvt	*	2,000-3,000	3,000-4,000

* Purchase only in good or excellent condition

1984 Dodge Daytona Turbo Z hatchback coupe

1984 Dodge 600 convertible coupe

1984 Dodge Charger 2.2 hatchback coupe

1985 Dodge 600 ES convertible coupe

1984

Daytona, Dodge's version of the G-24 sports coupe, paralleled the Chrysler Laser. The Turbo Z performance model came with ground-effects front air dam, side skirts and unique rear spoiler, tape stripes, and bodyside moldings. Chrysler's ohc 2.2 was standard, with Turbo and Turbo Z Daytonas carrying fuel injection and a Garrett turbocharger. All Turbos had the handling package as standard. Of the 49,347 Daytonas produced, 27,431 were Turbo and Turbo Z models. Chargers carried new instrument panels and cleaner front ends; the Shelby Charger came standard with a 110-bhp high-output 2.2 and the usual Shelby graphics. The Charger breakdown was 34,763 base coupes, 11,949 2.2s, and 7552 Shelbys. With a simple nameplate change, Dodge's convertible moved into the 600 line, using the 99-bhp 2.2-liter engine as standard. This really wasn't enough, but a Turbo 2.2 with 142 horsepower or Mitsubishi's 101-bhp 2.6 were optional. The convertible's rear seat was wider and the rear window was now glass; power rear quarter windows were also added. A $3378 ES package introduced at mid-year gave the ragtop the Turbo, handling package, upgraded leather interior, and more. Of the 10,960 convertibles built, 1786 were ES Turbos. Dodge's recovery was now well underway—production leaped to 375,513 units, and all of these were front-drive models save for 22,163 Diplomats. The production figure would look even better if the ultra-successful Caravan minivan, which was introduced this year, was counted (industry tallies list it as a truck).

	Restorable	Good	Excellent
Daytona Turbo Z	*	$1,500-2,500	$2,500-3,500
Charger 2.2	*	1,000-2,000	2,000-3,000
Shelby Charger	*	1,500-2,500	2,500-3,500
600 cvt	*	2,000-3,000	3,000-4,000
600 ES cvt	*	2,500-3,500	3,500-4,500

* Purchase only in good or excellent condition

1985

The Shelby Charger received a 2.2 Turbo packing 146 horsepower as standard equipment. It attracted 7709 customers, while 10,605 buyers opted for the 2.2 model. Meanwhile, the 600 convertible continued in base and ES guise. The carbureted 2.2 engine was dropped. In base form, the 600 soft top was mild mannered with adequate acceleration and family car handling traits. With the 2.2 Turbo it had a much different character—faster (0-60 in about 8.5 seconds), tauter, louder, more fun to drive. Collectors should look for the optional handling suspension standard with Turbos, which greatly improves road manners, but avoid the digital instrument display in favor of good old-fashioned needle gauges. Output this year was 8188 base convertibles and 5621 ES models. All Daytonas wore a three-piece spoiler this year, and there was a host of detail improvements. Out of 47,519 Daytonas built, enthusiasts selected 9509 Turbos and 8023 Turbo Zs. Total Dodge output took another healthy jump this year, to 440,043 cars. Included in this total were 45,583 Lancers, five-door sport sedans riding the 103.3-inch wheelbase. An ES model found favor with 15,286 buyers.

	Restorable	Good	Excellent
Daytona Turbo Z	*	$2,000-2,750	$2,750-3,750
Charger 2.2	*	1,000-2,000	2,000-3,000
Shelby Charger	*	2,000-3,000	3,000-4,000
600 cvt	*	2,500-3,500	3,500-4,500
600 ES cvt	*	3,000-4,000	4,000-5,000

* Purchase only in good or excellent condition

1985 Dodge Charger 2.2 hatchback coupe

1986 Dodge Daytona Turbo Z hatchback coupe

1986 Dodge 600 convertible coupe

1986

The Daytona's handling package—which is recommended—was called "C/S" in honor of Carroll Shelby, who had been injecting Dodge with a performance image of late. Included were wide unidirectional tires on cast aluminum wheels, large stabilizer bars, and firmer shocks. A T-bar roof was available, and worth looking for. A similar spec applied to the Shelby Charger, with its standard turbocharged engine. The blown engine was standard again on the ES model, along with sport suspension, leather-wrapped steering wheel, power windows, electronic instruments, Eagle GT tires on cast aluminum wheels, etc. The 600 convertible, meanwhile, was restyled front and rear. A Chrysler-built 2.5-liter four with twin balance shafts replaced the Mitsubishi 2.6 in the engine lineup, though neither of these engines is of any real interest to collectors. Omni strutted a five-door model of some interest this year, the GLH—Goes Like Hell—described as "a well-behaved savage." This model was dressed to a boy racer's delight with black-out trim everywhere and came with the 110-bhp 2.2 four or, more to the point, the 146-bhp Turbo 2.2 with functional hood louvers. It found 3629 buyers. With customers lined up to buy minivans, Dodge dealers probably hardly noticed that car sales slipped to 404,496 units. Some production figures: 4814 Charger 2.2s, 7669 Shelby Chargers, 17,595 Daytona Turbo Zs, 17,888 Lancer ES five-doors (a true bargain sportabout), 11,678 600 convertibles, and 4759 600 ES ragtops.

	Restorable	Good	Excellent
Daytona Turbo Z	*	$2,500-3,250	$3,250-4,250
Charger 2.2	*	1,500-2,500	2,500-3,500
Shelby Charger	*	2,500-3,500	3,500-4,500
600 cvt	*	3,000-3,750	3,750-5,000
600 ES cvt	*	3,500-4,250	4,250-5,500

* Purchase only in good or excellent condition

1987

This is the year Dodge abandoned the convertible market. Chrysler offered a new aero-look LeBaron ragtop, but Dodge didn't get a version. So Dodge concentrated on an attractive facelift of the Daytona,

1987 Dodge Shelby Charger hatchback coupe

1987 Dodge Daytona Shelby Z hatchback coupe

1988 Dodge Lancer Shelby hatchback sedan

which featured an aero-look front with hidden headlamps and revised rear styling. The Daytona line comprised a base coupe, a new luxury Pacifica, and the high-performance Shelby Z, the last being the obvious collectible. Pacifica, at $13,912, included the 146-bhp Turbo engine and a long list of goodies including even an Electronic Navigator computer. Z's came standard with the Turbo II 2.2 engine, with stronger internals, higher-boost pressure, an intercooler, and 174 horses, hooked to a beefed-up five-speed manual gearbox. Also featured was a more overtly aerodynamic package. Ignore Shelby Zs equipped with automatic and the 146-bhp Turbo I engine. Although Daytona production was down 25 percent, 7467 Pacificas and 7152 Shelby Zs were produced. The Shelby Charger continued pretty much unchanged, and output crashed to just 2011 units. Also suffering was the Lancer ES, which dropped to 9579 units. New this year was the 97-inch-wheelbase Shadow subcompact, offered in three- and five-door hatchback varieties. Though not collectible, they could be entertaining with the Turbo I engine and various performance-oriented options. In total, Dodge production slipped to 395,289 units.

	Restorable	Good	Excellent
Daytona Shelby Z	*	$3,000-3,750	$3,750-5,000
Daytona Pacifica	*	2,500-3,250	3,250-4,250
Shelby Charger	*	2,750-3,750	3,750-4,750

* Purchase only in good or excellent condition

1988

A lighter turbocharger, a new performance package option, and improved sound system were changes for Daytona, which continued as a base, Pacifica luxury, and Shelby Z performance coupe. A new blower was installed on the Turbo I engine, part of a new C/S Performance Package available on the base Daytona—similar to '87 C/S components but including four-wheel disc brakes. The discs, special trim inside and out, performance seats, stiff suspension, and wide tires on aluminum wheels were standard on Shelby Zs. Base coupes tripled to 54,075 units, some of them nicely optioned, but the Pacifica fell back to 4752 examples, while the Turbo Z increased slightly to 7580. The Charger was dropped after 1987. Meanwhile, the Lancer Shelby—a high-performance, limited-edition of Dodge's five-door hatchback—carried Carroll Shelby's image to another model. A body-color grille, outside mirrors, spoilers, and driving lights were fitted, along with the Turbo II 2.2-liter engine and five-speed manual gearbox. An automatic mated to the Turbo I engine was available, but avoid it. Shelby had already run off about 800 Shelby Lancers (note the all-important name difference), but Dodge's imitation, available in red or white color schemes, saw only 279 produced. Though production increased this year to 430,902 units, Dodge's concentration was now more on value-for-dollar models, the Omni and Aries Americas, and the new Dynasty, another K-car offshoot on a 104.3 wheelbase. The last would find happiness with fleet buyers.

	Restorable	Good	Excellent
Daytona Shelby Z	*	$4,500-5,500	$5,500-6,500
Daytona Pacifica	*	4,000-5,000	5,000-6,000
Daytona C/S	*	3,500-4,500	4,500-5,750
Lancer Shelby	*	5,000-6,500	6,500-8,000

* Purchase only in good or excellent condition

1989

A standard 174-bhp Turbo II engine, five-speed manual transmission, special handling package, and unique exterior trim were part of the '89 Lancer Shelby limited edition, available this year in white, red, or black. Also standard were leather-trimmed upholstery, air conditioning, and a six-way power driver's seat. The front-drive Daytona sport coupe featured freshened front and rear styling. An ES Turbo model replacing the Pacifica debuted with a 150-bhp 2.5-liter Turbo I engine. The Daytona Shelby lost its previous "Z" suffix but featured the Turbo II engine and received unique paint treatment that graduated from charcoal tint on the lower panels to body color in the upper panels. Shelbys also had new "pumper" alloy 16-inch wheels mated to unidirectional tires. The automatic transmission option remained, but with it a Shelby could only be had with the Turbo I engine. Calendar year sales came to 64,097 Daytonas of all types. The Lancer Shelby was now in its final year, and only 3113 were sold during the year, and 1081 leftovers would be sold in 1991. Spirit came on board for 1989 only as a four-door sedan, but it could be reasonably spirited with the 150-bhp Turbo four or 141-bhp Mitsubishi 3.0-liter V-6. All in all, however, there weren't very many Dodges to excite enthusiasts or collectors. Calendar year sales came to 410,995 units.

1989 Dodge Daytona Shelby hatchback coupe

1989 Dodge Daytona ES hatchback coupe

	Restorable	Good	Excellent
Daytona Shelby Turbo	*	$5,500-6,500	$6,500-8,000
Daytona ES Turbo	*	5,000-6,000	6,000-7,000
Daytona C/S	*	4,500-5,500	5,500-6,500
Lancer Shelby	*	5,500-7,000	7,000-8,500

* Purchase only in good or excellent condition

1990

The performance-leading Daytona received a new interior and two new engines, including the important 3.0-liter, 141-bhp V-6 by Mitsubishi—its first appearance in a front-drive sport coupe. It was optional on base and ES models, and was available with Chrysler's upgraded five-speed manual or automatic transmission. Standard in the Daytona Shelby, optional in the C/S package, was the 2.2-liter, 174-bhp four with variable-nozzle turbocharging, the Turbo IV, sold only with five-speed manual. It claimed reduced turbo lag. A throttle-body injected 2.5 with 100 bhp remained standard on the base and ES Daytonas. The new and more user-friendly interior housed an air bag for the driver. Shelbys sported exterior trim changes and a variable suspension option, allowing three shock damping settings via console switches. Gone this year were the Aries, Lancer, and rear-drive Diplomat, leaving

1990 Dodge Daytona Shelby hatchback coupe

Dodge selling only front-drivers. Sales fell for the calendar year to 334,839 Dodges of all types, including 34,253 Daytonas. As Dodge entered the '90s, it was desperately in need of new products.

	Restorable	Good	Excellent
Daytona Shelby Turbo	*	$6,500-8,000	$8,000-9,500
Daytona ES Turbo	*	6,000-7,000	7,000-8,500
Daytona ES	*	5,500-6,500	6,500-8,000
Daytona C/S	*	5,000-6,000	6,000-7,000

* Purchase only in good or excellent condition

1930 Duesenberg Model J Sport Berline by Murphy

Duesenberg Model J Convertible (Greta Garbo car)

1931 Duesenberg Model J convertible/aluminum top

Duesenberg

The greatest cars ever built in America are the nearest thing on wheels to blue chip stocks and bonds—only slightly affected by seasonal pitches in the collector car market, steadily rising in value all the time. Since only one basic model is involved, mechanical parts supply through specialists is surprisingly good. Body parts are scarce, but at these price levels almost anything can be fabricated. Club support is excellent.

1930-37

Announced in late 1928, the Model J Duesenberg was powered by a 32-valve, 420-cid Lycoming straight-eight engine with between 200 and 265 horsepower (the latter the company's figure), capable of 90 mph in second gear and about 115 in top—pretty good by 1992 standards, let alone 1930. Bodywork was anything the customer desired, supplied by coachbuilders for the $8500 ($9500 in 1931) 142-inch-wheelbase chassis. A total of about 470 were built, including 36 SJs and other variants mentioned here. The SJ, a supercharged J, arrived in 1932 boasting 320 bhp or, with engineer Augie Duesenberg's ram's horn manifolds, 400 bhp. A stock SJ could do 140 mph; racers added 20 mph to that. Tremendous in size, Duesies nevertheless had balance, precision, and finesse, and were remarkably docile at low speeds. Among the offshoots of the Model J were two short 125-inch-chassis SSJ roadsters built for and purchased by actors Gary Cooper and Clark Gable, and the 153.5-inch long-wheelbase Model JN, which appeared in 1935 (only 15 were built). Both SSJs and at least two JNs have survived. The chief caveat any Duesenberg immediately suggests to prospective purchasers is: be sure of the car's provenance. There are more open Duesenbergs around now than there were new, because so many closed models have been rebodied with open styles—usually with very excellent workmanship. The question of when a much-altered car becomes, like a much-fixed piece of antique furniture, a "married piece," varies according to the expert. But a Duesenberg that began life as a sedan and is now a convertible is not an original object, however valuable it may still be. Prices here are based on expert testimony for verified originals.

	Restorable	Good	Excellent
Closed bodies	$350,000-700,000	$500,000-1.0m	$1.0m-1.5m
Open bodies	650,000-1.0m	850,000-1.5m	1.5m-2.5m

Known auction high: $2,000,000
Highest known private sale: $3,000,000

Edsel

Long the butt of comedians' jokes, Ford's most famous flop is almost beneath notice by the money-losing standards of the 1990s—there have been years lately when Ford Motor Company could only wish its losses were confined to $100 million (or was it $250 million?). Furthermore, the Edsel is seen by the more even-minded as an intriguing car from a technical standpoint. Despite its brief life and scarcity, however, values are no higher than comparable 1958-60 makes. Club support is excellent, mechanical parts supply fair, body parts scarce.

1958 Edsel Citation hardtop coupe

1958 Edsel Pacer Bermuda four-door station wagon

1958 Edsel Citation hardtop coupe

1958

Aiming to sell at least 100,000 cars, Edsel hit the market with four separate lines comprising 18 models on three wheelbases: 116 inches for wagons, 118 for Rangers and Pacers, 124 for Corsairs and Citations. All Edsels came with V-8s: a 361-cid, 303-bhp unit for junior models, a 410-cid, 345-bhp powerhouse for seniors. Though initial sales were good (50,000 were built before the end of 1957), Edsel soon ran head-on into the 1958 recession, and 1958 calendar year production barely topped 25,000. The '58 is by far the most plentiful model, but the desirable convertibles are scarce: only 1876 Pacers and 930 Citations were produced. Several wagon models also saw under 1000 units: the two-door Ranger Roundup (936), the nine-passenger Ranger Villager (978, plus 2294 six-passenger models), and nine-passenger Pacer Bermuda (779, plus 1456 six-passenger models). But wagons are not investment-grade Edsels; if you can't afford the convertible, go for the two-door hardtops, available in all four series but best in the upper-end Corsair and Citation series. Their production figures were: Ranger, 5546; Pacer, 6139; Corsair, 3312; Citation, 2535. All series also offered four-door hardtops, though only Ranger and Pacer listed four-door sedans. In all, 63,110 Edsels were produced for the '58 model run.

	Restorable	Good	Excellent
Ranger & Pacer 2d htp	$2,500-6,000	$6,000-9,000	$9,000-12,000
Pacer cvt	5,000-8,000	8,000-15,000	15,000-20,000
Corsair 2d htp	3,000-6,000	6,000-10,000	10,000-13,000
Citation 2d htp	3,500-6,500	6,500-11,000	11,000-14,000

	Restorable	Good	Excellent
Citation cvt	7,000-12,000	12,000-18,000	18,000-25,000
Other models	2,000-5,000	5,000-7,000	7,000-9,500

1959 Edsel Ranger hardtop coupe

1959 Edsel Villager 9-passenger station wagon

1959 Edsel Corsair convertible coupe

1960 Edsel Ranger convertible coupe

1960 Edsel Villager four-door station wagon

1959

With sales dropping, the Edsel lineup was radically cut from 18 models to 10 in three series—Ranger, Corsair, and Station Wagon—all on a 120-inch wheelbase. The luxurious Citation was dropped, its name to be revived in 1980 by a Chevrolet; the bottom-rung Pacer was also killed, though American Motors adopted the name for a new "wide subcompact" in 1975. Only one convertible, a Corsair, was offered. Engines were a 292 V-8 for the Ranger and a 332 V-8 for the Corsair (optional on Rangers), though a delete-option 145-bhp six was available on Rangers and wagons, and the 361 V-8 from 1958 was optional on all models. Style-wise, the '59s were much less distinctive because the "horse collar" grille was blended into a more muted front end, though still with a vertical center section. Four-door sedans sold best, but among Rangers 2352 hardtop sedans and 5474 hardtop coupes were produced. In the Corsair line, 1694 hardtop sedans, 2315 hardtop coupes, and 1343 ragtops rolled off the line. Wagons numbered just 7820 out of total '59 Edsel production of 44,891 units.

	Restorable	Good	Excellent
Corsair cvt	$6,000-10,000	$10,000-17,500	$17,500-22,500
2d hardtops	3,000-7,000	7,000-10,000	10,000-13,000
Other models	1,000-4,000	4,000-6,000	6,000-8,500

1960

The '60 Edsel abandoned the trademark upright grille for a horizontal motif, divided in the center in a manner that looked suspiciously similar to the '59 Pontiac. Wagons were called Villagers, while all other body styles were Rangers. Heavy chrome accents outlined the fenders and bodysides, and the overall shape closely resembled the new '60 Ford aside from quad vertical taillights. The standard engine was a 185-bhp 292 V-8, but the six was again a no-cost option; only $58 bought a 352 "Super Express" V-8 with 300 horses. Two- or three-speed automatic transmission, power steering, and air conditioning were among the options. Extremely low production makes these models the scarcest of all three Edsel years. There were only 76 convertibles, 135 four-door hardtops, and 295 two-door hardtops, while output of Villager wagons came to 216 six-passenger and 59 nine-passenger models. Production was halted in November 1959 after 2846 cars had been built—after that the Edsel was history.

	Restorable	Good	Excellent
Ranger cvt	$6,000-10,000	$10,000-17,500	$17,500-22,500
Ranger 2d htp	3,000-7,000	7,000-11,000	11,000-14,000
Villager wgns	1,500-4,500	4,500-7,000	7,000-10,000
Other models	1,000-4,000	4,000-6,000	6,000-8,500

Essex

A Hudson offshoot (see also Terraplane), which started strong but was a negligible factor by the depths of the Depression, Essex has the benefit of a loyal marque club. Support is excellent, but the parts supply is low and investment potential is negligible.

1930-33

When introduced in 1919, the low-priced Essex ($1395) rode a 108½-inch wheelbase—just five inches more than a Ford Model T—and had a 55-horsepower F-head four. Its original claim to fame came via a number of performance records, among them covering 3037.4 miles in 50 hours at the Cincinnati Speedway. That translated to an average of 60.75 mph, pretty hot stuff in the days when the best a Model T could do was about 45 mph. More to the point, Essex achieved lasting fame by being one of the earliest affordable closed cars, just $1495 for a two-door Coach in 1922 (the price would drop rapidly). In 1924, a little 130-cubic-inch L-head six was introduced, though this was almost immediately upped to 144.6 cid and about 40 horsepower. Unfortunately, this engine (unlike the four) earned a poor reputation for durability. No matter, production nudged 230,000 units per year in 1928 and '29. By 1930, the six developed 58 horsepower via 161.4 cubic inches, finding its happiest home in an attractive Sun Sedan, a two-door convertible based on the Challenger two-door coach. That didn't matter, however, because the Depression knocked calendar-year output to 76,158 units, and to just 40,338 in 1931. In 1932, the bored-and-stroked 193.1-cid six yielded 70 horsepower. It powered the 113-inch-wheelbase Pacemaker and cheaper Standard—and at mid-year it went into a 106-inch chassis for a new car called Terraplane. The 1932-33 Essex Terraplane, hyped by no less than famed aviatrix Amelia Earhart, turned Hudson's fortunes around. It was fast (up to 80 mph), economical (up to 25 mpg), and cheap (as little as $425 in 1932). In its first half year, output nearly equaled the 17,425 Essex cars built. In 1933 a straight-eight engine was evolved from the original six. At 243.9 cid, it cranked out a healthy 94 horsepower—and showed its exhaust pipe to many a Ford V-8. Terraplanes set numerous speed and hill-climbing marks, including victories at Pikes Peak in 1932 and '33. It was so popular by 1934 that Hudson registered Terraplane as a separate make, replacing Essex. Production in 1933 came to 38,150 units.

	Restorable	Good	Excellent
'30 roadster	$2,500-6,000	$6,000-12,000	$12,000-17,500
'30 Sun sedan	1,500-3,000	3,000-7,500	7,500-12,000
'31 rdstr/phtn	7,000-12,500	12,500-22,500	22,500-35,000
'31 coupes	1,500-3,000	3,000-6,500	6,500-10,000
'30-31, other	500-2,000	2,000-4,000	4,000-7,000
'32 phtn/cvt	2,500-6,000	6,000-11,000	11,000-15,500

1930 Essex Sun Sedan

1931 Essex 2-passenger coupe

1932 Essex Series E convertible coupe

	Restorable	Good	Excellent
'32 Series EC clsd	1,000-3,000	3,000-5,000	5,000-6,500
'32 Pacemaker clsd	1,500-4,500	4,500-7,000	7,000-10,000

1932-33 Essex Terraplane (see also "Terraplane")

Open	3,000-7,500	7,500-14,000	14,000-19,000
Closed	1,500-4,000	4,000-6,500	6,500-9,500

1964 Studebaker SS Roadster (Excalibur prototype)

1965-69 Excalibur Series I SSK Roadster

1966-69 Excalibur Series I SS Phaeton

Excalibur

America's most successful replicar has had a small but enthusiastic following, the Series I being especially collectible for its close resemblance to the classic Mercedes-Benz SSK of 1928. Studebaker (1965 only) and Corvette drivetrains make mechanical parts readily available, though body parts are scarce. Club support is fair.

1965-69

The Excalibur Series I began with a Studebaker Lark Daytona chassis and 290-horsepower supercharged Avanti V-8. Studebaker's demise caused Excalibur's principals—designer Brooks Stevens and his sons—to substitute a 327 Corvette V-8. After 1966, Excaliburs were also offered with a 400-bhp Paxton supercharged engine and various Corvette high-performance mills. David Stevens handled the engineering; his father styled the roadster body, a remarkable likeness of the SSK. For 1966, a more elaborate roadster sporting full fenders and running boards and a phaeton were introduced, also on the SSK's 109-inch wheelbase. Equipment proliferated, and by 1969 included air conditioning, power steering, tilt steering wheel, disc front brakes, Posi-traction rear axle, chrome wire wheels, AM-FM stereo, Turbo Hydra-Matic transmission, radial tires, and self-leveling rear shock absorbers. Production out of the small Milwaukee factory from 1965-69 was predictably modest: 168 SSK roadsters, 59 full-fendered roadsters, and 89 phaetons.

	Restorable	Good	Excellent
SSK roadster	$7,500-15,000	$15,000-25,000	$25,000-35,000
Other models	5,000-10,000	10,000-18,000	18,000-27,500

1970-74

The Series II Excalibur rode a longer 111-inch wheelbase and was powered by a larger 350-cid Corvette engine. Though the same body styles were offered, the old Lark frame was replaced by a new box-section chassis designed by David Stevens around Corvette components. GM's "Muncie" four-speed gearbox was standard, Turbo Hydra-Matic optional. Independent suspension and four-wheel disc brakes delivered good ride, handling, and stopping power. The factory's 0-60 figure for the Series II was six seconds; its top speed was 150 mph. The price, which had begun at $7250 in 1965 had escalated to $17,000 in 1974. Production during the 1970-74 period totaled 72 roadsters and 270 phaetons, and Excalibur records show no production for 1971.

	Restorable	Good	Excellent
Roadster	$7,500-12,000	$12,000-20,000	$20,000-28,000
Phaeton	5,000-10,000	10,000-15,000	15,000-23,000

1975-80

Prices and production began rising with the Series III, announced in 1975 (Excalibur did not adhere strictly to a model year cycle). This was essentially a Series II modified to meet federal safety and emissions regulations—but not so much as to compromise styling or roadability. Besides shock-absorbing aluminum alloy bumpers, the Series III had fuller, clamshell-style fenders and standard high-back leather bucket seats. The engine was Chevy's 215-bhp Mark IV V-8 through 1978, more amenable to emissions tuning than the 350. The 350 nonetheless returned for 1979 with 180 horses, but was replaced by a 155-bhp 305 for 1980. Production hit a record 367 in the 1979 model year; the vast bulk of Series III production was of phaetons: 983 compared to 76 roadsters. This partly explains why the roadsters are worth more these days.

	Restorable	Good	Excellent
Roadster	$7,500-12,000	$12,000-20,000	$20,000-28,000
Phaeton	5,000-10,000	10,000-15,000	15,000-23,000

1981-90

The Series IV, introduced in January 1981, was more a luxury tourer than a lightweight sports machine, not surprising given a $37,700 base price. It was the most radically changed Excalibur since the beginning, and the best yet. Wheelbase was extended to near limousine length—125 inches—and the Series IV carried more standard equipment than any of its predecessors. Styling remained firmly in the classic tradition, but was smoother, sleeker, and evolutionary. The phaeton acquired a lift-off hardtop and a power soft top. Sales were good during the first three years: 444 phaetons and 96 roadsters. Sedans and limousines were introduced later in the decade, and other changes were made over the years to comply with Federal requirements. Unfortunately, sales reverses eventually put Excalibur into receivership, and two changes of ownership. Its revival at this writing is problematic, although as of late October 1992 new owners were planning to resume production.

	Restorable	Good	Excellent
1981-82 rdstr	*	$18,000-25,000	$25,000-33,000
1981-82 phtn	*	15,000-22,500	22,500-30,000

1979 Excalibur Series III Phaeton

1975-79 Excalibur Series III Phaeton

1980-85 Excalibur Series IV Phaeton

1981 Excalibur Series IV Roadster

	Restorable	Good	Excellent
1983-84 rdstr	*	20,000-30,000	30,000-40,000
1983-84 phtn	*	18,000-27,500	27,500-35,000
1985-86 rdstr	*	25,000-35,000	35,000-45,000
1985-86 phtn	*	22,500-30,000	30,000-40,000
1987-89 rdstr	*	30,000-40,000	40,000-50,000
1987-89 phtn	*	27,500-35,000	35,000-45,000
1988-89 sdn	*	25,000-35,000	35,000-45,000
1989 limo	*	30,000-40,000	40,000-50,000

* Purchase only in good or excellent condition

1930 Ford Model A DeLuxe 2-passenger coupe

1931 Ford Model A Victoria coupe

1932 Ford V-8 Victoria coupe

Ford

The Model T and Model A Fords were among the standard collectibles in the early days of the old car movement 40 years ago. But as the Classics—as defined by the Classic Car Club of America—became popular and postwar special interest cars after them, Ford was left behind by its erstwhile rival Chevrolet. Ford is now catching up; still, while '30s Fords remain more highly prized than comparable Chevys, Fords of the Fifties and Sixties tend to be cheaper. They thus provide good value for money and, usually, sound investment potential. Club support is excellent—there's at least 20 major groups. Body and mechanical parts supply is also generally good, with much new old stock (NOS) remanufacturing going on. Investment value: good to excellent.

1930-39

Prewar Fords are hobby cars for drivers and collectors, not investors. Since cars in this category mainly appeal to those who grew up with them, '30s Fords have peaked on the old car market. On the other hand, Ford V-8 prices will not drop precipitously because they're intrinsically fun to drive and offer a fine turn of performance. The editors recommend paying the higher price demanded for desirable body styles, which are not only the best investments but also the most fun to own.

Knowledgeable collectors we consulted name the following best current investments among Ford V-8s (Model A bodies follow the same general hierarchy, but generally the prices they command aren't as high): First, cabriolets or convertibles: best year 1939, then 1936, 1933-34, 1932. Second, woody wagons: best year 1939, then 1940, 1936, 1941, 1933-34. Third, roadsters: all years good, but relatively high current prices limit future appreciation. Fourth, convertible sedans and phaetons: best year 1932, then 1936, 1935, 1939, 1937, 1938. Fifth, coupes, especially the three-window versions, which limits your choice through 1936: best year 1932, then 1934, 1933, 1936, 1935—the '32 is a five-window style with cloth top and suicide doors, factors that put it ahead of the rest. Everything else, including sedans and Victorias, is bunched at the bottom of the collectible heap. Victorias tend to be overvalued in hobby price guides.

As the decade opened, Ford's Model A flathead four developed 40 horsepower from 200.5 cubic inches. In 1932, that was upped to 50 bhp for the Model B, and fours were available through 1934—though in tiny numbers during the last two years. The 221-cubic-inch V-8 came on stream in 1932 with 65 horsepower, but that was upped to 75 the following year, and to 85 for 1934, where it remained for the rest of the decade (some sources quote 90 bhp). In 1937, a tiny 136-cubic-inch V-8 debuted. Developing only 60 horsepower, it wasn't very popular, and because it was available only in sedans and coupes (and wagons in 1937), it isn't much sought after. This engine was withdrawn from the American market after 1940, though it would soldier on in Europe for another two decades.

During the '30s, Fords came in Standard and DeLuxe trim. The latter is the one to look for as it offered goodies—depending on model year—such as better upholstery and woodgrain dashboards, twin cowl lights, chromed exterior horns, more exterior chrome trim, and dual windshield wipers, sun visors, arm rests, and the like. Style-wise, the 1938-40 Standard models were slightly touched-up DeLuxes from the year before, making them visually quite different from the top-line models.

Fords, like competing cars, grew larger and heavier during the decade. The 1930-31 Model A rode a 103.5-inch wheelbase, but this was upped to 106.5 inches with the advent of the V-8. Then, in 1933, the Model 40 V-8 got a further stretch to 112 inches, where it would remain though 1940. A 1930 Model A four-door sedan weighed in at 2441 pounds, but by 1939 a DeLuxe Fordor tipped the scales at 2898 pounds.

Chevrolet outproduced Ford during much of the '30s, but Ford built more open cars, a boon to collectors. Ford's best year during the decade was 1930, when 1,140,710 Model As rolled off the line. The low point came in 1932, when the firm was hampered by both the Depression and delays in getting the new V-8 into production. Only 210,824 cars were assembled for the model year. Both 1936 and '37 were good years for Ford—output was well above 900,000 units. As an example of open-car production, take 1936, when Ford built the following (all in DeLuxe trim): 3862 rumble-seat roadsters, 5555 phaetons, 14,068 cabriolets, 4616 club cabriolets, and 5601 convertible sedans. In addition, 7044 woody wagons were sold that year. Taking the decade as a whole, Chevy beat Ford in calendar-year production 6,494,942 to 6,353,351.

	Restorable	Good	Excellent
1930-32 Model A & B (4-cyl)			
Open bodies	$2,500-7,500	$7,500-14,000	$14,000-20,000
Station wagons	3,500-7,500	7,500-12,000	12,000-17,500
Coupes	1,500-5,000	5,000-7,500	7,500-11,000
Other models	1,000-4,000	4,000-6,500	6,500-9,000
1932-39 V-8			
1932 cvt sdn	5,000-10,000	10,000-18,000	18,000-25,000
1932 phaeton	5,000-10,000	10,000-18,000	18,000-27,500
1932 roadster	6,000-12,000	12,000-18,000	18,000-30,000
1932 spt cpe	2,000-4,500	4,500-10,000	10,000-15,000

1933 Ford V-8 four-door station wagon

1934 Ford V-8 convertible coupe

1935 Ford DeLuxe 2-passenger coupe

1936 Ford DeLuxe 2/4-passenger roadster

1937 Ford DeLuxe 5-passenger Club Coupe

1939 Ford DeLuxe Fordor sedan

1940 Ford DeLuxe convertible coupe

1940 Ford DeLuxe Fordor sedan

1941 Ford Super DeLuxe Fordor sedan

	Restorable	Good	Excellent
1933-34 cabrio	4,000-7,500	7,500-15,000	15,000-23,000
1933-34 cpe	2,000-4,000	4,000-8,000	8,000-13,000
1933-34 rdstr	5,000-10,000	10,000-18,000	18,000-28,000
1933-34 wgn	3,500-8,000	8,000-14,000	14,000-21,000
1933-36 phtn	6,500-12,000	12,000-17,000	17,000-27,500
1934-36 cpe 3W	2,000-4,250	4,250-9,000	9,000-15,000
1935 cabrio	5,000-10,000	10,000-15,000	15,000-20,000
1935-36 cvt sdn	4,000-8,000	8,000-15,000	15,000-25,000
1935 roadster	5,000-9,000	9,000-17,000	17,000-25,000
1936 cabrio	3,000-7,500	7,500-15,000	15,000-26,000
1936 roadster	6,500-14,000	14,000-20,000	20,000-28,000
1936 wagon	3,500-8,000	8,000-13,000	13,000-20,000
1937 cabrio	5,000-10,000	10,000-15,000	15,000-20,000
1937 roadster	3,500-8,000	8,000-12,000	12,000-20,000
1937-38 cvt sdn	4,000-8,000	8,000-15,000	15,000-22,000
1937-38 phtn	4,000-8,000	8,000-15,000	15,000-23,000
1938 cvt	4,000-7,500	7,500-13,000	13,000-22,000
1939 cvt	5,000-12,000	12,000-20,000	20,000-30,000
1939 cvt sdn	6,000-13,000	13,000-18,000	18,000-30,000
1939 wagon	4,000-7,500	7,500-12,000	12,000-22,500
Other models	1,000-4,000	4,000-7,000	7,000-10,000

1940

The famous '40 Ford has become one of the most desirable single vintages, thanks to its brilliant styling on the DeLuxe models: a crisp, pointed hood meeting a handsome grille composed of delicate horizontal bars, flowing smoothly back to a rakishly angled windshield. The headlamps—Ford's first sealed beams—were faired into the fenders, which were beautifully shaped to complement body contours, and often skirted at the rear. Also well-liked were the chevron taillights. As since 1937, Ford offered two different V-8s—still rated at 60 and 85 horsepower and both installed on the same 112-inch wheelbase. The V-8/85 was far more popular then, and remains so today. This would be the last year that the Standard models looked similar to the DeLuxes of the previous year. Of the 575,085 cars built for the model run, 61,612 were two/three-passenger coupes, 36,968 were four/five-passenger coupes, 13,199 were woody wagons, and 23,704 were DeLuxe convertibles. Well over half of total production was devoted to two- and four-door sedans.

	Restorable	Good	Excellent
Convertible	$6,000-12,000	$12,000-22,500	$22,500-32,000
Station wagon	3,000-6,000	6,000-12,000	12,000-22,500
Coupe	2,000-4,000	4,000-8,000	8,000-12,000
Other models	1,000-3,000	3,000-6,000	6,000-9,000

1941

An L-head six was brought out this year to replace the little V-8/60, which must have been heresy to old Henry Ford even though he allowed it. That well-built flathead displaced 226 cubic inches, 90 more than the V-8/60, and had 50 percent more horsepower—five more in fact than the slightly smaller V-8/85. A vast array of six and V-8 Specials, DeLuxes, and Super Deluxes was offered. Styling, if not entirely new-looking in the middle, was quite different at each end with wider and more integrated front fenders, a busier vertical-bar grille flanked by auxiliary grilles, and larger rear fenders. With the larger new body and longer 114-inch wheelbase, this year's Fords were roomier inside. None of these changes did much for Ford volume, which at 691,455 units remained about two-thirds that of Chevrolet, which crossed the million mark this year. Collector prices for '41s are a hair off the level of comparable 1940 models. Ford built 30,240 convertibles (Super DeLuxe only) for the model run, as well as 66,299 three-passenger coupes (all series), 23,640 four-passenger coupes (DeLuxe and Super DeLuxe), 45,977 Super DeLuxe six-passenger Sedan Coupes (a new club coupe with longer rear side windows than other coupes), and 15,601 woody wagons (Super DeLuxe and DeLuxe).

	Restorable	Good	Excellent
Convertible	$6,000-12,000	$12,000-22,500	$22,500-30,000
Station wagon	3,000-6,000	6,000-12,000	12,000-21,000
V-8 coupes	2,000-4,000	4,000-8,000	8,000-11,000
Other models	1,000-3,000	3,000-6,000	6,000-9,000

1942

A wider, more cohesive rectangular-framed grille with fine vertical bars was introduced for '42, and taillights switched from vertical rectangles to horizontal ovals. But Ford produced only 160,432 cars through February 10, when civilian car production ended because of the war emergency. Those built in calendar '42 received painted bumpers and trim per government edict. By a stroke of the pen, the V-8 gained five horsepower to equal the output of the six, which was now the only engine available for bottom-rung Specials. Otherwise the model lineup was unchanged, save for the addition of a DeLuxe Sedan Coupe. All '42s were relatively scarce: just 2920 convertibles, 6050 wagons, 18,962 Sedan Coupes, 12,953 three-passenger coupes. As usual, the bulk of production was devoted to Tudor and Fordor sedans. Curiously, despite their scarcity, these Fords tend not to carry quite the values of comparable 1941 models, which are more plentiful—an inversion from the normal collector situation.

	Restorable	Good	Excellent
Convertible	$5,000-10,000	$10,000-20,000	$20,000-28,000
Station wagon	3,000-6,000	6,000-12,000	12,000-21,000
V-8 coupes	2,000-4,000	4,000-7,500	7,500-10,000
Other bodies	1,000-3,000	3,000-5,500	5,500-8,500

1946

The first postwar Fords used the '42 body with minor styling changes that included a grille with three husky horizontal bars topped by an even heavier bar sporting the Ford oval and script. Minor trim was also shuffled about. More important perhaps was a more powerful V-8—the 239.4-cid, 100-bhp Mercury engine. The cheaper Special line was eliminated, leaving DeLuxe and Super DeLuxe series. Now, however, there were two convertibles: regular and Sportsman (both Super DeLuxe V-8s). The latter—with its beautiful white ash and mahogany body trim produced in the firm's Iron Mountain, Michigan, plant—was sporty and interest-

1942 Ford Super DeLuxe four-door station wagon

1942 Ford Super DeLuxe Fordor sedan

1942 Ford Super DeLuxe Club Coupe

1946 Ford Super DeLuxe Tudor sedan

1946 Ford Super DeLuxe Sportsman convertible coupe

1946 Ford Super DeLuxe Fordor sedan

1947½ Ford Super DeLuxe Fordor sedan

1948 Ford Super DeLuxe convertible coupe

1948 Ford Super DeLuxe Fordor sedan

ing, but it came at a $494 premium ($1982). Naturally, among collectors, it has become the most sought after early postwar Ford. Only 1209 Sportsman convertibles were produced for the model year, compared to 16,359 regular ragtops. Ford got into postwar production more quickly than anyone, so it outdid Chevy this year 468,022 to 398,028. Station wagons numbered 16,960, while 70,826 Sedan Coupes and 22,919 three-passenger coupes were snapped up by car-hungry buyers.

	Restorable	Good	Excellent
Sportsman cvt	$10,000-20,000	$20,000-35,000	$35,000-50,000
Convertible	5,000-9,000	9,000-18,000	18,000-25,000
Station wagon	7,000-13,000	13,000-22,000	22,000-30,000
V-8 coupes	2,000-4,000	4,000-7,500	7,500-10,000
Other models	1,000-3,000	3,000-5,500	5,500-8,500

1947

Ford received a mild facelift for 1947½: smoother grille bars lacking the painted stripes of 1946-early '47 models, small round parking lights mounted beneath the headlights replacing rectangular units placed above the grille between the headlights, and a new wide chrome molding with Ford lettering sitting high on the decklid. Prices were up about $100 across the board, ranging now from $1154 to $2282. Sportsman production for the model year was 2250, and the regular ragtop increased to 22,159 units. Station wagon output eased slightly to 16,104. With 176,649 produced, the Tudor sedan was the year's most popular offering, followed by 161,307 Fordors. Due to material shortages and labor unrest industry-wide during this period, Ford production rose only modestly to 429,674 units, far behind Chevy's increase to 671,546.

	Restorable	Good	Excellent
Sportsman cvt	$10,000-20,000	$20,000-35,000	$35,000-50,000
Convertible	5,000-9,000	9,000-18,000	18,000-25,000
Station wagon	7,000-13,000	13,000-22,000	22,000-30,000
V-8 coupes	2,000-4,000	4,000-7,500	7,500-10,000
Other models	1,000-3,000	3,000-5,500	5,500-8,500

1948

Ford didn't bother to alter the '48s one iota because it quit building them early to shift over to the all-new '49s. As a result, only 429,674 were built despite labor peace and better materials availability. Identification is by serial number. Sportsman production was only 28 units (leftover '47s apparently), although 12,033 standard convertibles were built. Wagons numbered 8912. During the early postwar days, Ford Motor Company had been losing money heavily, and so the company was striving to return to profitability with all-new and more modern products, a drive spearheaded by Henry Ford II and the group of "Whiz Kids" he hired after World War II.

	Restorable	Good	Excellent
Sportsman cvt	$10,000-20,000	$20,000-35,000	$35,000-50,000
Convertible	5,000-9,000	9,000-18,000	18,000-25,000

	Restorable	Good	Excellent
Station wagon	7,000-13,000	13,000-22,000	22,000-30,000
V-8 coupes	2,000-4,000	4,000-7,500	7,500-10,000
Other models	1,000-3,000	3,000-5,500	5,500-8,500

1949

The brilliant new slabsided '49 Ford was styled by Dick Caleal for George Walker, who sold the package to management—including a Studebaker-like bullet nose influenced by Bob Bourke of Raymond Loewy Studios at South Bend, who had helped Caleal develop his clay model. The '49s used the 100-bhp V-8 in an improved form, but styling was the new Ford's strength and the design was a good one. Engineers also updated the chassis with independent front suspension and parallel leaf springs up back. These, of course, were standard throughout the industry, but a first for Ford as it discarded old Henry's beloved transverse leaf springs. The woody Sportsman body style was eliminated (though it had been considered), but 51,133 convertibles were built, all of them V-8s. They later became the darlings of hot-rodders and customizers. Originals are highly valued by collectors today. Other models of interest were the station wagon, now with only two doors and less wood, but it still attracted 31,412 buyers. A new club coupe with a sporty long rear deck fared poorly as a lower-line Standard, just 4170 sold, but suited 150,254 customers in fancier Custom form. There was even a similar business coupe in the Standard series, and it went on to record output of 28,946 units. But when all was said and done, Tudors and Fordors—Standard and Custom—accounted for 852,825 of the 1,118,308 Fords built for the long 1949 model year. Due to its length, Ford topped Chevy this year by a little over 100,000 units.

1949 Ford Custom convertible coupe

1949 Ford Custom Tudor sedan

1949 Ford Custom two-door station wagon

	Restorable	Good	Excellent
Convertible	$5,000-10,000	$10,000-17,000	$17,000-23,000
Station wagon	5,000-10,000	10,000-17,000	17,000-23,000
Club coupe	3,000-5,000	5,000-8,000	8,000-10,000
Other models	1,000-3,000	3,000-5,500	5,500-8,500

1950

Though the '49s sold extremely well, early examples were plagued with quality problems as a result of being rushed into production. Ford made many running changes during the model year and for 1950, enough to claim that the '50s were "50 Ways Better." Most changes were unseen, because the '50s didn't look much different, though the grille bar was wrapped around the fenders and the parking lights moved below it. The rear deck sported a new latch/license plate housing, the gas filler cap was hidden behind a door, side trim was modified slightly, and both hood and decklid flaunted a Ford crest. The model lineup still listed nine models (now in DeLuxe and Custom series), but the low-line club coupe was dropped and the Crestliner was added. An interesting model to look for, the latter was a limited-edition Custom Tudor distinguished by a vivid

1950 Ford Custom convertible coupe

1950 Ford Custom Crestliner two-door sedan

1951 Ford Custom Fordor sedan

1951 Ford Custom Victoria hardtop coupe

1951 Ford Custom Country Squire two-door wagon

1952 Ford Mainline Tudor sedan

contrasting color sweep on its lower body, special gold identification script, padded vinyl top, and luxurious interior. Though intended to compete with Chevy's new Bel Air hardtop, only 17,601 were sold, but with their convertible-like interiors and bright colors, Crestliners are highly prized today. Ford built 1,208,912 cars this year, its highest total since Model T days. Convertibles held steady at 50,299 units, though wagons fell to 22,929 and Custom club coupes skidded to 85,111.

	Restorable	Good	Excellent
Convertible	$5,000-10,000	$10,000-17,000	$17,000-23,000
Station wagon	5,000-10,000	10,000-17,000	17,000-23,000
Crestliner	3,000-5,000	5,000-8,500	8,500-12,000
Club coupe	3,000-5,000	5,000-8,000	8,000-10,000
Other models	1,000-3,000	3,000-5,500	5,500-8,500

1951

In the final year for this generation, Ford added its first "hardtop convertible," the Victoria. Styled by Gordon Buehrig of Cord 810 fame, it was offered as a Custom V-8 only. This neat alteration of the two-door coupe sold much better than the Crestliner, and despite a late introduction the 110,286 produced beat out the Chevy Bel Air. The '51 was distinguished by a "two-bullet" grille, chrome bodyside "jet tubes" leading up to the twin-tipped taillights, and a new asymmetrical dashboard grouping the controls in a grid on the left-hand side of the cockpit. As since 1948, horsepower ratings were 95 for the venerable L-head six, now in its last year, and 100 for the V-8. Total production slipped to 1,013,381, the convertible to 40,934. The wagon, now badged Country Squire, managed an increase to 29,017 units. The Crestliner, with modified "Duesenberg-sweep" two-toning, fell back to 8703 units and was dropped before the model year ended.

	Restorable	Good	Excellent
Convertible	$5,000-10,000	$10,000-17,000	$17,000-23,000
Cntry Squire wgn	5,000-10,000	10,000-17,000	17,000-23,000
Victoria htp	2,500-4,500	4,500-8,000	8,000-11,000
Crestliner	3,000-5,000	5,000-8,500	8,500-12,000
Club coupe	3,000-5,000	5,000-8,500	8,000-10,000
Other models	1,000-3,000	3,000-5,500	5,500-8,500

1952

Ford beat both Chevrolet and Plymouth to market with its second major postwar restyling, though it didn't much matter because the government severely restricted production because of US commitments in the Korean conflict. No matter, a handsome new body, on a one-inch-longer 115-inch wheelbase, debuted. Looking longer, lower, and wider as Ford proudly proclaimed, it was the work of Frank Hershey, George Walker, and others. Series names were now Mainline, Customline, and Crestline. The last were all V-8s in the top-end series: Victoria hardtop, Sunliner convertible, and Country Squire, Ford's first all-steel wagon. This top-end wagon sported wood-like side trim, but other wagons could be had without the fake wood as either a two-door Ranch Wagon or four-door Country Sedan. Wagon output more than doubled to 49,919 units. Given a drop to 671,733 cars for the model run, the Victoria and convertible did well to come in at 77,320 and 22,534 units. Ford's V-8 was boosted to 110 bhp this year, but a new short-stroke, overhead-valve six debuted. Though rated at 101 horsepower, some road tests indicated it was as fast or faster from 0-60 mph than the old V-8.

	Restorable	Good	Excellent
Sunliner cvt	$4,000-9,000	$9,000-15,000	$15,000-22,500
Victoria htp	2,000-4,500	4,500-6,500	6,500-9,500
Cntry Squire wgn	1,000-4,000	4,000-7,000	7,000-10,000
Other models	500-3,000	3,000-5,000	5,000-7,500

1953

The model lineup was unchanged and styling alterations were confined to details: a cleaner bullet-nose grille, slightly larger round taillights, an extra dash of chrome trim on the flanks. This year, however, Ford celebrated its Fiftieth Anniversary, and went on to produce 1,247,542 cars as it flooded the market in a bid to unseat Chevy from first place (it didn't). Horsepower was unchanged for both six and V-8. Crestline remained the high-priced series, and is the source of the most collectible '53 Fords. They were the Victoria hardtop, which saw output spurt to 128,302; the Sunliner, which enjoyed a production run of 40,861; and the Country Squire, which doubled to 11,001 units. The long-deck club coupe was still around, too, in the Customline series. Output was 43,999, up from 26,550 in 1952.

	Restorable	Good	Excellent
Sunliner cvt	$4,000-9,000	$9,000-15,000	$15,000-22,500
Victoria htp	2,000-4,500	4,500-6,500	6,500-9,500
Cntry Squire wgn	1,000-4,000	4,000-7,000	7,000-10,000
Other models	500-3,000	3,000-5,000	5,000-7,500

1954

Ford made history this year with the first overhead-valve V-8 in the low-price field: a "Y-block" with 130 horsepower, the hottest engine anywhere near its price. Together with ball-joint front suspension—which caused the wheelbase to increase slightly to 115.5 inches—the Y-block narrowed the gap between expensive and inexpensive American cars. Though it displaced the same 239 cubic inches as the old L-head, it was entirely different internally and of short-stroke design. Styling was a continuation of 1953, identification being a slotted spinner grille, full-length bodyside moldings (except Mainline), and chrome radius arms in the round taillights. New among Crestliners was a four-door sedan and—more to the point—the Skyliner, a hardtop with a front roof section made of transparent, green-tinted plexiglas, a forebear of the moon roof and very collectible. Though a down year for the industry, Ford production fell less than Chevy's, enabling Ford to claim a model year victory at

1952 Ford Country Sedan four-door station wagon

1952 Ford Crestline Sunliner convertible coupe

1953 Ford Customline four-door sedan

1953 Ford Crestline Victoria hardtop coupe

1953 Ford Crestline Country Squire four-door wagon

1954 Ford Mainline Tudor sedan

1955 Ford Thunderbird convertible coupe

1955 Ford Fairlane Town Sedan four-door

1955 Ford Fairlane Crown Victoria hardtop coupe

1,165,942 units to 1,143,561 (Chevy claimed a sales victory). Among Crestliners, the Skyliner found 13,344 buyers; Victoria, 95,464; Sunliner, 36,685; sedan, 99,677 (a nice budget collectible); and Country Squire, 12,797. The Customline club coupe came in at 33,951 units for its last year.

	Restorable	Good	Excellent
Sunliner cvt	$4,000-9,000	$9,000-15,000	$15,000-22,500
Skyliner plexi-top	3,000-6,000	6,000-9,000	9,000-12,000
Victoria htp	2,000-4,500	4,500-6,500	6,500-9,500
Cntry Squire wgn	1,000-4,000	4,000-7,000	7,000-10,000
Other models	500-3,000	3,000-5,000	5,000-7,500

1955

Ford launched the Thunderbird, a two-seat sporty "personal" car priced at $2944 and powered by a 292-cid Y-block V-8 with 193/198 horsepower (stick/Fordomatic). A detachable hardtop was optional. The 102-inch-wheelbase T-Bird swamped the Corvette, selling 16,155 units compared to a mere 674. So heavily facelifted it looked all-new, the 1955 Ford was swoopy and colorful. Featured were a wraparound windshield, full-width eggcrate grille, sculptured wheel openings, and larger, lower-set round taillights. Wagons, now five models strong, were rolled into a series of their own, though model names remained the same. At the top of the line, Crestlines became Fairlanes (named for Henry Ford's Dearborn estate), and the lineup expanded with a two-door sedan and Crown Victoria. The latter used Mercury's lower, longer roofline embellished with a rakish "basket-handle" B-pillar that wasn't structural. Crown Vics with the 1954-style plastic front roof section were called "Crown Victoria with transparent roof" in the sales brochure, though they're commonly referred to as Skyliners like the '54s. Engines this year consisted of a 120-bhp Mileage Maker Six, 272 V-8s with 162 and 182 bhp, and—late in the year—a 292 with 198 and 205 bhp. The last are rare in full-size Fords. In a boom year for the industry, Ford produced 1,451,157 cars, though this wasn't enough to stay ahead of Chevrolet. Even so, Fairlanes rolled out the factory door to the tune of 113,372 Victorias, 33,165 Crown Victorias, 1999 Crown Vics with the plastic roof, 49,966 Sunliners, and 427,748 Club Sedans and Town Sedans. Mainlines and Customlines also sold well, though they consisted only of sedans and a rare business coupe (8809 built).

	Restorable	Good	Excellent
Thunderbird	$7,000-15,000	$15,000-27,500	$27,500-37,500
Sunliner cvt	5,000-12,000	12,000-20,000	20,000-30,000
Crn Vic plexi-top	4,000-10,000	10,000-17,500	17,500-25,000
Crn Vic steel top	3,000-8,000	8,000-15,000	15,000-22,500
Victoria htp	2,000-6,000	6,000-9,000	9,000-14,000
Cntry Squire wgn	1,500-5,000	5,000-8,000	8,000-12,500
Other models	500-3,000	3,000-5,000	5,000-7,500

1956

Ford retained its basic lineup for 1956, stressing safety as a sales point, with standard deep-dished steering wheel, break-away rearview mirror, and crashproof door locks. A padded dash and sun visors cost $16 extra, factory seat belts $9 (supplied on about one '56 Ford in five). The facelift was mild, consisting of a nicely revised grille, new side trim, and what looked like larger taillights. A four-door hardtop, the Fairlane Victoria Fordor, was now available, as was a two-door Customline Victoria. The Crown Victoria was in its last year: production totaled 9209 steel-top models and only 603 plexi-top versions. Total production slipped slightly to 1,408,478 units, highlighted by the following Fairlanes: 177,735 Victorias, 32,111 Victoria Fordors, and 58,147 Sunliners. The Customline Victoria scored with 33,130 buyers, and with its unique side trim and two-toning is worth consideration. Station wagon fanciers might be interested in the Parklane, a luxuriously trimmed two-door that attracted 15,186 customers. Thunderbird, meanwhile, returned with a continental spare tire created to yield more cargo space and vent flaps on the front fenders to improve interior cooling. There were three engines: a 202-bhp 298 V-8 (stick shift), 215-bhp 312 (overdrive), and a 225-bhp 312 (Fordomatic). A popular no-cost option was portholes for the removable hardtop, which improved rear quarter visibility and added a novel touch. Sales slipped slightly to 15,631 units.

1956 Ford Fairlane Victoria Fordor hardtop

1956 Ford Fairlane Victoria hardtop coupe

1956 Ford Fairlane Sunliner convertible coupe

	Restorable	Good	Excellent
Thunderbird	$8,000-18,000	$18,000-30,000	$30,000-40,000
Sunliner cvt	5,000-12,000	12,000-20,000	20,000-30,000
Crn Vic plexi-top	5,000-10,000	10,000-18,000	18,000-27,500
Crn Vic steel top	3,000-8,000	8,000-16,000	16,000-24,000
Fairlane 2d htp	2,000-5,000	5,000-8,000	8,000-12,000
Cstmline 2d htp	1,500-4,000	4,000-7,000	7,000-10,000
Cntry Squire wgn	1,500-5,000	5,000-8,000	8,000-12,500
Other models	500-3,000	3,000-5,000	5,000-7,500

1956 Ford Thunderbird convertible coupe

1957

An all-new lineup offered a 144-bhp six plus an array of V-8s from a 190-bhp 272 to a 300-bhp supercharged 312. Dimensions increased, grouped around longer 116- and 118-inch wheelbases, the first for Customs, Custom 300s, and Station Wagons, the latter for Fairlanes and Fairlane 500s. Styling was highlighted by "frog-eye" headlights; crosshatch grille; various bodyside trim combinations and two-tones; short, canted tailfins; and big pie-plate taillights. The top-line Fairlane 500s included the Sunliner convertible and a new novelty, the Skyliner retractable hardtop. A mid-1957 addition, the "retrac" had an all-steel roof that folded under the decklid through a series of servo motors (and took up most of the room back there). Though some feel they look gorpy with the top up and tail-heavy with it down, Skyliners are avidly sought after by collectors, and they have their own club. Some 20,766 were produced, compared to 77,726

1957 Ford Custom 300 Tudor sedan

1957 Ford Country Squire 9-passenger station wagon

1958 Ford Fairlane 500 Skyliner retractable convertible

1958 Ford Custom 300 Tudor sedan

1958 Ford Fairlane 500 Town Sedan four-door

1958 Ford Thunderbird hardtop coupe

Sunliners. Victorias were popular: 183,202 Fairlane 500s and 44,127 Fairlanes. Victoria four-doors didn't fare nearly as well: 68,550 Fairlane 500s, 12,695 Fairlanes. The cheaper Customs and Custom 300s came only as sedans, so they've been of little interest to collectors. All in all, however, 1957 was a triumphant year as Ford topped Chevy 1,676,449 to 1,505,910. The 1957 Thunderbird, restyled with a combination bumper-grille and modest tailfins, was available with all the performance engines starting with a 212-bhp 292 up to the supercharged 312, though such examples are rare. In a longer than usual model year, output came to 21,380 units.

	Restorable	Good	Excellent
Thunderbird	$9,000-18,000	$18,000-32,500	$32,500-42,500
T-Bird 270/285 bhp	10,000-20,000	20,000-35,000	35,000-50,000
T-Bird s'chgd	15,000-22,500	22,500-40,000	40,000-60,000
Fairlane 500 cvt	5,000-10,000	10,000-18,000	18,000-24,000
Skyliner retrac	7,500-14,000	14,000-20,000	20,000-29,000
Frlane 500 2d htp	2,000-6,000	6,000-9,000	9,000-12,000
Frlane 2d htp	1,500-5,000	5,000-8,000	8,000-10,000
Cntry Squire wgn	1,500-4,000	4,000-8,000	8,000-10,000
Other models	500-3,000	3,000-5,000	5,000-7,500

1958

The all-new Thunderbird was now a trend-setting four-seater "personal-luxury" car, and as such it appealed to a much broader market: 37,892 were produced, including 2134 convertibles. It was larger, riding a 113-inch wheelbase, and much heavier, 3631 pounds for the hardtop. The big Fords were heavily facelifted, sporting quad headlamps and a combination bumper-grille based on Thunderbird's. Quad oval taillights, bodyside trim, and two-toning were also new. A 300-bhp 352 V-8 now topped the engine offerings, and a new dual-range Cruise-O-Matic transmission debuted. No matter, whatever the engineering advances the styling didn't catch on and that, coupled to a sharp economic recession, sent production tumbling to 987,945 units. The '58 Ford was what Lee Iacocca would later reflect on as the worst product of the Fifties—quality control slipped, doors would fly open over rough surfaces, and early rust-out was a problem. Perhaps for these reasons, collectors haven't responded as much to the '58 line. Fairlane 500 production included 14,713 Skyliners, 80,439 Victorias, 35,029 Sunliners, and 36,509 Victoria four-doors. Among Fairlanes, Ford built 16,416 Victoria two-doors and 5868 Victoria four-doors.

	Restorable	Good	Excellent
Thunderbird cvt	$5,000-10,000	$10,000-17,500	$17,500-25,000
Thunderbird htp	3,000-7,500	7,500-12,500	12,500-18,000
Frlane 500 cvt	5,000-8,000	8,000-14,000	14,000-20,000
Skyliner retrac	6,000-10,000	10,000-18,000	18,000-22,500
Frlane 500 2d htp	2,000-6,000	6,000-9,000	9,000-12,000
Fairlane 2d htp	1,500-5,000	5,000-8,000	8,000-10,000
Cntry Squire wgn	1,000-3,000	3,000-6,000	6,000-8,500
Other models	500-3,000	3,000-5,000	5,000-7,500

1959

The redesigned '59 Fords rode a single 118-inch wheelbase and used the basic '57 body completely reskinned with very conservative exterior sheetmetal. Bizarre two-tone patterns and radical fins were avoided in favor of a squared-off grille with floating, starlike ornaments and simple side moldings reminiscent of 1957. Tiny fins were featured, and round taillights returned larger than ever. A new Galaxie series with a T-Bird-like roofline was added, including sedans, hardtops, and convertible. Engine choices were very similar to 1958. The public took to the conservative look, pumping production to 1,450,953, and though this was 11,000 units short of Chevy for the model year, Ford took calendar year honors. Some Galaxie figures (which include some early Fairlane 500s): 12,915 Skyliners, 45,868 Sunliners, 121,869 Victoria coupes, 47,728 Victoria sedans. A snazzy two-door wagon, the Del Rio, rang up 8663 sales, and the woody-look Country Squire attracted 24,336 admirers. The Thunderbird changed only in detail: a horizontal-bar grille, air scoop, and taillight panels; projectile-like door moldings; reworked Thunderbird script; and a 'Bird emblem for the hardtop's rear roof pillars. After a short '58 model year, production hit full stride this year, resulting in 57,195 hardtops and 10,261 ragtops.

	Restorable	Good	Excellent
Thunderbird cvt	$5,000-10,000	$10,000-17,500	$17,500-25,000
Thunderbird htp	3,000-7,500	7,500-12,500	12,500-18,000
Galaxie cvt	4,000-7,000	7,000-12,000	12,000-18,000
Frlane 500 cvt	4,000-7,000	7,000-10,000	10,000-15,000
Skyliner retrac	6,000-10,000	10,000-18,000	18,000-22,500
Galaxie 2d htp	2,000-6,000	6,000-9,000	9,000-12,000
Frlane 500 2d htp	1,500-5,000	5,000-7,000	7,000-10,000
Cntry Squire wgn	1,000-3,000	3,000-6,000	6,000-8,000
Other models	500-3,000	3,000-5,000	5,000-7,000

1960

Falcon, Ford's new compact, rode a 109.5-inch wheelbase and was powered by a small 144-cid, 90-bhp six. Sedans and wagons with two or four doors were offered, along with a deluxe trim package. Styling was plain but smooth, and the public responded by snapping up 435,676 Falcons in its first year out. Alas, there was little in these initial offerings to interest collectors. The big Fords, however, were restyled and much more streamlined—the new body had been hastily developed to keep pace with the redesigned 1959 "batwing" Chevrolet. Features included a sloping hood, wide grille incorporating quad headlights, lower beltline, glassier greenhouse, flat "fins," and half-moon taillights. The series lineup remained the same, but a new Starliner semi-fastback hardtop replaced the notchback model, and the Skyliner retractable was gone. Engines offerings embraced a 145-bhp 223 six, 185-bhp 292 V-8, and a 352 with 235, 300, or 360 horsepower (the last being quite rare). Despite the handsome new styling, it apparently didn't appeal to Ford traditional-

1959 Ford Country Squire 9-passenger station wagon

1959 Ford Fairlane 500 Fordor sedan

1959 Ford Fairlane 500 Skyliner retractable hardtop

1959 Ford Thunderbird convertible coupe

1960 Ford Falcon four-door sedan

1960 Ford Galaxie Sunliner convertible coupe

1960 Ford Thunderbird hardtop coupe

1961 Ford Galaxie Starliner hardtop coupe

1961 Ford Thunderbird hardtop coupe

1961 Ford Falcon two-door sedan

ists—full-size Ford production tumbled to 910,851 units. The Starliner found 68,461 buyers, far fewer than the '59 notchback hardtop. Sunliner sales held steady at 44,762 units, the Galaxie Victoria four-door hardtop attracted 39,215 customers, and the woody-look Country Squire went to 22,237 new homes. Thunderbird, with an all-new design in the wings for 1961, was little changed for 1960, the main changes being a new grille with a large main horizontal bar and three uprights complemented by a fine-mesh background, triple taillight clusters, and minor trim revisions. A 300-bhp, 352-cid V-8 was standard, though the 350-bhp, 430-cid Lincoln V-8 remained optional as since 1958; hardtops could be ordered with a sunroof. Despite the few changes, production soared to 76,447 coupes, 11,860 convertibles, and 2536 specially trimmed "Gold Top" hardtops.

	Restorable	Good	Excellent
Thunderbird cvt	$5,000-10,000	$10,000-17,500	$17,500-25,000
Thunderbird htp	3,000-7,500	7,500-12,500	12,500-18,000
T-Bird sunroof	3,500-8,500	8,500-15,000	15,000-20,000
Galaxie cvt	4,000-7,000	7,000-12,000	12,000-18,000
Galaxie 2d htp	2,000-6,000	6,000-9,000	9,000-12,000
Falcon	500-2,000	2,000-3,500	3,500-5,000
Other models	500-3,000	3,000-5,000	5,000-7,000

1961

The new Thunderbird, sharing a Lincoln platform, offered rakish, rounded lines highlighted by a sharply pointed "projectile" front profile. A 300-bhp 390 V-8 was the only engine offered. Extensive use of rubber suspension bushings made it one of the best riding cars of its day, and a novel new feature was its "Swing-Away" steering wheel. Output nonetheless cooled off to 62,535 hardtops and 10,516 ragtops. The big Fords were modified again, squared up in the front and looking more Ford-like up back with huge round taillights topped by discreet blades. A full-width concave grille appeared. Joining the Galaxie Starliner semi-fastback hardtop was a notchback Victoria; the public preferred the T-Bird look 75,437 to 29,699, so the Starliner was dropped after the model run. Sunliner output again held steady at 44,614 units, while the Country Squire (now a six-passenger model) fell to 16,961 units. Overall, big Ford production dropped to 791,498. On the other hand, Falcon production rose to 474,241 even though a new fine-mesh convex grille was about the only noticeable exterior change. Ford, however, did respond to the popular Chevrolet Corvair Monza by offering a Falcon Futura coupe with bucket seats, color-keyed interior, and a few exterior embellishments. In addition, a 101-bhp, 170-cid six became available, and it could be mated to a European Ford four-speed manual transmission. Futura sales were brisk: 44,470 units.

	Restorable	Good	Excellent
Thunderbird cvt	$5,000-8,000	$8,000-15,000	$15,000-22,500
Thunderbird htp	2,000-5,000	5,000-8,000	8,000-12,000
Galaxie cvt	3,000-6,000	6,000-10,000	10,000-15,000

	Restorable	Good	Excellent
Galaxie 2d htp	2,000-4,000	4,000-7,000	7,000-9,000
Falcon Futura	1,000-3,000	3,000-5,000	5,000-8,000
Falcon, other	500-2,000	2,000-3,500	3,500-5,000
Other models	500-3,000	3,000-5,000	5,000-7,000

1962 Ford Country Sedan four-door station wagon

1962 Ford Galaxie 500 four-door sedan

1962 Ford T-Bird Sports Roadster convertible coupe

1962 Ford Fairlane 500 four-door sedan

1962 Ford Thunderbird convertible coupe

1962

The new Thunderbird Sports Roadster used a fiberglass tonneau to cover the area behind the front seats and form twin headrests, resulting in a long, sleek look with the top down. Kelsey-Hayes chrome wire wheels were standard. (The stock rear fender skirts were left off because they wouldn't clear the pseudo knock-off hubs.) Limited demand made the Sports Roadster rare—only 1427 were built this year. At $5439, it sold for about $650 more than the standard T-Bird ragtop. A more popular offering this year was the Landau, with vinyl-covered roof and fake landau bars on roof quarters—but the Sports Roadster is most desirable today. Hardtop output of 69,554 units included Landaus, and 7030 ragtops were built. Also offered this year was a 340-bhp version of the 390 with triple Holley two-barrel carbs, and reportedly it went into 230 Sports Roadsters. New also was Ford's 115.5-inch-wheelbase intermediate, the Fairlane, which introduced the famous small-block 260 V-8 (shortly after the introductory 221-cid version)—an engine destined to power some of the greatest sports cars of the Sixties. Fairlane production hit 297,116, but the only model of interest was the 500 Sport Coupe with bucket-seat interior. This pillared sedan attracted 19,628 buyers. Falcon, lightly facelifted, saw output slip to 396,129, and only 17,011 were Futura coupes. The full-size cars—now in Galaxie, Galaxie 500, and Station Wagon series—received an attractive facelift featuring a crosshatch grille and large round taillights sunk partway into the rear bumper. Galaxie 500/XLs with sporty bucket-seat interiors are highly desirable. They accounted for 28,412 Victoria hardtops and 13,183 Sunliners, compared to 87,562 regular Victorias and 42,646 Sunliners. Late in the year a 385/405-horse 406 V-8 debuted. It's rare and demands a hefty premium these days. Ford production for '62 totaled 1,476,031 units.

	Restorable	Good	Excellent
Thunderbird cvt	$5,000-8,000	$8,000-15,000	$15,000-22,500
Thunderbird htp	2,000-5,000	5,000-8,000	8,000-12,000
T-Bird Rdstr	7,000-12,000	12,000-20,000	20,000-32,500
T-Bird Landau	2,500-6,000	6,000-10,000	10,000-15,000
Galaxie 500/XL cvt	4,000-7,500	7,500-10,000	10,000-14,000
Galaxie 500/XL htp	2,500-5,000	5,000-7,500	7,500-9,500
Galaxie cvt	3,000-6,000	6,000-10,000	10,000-13,000
Galaxie 2d htp	2,000-4,000	4,000-7,000	7,000-10,000
Falcon Futura	1,000-3,000	3,000-5,000	5,000-8,000
Falcon, other	500-2,000	2,000-3,500	3,500-5,000
Other models	500-3,000	3,000-5,000	5,000-7,000

1963

The mildly changed '63 T-Birds included 2000 examples of a limited-edition "Monaco," introduced in

1963 Ford Galaxie 500/XL "Scatback" hardtop coupe

1963 Ford Fairlane 500 Sport Coupe hardtop

1963 Ford Falcon Futura convertible coupe

1963 Ford Thunderbird hardtop coupe

1964 Ford Thunderbird convertible coupe

the spring and identified by white paint, rose beige padded top, special Landau bars, knock-off-style wheel covers, white leather interior and steering wheel, simulated rosewood trim—and a special numbered plaque on the console. The Sports Roadster made its last appearance, with only 455 built (37 with the 340-horse 390), and regular ragtops were down to 5913 units. Landaus, including the Monaco, totaled 14,139. Though a new grille was the major styling change, this was to be Falcon's finest year due to the arrival of a convertible and hardtop and the sporty bucket-seat Sprint. Look for Sprints with the 260 V-8 fitted with manual gearbox—neat little bargain rockets. Buyers drove home 10,479 hardtops and 4602 ragtops. Futuras, which got full-length bodyside chrome spears, had vinyl bench-seat interiors and could be ordered with the V-8. They were more numerous: 28,496 hardtops, 31,192 convertibles. A Fairlane 500 hardtop coupe with bucket seats appeared, and 28,268 were built (plus 41,641 bench-seat hardtops). The reskinned and more aggressive-looking Galaxie 500 and 500/XL two-door hardtops came in conventional notchback and fastback form; the latter are slightly more collectible. Production was 29,713 and 3,870 units, respectively, plus 18,551 500/XL Sunliners. Regular 500s numbered 49,733 Victorias, 100,500 fastbacks, and 36,876 Sunliners. Add 25 percent for Galaxies packing the 427 V-8 with 410-425 bhp, the first of Ford's jumbo blocks, and 20 percent for Fairlanes equipped with the new 271-bhp small-block 289.

	Restorable	Good	Excellent
Thunderbird cvt	$5,000-8,000	$8,000-15,000	$15,000-22,500
Thunderbird htp	2,000-5,000	5,000-8,000	8,000-12,000
T-Bird Rdstr	7,000-12,000	12,000-20,000	20,000-32,500
T-Bird Landau	2,500-6,000	6,000-10,000	10,000-15,000
Galaxie 500/XL cvt	4,000-7,500	7,500-10,000	10,000-14,000
Galaxie 500/XL htp	2,500-5,000	5,000-7,500	7,500-9,500
Galaxie fstbk htp	3,000-6,000	6,000-8,500	8,500-11,000
Galaxie cvt	3,000-6,000	6,000-10,000	10,000-13,000
Galaxie 2d htp	2,000-4,000	4,000-7,000	7,000-10,000
Fairlane 500 2d htp	2,000-4,000	4,000-6,000	6,000-8,000
Falcon Futura cvt	2,500-4,500	4,500-7,000	7,000-10,000
Falcon Futura htp	1,000-3,000	3,000-5,000	5,000-8,000
Falcon Sprint cvt	3,000-6,000	6,000-9,000	9,000-12,000
Falcon Sprint htp	2,000-4,000	4,000-7,000	7,000-10,000
Falcon, other	500-2,000	2,000-3,500	3,500-5,000
Other models	500-3,000	3,000-5,000	5,000-7,000

1964

Ford's entire line won the *Motor Trend* "Car of the Year" award on the basis of its "Total Performance" image. The big Galaxie 500/XLs, looking even more aggressive this year, would rocket to 60 mph in seven seconds and turn in standing quarter-mile runs at nearly 100 mph with big-block power. Enthusiasts bought 58,306 fastbacks, 15,169 ragtops, and even 14,661 hardtop sedans. Added to that were 206,998 Galaxie 500 hardtops, 37,311 Sunliners, and 49,242 hardtop sedans, which also had a fastback—or "Scatback"—look this year. The compact Falcon was reskinned with a more conventional, squarer shape. Sprints numbered 13,830 hardtops and 4278 ragtops, and Futura added 32,608 hardtops and 13,220 soft tops. The Thunderbird featured new heavily sculptured sheetmetal. Luxury, silence, and refinement were the main T-Bird goals now; among its new features was flow-through ventilation. As before, the offerings were hardtop, Landau, and convertible; production was 60,552, 22,715, and 9198, respectively. The drag-race-ready Fairlane Thunderbolt, with its highly tuned 427, must be a documented factory original to command the figures shown here. Only 100 were built for Ford by Dearborn Steel Tubing Company. Regular Fairlanes were shorn of their little fins, and 21,431 bucket-seat Sport Coupes were built, along with 42,733 bench-seat models. Though 1,594,053 Fords were built this year, that was still more than 700,000 units behind Chevy.

	Restorable	Good	Excellent
Thunderbird cvt	$4,000-7,000	$7,000-14,000	$14,000-20,000
Thunderbird htp	2,000-4,000	4,000-7,000	7,000-10,000
Galaxie 500/XL cvt	4,000-8,000	8,000-12,000	12,000-18,000
Galaxie 500/XL htp	2,500-5,000	5,000-9,500	9,500-12,000
Galaxie 500 cvt	3,000-6,000	6,000-10,000	10,000-13,000
Galaxie 500 2d htp	2,000-4,000	4,000-7,000	7,000-10,000
Fairlane T'Bolt	25,000-50,000	50,000-75,000	75,000-100,000
Fairlane Spt htp	2,000-4,000	4,000-6,000	6,000-9,000
Falcon cvt	2,500-4,500	4,500-7,000	7,000-10,000
Falcon htp	1,000-3,000	3,000-5,000	5,000-8,000
Falcon Sprint cvt	3,000-6,000	6,000-9,000	9,000-12,000
Falcon Sprint htp	2,000-4,000	4,000-7,000	7,000-10,000
Falcon, other	500-2,000	2,000-3,500	3,500-5,000
Other models	500-3,000	3,000-5,000	5,000-7,000

1965

Lee Iacocca's dream sales-machine, the Mustang, debuted to rave reviews on April 17, 1964—and contrary to some sources, all first-year Mustangs are 1965 models. A hardtop, convertible, and semi-fastback coupe were offered, all on a 108-inch wheelbase and with a long list of options and engines from the 170-cid Falcon six to the small-block 289 V-8 with up to 271 bhp. Look for Mustangs with the deluxe "Pony" interior and the "Rallye" instrument pack—extra gauges hung around the steering wheel makes this obvious. Production during the first long model year was amazing: 501,965 hardtops, 101,945 convertibles, and 77,079 fastbacks. Overshadowed by the new Mustang, Falcon was now in its last year of offering hardtops and convertibles—Futuras numbered 25,754 and 6315, respectively, Sprints 2806 and 300. Fairlanes received an inept facelift, but 15,141 Sport Coupes and 41,405 regular hardtops were built. Big Fords were new from the ground up with longer, sleeker lines and a new, sophisticated front suspension and coil rear suspension. Important historically was the first LTD, an ultra-luxurious Galaxie hardtop in coupe and sedan guise. First year output was 37,691 two-doors and 68,038 four-doors. 500/XLs were still around, too: 28,141 hardtops and

1964 Ford Falcon Sprint convertible coupe

1964 Ford Galaxie 500/XL convertible coupe

1964 Ford Fairlane 500 Sport Coupe hardtop

1965 Ford Mustang convertible coupe

1965 Ford Mustang 2+2 fastback coupe

1965 Ford Falcon Futura hardtop coupe

1965 Ford Thunderbird hardtop coupe

1965 Ford Galaxie 500/XL hardtop coupe

1965 Ford Fairlane 500 Sports Coupe hardtop

1966 Ford Mustang hardtop coupe

9849 ragtops; so were regular Galaxies: 157,284 hardtops, 31,930 soft tops. Thunderbirds finally had front disc brakes; this year 42,652 hardtops, 20,974 Landaus, and 6846 convertibles were produced. In a banner year, Ford production shot up to 2,170,795 units, narrowing the gap with Chevrolet to 200,000.

	Restorable	Good	Excellent
Mustang 2d htp	$1,500-5,000	$5,000-7,000	$7,000-10,000
Mustang fastback	2,500-7,000	7,000-10,000	10,000-15,000
Mustang cvt	3,500-9,000	9,000-14,000	14,000-20,000
(add 25% for 271 bhp, 15% for GT equipment)			
Thunderbird cvt	4,000-7,000	7,000-14,000	14,000-20,000
Thunderbird htp	2,000-4,000	4,000-7,000	7,000-11,000
Galaxie 500/XL cvt	4,000-7,000	7,000-11,000	11,000-15,000
Galaxie 500/XL htp	2,000-4,000	4,000-8,500	8,500-11,000
Galaxie 500 cvt	3,000-6,000	6,000-10,000	10,000-13,000
Galaxie 500 2d htp	2,000-4,000	4,000-7,000	7,000-10,000
Fairlane Spt Cpe	2,000-4,000	4,000-6,000	6,000-9,000
Falcon Futura cvt	2,500-4,500	4,500-7,000	7,000-10,000
Falcon Futura htp	1,000-3,000	3,000-5,000	5,000-8,000
Falcon Sprint cvt	3,000-6,000	6,000-9,000	9,000-12,000
Falcon Sprint htp	2,000-4,000	4,000-7,000	7,000-10,000
Falcon, other	500-2,000	2,000-3,500	3,500-5,000
Other models	500-3,000	3,000-5,000	5,000-7,000

1966

Falcon was restyled for the third time, with a longer 110.9-inch wheelbase (wagons 113) and long-hood, short-deck proportions like Mustang's. But there were only pillared sedans and wagons, although the Futura Sport Coupe came with a bucket-seat interior; 20,290 examples were sold. Mustang continued its winning ways with a simplified engine lineup, minor trim changes, and an upgraded dash. Output this year was 499,751 hardtops, 72,119 ragtops, and 35,698 fastbacks. Fairlane was also completely restyled—producing some of the most desirable Fords of the decade in the process. Mounted on a 116-inch wheelbase (wagons 113), this longer, sleeker intermediate with smooth lines, curved side glass, and vertical taillights was distinctive—especially when decked out as a 500/XL hardtop or convertible in standard or GT trim. Most XLs had the small-block V-8, but GTs boasted the 335-bhp 390 as standard. Some production figures: XL hardtop, 23,942; XL ragtop, 4560; XL GT hardtop, 33,015; XL GT soft top, 4327; regular 500 hardtop, 75,947, 500 convertible, 9299. The big Fords received a modest facelift with a revised grille and square taillights. A new addition was the 7-Liter, a bucket-seat hardtop and convertible with a standard 345-bhp 428 V-8; sales were 8705 and 2368. Galaxie 500/XL sales slipped to 25,715 hardtops and 6360 ragtops, as buyers snapped up more than 100,000 LTDs. Thunderbirds wore their first "wall-to-wall" taillights, including sequential turn signals, and a "Town" formal roofline (blanked rear quarter windows) for the Landau and hardtop. T-Bird convertible production ceased after 5049 were built this year. Look for the uncommon 428 V-8 with 345 bhp, optional but rarely ordered.

	Restorable	Good	Excellent
Mustang 2d htp	$1,500-5,000	$5,000-7,000	$7,000-10,000
Mustang fastback	2,500-7,000	7,000-10,000	10,000-15,000
Mustang cvt	3,500-9,000	9,000-14,000	14,000-20,000
(add 25% for 271 bhp, add 15% for GT equipment)			
Thunderbird cvt	4,000-7,000	7,000-14,000	14,000-20,000
Thunderbird htp	2,000-4,000	4,000-7,000	7,000-11,000
Galaxie 7-Litre cvt	4,000-7,000	7,000-11,000	11,000-15,000
Galaxie 7-Litre htp	2,000-4,000	4,000-8,500	8,500-11,000
Galaxie 500 cvt	3,000-6,000	6,000-10,000	10,000-13,000
Galaxie 500 2d htp	2,000-4,000	4,000-7,000	7,000-10,000
Fairlane 500/XL cvt	2,500-4,000	4,000-6,500	6,500-9,000
Fairlane 500/XL htp	1,500-3,000	3,000-5,000	5,000-7,000
Fairlane 500 GT cvt	2,500-4,500	4,500-7,000	7,000-10,000
Fairlane 500 GT htp	2,000-3,500	3,500-5,500	5,500-8,000
Fairlane cvt	2,000-4,000	4,000-6,000	6,000-9,000
Falcon	500-2,000	2,000-3,500	3,500-5,000
Other models	500-2,000	2,000-4,000	4,000-6,000

1967

A restyled line of Thunderbirds, all with a wide eggcrate grille featuring hidden headlights, now included a Landau four-door sedan on a longer 117.2-inch wheelbase. The hardtop and Landau coupe continued on a shorter 114.7-inch span. Though the 428 V-8 remained optional, the 315-bhp 390 was still standard. Initial reaction to the four-door was good, 24,967 units sold, but the Landau was still on top with 37,422 sales, while the base hardtop trailed at 15,567. In addition to a true fastback coupe, the '67 Mustang was given all-new lower sheetmetal that made it look bigger and more aggressive. A larger, deeper grille, sculptured side panels ending in twin simulated air scoops, concave rear panel, and new wheel covers with a blade motif provided instant recognition. More power was available in the form of an optional 320-bhp 390 V-8. Despite the added competition from Camaro, Firebird, and Cougar, 472,121 Mustangs were built, including 71,042 fastbacks and 44,808 ragtops. Falcon still offered a pillared Futura Sport Coupe, but only 7053 buyers noticed. Fairlane wasn't too much different this year, either, cranking out 14,871 500/XL hardtops and 1943 convertibles, plus 18,670 500/XL GT hardtops and 2117 ragtops. In Ford talk, a GT/A badge meant that a GT had an automatic transmission. The big Ford Galaxies got a major facelift with faster rooflines for two-door hardtops, but 500/XL production slipped to 18,174 hardtops and 5161 ragtops. Regular Galaxie 500s did much better: 197,388 hardtops and 19,068 convertibles.

	Restorable	Good	Excellent
Mustang 2d htp	$1,500-4,000	$4,000-6,000	$6,000-9,000
Mustang fastback	2,500-6,000	6,000-9,000	9,000-14,000
Mustang cvt	3,500-8,000	8,000-13,000	13,000-18,000
(add 25% for 271 bhp, add 15% for 390 bhp and/or GT equipment)			
Thunderbird 4d	1,000-2,500	2,500-4,500	4,500-6,500
Thunderbird 2d	1,500-4,000	4,000-6,000	6,000-8,000
Galaxie 500/XL cvt	4,000-6,000	6,000-9,000	9,000-13,000
Galaxie 500/XL htp	2,000-3,000	3,000-7,500	7,500-9,500
Galaxie 500 cvt	3,000-5,000	5,000-7,000	7,000-10,000
Galaxie 500 2d htp	1,500-2,500	2,500-5,000	5,000-7,500
Fairlane 500/XL cvt	2,500-4,000	4,000-7,500	7,500-10,000
Fairlane 500/XL htp	1,500-3,000	3,000-5,000	5,000-7,000

1966 Ford Galaxie 500 hardtop coupe

1966 Ford Thunderbird Landau hardtop coupe

1967 Ford Mustang convertible coupe

1967 Ford Thunderbird Landau four-door sedan

1967 Ford Galaxie 500/XL convertible coupe

1967 Ford Fairlane GT/A convertible coupe

1968 Ford Torino GT 428 Cobra Jet Official Pace Car

1968 Ford Thunderbird Landau hardtop coupe

1968 Ford Torino GT fastback hardtop coupe

1968 Ford Galaxie 500 convertible coupe

	Restorable	Good	Excellent
Fairlane GT/GTA cvt	3,000-5,500	5,500-8,000	8,000-12,000
Fairlane GT/GTA htp	2,000-3,500	3,500-5,500	5,500-8,000
Fairlane 500 cvt	2,000-4,000	4,000-6,000	6,000-9,000
Falcon	500-2,000	2,000-3,500	3,500-5,000
Other models	500-2,000	2,000-4,000	4,000-6,000

1968

Stroked to 302 cubes, the small-block V-8 now delivered 230 horsepower with a four-barrel carb. Fairlane, restyled to look bulkier and now sporting horizontal quad headlamps, was one-upped by a new top-line Torino series. Base Torinos had a six, but GTs featured V-8s plus bucket seats, console, paint striping, and a long list of performance options. With 74,135 built, the fastback coupe was the favorite, followed by the notchback hardtop and ragtop with 23,939 and 5310 buyers. A Torino GT paced this year's Indy 500 race. Mustang coasted along style-wise, but a 390-bhp 427 V-8 and 335-bhp 428 were seen this year. Production fell from 472,121 in 1967 to 317,404—the ponycar market had already peaked and would drop quickly from here. Among the full-size Fords, LTDs and XLs sported hidden headlights; models with exposed units wore them in a horizontal position. LTDs were ever more popular, but buyers nonetheless selected 50,048 XL fastback hardtops and 6066 convertibles. Equivalent Galaxie 500 models scored with 84,332 and 11,832 customers. Thunderbirds received a new 360-bhp 429 V-8 as an option (it would be standard in 1969), plus a rectangular eggcrate grille pattern. Sales were down, however, to 33,019 Landau hardtops, 21,925 Landau four-doors, and 9977 base hardtops. Falcon, practically forgotten by now, found 10,077 buyers for the Futura Sport Coupe. Total Ford production this year totaled 1,753,334, up slightly from 1967.

	Restorable	Good	Excellent
Mustang 2d htp	$1,500-4,000	$4,000-6,000	$6,000-9,000
Mustang fastback	2,500-6,000	6,000-9,000	9,000-14,000
Mustang cvt	3,500-8,000	8,000-13,000	13,000-18,000
(add 15% for 390 bhp and/or GT equipment)			
Thunderbird 4d	1,000-2,500	2,500-4,500	4,500-6,500
Thunderbird 2d	1,500-4,000	4,000-6,000	6,000-8,000
Galaxie 500/XL cvt	4,000-6,000	6,000-9,000	9,000-13,000
Galaxie 500/XL htp	2,000-3,000	3,000-7,500	7,500-9,500
Galaxie 500 cvt	3,000-5,000	5,000-7,000	7,000-10,000
Galaxie 500 2d htp	1,500-2,500	2,500-5,000	5,000-7,500
Torino GT cvt	3,000-6,000	6,000-8,500	8,500-12,000
Torino GT 2d htp	1,000-3,000	3,000-5,000	5,000-7,500
Fairlane 500 cvt	2,000-4,000	4,000-6,000	6,000-9,000
Falcon	500-2,000	2,000-3,500	3,500-5,000
Other models	500-2,000	2,000-4,000	4,000-6,000

1969

Torino was little changed except for two new arrivals that were actually package options, the fastback and hardtop Torino Cobra, packing Ford's 335-horsepower 428 V-8 also available in the Mustang Mach I. Ram-Air was an option: a fiberglass hood scoop with a special air cleaner that ducted incoming air directly into the carb via a special valve. Four-speed gearbox, stiff suspension, and hood locking pins were standard. Torinos, led by the more aerodynamic, longer-nose Talledega (754 street models built) dominated stock car racing, regularly running about 190 mph. Torino GT production was 61,319 fastbacks, 17,951 notchbacks, and 2552 ragtops. Full-size Fords were redone on a longer 121-inch wheelbase. SportsRoof (fastback) models featured a tunneled rear window. A 320/360-bhp 429 V-8 was available, and some of the 54,557 500/XL hardtops and 7402 convertibles had it. Thunderbirds sported an eight-element rectangular grille and divided taillights instead of the wall-to-wall types. A power sun roof was optional. Production was down again to 27,664 Landaus hardtops, 15,695 Landau four-doors, and 5913 base hardtops. Mustang added muscle: the Trans Am racing-inspired Boss 302 fastback with a rated 290 horsepower (really much more) and the Mach 1 fastback, packing a 250-bhp 351 V-8, with larger engines available up to the 335-bhp Ram Air 428. Only 6319 Boss 302s were built, but the Mach 1 in all guises appealed to 72,458 buyers. A luxury Mustang, the Grandé, was also added, but only 13,581 examples were ordered. It hasn't become particularly collectible. Rare but exciting: the Boss 429, with 360/375 horsepower and the mightiest engine of all. Only 498 copies were produced, the goal being to homologate the V-8 for NASCAR racing. Total Ford production this year perked up to 1,826,777 units.

	Restorable	Good	Excellent
Mustang 2d htp	$1,500-4,000	$4,000-6,000	$6,000-9,000
Mustang fastback	2,000-5,000	5,000-7,000	7,000-10,000
Mustang cvt	3,500-7,000	7,000-10,000	10,000-14,000
Mustang Grandé	1,500-4,000	4,000-6,500	6,500-10,000
Mustang Mach I (351)	2,500-8,000	8,000-12,000	12,000-16,000
Mustang Boss 302	4,000-9,500	9,500-17,500	17,500-25,000
Mustang Boss 429	8,000-20,000	20,000-35,000	35,000-48,000
(add 25% for Cobra Jet engines, 15% for 390 bhp and/or GT equipment)			
Thunderbird 4d	1,000-2,500	2,500-4,500	4,500-6,500
Thunderbird 2d	1,500-4,000	4,000-6,000	6,000-8,000
Galaxie 500/XL cvt	3,000-5,000	5,000-7,500	7,500-10,000
Galaxie 500/XL htp	1,500-3,000	3,000-5,000	5,000-7,500
Galaxie 500 cvt	2,000-4,000	4,000-6,000	6,000-8,000
Galaxie 500 2d htp	1,000-2,500	2,500-4,000	4,000-6,000
Torino GT cvt	3,000-6,000	6,000-8,500	8,500-12,000
Torino GT 2d	1,000-3,000	3,000-5,000	5,000-7,500
Torino GT Cobra	3,000-6,500	6,500-9,000	9,000-13,500
Fairlane 500 cvt	2,000-3,000	3,000-5,000	5,000-8,000
Falcon	500-2,000	2,000-3,500	3,500-5,000
Other models	500-2,000	2,000-4,000	4,000-6,000

1970

Ford held pat with a Falcon similar to the '69 until mid-year, when a stripper model of the larger Torino became the '70½ Falcon, but this was axed at the end of the year. Falcon was displaced by a new offering, the compact Maverick that had been intro-

1969 Ford Thunderbird Landau hardtop coupe

1969 Ford Galaxie 500 "fastback" hardtop coupe

1969 Ford LTD hardtop sedan

1969 Ford Mustang Boss 302 fastback hardtop coupe

1970 Ford Galaxie 500/XL convertible coupe

1970 Ford Thunderbird hardtop coupe

1970 Ford Mustang Boss 302 fastback coupe

1970 Ford Torino GT SportsRoof hardtop coupe

1970 Ford Falcon two-door sedan

1971 Ford LTD hardtop coupe

duced in mid-1969 as a 1970 model. The Fairlane 500 badge was applied to the base Torino series. The Torino's new aerodynamic styling rode a slightly longer 117-inch wheelbase (wagons 114). GTs got hidden headlights; 56,819 hardtops and 3939 convertibles were called for. The muscle-car Cobra, with its standard 360-bhp 429 (375 bhp optional), sold to 7675 diehard performance buffs. The big Fords received refined versions of the "poke-through" center-section grille on LTDs and XLs, along with low-mounted horizontal taillamps. Four series were offered, with the LTD Brougham leading the line. LTD production hummed along at 373,934 units, but XLs appealed to 27,251 hardtop and 6348 ragtop buyers. There was no longer a Galaxie 500 convertible. Thunderbird was restyled on the same wheelbases, gaining a more prominent hood, snout-like grille, and exposed headlamps. Output came to 36,847 Landau coupes, 5116 base coupes, and 8401 four-door Landaus. Total production passed the two-million mark this year, enabling Ford to beat Chevy in the model-year production race.

	Restorable	Good	Excellent
Mustang 2d htp	$1,500-4,000	$4,000-6,000	$6,000-9,000
Mustang fastback	2,000-5,000	5,000-7,000	7,000-10,000
Mustang cvt	3,500-7,000	7,000-10,000	10,000-14,000
Mustang Grandé	1,500-4,000	4,000-6,500	6,500-10,000
Mustang Mach I (351)	2,500-8,000	8,000-12,000	12,000-16,000
Mustang Boss 302	4,000-9,500	9,500-17,500	17,500-25,000
Mustang Boss 429	8,000-20,000	20,000-35,000	35,000-48,000
(add 25% for Cobra Jet engines, 15% for 390 bhp and/or GT equipment)			
Thunderbird, all	1,000-2,500	2,500-5,000	5,000-7,000
Galaxie 500/XL cvt	3,000-5,000	5,000-7,500	7,500-10,000
Gal 500/XL 2d htp	1,000-$2,000	2,000-3,000	3,000-6,000
Galaxie 500 2d htp	500-1,500	1,500-2,500	2,500-4,500
Torino GT cvt	3,000-6,000	6,000-8,500	8,500-12,000
Torino GT 2d	1,000-3,000	3,000-5,000	5,000-7,500
Torino Cobra	3,000-6,500	6,500-9,000	9,000-14,000
Fairlane 500 cvt	2,000-3,000	3,000-5,000	5,000-8,000
Falcon/Maverick	500-2,000	2,000-3,000	3,000-4,500
Other models	500-2,000	2,000-4,000	4,000-6,000

1971

Because Ford dropped its XL models this year, the full-size convertible became an LTD. It's definitely collectible today, but only 5750 were built. The subcompact Pinto, a $1919 "throw-away" car, was introduced; none have become collectible, though there were a few interesting variations over the years. A new Mustang arrived on a 109-inch wheelbase: eight inches longer overall, six inches wider, and nearly 600 pounds heavier than in 1964. Mach 1 Cobra Jet 429s, rated at 370 horsepower, could now be ordered with air conditioning and automatic transmission—they were still quick, easily thundering from 0-60 in under seven seconds. A new kind of Boss Mustang, the 351 (with a 330-bhp 351 V-8), debuted, but production was halted after an estimated 1800 were built. Mach 1s, with 302, 351, or 429 V-8s, were far more popular, appealing to

36,499 buyers. Mustang convertible output, however, continued to slide, down to 6121 units. Though it kept its "Bunkie beak" front end, the T-Bird received a modest facelift. Buyers drove home in 20,356 Landau coupes and 9146 hardtops. They also purchased 6553 Landau four-doors, but because sales had been falling ever since the 1967 debut, T-Bird wouldn't offer a four-door after 1971. Torino, 14 models strong, was mainly a carryover. The Cobra fastback coupe remained the most exciting model, although it was downgraded from the 429 to the 351 engine in this, its last year. Output was only 3054, and only a few had the 370-bhp 429. Properly optioned GTs are also of interest, and 31,641 hardtops reached customers, though the ragtop was very rare as only 1613 were ordered. Maverick added a four-door sedan, which is of no particular interest, but the sporty-looking Grabber fastback with the optional 302 V-8 could make for a low-bucks daily driver. For the second year in a row, Ford out-produced Chevy; the tally this year was 2,054,351 units.

	Restorable	Good	Excellent
Mustang htp/Grandé	$1,500-4,000	$4,000-6,000	$6,000-9,000
Mustang fastback	2,000-5,000	5,000-7,000	7,000-10,000
Mustang cvt	3,500-7,000	7,000-10,000	10,000-14,000
Mustang Mach 1	2,500-6,000	6,000-10,000	10,000-14,000
Mustang Boss 351	4,000-9,500	9,500-17,500	17,500-25,000
Thunderbird	1,500-2,500	2,500-5,000	5,000-7,000
Torino Cobra htp	2,500-5,000	5,000-10,000	10,000-15,000
Torino 500 cvt	3,000-5,000	5,000-7,000	7,000-9,000
Torino GT htp	2,000-4,000	4,000-6,000	6,000-7,500
LTD convertible	2,000-4,500	4,500-7,000	7,000-9,000
Maverick Grabber V-8	500-1,000	1,000-2,000	2,000-3,500

1972

Mustang wasn't much changed, but there were fewer engine options and the Boss 351 vanished. Look for the Sprint decor option: white paint with broad blue racing stripes edged in red, with complementary interior colors, and mag wheels. Mach 1s numbered 27,675, convertibles 6401. Thunderbird was new, the largest and heaviest 'Bird before or since, sharing its basic 120.4-inch-wheelbase structure with the Continental Mark IV. A 212-*net*-horsepower 429 V-8 was standard, a 224-bhp 460 optional. Though available only as a hardtop, 57,814 were sold. A new, larger, gawky Torino appeared, without Cobras or ragtops. The "formal" two-door hardtop enticed 165,814 buyers (most preferring the more expensive Gran Torino version), while 31,239 chose the Sport fastback hardtop, and 60,794 bought the sportier GT Sport fastback. Though this was the last year for the full-size LTD convertible, only 4234 buyers took advantage. Over a quarter of a million customers, however, bought a full-size hardtop coupe. Though Chevy regained the lead in production, Ford nonetheless built 2,246,563 cars for the model year.

1971 Ford Torino Brougham hardtop sedan

1971 Ford Mustang Mach 1 fastback hardtop coupe

1972 Ford LTD convertible coupe

1972 Ford Gran Torino four-door sedan

1972 Ford Thunderbird hardtop coupe

1973 Ford Mustang Mach 1 fastback hardtop

1973 Ford Gran Torino Brougham four-door sedan

1973 Ford Thunderbird coupe

1974 Ford Mustang II "Grandé" coupe prototype

1974 Ford Mustang hatchback coupe

	Restorable	Good	Excellent
Mustang htp/Grandé	$1,500-4,000	$4,000-6,000	$6,000-9,000
Mustang fastback	2,000-5,000	5,000-7,000	7,000-10,000
Mustang cvt	3,500-7,000	7,000-10,000	10,000-14,000
Mustang Mach I	2,500-6,000	6,000-10,000	10,000-14,000
Thunderbird	1,500-2,500	2,500-5,000	5,000-7,000
Gran Torino Spt htp	1,000-2,500	2,500-4,000	4,000-6,000
LTD convertible	2,000-4,500	4,500-7,000	7,000-9,000
Maverick Grabber V-8	500-1,000	1,000-2,000	2,000-3,500

1973

The hefty Mustang remained as before, with most changes designed to meet Federal regulations: five-mph bumpers, rubber control knobs, fire-retardant upholstery, EGR system to cope with emissions. Production continued to slide, this year to 125,093; 27,675 were Mach 1s, and even though it was no secret that the convertible was about to be dropped, just 6401 were sold. Modest changes attended the Thunderbird; up front, headlights were set into square holes, an eggcrate grille replaced horizontal bars, and an opera window was added. Output jumped to 87,269. Pinto introduced a Squire station wagon with dummy wood on the body sides, and Maverick continued with the Grabber (32,350 built this year) and V-8 option. Torinos looked particularly clumsy with the new crash bumpers, and the GT model was gone. The Sport fastback hardtop was still available, however, and could still be optioned with the 429 V-8, now at 201 net bhp. Big Fords adopted a more Thunderbird-like grille; hardtop coupes and sedans continued to sell well, and the 429 plus a 460 Lincoln V-8 (202 bhp) were offered. Total Ford production was up by just over 100,000 cars.

	Restorable	Good	Excellent
Mustang htp/Grandé	$1,500-4,000	$4,000-6,000	$6,000-9,000
Mustang fastback	2,000-5,000	5,000-7,000	7,000-10,000
Mustang cvt	3,500-7,000	7,000-11,000	11,000-15,000
Mustang Mach 1	2,500-6,000	6,000-10,000	10,000-14,000
Thunderbird	1,000-2,000	2,000-4,000	4,000-6,000
Gran Torino Spt htp	1,000-2,500	2,500-4,000	4,000-6,000
Maverick Grabber V-8	500-1,000	1,000-2,000	2,000-3,500

1974

The smaller, lighter—and partly Pinto-based—Mustang II was well timed, coinciding with the national fuel crisis, and sold nearly 400,000 units in its first year out. Riding a 96.2-inch wheelbase, it was 20 inches shorter and 400-500 pounds lighter than the '73 Mustang. To its credit, it had a unit body, conventional suspension, and precise steering. No convertible was offered, nor was there a V-8, though the 2.8-liter V-6 option was reasonably quick. Ghia luxury notchbacks and a Mach 1 fastback (now with hatch) remained available, the latter attracting 44,406 buyers. Thunderbirds looked clumsier than ever with Federal bumpers front and rear, and the 460 V-8 was standard equipment. Look for the Gold Tint moonroof option or the Burgundy or White-on-Gold decor packages. Sales this year numbered 58,443 units. Maverick introduced an optional $322 LDO (Luxury Decor Option) package, and while it made the car more palatable it's of little interest to collectors, even with the 302 V-8. Torino marked time, but the Gran Sport hardtop fell to 23,142 sales. A gussied-up Torino coupe—with formal grille, twin opera windows, and stand-up hood ornament—debuted at mid-year to do battle with the extremely successful Chevy Monte Carlo. Called Gran Torino Elite, it found 96,604 buyers despite its superficial luxury cues. The big Fords didn't change much, though it should be noted that this would be the last year for the Galaxie 500 nameplate and for the true two-door hardtop. This body style, around since 1951, ended its career thusly: 34,214 Galaxie 500s, 73,296 LTDs, and 39,084 LTD Broughams. With a total of 2,179,791 cars built, Ford wasn't suffering too badly from the first Arab oil embargo.

Restorable	Good	Excellent	
Mustang II Mach 1	$1,000-2,000	$2,000-3,500	$3,500-4,500
Mustang II	500-1,000	1,000-2,000	2,000-3,500
Thunderbird	1,000-2,000	2,000-3,500	3,500-5,500
Gran Torino Sport htp	1,000-2,500	2,500-4,000	4,000-6,000
Maverick Grabber V-8	500-1,000	1,000-2,000	2,000-3,500

1974 Ford Gran Torino Brougham coupe

1974 Ford Thunderbird coupe

1975

Ford's new Granada "luxury compact" appeared as a four-door sedan and opera-windowed coupe. This was an excellent product that was deservedly praised and sold well, but it hasn't become a collector car. Top-line Ghias are the most interesting, with 43,652 four-doors and 40,028 two-doors built. Mustang received a V-8 option: the workhorse 302, now down to 122 net bhp. The sportiest model was still the Mach 1; 21,062 were sold. Thunderbird was detuned again (the 460 V-8 was down to 194 bhp), but useful options were four-wheel disc brakes and "Sure-Track," an early anti-lock braking device. Decor packages were Copper, Jade, and Silver, with velour or leather upholstery. All had a padded vinyl roof and opera windows, though the windows were deleted if a moonroof was added. T-Bird output dropped to 42,685 units. Pinto added a V-6 option on some models, and Maverick carried on, though Grabber production was down to 8473 units. Among Torinos, the Sport hardtop stumbled to 5126 sales; it would not return for 1976. The Elite saw production increase to 123,372 units even though the car itself changed hardly at all. Full-size Fords lost their four-door hardtops this year, which pretty much put an end to any interesting models among big Fords. LTD Broughams were the new top-line models for '75. Total production was way down this year to 1,569,608 units.

1975 Ford Granada two-door coupe

1975 Ford Mustang II V-8 Ghia coupe

1975 Ford Thunderbird with Copper Luxury Group

1976 Ford Thunderbird with glass "Moonroof"

1976 Ford Granada Ghia with Luxury Decor option

1976 Ford Mustang II fastback with Stallion option

1977 Ford Granada with Sports Coupe option

	Restorable	Good	Excellent
Mustang II			
Mach 1	$1,000-2,000	$2,000-3,500	$3,500-4,500
Mustang II	500-1,000	1,000-2,000	2,000-3,500
Thunderbird	1,000-2,000	2,000-3,500	3,500-5,500
Maverick			
Grabber V-8	500-1,000	1,000-2,000	2,000-3,500
Granada Ghia sdns	500-1,000	1,000-2,000	2,000-3,000

1976

Mustang now offered the Cobra II, a $325 trim option for hatchbacks, boasting sport steering wheel, dual remote control rearview mirrors, brushed aluminum dash and door panel appliqués, black grille, styled steering wheel, radial tires, flip-out rear side windows with add-on louvers, front air dam, spoiler, simulated hood scoop, and boy-racer stripes. Only white paint jobs were available. The Mach 1 was down to just 9232 sales. Thunderbird explored the depths of fashion with its Lipstick, Bordeaux, and Creme & Gold luxury decor groups. Output rose to 52,935 units, and 30 were Commemorative Editions. Pintos, Mavericks, and Mustang IIs could be had with a Stallion package: silver paint with black-out trim plus black lower bodysides, hood, and roof and big Stallion decals on the front fenders. Pinto also offered Squire fake wood trim on the three-door hatchback. Granadas carried on much as before, though there was a $482 Sport Sedan option. Elite became a separate nameplate this year, and output increased to 146,475 units, but ironically this would be its last year. Bucket seats and floor shift were offered. The big Fords featured optional four-wheel power disc brakes and half-vinyl tops for two-door models. As buyers forgot about the oil embargo, production of all models increased to 1,861,537 cars.

	Restorable	Good	Excellent
Cobra II	$1,000-2,500	$2,500-3,500	$3,500-6,000
Mustang II			
Mach 1	1,000-2,000	2,000-3,000	3,000-4,500
Mustang II	500-1,000	1,000-2,000	2,000-3,500
Thunderbird	1,000-2,000	2,000-3,000	3,000-5,000
Granada Ghia sdns	500-1,000	1,000-2,000	2,000-3,000

1977

Torino received cleaner exterior sheetmetal and was "badge engineered" to pass as a new car, the LTD II. It wasn't, but output moved up 20 percent to 232,324 units. Hardtops, with small rear quarter windows and C-pillar opera windows numbered 87,959 in S, base, and Brougham form. The new Thunderbird was much smaller and lighter (1800 pounds), downsized by moving it to the intermediate LTD II platform. In reality, it was an Elite replacement. The top-line 'Bird was the Town Landau, with many standard features including a "Tiara" roof band. Production exploded to 318,140 units, helped by lower prices. Standard power was the 302 V-8, or the 351 in California. The Cobra II could be ordered in a number of different colors this year and its appearance was altered at mid-year with new tri-color tape striping. The big news regarding the Mustang II was an optional T-top roof, a Rallye Appearance Package replacing the Stallion option, and continuation of the Rallye package with competition suspension, Traction-Lok differential, "extra-cooling package," and dual exhausts with chrome tips. Mustang production declined to 153,173 units. Big Fords soldiered on, and despite the all-new downsized big Chevys scored a sales increase of about 24,000 units. Granada offered some new options, among them a four-speed overdrive manual transmission and leather upholstery for Ghia models, which found 69,896 buyers. Maverick was in its last year, so there was little change. Pinto, meanwhile, received revised front and rear styling and an interesting Cruising Wagon, a youth-oriented station wagon package with front spoiler, styled wheels, blanked-off rear quarter windows with portholes, and wild colors. Though Chevy showed a healthy sales increase, total Ford output dipped slightly to 1,840,427 units.

	Restorable	Good	Excellent
Cobra II	$1,000-2,500	$2,500-3,500	$3,500-6,000
Mustang II Mach 1	1,000-2,000	2,000-3,000	3,000-4,500
Mustang II	500-1,000	1,000-2,000	2,000-3,500
Thunderbird	1,000-2,000	2,000-3,000	3,000-5,000
Granada Ghia sdns	500-1,000	1,000-2,000	2,000-3,000

1978

An "instant collectible," the Thunderbird Diamond Jubilee model was painted Diamond Blue or Ember metallic and came with the owner's initials on the door and a 22-carat gold nameplate on the dash. Some 18,994 paid $10,106 to have one, while 333,757 more conservative buyers settled for the base and Town Landau coupe. Ford tried paint-on-performance with the Mustang II's "King Cobra" package: the usual Cobra II equipment plus a snake decal on the hood and fore-to-aft tape stripes; the package cost $1300 and included a 302 V-8, power steering, handling suspension, and radials. Total Mustang output was 192,410 units. Fairmont, replacement for the unlamented Maverick, was a ground-up redesign on the new Fox platform, which would influence Ford products through the mid-1980s. Notable was its all-coil-spring, MacPherson-strut suspension, which produced excellent handling and service access. A Futura coupe, of which 116,966 were built, featured Thunderbird-style looks for just $4103, and a 139-bhp 302 V-8 was available. Pinto didn't change much, but Granada now offered rectangular headlights plus two- and four-door ESS—European Sport Sedan—packages with heavy-duty suspension, dual sport mirrors, leather-wrapped steering wheel, and unique black-out trim and badges. LTD II lost its wagons, and the full-size Ford marked time while its replacement was readied for 1979. Production for 1978 increased a bit to 1,923,655.

	Restorable	Good	Excellent
King Cobra	$2,000-3,000	$3,000-5,000	$5,000-7,000

1977 Ford Mustang II with Cobra II package

1977 Ford Thunderbird Town Landau coupe

1978 Ford Thunderbird with T-Roof Convertible option

1978 Ford Granada Ghia coupe

1978 Ford Mustang II Ghia coupe

1979 Ford Mustang three-door with Cobra package

1979 Ford Granada with ESS package

1980 Ford Mustang three-door with Cobra package

1980 Ford Thunderbird coupe

	Restorable	Good	Excellent
Cobra II	1,000-2,500	2,500-3,500	3,500-6,000
Mustang II Mach 1	1,000-2,000	2,000-3,000	3,000-4,500
Mustang II	500-1,000	1,000-2,000	2,000-3,500
Thunderbird	1,000-2,000	2,000-3,000	3,000-5,000
T-B Diamond Jubilee	2,000-3,000	3,000-4,500	4,500-6,000
Granada Ghia sdns	500-1,000	1,000-2,000	2,000-3,000

1979

The third-generation Mustang was announced—a major improvement on the Mustang II. Clean and lean, it had little superfluous ornamentation, and despite more interior space it weighed 200 pounds less than the Mustang II. Its suspension, borrowed from the Fairmont/Zephyr, used modified MacPherson-struts in front, four-bar-link rear axle location, sway bars at both ends, and coil springs all around. The top engine was a 140-bhp 302 V-8. Mustang paced the 1979 Indy 500, so a mid-year Pace Car Replica was issued with spoilers fore and aft, integral fog lamps, slatted grille, and dummy hood scoop. Two other interesting offerings were the boy-racer Cobra package and the 140-bhp Turbo 2.3 four-cylinder engine. Output jumped 92 percent to 369,936 coupes and hatchbacks. The '78 Thunderbird Jubilee edition was back as the $10,687 Heritage model, offered with special maroon or light blue paint jobs. T-Bird production totaled 284,141. The luxury-leader LTD was now downsized, becoming much trimmer and vastly lighter, though boxy looking. There wasn't much to interest collectors. Granada and LTD II continued much as before, though sales were down sharply for both. Pinto sported new front-end styling. Total Ford output this year was 1,835,937 units.

	Restorable	Good	Excellent
Mustang	$1,000-2,000	$2,000-3,000	$3,000-4,500
Must Pace Car Replica	1,500-2,500	2,500-3,500	3,500-5,000
Thunderbird	1,000-2,000	2,000-3,000	3,000-5,000
T-Bird Heritage	1,000-2,500	2,500-3,500	3,500-5,500
Granada Ghia sdns	500-1,000	1,000-2,000	2,000-3,000

1980

Thunderbird was downsized again, losing 16 inches in length. Using the Fairmont's "Fox" platform, it was a half-ton lighter than the '79: a nicely executed package, with a handsome interior, though styling was on the baroque side. Options included Recaro seats and the 302 V-8 (a 255 was now standard). Four-speed overdrive automatic, rack-and-pinion steering, and all-coil springs were standard. A coupe, Town Landau coupe, and Silver Anniversary Edition were offered, but output skidded to 156,803. Mustang's 1979 Pace Car Replica's special styling was applied to a revised Cobra package, equipped with a TRX handling suspension. The new 118-bhp 255 V-8 was optional on all Mustangs, good on gas while still providing decent performance. The Turbo was still available, too. Production fell to 271,322 units. An old name, Crown Victoria, returned to grace a luxury edition of the LTD, though only 7725 coupes were called for. Granada was still available in ESS guise; Pinto was now in its last year. Due in good part to the recession following the second oil embargo, total Ford production plummeted to 1,162,275 units.

	Restorable	Good	Excellent
Mustang	$1,000-2,000	$2,000-3,000	$3,000-4,500
Thunderbird	1,000-2,000	2,000-3,000	3,000-5,000
T-Bird Silver Ann	2,000-3,000	3,000-4,000	4,000-6,000
Granada ESS	500-1,000	1,000-2,000	2,000-3,000
LTD Crown Vic	500-1,000	1,000-2,000	2,000-3,500

1981 Ford LTD Crown Victoria four-door sedan

1981 Ford Thunderbird Town Landau coupe

1981

Ford's new front-drive Escort debuted, replacing the imported Fiesta and Pinto simultaneously. The most interesting models were the sporty SS hatchbacks, though they're hardly collectible. First year Escort output was 320,727. Granada was completely redone by reworking the Fairmont's body and chassis to give it a more massive look. The top model was the GLX, available with two or four doors. Granada attracted 121,341 buyers. Mustang was little changed; Turbos were no longer available with automatic, but few wanted that combination. Buyers drove 182,552 Mustangs home this year. A Heritage T-Bird returned, essentially the same as the '80 anniversary model, but Heritage Birds are worth no premium on the current collector market. Output dropped to 86,693. The recession continued, and so did the sales slide, down to 1,054,976.

	Restorable	Good	Excellent
Mustang (incl Cobra)	*	$2,000-3,000	$3,000-4,500
Thunderbird	*	2,000-3,000	3,000-5,000
LTD Crown Vic	*	1,000-2,000	2,000-3,500
Granada GLX	*	1,000-2,000	2,000-3,000

*Purchase only in good or excellent condition

1982 Ford EXP 2-passenger hatchback coupe

1982 Ford Mustang GT hatchback coupe

1982

The Escort-based EXP was a sports derivation with low seating, no back seat, peculiar styling (with "bug-eye" headlights), and a choppy ride. Even so, it attracted 98,256 buyers. A better choice is the Escort GT, a three-door hatchback with sport suspension and deluxe trim. Escort production increased to 385,182 units. After a two-year absence, the 302 V-8 (5.0 liter) returned as a performance option for Mustang, teamed with four-speed overdrive manual transmission in a new GT hatchback coupe that replaced 1981's Cobra; 0-60 took eight seconds. Though Mustang output dipped to 130,448, some 23,447 GTs were ordered. Thunderbird, only lightly facelifted and still offering the luxurious Heritage model, continued its slide to just 45,142 units. Total Ford production was down slightly to 1,035,093 units.

1983 Ford Mustang GLX convertible coupe

1983 Ford Thunderbird coupe

1983 Ford LTD Crown Victoria four-door sedan

1984 Ford LTD LX four-door sedan

	Restorable	Good	Excellent
Mustang	*	$2,000-3,000	$3,000-4,500
Thunderbird	*	2,000-3,000	3,000-5,000
LTD Crown Victoria	*	1,000-2,000	2,000-3,500
Escort GT	*	1,000-2,500	2,500-4,000
Granada GLX	*	1,000-2,000	2,000-3,000
EXP	*	1,500-2,500	2,500-4,500

*Purchase only in good or excellent condition

1983

The brand-new, aerodynamic Thunderbird was slightly smaller and much sportier than its predecessor, though still in front-engine, rear-drive format. Collectors tend to emphasize the Turbo Coupe, with its 145-bhp blown version of the Mustang 2.3-liter, fuel-injected four and manual five-speed. Also offered was a base coupe and Heritage model; production increased to 121,999 total 'Birds. A flashy new Mustang convertible returned for the first time in a decade, with four-barrel power for the optional V-8 and a new five-speed manual transmission; a Turbo four was added later. The GT package included wide tires, handling suspension, fog lamps, lots of black accents, spoilers, deep buckets, and console. Of the 120,873 Mustangs produced, 23,488 were GLX and GT ragtops. Escort GTs got a horsepower boost to 88. Fairmonts were all Futuras now, including the still-available coupe. Granada was replaced by a restyled aero-look Fairmont called LTD, which meant that all big Fords became LTD Crown Victorias. Despite all the changes, Ford output bottomed out at 928,137 units.

	Restorable	Good	Excellent
Mustang coupe	*	$2,000-3,000	$3,000-3,500
Mustang GT coupe	*	3,000-4,000	4,000-4,500
Mustang GT cvt	*	4,000-6,000	6,000-8,000
T-Bird Turbo cpe	*	2,500-3,500	3,500-6,500
Thunderbird	*	2,000-3,000	3,000-5,000
LTD Crown Vic	*	1,000-2,000	2,000-3,500
Escort GT	*	1,000-2,500	2,500-4,000
Granada GLX	*	1,000-2,000	2,000-3,000
EXP	*	1,500-2,500	2,500-4,500

*Purchase only in good or excellent condition

1984

Turbocharging gave the Escort and EXP something they had always lacked: power. The EXP, however, retained many shortcomings, including its bathtub driving position and dreadful ride. The Escort wasn't the most habitable creation either, but it did offer roominess and, with the 120-bhp turbo setup, driving fun. Total Escort output was 372,523, while EXP struggled at 23,016. Mustang's new SVO was king of the performance hill, with its turbocharged 2.3-liter four boasting intercooler, port fuel injection, and 175 horses. The SVO (Special Vehicle Operations) was a complete package with four-wheel discs, Koni shocks, wide tires on aluminum wheels, Hurst five-speed, functional hood scoop—and a $15,596 price tag. Its top speed was over 130 mph and it would do 0-60 in 7.5 seconds. Only 4508 were built. Also offered was a 145-bhp Mustang Turbo hatchback and ragtop, and the 175-bhp 302 V-8 in GT models. Total Mustang production was 141,580, including 17,600 Turbo and GT soft tops. The Thunderbird Turbo Coupe was now available with automatic transmission. Among V-6 'Birds, look for the élan and Fila special editions, the latter named for the leisure sportswear manufacturer, and decorated to match. T-Birds numbered 170,533 this year. A new offering was Tempo, a front-drive compact offered as a coupe and four-door sedan. It got off to a good start: 402,214 units. Economic times were improving, helping Ford to increase total production to 1,497,097 units.

	Restorable	Good	Excellent
Mustang coupe	*	$2,000-3,000	$3,000-4,500
Mustang GT cpe	*	3,000-4,000	4,000-5,000
Mustang SVO cpe	*	4,500-5,500	5,500-6,000
Mustang cvt	*	4,000-6,000	6,000-8,000
T-Bird Turbo cpe	*	2,500-3,500	3,500-6,500
Thunderbird	*	2,000-3,000	3,000-5,000
Escort Turbo GT	*	1,000-2,500	2,500-3,500
EXP Turbo	*	1,500-2,500	2,500-4,000

*Purchase only in good or excellent condition

1984 Ford Thunderbird Fila coupe

1985 Ford Mustang GT convertible

1986 Ford Mustang GT convertible coupe

1985

All Mustangs adopted an SVO-like front fascia and grille. The Turbo GT was still in the lineup (barely) and the 5.0-liter V-8 was fortified to 210 horsepower with a high-lift camshaft and roller tappets for reduced friction. The '85 SVO, released late, sported 50-series tires on 16-inch wheels. SVO sales slid to 1954 units, while Mustang as a whole increased to 156,514, including 15,110 LX and GT convertibles. A new dashboard, revised grille, and wrapped taillights gave the Thunderbird a different look—the Turbo Coupe retained analog instruments. A graphic equalizer for the stereo system and new power front seat recliners were among the options; a shorter console allowed three to sit in the back seat. Ford trotted out a few thousand 30th Anniversary Edition 'Birds, basically the élan in Medium Regatta Blue, with matching interior and appropriate badging. Production eased to 151,851 'Birds. Escort was handsomely restyled at mid-year with aero headlights, and the three-door GT was still offered with the 120-bhp Turbo engine. A larger 1.9-liter four appeared with the mid-year restyle. Escort output rose to 407,083 units, while EXP increased to 26,462. Total Ford production came to 1,485,633 cars.

	Restorable	Good	Excellent
Mustang coupe	*	$1,500-2,500	$2,500-3,500
Mustang GT cpe	*	3,000-4,000	4,000-5,000
Mustang SVO cpe	*	5,000-6,000	6,000-7,000
Mustang cvt	*	4,000-5,000	5,000-7,000
T-Bird Turbo cpe	*	2,500-3,500	3,500-5,000
Thunderbird	*	2,000-3,000	3,000-4,500
Escort Turbo GT	*	1,000-2,500	2,500-3,500
EXP Turbo	*	500-2,000	2,000-3,000

*Purchase only in good or excellent condition

1986

Ford's slick, aerodynamic new Taurus sedan and wagon debuted, with front-wheel-drive and, initially, a 3.0-liter V-6 with automatic as standard. Later, a

1987 Ford Escort GT hatchback coupe

1987 Ford EXP 2-passenger hatchback coupe

1987 Ford Mustang GT convertible coupe

1987 Ford Taurus LX four-door sedan

2.5-liter four was offered for the sporty MT5 model, though with only 88 bhp it was underpowered. (Taurus' collectibility is by no means established; we list the most likely models.) First year output was 178,737 sedans and 57,625 wagons. Thunderbird was little changed—the V-6 élan is higher-valued than the Turbo Coupe by used car market reports, but the latter is more collectible. The Fila luxury package was dropped. Production increased to 163,965 units. All Mustang V-8s had fuel injection and the SVO made its final appearance, disappearing after just 3382 were built. In all, 224,410 buyers chose Mustangs. EXP was restyled at mid-year, and looked much better with smooth aero headlights, but it was still far from beautiful. EXP and Escort were not offered with turbochargers, but the Escort GT's injected 1.9 four gave that model good acceleration; collectibility of any post-1985 Escorts and EXPs is questionable. A total of 430,053 Escorts and 30,978 EXPs were produced for the model run. Tempo received a two-slot grille and aero headlights this year, while the LTD Crown Victoria adopted an injected 150-bhp version of the 302 V-8. The two-door Crown Vic coupe was still available, though only 6559 were sold (base and LX). For the model run, 1,559,959 Fords were built.

	Restorable	Good	Excellent
Mustang LX 5.0 cpe	*	$2,500-3,500	$3,500-5,000
Mustang SVO coupe	*	5,500-6,500	6,500-7,500
Mustang LX 5.0 cvt	*	4,500-6,500	6,500-7,500
Mustang GT coupe	*	3,500-4,500	4,500-6,000
Mustang GT cvt	*	5,000-7,000	7,000-8,000
Taurus MT5 4-cyl sdn	*	1,500-2,250	2,250-3,000
Taurus LX V-6 sdn/wgn	*	2,500-3,750	3,750-5,000
T-Bird Turbo Cpe	*	3,000-4,500	4,500-6,000
Escort GT & EXP	*	1,000-2,000	2,000-3,000

*Purchase only in good or excellent condition

1987

Ford managed to keep the eight-year-old Mustang up to date with a grilleless front end and aero headlights and, for GTs, extensive body cladding and "decorator" louvered taillights. Inside resided a new instrument panel. Though the SVO was gone, its intercooler turbo engine lived on in the Thunderbird Turbo Coupe: 190 bhp and, with automatic, 150 bhp. The TC also boasted standard antilock brakes. T-Bird also had new styling, but of the same genre—Ford was emphasizing a consistent look, and T-Bird styling had won many accolades. Most noticeable changes on the personal-luxury flagship were aero headlamps, a longer snout, and flush-mounted side glass. Output this year was 159,145 Mustangs (including about 20,000 convertibles) and 128,135 T-Birds. Taurus was carried over with only minor mechanical changes. Escort GT and EXP still came with the high-output 1.9-liter four with multi-point injection. EXP reached just 25,888 buyers. Escort, with motorized seat belts this year, came in at 374,765. Tempo received an All-Wheel-Drive option. LTD Crown Victoria coupe sales were down to just 5527, so the two-door was dropped at the end of the model year. Production came in at 1,474,666 Fords, not counting the new mini Festiva imported from Korea.

	Restorable	Good	Excellent
Mustang LX 5.0 cpe	*	$3,500-5,000	$5,000-6,500
Mustang LX 5.0 cvt	*	6,000-7,500	7,500-9,000
Mustang GT coupe	*	5,500-7,000	7,000-8,000
Mustang GT cvt	*	6,000-7,500	7,500-9,000
Taurus MT5 4-cyl sdn	*	2,000-3,000	3,000-3,500
Taurus LX V-6 sdn/wgn	*	3,500-5,000	5,000-6,000
T-Bird Turbo Coupe	*	4,000-5,500	5,500-6,500
Escort GT & EXP	*	1,500-2,500	2,500-3,500

*Purchase only in good or excellent condition

1988 Ford Mustang GT hatchback coupe

1988

The EXP Sport Coupe was discontinued, but the Luxury Coupe model lived on officially listed as an Escort. Only the Escort GT, however, got the 1.9 multi-port injected performance engine, still rated at 115 bhp. At mid-year, Escort received a restyled rear end. Production, including EXP, was 422,035. The unchanged Mustang found 179,565 buyers, including 33,344 who preferred convertibles. A 3.8-liter V-6 was a new Taurus engine option, giving the same 140 horsepower as the 3.0 unit, but considerably more torque, 215 lbs/ft at a useful 2200 rpm. The still-underpowered MT5 came only as a sedan this year, after which it became history. Taurus output this year was 387,577 units. Turbo Coupe Thunderbirds had a five-speed manual gearbox, analog gauges, anti-lock brakes, electronic ride control, and 16-inch wheels—all standard. T-Birds this year numbered 147,243. LTD Crown Victorias were freshened up this year front and rear via slightly rounded corners and Oldsmobile-like taillights. About 125,000 customers liked the new look. Tempo, though the same underneath, was reskinned to look more like the Taurus. Model year Ford production was 1,606,531 cars.

	Restorable	Good	Excellent
Mustang LX 5.0 cpe	*	$4,000-6,000	$6,000-8,000
Mustang LX 5.0 cvt	*	7,000-9,000	9,000-11,000
Mustang GT cpe	*	6,500-8,000	8,000-9,000
Mustang GT cvt	*	8,500-10,000	10,000-11,500
Taurus MT5 sdn	*	3,000-4,000	4,000-5,000
Taurus LX V-6 sdn/wgn	*	4,500-5,500	5,500-6,500
T-Bird Turbo Cpe	*	5,000-6,500	6,500-8,000
Escort GT	*	2,500-3,500	3,500-4,500

*Purchase only in good or excellent condition

1989

Ford's exotic new front-wheel-drive Probe shared a chassis/drivetrain and five-speed gearbox with

1989 Ford Probe GT hatchback coupe

1989 Ford Thunderbird Super Coupe

1990 Ford Taurus LX four-door sedan

1990 Ford Taurus SHO four-door sedan

Mazda's MX-6, which looked far more conservative than the Probe. Most potentially collectible is the Probe GT, with a 145-bhp turbo four, firm suspension, alloy wheels, and unique front and rear styling. Mustang, which was originally to have been replaced by the Probe, continued with few changes, as did Tempo and LTD Crown Victoria. Thunderbird, however, was completely restyled, remindful of a 6-series BMW. Riding a longer 113-inch wheelbase, it retained rear-wheel drive; underneath was the 'Bird's first independent rear suspension. Topping the line was the Super Coupe with a 210-bhp supercharged 3.8-liter V-6. An important Taurus, the 140-mph SHO performance sedan, offered a 220-bhp V-6 with dual overhead cams and four valves per cylinder, a special handling suspension, and all-wheel disc brakes. SHOs came with five-speed manual transmission only, and were visually identifiable with modest ground-effects body panels, including a front air dam with fog lamps. Production was about 12,000 units per year. A total of 1,433,550 Fords were sold during calendar year 1989, among them 161,148 Mustangs, 348,061 Taurus, 120,634 Thunderbirds, and 133,650 Probes.

	Restorable	Good	Excellent
Probe, 4-cyl	*	$4,500-5,750	$5,750-7,000
Probe GT Turbo	*	6,000-7,250	7,250-8,500
Mustang LX 5.0 cpe	*	6,000-7,500	7,500-9,500
Mustang LX 5.0 cvt	*	8,500-10,000	10,000-12,000
Mustang GT cpe	*	7,500-9,000	9,000-11,000
Mustang GT cvt	*	10,000-12,000	12,000-13,500
Taurus SHO	*	7,500-9,000	9,000-10,500
T-Bird Super Cpe	*	8,000-10,500	10,500-13,000

*Purchase only in good or excellent condition

1990

Probes now came with four-wheel disc brakes; anti-lock brakes were optional. The GT retained its turbocharged engine, but a Ford V-6 was available for the LX. All Probes received subtle styling alterations, and an automatic transmission option. Mustang was hardly changed at all, continuing with its LX and GT coupe and convertible lineup. Thunderbird made few changes to its one-year-old body which, despite being slightly shorter, lower, and narrower, rode a nine-inch-longer wheelbase than the 1983-88 generation. The hot Super Coupe continued; both five-speed manual and four-speed automatic were available. The Escort, Tempo, Taurus, and LTD Crown Victoria were carryovers, though driver-side air bags were becoming available on some models. Calendar year sales were down to 1,268,629, with only the Crown Vic moving upward. Sales slipped to 124,135 for Mustang, to 313,274 for Taurus, 103,062 for Probe, and 106,124 for Thunderbird. The early '90s would be a difficult time in the U.S. auto market as the country once again moved into recession.

	Restorable	Good	Excellent
Probe LX (V-6)	*	$6,000-7,500	$7,500-8,500
Probe GT Turbo	*	7,500-8,500	8,500-10,000

	Restorable	Good	Excellent
Mustang LX 5.0 cpe	*	6,500-7,500	7,500-9,000
Mustang LX 5.0 cvt	*	9,000-10,500	10,500-12,000
Mustang GT cpe	*	8,000-9,500	9,500-11,000
Mustang GT cvt	*	10,000-12,500	12,500-15,000
Taurus SHO	*	9,000-10,500	10,500-12,500
Thunderbird LX	*	7,000-9,000	9,000-11,000
T-Bird Super Cpe	*	10,000-12,500	12,500-14,000

*Purchase only in good or excellent condition

Franklin

Long a respected Classic car, appropriately honored by the Classic Car Club of America, Franklin has a small but enthusiastic following with excellent club support. The cars have a reputation as blue chip investments with slow but steady growth in value over the years. Parts supply is problematic, however.

1930 Franklin Six Pirate 7-passenger phaeton

1930-34

As the only U.S. luxury make to achieve any real success with air-cooled engines, Franklin—established in 1902 in Syracuse, New York—produced interesting, high-tech sixes and V-12s until finally wiped out by the Depression in 1934. The 125-inch-wheelbase Transcontinent Six, introduced at $2395 in 1930, was the cheapest Franklin to date; above it were 125-inch and 132-inch-chassis Sixes (all with 95 bhp). They were strikingly handsome with more rakish clamshell fenders and flowing body lines designed by Ray Dietrich. The last grand hurrah came in 1932: a supercharged, air-cooled V-12 with 398 cubic inches and 150 bhp, mounted on the 132-inch wheelbase Airman chassis. Coachwork was by Franklin's own factory, distinguished by a sharply vee'd hood and rakish windshield. Only about 300 Twelves were built, making them rare and desirable today—even though no production open bodies were built. Sixes numbered 12,000 from 1930-34. The final Franklin series was the low-priced Olympic, sharing its body with the Reo Flying Cloud—a very good car, but not enough to save the company. The most sought-after Franklin Sixes are the 1930 Pirate phaeton and touring, the 1930-32 DeLuxe and Transcontinent convertibles, and the 1933-34 Olympic convertibles.

1932 Franklin Airman Six convertible coupe

1933 Franklin Supercharged Twelve four-door sedan

1933 Franklin Olympic four-door sedan

	Restorable	Good	Excellent
1930-32 Six, open	$7,500-18,000	$18,000-30,000	$30,000-45,000
1930-34 Six, clsd	3,500-10,000	10,000-15,000	15,000-25,000
Twelve	5,000-12,000	12,000-18,000	18,000-30,000
Olympic, open	3,500-10,000	10,000-17,500	17,500-27,500

1948 Frazer Manhattan four-door sedan

1948 Frazer four-door sedan

1949-50 Frazer four-door sedan

Frazer

A quirky car with several interesting permutations, the Frazer is mainly of interest to Kaiser-Frazer collectors, except for the four-door convertible models, which have broad collector appeal. Colorful interiors and low prices make Frazers good entry-level collector cars. Club support is good, but body parts are scarce. Fortunately, mechanical parts supplies are generally good. Investment potential is low, except for convertibles, which are good.

1947-48

Frazer output during this period consisted of only two models: the standard four-door sedan and the up-market Frazer Manhattan sedan, the latter distinguished by elaborate interiors of two-tone Bedford and other broadcloth, or quality pleated leather. One-piece hood/deck nameplates generally adorn the '48 models, individual-letter nameplates the '47s—but there was some overlap. The most collectible cars from this period are the 8940 early '47s manufactured as products of Graham-Paige in Detroit, which was duly noted on the firewall plate. Later plates say Kaiser-Frazer. These were all standard Frazers, from serial number F47-001001 to F47-009940. Frazers weighed in at around 3400 pounds, and were thus a bit underpowered given the Continental L-head six rated at 100 horsepower, or 112 via a dual downdraft Carter carburetor. This didn't matter too much in the early postwar years, but it did become important later as other makers switched over to high-output overhead-valve V-8s. Riding a generous 123.5-inch wheelbase, the smooth-sided Frazers boasted tremendous interior space; the 64-inch front seat, for example, was the widest in the industry. The transmission was the usual three-speed stick, but for about $80 a buyer could specify Borg-Warner overdrive, a useful extra worth seeking out now. At $2295 and $2712 in 1947, prices were high, especially considering that a Series Sixty-One Cadillac sedan started at $2324. In the booming early postwar years, that didn't matter either because production was satisfyingly high: 36,120 base and 32,655 Manhattans for 1947, plus 29,480 base models and 18,951 Manhattans for 1948.

	Restorable	Good	Excellent
Frazer 4d sedan	$500-2,000	$2,000-4,000	$4,000-7,500
Frazer, Graham-Paige	1,500-2,500	2,500-5,000	5,000-8,500
Manhattan 4d sedan	1,000-3,000	3,000-6,000	6,000-9,000

1949-50

The 1949 Frazers were facelifted with a bold and handsome eggcrate grille, large flanking parking lights, and vertical taillights. Hood ornaments are commonly seen, but they were actually made available retroactively. Interiors continued to be striking, consisting of long-wearing houndstooth patterns for the base Frazer and a wide variety of luxury cloth and leather for the Manhattan. Almost as an afterthought came the Manhattan four-door convertible, cobbled out of beefed-up sedan bodyshells with hardtop-like side window frames that did not crank down with the glass. Convertibles featured magnificent leather or leather-and-cloth interiors and vacuum-powered top and window lifts. Only about 70 1949-50 convertibles were built; they rocketed in value during the Eighties, but haven't gained much for the past five years. Frazers for 1950 were simply '49 models with new VIN plates bearing 1950 instead of 1949 prefixes, this a result of overly optimistic production schedules in 1949. Combined output for the two years was approximately 14,700 standard sedans, 9950 Manhattan sedans, and the 70 ragtops.

	Restorable	Good	Excellent
Frazer sedan	$500-2,000	$2,000-5,000	$5,000-8,000
Manhattan sedan	1,000-3,000	3,000-6,500	6,500-9,500
Manhattan cvt	3,000-10,000	10,000-17,500	17,500-25,000

1951

Kaiser-Frazer Corporation rounded up all the unsold 1949-50 K-F bodies and retrofitted them with new Frazer sheetmetal fore and aft: elongated front fenders with a prominent cross-bar grille wearing an elaborate lucite badge and "charging-knight" hood ornament and stretched rear fenders with shallow, flush-fitting taillights sitting on top. The Frazer standard line comprised a four-door sedan and Vagabond utility car, the latter a precursor to the hatchback in which a double hatch opened and the rear seat folded down. The spare tire was bolted to the left rear door, which was welded shut (at least in most cases). The Manhattan line included about 130 leftover four-door convertibles and 150 leftover Kaiser Virginians, the latter convertible-style cars with a hard steel roof. A handful of the Manhattan hardtops sported nylon-covered roofs, but the majority were steel, painted a contrasting color to the lower bodywork. Prototype nameplates read "Hardtop," but didn't appear on production models. Fitted as standard with the optional Hydra-Matic transmission, the Manhattans are highly desirable. The '51 convertible is generally preferred over the 1949-50 ragtop because of its one-year-only styling and last-of-the-line status. In addition to the Manhattans, about 6900 sedans and 3000 Vagabonds were produced. Interestingly enough, dealers ordered about 50,000 '51s, but there were only 10,000 leftover bodies to go around.

	Restorable	Good	Excellent
Frazer sedan	$1,000-3,000	$3,000-6000	$6,000-8,500
Vagabond utility	1,500-4,000	4,000-7,000	7,000-9,500
Manhattan 4d cvt	3,500-12,000	12,000-20,000	20,000-27,500
Manhattan 4d htp	2,500-7,500	7,500-14,000	14,000-20,000

1949-50 Frazer with Kaiser hubcaps

1951 Frazer Manhattan hardtop sedan

1951 Frazer four-door sedan

1933 Graham second series Standard Six four-door

1935 Graham first series Supercharged Custom Eight

1936 Graham Series 110 Supercharger Touring Sedan

Graham

Graham has a limited collector following; only a handful are considered Classics by the Classic Car Club of America (1929-30 Series 837 models), and relatively few have survived. Open models, the later Supercharger series, and the Hollywoods of 1940-41 are the best choices. Club support is fair, body parts very scarce, mechanical parts supplies variable.

1930-39

Graham began the Thirties with a wide variety of L-head sixes and eights featuring Graham-Paige's famous four-speed transmission, which was dropped after 1931. Widely admired were the Custom Eight roadster, phaeton, and 137-inch wheelbase LeBaron town car on wheelbases of 127 and 137 inches. This and other long-wheelbase models were produced in the Custom series only through 1931, and total production of the three models mentioned probably didn't exceed 100. A cut-rate Prosperity Six on a 113-inch chassis was launched in 1931, but didn't prosper much as only about 1000 were produced. Embattled Graham offered one of its finest designs in 1932: the 123-inch-wheelbase Blue Streak Eight, with skirted fenders, "banjo" frame, and outboard-mounted springs. Stylistically, it was a sensation—and widely copied. Only 9714 were built for '32. The Supercharged Custom Eight, appearing in 1934, was another fine car, though with a late introduction only 89 were built. Styling slipped in 1935, when 15,965 cars were built. In 1936, the straight eight was dropped, but Graham now offered America's first supercharged six. The blown six remained a Graham engine through 1941, and it should be noted that in the prewar era Graham built as many supercharged cars as the rest of the industry combined, 5500 in 1936 alone. Crusader and Cavalier were small sixes riding 111- and 115-inch wheelbases, all sedan or coupe models save for a Cavalier convertible in 1937. Total output rose to 19,225 units for 1936, and then slipped slightly to 18,219 for 1937.

Among the best remembered and most collectible Grahams are the "Spirit of Motion" designs beginning in 1938, dominated by a sharply undercut front end that earned it the nickname "sharknose." This art deco masterpiece was another contribution by Amos Northup, who had designed the Blue Streak. There was no shortage of opinion about this car, but everyone agreed (and still agrees) that it was distinctive. The lineup comprised four-door trunkback sedans in 1938, in two models, Six and "Supercharger," each with two different levels of trim. For 1939, a two-door sedan and combination-coupe body were added, yielding twelve different models/body styles. Sharknoses are still around: they're wild, they're fun, and they don't cost a king's ransom. In our opinion, they're the most collectible

Thirties Grahams (except perhaps for some of the drop tops) and will appreciate faster than most. Look for the '39 coupe. Unfortunately, by 1938 Graham was fading fast as only 5020 cars were produced, and although the 1939 figure improved to 5392 units, that clearly wasn't enough.

	Restorable	Good	Excellent
1930-31 Cust open	$7,500-20,000	$20,000-33,000	$33,000-48,000
1930-32 Cust clsd	5,000-8,000	8,000-14,000	14,000-20,000
1930-37 open	5,000-12,000	12,000-20,000	20,000-27,500
1930-36 closed	1,000-3,000	3,000-7,000	7,000-10,000
1936-37 Crusader	500-2,500	2,500-5,000	5,000-7,500
1936-37 Cavalier clsd	500-2,500	2,500-5,500	5,500-8,500
Blue Streak			
1932-33 cvt	6,000-15,000	15,000-25,000	25,000-32,500
1932-33 other	1,000-4,000	4,000-8,000	8,000-12,000
Supercharged Custom Eight			
1934 cvt	5,000-12,000	12,000-22,500	22,500-30,000
1935 cvt	4,000-10,000	10,000-18,000	18,000-25,000
1934-35 clsd	1,000-3,000	3,000-6,500	6,500-9,500
Supercharged Custom Six			
1936-37 cvt	3,500-11,000	11,000-17,500	17,500-25,000
1936-37 other	1,000-3,000	3,000-6,500	6,500-9,500
"Spirit of Motion"			
1938-39 Six	1,000-3,000	3,000-5,000	5,000-8,500
1938-39 Supercharger	2,000-5,000	5,000-8,000	8,000-12,000

1937 Graham Custom Supercharger business coupe

1940 Graham Supercharger Custom four-door sedan

1941 Graham Custom Hollywood four-door sedan

1940-41

Although the "sharknose" cars continued with or without supercharger, only about 1000 were made for the 1940 model year, even though prices started at just $995 for the DeLuxe sedan. Graham's grand finale was the Hollywood, introduced in 1940 as a convertible and sedan, although only a couple of convertible prototypes were actually constructed. Built from old Cord 810/812 Beverly body dies, the Hollywood looked very similar, but sported a distinctive front end (and got rear-wheel drive). Most were powered by the supercharged 120-horsepower six. Despite a price starting at $968 for the 93-bhp Custom Hollywood sedan in 1941, the public had lost confidence in Graham-Paige, and the Hollywood didn't sell. Total production for the two model years was just 1859. Today, Hollywoods are uncommon and sought after, but do not bring the price of their Cord Beverly forebears. They're a budget Cord, sort of—all you have to do is find one....

	Restorable	Good	Excellent
1940 Standard	$1,000-3,000	$3,000-5,000	$5,000-8,500
1940 Supercharger	2,000-5,000	5,000-8,000	8,000-12,000
1940-41 Hollywood	4,000-7,000	7,000-10,000	10,000-17,500

1951 Henry J two-door fastback sedan

1953 Henry J Corsair two-door fastback sedan

1953 Henry J Corsair DeLuxe two-door fastback

Henry J

Like Frazer, the Henry J is largely of interest to the 2000 Kaiser-Frazer collectors, especially since no hardtop or convertible models exist except for the odd custom. Club support is good, body parts supply low, mechanical parts supply good, investment potential low.

1951-54

The compact Henry J was available with either a four or six, both L-heads from Willys. The four-banger was a 134.2-cid unit with 68 horsepower, the six pot a 161-cid mill cranking out 80 horses. If you're buying one today, the six is highly desirable because the economical four is distinctly underpowered. The same fastback two-door body—which road tester Tom McCahill from *Mechanix Illustrated* said "looks like a Cadillac that started smoking too young"—was applied to all models. The only facelift occurred in mid-1952, when a handsomer full-width grille and tailfin-mounted taillights were adopted. Although generally not much sought after, certain Henry J models are worth keeping in mind. The few '51s upholstered by special order in full leather or "Dinosaur vinyl," and the early '52 Vagabond (a reserialed '51 with exterior spare tire but lacking an opening hatch like the Kaiser-Frazer Vagabonds) are particularly desirable. One of these in absolutely perfect 98-point show condition would clear five figures in value. The rarest model year is 1954, but since these were just reserialed '53s, nobody much cares one way or the other. Production started out at an encouraging 81,942 units for 1951, then plummeted to 30,585 in 1952 (including 7017 Vagabonds actually built in 1951), fell further to 16,672 in 1953, and finally crashed to 1123 in 1954. Sears-Roebuck sold a slightly modified Henry J as the Allstate (see entry).

	Restorable	Good	Excellent
Four	$500-2,000	$2,000-4,000	$4,000-6,500
Six	1,000-2,500	2,500-5,000	5,000-8,000

(add 20% for 1952 Vagabond, 20% for all-vinyl or leather upholstery)

1930 Hudson Great Eight Club Sedan by LeBaron

Hudson

Backed by a strong marque club producing highly professional publications and offering varied activities and research and restoration aids, Hudson is a solid choice among independent makes for collectors who want specialist vendors and kindred souls. Postwar Hudsons, which dominate the collector field today, are unique and interesting, with a great competition heritage including winning the NASCAR stock-car title in 1952-53-54. Club support is excellent, body and parts supplies reasonably good, investment potential modest. The 1929 Model L is considered a Classic by the Classic Car Club of America.

1930-39

The best 1930 Hudsons were phaetons and speedsters by Murray, Briggs, and LeBaron. All of these were eights; Hudson did not field a six until 1933, which was essentially a Terraplane in a short-wheelbase Hudson chassis. "Terraplane" was a separate make for 1934-37, an Essex Terraplane in 1932-33, and a Hudson in 1938. Whatever the badge, they were generally fast, always well built, came in a wide range of body styles, and sold as many as 90,253 units in 1937.

The last of the four-square or "classic"-style Hudsons ended in 1933; the 1934-35s were transitional designs, and quite handsome. New styling for 1936 could be compared to the Chrysler and DeSoto Airstreams (but not Airflows), with smooth, art deco curves, bright metal embellishments, skirted rear fenders, and rounded grilles. By 1938, facing a severe recession, Hudson reversed its emphasis on performance and concentrated on economy, adding a low-end Terraplane model and the underwhelming 112 Six, named for its wheelbase. In 1939, Hudson launched the 118-inch-wheelbase Pacemaker Six and replaced the 122-inch Custom Six and Eight with the Country Club Six and Eight, powered by the 101-bhp, 212-cid former Terraplane six and 122-bhp, 254.4-cid straight eight. Two large closed models riding a 119-inch wheelbase were offered under a Big Boy badge, and a Country Club Eight on an extra-long 129-inch wheelbase topped the lineup. The '39s were the best looking Hudsons in years, with horizontal-bar grilles and faired-in headlamps. As with most makes, Hudson rode a roller coaster during the Thirties, with calendar-year production sinking to a low of 2852 cars in 1933 and rising to a high of 81,521 in 1939, the last after the Terraplane was dropped. Prices at the end of the decade ranged from $695 for the 112 DeLuxe Six Traveler coupe to $1430 for a Country Club Eight seven-passenger sedan. Though built in small numbers, Hudson offered both a convertible coupe and brougham in the 112 DeLuxe Six, Six, Country Club Six, and Country Club Eight series.

	Restorable	Good	Excellent
1930-31, open	$7,500-17,500	$17,500-30,000	30,000-45,000
1930-32, closed	2,000-5,000	5,000-8,000	8,000-12,000
1932, open	5,000-12,500	12,500-20,000	20,000-30,000
1933-39, closed	1,000-3,000	3,000-6,000	6,000-9,000
1933, open	3,000-10,000	10,000-17,500	17,500-25,000
1934-37, open	4,000-12,000	12,000-20,000	20,000-30,000
1938-39, open	5,000-17,500	17,500-25,000	25,00-35,000

1940

Since Hudson had restyled in 1939, the '40s were merely facelifted, with very nice results: a rakish, pointed nose; divided horizontal-bar grille; modest side ornamentation. There were seven series on

1934 Hudson DeLuxe Eight 5-window coupe

1935 Hudson Custom Eight Brougham sedan

1936 Hudson Custom Eight Touring Sedan

1938 Hudson DeLuxe Eight four-door sedan

1939 Hudson Series 92 Convertible Brougham

1940 Hudson Eight Convertible Sedan two-door

1941 Hudson Super Six four-door station wagon

1941 Hudson Commodore Eight "Convertible Sedan "

three wheelbases with three different engines: 92- and 98-bhp sixes and 102- and 128-bhp eights. The small six powered the Traveler and DeLuxe on the shorter 113-inch wheelbase; the other engines powered a wide variety of body styles on the Six and Eight and their Country Club (longer wheelbase) derivations. The Big Boy included a Carry-All and seven-passenger sedan running with the 98-bhp six on the Country Club chassis. The main thing to remember here is that convertible coupes and sedans lead all the other body styles; they came on the 118-inch-wheelbase Six and Eight, and the 113-inch-wheelbase DeLuxe. Model year production was 77,295 sixes and 10,620 eights.

	Restorable	Good	Excellent
DeLuxe cvt	$4,000-10,000	$10,000-18,000	$18,000-25,000
Six/Eight cvt	5,000-12,000	12,000-20,000	20,000-30,000
Closed models	1,000-3,000	3,000-6,000	6,000-9,000

1941

Another facelift was performed, most notable for more grille bars, revised hood trim, and parking lights mounted in large fendertop housings on all models. Hudson's unit body was revised for new, longer wheelbases (now 116, 121, or 128 inches), and the Commodore series debuted, listing a wide range of body styles on the 121-inch wheelbase. Commodores could be ordered with the 212-cid six or 255.4-cid eight, except that only the eight was offered on the 128-inch-wheelbase sedans and Commodore station wagon. The Big Boy seven-passenger sedan put in its final appearance, still with six-cylinder power. The '41s were pretty Hudsons, probably the purest from a design standpoint until the famous Step-down series of 1948. Total output increased to 91,769 sixes and 9718 eights. Production estimates for convertibles: 140 DeLuxes, 300 Supers, 200 Commodore Sixes, and 200 Commodore Eights. Wagons were rare, too, with only about 100 Supers and 80 Commodore Eights built.

	Restorable	Good	Excellent
DeLuxe cvt	$4,000-10,000	$10,000-18,000	$18,000-25,000
Super cvt	5,000-12,000	12,000-20,000	20,000-30,000
Commodore cvt	6,000-15,000	15,000-22,500	22,500-32,500
Super/ Commodore wgn	3,000-8,000	8,000-12,000	12,000-18,000
Closed models	1,000-3,000	3,000-6,000	6,000-9,000

1942

Announced in August 1941, the '42 Hudson was one of the nicest looking ever. Running boards were hidden, the grille was low and very clean, and optional parking lights rode atop the fenders. Hudson's famous white triangle logo, placed on either side of the hood, was illuminated after dark. Soundly built and richly appointed, these were excellent cars for the money: $828 to $1451. Most rode the 121-inch chassis, though a 128-inch-wheelbase Commodore Custom Eight sedan was offered in limited quantities and Travelers and DeLuxes still shared a 116-inch span. The war put an end to car production the following February, and only 5396 Hudsons were registered during calendar 1942, though model year production ended at 34,069 Sixes and 6592 Eights.

	Restorable	Good	Excellent
DeLuxe cvt	$4,000-10,000	$10,000-18,000	$18,000-25,000
Super Six cvt	5,000-12,000	12,000-20,000	20,000-30,000
Commodore cvt	6,000-15,000	15,000-22,500	22,500-32,500
Super wagon	3,000-6,000	6,000-9,000	9,000-14,000
Closed models	1,000-3,000	3,000-6,000	6,000-9,000

1942 Hudson Super Six Convertible Sedan two-door

1946

Hudson built airplanes, landing craft, and naval munitions for four years, then resumed passenger car production after the war with a slight but busy facelift of the 1942 bodies featuring a recessed center section of the grille and revised trim along the sides of the hood. As before, sixes and eights were offered, but only in horsepower ratings of 102 and 128. The small 92-bhp, 175-cid six that had powered the Traveler and DeLuxe in prewar years was eliminated. All models were now confined to the 121-inch wheelbase, as production was too small to support the rest. This resulted in four lines: Super Six and Eight, Commodore Six and Eight. Four body styles were offered: four- and two-door sedans, "Brougham" convertible coupe, and club coupe (plus a three-passenger coupe variant). The woody station wagon was dropped. Value-wise, there is little to choose from between Six and Eight. Convertibles were few, only 1177, most of them Supers. Model year production totaled 91,039 units.

	Restorable	Good	Excellent
Commodore cvt	$5,000-12,000	$12,000-22,000	$22,000-32,000
Super cvt	4,000-10,000	10,000-17,500	17,500-25,000
Other models	1,000-3,000	3,000-6,000	6,000-9,000

1946 Hudson Commodore Eight four-door sedan

1946 Hudson Super Six Convertible Brougham

1947

The '47 Hudsons were unchanged except in details, such as a new chrome nameplate on the trunk, right-hand as well as left-hand door locks, and a small lip around the center grille emblem housing. Engines remained a 212-cid six with 102 bhp and a 254.4-cid eight with 128 bhp. Transmission options comprised Vacumotive Drive (automatic clutch operation) and Drive-Master (eliminating both clutch and gear lever motion). Overdrive was also listed. Hudson built 92,083 cars, including just 1823 convertibles; Supers accounted for two-thirds of ragtop output. Production by series was 49,276 Super Sixes, 25,138 Commodore Sixes, 5076 Super Eights, and 12,593 Commodore Eights.

	Restorable	Good	Excellent
Commodore cvt	$5,000-12,000	$12,000-22,000	$22,000-32,000
Super cvt	4,000-10,000	10,000-17,500	17,500-25,000
Other models	1,000-3,000	3,000-6,000	6,000-9,000

1948 Hudson Commodore Eight Convertible Brougham

1949 Hudson Commodore Custom convertible

1949 Hudson Commodore Eight Custom convertible

1948

Hudson's low, sleek Step-down unit body, one of the great postwar designs, was introduced this year. Its dropped floor—hence the Step-down name—was anchored between heavy frame girders, providing outstanding passenger protection. This Hudson handled exceptionally well thanks to its radically low center of gravity. Designed by a team led by Frank Spring, it was beautiful in an understated way, with clean sides, low grille, and modest taillights. The four usual series—Commodore and Super, Six and Eight—were offered on a 124-inch wheelbase. A new 262-cid Super Six developed 121 horsepower, only seven less than the old straight eight that was continued. Convertible production was estimated at about 200: 88 Super Sixes, 48 Commodore Sixes, and 64 Commodore Eights. Total output for the model run was a healthy 117,200 units.

	Restorable	Good	Excellent
Commodore cvt	$5,000-12,000	$12,000-22,000	$22,000-30,000
Super cvt	4,000-10,000	10,000-17,500	17,500-25,000
Other models	1,000-3,000	3,000-6,000	6,000-10,000

1949

The Step-down Hudson for 1949 was identical to the 1948 model except for serial numbers, and indeed it would look pretty much the same for the rest of its long history, lasting until 1954. Although Hudson would create several interesting permutations, the firm lacked the finances to make wholesale design revisions that were needed to produce, for example, a wagon. This, plus reliance on L-head engines and sixes in particular, were to prove damaging for Hudson as competition intensified in the Fifties. An estimated 3119 Brougham convertibles were built this year: 1870 Super Sixes, 655 Commodore Sixes, and 595 Commodore Eights. Production peaked this model year at 159,100 units. Never again would Hudson have it so good.

	Restorable	**Good**	**Excellent**
Commodore cvt	$5,000-12,000	$12,000-22,000	$22,000-30,000
Super cvt	4,000-10,000	10,000-17,500	17,500-25,000
Other models	1,000-3,000	3,000-6,000	6,000-10,000

1950

Hudson produced 121,408 cars this year, including 61,752 copies of its new 119-inch shorter-wheelbase Pacemaker and Pacemaker DeLuxe. Priced a little under $2000 before extras (except for the $2500 convertible), the Pacemaker ran with a destroked 232-cid, 112-bhp version of the Super Six, which still gave it above average performance for its class—equal to a Nash Ambassador, for example. Transmission options were stick-overdrive, Drive-Master (see 1947), and Supermatic Drive. With Supermatic, a high cruising gear was added to Drive-Master—the shift to high occurred automatically at 22 mph when a dashboard button was engaged. The 1950 Hudsons looked much like the

1948-49s, but can be told at a glance by an inverted "V" running down from the Hudson badge atop the grille. Estimated ragtop production was 3322, divided thusly: 1100 Pacemakers, 630 Pacemaker DeLuxes, 465 Super Sixes, 700 Commodore Sixes, and 700 Commodore Eights. In addition to the Pacemakers, Hudson built 17,246 Super Sixes, 24,605 Commodore Sixes, 1074 Super Eights, and 16,731 Commodore Eights.

	Restorable	Good	Excellent
Commodore cvt	$5,000-12,000	$12,000-22,000	$22,000-30,000
Super cvt	4,500-11,000	11,000-20,000	20,000-27,500
Pacemaker cvt	4,000-10,000	10,000-17,500	17,500-25,000
Other models	1,000-3,000	3,000-6,000	6,000-10,000

1951

Although the bodyshell didn't change a whit, this was a momentous year for Hudson—at least for collectors. This was the year of the first Hornet, with its powerful 308-cubic-inch, 145-horsepower L-head six (with a super tough cast iron/chromium block). The Hornet was introduced in four body styles, replacing the Super Eight and priced equal to the Commodore Eight. It soon began winning stock car races, although Oldsmobile was the NASCAR champion in 1951. Hudson also introduced a hardtop, the Hollywood, available on all of the longer 123-inch-wheelbase series. All Hudsons received a modest facelift, with simpler, heavier grille bars, and the four-speed Hydra-Matic automatic transmission from General Motors became an option (Drive-Master and Supermatic were continued only through the model year). The most desirable Hornet body styles remain scarce: only about 500 Brougham convertibles and 2100 Hollywood hardtops were built. However, the Hornet apparently helped, as total Hudson production increased modestly to 131,915 units. Production of the desirable convertible models was an estimated 430 Pacemaker Customs, 280 Super Six Customs, 210 Commodore Six Customs, and 180 Commodore Eight Customs (Custom was "in" this year). Hollywood hardtops weren't very plentiful, either: 1100 Super Six Customs, 820 Commodore Six Customs, and 670 Commodore Eight Customs.

	Restorable	Good	Excellent
Hornet/Comm cvt	$5,000-12,000	$12,000-22,000	$22,000-32,000
Super/Pacemkr cvt	4,500-11,000	11,000-20,000	20,000-27,500
Hollywood htps	2,500-5,000	5,000-9,000	9,000-14,000
Other models	1,000-3,000	3,000-6,000	6,000-10,000

1952

Hudson won both the AAA (American Automobile Club) and NASCAR (National Association for Stock Car Auto Racing) championships. Top driver Marshall Teague led his nearest AAA rival by 1000 points, and Hudsons won 27 NASCAR Grand Nationals. This was the chief news for 1952, since

1950 Hudson Pacemaker four-door sedan

1950 Hudson Commodore Eight Custom convertible

1951 Hudson Commodore Eight Custom Hollywood

1951 Hudson Commodore Eight Custom Hollywood

1951 Hudson Hornet Convertible Brougham

1952 Hudson Hornet Club Coupe

1952 Hudson Hornet four-door sedan

1953 Hudson Hornet Club Coupe

1953 Hudson Super Wasp four-door sedan

the product was again little changed, though a minor trim shuffling took place. The Wasp—a sort of glorified Pacemaker with a more memorable name—replaced the old Super Six, and the Pacemaker convertible was dropped. The Pacemaker and Commodore put in their last appearance this year. Production was way down to 70,000 cars, partly because of an unchanged product and more so, perhaps, because the government severely restricted production because of defense production for the Korean conflict. What it all boiled down to was an extremely limited supply of the most desirable models: 636 soft tops and 3777 Hollywood hardtops, this spread over four model lines. The rarest was the Commodore Eight convertible—only about 30 were produced. Among Hornets, an estimated 360 Brougham convertibles and 2160 Hollywood hardtops were ordered.

	Restorable	Good	Excellent
Hornet/Comm cvt	$5,000-12,000	$12,000-22,000	$22,000-32,000
Wasp/Pacemaker cvt	4,500-11,000	11,000-20,00	20,000-27,000
Hollywood htps	500-5,000	5,000-9,000	9,000-14,000
Other models	1,000-3,000	3,000-6,000	6,000-10,000

1953

"Twin-H Power"—twin carbs and dual-manifold induction—were offered this year on the Hornet and Hudson's new Jet, a well-engineered performance compact riding a 105-inch wheelbase and powered by a 202-cid six. With Twin-H Power, the up-market Super Jet developed 114 bhp, distinctly better than anything in its price class at the time. The base horsepower rating was 104. Unfortunately, the Jet's dowdy looks and relatively high price ($1858 and up) killed it among buyers. Availability of only two- and four-door sedans didn't help, either. Racing Hornets could be had with the special 7-X engine, using .020 overbore cylinders, special cam and head, larger valves, higher compression, Twin-H Power and headers; they developed about 210 bhp. Regular Twin-H Hornets cranked out 160 horsepower (this option had actually become available in mid-1952). The big Hudsons were modestly facelifted with a new dummy hood scoop and a cleaner grille, and a new Super Wasp model arrived in place of the departed Commodores. Super Wasps included hardtops and convertibles, but retained the smaller, 119-inch wheelbase, and were a bit chunkier by comparison to the longer Hornets. Look for Twin-H Hornets and Jets, the rare Super Wasp convertible (only about 50 built) and, of course, the 7-X engine, as esoteric as any six of its time. Production slipped this year to 66,143 units: 21,143 Jets, 17,792 Wasps and Super Wasps, and 27,208 Hornets. Hollywood hardtops numbered 1501, about 910 of them Hornets.

	Restorable	Good	Excellent
Hornet cvt	$5,000-12,000	$12,000-22,000	$22,000-32,000

	Restorable	Good	Excellent
Super Wasp cvt	4,500-11,000	11,000-20,000	20,000-27,500
Hollywood htp	2,500-5,000	5,000-9,000	9,000-14,000
Jet, with Twin-H	1,500-3,000	3,000-5,000	5,000-8,500
Jet, other	1,000-2,500	2,500-4,000	4,000-7,000
Other models	1,000-3,000	3,000-6,000	6,000-10,000

1954

Hudson's last year as an independent saw a new luxury model Jet-Liner and a Hornet Special priced $150 under the Hornet, but available only as a four-door sedan, two-door club sedan, and club coupe. The other Jets and Wasps continued. Wasps and Hornets were easily distinguished by their broad hood scoop, single-bar grille, and high-riding, triangular taillamps fitted to newly squared-up rear fenders. The Jet also sparked Hudson's Italia, a four-seat grand touring coupe designed by Frank Spring and built by Carrozzeria Touring of Milan, Italy. Italias had wrapped windshields, doors cut into the roof, fender scoops that ducted cooling air to the brakes, flow-through ventilation, and form-fitting leather seats—and a high $4800 price tag. Wild looking for the mid-Fifties, Italias are avidly sought after by Hudson fans, but only 25 "production" versions and one prototype were built; 20 are believed to be 1954 models. A four-door Hornet Italia prototype was also built, and still exists. Model year production fell to 50,670 units: 14,224 Jets, 11,603 Wasps and Super Wasps, and 24,833 Hornets and Hornet Specials. Due to a fire at GM's Hydra-Matic plant, some Hudsons were equipped with a Borg-Warner automatic this year. Hudson took the NASCAR championship again in 1954, and from 1951-54 had won 78 NASCAR events; runner-up Oldsmobile had won only 43. Hudson, very much the junior partner, merged with Nash on May 1, 1954, to form American Motors. Henceforth all Hudsons would be Nash-based and built in Kenosha, Wisconsin.

1954 Hudson Hornet Convertible Brougham

1954 Hudson Wasp four-door sedan

1954 Hudson Super Jet Club Sedan

1954 Hudson Italia coupe

	Restorable	Good	Excellent
Italia	$10,000-20,000	$20,000-30,000	$30,000-40,000
Hornet cvt	$5,000-12,000	12,000-22,000	22,000-32,000
Super Wasp cvt	4,500-11,000	11,000-20,000	20,000-27,500
Hollywood htps	2,500-5,000	5,000-9,000	9,000-14,000
Jet, with Twin-H	1,500-3,000	3,000-5,000	5,000-8,500
Jet, other	1,000-2,500	2,500-4,000	4,000-7,000
Other models	1,000-3,000	3,000-6,000	6,000-10,000

1955

After Hudson merged with Nash to form American Motors in 1954, Hudson's Detroit plant was closed and the Jet and big Step-down models were scrapped. Hudson appeared as a differently styled Nash, using Nash bodyshells but with Hudson ornamentation and the familiar '54 Hudson dashboard. Engines were familiar, too: the 202-cid Jet six for the Wasp and the 308-cid six (with or without Twin-H) for the Hornet. As before, the Wasp was distinctly

1955 Hudson Hornet Custom Hollywood hardtop coupe

1955 Hudson Wasp four-door sedan

1956 Hudson Hornet V-8 Hollywood hardtop coupe

1956 Hudson Wasp four-door sedan

chunkier than the Hornet, with a shorter wheelbase: 114.3 inches versus 121.3. There was now a Hornet V-8, a 208-bhp, 320-cid unit built by Packard. The '55 big Hudsons were quite nice styling workouts based on the Nash body, though entirely different from the old Step-down. A bold eggcrate grille topped by the Hudson triangle and bodyside two-toning were featured. Body styles consisted of a four-door sedan and two-door hardtop, still named Hollywood. Hudson dealers also sold Nash Metropolitans and Ramblers wearing Hudson badges, and a few leftover Italias (five Italias are said to be 1955 models). Production this year was estimated at 46,000 units, about half of them Ramblers. Hornets and Wasps totaled 20,321. Hollywood hardtops included 1640 Wasps, 1554 Hornet Sixes, and 1770 Hornet V-8s.

	Restorable	Good	Excellent
Italia	$10,000-20,000	$20,000-30,000	$30,000-40,000
Wasp/Hornet sdns	750-1,500	1,500-4,000	4,000-7,500
Wasp Hollywood htp	1,500-3,000	3,000-7,000	7,000-11,000
Hornet Hollywood htp	2,000-4,000	4,000-8,500	8,500-13,000
Metropolitan	500-1,500	1,500-3,500	3,500-5,500
Rambler	500-1,500	1,500-4,000	4,000-6,000

1956

American Motors introduced its own 250-cid, 190-bhp V-8 this year, replacing the Packard V-8 in mid-season for the Hornet Special. The small Wasp remained, as did the Hornet Six, along with the usual assortment of Hudson Ramblers and Metropolitans. AMC called Hudson's 1956 design "V-Line Styling," but customers called it a lot of other things, and collector consensus since is that it represented the ugliest Hudson in a generation. Featured were a fine mesh grille with the "V" theme top and bottom, rear fender peaks combined with new taillights, and three-tone paint and anodized aluminum side trim on Hornets. The small AMC V-8 was not nearly the performer the Packard V-8 had been. Only a little over 10,000 big Hudsons were built this year, most of them Hornets and Hornet Specials; the only Wasp was a four-door sedan on the 114.3-inch wheelbase. Ramblers were completely restyled this year, and the Custom series listed a four-door hardtop sedan and Cross Country hardtop wagon. Hudson model year output fell to 35,671 units, 10,671 of them Wasps and Hornets. Hollywood hardtop production came to just 229 Hornet Specials, 358 Hornet Sixes, and 1053 Hornet V-8s.

	Restorable	Good	Excellent
Wasp	$500-1,500	$1,500-3,000	$3,000-6,000
Hornet sedans	750-1,500	1,500-4,500	4,500-8,000
Hornet Hollywood htp	2,000-4,000	4,000-8,500	8,500-13,000
Metropolitan	500-1,500	1,500-3,500	3,500-5,500
Rambler	500-1,500	1,500-4,000	4,000-6,000

1957

The Hornet Super and Custom—sedans and Hollywood hardtops—were all mounted on the Nash Ambassador's big 121.3-inch wheelbase and powered by AMC's new 327 V-8 with 255 horsepower, a distinct improvement on 1956's 190 bhp. Styling was somewhat better too, or at least more unified, though the "V-Line" theme was still apparent. Deluxe interiors, neat little vestigial fins, and broad, spear-like panels trimmed in anodized aluminum were featured. Only 4180 of these Hudsons were built, most of them four-door sedans, making them extremely scarce today. Their status as the very last of a respected badge has helped their value. The Rambler was listed as a separate make starting this year, but a few Hudson Metropolitans were still sold. Originally, a stretched Rambler was to become the '58 Hudson (and '58 Nash), but at the last moment it was decided to kill both grand old names. Instead, the long Rambler became the Rambler Ambassador.

1957 Hudson Hornet Custom Hollywood hardtop coupe

	Restorable	Good	Excellent
Hornet sedan	$1,500-3,000	$3,000-6,500	$6,500-11,000
Hornet Hollywood htp	3,000-5,000	5,000-10,000	10,000-15,000
Metropolitan	500-1,500	1,500-3,500	3,500-5,500

Hupmobile

General comments on Hupp follow those for Graham: a limited collector following in an era of diminishing interest—the late prewar years. Open models and Skylarks are the best choices for investment. Club support is nil, body parts are very scarce, mechanical parts scarce.

1930 Hupmobile Model C rumble-seat coupe

1930-39

Hupmobile had been a respected nameplate since 1908, and in 1928 the firm enjoyed its best-ever year as more than 50,000 registrations were recorded. Hupp's 1930 line comprised the six-cylinder S series and three straight eights, the C, H, and U series. The S and C were bread-and-butter models riding a 111- and 121-inch wheelbase, respectively. The first had a 211.6-cid, 70-bhp six, the latter a 268.6-cid, 100-bhp six, both L-heads. The H and U shared the same 365.6-cid, 133-bhp straight eight, though the H rode a 125-inch wheelbase, the U a stretched 137-inch chassis for a luxurious limousine and seven-passenger sedan. Hupp built 22,183 cars in calendar 1930. Similar things happened in 1931, when the 118-inch-wheelbase L-series Century was added. It had a smaller straight eight: 240.2-cid, 90-bhp. No matter, the Depression saw to it that output dropped to 17,451. Beginning in 1932, Hupp designated model year and wheelbase in series codes; thus, B-216 indicated a 1932 six-cylinder

1932 Hupmobile F-222 Sport Coupe with rumble seat

1934 Hupmobile Model J-421 "Aerodynamic" four-door

1937 Hupmobile Six Model 822-E four-door sedan

series on a 116-inch wheelbase. This same year saw Raymond Loewy arrive to style the graceful F-222 and I-226 eight-cylinder models with tire hugging cycle-type fenders, vee'd radiator grilles, sloping windshields, and chrome wheel discs. Despite this, production fell to 10,476 units. The '33s were '32 carryovers with a more sloping grille. Two new cycle-fender Sixes, the K-321 and K-321A, had stationary hood louvers and single wiper and taillight, as Hupp tried to cut prices to the bone to garner a handful of sales. It didn't help—production tumbled to 7313. Loewy's radical "Aerodynamic" model debuted on an eight-cylinder chassis for 1934 with its three-piece wrapped windshield, faired-in headlights, and flush-mounted spare tires—an interesting, highly collectible car. Calendar-year output rallied a bit to 9420 units. A smaller Aerodynamic Six with a flat windshield and a Model O Eight arrived in 1935, helping boost production to 10,781. No matter, Hupmobile closed in 1936 after 1556 cars had been built (and supposedly there were 138 cars assembled in 1937), but then reopened in 1938 with the conventional 822-E Six and 825-H Eight, which carried on into 1939. As since 1936, there were only two engines: a 101-bhp, 245.3-cid six and a 120-bhp, 303.2-cid eight. Industry sources disagree as to the existence of 1937 models—if there are any, they would be identical to 1936.

Some collector generalities: 1) Through 1934, the classic, crisp styling and smooth performance, of Eights especially, makes open Hupps quite desirable. 2) The open cars were very low-volume items and are today almost impossible to find. 3) The 1935-39 cars are very cheap and will certainly remain that way. 4) Hupps are not common on the auction circuit, so collectors who despise auctions can shop happily in the classifieds. 5) Later Hupps are ideal for collectors without much to spend, but who want a good car they can enjoy for a long time.

	Restorable	Good	Excellent
1930-31 Six, open	$7,500-15,000	$15,000-25,000	$25,000-35,000
1930-31 Eight, open	10,000-20,000	20,000-28,000	28,000-42,500
1930-32, closed	4,000-8,000	8,000-15,000	15,000-23,000
1932, open	10,000-20,000	20,000-28,000	28,000-45,000
1933-34, open	9,000-18,000	18,000-32,500	32,500-40,000
1933-35, closed	3,000-7,500	7,500-12,000	12,000-18,000
1936-39	2,000-4,500	4,500-7,000	7,000-10,000
1934-35 Aerodynamic			
427-T, 527-T (8)	4,000-9,000	9,000-15,000	15,000-22,500
521-J (6)	2,500-5,000	5,000-7,500	7,500-11,000

1940

In partnership with Graham, Hupp revived the old Cord Beverly sedan, using the old Cord body dies and a 115-inch wheelbase (10 inches shorter than Cord's). Hupp's version of this famous four-door fastback was called the Skylark, with a unique front end (not unlike that of the original Cord) and the 101-bhp six-cylinder powerplant. The Hupp Six was livelier than the standard Graham Six, but the supercharged Graham Hollywood was faster. Skylarks—

production 319—are far scarcer than Hollywoods—1859 built—although collectors given the choice tend to prefer the supercharged version of the Hollywood, for obvious reasons. But finding a Skylark is a challenge.

	Restorable	Good	Excellent
Skylark	$2,000-5,000	$5,000-8,000	$8,000-15,000

1941 Hupmobile Skylark Custom four-door sedan

1941

Delays in getting the assembly operation going—partly because of the complex, multi-piece Cord dies—condemned both Hupmobile and Skylark. Hupp officially quit automaking in October 1940, after the final Skylarks had been built in July. Only 103 Hupps were registered in 1941. The 1941 models were identical to the '40s. After reorganization under bankruptcy, Hupp became a components producer, and today makes industrial heating and air conditioning units as a subsidiary of White Consolidated Industries.

	Restorable	Good	Excellent
Skylark	$2,000-5,000	$5,000-8,000	$8,000-15,000

Imperial

1955 Imperial four-door sedan

Imperial's fate as a separate make from 1955-75 and 1981-83 varies directly with the topsy-turvy history of Chrysler Corporation itself, and its standing among car collectors is just as uneven. Recently, an Imperial club was organized to cater to the make alone, but most everybody considers the Imperial a model of the Chrysler (as it was before 1955 and is again), and Chrysler's top marque has never rivaled the market values of comparable Cadillacs. Club support is good, however, and so is the mechanical parts supply, though body parts are scarce.

1955 Imperial Newport hardtop coupe

1955

Imperial's first year as a declared separate make was a fine start, with styling based on Virgil Exner's K-310 show car and outstanding engineering with the famous Chrysler 331-cid Hemi V-8, this year with 250 horsepower. A divided eggcrate grille, enormous eagle hood ornament, and stand-up "gunsight" taillamps were identifying features. A four-door sedan and Newport hardtop were offered, both riding a 130-inch wheelbase (four inches longer than the Chrysler New Yorker). First-year production was modest: 7840 sedans and 3418 Newports. The traditional Crown Imperial rode a 149.5-inch wheelbase, though only 45 eight-passenger sedans and 127 limousines were built.

1956 Imperial four-door sedan

1957 Imperial LeBaron Southampton hardtop sedan

1957 Imperial Crown convertible coupe

	Restorable	Good	Excellent
4d sedan	$2,000-5,000	$5,000-8,000	$8,000-12,000
Newport 2d htp	3,500-7,500	7,500-11,000	11,000-16,500
Crown Imp limo	3,000-7,500	7,500-11,000	11,000-17,500
Crown Imp 8P sdn	2,500-6,000	6,000-8,000	8,000-11,000

1956

The hardtop and sedan wheelbase was stretched to 133 inches, identical to the Cadillac Sixty Special sedan and four inches longer than the mainstream Cadillac Series Sixty-Two models. For 1956, the Imperial sprouted modest tailfins, but was otherwise of much the same design. The two-door hardtop was now called Southampton, and was joined by a four-door hardtop of the same name. They accounted for 2094 and 1543 sales, but were overshadowed by the 6821 sedans called for. The only significant option was air conditioning. Crown Imperial long-wheelbase models continued to be built in very limited numbers: just 51 sedans and 175 limousines for the model year. All models were boosted to 280 horsepower for '56.

	Restorable	Good	Excellent
4d sedan	$2,000-5,000	$5,000-8,000	$8,000-11,000
Southampton 2d htp	3,500-7,500	7,500-11,000	11,000-16,500
Southampton 4d htp	2,500-6,000	6,000-9,000	9,000-13,500
Crown Imperial limo	3,000-7,500	7,500-11,000	11,000-17,500
Crown Imp 8P sdn	3,500-6,000	6,000-8,000	8,000-11,000

1957

Virgil Exner's "Forward Look" bestowed huge tailfins and a complicated, full-width grille on the new Imperial, which nearly outsold Lincoln and enjoyed its highest production ever in history: 37,593 units. Two new series—Crown and LeBaron—were added. In addition to the four-door sedan and hardtop, the Crown included a new convertible model, while the luxury-laden LeBaron sedans were priced considerably higher than the other models: about $900 more than the base four-doors and nearly $350 above the Crowns. An enlarged 392-cid Hemi rated at 325 horsepower was standard on all models, which now rode a shorter 129-inch wheelbase. Beginning in 1957, Crown Imperial limousines were built by Ghia of Turin, who began by extending unfinished two-door hardtop bodies, adding 20.5 inches to the wheelbase, and finishing off the exterior using 1560 pounds of lead filler. Production was infinitesimal—only 36 this year. By the time Ghia quit building them in 1965, Crown Imperial volume had amounted to only 132 units. Despite their size, the '57 Imperials were roadworthy cars, benefitting from Chrysler's new torsion-bar front suspension. The top-shelf Crowns were rare: 1729 sedans and 911 Southampton hardtop sedans. The Crown convertible found only 1167 takers. Southampton hardtop coupes were more common: 4885 base models and 4199 Crowns.

	Restorable	Good	Excellent
4d sedans	$2,000-5,500	$5,500-9,000	$9,000-12,000
4d hardtops	2,500-6,000	6,000-9,500	9,500-13,500
2d hardtops	3,500-7,500	7,500-11,000	11,000-17,500
Crown convertible	7,500-15,000	15,000-22,500	22,500-30,000
Crown Imp limo	3,500-9,000	9,000-17,500	17,500-25,000

1958

Changed only slightly from 1957, Imperial gained circular parking lights and a more complex grille filled with four rows of wide, low rectangles. Models and body styles were unaltered, but prices were up a bit and horsepower climbed to 345. The luxurious LeBaron four-door sedan and hardtop were very rare in this model year—just over 500 of each were built. Crown convertibles were also scarce, totaling just 675 units, and the Crown Imperial saw just 31 limos constructed. With 4146 built, the most popular model of the year was the Crown Southampton hardtop sedan. Overall, production nosedived to just 16,133 units, partly due to a sharp recession in 1958.

1958 Imperial Crown convertible coupe

1958 Imperial Crown Southampton hardtop sedan

	Restorable	Good	Excellent
4d sedans	$2,000-5,500	$5,500-9,000	$9,000-12,000
4d hardtops	2,500-6,000	6,000-9,500	9,500-13,500
2d hardtops	3,500-7,500	7,500-11,000	11,000-17,500
Crown convertible	7,500-15,000	15,000-22,500	22,500-30,000
Crown Imp limo	3,500-9,000	9,000-17,500	17,500-25,000

1959

Imperial styling was more extensively facelifted, featuring a toothy grille (looking for all the world like it had been ripped off a '54 Chevy) and added brightwork adorned the sides, particularly on the lower rear quarter panels. The standard series was now designed Custom, but the 10-model lineup was otherwise unchanged. Departing from Hemi engines, Imperial adopted a 413-cubic-inch wedgehead V-8, which with 350 horsepower provided performance comparable to the Hemi but was more economical to build and maintain. Hardtops offered three roof options. With a production run of 17,719 units, Imperial finally outsold Lincoln this year (but only if the Mark IV Continentals are not counted in). LeBarons totaled 1132 four-door hardtops and sedans, and only 555 Crown convertibles were built. Southampton two-doors weren't common, either: 1743 Customs and 1728 Crowns.

1959 Imperial Crown Southampton hardtop coupe

	Restorable	Good	Excellent
4d sedans	$2,000-5,500	$5,500-9,000	$9,000-12,000
4d hardtops	2,500-6,000	6,000-9,500	9,500-13,500
2d hardtops	3,500-7,500	7,500-11,000	11,000-17,500
Crown convertible	7,500-15,000	15,000-22,500	22,500-30,000
Crown Imp limo	3,500-9,000	9,000-17,500	17,500-25,000

1960

Though Imperial again outsold Lincoln (not counting the Mark V Continentals), it was far behind

1960 Imperial Crown convertible coupe

1960 Imperial LeBaron Southampton hardtop sedan

1961 Imperial Crown convertible coupe

1961 Imperial Custom Southampton hardtop coupe

1962 Imperial Crown Southampton hardtop sedan

Cadillac. The tally was 142,184 units versus 17,719. Though the Imperial received new lower sheetmetal, more humped fins, revised grille, and a vee'd front bumper, the heroically finned models had already fallen behind the styling curve of 1960. Swivel front seats were optional in some models, as was a simulated spare tire cover for the rear deck. The 413 wedge V-8 continued to provide 350 bhp, and Imperial stuck to body-and-frame construction even though the rest of the corporation went Unibody. Southampton hardtop sedans were the best sellers: 3953 Customs, 4510 Crowns, and 999 LeBarons. Crown convertible output increased slightly to 618, and after only seven units in 1959, Crown Imperial limo production shot up to 16 units.

	Restorable	Good	Excellent
4d sedans	$2,000-4,500	$4,500-7,000	$7,000-9,000
2d hardtops	2,500-5,000	5,000-8,500	8,500-12,000
Crown convertible	5,000-10,000	10,000-17,500	17,500-25,000
Crown Imp limo	3,500-9,000	9,000-17,500	17,500-25,000

1961

Retaining the 1960 shell, the '61 Imperial was the most extroverted yet, with yet taller tailfins, free-standing headlamps pocketed in the curve of the front fenders, and free-standing taillights to match. These were the idea of Virgil Exner, who was influenced by classic cars. This odd feature was retained through 1963—check these out on prospective purchases because new-old-stock replacements are extinct and restoration is expensive. Four-door sedans were eliminated from the Custom, Crown, and LeBaron lines, dropping the model count to seven. The old "classic" styling touches were controversial, which may explain why production fell to just 12,258 units for the model year. Only 889 Custom and 1007 Crown Southampton hardtop coupes were built, and the Crown convertible fell to just 429 units. The Crown Imperial limo attracted only nine orders.

	Restorable	Good	Excellent
Hardtops, all	$2,000-4,000	$4,000-7,500	$7,500-9,500
Crown convertible	5,000-10,000	10,000-17,500	17,500-25,000
Crown Imperial limo	3,500-9,000	9,000-17,500	17,500-25,000

1962

Small styling changes added up to a much less controversial appearance this year. Tailfins were pared down to mere nubs of what they had been, and the new, elongated bullet taillamps, still free-standing but now returned to the fender tops, blended better with the rear fenders. Up front, the free-standing headlamps returned, and the grille was now split down the middle. Sales improved commensurately to 14,337, but the lion's share went to the Southampton four-door hardtops. The Crown convertible was very scarce with just 554 built, and the Southampton two-door hardtops were far behind with 826 Customs and 1010 Crowns produced.

	Restorable	Good	Excellent
Hardtops, all	$2,000-4,000	$4,000-7,500	$7,500-9,500
Crown convertible	5,000-10,000	10,000-15,000	15,000-22,500
Crown Imp limo	3,000-7,000	7,000-13,000	13,000-20,000

1962 Imperial Custom hardtop coupe

1963

Imperial received a mild facelift, highlighted by a new grille composed of elongated rectangles, a crisp new roofline, and a restyled rear deck with the free-standing taillights replaced by thin, built-in lenses. The lineup was unchanged and production was about the same: 14,121 units. Broken down, there were 749 Custom and 1067 Crown Southampton hardtop coupes; 3264 Custom, 6960 Crown, and 1537 LeBaron Southampton hardtop sedans, 531 Crown convertibles, and 13 Crown Imperial limos. Prices this year ranged from $5058 for a Custom hardtop coupe to $18,500 for the Ghia-built limo.

1963 Imperial Crown Southampton hardtop sedan

	Restorable	Good	Excellent
Hardtops, all	$2,000-4,000	$4,000-7,500	$7,500-9,500
Crown convertible	5,000-10,000	10,000-15,000	15,000-22,500
Crown Imp limo	3,500-7,000	7,000-13,000	13,000-18,000

1963 Crown Imperial limousine

1964

Still riding a 129-inch wheelbase, the Imperial was treated to a complete restyling under the direction of Elwood Engel, making the '64 reminiscent of his beautiful 1961 Lincoln Continental. A divided grille recalled the appearance of the '55s, while the remains of a spare tire outline was left on the deck. The roofline was angular and formal, the bodysides flat. The bottom-line Custom series was eliminated, along with the Southampton designation for hardtop body styles—all Imperials except the Ghia Crowns were again pillarless. Customers responded to the improved looks of the '64 Imperials, causing production to jump to 23,295 units. The Crown convertible reached 922 buyers this year, well up from its usual 500. Output of the other four models was 5233 hardtop coupes and 14,181 hardtop sedans in the Crown series, 2949 LeBaron hardtop sedans, and 10 Crown Imperial limos.

1964 Imperial Crown convertible coupe

	Restorable	Good	Excellent
Hardtops, all	$1,500-3,000	$3,000-4,500	$4,500-7,500
Crown convertible	4,000-8,000	8,000-12,000	12,000-17,500
Crown Imp limo	3,500-7,000	7,000-13,000	13,000-18,000

1965 Crown Imperial limousine

1965

The Crown and LeBaron line received a mild facelift, most notably a new grille with glass-enclosed quad headlamps. Stylist Engel had now perfected the formal look he wanted for Chrysler Corporation's luxury line leader, but production sank somewhat to 18,409 units. In Italy, Ghia assembled its last 10 Crown Imperial limousines this year. They

1965 Imperial Crown convertible coupe

1966 Imperial Crown convertible coupe

1966 Imperial Crown convertible coupe

1967 Imperial Crown hardtop sedan

remained priced at $18,500. With 11,628 built, the $5772 Crown hardtop sedan was easily the year's best seller, followed by the $5930 Crown hardtop coupe at 3974 units. The LeBaron hardtop sedan, which listed at $6596, came in at 2164.

	Restorable	Good	Excellent
Hardtops, all	$1,500-3,000	$3,000-4,500	$4,500-7,500
Crown convertible	4,000-8,000	8,000-12,000	12,000-16,000
Crown Imp limo	3,500-7,000	7,000-13,000	13,000-18,000

1966

Once more, the Engel-styled Crowns and LeBarons were offered with only detail changes. The grille was a cellular affair, each cell housing the familiar elongated rectangle. Back-up lights and taillights were inset into the rear bumper as before. The 413 V-8 was bored out to 440 cubic inches; running with 10.0:1 compression, it was rated at 350 bhp. Production dropped considerably to 13,742 units, with the Crown convertible sinking to a more normal 514 units. Crown hardtop sedans and coupes came in at 8977 and 2373, respectively, while the LeBaron hardtop sedan fell back to 1878. All of the above models measured 227.8 inches in length. Although Ghia limousine production had stopped, 10 Crown Imperials were constructed in Spain using 1966 grilles and rear decks.

	Restorable	Good	Excellent
Hardtops, all	$1,500-3,000	$3,000-4,500	$4,500-7,500
Crown convertible	4,000-8,000	8,000-12,000	12,000-16,000
Crown Imp limo	3,500-7,000	7,000-13,000	13,000-18,000

1967

Chrysler's experience with unit body/chassis production was sufficient now to include the Imperial, which—unlike all other Chrysler cars since 1960—had continued with separate body-on-frame construction in order to assure stress strength and good assembly quality. As Unibody cars, the all-new '67 Imperials were completely restyled, featuring prominent block-letter badging in the center of a fine-mesh grille, pointed front fenders housing parking lights, vertical rear bumper ends, and strong horizontal "character lines" along clean bodysides. Basically a glorified Chrysler again, wheelbase contracted to 127 inches (three inches longer than Chrysler), and a price-leader four-door pillared sedan returned. Priced at $5374, it was $359 cheaper than the least expensive '66 model. Production increased to 17,620 units, broken down thusly: 2193 four-door sedans, 577 convertibles, 3235 Crown hardtop coupes, 9415 Crown hardtop sedans, and 2194 LeBaron hardtop sedans. In addition, Stageway (a Fort Smith, Arkansas, firm) produced a half-dozen limos on a stretched 163-inch wheelbase. Overall length of these monsters was 260 inches.

	Restorable	Good	Excellent
Sedan & 4d htps	$1,500-3,000	$3,000-4,000	$4,000-7,000
Crown 2d hardtop	2,000-3,500	3,500-5,000	5,000-8,500
Crown convertible	4,000-7,000	7,000-11,000	11,000-15,000

1968 Imperial Crown hardtop sedan

1968

Imperial was only slightly altered this year. Highlights included a more massive-looking grille extending around the front fenders to enclose parking and cornering lights and dual moldings on lower bodysides. Rear side marker lights—required by government mandate—were also new. Narrow paint stripes were applied along the beltline on all models. The 350-bhp 440 V-8 was still standard, though dual exhausts and twin-snorkel air cleaners were optional, upping output to 360 horses. This year marked the final appearance of the Imperial convertible, 474 of which were built. Total output this year was 15,367, which included 2656 hardtop coupes and another half-dozen Stageway limo conversions. The balance of production was four-door hardtops, save for 1887 pillared sedans.

1969 Imperial Crown hardtop coupe

	Restorable	Good	Excellent
Sedans & 4d htps	$1,500-3,000	$3,000-4,000	$4,000-7,000
Crown 2d htp	2,000-3,500	3,500-5,000	5,000-8,500
Crown convertible	5,000-8,000	8,000-13,000	13,000-17,500

1969 Imperial LeBaron hardtop sedan

1969

Though the Imperial retained its exclusive 127-inch wheelbase, declining sales forced a decision calling for Chrysler Corporation's flagship to share more Chrysler sheetmetal. This marked the beginning of a reabsorption of Imperial into the Chrysler model ranks, though it wouldn't occur formally for another six years. Lacking a convertible, the line consisted of Crown and LeBaron two- and four-door hardtops (the first two-door LeBaron), and a Crown four-door sedan. New styling stretched overall length by five inches, yet weight was down by about 100 pounds. Neater front and rear styling provided a wide, wide look, emphasized up front by hidden headlights. Sales were good—22,103 units made 1969 the third best year in Imperial history. LeBaron hardtop sedans took the bulk of sales, 14,821 units, leaving the remaining models relatively rare: 224 Crown two-door hardtops, 823 four-door hardtops, 1617 four door sedans. The LeBaron hardtop coupe found 4592 customers. An estimated half-dozen LeBaron limousines were again turned out by Stageway.

	Restorable	Good	Excellent
Sedans & htps	$1,500-3,000	$3,000-4,000	$4,000-6,000
LeBaron limo	3,500-7,000	7,000-12,000	12,000-16,000

1970 Imperial Crown hardtop coupe

1971 Imperial LeBaron hardtop sedan

1972 Imperial LeBaron hardtop coupe

1972 Imperial LeBaron hardtop coupe

1973 Imperial LeBaron hardtop sedan

1970

A simpler rectangle-theme grille (again with hidden headlamps) highlighted the '70 Imperial up front. Segmented taillights lens identified the rear end. All in all, the '70s were arguably the cleanest Imperials in history. Ventless side glass was a feature of air conditioned coupes. This was the last year for the Crown series, which was losing most Imperial sales to the LeBaron. The pillared sedan had been eliminated this year, and only 254 Crown two-door hardtops and 1333 four-door hardtops were produced. LeBarons numbered 1803 hardtop coupes and 8426 hardtop sedans. Stageway built a few more limos.

	Restorable	Good	Excellent
Sedans & htps	$1,500-3,000	$3,000-4,000	$4,000-6,000
LeBaron limo	3,500-7,000	7,000-12,000	12,000-16,000

1971

With a single LeBaron series consisting only of two- and four-door hardtops, the Imperial sported a somewhat busier grille and revised trim. More importantly, Imperial moved into the Chrysler lineup, losing its independent status. Production came in at 1442 LeBaron hardtop coupes and 10,116 LeBaron hardtop sedans. The 440 V-8, detuned to meet emission standards, now developed 335 bhp.

	Restorable	Good	Excellent
2d & 4d htp	$1,000-2,500	$2,500-3,500	$3,500-5,000

1972

The '72 was facelifted, with crisper lines and bold upright grillework. Electronic ignition was new and horsepower, now expressed in *net* bhp, was 225. Bendix anti-skid brakes were optional at $250; an electric sunroof cost an extra $584.75. Prices for both LeBarons still began under $7000, and 15,804 were built, just 2332 of them hardtop coupes.

	Restorable	Good	Excellent
2d & 4d htp	$1,000-2,500	$2,500-3,500	$3,500-5,000

1973

Imperial received a new, finer, horizontal-mesh grille, which gave it a cleaner look, but mandatory five-mph "crash" bumper guards spoiled the effect. A vinyl roof and "power everything" was standard. Net horsepower was down to 215, while overall length increased slightly to 229.6 inches. Output was 2563 LeBaron hardtop coupes and 14,166 LeBaron hardtop sedans.

	Restorable	Good	Excellent
2d & 4d htp	$1,000-2,500	$2,500-3,500	$3,500-5,000

1974

The LeBaron was completely restyled, now sporting a split "waterfall" grille composed of fine vertical bars and vertical parking lights in the style of Lincoln's popular Continental. Headlights remained hidden. Ribbed velour upholstery and four-wheel power disc brakes were among the long list of standard equipment. The body, shared again with the New Yorker, rode a shorter, 124-inch wheelbase, but overall length was up to 231.1 inches, partly because five-mph bumpers were now required front and rear. The same pair of LeBaron hardtops was offered, now priced at $7673 and $7804. Two-door production was up to 3850 units, but the four-door dropped to 10,576.

1974 Imperial LeBaron hardtop sedan

	Restorable	Good	Excellent
2d & 4d htp	$1,000-2,500	$2,500-3,500	$3,500-5,000

1975

The last Imperial (until 1981, that is) was introduced on October 1, 1974, part of 6102 LeBaron hardtop sedans and 2728 LeBaron coupes that made up 1975's model year output. Styling was unchanged from 1974, though the base price of the two-door was up to $8698. An ultra-luxurious Crown Coupe option, $569 worth of extra interior and exterior embellishments, was the most desirable version. Though the Imperial nameplate was gone, the car itself would live on for several years badged as the Chrysler New Yorker Brougham. With less standard equipment and a base price of $6641, Chrysler sold nearly 40,000 of them for 1976.

1975 Imperial LeBaron Crown Coupe

1975 Imperial LeBaron Crown Coupe

	Restorable	Good	Excellent
2d & 4d htp	$1,000-2,500	$2,500-3,500	$3,500-5,000
Crown Coupe	$1,500-3,000	$3,000-4,000	$4,000-6,000

1981

Chrysler relaunched the Imperial as a separate make, now in the form of a limited-production personal-luxury coupe weighing nearly two tons and equipped with everything in the options book—and base-priced at nearly $20,000. The formal styling was of the "razor-edge" school, reminiscent of mid-century British coachwork, as well as the 1980-85 Cadillac Seville and 1982-87 Lincoln Continental. Power came from a new fuel-injected version of Chrysler's venerable 318 V-8 rated at 140 bhp. No-cost options included Mark Cross leather or cloth upholstery, digital instruments, clearcoat paint, and a variety of sound systems. An oddball of minor collector interest is the "Frank Sinatra" package, with special trim and a load of Sinatra tape cassettes—148 Imperials were so designated out of the 7225 built.

1981 Imperial coupe

	Restorable	Good	Excellent
Standard edition	*	$2,500-4,000	$4,000-5,000
FS edition	*	3,000-4,500	4,500-6,000

*Purchase only in good or excellent condition

1981 Imperial coupe

1982 Imperial Frank Sinatra Edition

1982 Imperial Frank Sinatra Edition

1983 Imperial coupe

1982

Guess what? The reincarnated Imperial didn't sell. Thus little change was made for 1982, although new interiors were offered using Kimberley velvet cloth upholstery in six choices of color. Colors were Sterling Silver, Golden Tan, and Light Blue "Crystal Coat." A mere 2329 Imperials were built, and of those just 279 had the Sinatra package. Their future scarcity suggests some collector potential, although there are scarcer cars that are going nowhere. Our guess is that you should buy this car only if it appeals to you for its own character, and not as an alternative IRA.

	Restorable	Good	Excellent
Standard edition	*	$2,500-4,000	$4,000-5,000
FS edition	*	3,000-4,500	4,500-6,000

* Purchase only in good or excellent condition

1983

Attempting to use up what was left of this singularly unsuccessful Imperial, Chrysler cut its price from $20,988 in 1982 to $18,688 in 1983, offered new colors inside and out, and dropped the Sinatra edition. Upholstery was Kimberley velvet, Mark Cross cloth, or Corinthian leather. Production was only 1427 units, making the '83 the rarest of this three-year series; as the most recent, it's also the one you are likely to find in the best possible condition—and it doesn't pay to bother about "restorable" ones. Although dropped at the end of the 1983 model run, the Imperial would resurface again in 1990, this time as a more luxurious and stretched version of the 1989 Chrysler New Yorker sedan.

	Restorable	Good	Excellent
2d coupe	*	$3,000-4,500	$4,500-6,000

1947½-48 Kaiser Special four-door sedan

Kaiser

Henry J. Kaiser's namesake offers modest investment potential—and plenty of entertainment through its variety of interesting features, imaginative color combinations, and innovative styling. Club support is good, body parts supply problematic, mechanical parts supply good. Investment potential is modest.

1947-48

Intended to break ground with front-wheel drive, the production Kaiser was a conventional front-engine, rear-drive sedan sharing its body and mechanical components with the Frazer. The difference was that the Kaiser was more affordable, if more cheaply finished. Styling was slab-sided, setting a postwar trend, with generous glass area for the time. The interior of the base K-100 Kaiser Special was spartan;

the up-market K-101 Custom was better, but this model is extremely rare: fewer than 7000 were built over two years. Offered as a conventional four-door sedan with a 100-bhp Continental-based L-head six, the Kaiser was no powerhouse (the Custom had 112 horses, and needed it). A long 123.5-inch wheelbase provided a good ride. The 1947-48 model years are virtually the same, but can often be told apart by the presence of individual hood/deck letters on '47s and one-piece letters on '48s—there is some overlap, however, so it's safest to check VIN plates. For 1947, 65,062 Specials and 5412 Customs were built; for 1948 the figures were 90,588 and 1263.

	Restorable	Good	Excellent
Special 4d	$1,000-3,000	$3,000-5,000	$5,000-8,000
Custom 4d	3,000-4,500	4,500-7,500	7,500-12,000

1949-50

Restyled to provide a more massive look, the '49 Kaiser sported broad horizontal grille bars, rectangular parking lights, and more prominent taillights. As before, there were two series with 100 and 112 bhp, but the up-market DeLuxe expanded with three new body styles: the Vagabond utility sedan with a double-opening rear hatch and fold-down back seat; a four-door convertible, with permanent chrome frames for the power side windows; and a Virginian hardtop version of the convertible (which was launched just before GM's new two-door hardtops). Both the ragtop and Virginian had a little fixed, framed window in lieu of a B-pillar. The base Kaiser line also contained a Traveler hatchback, but the DeLuxe Vagabond is the one to look for, being much better trimmed inside. Virginians came with padded and painted tops; the latter is less common. For the 1950 model year, leftover Kaisers were re-serialed with 1950 VIN plates—but this model year lasted less than six months because the '51s were introduced in March 1950. Virginians and convertibles are scarce: Kaiser produced only 946 Virginians and perhaps 60 ragtops. An estimated 22,000 Travelers and 4500 Vagabonds were built out of a total 1949-50 run of 95,175 cars (about 16 percent were considered 1950 models).

	Restorable	Good	Excellent
4d sedans	$1,000-3,000	$3,000-6,000	$6,000-9,500
Traveler utility	1,000-3,500	3,500-7,000	7,000-11,000
Vagabond utility	1,500-4,500	4,500-8,500	8,500-13,000
Virginian 4d htp	2,500-7,000	7,000-13,000	13,000-20,000
4d convertible	3,000-10,000	10,000-17,500	17,500-25,000

1951

An all-new Kaiser styled by Dutch Darrin and Duncan McRae set a new standard for lowness and visibility, but the underpinnings were conventional and the 226.2-cubic-inch L-head six was still the only powerplant, now rated at 115 horsepower. At 118.5 inches, the wheelbase was five inches shorter than before. The restyled Kaiser offered a genuine

1949-50 Kaiser DeLuxe Virginian hardtop sedan

1949 Kaiser DeLuxe Vagabond utility sedan

1949-50 Kaiser Special Traveler utility sedan

1949 Kaiser DeLuxe "Glass Green" four-door sedan

1951 Kaiser Special Traveler two-door utility sedan

1951 Kaiser DeLuxe four-door sedan

1952 Kaiser DeLuxe four-door sedan

1953 Kaiser Carolina two-door sedan

1953 Kaiser "Hardtop" Dragon four-door sedan

1953 Kaiser "Hardtop" Dragon four-door sedan

safety interior and some of the best handling on a separate body-and-frame Detroit automobile at that time. A wide variety of body styles was offered, but two-door models, club coupes, and Travelers in particular, are extremely rare and thus more desirable. Several specially trimmed show cars exist, along with a limited edition called the Dragon, with exotic pleated vinyl upholstery and, in some cases, padded vinyl tops. Hydra-Matic transmission was optional for the first time on all Kaiser models. Model year production was an encouraging 139,452 units. Traveler two-doors numbered about 2500, four-door Travelers about 3000, two-door sedans about 21,000, club coupes about 7500.

	Restorable	Good	Excellent
Dragon	$2,000-4,000	$4,000-8,000	$8,000-13,000
2d models	1,500-3,000	3,000-7,000	7,000-11,000
4d models	1,000-2,500	2,500-5,500	5,500-9,500

1952

A number of leftover '51 Kaisers were reserialed as early 1952 models and called Virginians. Aside from black plastic-embellished hood ornaments, they were identical to 1951 production, although many featured exterior spare tires. In mid-1952, the "genuine" '52s were announced, slightly restyled, with one-piece windshields and teardrop taillights. These later '52s comprised a base DeLuxe and luxury Manhattan series. Whether they included Traveler utility models is questionable, but if these exist they were probably DeLuxes. A handful of Dragons was built out of Manhattans sedans, usually painted bright blue with tan vinyl interiors. These are virtual show models and would, of course, command a premium. Total Virginian production was 5579, and DeLuxe/Manhattan output was 26,552. Estimated model breakdowns are 5000 four-door sedans, 2000 two-door sedans, and 500 club coupes in the DeLuxe range, plus 16,500 four-doors, 2000 two-door sedans, and 500 club coupes in the Manhattan line.

	Restorable	Good	Excellent
2d models	$1,500-3,000	$3,000-7,000	$7,000-11,000
4d models	1,000-2,500	2,500-5,500	5,500-9,500

1953

Kaiser introduced the "Hardtop Dragon," in reality a four-door sedan, but comprehensively equipped and luxuriously trimmed with special interior cloth-and-vinyl upholstery and padded vinyl or canvas tops. All Dragons featured Hydra-Matic transmission, whitewalls, dual-speaker radio, Calpoint custom carpeting on floor and trunk, and a gold dashboard medallion engraved with the owner's name. The '53 Dragon sold for $4000 (as much as a Cadillac Coupe de Ville!) and was instantly identifiable by its gold-plated exterior trim—but at the price K-F managed to unload only 1277 of them. Aside from the Dragon, and a stripped model called the

Carolina, 1953 changes were slight, though horsepower went up to 118 and power steering was offered late in the season as an option. Instant model-year identification is the "sabre jet" hood ornament and the small chrome tailfins on rear fenders. Production came to 7883 DeLuxes, 17,957 Manhattans, and 1182 Carolinas. About 1000 Travelers and 4400 two-door sedans were built.

	Restorable	Good	Excellent
Dragon sedan	$2,500-5,000	$5,000-9,000	$9,000-15,000
2d models	1,500-3,000	3,000-7,000	7,000-11,000
4d models	1,000-2,500	2,500-5,500	5,500-9,500

1954

Kaiser reduced its passenger car line to two- and four-door sedans only, elegantly facelifted with a concave vertical-bar grille, combination headlamp/parking lamp panels, and glitzy, all-way-visible taillights with illuminated strips running along the rear fenders. Models consisted of a Special and the more luxurious Manhattan. The latter was equipped with a McCullough supercharger, the first blown production car since the prewar Graham; it developed 140 horsepower and offered much improved performance from the 226.2-cid six. Early Specials were leftover 1953 Manhattans with the '53 dash and "Bambu" vinyl/Boucle cloth upholstery. Later Specials and Manhattans featured a new aircraft-inspired dashboard and fully wrapped rear windows. Kaiser also produced the fiberglass Darrin two-seat sports car with its novel sliding doors, an imaginative design by Dutch Darrin using Henry J underpinnings, 100-inch wheelbase, and a Willys F-head 161-cid six developing 90 bhp. Unfortunately, the company was dying, and production of all these interesting vehicles was slight: 435 Darrins, about 4110 Manhattans, 3500 early Specials, and 929 late Specials. Two-door sedans were rare: 250 Manhattans, 500 early Specials, and 125 late Specials.

	Restorable	Good	Excellent
Darrin	$10,000-18,000	$18,000-27,500	$27,500-32,500
Manhattan 2d	2,000-4,000	4,000-9,000	9,000-13,000
Other models	1,500-3,000	3,000-7,000	7,000-12,000

1955

The Kaiser line was reduced to Manhattan two- and four-door sedans, but the majority of production was exported to Argentina, where Henry Kaiser had gone to set up a vehicle facility. Only 226 Manhattan four-doors and 44 two-doors were built for the American market. These are easily distinguished from the '54s by their hood ornament/scoop, which contains a high center "sail" and four small flanking sails, distinct from the plainer '54 version. These, of course, can be switched, so look for serial numbers. Prefixes are 51367 for the four-door, 51467 for the two-door. The rare '55s are worth a premium.

	Restorable	Good	Excellent
Manhattan 2d	$2,500-4,500	$4,500-10,000	$10,000-14,000
Manhattan 4d	2,000-3,500	3,500-11,000	11,000-13,000

1953 Kaiser DeLuxe Traveler four-door utility sedan

1954 Kaiser Special four-door sedan

1954 Kaiser-Darrin 2-passenger roadster

1955 Kaiser Manhattan four-door sedan

1930 LaSalle 7-passenger sedan

1932 LaSalle convertible coupe

1934 LaSalle Series 350 Club Sedan four-door

1936 LaSalle Series 50 Stationary Coupe

1937 LaSalle Series 50 2-passenger coupe

LaSalle

As Cadillac's prewar companion make from 1927, LaSalle has a strong following, especially for the pre-1934 "Classic" models (as defined by the Classic Car Club of America), but these tend to be pricey. The '27 is generally credited with being the first American car to actually be "styled," and by none other than the legendary Harley Earl, who set up GM's famed Art & Colour Section. LaSalles are interesting cars, usually handsome, with many winning qualities. LaSalle was also one of the first makers to offer a true convertible, this way back in 1927. Club support is excellent, body parts scarce, mechanical parts supply fair. Investment potential is good to excellent.

1930-40

Planned before the Depression, the '30 LaSalles were longer, heavier, and costlier than the 1929 models, offering Fisher and Fleetwood lines from coupes and sedans up to elaborate phaetons and cabriolets. Cost cutting occurred in 1931, and LaSalle received a single 353-cid flathead V-8 through 1933 (when it had 115 bhp), using 130-, 134- and 136-inch wheelbases and a smaller array of body styles. A new approach was tried in 1934, when LaSalle abandoned the luxury market and slashed prices, using a 240.3-cid, 95-bhp Oldsmobile L-head eight and GM's new "Knee-Action" independent front suspension. Through 1936, models comprised coupes, convertibles, and sedans and shorter wheelbases (119 and 120 inches). Then in 1937, the wheelbase was stretched to 124 inches and the Olds engine dropped in favor of a 125-bhp V-8 from the Cadillac Series Sixty. The public responded and LaSalle production set a record, but sales plummeted again in recession year 1938. By 1939, dual-make lineups such as Pontiac-Oakland, Olds-Viking and Buick-Marquette had long disappeared, except at Cadillac. Trying to keep LaSalle going, designers reworked the car with more glass, a shorter 120-inch wheelbase, even an optional metal sunroof for sedans. Styling was revised again for 1940, and quite good, thanks in part to a three-inch wheelbase increase, but a marketing decision had already been made, so LaSalle was replaced for 1941 by the bottom-line Cadillac Sixty-One. Today's collectors are divided. Through 1933, LaSalle produced grand, luxurious cars that are rare and desirable; from 1934, it produced upper-medium-priced cars with attractive attributes but by no means the exclusivity of the earlier years. Both in their way are worth considering. From 1934 through 1940, all open LaSalles were convertible coupes with the addition of a convertible sedan from 1937; the latter is worth marginally more than a convertible coupe in the same condition. Production from 1930-40 ranged from a low of 3482 units in 1933, and hit a high of 32,000 units in 1937, then dropped back to

14,635 in 1938, bounced back to 21,127 in 1939, and ended at 24,130 in 1940. Convertible sedans were rare: 265 in 1938, 185 in 1939, and 200 in 1940. During the same period, 855, 1056, and 1024 convertible coupes were built. Sunroof sedans numbered 72 in 1938, 427 in 1939 (23 of them two-doors).

	Restorable	Good	Excellent
1930-33, open	$15,000-30,000	$30,000-70,000	$70,000-110,000
1930-33, closed	7,500-15,000	15,000-35,000	35,000-50,000
1934-35, open	10,000-25,000	25,000-50,000	50,000-75,000
1934-35 coupes	5,000-12,500	12,500-25,000	25,000-35,000
1934-35 sedans	3,500-9,000	9,000-15,000	15,000-25,000
1936-40 cvt cpe	7,500-17,500	17,500-40,00	40,000-60,000
1937-40 cvt sdn	10,000-20,000	20,000-50,000	50,000-65,000
1936-40 coupes	4,000-9,000	9,000-15,000	15,000-25,000
1936-40 sedans	4,000-7,500	7,500-12,500	12,500-20,000

1940 LaSalle Series 52 Special 2/4-passenger coupe

Lincoln

Though a long way from Cadillac in collector acceptance and even esteem, Lincoln offers many high points throughout its seven-decade-long history. Its products are firmly ensconced among the most highly sought-after American cars: the K-series customs of the Thirties, Zephyrs, Continentals, "Road Race" Lincolns, the finned monsters of the late Fifties, and Sixties Continentals. Club support is excellent, but body and mechanical parts supplies are scarce through 1960, spotty thereafter. Investment potential is generally good except for workaday four-door sedans. (Note: For the 1956-58 Continental Mark II and III, see "Continental.")

1930-39

Lincoln began building cars in the summer of 1920 with the Model L, a well-engineered but conservatively styled luxury car. After only 3407 cars were built, Henry Ford bought the company in 1922, and son Edsel soon became involved in running the division. Power during the '20s came from a 357.8-cid, 81-bhp L-head V-8, but by 1930 90 bhp was being developed from 385 cid. The lavish but anachronistic Model L was replaced in 1931 by the Model K, with a modernized 120-bhp V-8. Its new chassis was actually designed for the V-12 that arrived in 1932 as the Model KB, a magnificent city and highway car with great roadability and impressive appearance. A smaller 382-cid V-12 (the KA) succeeded the V-8 in 1933, on a shorter chassis topped by Murray-built bodies sporting a rakish vee'd radiator and skirted fenders. In 1934, KA and KB both switched to a bored-out, 414-cid version of the smaller V-12, retaining their separate 136- and 145-inch wheelbases. In this form, the Model K—as it was called from 1935—carried on through the 1930s, updated in styling and produced in increasingly small quantities.

1930 Lincoln Series L 3-window Town Sedan

1931 Lincoln Series K 2-passenger coupe by Judkins

1932 Lincoln Series KA Sport Phaeton

1933 Lincoln Series KB 2-window Berline by Judkins

1934 Lincoln Series KB Convertible Victoria by Brunn

1935 Lincoln Series K Convertible Sedan by Brunn

1936 Lincoln Series K 3-window four-door sedan

1936 Lincoln-Zephyr four-door sedan

1939 Lincoln non-collapsible Cabriolet by Brunn

An answer to LaSalle and the Packard One Twenty was the 1936 Lincoln-Zephyr, a radical unibody design by John Tjaarda with a genuinely aerodynamic shape, powered by a small L-head V-12 (based on the Ford V-8). Zephyr styling was pure art deco and some of it was among the best of the late Thirties. Especially desirable are the coupe and convertible sedan, added to the line in 1937, and the convertible coupe, added a year later. Hydraulic brakes didn't appear until 1939. Zephyr V-12s are prone to problems stemming from overheating, a product of inadequate water passages, and excessive internal wear, the result of inadequate oil flow. Hydraulic lifters (1938) helped, but collectors should be very careful to check prospective purchases. Nonetheless, non-stock engine swaps are undesirable, even though many have been made over the years.

Production during the '30s went from a low of 1434 Lincolns in 1935 to a high of 30,875 in 1937, most of these Lincoln-Zephyrs. Many of the Lincolns of the '20s and '30s carried custom bodies made by the finest coachbuilders in the business, and production runs were often extremely tiny.

	Restorable	Good	Excellent
1930 L, open	$20,000-50,000	$50,000-80,000	$80,000-110,000
1930 L, closed	10,000-25,000	25,000-50,000	50,000-75,000
1932-34 KA, open	20,000-50,000	50,000-90,000	90,000-125,000
1932-34 KA, closed	7,500-20,000	20,000-35,000	35,000-50,000
1930-34 KB			
Open customs	40,000-80,000	80,000-125,000	125,000-200,000
Open factory body	30,000-70,000	70,000-100,000	100,000-150,000
Closed bodies	10,000-25,000	25,000-50,000	50,000-75,000
1935-39 K			
K, open	15,000-30,000	30,000-60,000	60,000-100,000
K, closed	10,000-20,000	20,000-45,000	45,000-70,000
Zephyr			
1936-39 sedans	5,000-10,000	10,000-17,500	17,500-25,000
1937-39 coupe	6,000-12,000	12,000-20,000	20,000-27,500
1937-39 cvt sdn	8,000-15,000	15,000-30,000	30,000-45,000
1938-39 cvt cpe	7,500-12,500	12,500-27,500	27,500-42,500

1940

The Lincoln-Zephyr Continental, one of the most stunning designs of the Forties, was conceived by Edsel Ford in 1939 and brought to life as a production car by the ingenious stylist Bob Gregorie. A club coupe and convertible were offered, both priced under $3000, which was remarkable—404 were built, only 54 of them soft top models. The rest of the Zephyr line comprised two series with standard or Custom interiors, the latter including a special five-passenger Town Limousine. The Zephyr convertible sedan was dropped after only 302 had been produced for 1939. Brunn also built four Zephyr Custom Town Cars, three of which went to the Ford family, and four Town Limousines. The Model K continued, but a much smaller array of models was offered, including only two open models, a Brunn convertible victoria and a LeBaron roadster. Only 133 K's were built. Zephyr and Continental had a bored out version of the little V-12, now displacing 292 cubic inches with 120 bhp; K's had the familiar 150-bhp, 414-cid V-12, but this was its last year. Zephyr production included 3500 club coupes, 1256 three-passenger coupes, 700 convertibles, and 15,764 four-door sedans.

	Restorable	Good	Excellent
Continental cvt	$10,000-20,000	$20,000-40,000	$40,000-60,000
Continental cpe	7,500-15,000	15,000-27,500	27,500-40,000
Model K, open	15,000-25,000	25,000-50,000	50,000-75,000
Model K, closed	7,500-15,000	15,000-27,500	27,500-40,000
Zephyr cvt cpe	10,000-17,500	17,500-27,500	27,500-40,000
Zephyr coupes	5,000-10,000	10,000-17,500	17,500-25,000
Zephyr sedans	3,500-8,000	8,000-14,000	14,000-20,000

1940 Lincoln-Zephyr 3-passenger coupe

1940 Lincoln-Zephyr Continental Club Coupe

1941

Continental became a separate and distinct Lincoln series for '41, and production increased to 400 convertibles and 850 coupes. The big K series was dropped in favor of Zephyr-engined, long-wheelbase Lincoln Customs, a limousine and long sedan on a 138-inch wheelbase (an increase of 13 inches). Output was 295 and 355 units, respectively. Zephyr sedans and club coupes remained Lincoln's chief breadwinners with 14,469 and 3750 sales. The Zephyr Town Limousine was dropped, but the convertible and three-passenger coupe remained, though only 725 and 972 were built. As in 1940, some Zephyrs were available with custom interiors. Styling changes were slight, but '41 Zephyrs can be identified by their fender-mounted parking lights, Continentals by their pushbutton exterior door knobs and combination parking lights/directional signals.

1941 Lincoln Continental Cabriolet

	Restorable	Good	Excellent
Continental cvt	$10,000-20,000	$20,000-40,000	$40,000-55,000
Continental cpe	7,500-15,000	15,000-27,500	27,500-37,500
Custom lwb	5,000-9,000	9,000-15,000	15,000-22,500
Zephyr cvt cpe	10,000-17,500	17,500-27,500	27,500-40,000
Zephyr coupes	5,000-10,000	10,000-17,500	17,500-25,000
Zephyr sedans	3,500-8,000	8,000-14,000	14,000-20,000

Franklin D. Roosevelt's Lincoln K "Sunshine Special" with 1942 front styling

1942

Though truncated because of the halt in car production following American entry into World War II, 1942 was significant for design and engineering changes. Lincoln adopted a bored 305-cid V-12 with 130 horsepower and offered Liquamatic semi-automatic transmission (it was so troublesome it was quickly dropped). It also featured a flashy facelift that prefigured the look of its first postwar cars in 1946. All models had longer, higher fenders, which increased the Continental's length by more than seven inches. Height was down, but weight was up about 200 pounds. Front ends wore a bold two-tier, horizontal-bar grille, and the front fenders were decorated by parking lights flanking both sides of each headlamp. The last prewar Lincoln left the factory on February 10, 1942, after only 6547 cars had been

1942 Lincoln Custom 8-passenger sedan

1942 Lincoln Continental Cabriolet

1946 Lincoln Club Coupe

1946 Lincoln convertible coupe

1946 Lincoln convertible coupe

1946 Lincoln Continental Cabriolet

assembled. Continentals numbered 136 convertibles and 200 club coupes, while the long-wheelbase Custom saw just 47 eight-passenger sedans and 66 limos built. The three-passenger coupe put in its last appearance, and only 273 were bought (just 20 of them with auxiliary seats). In addition, 1236 club coupes, 4418 four-door sedans, and 191 convertibles were produced.

	Restorable	Good	Excellent
Continental cvt	$10,000-20,000	$20,000-40,000	$40,000-55,000
Continental cpe	7,500-15,000	15,000-27,500	27,500-40,000
Custom lwb	5,000-9,000	9,000-15,000	15,000-22,500
Zephyr cvt cpe	10,000-17,500	17,500-27,500	27,500-40,000
Zephyr coupes	5,000-10,000	10,000-17,500	17,500-25,000
Zephyr sedans	3,500-8,000	8,000-14,000	14,000-20,000

1946

Long-wheelbase Customs were dropped for 1946, along with the three-passenger coupe. The Zephyr name was dropped, too, so the standard passenger cars—sedan, club coupe, and convertible—were simply called Lincoln. The closed models were available with standard or custom interiors. A bold two-tier eggcrate grille was the main identification point, though trim had also been shuffled about. Continentals again appeared as a coupe or cabriolet (convertible), also with the new grille. A winged globe was adopted for the hood ornament. All Lincolns continued to ride on the 125-inch wheelbase, but reverted to the 120-bhp 292 V-12 after less than 2000 305 V-12s had been produced, this because of problems in casting the block of the 130-bhp 305. Continental production was 201 cabriolets and 265 coupes, quite low compared to the 16,179 Lincolns built.

	Restorable	Good	Excellent
Continental cvt	$10,000-20,000	$20,000-37,500	$37,500-47,500
Continental cpe	7,500-15,000	15,000-25,000	25,000-32,500
Lincoln cvt	10,000-17,500	17,500-27,500	27,500-37,500
Lincoln coupe	4,000-7,500	7,500-12,500	12,500-17,500
Lincoln sedan	3,000-6,000	6,000-10,000	10,000-14,000

1947

The '47 Lincolns were not introduced until the spring of that year. They were virtually identical to the '46 models, but for quick identification they had pull-out door handles rather than pushbuttons, a longer wing on the hood ornament, pocket-type interior armrests, and Lincoln script on the rear sides of the hood. Horsepower of the 292 V-12 was up by five, to 125. Continentals were virtually unchanged, but production increased to 452 cabriolets and 847 coupes; they were priced at $4746 and $4662. The three Lincoln body styles, which listed at $2533 to $3142, saw 19,891 total examples built. Custom interiors were still offered on the sedan and club coupe.

	Restorable	Good	Excellent
Continental cvt	$10,000-20,000	$20,000-37,500	$37,500-47,500

	Restorable	Good	Excellent
Continental cpe	7,500-15,000	15,000-25,000	25,000-32,500
Lincoln cvt	10,000-17,500	17,500-27,500	27,500-37,500
Lincoln coupe	4,000-7,500	7,500-12,500	12,500-17,500
Lincoln sedan	3,000-6,000	6,000-10,000	10,000-14,000

1948

For one last time, Lincoln appeared with its prewar designs and low revving V-12 engine. Both Lincoln and Continental were identical to 1947, and can be told only by serial numbers. The reason for the lack of change was that the all-new 1949 Lincolns were set to debut in April 1948. For that reason, production was down to 6470 Lincolns, plus 452 Continental cabriolets and 847 club coupes.

	Restorable	Good	Excellent
Continental cvt	$10,000-20,000	$20,000-37,500	$37,500-47,500
Continental cpe	7,500-15,000	15,000-25,000	25,000-32,500
Lincoln cvt	10,000-17,500	17,500-27,500	27,500-37,500
Lincoln coupe	4,000-7,500	7,500-12,500	12,500-17,500
Lincoln sedan	3,000-6,000	6,000-10,000	10,000-14,000

1949

Lincoln considered—but dropped—the idea of continuing the Continental series within its all-new '49s. Instead, it concentrated on the higher selling models, bringing out a standard and Cosmopolitan series on 121- and 125-inch wheelbases. The smaller Lincoln shared many body components with Mercury, while the Cosmopolitan was unique unto itself. Each line contained a coupe, sedan, and convertible; the Cosmo also had a Town Sedan. Styling was of the bar-of-soap school, but dignified, with "frenched" head- and taillights, conservative grilles, and smooth, rounded lines. Cosmopolitans were recognizable by a large curved one-piece windshield, broad chrome gravel deflectors over the front wheelwells, and thin window frames. Lincoln discarded the V-12 this year, switching to a 336.7-cid L-head V-8 with 152 bhp (an engine borrowed with modifications from the Ford F7 and F8 heavy truck lines). Also featured (finally) was independent front suspension. Beginning in June 1949, GM's Hydra-Matic became available. Convertibles, as always, are the cars to look for, but there is a value difference between the standard and Cosmopolitan versions. Due to an early April 22, 1948, introduction, the model year was a long one, thus the record production figure of 73,507 cars. The Cosmopolitan contributed with 18,906 Sport Sedans (notchbacks), 7302 Town Sedans (fastbacks), 7685 coupes (two-door sedans), and 1230 convertibles. The three-model little Lincoln lineup saw production reach 38,384 units.

	Restorable	Good	Excellent
Cosmo cvt	$5,000-12,000	$12,000-18,000	$18,000-25,000
Cosmo sdn/cpe	2,500-6,000	6,000-8,000	8,000-12,000
Standard cvt	4,000-10,000	10,000-15,000	15,000-20,000
Standard sdn/cpe	2,500-6,000	6,000-8,000	8,000-11,000

1946 Lincoln four-door sedan

1949 Lincoln Sport Sedan four-door

1949 Lincoln Cosmopolitan Town Sedan fastback

1950 Lincoln Cosmopolitan Sport Sedan

1951 Lincoln club coupe

1951 Lincoln Cosmopolitan convertible coupe

1951 Lincoln Lido club coupe

1952 Lincoln Cosmopolitan four-door sedan

1950

A new dashboard created by Tom Hibbard was introduced: an attractive rolled affair with an oblong window covering the instruments; variations of that design survived on Lincolns through 1956. The grille was simpler, with one instead of two horizontal bars. Special limited-edition coupes were offered with custom interiors and padded tops: the Lincoln Lido in the base series, the Capri in the Cosmopolitan line. These cars featured glamorous interiors and usually a choice of canvas or vinyl roof topping. Lidos also sported fender skirts, which were standard on all Cosmopolitans, including the Capri. Gone this year were the base Lincoln convertible and the Cosmopolitan Town Sedan. Partly due to a normal-length model year, production fell back to 28,190 units, still good by Lincoln standards. The breakdown was 5748 Lincoln coupes and Lidos and 11,741 Sport Sedans. In the case of the Cosmopolitan, 1824 coupes and Capris, 8341 Sport Sedans, and 536 convertibles were built.

	Restorable	Good	Excellent
Cosmo cvt	$5,000-12,000	$12,000-18,000	$18,000-25,000
Cosmo sdn/cpe	2,500-6,000	6,000-8,000	8,000-12,000
Capri/Lido cpes	3,500-7,500	7,500-11,000	11,000-15,000
Standard sdn/cpe	2,500-6,000	6,000-8,000	8,000-11,000

1951

The 1951 grille was simplified, wheel covers were changed, and horsepower was increased by two to 154. The Cosmopolitan, though still distinctly longer and more luxurious, lost its curious front wheelwell gravel shields and acquired a body-length bright metal strip similar to that of the standard Lincoln. Production increased nicely to 32,574 units: 4482 Lincoln coupes and Lidos and 12,279 sedans, plus 2727 Cosmopolitan coupes and Capris, 12,229 sedans, and 857 convertibles.

	Restorable	Good	Excellent
Cosmo cvt	$5,000-12,000	$12,000-18,000	$18,000-25,000
Cosmo sdn/cpe	2,500-6,000	6,000-8,000	8,000-12,000
Capri/Lido cpes	3,500-7,500	7,500-11,000	11,000-15,000
Standard sdn/cpe	2,500-6,000	6,000-8,000	8,000-11,000

1952

The all-new '52 line comprised two series: the Cosmopolitan (now the base version) and the upmarket Capri. For these cars, Lincoln brought out a fine new valve-in-head V-8 (317.5 cid, 160 bhp), carefully designed for smoothness and longevity, along with ball-joint front suspension, an industry first and the forerunner of suspensions used by many cars for years afterward. Recirculating-ball power steering, oversize drum brakes, power seats, and liberal sound deadening were featured. Smooth styling on a new 123-inch wheelbase chassis was unfortunately a bit too close to that of Mercury for Lincoln's good, but at least Lincoln finally had a true hardtop to compete with Cadillac's Coupe de Ville.

The '52 was the first of the famous "Road Race" Lincolns, which dominated their class in the Mexican *Carrera Panamericana,* winning the top five places and finishing high overall. Because of defense production for the Korean War, output was restricted this year by the government. Total Lincoln output thus fell to 27,271 units: 4545 Cosmopolitan hardtops, 5681 Capri hardtops and 1191 convertibles, plus 15,854 four-door sedans from both series.

	Restorable	Good	Excellent
Capri convertible	$5,000-12,000	$12,000-17,000	$17,000-24,000
2d hardtops	2,500-6,500	6,500-9,000	9,000-12,500
Sedans	1,500-4,000	4,000-6,500	6,500-9,000

1952 Lincoln Capri hardtop coupe

1953 Lincoln Capri hardtop coupe

1953

The '53 Lincoln was almost a direct repeat of the year before. For instant identification, the '53s had the marque name spelled out on the hood and the Lincoln badge moved from the hood to the center of the grille. There was a significant increase in horsepower, which was now 205 against 160 the year before. Lincoln again triumphed in the Mexican Road Race, taking the first four positions in its class. Production was up strongly to 40,762 units, which included 6562 Cosmopolitan hardtops, 12,916 Capri hardtops, and 2372 Capri ragtops.

	Restorable	Good	Excellent
Capri convertible	$5,000-12,000	$12,000-17,000	$17,000-25,000
2d hardtops	2,500-6,500	6,500-9,000	9,000-13,500
Sedans	1,500-4,000	4,000-6,500	6,500-9,000

1954 Lincoln Capri convertible coupe

1954 Lincoln Capri convertible coupe

1954

The best styled of the three-year run of Road Race Lincolns was the '54, with its ultra-clean bar grille and oversize, three-way-visible taillights. Though fractionally longer and wider, these Lincolns really bucked the Fifties Detroit trend toward outlandish bodies swathed in chrome, and as such they are admired today. The same combination of body styles—Cosmo and Capri sedans and hardtops, Capri convertible—was offered, and there was no change in horsepower. Lincoln was first in the industry this year with a four-way power seat, and air conditioning became available in the spring. Lincoln finished first and second in its class in the 1954 Mexican Road Race, the last one that would be run. Output edged downward to 36,993: 2994 Cosmopolitan hardtops, 14,003 Capri hardtops, and 1951 Capri convertibles. Sedans totaled a bit over 14,000 units.

	Restorable	Good	Excellent
Capri convertible	$5,000-12,500	$12,500-20,000	$20,000-27,500
2d hardtops	2,500-7,500	7,500-10,000	10,000-14,000
Sedans	1,500-4,000	4,000-6,500	6,500-10,000

1955 Lincoln Capri convertible coupe

1955 Lincoln Capri hardtop coupe

1955 Lincoln Capri sedan (with air conditioning)

1956 Lincoln Premiere hardtop coupe

1956 Lincoln Premiere convertible coupe

1957 Lincoln Capri four-door sedan

1955

Lincoln wasn't ready with a total redesign, so its 1955 line was the most conservative in the industry, and one of only three makes without a wraparound windshield. Lincoln now offered its own automatic transmission, Turbo-Drive, and horsepower was bumped to 225. Instead of Cosmopolitan, the bottom line was called Custom; Capri remained with the same three body styles as before. Styling was crisp, clean, and elegant, with a neater grille and extended rear fenders. As before, the interiors featured a fine combination of fabrics and leather. Sales, however, were down to 27,222 units because the '55 wasn't "new" enough, but for admirers of good design, the '55 has much to recommend it. This year, 1362 Custom and 11,462 Capri hardtops were built, along with 1487 Capri ragtops.

	Restorable	Good	Excellent
Capri convertible	$5,000-12,000	$12,000-17,000	$17,000-24,000
2d hardtops	2,500-6,500	6,500-9,000	9,000-12,500
Sedans	1,500-4,000	4,000-6,500	6,500-9,000

1956

The ads read, "Unmistakably Lincoln," and so it was—the '56 was completely changed. Gone were the short wheelbase and conservative styling, replaced by a much longer and wider body (on a 126-inch wheelbase) with peaked fenders and lots of glass—very clean up front with a bisected horizontal-bar grille. Up back were large vertical taillights along the lines of the '55, dual exhaust outlets in the bumper, and grille pattern trim above the bumper. Capri became the lower line, and the top Lincoln was now named Premiere. Body styles remained the same. The engine was also new: a 368-cid V-8 with 285 horsepower. In line with its bulk, the '56 weighed about 600 pounds more than in 1955. Apparently the public liked what it saw, because production jumped to 50,322 units, including 4355 Capri and 19,619 Premiere hardtops and 2447 Premiere convertibles.

	Restorable	Good	Excellent
Premiere cvt	$6,000-14,000	$14,000-20,000	$20,000-28,000
Premiere sedan	1,500-4,500	4,500-7,000	7,000-10,000
2d hardtops	2,500-7,500	7,500-12,500	12,500-16,500

1957

Despite an all-new car introduced in 1956, Lincoln charged into 1957 strutting a major facelift. Among changes was the addition of a four-door hardtop body style, called Landau, offered as both a Capri and Premiere. Most noticeable, however, were tall tailfins borrowed from the Futura dream car and four-lamp front-end styling (two regular seven-inch units above two smaller lights). With 10.0:1 compression, the 368 V-8 now delivered 300 horsepower. The car to watch for, of course, is the Premier convertible, which is very much in demand as a sort of Fifties cult symbol. Given the all-new

Cadillacs and Imperials, it's not surprising that production fell back to 41,123 units, though convertible output was up smartly to 3676 units. The Landaus attracted 1451 Capri and 11,223 Premiere buyers, while the two-door hardtops found favor with 2973 and 15,185 shoppers. Four-door sedans in both lines totaled less than 7000.

	Restorable	Good	Excellent
Premiere cvt	$6,000-14,000	$14,000-20,000	$20,000-28,000
2d hardtops	2,500-7,500	7,500-12,500	12,500-16,500
Landau 4d htps	2,000-5,000	5,000-8,000	8,000-12,000
Sedans	1,500-4,500	4,500-7,000	7,000-10,000

1958

Sales were down despite millions invested in new tooling. That's because the Lincoln restyle ended up opposite from what the market wanted: The '58 was six inches longer, with a 131-inch wheelbase, and featured radical styling with sharp tailfins, pointed fenders, and slanted quad headlamps. Under the hood was the largest engine in the industry, the 430-cid Continental V-8 with 375 horses. The Capri and Premiere lineups were unchanged except that there was no convertible, this body style being reserved for the Lincoln-based Continental Mark III (see "Continental"). Lincoln output plummeted to 17,134 units. For Capris, that translated to 1184 sedans, 3084 Landau hardtops, and 2591 two-door hardtops; for Premieres, it was 1660, 5572, and 3043 units.

	Restorable	Good	Excellent
Sedans	$1,500-3,500	$3,500-5,000	$5,000-7,500
Landau 4d htps	2,000-5,000	5,000-6,500	6,500-8,500
2d hardtops	2,500-5,000	5,000-7,500	7,500-10,000

1959

Continental was melded back into Lincoln Division as a Lincoln model: the 1959 Mark IV, a stalwartly priced, heroically decorated, tailfinned luxury line-leader included a sedan, two- and four-door hardtops, a new Town Car and limousine, and Lincoln's only convertible. Hess & Eisenhardt of Cincinnati constructed 49 Limousines and 78 Town Cars for Lincoln. Though using the standard 131-inch wheelbase, they featured padded tops and blind rear quarters, inside divider glass for the limo, super deluxe interiors, every option in the book—and $10,000 price tags. Styling for '59 was a facelift of 1958: the bodyside scallops now flowed into the front doors and grilles and taillights were tinkered with. The Capri and Premiere received similar changes. Horsepower was cut to 350 in an attempt to improve fuel economy. Lincoln output totaled 15,780, and 11,125 Continentals were built, including 2195 convertibles.

	Restorable	Good	Excellent
Mark IV cvt	$5,000-14,000	$14,000-20,000	$20,000-30,000
Mark IV 2d htp	3,000-7,000	7,000-11,000	11,000-15,000

1958 Lincoln Capri Landau hardtop sedan

1958 Lincoln Premiere hardtop coupe

1959 Lincoln Continental Mark IV hardtop coupe

1959 Lincoln Continental Mark IV hardtop coupe

1959 Lincoln Premiere hardtop sedan

1960 Lincoln Continental Mark V Landau hardtop sedan

	Restorable	Good	Excellent
Mk IV Town Car/limo	3,000-7,000	7,000-11,000	11,000-15,000
Mark IV sedan	2,500-5,000	5,000-7,500	7,500-10,000
Other sedans	1,500-3,500	3,500-5,000	5,000-7,500
Other 4d htps	2,000-5,000	5,000-6,500	6,500-8,500
Other 2d htps	2,500-6,000	6,000-7,500	7,500-10,000

1960

The two-year-old bodyshell was again facelifted with a revised grille and front bumper, with the massive bumper guards moved inboard of the canted headlamps. Also, the rear end was reworked to give it model-year identification. Continentals continued for the last year with the unique reverse-slant rear window that could be lowered. Curiously, horsepower was reduced again, to 315. Production came to 13,734 Lincolns and 11,086 Continentals, including 2044 ragtops. The Limousine and Town Car were continued, with 34 and 136 built.

1960 Lincoln Premiere Landau hardtop sedan

	Restorable	Good	Excellent
Mark V cvt	$5,000-14,000	$14,000-20,000	$20,000-30,000
Mark V 2d htp	3,000-7,000	7,000-11,000	11,000-15,000
Mk V Town Car/limo	3,000-7,000	7,000-11,000	11,000-15,000
Mark V sedan	2,500-5,000	5,000-7,500	7,500-10,000
Other sedans	1,500-3,500	3,500-5,000	5,000-7,500
Other 4d htps	2,000-5,000	5,000-6,500	6,500-8,500

1961 Lincoln Continental convertible sedan

1961

Lincoln made history with the classically beautiful and brilliantly engineered Lincoln Continental four-door sedan and convertible sedan, styled by an award-winning cadre of top Ford designers with ultra-clean lines picked out by bright metal accents along the fender tops. Wheelbase was a more compact 123 inches, but weight was surprisingly high: 4927 pounds for the sedan, 5215 for the ragtop. Sales reached 25,164, about 85 percent of them sedans (which had frameless door glass like a hardtop, though there was a thin B-pillar). The convertible sedan (2857 built) is an exotic affair, but a restoration nightmare with its spaghetti bowl of electrical circuits, wiring, and servos. Both cars had a rigid unit body-chassis, impressive sound insulation, extremely close machining tolerances, and lots of long-service components. In addition, each car was thoroughly tested before leaving the factory. But these are complicated cars, the very devil to restore, and we strongly recommend buying the finest possible example and paying the price—it will be much cheaper in the long run than a full or partial restoration. For its present price, a sedan in top condition is a remarkable value. The '61 was Lincoln's turnaround car, though it would take some years of "sticking with it" before sales would really rebound.

1961 Lincoln Continental four-door sedan

	Restorable	Good	Excellent
Continental cvt	$4,000-9,000	$9,000-14,000	$14,000-18,500
Continental sdn	2,500-4,000	4,000-6,000	6,000-8,500

1962

Lincoln had promised an end to "dynamic obsolescence" on Continentals, so the '62s were hardly changed. There was a cleaner grille with a narrower center crossbar, headlamps were no longer sunk into the grille but carried prominently on each side, and the bumper was more conventional. The grille texture featured little floating rectangles. Specifications were exactly the same, with the 430-cid V-8 developing 300 horsepower. Production totaled 31,061 units, 3212 being convertible sedans.

	Restorable	Good	Excellent
Continental cvt	$4,000-9,000	$9,000-14,000	$14,000-18,500
Continental sdn	2,500-4,000	4,000-6,000	6,000-8,500

1963

Horsepower was raised to 320 this year, a square-textured grille and new back panel appliqué were featured, and the trunk was redesigned to provide more space. Lehmann-Peterson of Chicago built two eight-passenger Executive Limousine models on a 159-inch wheelbase. They came with padded top and small back window, drop-leaf table, and optional anything a buyer wanted. Base price was announced at $13,400, compared to $6270 for the regular sedan. Output this year was 28,095 sedans and 3138 ragtops.

	Restorable	Good	Excellent
Continental cvt	$4,000-9,000	$9,000-14,000	$14,000-18,500
Continental sdn	2,500-4,000	4,000-6,000	6,000-8,500
Continental limo	3,500-5,000	5,000-8,000	8,000-12,500

1964

The wheelbase was extended to 126 inches, a length retained into the 1970s. The basic styling theme, however, remained the same. A convex grille with vertical bars, a wider roof, a broader rear window, and a low-contour convertible top were the only major alterations. As usual, convertibles accounted for about 10 percent of total sales—3328 for '64, compared to 32,969 sedans. This year, the Lehmann-Peterson Executive Limousine rode a 160-inch wheelbase and cost $15,153; 15 were built.

	Restorable	Good	Excellent
Continental cvt	$4,000-9,000	$9,000-14,000	$14,000-18,500
Continental sdn	2,500-4,000	4,000-6,000	6,000-8,500
Continental limo	3,500-5,000	5,000-8,000	8,000-12,500

1965

A new horizontal-theme grille, combination parking and turn signals in the front fenders, and ribbed taillights were found on the '65 Lincolns, which continued otherwise much as before. The big 430 V-8 still cranked out 320 horsepower. Production this year was 36,824 sedans, 3356 convertibles, and 85

1962 Lincoln Continental four-door sedan

1962 Lincoln Continental convertible sedan

1963 Lincoln Continental convertible sedan

1964 Lincoln Continental convertible sedan

1964 Lincoln Continental convertible sedan

1965 Lincoln Continental four-door sedan

1966 Lincoln Continental four-door sedan

1966 Lincoln Continental convertible sedan

1966 Lincoln Continental hardtop coupe

1968 Lincoln Continental Mark III hardtop coupe

Executive Limousines. Ford, incidentally, honored warranties on the Lehmann-Peterson cars and presented them in the Lincoln brochure this year.

	Restorable	Good	Excellent
Continental cvt	$4,000-9,000	$9,000-14,000	$14,000-18,500
Continental sdn	2,500-4,000	4,000-6,000	6,000-8,500
Continental limo	3,500-5,000	5,000-8,000	8,000-12,500

1966

Lincoln had long wanted a two-door hardtop, which it added this year, while cutting prices to spur sales. The result was a production run of 54,755 '66 models—still only a fourth of Cadillac's total, but hardly bad. The V-8 was also enlarged this year, bored and stroked to 462 cid, whence it developed 340 bhp. The hood was lengthened, adding five inches to overall length. Rear wheel cutouts were enlarged and a slight hop-up appeared in the rear beltline. A new fine horizontal-bar grille was applied and the front bumper wrapped all the way back to the front-wheel cutouts. Up back, wide horizontal taillights were mounted in the bumper. Production this year was 35,809 sedans, 3180 convertible sedans, and 15,766 two-door hardtops. The Executive Limo was up to nearly 6000 pounds now, but the price was a bit lower at $14,666, which helped spur sales to 130 units.

	Restorable	Good	Excellent
Continental cvt	$4,000-9,000	$9,000-14,000	$14,000-18,500
Continental sdn	2,500-4,000	4,000-6,000	6,000-8,500
Continental 2d htp	3,000-4,500	4,500-7,000	7,000-9,500
Continental limo	3,500-5,000	5,000-8,000	8,000-12,500

1967

Another grille and taillight shuffle and a spring-loaded hood emblem distinguished the '67 Lincolns. The convertible put in its last appearance, and saw only 2276 copies. The sedan was down a bit to 33,331 units, the hardtop to 11,060. Lehmann-Peterson Executive Limousines this year featured broad front B-pillars. Also, Lincoln delivered two custom convertibles to the U.S. Secret Service for official functions.

	Restorable	Good	Excellent
Continental cvt	$4,000-9,000	$9,000-14,000	$14,000-18,500
Continental sdn	2,500-4,000	4,000-6,000	6,000-8,500
Continental 2d htp	3,000-4,500	4,500-7,000	7,000-9,500
Continental limo	3,500-6,000	6,000-9,000	9,000-13,000

1968

Lincoln reintroduced the Continental at midyear—this time as a Lincoln model. Ignoring the series of Marks it had built during 1958-60, Lincoln dubbed this new version the Mark III, establishing a direct lineal relationship to the 1956-57 Mark II. But the two-door hardtop Mark III was not planned as a money-losing "statement." It was designed to sell in volume. Priced at only $6585 base and riding a 117.2-inch wheelbase (borrowed from the four-door

Thunderbird), it was a personal-luxury rival to the Cadillac Eldorado coupe, but with conventional rear-wheel-drive and a 365-bhp 460 V-8. There was a wide choice of luxury interiors and 26 exterior colors. The Continental sedan and coupe continued, with horizontal grillework front and rear and government-mandated side marker lights. Production was 9415 hardtops, 29,719 four-doors, 7770 Mark IIIs, and 56 Lehmann-Peterson Executive Limousines.

	Restorable	Good	Excellent
Mark III	$3,000-6,000	$6,000-9,000	$9,000-12,000
Continental sdn	2,000-3,000	3,000-4,500	4,500-6,500
Continental 2d htp	2,500-4,000	4,000-5,500	5,500-7,500
Continental limo	3,500-6,000	6,000-9,000	9,000-13,000

1969

A new Mercedes-inspired squarish grille with raised center section extending into the hood and a Town Car interior option for the sedan marked the new Continentals. The Mark III was unchanged, though a Sure-Lock anti-skid brake system was offered at mid-year, the first for a domestic make. Lehmann-Peterson's Presidential limo was updated to 1969 styling. Continental hardtop and sedan production held steady at 9032 and 29,258 units, but the Mark III shot up to 23,088 deliveries.

	Restorable	Good	Excellent
Mark III	$3,000-6,000	$6,000-9,000	$9,000-12,000
Continental sdn	2,000-3,000	3,000-4,500	4,500-6,500
Continental 2d htp	2,500-4,000	4,000-5,500	5,500-7,500

1970

The '70 Lincoln Continental was all-new with a 127-inch wheelbase and body-on-frame construction. Aside from hidden headlamps and a strong horizontal-bar grille design, the 1970 Lincoln Continental maintained styling continuity with the '69 version. Ventless side glass, concealed wipers, wider doors, more prominent B-pillars and forward-hinged rear doors for the sedan, and full-width taillamps were the major differences. The 460 V-8 with appropriate emissions controls remained the sole powerplant, still rated at 365 bhp. The Mark III now had hidden windshield wipers, too, plus new wheelcovers and parking/taillights. Lincoln dropped its cooperative sales relationship with Lehmann-Peterson this year. Due to a recession, production was down to 9073 hardtops, 28,622 sedans, and 21,432 Mark IIIs.

	Restorable	Good	Excellent
Mark III	$3,000-6,000	$6,000-9,000	$9,000-12,000
Continental sdn	1,500-3,000	3,000-4,000	4,000-6,000
Continental 2d htp	2,000-4,000	4,000-5,000	5,000-7,000

1971

Continentals were little changed, but the grille was made more prominent and classical-looking by eliminating the extensions over the headlamp cov-

1968 Lincoln Continental hardtop coupe

1969 Lincoln Continental hardtop coupe

1969 Lincoln Continental four-door sedan

1969 Lincoln Continental Mark III hardtop coupe

1970 Lincoln Continental four-door sedan

1970 Lincoln Continental Mark III hardtop coupe

1971 Lincoln Continental Mark III hardtop coupe

1971 Lincoln Continental hardtop coupe

1972 Lincoln Continental four-door sedan

1972 Lincoln Continental Mark IV hardtop coupe

1973 Lincoln Continental Mark IV coupe

ers. The Mark III was unchanged, and was in its final year now. Look for the Golden Anniversary Town Car option package, comprising special leather inserts for the seats, wood-like panels on the backs of the front seats, deeper carpets, soft nylon headliner, special dash and fender nameplates, plus keys and door-mounted owner initials in 22-carat gold. Output was up this year: 8205 hardtops, 27,346 sedans, and 27,091 Mark IIIs.

	Restorable	Good	Excellent
Mark III	$3,000-6,000	$6,000-9,000	$9,000-12,000
Continental sdn	1,500-2,500	2,500-3,500	3,500-5,000
Continental 2d htp	2,000-3,500	3,500-4,500	4,500-6,000

1972

Longer, lower, and wider, the new Continental Mark IV racked up double the sales of the previous year's Mark III. Riding a longer 120.4-inch wheelbase and measuring 220.1 inches overall, it offered a bit more passenger room. But it was less agile and thirstier, the latter because of tightening emissions rules (this despite a 200-pound weight loss). Though the Mark IV shared basic structure with the contemporary Thunderbird, this wasn't immediately apparent. Oval opera windows, at first standard, were later made optional. The Town Car package was continued, and revised at mid-year. Continentals featured a grille more akin to 1969, and Moloney Standard Coach Builders of Rolling Meadows, Illinois, was producing Executive Limousines with a 36-inch stretch. A new Presidential limo was built in-house by Ford for White House use. The 460 V-8 was standard in all models, but this year horsepower ratings were net: 224 for Continental, 212 for the Mark IV. Total output set a record: 94,560 units. Mark IVs numbered 48,591, Continental hardtops 10,408, sedans 35,561.

	Restorable	Good	Excellent
Mark IV	$3,000-5,000	$5,000-7,000	$7,000-9,000
Continental sdn	1,000-2,000	2,000-3,500	3,500-5,000
Continental 2d htp	1,500-3,000	3,000-4,000	4,000-6,000

1973

Town Car treatment was now applied to the Continental two-door hardtop as well as the sedan, resulting in a Town Coupe. A Silver Luxury Group Option was extremely popular this year. It featured Silver Moondust Metallic exterior paint (with matching vinyl roof) and a Cranberry Victoria Velour interior. A dark red leather interior was added later in the year. With 69,437 built, the Mark IV was enjoying a sales lead over the Cadillac Eldorado, but this hasn't shown up in latterday collector preferences. Horsepower was down to 219, 208 for the Mark IV. Total Lincoln production set a record of 128,073 units; Continental was up to 13,348 hardtops and 45,288 sedans.

	Restorable	Good	Excellent
Mark IV	$3,000-5,000	$5,000-7,000	$7,000-9,000

	Restorable	Good	Excellent
Continental sdn	1,000-2,000	2,000-3,500	3,500-5,000
Continental 2d htp	1,500-3,000	3,000-4,000	4,000-6,000

1974

Lincoln marked time, the only noteworthy changes being a vertical-bar grille, heavier bumpers at the rear to match the beefy front units adopted in 1973, new taillights, plus a brace of Luxury Group interior/exterior trim packages. New sound insulation and thicker carpeting made the Mark IV a bit quieter this year, and a Saddle and White Luxury Group was available, as was a Gold group. Look for these on Mark IVs. A solid-state ignition system aided reliability, though horsepower ratings were little changed at 215 and 220. Weight of the Mark was way up—to 5361 pounds and overall length was now 228.3 inches. The Arab oil embargo hampered sales this year, which were down to 7318 Continental coupes and 29,351 sedans, plus 57,316 Mark IVs.

1974 Lincoln Continental hardtop coupe

1974 Lincoln Continental Mark IV coupe

	Restorable	Good	Excellent
Mark IV	$3,000-5,000	$5,000-7,000	$7,000-9,000
Continental sdn	1,000-2,000	2,000-3,500	3,500-5,000
Continental 2d htp	1,500-3,000	3,000-4,000	4,000-6,000

1975

A revamped Continental sedan and coupe for 1975 brought the first opera window rooflines, with heavy fixed B-posts (with coach lights) and padded vinyl tops. These models continued largely unchanged through 1979 and are distinctly uncollectible. The Mark IV was pretty much the same, although there was a new Landau roof option with an inset backlight and a broad chrome "tiara," and weight was down about 150 pounds. Various luxury series continued, this year including Lipstick and White, Versailles, Blue Diamond, and Jade. Catalytic converters were also new. Production was up to 101,843 Lincolns: 21,185 Continental coupes, 33,513 sedans, and 47,145 Mark IVs.

1975 Lincoln Continental Mark IV coupe

1975 Lincoln Continental Coupé

	Restorable	Good	Excellent
Mark IV	$3,000-5,000	$5,000-7,000	$7,000-9,000
Continental, all	1,500-2,500	2,500-3,500	3,500-4,500

1976

The Lincoln line continued unchanged, except for color and trim variations. The 460-cid V-8 with 202 net horsepower was standard on all models. Designer Series Mark IVs were the big news this year: Cartier (dove grey color scheme), Bill Blass (navy blue and cream), Givenchy (turquoise and white), and Pucci (burgundy and silver). And if that wasn't enough, there were others: Gold and Cream, Red and Rosé, two-tone Jade, Jade and White, and Black Diamond. Sales were up again, to 24,663 Continental coupes, 43,983 sedans, and 56,110 Mark IVs.

1976 Lincoln Continental Mark IV coupe

1977 Lincoln Continental Mark V coupe

1978 Lincoln Versailles four-door sedan

1978 Lincoln Continental Mark V Diamond Jubilee

1979 Lincoln Continental Mark V Bill Blass Edition

1979 Lincoln Continental Mark V coupe

	Restorable	Good	Excellent
Mark IV	$3,000-5,000	$5,000-7,000	$7,000-9,000
Continental	1,500-2,500	2,500-3,500	3,500-4,500

1977

Versailles, a new luxury compact, was introduced as a reply to Cadillac's Seville. It was little more than a gussied-up Ford Granada carrying a Continental-style square grille, stand-up hood ornament, and humped trunklid, plus an extensive array of standard equipment. Priced at $11,500 ($1864 more than the Continental sedan), it was doomed to be a failure. It scored 15,434 sales in its first year. The big news at Lincoln this year was the new Continental Mark V. Though still riding a 120.4-inch wheelbase, it was 400 pounds lighter and boasted 21 percent more trunk space. Styling was very much in the Mark mode, though crisper this time around. Buyers liked it, as output soared to 80,321 units. Luxury and Designer groups were continued. The ponderous big Continentals got a Mark-style grille this year, and there were now two engines (also for the Mark V): a 179-bhp, 400-cid V-8 and a 208-bhp 460. Production increased to 27,440 coupes and 68,160 sedans. Total Lincoln output of 191,355 cars set yet another record.

	Restorable	Good	Excellent
Mark V	$2,000-4,000	$4,000-5,000	$5,000-7,000
Continental	1,500-2,500	2,500-3,500	3,500-4,000
Versailles	1,000-2,000	2,000-3,000	3,000-4,000

1978

The Continental-substitute Versailles switched from a 135-bhp 351 V-8 to a smaller, 133-bhp 302, but its styling was little changed. Sales skidded to 8931. Continentals and Mark Vs were also little changed, though a Diamond Jubilee Edition Mark V celebrated Ford's 75th anniversary. This car came in Diamond Blue or Jubilee Gold clearcoat metallic paint, Valino grain landau vinyl roof, color-keyed grille bars, and a unique hood ornament. Production was down this year to 20,977 Continental coupes, 67,110 sedans, and 72,602 Mark Vs.

	Restorable	Good	Excellent
Mark V	$2,000-4,000	$4,000-5,000	$5,000-7,000
Mark V Dia. Jub.	3,500-5,000	5,000-7,000	7,000-9,000
Continental	1,500-2,500	2,500-3,500	3,500-4,000
Versailles	1,000-2,000	2,000-3,000	3,000-4,000

1979

Some features of the Diamond Jubilee Mark V were applied to the Continental "Collectors Series" sedan, including special paint and a gold-colored grille. The Versailles roof was restyled to a more formal appearance and new colors and trims were offered, which helped push sales up to 21,007 units. The Mark V also added a Collector's Series with gold grille, landau vinyl roof, and blind roof quarters. The usual quartet of Designer Series Marks were still available, among which the Bill Blass edition was most memorable: two-toned in white and midnight blue metallic, with dark blue bodyside moldings and gold striping. An optional full-vinyl roof gave Marks the appearance of a convertible. Production was robust: 16,142 Continental coupes, 76,458 sedans, and 75,939 Mark Vs.

	Restorable	Good	Excellent
Mark V	$2,000-4,000	$4,000-5,000	$5,000-8,000
Continental	1,500-2,500	2,500-3,500	3,500-4,000
Versailles	1,000-2,000	2,000-3,000	3,000-4,000

1979 Lincoln Versailles four-door sedan

1980

Continental and the new Mark VI were drastically downsized, each weighing nearly 800 pounds less and sharing the same 117.3-inch wheelbase. For the first time, a Mark-series four-door sedan was offered. This smaller size was now crowding the Versailles, which was getting long in the tooth anyway, and was putting in its final appearance this year. Hardly anyone noticed, as only 4784 were sold. New, soft-riding suspension systems, electronic engine controls, and four-speed overdrive automatic transmission were standard; digital instruments, keyless entry, and a vast array of audio systems were available. Collectibility of Mark VI four-doors and Continentals is near negligible from this point on, and they are omitted from our listings. The downsizing wasn't popular—that and a severe recession held production down to 7177 Continental coupes, 24,056 sedans, and 38,891 Mark VIs (two- and four-door).

	Restorable	Good	Excellent
Mark VI 2d	*	$3,000-4,000	$4,000-5,000
Versailles	*	2,000-3,000	3,000-4,000

* Purchase only in good or excellent condition

1980 Lincoln Versailles four-door sedan

1980 Lincoln Continental Mark VI coupe

1981

All Lincolns dropped the previously optional carbureted 140-bhp 351 V-8 in favor of a fuel-injected 302 with 130 horsepower. Signature Series, Designer Series, and standard Marks were again offered in two-door coupe and four-door sedan body styles; 18,740 and 17,958 were built. The existence of four-door Mark VIs cuts collector interest in Lincolns, which officially became known as Town Cars this year. Even the coupe was called Town Car, though only 4935 were built (plus 27,904 sedans). Lincoln limousines resumed production in reasonable quantity this year, specially built on an extended wheelbase.

	Restorable	Good	Excellent
Mark VI 2d	*	$3,000-4,000	$4,000-5,000
Limousine	*	5,000-7,000	7,000-9,000

* Purchase only in good or excellent condition

1981 Lincoln Continental Mark VI coupe

1982

The Continental four-door sedan, with a bustle-back tail probably influenced by the Cadillac Seville,

1982 Lincoln Continental Signature Series four-door

1983 Lincoln Continental four-door sedan

1983 Lincoln Continental Mark VI four-door sedan

1983 Lincoln Town Car four-door sedan

1984 Lincoln Continental Mark VII LSC coupe

arrived as Lincoln's new luxury compact (on a 108.7-inch wheelbase), a replacement for the Versailles. It was based on the Thunderbird/Cougar platform and shared their suspension design, but with adjustments for a softer ride and two standard items: gas shock absorbers and radial tires. First year output was an encouraging 23,908 units. Base, Signature, and Givenchy Designer Series trim levels were offered. The big Mark VI continued to come as a sedan or coupe with base, Signature, Givenchy, Bill Blass, and Pucci editions. A total of 11,532 two-doors and 14,804 four-doors were produced. The standard Town Car series lost its coupe, leaving just the sedan, which came in base, Signature, and Cartier versions. Output was 35,069 units.

	Restorable	Good	Excellent
Mark VI 2d	*	$3,000-4,000	$4,000-5,000
Limousine	*	7,000-8,500	8,500-10,000
Continental	*	2,500-3,500	3,500-4,500

* Purchase only in good or excellent condition

1983

Electronic fuel injection was adopted by the bustle-back Lincoln Continental luxury compact, which looked virtually the same as the '82 version. This really was quite a good job, extremely quiet, smooth, and refined—and loaded with convenience features. But its collectibility, if any, lies mainly in its novel rear-end styling. The Signature series was replaced this year by a Valentino edition. Sales fell to 16,831. The Mark VI was little changed, still big, thirsty, and overdecorated. Output ended at 12,743 two-doors and 18,113 four-doors. The Givenchy edition was dropped. The Town Car saw only detail changes, but production shot up to 53,381 units.

	Restorable	Good	Excellent
Mark VI	*	$3,000-4,000	$4,000-6,000
Limousine	*	8,000-9,500	9,500-11,000
Continental	*	3,000-4,000	4,000-5,000

* Purchase only in good or excellent condition

1984

The ponderous and obsolete Mark VI was finally dumped in favor of the sleek, modern Mark VII coupe. The newcomer was over a foot shorter and 400 pounds lighter, sharing its short, 108.6-inch wheelbase with the Continental sedan. Base, Bill Blass, Versace, and LSC (Luxury Sport Coupe) models were offered, the last being the most interesting. It featured a handling suspension, quick-ratio power steering, high-performance tires on six-inch-wide wheels, a shorter final drive ratio for quicker acceleration, fog lamps, and a leather interior. Electronic air suspension was standard on all models. Though it didn't match such vaunted European rivals as the Mercedes 380SEC, it came extremely close, and is by far the most collectible Lincoln of the later Eighties. Sales totaled 33,344 units. The Continental sedan received a swept-back grille, electronic air suspension, and an optional BMW turbo diesel engine (avoid it)—and saw production nearly double to 30,468. A largely unchanged Town Car found 93,622 customers.

	Restorable	Good	Excellent
Mark VII	*	$3,500-4,500	$4,500-5,500
Mark VII LSC	*	4,000-5,000	5,000-6,500
Limousine	*	8,500-10,000	10,000-12,000

* Purchase only in good or excellent condition

1985

The Mark VII's most significant addition was an anti-skid braking system, using a computer to monitor all four wheels to prevent lock-up in hard stops. This was standard on all V-8 Designer Series models. The LSC now had a 180-bhp high-performance version of Ford's 5.0-liter V-8 with tubular exhaust headers and multi-adjustable articulated sport seats. Production, however, tumbled to 18,355 units. The Town Car received its first freshening, notable for a softer, more rounded look. Output jumped to 119,878. Anti-lock brakes were also new to the Continental, which enjoyed a production run of 28,253 units.

	Restorable	Good	Excellent
Mark VII	*	$3,800-4,800	$4,800-5,800
Mark VII LSC	*	5,000-6,000	6,000-7,000
Limousine	*	9,500-12,000	12,000-14,000

* Purchase only in good or excellent condition

1986

Sequential port fuel injection, fast-burn combustion chambers, higher compression, low-tension piston rings, and roller tappets were the changes made to standard V-8s (now 150 bhp); anti-lock brakes were standard on all models. The Mark VII LSC had a new tuned intake manifold and tubular exhaust headers (for 200 bhp), and an analog instrument cluster to replace the previous year's electronic display. Continental lost its Valentino edition, Mark VII its Versace version. Production came in at 19,012 Continentals, 20,056 Mark VIIs, and 117,771 Town Cars.

	Restorable	Good	Excellent
Mark VII	*	$5,000-6,500	$6,500-7,500
Mark VII LSC	*	6,000-7,500	7,500-8,500
Limousine	*	10,000-13,000	13,000-16,000

* Purchase only in good or excellent condition

1987

The '87 Mark VII lasted only until March, when it was replaced by the 1988 model. Minor equipment changes only were made on the '87, the most roadable version of which continued to be the LSC with its high-output V-8. The LSC's price was quite reasonable compared to European rivals like the BMW 635CSi, Jaguar XJS, and Mercedes 560SEC; in CONSUMER GUIDE®'s opinion, the LSC outperformed its GM rivals: Eldorado, Riviera, and Toronado. Top examples of the Mark VII, and the

1984 Lincoln Continental Mark VII

1985 Lincoln Continental Mark VII LSC coupe

1987 Lincoln Mark VII LSC coupe

1988 Lincoln Mark VII LSC coupe

LSC in particular, will almost certainly be collectible in the future. Also worthy of note was the new Bill Blass package, with gold interior, gold clearcoat metallic paint, six-way power seats, leather trim, wire spoke aluminum wheels, and premium sound system. Mark VII output fell to 15,286. The Continental was now in the last year of its styling generation; 17,597 found homes. Detail improvements attended to the Town Car; production came in at 76,483 units.

	Restorable	Good	Excellent
Mark VII	*	$5,500-7,000	$7,000-8,000
Mark VII LSC/Bill Blass	*	6,500-8,000	8,000-9,000
Limousine	*	12,000-15,000	15,000-18,000

* Purchase only in good or excellent condition

1988

Introduced early with a more powerful engine, the Mark VII gained a new standard sound system with 18-station preset memory later in the year; a compact disc player was optional. The base model was dropped, leaving the LSC high-performance touring coupe and the Bill Blass Designer Series, both powered by a 225-bhp 5.0-liter V-8 out of the Mustang GT. The Bill Blass had Prairie Mist metallic clearcoat paint; bodyside and decklid paint stripes; leather, suede, or cloth interior; wire-spoke aluminum wheels; and electronic instrument cluster (nobody's perfect). Production this year totaled 38,259. The Continental was all-new, based on a stretched Ford Taurus front-drive platform. It had a 109-inch wheelbase and a 140-bhp V-6, plus an extensive list of standard equipment. Some 41,287 were sold. The Town Car featured a new grille and taillights; output soared to 201,113.

	Restorable	Good	Excellent
Mark VII LSC/Bill Blass	*	$7,000-9,000	$9,000-11,000
Limousine	*	$13,000-19,000	$19,000-24,000

* Purchase only in good or excellent condition

1989

The Mark VII was carried over virtually unchanged from 1988, its only alteration being an engine-management computer malfunction warning light (previously standard in California only). The LSC and luxury Bill Blass models were retained, along with the 225-bhp V-8. The LSC had black sidewall high-performance tires on alloy wheels, quick steering, handling suspension, and leather upholstery. The Bill Blass threw in some chrome trim to remind you of 1960, and offered a choice of leather or cloth interior. Both models featured automatic climate control, self-leveling suspension, remote decklid release, and six-way power seats. A power glass moonroof was optional. Town Car and Continental were left largely unchanged. Calendar-year sales were: Continental, 56,441; Mark VII, 24,620; Town Car, 119,254.

	Restorable	Good	Excellent
Mark VII			
LSC/Bill Blass	*	$9,000-12,000	$12,000-14,000
Limousine	*	15,000-21,000	21,000-28,000

* Purchase only in good or excellent condition

1990 Lincoln Mark VII LSC coupe

1990

A revised grille, new dashboard, and driver-side air bag marked the 1990 edition of the Mark VII. The sporty LSC version had standard BBS alloy wheels and revised seats; the Bill Blass Designer Series sported whitewall tires and metallic clear coat paint. Rear shoulder belts were added to both models, and anti-lock brakes were standard. The broad '89 array of standard equipment continued. Calendar-year sales were 20,239. Continental found 62,732 buyers, the Town Car 148,689. Lincoln at this point was doing very well indeed, and during the Eighties had become serious competition to Cadillac.

1990 Lincoln Mark VII LSC coupe

	Restorable	Good	Excellent
Mark VII			
LSC/Bill Blass	*	$11,000-14,000	$14,000-18,000
Limousine	*	25,000-30,000	30,000-35,000

* Purchase only in good or excellent condition

Marmon

A notable Classic car (according to the Classic Car Club of America), Marmon appeals to the cognoscenti, the technically sophisticated. The supply of available vehicles is severely limited, and these beautiful machines have all the attributes of the obscure Classics: impossible-to-find body parts, almost irreplaceable mechanical parts. For Marmon owners, what breaks often has to be made by hand, and they say it's worth it. Investment potential is excellent for the magnificent Sixteen, very good for the Big Eight and 88, and modest for other models.

1930 Marmon Roosevelt Eight four-door sedan

1932 Marmon Sixteen convertible sedan

1930-33

Packing 200 horsepower from an overhead-valve engine of 490.8 cubic inches, the mighty Marmon Sixteen cost a cool $5200 to $5400 upon introduction in 1931—a time when few people had that kind of money to spend on a house, let alone a car. Worse, the Sixteen's limited sales potential was rendered almost meaningless through a long delay in deliveries. Lightweight construction was achieved thanks to extensive use of aluminum, and few cars could touch the Sixteen's performance. Body design, by Walter Dorwin Teague, was generally superior. Marmon's stock in trade was, of course, its array of eights, three in all in 1930-31 (84, 100, and 125 bhp). The most luxurious bodies came on the 136-inch wheelbase Big Eight of 1930-31 and the Model 88 (130- and 136-inches) in 1931. Only three series were fielded for 1932: the Sixteen (with a

1932 Marmon Sixteen limousine

huge variety of custom bodies, few if any of which were built), the eight-cylinder 70, and a 315.2-cid straight-eight series called the 125 (named for its wheelbase). The Sixteen was the only line listed for 1933, and its price was cut to as low as $4825 for the closed models, but in the depths of the Depression it hardly mattered. Marmon's assets were ultimately liquidated in 1937. Registrations were as follows: 12,369 in 1930, 5687 in 1931, 1365 in 1932, and just 86 in 1933. Needless to say, the open models in particular are practically non-existent—but an absolute prize when found.

	Restorable	Good	Excellent
1930-32 Roosevelt & Model 70			
Open bodies	$6,000-12,000	$12,000-20,000	$20,000-27,500
Closed bodies	3,000-7,000	7,000-11,000	11,000-14,000
1930-31 Models 8-69 & 8-79; 1932 Model 125			
Open bodies	7,500-18,000	18,000-32,500	32,500-45,000
Closed bodies	3,000-7,000	7,000-11,000	11,000-14,000
1930-31 Big Eight			
Open bodies	20,000-35,000	35,000-50,000	50,000-75,000
Closed bodies	5,000-12,500	12,500-20,000	20,000-30,000
1931 Model 88			
Open bodies	15,000-27,500	27,500-40,000	40,000-55,000
Closed bodies	5,000-12,500	12,500-20,000	20,000-30,000
1931-33 Sixteen			
Convertible coupe	40,000-75,000	75,000-110,000	110,000-150,000
Convertible sedan	45,000-85,000	85,000-125,000	125,000-175,000
Closed bodies	15,000-30,000	30,000-55,000	55,000-75,000

1939 Mercury convertible coupe

Mercury

A late arrival into both the auto industry and the collector car field, Mercury has never built up a broad collector following. Interest is compartmentalized around specific models, like the muscle cars of the Sixties. This makes for lots of bargains, but only moderate investment potential. Club support is fair, parts supplies more often than not are scarce.

1939

Conceived by Edsel Ford to fill a gap between Ford and the Lincoln-Zephyr, Mercury—priced around $1000 in its initial year—competed with Pontiac, Olds, Dodge, DeSoto, and low-end Buicks. A convertible, six-passenger coupe, and two- and four-door sedans were offered, all powered by a 239-cid V-8 rated at 95 horsepower and mounted on a 116-inch wheelbase. The convertible is clearly the most desirable, and 7102 were built. The open model is underrated as an investment. Not having risen in value as fast as contemporary Fords, it stands to have farther to go upward and will thus enjoy a rather steeper price spiral over the long term. The Sedan-Coupe was nearly as rare as the ragtop, as only 7664 were produced. Altogether, 70,835 cars rolled off the line the first year, though that included 10,621 foreign assemblies.

	Restorable	Good	Excellent
Convertible cpe	$4,000-12,000	$12,000-18,000	$18,000-25,000
Coupe	2,000-5,000	5,000-8,000	8,000-12,000
Sedans	1,000-4,000	4,000-6,500	6,500-9,000

1939 Mercury four-door sedan

1940

Like the '40 Ford, Mercury's styling was crisp, featuring a pointed nose, flush-mounted headlamps, and smoothly rounded lines. A new body style that has since become highly desirable was the four-door convertible, but this is unfortunately very rare—only 1083 were built during the model year, after which it was dropped. With their sleek art deco styling, the '40 Mercurys are fine examples of pre-war industrial design and still fun to drive and to show. Total production increased to 86,062, including 9741 convertibles and 16,189 coupes. The 1939-40 Sedan-Coupes (six-passenger) had narrow B-pillars and chrome-framed side windows, giving them an attractive semi-hardtop look.

1940 Mercury convertible coupe

	Restorable	Good	Excellent
Convertible sdn	$5,000-13,000	$13,000-20,000	$20,000-27,500
Convertible cpe	4,000-12,000	12,000-18,000	18,000-25,000
Coupe	2,000-5,000	5,000-8,000	8,000-12,000
Sedans	1,000-4,000	4,000-6,500	6,500-9,000

1941 Mercury coupe

1941

Mercury mounted a seven-car lineup for its third year, including a 2/4-passenger coupe, business coupe, and woody station wagon. Styling was much changed, again following Ford lines, and not nearly as singular as it had been in 1940. For this reason, there is no premium value attached to coupe body styles over sedans. Longer, higher, squared-off fenders were accompanied by a divider-bar grille and fender-mounted parking lights. The bigger body now rode a 118-inch wheelbase and was noticeably roomier inside. The convertible coupe and woody wagon are about equal in collector preference. Out of a total run of 82,391 cars, only 2291 wagons and 8556 ragtops were produced, plus 18,263 Sedan-Coupes and 1954 2/4-passenger coupes with auxiliary seats.

	Restorable	Good	Excellent
Convertible cpe	$4,000-12,000	$12,000-18,000	$18,000-25,000
Station wagon	5,000-14,000	14,000-20,000	20,000-27,500
Other models	1,000-4,000	4,000-6,500	6,500-9,000

1942

A serious facelift was accompanied by a 100-horsepower V-8 and a semi-automatic transmission

1942 Mercury coupe

1942 Mercury four-door station wagon

1942 Mercury two-door sedan

1946 Mercury Sportsman convertible coupe

called Liquamatic, but it proved so troublesome that Ford retrofitted most cars with standard transmissions. The war, of course, prevented a full model run, so production was halted in early February after only 22,816 cars had been built. The '42 Merc is easily distinguished by its two-tier, horizontal-bar grille (similar to the Lincoln-Zephyr and Continental), double chrome bands on all four fenders, and a bright beltline molding running completely around the hood. Parking lights were shifted inboard atop the fenders, and directional signals were made optional this year. Except for the elimination of the 2/4-passenger auxiliary-seat coupe, there was no change in body styles. Output this year included 800 three-passenger coupes, 857 woody wagons, 969 convertibles, and 5345 Sedan-Coupes. Cars built after December 31, 1941, had painted trim by government edict. These cars would be really rare as they were in production for only a month.

	Restorable	Good	Excellent
Convertible cpe	$4,000-12,000	$12,000-18,000	$18,000-25,000
Station wagon	5,000-14,000	14,000-20,000	20,000-27,500
Other models	1,000-4,000	4,000-6,500	6,500-9,000

1946

The prewar business coupe was dropped, but the novel Sportsman convertible arrived for '46. Comparable to Ford's Sportsman, it was trimmed with maple or yellow birch framing and mahogany inserts on the doors, rear bodyside panels, and rear deck. The wood paneling was structural, not merely decorative, creating problems at the rear end, where standard production fenders could not be fitted. To solve this, Mercury used '41 Ford sedan delivery fenders, and designed the wooden structure around them. The body was framed out in solid wood, beautifully mitered and glued together and covered with multiple coats of varnish. At $2209, Sportsman convertibles cost nearly $500 more than the regular soft top—Mercury made only 200, then dropped the model for 1947. As a result, the Mercury Sportsman is extremely rare and desirable. The grille, sporting fine vertical bars, was new. Among the 86,608 cars produced were 24,163 Sedan-Coupes, 6044 convertibles, and 2797 wagons.

	Restorable	Good	Excellent
Sportsman cvt	$10,000-20,000	$20,000-35,000	$35,000-55,000
Convertible cpe	4,000-12,000	12,000-18,000	18,000-25,000
Station wagon	5,000-14,000	14,000-20,000	20,000-27,500
Other models	1,000-4,000	4,000-6,500	6,500-9,000

1947

Though it looked about the same, Mercury made a number of changes for 1947. Bodies demonstrated the improved supply of raw materials after the strain of the war. Aluminum pistons and hood ornament, chrome-plated interior hardware, and a chrome instead of painted grille frame were all new features. Dashboard gauges were more legible, in black with silver letters. The beltline molding no longer wrapped around the hood, but stopped just ahead of the cowl. Body styles decreased to five with the deletion of the Sportsman. Production of the "true" '47s didn't begin until February that year (and without the two-door sedan), so they are no more common than '46s. Among the 85,383 cars produced were 3558 wagons, 10,221 ragtops, 29,284 Sedan-Coupes, and 43,281 four-door Town Sedans.

	Restorable	Good	Excellent
Convertible cpe	$4,000-12,000	$12,000-18,000	$18,000-25,000
Station wagon	5,000-14,000	14,000-20,000	20,000-27,500
Other models	1,000-4,000	4,000-6,500	6,500-9,000

1946 Mercury Sedan Coupe

1948

No changes at all were made on the '48 models, their only identification being their serial numbers. Mercury offered the same body styles and prices, and sold 1948 model cars from November 1947 until mid-April 1948, when the all-new '49s appeared. As a result, 1948 model year production was the lowest for any postwar year—only 50,268: 16,476 Sedan-Coupes, 24,283 Town Sedans, 7586 convertibles, and 1889 woody wagons (plus a few chassis).

	Restorable	Good	Excellent
Convertible cpe	$4,000-12,000	$12,000-18,000	$18,000-25,000
Station wagon	5,000-14,000	14,000-20,000	20,000-27,500
Other models	1,000-4,000	4,000-6,500	6,500-9,000

1949 Mercury Sport Sedan four-door

1949

The completely restyled '49 was longer than before, though it still rode a 118-inch wheelbase. Initial planning had called for a much larger new Ford, but this ended up ultimately being the new Merc, which now shared its bodyshell with the equally new junior Lincoln (which got a 121-inch wheelbase). Styling was clean, massive, and streamlined, and performance benefitted by a displacement increase to 255.4 cubic inches. With a dual-downdraft Holley carburetor, horsepower rose to 110. A genuine 100-mph car, Mercury quickly became the darling of the hot-rod set, and tail-dragging custom Mercs with cruiser skirts and cowl-mounted spotlights became a common sight at high schools and soda fountains. The chassis was all-new, too, discarding the old transverse leaf springs in favor of a coil-spring independent setup in front and conventional twin leaf springs up back. Introduced on April 18, 1948, a long model year helped Mercury to a record production run of 301,319 units and sixth place in industry standings. This broke down to 120,616 two-door sedans (Mercury called them coupes), 155,882 four-door Sport Sedans, 16,765 convertibles, and 8044 station wagons. The last, now a two-door model, featured less structural wood and had a steel roof.

1949 Mercury two-door station wagon

1949 Mercury convertible coupe

	Restorable	Good	Excellent
Convertible cpe	$4,000-12,000	$12,000-18,000	$18,000-23,000
Station wagon	4,000-12,000	12,000-18,000	18,000-23,000

1950 Mercury convertible coupe

	Restorable	Good	Excellent
Coupe 2d	2,500-6,000	6,000-10,000	10,000-15,000
Sedan 4d	1,500-4,500	4,500-6,500	6,500-9,000

1950

The '50 model was a near twin to the '49, except for a chrome strip at the leading edge of the hood carrying the Mercury name and crest and much larger parking light surrounds. There were three new models: a stripped economy coupe (Model M-72A) and two special sport coupes called Montereys (M-72C). The latter had colorful, luxurious, convertible-like interiors, and came with a padded top of either canvas or leather. Like the Lincoln Lido and Capri and Ford Crestliner of the same years, they were substitute hardtops—a body style Mercury wouldn't get until 1952. Production fell slightly to 293,658 due to a normal length model year. Coupes (including Montereys) totaled 151,489, Sport Sedans 132,082, ragtops 8341, and wagons 1746.

1951 Mercury two-door station wagon

	Restorable	Good	Excellent
Convertible cpe	$4,000-12,000	$12,000-18,000	$18,000-23,000
Station wagon	4,000-12,000	12,000-18,000	18,000-23,000
Monterey	3,000-7,000	7,000-10,000	10,000-15,000
Coupe 2d	2,500-6,000	6,000-9,000	9,000-13,000
Sedan 4d	1,500-4,500	4,500-6,500	6,500-9,000

1951

Using the previous body but sporting slightly more glitzy trim, the '51 Mercury featured a bolder grille that wrapped around at the sides and prominent vertical taillamps riding squared-up rear fenders. The economy coupe was dropped, but the other models remained. Horsepower was raised slightly to 112, and the old flathead V-8 could now be mated to a three-speed Merc-O-Matic automatic transmission (developed with Borg-Warner). Convertible production dropped to 6759, but wagons recovered to 3812 units. The remainder of the 310,387 cars produced consisted of 142,168 coupes (including Montereys) and 157,648 Sport Sedans.

1952 Mercury Monterey convertible coupe

	Restorable	Good	Excellent
Convertible cpe	$4,000-12,000	$12,000-18,000	$18,000-23,000
Station wagon	4,000-12,000	12,000-18,000	18,000-23,000
Monterey cpe	3,000-7,000	7,000-10,000	10,000-15,000
Coupe 2d	2,500-6,000	6,000-9,000	9,000-13,000
Sedan 4d	1,500-4,500	4,500-6,500	6,500-9,000

1952 Mercury Sport Coupe hardtop

1952

Like Ford and Lincoln, the '52 Mercury was completely new, with tight, elegant lines on the same 118-inch wheelbase of the previous generation. The L-head V-8 was retained, but boosted to 125 horsepower. There were three top-line Monterey models: luxury four-door sedan, convertible, and (finally) a true two-door hardtop. The lower-line Custom (though not badged as such) consisted of two- and four-door sedans and a hardtop. Mercury offered quality, performance, and understated good looks led off by a massive Lincoln-like bumper-grille and

1952 Mercury four-door station wagon

ending with massive vertical chrome housings for taillights and back-up lights. Body style and condition being equal, there isn't much to separate values of the top-line Monterey and the cheaper Custom—Monterey might have a 10 percent edge but condition is far more important. Station wagons, six- and eight-passenger, now had all-steel bodies, though the bodysides were trimmed with simulated wood. Government-imposed cutbacks brought on by the Korean War forced production down to 172,087 units, including 30,559 Custom Sport Coupes (hardtops), 30,599 Monterey hardtops, 5261 convertibles, and just 2487 wagons.

	Restorable	Good	Excellent
Monterey cvt	$4,000-12,000	$12,000-18,000	$18,000-23,000
Monterey 2d htp	2,000-5,000	5,000-7,500	7,500-10,000
Custom 2d htp	2,000-5,000	5,000-7,000	7,000-9,000
Other models	1,500-3,000	3,000-5,000	5,000-8,000

1953

Mercury continued with two lines, Custom and Monterey, the latter priced about $150 higher and more elaborately trimmed. Hardtops came standard with two-tone paint. Identifying points this year were a grille with big Dagmar-style bumper guards and full-length side trim. The dashboard, similar to 1952, was interesting, with aircraft-style toggle levers for heating and ventilation and a cockpit-like instrument cluster. This was the last year for the L-head V-8. With production restrictions lifted, output shot up to 305,863 units, among them 39,547 Custom Sport Coupes, 76,119 Monterey hardtops, 8463 soft tops, and 7719 wagons.

	Restorable	Good	Excellent
Monterey cvt	$4,000-12,000	$12,000-18,000	$18,000-23,000
Monterey 2d htp	2,000-5,000	5,000-7,500	7,500-10,000
Custom 2d htp	2,000-5,000	5,000-7,000	7,000-9,000
Other models	1,500-3,000	3,000-5,000	5,000-8,000

1954

Mercury joined Ford in a switch to an overhead valve V-8. Mercury's version displaced 256 cubic inches and developed 161 horsepower with the standard four-barrel carburetor. Styling was measurably improved by the addition of wraparound taillights (eliminating the big chrome blobs of 1952-53) and an ultra-clean grille with a vertical-bar theme between the front bumper guards. A new Monterey, the Sun Valley, featured a transparent plastic front roof section like the Ford Skyliner. This created a mini-greenhouse effect, and Sun Valleys came with a shade to screen out the sun on hot days. Painted mint green or yellow with a dark green roof, the car came with a deluxe interior and special gold anodized Sun Valley script. The '54 Sun Valley, probably because of its evocative name, fine styling, and performance, is the most collectible of Ford's mid-Fifties glass-top models—9761 were built. In a down year for the industry, production fell to 259,305 cars. The Custom hardtop tumbled to 15,234, though the Monterey hardtop was up a bit to 79,533 units. Also

1953 Mercury prototype with 1952 grille

1954 Mercury Monterey Sun Valley hardtop coupe

1954 Mercury Monterey convertible coupe

1954 Mercury Monterey four-door station wagon

1954 Mercury Custom four-door sedan

1955 Mercury Monterey four-door sedan

1955 Mercury Montclair hardtop coupe

1955 Mercury Custom four-door station wagon

1955 Mercury Montclair four-door sedan

1955 Mercury Montclair convertible coupe

down was the Monterey ragtop, to 7293, while the wagons spurted to 11,656.

	Restorable	Good	Excellent
Sun Valley 2d htp	$3,000-7,000	$7,000-12,000	$12,000-18,000
Monterey cvt	4,000-12,000	12,000-18,000	18,000-23,000
Monterey 2d htp	2,000-5,000	5,000-7,500	7,500-10,000
Custom 2d htp	2,000-5,000	5,000-7,000	7,000-9,000
Other models	1,500-3,000	3,000-5,000	5,000-8,000

1955

All-new styling (with the obligatory wraparound windshield), a larger 292 V-8, and a longer 119-inch wheelbase (118 for wagons) marked these handsome Mercurys, which sold a record 329,808 copies. Line leader was the new Montclair series, offered in Sun Valley guise as well as other body styles. These Mercurys are very strong on the collector market, especially the rare Sun Valley (only 1787 built). Though they lack tailfins, the "Big M" has all the other neo-classic features: flashy paint jobs, rakish lines, and big engines (188 and 198 horsepower). At mid-year, a Montclair thin-pillar four-door sedan with a hardtop roofline appeared. Looking much like a hardtop, it enjoyed a production run of 20,624. Montclairs slightly lead Custom and Monterey models in values for the same body style. Hardtop output was 7040 Customs, 69,093 Montereys, and 71,588 Montclairs, the last having a lower roofline. Montclair also attracted 11,968 ragtop buyers.

	Restorable	Good	Excellent
Montclair cvt	$5,000-14,000	$14,000-19,000	$19,000-27,500
Sun Valley 2d htp	4,000-10,000	10,000-18,000	18,000-22,000
Montclair 2d htp	2,500-7,500	7,500-11,000	11,000-15,000
Other 2d htps	2,000-6,000	6,000-9,000	9,000-12,500
Other models	1,500-3,000	3,000-5,000	5,000-8,000

1956

Mercury expanded into somewhat uncharted territory, with a price-leading Medalist series starting at $2254, $200 more than a Ford Fairlane two-door sedan. Also new was a four-door hardtop body style called Phaeton, based on the '55 Montclair thin-pillar sedan. The facelift was a mild update, featuring a fussier grille and lightning-bolt side moldings that provided a flashier two-toned look. This year, Mercury got an enlarged 312-cid V-8 with 210, 225, or 235 bhp depending on model and transmission. There was even a mid-year 260-bhp hot-rod engine that's extremely rare (it was intended mainly for racing). The Sun Valley was dropped. In a down year for the industry, Mercury held steady at 327,943 units, among them the following hardtops: 11,982 two-door and 6685 Phaeton Medalists; 20,857 two-door and 12,187 Phaeton Customs; 11,765 two-door and 10,726 Phaeton Montereys; and 50,562 two-door and 23,493 Phaeton Montclairs. In addition, Mercury built 2311 Custom and 7762 Montclair convertibles. Wagon sales were up: 17,770

Customs and 13,280 Montereys, the latter still flaunting fake wood on the bodysides.

	Restorable	Good	Excellent
Montclair cvt	$5,000-14,000	$14,000-19,000	$19,000-27,500
Custom cvt	4,000-10,000	10,000-16,000	16,000-23,000
Montclair 2d htp	2,500-7,500	7,500-11,000	11,000-15,000
Other 2d htps	2,000-6,000	6,000-9,000	9,000-12,500
Phaeton 4d htps	2,000-5,000	5,000-8,000	8,000-11,000
Other models	1,500-3,000	3,000-5,000	5,000-8,000

1957

"A dramatic expression of dream car design," the Mercury Turnpike Cruiser was introduced as a two- and four-door hardtop and convertible. Equipment-wise, it was loaded, from its "skylight dual curve windshield" to its retractable, nearly vertical backlight. There were quad headlamps, dual air intakes over the windshield corners that housed little protruding radio antennas, a "Seat-O-Matic" power seat that automatically moved the seat rearward for exit and returned to any of 49 preset positions when the ignition was turned on, and pushbutton controls for the standard Merc-O-Matic transmission. The convertible was a replica of the Indianapolis Pace Car that year. The rest of the Mercury line followed the Cruiser's bigger, bolder new styling, all on a longer 122-inch wheelbase. Convertibles were offered in both Monterey and Montclair lines. Station wagons, meanwhile, were broken out as a separate series and were all hardtops, with two or four doors. The public didn't take to the new styling, so output fell back to 286,183. Monterey and Montclair two- and four-door hardtops and convertibles were called Phaetons and numbered 42,199, 22,475, and 5033 Montereys, respectively, and 30,111, 21,567, and 4248 Montclairs. Turnpike Cruisers were a sales disappointment: 7291 hardtop coupes, 8305 hardtop sedans, and 1265 ragtops. Two-door hardtop wagons (Commuter and Voyager) totaled 7168, four-doors (Commuter, Voyager, and Colony Park) 28,744.

	Restorable	Good	Excellent
Tpk Cruiser cvt	$5,000-14,000	$14,000-20,000	$20,000-27,500
Tpk Cruiser 2d htp	3,500-7,500	7,500-12,000	12,000-15,000
Tpk Cruiser 4d htp	2,500-6,000	6,000-8,000	8,000-11,000
Other convertibles	3,500-8,000	8,000-13,000	13,000-18,500
Other 2d htps	2,000-6,000	6,000-9,000	9,000-12,500
Phaeton 4d htps	1,500-4,000	4,000-6,000	6,000-9,000
Other models	1,500-3,000	3,000-5,000	5,000-8,000

1958

Slightly more conservative styling was offered for 1958, the year a recession clobbered sales of all medium-priced cars, including Mercury—making the '58s relatively rare today. Featured were twin grilles within a more massive bumper, dual headlights, and bodyside sculptures that rarely wore two-toning. The Turnpike Cruiser lost its convertible and became an upper-level sub-series within the Montclair line, but only 2864 two-door and 3543 four-door hardtops

1957 Mercury Montclair hardtop coupe

1957 Mercury Montclair Phaeton hardtop sedan

1957 Mercury Turnpike Cruiser convertible coupe

1958 Mercury Monterey hardtop coupe

1958 Mercury Monterey hardtop coupe

1958 Mercury Montclair Turnpike Cruiser hardtop

1958 Mercury Colony Park four-door hardtop wagon

1959 Mercury Park Lane convertible coupe

1959 Mercury Montclair Cruiser hardtop coupe

1960 Mercury Montclair Cruiser hardtop sedan

were built. The Medalist, which had disappeared in '57, was back for a short encore as a two- or four-door sedan to fight the recession—prices started at $2547. A 230-bhp 312 V-8 was the only engine offered. Ranked above the Montclair now were the Park Lane Phaeton two- and four-door hardtops and a convertible, all packing a 360-bhp, 430-cid Lincoln V-8 and riding a three-inch-longer 125-inch wheelbase. Automatic dual-range Multi-Drive Merc-O-Matic transmission made its debut. Another new engine was a 383 V-8 with 312 or 300 bhp, standard on Montclairs and wagons. Most collectible: the big, flashy Park Lane convertible, but only 853 were built. The Montclair ragtop did even worse, only 844 units, though the Monterey managed 2292. With only 153,271 cars built over a wide range of models, even four-door sedans were fairly rare; with 29,892 produced, the Monterey was '58's best selling model.

	Restorable	Good	Excellent
Park Lane cvt	$3,000-8,000	$8,000-15,000	$15,000-22,500
Other cvts	3,000-7,000	7,000-12,000	12,000-19,000
2d hardtops	2,000-6,000	6,000-10,000	10,000-15,000
Other models	1,500-3,000	3,000-6,000	6,000-9,000

1959

The '59 Mercurys rode a longer chassis with 126- and 128-inch wheelbases, wore a more conventional, full-width grille filled with small rectangles, and sported an extension of the odd concave rear fender styling of 1957-58 with even larger wedge-shaped taillights. The Medalist and Turnpike Cruiser were dropped, leaving a line thinned to Monterey, Montclair, Park Lane, and wagons. The last were still two- or four-door hardtops, referred to as Country Cruisers. Engines ranged from a 210-bhp 312 V-8 to a 345-bhp 430. Convertibles were cut to just two, the Monterey and Park Lane (4426 and 1254 built). These were more conventional-looking Mercurys than any that had appeared since 1954; because they are more ordinary, they have not garnered much latterday collector enthusiasm. They didn't garner much enthusiasm when new, either, as production dipped to 149,987 units.

	Restorable	Good	Excellent
Park Lane cvt	$3,000-7,000	$7,000-13,000	$13,000-20,000
Monterey cvt	3,000-7,000	7,000-11,000	11,000-15,000
2d hardtops	2,000-6,000	6,000-10,000	10,000-15,000
Other models	1,500-3,000	3,000-6,000	6,000-9,000

1960

Beginning at mid-year, the Comet brought Mercury a version of the Ford Falcon, wearing styling originally intended for the Edsel, which by then had been phased out. Comets rode a longer 114-inch wheelbase (wagons 109.5), featured better trim than Falcons, and sold quite well (over 100,000 in a short model year). The full-size Montclair and Park Lane packed the Lincoln 430 V-8 (this year with a two-barrel carb) and received a fairly ambitious facelift that shed the old "dream-car look." Most noticeable were a wide, closely-spaced, vertical-bar grille housing quad headlights and canted fins and taillights at the rear. Montereys and Commuter wagons carried 312 and 383 V-8s. Though Monterey dominated sales, the senior Park Lane is definitely more collectible. The big Mercs saw a small improvement in sales, including 6062 Monterey and 1525 Park Lane ragtops, 2974 Park Lane Cruiser two-door hardtops, and 5788 Park Lane Cruiser four-door hardtops. This was the last year for hardtop wagons, now only with four doors; Commuter and Colony Park output totaled 22,360 units. With Comet's help, total Mercury output jumped to 271,331.

	Restorable	Good	Excellent
Park Lane cvt	$3,000-7,000	$7,000-12,000	$12,000-18,000
Monterey cvt	3,000-6,000	6,000-10,000	10,000-15,000
Comet	1,000-2,000	2,000-4,000	4,000-6,500
Other models	1,500-3,000	3,000-6,000	6,000-8,500

1961

Responding to the '58 recession and the demise of Edsel, the '61 Mercury moved downward to the Ford bodyshell, though on a one-inch-longer 120-inch wheelbase. Montclair and Park Lane were dropped, as was the Lincoln engine. A 175-bhp 292 V-8 became standard, though a new budget-priced Meteor 600 and 800 series could be had with Ford's 135-bhp, 223-cid six. All were sedans, save for a $2774 800 hardtop coupe. The top-line Merc was now the Monterey, though with prices starting at $2871 the big Mercury was reduced to a lower-medium-priced niche at best. Optional V-8s were the 220-bhp 352 and 300-bhp 390. Aside from the four-door models, Monterey output reached 10,942 hardtop coupes and 7053 convertibles. The Comet received a new grille, plus the $2284 S-22 pillared coupe sporting bucket seats and a deluxe interior, as well as an optional 101-bhp, 170-cid six (which still left the Comet rather sluggish, especially with the two-speed automatic). The S-22 is mildly collectible, but scarce. Though total Mercury output rose smartly to 317,351 units (much of that because of the Comet), this was not a good year for Mercury collectors.

	Restorable	Good	Excellent
Monterey cvt	$2,500-5,000	$5,000-7,500	$7,500-11,000
Comet S-22	2,000-4,000	4,000-6,000	6,000-8,500
Other models	1,000-2,500	2,500-5,000	5,000-8,000

1962

Almost forgotten by the investor crowd today, the intermediate Meteor (116.5-inch wheelbase) was introduced as Mercury's version of the Ford Fairlane, though only with two- and four-door sedans. Aside from the puny 170-cid six, Meteors could be had with a 145-bhp lightweight 221 V-8 or a 164-bhp version bored to 260 cid. The Meteor to look for is the sporty S-33, a two-door with bucket seats and

1960 Mercury Comet four-door sedan

1960 Mercury Comet four-door station wagon

1961 Mercury Colony Park four-door station wagon

1961 Mercury Monterey convertible coupe

1961 Mercury Monterey hardtop sedan

1962 Mercury Monterey two-door sedan

1963 Mercury Monterey Breezeway hardtop

1963 Mercury Monterey Custom hardtop sedan

1963 Mercury Meteor S-33 hardtop coupe

1963 Mercury Comet Custom Sportster hardtop coupe

1963 Mercury Comet S-22 convertible coupe

sportier trim (red-white-blue hubcap centers, for example). Only 5900 were called for. The still-languishing full-size Mercurys featured a new convex grille and high-mounted "jet-tube" taillights, as well as a slightly more upmarket Monterey Custom series. Within this came the sporty S-55 hardtop and convertible, with bucket seats, and particularly desirable with the optional (and very rare) 406 V-8 performance engine. Two-door hardtops included 5328 Montereys, 10,814 Monterey Customs, and 2772 S-55s. The Monterey Custom convertible found 5489 buyers, the S-55 just 1315. Comet was only lightly facelifted, mainly at the rear end. The S-22 remained a two-door sedan. Total production increased to 341,366 units and found Mercury in seventh place in the sales race.

	Restorable	Good	Excellent
Monterey, S-55 cvt	$3,000-6,000	$6,000-8,500	$8,500-13,500
Meteor S-33 2d sdn	2,000-3,000	3,000-5,000	5,000-6,500
Comet S-22 2d sdn	2,000-4,000	4,000-6,000	6,000-8,500
Meteor, other	1,000-2,000	2,000-3,500	3,500-5,000
Other models	500-2,000	2,000-4,000	4,000-6,000

1963

A new '63 styling feature, Mercury's "Breezeway" reverse-slant retractable rear window, was an interesting idea that collectors find uninteresting—different and practical though it might have been. Though available on all models including the hot Monterey Custom S-55 hardtop (3863 built), collectors prefer the mid-year S-55 Marauder semi-fastback version (2319 built). Also consider the S-55 hardtop sedan (1203 built), and look for the convertible (1379 produced). All Montereys and Monterey Customs came with a 250-bhp Marauder 390 V-8 this year, S-55s with a 300-bhp version (330 bhp optional). Look especially for the rare 406- or 427-cid V-8 engines; they packed 385/405 and 410/425 horsepower. Station wagons were pared down to just the Colony Park this year, and 13,976 were built. Monterey Customs are also worth considering, and there were 10,693 Breezeway hardtop coupes, 7298 Marauder hardtops, and 3783 ragtops. Though this would be its last year, a modestly changed Meteor got a true two-door hardtop; 7565 Customs and 4865 S-33s found buyers. A mildly facelifted Comet finally introduced a convertible and a two-door semi-fastback hardtop, with S-22 versions of both—and V-8 power, too, via the 145-bhp 221 and 164-bhp 260. Custom hardtops and ragtops numbered 9432 and 7354, S-22s 5807 and 5757. Despite far more cars of interest to collectors, total output fell to 301,581 units.

	Restorable	Good	Excellent
S-55 convertible	$3,500-7,000	$7,000-10,000	$10,000-14,000
S-55 hardtop	2,500-4,000	4,000-6,500	6,500-9,500
Meteor S-33 2d htp	2,500-3,500	3,500-5,000	5,500-7,500
Meteor, other	1,000-2,000	2,000-3,500	3,500-6,000
Comet S-22 cvt	2,500-5,000	5,000-8,000	8,000-12,500

	Restorable	Good	Excellent
Comet S-22 2d htp	2,000-4,000	4,000-6,000	6,000-8,500
Comet convertible	2,000-4,000	4,000-6,000	6,000-9,000
Other models	500-2,000	2,000-4,000	4,000-6,000

1964

Following lackluster sales, the Meteor was dropped for '64. Comet, meanwhile, received a squarish facelift, and the S-22 was renamed Caliente (hot). Any Comet could be ordered with the 260 (later 289) small-block V-8, but the best version was the Cyclone hardtop, powered by a 210-bhp 289. There is little spread in today's market between the Comet convertible and hardtop—9039 and 31,204 built—which makes the ragtop a bargain. Calientes constitute undiscovered territory—maybe they always will—while the muscle-bound Cyclone hardtop found 7454 buyers, and sells for about the same as a Caliente convertible. The big Mercs, still moving back upmarket, reverted to a Monterey, Montclair, and Park Lane lineup, and Breezeways were less popular. A notable addition was the Marauder semi-fastback hardtop sedan in all three series. The 390 V-8 was still standard, with 250 and 266 bhp for Montereys/Montclairs, 300 and 330 bhp for Park Lanes. The 410/425-bhp 427 was optional across the line. Marauders, with the 425-bhp version of this huge mill are awesome performers, and quite desirable. Monterey production included 2592 convertibles, 8760 Marauder hardtop coupes, and 4143 Marauder hardtop sedans. Equivalent figures for Montclairs were 2329, 6459, and 8655; for Park Lanes it was 1967, 1052, and 4505. Total Mercury output dipped slightly to 298,609.

	Restorable	Good	Excellent
Park Lane cvt	$2,500-6,000	$6,000-9,000	$9,000-12,000
Monterey cvt	2,500-5,000	5,000-8,000	8,000-10,000
Marauder 410 bhp	2,500-5,000	5,000-8,000	8,000-10,000
Super Marauder 425	4,000-8,000	8,000-12,000	12,000-15,000
Comet Cyclone htp	3,000-6,000	6,000-8,500	8,500-11,500
Comet Caliente cvt	3,000-6,000	6,000-8,500	8,500-11,500
Comet Caliente htp	2,500-5,000	5,000-7,500	7,500-9,500
Other models	500-2,000	2,000-4,000	4,000-6,000

1965

Mercury shared a complete restyle with Ford, but riding a 123-inch wheelbase (119 for wagons). Breezeway styling was now limited to four-door sedans in all series, and all two-door hardtops were semi-fastbacks. The usual line of 390 and 427 V-8s was offered with horsepower ranging from 250 to 425. "Torque Box" construction referred to frames tuned for each body style to minimize noise and vibration, and coil springs were adopted at the rear. Styling was crisp, formal, and attractive—almost Lincolnesque. Big cars had come back and the Lincoln image was again worth cultivating. Big Mercury output rose to 181,699 (the best since

1964 Mercury Montclair Marauder hardtop sedan

1964 Mercury Comet Cyclone hardtop coupe

1964 Mercury Comet Caliente convertible coupe

1965 Mercury Montclair Marauder hardtop coupe

1965 Mercury Park Lane Marauder hardtop coupe

1965 Mercury Comet Caliente convertible coupe

1965 Mercury Comet Caliente hardtop coupe

1966 Mercury Comet Caliente convertible coupe

1966 Mercury S-55 convertible coupe

1966 Mercury Montclair hardtop coupe

1957), which included 46,828 Breezeways, 33,355 two-door Marauder hardtops, and 41,235 hardtop sedans. Convertibles numbered 4762 Montereys and 3006 Park Lanes. Comets sported new front styling highlighted by vertical quad headlights and a base 200-cid six with 120 bhp. The 289 V-8 (200 and 225 horses) was optional in the 202, 404, and Caliente series, standard on the sporty Caliente hardtop. Comet output declined to 165,032, but was still enough to help Mercury to a record total of 346,751 units. Comet hardtop production was 29,247 Calientes and 12,347 Cyclones, and 6035 Caliente convertibles were built.

	Restorable	Good	Excellent
Park Lane cvt	$2,500-6,000	$6,000-9,000	$9,000-12,000
Monterey cvt	2,500-5,000	5,000-8,000	8,000-10,000
Marauder 427	2,500-5,000	5,000-8,000	8,000-10,000
Marauder Super 427	4,000-8,000	8,000-12,000	12,000-15,000
Comet Cyclone htp	3,000-6,000	6,000-8,500	8,500-11,500
Comet Caliente cvt	3,000-6,000	6,000-8,500	8,500-11,500
Other models	500-2,000	2,000-4,000	4,000-6,000

1966

A modestly restyled grille was adopted for the big Mercs; two-door models had new "sweep-style" roofs with a concave backlight, a dramatic break with the Breezeway design, which was now further restricted to Monterey and Park Lane sedans. The sporty bucket-seat S-55, now with a 345-bhp 428 V-8, was revived, though only 2916 hardtop coupes and 669 convertibles were sold. Other production figures included 22,870 total Breezeways, 3279 Monterey ragtops, 19,103 Monterey two-door hardtops, 11,290 Montclair hardtop coupes, 19,204 Park Lane hardtop coupes, 2546 Park Lane soft tops, and 18,894 woody-look Colony Park wagons, which this year introduced a Dual-Action tailgate that dropped down or opened like a door. Comet received its first complete restyle—as did the related Ford Fairlane—and become an intermediate riding a longer 116-inch wheelbase. Styling was curvier, especially at the "hips," and vertically stacked headlights returned. Four series were listed: 202, Capri, Caliente, and Cyclone. The last came as a base or GT hardtop and convertible powered by Ford's 335-bhp 390 V-8, and offered some useful suspension options. Cyclone production came to 6889 hardtops, 13,812 GT hardtops, 1305 convertibles, and 2158 GT ragtops. In addition, Mercury built 25,862 Caliente hardtops, 3922 Caliente soft tops, and 15,031 Capri hardtops.

	Restorable	Good	Excellent
Full-size cvt	$2,500-5,000	$5,000-7,500	$7,500-11,000
S-55 convertible	3,500-6,000	6,000-8,000	8,000-12,000
S-55 2d htp	2,000-4,000	4,000-6,000	6,000-8,000
Comet Cyclone GT cvt	3,500-7,500	7,500-10,000	10,000-13,000
Comet Cyclone GT htp	3,000-6,000	6,000-8,500	8,500-11,500
Comet Cyclone cvt	3,000-6,500	6,500-9,000	9,000-11,000

	Restorable	Good	Excellent
Comet Cyclone htp	2,500-5,000	5,000-7,000	7,000-9,000
Comet Caliente cvt	3,000-6,000	6,000-8,500	8,500-11,500
Other models	500-2,000	2,000-4,000	4,000-6,000

1967

Cougar, Mercury's version of the Mustang on a longer 111-inch wheelbase, offered more luxury and handsome looks; hidden headlights, sequential taillights, and the 289 V-8 were standard. The upmarket XR-7 version had a dummy wood dash full of dials and a leather interior, while the GT with a 320-bhp 390 V-8 was the sportiest model. First-year output totaled 116,260 hardtops, 27,221 XR-7s, and 7412 GTs. The Comet was only mildly facelifted. More impressive than ever, the Cyclone GT had as an option the 427 Ford V-8, providing 410/425 bhp. Cyclones were rare this year: 2682 hardtops and 431 convertibles plus 3419 GT hardtops and 378 GT ragtops. Full-size styling was revised again, now much curvier and hippier. A limited-production Marquis was announced—a $3989 two-door hardtop with broad rear roof pillars and a vinyl top. Only 6510 were built. Another newcomer was the vinyl-topped Park Lane Brougham ($3896-$3986); 3325 Breezeway sedans and 4189 hardtop sedans were sold. The S-55 was so rare—just 570 hardtops and 145 ragtops—that it would not reappear for 1968. Mercury also built 2673 Monterey and 1191 Park Lane soft tops. Total model year production was up slightly to 354,923 units.

	Restorable	Good	Excellent
Cougar, incl. XR-7	$2,000-4,000	$4,000-6,000	$6,000-8,000
Full-size cvt	2,500-5,000	5,000-7,000	7,000-10,000
S-55 convertible	3,500-6,000	6,000-8,000	8,000-12,000
S-55 2d htp	2,000-4,000	4,000-6,000	6,000-8,000
Cyclone GT cvt	3,500-7,500	7,500-10,000	10,000-12,000
Cyclone GT htp	3,000-6,000	6,000-8,500	8,500-11,000
Cyclone cvt	3,000-6,500	6,500-8,000	8,000-10,000
Cyclone htp	2,500-5,000	5,000-7,000	7,000-9,000
Caliente cvt	2,500-4,500	4,500-6,500	6,500-9,500
Other models	500-2,000	2,000-4,000	4,000-6,000

1968

Cougar GT and GT-Es powered by the brawny 345-bhp 427 V-8 were available this year, with a variety of handling and performance options. Another interesting model was the XR-7G, a racy package named after race driver Dan Gurney. A 210/230-bhp 302 small-block V-8 also became available. Cougar production was down this year to 113,726 units. The heavily facelifted mid-size Mercurys got horizontally mounted quad headlights and could be had with engines ranging from a 120-bhp 200 six to a 335-bhp 428 V-8. The lineup consisted of a hardtop Comet and the luxurious Montego in standard sedan and coupe plus MX sedan, coupe, convertible and wagon. A luxury Brougham trim option was available on the MX four-door sedan and hardtop coupe. There were no convertible Cyclones this year, only formal and fastback hardtops in base or GT guise.

1967 Mercury Cougar XR-7 hardtop coupe

1967 Mercury Cougar hardtop coupe

1967 Mercury Comet Cyclone GT hardtop coupe

1967 Mercury Monterey hardtop coupe

1967 Mercury Monterey S-55 convertible coupe

1968 Mercury Cougar XR-7 7.0 Litre GT-E hardtop

1968 Mercury Park Lane convertible coupe

1969 Mercury Cougar Eliminator hardtop coupe

1969 Mercury Cougar CJ 428 hardtop coupe

1969 Mercury Marauder X-100 hardtop coupe

Cyclones haven't risen in value as fast as many others of their type, particularly their Ford counterparts. New old stock parts are in short supply and club support is not tremendous. Still, the Cyclone is a good entry-level muscle car that won't cost a king's ransom. Cyclones numbered 6165 fastback hardtops and 1034 formal hardtops, plus 6105 GT fastbacks and 334 notchbacks. In the Montego MX line, Mercury produced 25,827 hardtops and 3248 ragtops. The big Mercs sported new two- and four-door hardtop rooflines and revised frontal styling, while Brougham became a package option for Park Lanes. Park Lane two-door hardtops and convertibles could also be had with "yacht-deck" simulated wood paneling on the bodysides (very rare). Ragtop output was 1515 Montereys and 1112 Park Lanes, while the luxurious Marquis hardtop found 3965 buyers. Total Mercury output edged up to 360,467 units.

	Restorable	Good	Excellent
Cougar, incl. XR-7	$2,000-4,000	$4,000-6,000	$6,000-8,000
Cougar GT/GT-E	2,500-5,000	5,000-7,500	7,500-10,000
Montego cvt	2,500-4,000	4,000-6,000	6,000-8,000
Cyclone cpe/htp	1,500-3,000	3,000-5,000	5,000-7,000
Cyclone GT	2,000-3,500	3,500-6,000	6,000-9,000
Cyclone GT 427	3,000-5,000	5,000-9,000	9,000-14,000
Full-size cvt	2,500-5,000	5,000-7,500	7,500-10,000
Full-size 427/428 V-8	3,500-7,500	7,500-11,000	11,000-16,000
Other models	500-2,000	2,000-4,000	4,000-6,000

1969

An exciting pair of street racers, the Cyclone and Cyclone CJ fastback hardtops, featured black-out grilles, clean sides without chrome, racing stripes, and special rear-end styling. Options included turbine-style wheel covers and racing-style outside mirrors. Most collectible is the CJ, carrying a functional hood scoop for its Ram-Air 428 Cobra-Jet engine, a star on the stock car racing circuit. CJs numbered 3261, the Cyclone 5882. A Cyclone Spoiler model joined the line at mid-year. Big Mercs, now on a 124-inch wheelbase (wagons 121) looked more Lincoln-like. Monterey Custom replaced the Montclair. Marquis became a full series—replacing Park Lane—with upmarket Brougham models. The Marauder fastback hardtop (on a 121-inch wheelbase) was a high-performance, low-production entry this year; it had clean bodywork, the Marquis grille with concealed headlights, and ventless side windows. Buyers requested 9031 base models and 5635 X-100s. Monterey and Marquis convertibles were offered (1297 and 2319 built), and a soft top was added to the Cougar line in base and XR-7 trim (5796 and 4024 produced). The hottest Cougar was the Eliminator with the 428 engine. All Cougars sported swoopier styling and were slightly larger. Base engine was now a 250-bhp 351 V-8. Total Mercury production shot up to 398,262.

	Restorable	Good	Excellent
Cougar htp coupe	$2,000-4,000	$4,000-6,000	$6,000-8,000

	Restorable	Good	Excellent
Eliminator (428)	3,000-8,000	8,000-11,000	11,000-15,000
Cougar convertible	3,000-5,000	5,000-7,500	7,500-10,000
Eliminator (428)	5,000-9,000	9,000-13,000	13,000-17,500
Montego cvt	2,500-4,000	4,000-6,000	6,000-8,000
Cyclone Spoiler	3,000-5,000	5,000-7,000	7,000-10,000
Cyclone CJ (428)	2,000-3,500	3,500-6,000	6,000-9,000
Full-size cvt	2,500-5,000	5,000-7,500	7,500-10,000
Full-size 428/429	3,500-7,500	7,500-11,000	11,000-16,000
Marauder 2d htp	1,500-4,000	4,000-6,000	6,000-8,500
Marauder X-100	2,500-5,000	5,000-7,500	7,500-10,000
Other models	500-2,000	2,000-4,000	4,000-6,000

1970

The full-size lineup was a repeat of 1969 with only minor styling changes. Monterey and Marquis convertibles (581 and 1233 built) were now in their final year. Marauder output dropped to 3397 base models and 2646 X-100s. In the heavily restyled midsize line, the Comet was dropped, leaving Montegos in base, MX, and MX Brougham form, but without any soft tops. However, an MX Brougham four-door hardtop was added. There were three Cyclones, now semi-fastbacks, which saw output of 1695 base models, 1631 Spoilers, and 10,170 GTs. The big-block 429 was broadly spread around the Mercury line, but usually in low states of tune. Top 429s with 370-375 bhp were found as standard in the Cyclone Spoiler and optional on other Cyclones. Cougar, little changed, could also be equipped with the "Boss 429," and the Eliminator package was still available. Cougar output was down to 49,479 base and 18,565 XR-7 hardtops plus 2322 base and 1977 XR-7 ragtops. The economy was down, and so were total Mercury sales, to 324,716 units.

	Restorable	Good	Excellent
Cougar htp cpe	$2,000-4,000	$4,000-6,000	$6,000-8,000
Cougar convertible	3,000-5,000	5,000-7,500	7,500-10,000
Cyclone Spoiler	2,000-3,500	3,500-6,000	6,000-8,000
	(add 50% for 428/429)		
Full-size cvt	2,500-5,000	5,000-7,500	7,500-10,000
	(add 25% for 429)		
Marauder 2d htp	1,500-3,000	3,000-5,000	5,000-7,000
Marauder X-100	2,000-4,000	4,000-6,000	6,000-8,000
Other models	500-2,000	2,000-4,000	4,000-6,000

1971

Cougar began to diverge from Ford's Mustang, adding two inches to its wheelbase, along with considerable weight and bulk. Headlights were exposed, windshield wipers hidden. In addition, the grille was bolder and more upright and the rear window was tunneled in. Hardtop production ended up at 34,008 base and 25,416 XR-7 models. Considering that Cougar now offered the only convertible with a Mercury nameplate, demand was modest: 1723 base models, 1717 XR-7s. The muscular Cyclone intermediates were putting in their last year; they came standard with the 351 V-8, but the 370-bhp 429 was optional—and desirable. Swoopy sheetmetal set it clearly apart from run-of-the-mill Montegos. Most desirable was the limited-edition 429 Spoiler. Cyclone sales were way down to 444

1969 Mercury Cyclone CJ 428 fastback hardtop coupe

1969 Mercury Cyclone Spoiler Cale Yarborough Special

1969 Mercury Cyclone Spoiler Dan Gurney Special

1970 Mercury Cyclone Spoiler 429 hardtop coupe

1970 Mercury Cougar XR-7 convertible coupe

1971 Mercury Cyclone Spoiler hardtop coupe

1971 Mercury Cougar XR-7 hardtop coupe

1972 Mercury Cougar XR-7 convertible coupe

1972 Mercury Cougar XR-7 hardtop coupe

base hardtops, 353 Spoilers, and 2287 GTs. Among the more luxury-oriented Montegos, two-door hardtops numbered 9623 base, 13,719 MX, and 2851 MX Brougham. The Comet name was revived for a Mercury version of Ford's compact Maverick. Though both cars are eminently forgettable, Mercury managed to move 83,000 units, some of them two-doors with the GT package. Among the reskinned big Mercurys, the Marauder series was dropped, and the Custom Montereys were blended into the Monterey lineup. Marquis still topped the line. Two-door hardtop sales were 9099 Montereys, 4508 Custom Montereys, 7726 Marquis, and 14,570 Marquis Broughams. Despite a shortening list of models of interest to collectors, total output increased to 365,310 units.

	Restorable	Good	Excellent
Cougar htp cpe	$1,000-3,000	$3,000-4,500	$4,500-6,500
Cougar convertible	2,000-4,000	4,000-6,000	6,000-8,500
Cyclone Spoiler	2,000-3,500	3,500-6,000	6,000-8,000
	(add 50% for 429)		

1972

There's not much to say about the '72 Mercurys from a collector viewpoint. By now, the combined effects of federal regulations, a dearth of buyers for muscle cars and high insurance rates on them, engine detuning, and *net* horsepower ratings had eliminated virtually all the interesting models. The only '72 Mercurys with a hint of collectibility are the Cougars, but even Mercury's ponycar turned personal-luxury car was muddling through a mundane period. A case in point is the fact that the only engine now available for the Cougar was a 351 V-8 tuned to 164, 262, or 266 net horsepower. The GT model disappeared at mid-season. Production was 23,731 standard and 26,802 XR-7 hardtops plus 1240 base and 1929 XR-7 ragtops. Montego was all-new this year, with a 114-inch wheelbase for two-doors, 118 for four-doors, including wagons. Though the distinctive Cyclones were gone, a Cyclone package was available for two-door hardtops. It had functional dual hood scoops, special striping, Traction-Lok rear axle, 70-series tires, and other goodies. Four-speed stick was available, and so was the 429 V-8, now rated at 205 net bhp. Hardtop coupes numbered 9963 standard models, 25,802 MXs, and 28,417 MX Broughams. Comet was a carryover, with the GT package and 302 V-8 (with 143 net bhp) still offered. Big Mercs changed little; Marquis two-door hardtop output included 5507 base models and 20,064 Broughams. Total production zoomed to 441,964 units.

	Restorable	Good	Excellent
Cougar htp cpe	$1,000-3,000	$3,000-4,500	$4,500-6,500
Cougar convertible	2,000-4,000	4,000-6,000	6,000-8,500

1973

This was the last year for the Cougar convertible. If you're floored by the prices of Fifties and Sixties convertibles, Cougars of the Seventies ought to seem like bargains—but always opt for the best one you can find because the cost of restoration of such complicated cars is formidable, and the finished product will cost much more than its market value. Because it was well known that the ragtop was about to be dropped, output increased to 1284 base models and 3165 XR-7s. Hardtops were of course far more common: 21,069 and 35,110. Beginning this year, all Mercurys looked clumsier (and weighed more) because of the federally mandated five-mph crash bumpers up front. Tighter emissions rules hurt fuel economy. The big Mercs were reskinned and looked more formal than ever. They could still be had with the 429 V-8 (198/200 net bhp), and—on special order—a Police Interceptor 460 V-8 with 202/267 horses. Top-line Marquis two-door hardtop production came to 5973 base models and 22,770 Broughams. Montegos and Comets changed only enough to keep the Feds happy. The GT package was still available for both, and just 4464 were applied to the Montego.

	Restorable	Good	Excellent
Cougar htp cpe	$1,000-3,000	$3,000-4,500	$4,500-6,500
Cougar convertible	2,000-4,000	4,000-6,000	6,000-8,500

1973 Mercury Montego GT fastback hardtop

1973 Mercury Cougar XR-7 hardtop coupe

1974 Mercury Cougar XR-7 coupe

1974 Mercury Cougar XR-7 coupe

1974

While Ford's Mustang evolved to a smaller, lighter sporty car, the Cougar became a kind of ersatz Thunderbird (complete with opera windows), built on the Montego platform with no convertible available. A 351 V-8 was standard, but 400 and 460 V-8s were optional, as were Twin Comfort Lounge Seats. Though available only as an XR-7, production took a healthy jump to 91,670 units. The full-size Mercurys sported restyled grilles and taillights and engines were 400 and 460 V-8s. Hardtop coupes numbered 2003 Montereys, 4510 Monterey Customs, 2633 Marquis, and 10,207 Marquis Broughams. The Montego lost the GT package, but a Sports Appearance Group and Custom Trim Option were offered. Two-door hardtop production was 7082 base models, 27,812 MXs, and 40,951 MX Broughams. The Comet retained its GT package. Five-mph bumpers were required at the rear this year, adding even more weight and length to most models. Due in part to the Arab oil embargo, Mercury saw output drop to 403,977 units.

	Restorable	Good	Excellent
Cougar XR-7 htp cpe	$500-1,500	$1,500-3,000	$3,000-5,000

1975

Monarch was the new Mercury version of the Ford Granada and may be interesting historically,

1975 Mercury Cougar XR-7 coupe

1975 Mercury Monarch Ghia four-door sedan

1976 Mercury Cougar XR-7 coupe

but is hardly a collector car. The most desirable Monarch is the sportier two-door, and the best trim version is the Ghia, which offered fake wood, velour upholstery, and thick carpets. That could even be upgraded via a Grand Monarch Ghia option. Two-door output reached 29,151 base and 17,755 Ghia models. Bobcat was Mercury's Ford Pinto wearing a more formal grille. It could be had as a three-door hatchback Runabout or two-door Villager wagon with four or V-6 and be dressed up with various trim packages, but it's not a collectible. Big Mercurys all carried the Marquis name now, in base, Brougham, or Grand Marquis versions. They received front and rear touch-ups, and the rear side windows on the two-door hardtops were now fixed, a minus for collectors. A 158-bhp 400 V-8 was standard on cheaper models, while the 460 V-8 was downgraded from 275 bhp to 216. Comet received an upgraded GT package, while Montego hardly changed. Cougars could be outfitted with special interiors: Dark Red and White, Blue and White. A Gold package offered Gold Metallic paint, Gold Landau Roof, and other gold trim. A power moonroof was a new option. Production fell to 62,987 units. Total Mercury output edged up to 404,650.

	Restorable	Good	Excellent
Cougar XR-7 htp cpe	$500-1,500	$1,500-3,000	$3,000-5,000
Monarch Ghia 2d cpe	500-1,000	1,000-2,000	2,000-3,500

1976

There were few changes in the Mercury lineup, which had evolved in five years from a star-studded cast to a host of mediocrities. The Cougar XR-7 continued as a one-car line; standard equipment included Landau vinyl roof and full instrumentation including clock; power was supplied by the 351 V-8, though the 400 and 460 were still optional. Output recovered to 83,765 units. Monarch threw in a few engineering refinements and offered more options. Coupe production was 47,466 base models and 14,950 Ghias. Big Mercs all had a standard 400 V-8 this year, though the 460 was available. Given an improved economic picture, Mercury production jumped to 480,361 units.

	Restorable	Good	Excellent
Cougar XR-7 htp cpe	$500-1,500	$1,500-3,000	$3,000-5,000
Monarch Ghia 2d cpe	500-1,000	1,000-2,000	2,000-3,500

1977

The Cougar name now replaced Montego on the entire intermediate line, with XR-7 being reserved for a top-of-the-line coupe. Styling was largely new, incorporating quad rectangular headlights, humped decklid, and revised opera windows. Also new was the instrument panel. The XR-7 is the only collectible model, and was equipped with the usual identifying bits and pieces: Landau vinyl roof, special moldings and identification, comprehensive instrumentation. Standard engine was now the 302, with a 400 optional. Output of the XR-7 was up by half to 124,799 units. Monarch deleted the Grand Ghia model and added a Grand Touring Sedan. A four-speed floor-mounted transmission replaced the old three-speed stick. Coupe output came to 44,509 base models and 11,051 Ghias. Mercury enjoyed a good year as production climbed to 526,254 units.

	Restorable	Good	Excellent
Cougar XR-7 cpe	$500-1,500	$1,500-3,000	$3,000-5,000
Monarch Ghia 2d cpe	500-1,000	1,000-2,000	2,000-3,500

1978

As Ford replaced Maverick with the more able Fairmont, Mercury replaced Comet with a Fairmont clone with a traditional name from Lincoln: Zephyr. A high-performance, sporty-looking Zephyr, the Z-7 coupe, received favorable reviews in the press. Its suspension involved a rear stabilizer bar, modified spring rates, and special shock valving. A black-out grille, "wrap-over roof" with wide B-pillars with Z-7 emblems, tape stripes, and vinyl interior (with lots of "woodtone") distinguished this special model. Little collector demand has yet developed for it, so prices will be low—providing cheap driving fun. But look for—insist on—the 139-bhp 302 V-8, not the plug-slow 88-bhp four-cylinder model (or 85-bhp 200-cid six), and buy only a mint original. Monarch received a styling update that included a new grille and rectangular headlights. Ghia became an option package, and a new one was added: ESS (Euro Sport Sedan). Coupes, of which 38,939 were built, got overlays on the opera windows to make them look like "twindows" on each side. Though basically unchanged, Cougar XR-7s could receive a Midnight/Chamois Decor option. XR-7 output was 166,508 units. Total Mercury production set a new record: 635,051.

	Restorable	Good	Excellent
Cougar XR-7 cpe	$500-1,500	$1,500-3,000	$3,000-5,000
Monarch Ghia 2d cpe	500-1,000	1,000-2,000	2,000-3,500
Zephyr Z-7 cpe	500-1,000	1,000-2,000	2,000-3,500

1979

Mercury Capri was a new line of cars based on the redesigned and larger Ford Mustang, once again giving Mercury a close counterpart (busier styling, fastback body style) to Ford's 100.4-inch-wheelbase ponycar. Base, Ghia, and RS packages were offered, and a Turbo RS was an interesting engine option. That 2.3 four developed 140 horsepower, same as the torquier 302 V-8, which was also optional. First year sales came to 92,432 coupes (including RS and RS Turbo) and 17,712 Ghias. A little-changed Cougar found 163,716 buyers. Zephyr was also little changed, though a Ghia

1977 Mercury Cougar XR-7 coupe

1977 Mercury Cougar XR-7 coupe

1978 Mercury Cougar XR-7 coupe

1979 Mercury Cougar XR-7 coupe

1979 Mercury Zephyr Z-7 coupe

1979 Mercury Capri RS hatchback coupe

1980 Mercury Cougar XR-7 coupe

1980 Mercury Cougar XR-7 coupe

1980 Mercury Capri RS hatchback coupe

1980 Mercury Zephyr Z-7 Turbo coupe

package was made available. Z-7 coupe production came to 42,923 units. Monarch soldiered on as before, though coupe output fell to 28,285. Bobcat received a modest facelift highlighted by an attractive new vertical-bar grille, but the big Mercs were all-new, downsized to a 114.3-inch wheelbase and weighing about 800 pounds less. Offered as two- and four-door sedans and wagons, they're of little interest to collectors.

	Restorable	Good	Excellent
Capri 3d cpe	$500-1,000	$1,000-2,000	$2,000-3,000
Capri RS 3d cpe	750-1,500	1,500-2,500	2,500-4,000
Cougar XR-7 cpe	500-1,500	1,500-3,000	3,000-5,000
Monarch Ghia 2d cpe	500-1,000	1,000-2,000	2,000-3,500
Zephyr Z-7 2d cpe	500-1,000	1,000-2,000	2,000-3,500

1980

Cougar XR-7 was now a genuine Thunderbird copy, a twin to this year's downsized 'Bird, now on a 108.4-inch wheelbase. Styling, best described as baroque, was one of the reasons production skidded to 58,028 (a severe recession was another reason). Standard power was a new 255-cid V-8 developing 115 bhp. The 131-bhp 302 V-8 was optional, and during the model year the 91-bhp 200-cid six became a delete option (avoid it). Option packages included Decor, Sport, and Luxury. The Zephyr Z-7 was particularly attractive and modern looking in this model year, with its upper bodyside accent stripe wrapping over the roof. Standard Z-7 equipment was black vinyl insert bodyside molding, wheel lip moldings, Z-7 ornaments on the "B" pillars, wrapped taillamps, vinyl upholstery, and tinted rear window glass. Only 19,486 Z-7s were called for this year. Capri's optional V-8 was now the 255 instead of the 302, and the Turbo four was still available. Model year production fell to 72,009 coupes and just 7975 Ghias. The big Mercurys were virtually unchanged (just 8308 two-doors were built), while Monarch and Bobcat were both in their last year. Total Mercury output was a dismal 347,711 units.

	Restorable	Good	Excellent
Capri 3d cpe	$500-1,000	$1,000-2,000	$2,000-3,000
Capri RS 3d cpe	750-1,500	1,500-2,500	2,500-4,000
Cougar XR-7 2d cpe	500-1,500	1,500-3,000	3,000-5,000
Monarch Ghia 2d cpe	500-1,000	1,000-2,000	2,000-3,500
Zephyr Z-7 2d cpe	500-1,000	1,000-2,000	2,000-3,500

1981

Basically a holdover, the Capri hatchback returned with a few drivetrain revisions and a new "Black Magic" interior/exterior color package. Look for the T-bar hatch roof, a new option that transformed the Capri into an "almost" convertible, and the 255 V-8, a smoother, quieter performance option than the turbocharged four; beware the five speed, which had a notoriously notchy shift linkage. The TRX suspension option is strongly recommended, as handling wasn't outstanding without it. Though the Ghia was gone, it was replaced by the GS. Output this year fell to 51,786 hatchback coupes and 7160 GS models. The Cougar name was placed on Ford Granada two- and four-door clones with the 2.3-liter four standard, these cars based on the Fairmont/Zephyr. For the "real" Cougar, the RX-7, a 3.3-liter (200-cid) inline six was now standard, but the 5.0-liter (302) V-8 was optional (and strongly recommended). Look for the GS/LS option package. Production skidded to 37,275. Zephyr saw only detail changes, and the Z-7 coupe found only 10,078 customers. The front-drive Lynx subcompact, a rebadged Ford Escort, replaced the Bobcat, but isn't of interest to collectors. The big Mercs carried on with 255, 302, and 351 V-8s available.

	Restorable	Good	Excellent
Capri 3d cpe	$500-1,000	$1,000-2,000	$2,000-3,000
Capri GS V-8	750-1,500	1,500-2,500	2,500-4,000
Cougar XR-7			
2d cpe	500-1,500	1,500-3,000	3,000-5,000
Zephyr Z-7 2d cpe	500-1,000	1,000-2,000	2,000-3,500

1981 Mercury Cougar XR-7 coupe

1981 Mercury Capri Black Magic hatchback coupe

1982

Introduced in the Spring of 1981 as an '82 model, the LN7 "bubbleback" two-seat coupe was a Mercury version of the Ford Escort-based EXP, with all the pros and cons (mostly cons) of that model. It featured a sports-tuned suspension and the Escort/Lynx 1.6 four-cylinder engine. Despite its "bug-eye" look up front, buyers drove 35,147 examples home. Cougar and Zephyr were little changed. New for Cougar was a station wagon and Ford's corporate 3.8-liter (232-cid) V-6 as the mid-range optional engine. The 302 V-8 was deleted, leaving just the 255 for V-8 power. XR-7s started out with the 200-cid inline six, but look for the V-6 or V-8. Production, GS and LS, totaled just 16,867 units. Capri saw the 5.0-liter V-8 again become available, this time with 157 horsepower. Models were base, L, GS, Black Magic, and RS. No matter—output of all five models was just 36,134 units. The Zephyr Z-7 coupe lost its V-8 option, and sales plummeted to only 7394.

1982 Mercury Capri RS 5.0 hatchback coupe

	Restorable	Good	Excellent
LN7 3d coupe	$500-1,000	$1,000-2,000	$2,000-3,000
Capri 3d cpe	500-1,000	1,000-2,000	2,000-3,000
Capri GS V-8	750-1,500	1,500-2,500	2,500-4,000
Cougar XR-7			
2d cpe	500-1,500	1,500-3,000	3,000-5,000
Zephyr Z-7 2d cpe	500-1,000	1,000-2,000	2,000-3,500

1982 Mercury LN7 2-passenger hatchback coupe

1983

Looking very smooth front and rear with a revised face and tail, the Capri retained its usual drivetrains, and gained a four-barrel carburetor instead of two-barrel for the 5.0-liter (302-cid) High Output V-8, boosting horsepower to 175. A Borg-Warner five-speed was available as an option with this engine later in the year—together, they make a desirable combination. Also new was a Crimson Cat model to

1983 Mercury Cougar LS coupe

1983 Mercury Capri GS hatchback coupe

1983 Mercury Capri GS hatchback coupe

1983 Mercury LN7 hatchback coupe

1983 Mercury Cougar XR-7 coupe

replace the Black Magic. Aside from the V-8, this year included the 2.3-liter four with 90 bhp (142 with turbo) and 3.8-liter V-6. None of this helped as output fell further to 25,376. Zephyr was scheduled to be replaced by the front-drive Topaz in the spring, so it was little changed in this final model year. Only 3471 Z-7 coupes were built. The two-seat LN7 now had an available 88-bhp HO (High Output) version of the 1.6-liter four, plus a notchy five-speed manual transmission. But sales were down to 4528, so it disappeared by the time the year was out. Cougar, like Thunderbird, was fully restyled, but differed in its notchback rear roofline (Thunderbird was a semi-fastback). Power came from the 3.8-liter V-6, but an injected 5.0L V-8 showed up later as an option. The XR-7 designation was scrubbed. This more aerodynamic Cougar was far more popular, attracting 75,743 buyers. The big Mercury became Grand Marquis this year to allow for a more aerodynamic mid-size Marquis based on the Zephyr, but it came only in four-door sedan and wagon form.

	Restorable	Good	Excellent
LN7 3d cpe	$500-1,000	$1,000-2,000	$2,000-3,500
Capri 3d cpe	500-1,000	1,000-2,000	2,000-3,500
Capri GS V-8	750-1,500	1,500-2,500	2,500-4,000
Cougar 2d cpe	500-1,500	1,500-3,000	3,000-5,000
Zephyr Z-7 2d cpe	500-1,000	1,000-2,500	2,500-4,000

1984

The sporty Capri continued with a simplified model lineup: base GS, high-performance RS, and RS Turbo, the latter featuring the turbocharged 2.3-liter reintroduced in 1983. Injection V-8s were also available. Still, production languished to 20,642 units in all series. The turbo engine was also optional in the Cougar (and found in the T-Bird Turbo Coupe)—cars so equipped were called XR-7, and also included five-speed gearbox, tachometer, special tires and wheels, and handling suspension. Although technically interesting, the XR-7s have not kept pace with the more conventional V-8 Cougars in used car values. Base and LN models were also offered, and total Cougar output came to a satisfying 131,190 units. Introduced in the spring of 1983 as an '84 model was Topaz, Mercury's version of the new aerodynamic Ford Tempo. It ran with an 84-horse 2.3-liter four (2.0-liter diesel optional) mated to four- and five-speed manuals or a three-speed automatic. Two- and four-door sedans were offered in GS or LS trim. Though a good seller (129,254 units for '84), it offered little to interest enthusiasts or collectors. Marquis and Grand Marquis received only modest changes, while the Lynx gained a Turbo RS three-door hatchback. With the recession gone and offering an attractive product line, total Mercury production for the model year came to 613,155 units.

	Restorable	Good	Excellent
Capri 3d cpe	*	$1,000-2,000	$2,000-3,000
Capri GS V-8	*	1,500-2,500	2,500-4,000
Cougar 2d cpe	*	1,500-3,000	3,000-5,000

* Purchase only in good or excellent condition

1985

A higher performance V-8, standard in the Capri RS, had roller tappets, higher-lift cam, and two-speed accessory drive system. It developed 180 bhp with throttle-body fuel injection, 210 with a four-barrel carb. Both are desirable. The GS, the only other model now listed, came with the 88-bhp four standard, but could be optioned with the 120-bhp V-6 or either V-8. The Turbo RS was discontinued this year, so look for the V-8s. Capri output fell further to 18,657 units. Cougar continued with modest exterior styling changes and a new instrument panel. The XR-7 turbocharged option was continued, now up to 155 bhp. On base and LS Cougars, look for the V-8 rather than the standard V-6. Production was a still healthy 117,274 units. At mid-year, Lynx received an aero front end and an 86-bhp 1.9-liter four. The model lineup was simplified, the Turbo RS being one victim. Marquis and Grand Marquis carried on much as before, though one could note that among the big Mercs the two-doors were relatively rare: 10,900 out of a total 161,258 Grand Marquis models built. Mercury output of all models totaled 597,754 units.

	Restorable	Good	Excellent
Capri 3d cpe	*	$1,000-2,000	$2,000-3,000
Capri GS cpe V-8	*	1,500-2,500	2,500-4,000
Cougar LS cpe V-8	*	1,500-3,000	3,000-5,000
Cougar XR-7 2d cpe	*	1,500-3,000	3,000-4,500

* Purchase only in good or excellent condition

1986

Daringly styled in the aero-jellybean school, Mercury's new Sable was a design sensation. Four-door sedans and wagons were offered in GS and up-market LS trim levels. All initially came with a new 140-bhp 3.0-liter V-6 and four-speed automatic; a manual transmission wasn't planned, and since no "performance" packages were offered it's hard to say whether early Sables will be collectible, but they are such interesting cars from a design standpoint that mint originals ought certainly to retain a value premium over ordinary used cars. Though introduced a bit late, first year production came to 105,638 cars. Capri received a new injection system for the V-8, now rated at 200 bhp, but no other significant changes; again, the V-8 is far preferable to the puny 2.3-liter four base engine, though the 120-bhp V-6 remains a reasonable compromise. Production rallied a bit to 20,869 units, but the Capri would be gone in 1987. During the last years of the Capri, a limited-edition ASC/McLaren was offered in coupe and convertible guise. Though not built by Mercury, 933 were sold (255 ragtops), many through selected Mercury dealers. Mint convertibles can go for about $15,000 or a bit more, coupes for $10,000. Cougars also featured the revised 5.0L V-8, plus a new electronic stereo radio with graphic equalizer and a power moonroof option. A total of 135,909 base, LS, and XR-7 models were sold. Marquis was phased out before the model year ended, while the Grand Marquis was little

1985 Mercury Cougar XR-7 coupe

1985 Mercury Capri RS 5.0 hatchback coupe

1986 Mercury Sable LS four-door station wagon

1986 Mercury Sable LS four-door sedan

1986 Mercury Cougar XR-7 coupe

1987 Mercury Sable LS four-door sedan

1987 Mercury Cougar LS coupe

1988 Mercury Sable LS four-door sedan

1988 Mercury Cougar XR-7 coupe

changed—and two-doors sales were down to just 5610. Mercury output dropped to 554,787 units.

	Restorable	Good	Excellent
Capri 3d cpe	*	$1,000-2,000	$2,000-3,000
Capri GS cpe V-8	*	1,500-2,500	2,500-4,000
Cougar LS cpe V-8	*	1,500-3,000	3,000-5,000
Cougar XR-7 2d cpe	*	1,500-3,000	3,000-4,500
Sable 2d sdn/wgn	*	2,000-4,000	4,000-5,000

* Purchase only in good or excellent condition

1987

Aerodynamic headlamps, flush glass, full-width taillamps, and a new greenhouse design marked the restyled-but-still-familiar Cougar for 1987. The XR-7 also got a new engine, the 150/155-bhp 5.0-liter V-8, replacing the previous Turbo four. The 120-bhp 3.8-liter V-6 was standard in the LS (the base model was dropped), and four-speed automatic was now the only transmission. Air conditioning became standard. Since this was Cougar's 20th Anniversary year, a limited-edition model celebrated the fact. It was a V-8-powered LS finished in Medium Cabernet complemented by gold cast alloy wheels and a Sand Beige Ultrasuede and leather interior featuring heated Twin Comfort Lounge seats. There were many other trim differences, plus special badges on the decklid, C-pillars, and on the dash. Despite the big styling change, Cougar output dropped to 104,526 units, which included 5000 Anniversary models. Sable, as expected, was virtually unchanged, though the anemic four-cylinder engine introduced later in the '86 model year was dropped because only 2000 buyers ordered it. Output jumped to 121,313. Topaz added an All-Wheel-Drive option, turned the not-so-sporty GS Sport option into cataloged models, and dropped the LS two-door and diesel engine. Grand Marquis dropped the base two-door sedan, leaving only the LS, which found just 4904 customers. Total Mercury output this year was 495,502 units.

	Restorable	Good	Excellent
Cougar LS 2d cpe	*	$2,500-4,000	$4,000-5,500
Cougar XR-7 2d cpe	*	3,000-5,000	5,000-6,500
Sable 2d sdn/wgn	*	2,500-4,500	4,500-6,000

* Purchase only in good or excellent condition

1988

Cougar's base V-6 was revised to produce 20 more horsepower, now 140, while the high-performance XR-7 sported monochrome exterior treatment on bumpers, grille, and outside mirrors, plus an analog instrument cluster. The 5.0-liter V-8, standard on XR-7 and optional on LS, got dual exhausts. For Sables, the same new 3.8-liter V-6 option and standard air conditioning arrived. The 3.0-liter V-6 was still standard, also rated at 140 bhp, but the larger engine had an additional 55 lbs/ft torque (210 in all). Topaz wore new sheetmetal, while the

Mexican-built, Mazda-based Tracer carried on. Introduced in the spring of '87 as an '88 model, it replaced the Lynx. Grand Marquis sported rounder front and rear styling, and dropped the two-door body style. Cougar output perked up to 119,162 units, while Sable jumped to 121,285.

	Restorable	Good	Excellent
Cougar LS			
2d cpe	*	$3,500-4,800	$4,800-6,500
Cougar XR-7			
2d cpe	*	4,000-6,000	6,000-8,000
Sable 4d sdn/wgn	*	3,000-5,000	5,000-7,000

* Purchase only in good or excellent condition

1989 Mercury Sable LS four-door sedan

1989

Cougar shared with the Ford Thunderbird an all-new mid-size coupe design, the Cougar again distinguished by its more formal notchback rear roofline. The '89 Cougar was 3.4 inches shorter, but its wheelbase was 8.8 inches longer (113 inches), giving much increased interior space. Both models had V-6s, the XR-7 now offering the supercharged, intercooled version of the 3.8 found in the T-Bird Super Coupe. It delivered 210 hp against 140 in the base LS model. XR-7 also got standard anti-lock brakes, which were optional on the LS. A five-speed manual was available, but most Cougars were ordered with the four-speed automatic. Sables were little changed, though the area between the headlights was now illuminated to create a "light-bar" grille. Mercury, celebrating its 50th Anniversary in 1989, announced an Anniversary Edition for the Grand Marquis, but for whatever reason later canceled it. Topaz offered a "sporty" XR-5 two-door model, but with a 100-bhp 2.3 four it was hardly that, even though it was nicely trimmed. Mercury sales for the calendar year came in at 407,943, including 110,962 Sables and 99,674 Cougars.

1989 Mercury Cougar XR-7 coupe

1989 Mercury Cougar XR-7 coupe

	Restorable	Good	Excellent
Cougar LS 2d cpe	*	$5,500-7,500	$7,500-9,000
Cougar XR-7			
2d cpe	*	6,500-9,000	9,000-11,000
Sable 4d sdn/wgn	*	4,000-6,500	6,500-8,000

* Purchase only in good or excellent condition

1990 Mercury Cougar LS coupe

1990

A Mercury Capri returned to the line, though whether this one should be included in a value guide for American collector cars is a question. Officially it was a '91 model, though many were sold and possibly registered as '90s. Also, this 2+2 convertible was built for Lincoln-Mercury by Ford Australia, though heavily based on Japanese Mazda 323 components. The two models were powered respectively by a 100-bhp 1.6-liter four and, for the high-performance XR-2, a 132-bhp turbocharged twin-cam 1.6, the latter available only with five-speed. A lift-off hardtop was optional. As a two-seat convertible (the +2 part was really tiny), the new Capri seems destined for collectibility of some kind; its main problem was its plug ugly front-end styling. Cougar returned

1991 Mercury Capri 2+2 convertible coupe

with few changes; Sable came with a driver-side air bag, while ABS was an option on sedans only. The 3.0- and 3.8-liter V-6s were retained. With industry sales in the doldrums, Mercury saw its calendar year sales fall to 345,606 units, with 96,803 of them going to Sable and 76,313 to Cougar.

	Restorable	Good	Excellent
'91 Capri cvt	*	$9,000-10,000	$10,000-11,500
Capri XR-2 cvt	*	10,000-11,500	11,500-13,000
Cougar LS 2d cpe	*	7,500-9,000	9,000-10,500
Cougar XR-7 2d cpe	*	9,500-11,500	11,500-13,000
Sable 4d sdn/wgn	*	5,000-8,000	8,000-10,000

* Purchase only in good or excellent condition

1930 Nash Twin Ignition Eight Touring 7-passenger

1931 Nash 880 two-door convertible sedan

Nash/AMC

Never strong among collectors, Nash offers low-priced collectible alternatives—but not prime investments. AMC built many interesting high performance rivals to Big Three muscle cars that are equally low priced relative to GM, Ford, and Chrysler products. Club support is relatively good via the Nash Car Club of America, American Motors Owners Association, AMC Rambler Club, and the specialist clubs for AMX, Javelin, and Nash Healey. Parts are scarce, except for the '70s and '80s cars. Investment potential is generally modest.

1930-39

Early Thirties Nashes were sumptuous, beautiful cars with many special features. Indeed, some have been accorded Classic status by the Classic Car Club of America: 1931 Series 8-90; 1932 Series 9-90, Advanced Eight, and Ambassador Eight; 1933-34 Ambassador Eight.

A 60/65-bhp, 201.3-cid sidevalve six powered low-line models through 1933, but the Twin Ignition sixes (242 and 234 cid) and straight eights (240, 260.8, 298.6, and 322 cid) were more interesting and gave good performance. They boasted double sets of spark plugs and were offered throughout the decade in one form or another with 74-125 bhp. Though the 1935-39 Twin Ignition eight was the smaller 260.8-cid engine with 102 or 115 bhp, all eights of the Thirties were nine-main-bearing engines.

Notable features of these luxurious Nashes were cowl vents, dash starter button, shatterproof glass, and automatic radiator vents (1930); downdraft carbs and Bijur automatic chassis lubrication (1931); dash-mounted shift lever and optional freewheeling (1932); the sumptuous 142-inch long-wheelbase Ambassador series (1933); aircraft-type instruments (1934). Collectors should note there were no open body styles in 1934-35, and any convertible coupe or sedan built in the other years of the decade is very rare.

A fine, art deco restyle called "Aeroform" appeared for 1935, featuring sweeping bodies, skirted fenders, swept-down decks and concealed spare tires, louvered hoods, vee'd radiators, and all-steel wheels. For 1935-39, there were three series: Six, Eight, and Ambassador Eight; the Six was called 400 through 1936, LaFayette thereafter. A dumpy facelift for 1938 was succeeded by ultra-sharp styling for 1939: a smooth, narrow grille flanked by vertical catwalk grilles and flush-fitting headlamps. An important 1938 innovation was the Weather-Eye combination heating and ventilation system, one of the best fresh-air heating units ever invented; it remained a Nash feature for the next 20 years.

Nash opened the decade by building 63,265 cars, but as the Depression deepened, this fell to just 14,973 in 1933, then improved to about 77,000 for 1937, the decade's high. Nash closed out the Thirties with a production run of 62,854 cars. These figures include the LaFayette, which was considered a separate companion make from 1934-36 (5000, 9400, and 27,860 built). It became the lowest-price Nash series from 1937-40, after which the nameplate was retired.

	Restorable	Good	Excellent
Sixes			
1930-31, open	$4,000-8,000	$8,000-13,000	$13,000-17,500
1930 TI, open	6,000-10,000	10,000-18,000	18,000-25,000
1932 960, open	6,000-12,000	12,000-20,000	20,000-30,000
1930-33, closed	1,000-4,000	4,000-6,000	6,000-9,000
1933 roadster	6,000-10,000	10,000-18,000	18,000-25,000
1934-36, closed	1,000-4,000	4,000-6,000	6,000-8,000
1936-37 cabrios	3,500-8,000	8,000-15,000	15,000-19,000
1937-39, closed	500-3,000	3,000-5,000	5,000-6,500
1938-39 cabrios	3,000-7,000	7,000-12,500	12,500-17,500
1939 Amb. cabrio	4,000-9,000	9,000-15,000	15,000-20,000
Twin Ignition Eights			
1930, open	$7,500-15,000	$15,000-22,500	$22,500-32,500
1930-31, closed	2,000-5,000	5,000-8,000	8,000-12,000
1931 890, closed	3,000-6,000	6,000-10,000	10,000-15,000
1931 880/890, open	8,000-18,000	18,000-30,000	30,000-45,000
1932 970, open	8,000-20,000	20,000-35,000	35,000-50,000
1932 970, closed	2,000-5,000	5,000-8,000	8,000-12,000
1932 980/990, open	10,000-20,000	20,000-35,000	35,000-50,000
1932 980/990, clsd	6,000-12,000	12,000-17,500	17,500-25,000
1933 Amb. cvt sdn	10,000-20,000	20,000-35,000	35,000-50,000
1933 other, open	7,500-15,000	15,000-27,500	27,500-40,000
1933 Adv. 8 cabrio	5,000-12,500	12,500-20,000	20,000-27,500
1933 Amb., closed	3,000-10,000	10,000-17,500	17,500-25,000
1933 other, closed	1,500-5,000	5,000-7,500	7,500-10,000
1934-37, closed	1,500-5,000	5,000-7,500	7,500-10,000
1937 Amb. cabrio	4,000-8,500	8,500-16,500	16,500-22,500
1938, closed	1,000-4,000	4,000-6,500	6,500-8,500
1938 Amb. cabrio	3,500-8,000	8,000-15,000	15,000-20,000
1939 Amb. cabrio	6,000-12,000	12,000-18,000	18,000-25,000

1933 Nash Advanced Eight Convertible-Roadster

1934 LaFayette Touring Sedan two-door

1935 Nash Ambassador four-door sedan

1936 LaFayette Model 3612 three-passenger coupe

1936 Nash 400 New Six four-door sedan

1940 Nash Ambassador Eight trunkback sedan

1940 Nash Ambassador Eight All-Purpose cabriolet

1940

This year saw the last Nash LaFayette ($795-$975). The line consisted of a LaFayette Six (234.8 cid, 99 bhp) and Nash Ambassador Six or Eight ($925-$1295). The Ambassador Six (234.8 cid, 105 bhp) cost about $150 more than the Lafayette and rode a four-inch-longer 121-inch wheelbase. The refined, nine-main-bearing Ambassador Eight was a valve-in-head powerplant with 260.8 cid and 115 bhp. All three series featured vertical, peaked grilles in a clean design and body styles were identical in all three series. These included one open model, the custom cabriolet, whose value depends greatly on the model—but all are scarce. This was the last year for the 125-inch wheelbase Ambassador Eight, which had been around since 1935. Nash built 62,131 cars for the model run, good for 1.5 percent of the market.

	Restorable	Good	Excellent
LaFayette cabrio	$3,500-8,000	$8,000-17,000	$17,000-25,000
LaFayette, other	1,000-2,500	2,500-4,000	4,000-6,000
Amb. Six cabrio	5,000-12,500	12,500-20,000	20,000-30,000
Amb. Six, other	1,500-3,500	3,500-5,000	5,000-7,000
Amb. Eight cabrio	6,500-15,000	15,000-25,000	25,000-35,000
Amb. Eight, other	2,000-4,000	4,000-6,000	6,000-9,000

1941 Nash Ambassador Six Slipstream Sedan two-door

1941 Nash 600 DeLuxe trunkback four-door sedan

1941 Nash Ambassador Six trunkback four-door sedan

1941

Nash's unit body/chassis for the 600 was an important breakthrough, which Nash and American Motors would continue to trumpet for many decades. Baseline model was the 600—named for delivering 600 miles from its 20-gallon tank. It rode a shorter 112-inch wheelbase and weighed about 600 pounds less than the LaFayette it replaced at the bottom of the line, and it cost a few bucks less. Its engine was smaller, too: an L-head six displacing 172.6 cubic inches and developing 75 horsepower. Styling was based on 1940, but quite different up front: the center grille was gone and there were prominent "electric shaver" grilles flanking the prow, with full-width horizontal bars underneath. Ambassador Six and Eight now shared the same 121-inch wheelbase and body styles, nor was there much difference in performance between the 105-bhp, 235-cid six and the 115-bhp, 261-cid eight. The 600 offered no convertible, but both Ambassador series listed an All-Purpose Cabriolet. Production rose to 84,007 units.

	Restorable	Good	Excellent
600, all closed	$1,000-2,500	$2,500-4,000	$4,000-5,500
Amb. Six cabrio	5,000-12,500	12,500-18,000	18,000-27,500
Amb. Six, other	1,500-3,500	3,500-5,000	5,000-7,000
Amb. Eight cabrio	6,500-15,000	15,000-22,500	22,500-30,000
Amb. Eight, other	2,000-4,000	4,000-6,000	6,000-9,000

1942

Rare indeed is the 1942 Nash—only 31,780 were built. Like other Detroit makes, the firm was cut off by the abrupt halt in auto production shortly after Pearl Harbor. This was unfortunate, since Nash had made a major facelift based on a strong horizontal frontal motif, including a narrow horizontal-bar center section atop another set of horizontal bars that wrapped around from front wheelwell to wheelwell. DeLuxe models had parking lights perched atop the front fenders. Mechanically there was no change and the three-series lineup continued, but with a simplified lineup dispensing with Special and DeLuxe in favor of a single trim level within each series. Unfortunately for collectors, the cabriolets, which had not been selling well, were dropped. Price ranges this year were: 600, $843-$918; Ambassador Six, $994-$1069; Ambassador Eight, $1084-$1119.

	Restorable	Good	Excellent
Nash 600	$1,000-2,500	$2,500-4,000	$4,000-6,000
Ambassador Six	1,500-3,000	3,000-5,000	5,000-7,000
Ambassador Eight	2,000-4,000	4,000-6,000	6,000-9,000

1946

Nash's '46s were slightly revamped '42s, distinguished by a pinched center grille and parking lights moved from the fender tops to a new position inboard of the headlamps. The Ambassador Eight was dropped, but horsepower of the sixes was increased marginally to 82 for the 600 and 112 for the Ambassador. Two-door models, as in late prewar years, were called Broughams. A new Ambassador that is highly collectible today was the Suburban, a four-door sedan lavishly trimmed with white ash and mahogany in the style of Chrysler's Town & Country. Unfortunately, only 272 were built this model year. Production for the model year was about 94,000 units, this despite only three body styles: two-door Brougham, plus four-door trunkback and fastback sedans.

	Restorable	Good	Excellent
Nash 600	$1,000-2,500	$2,500-4,000	$4,000-6,000
Amb. Suburban	5,000-12,000	12,000-18,000	18,000-25,000
Ambassador, other	2,000-4,000	4,000-6,000	6,000-8,500

1947

For 1947, the upper central grille was widened slightly and new raised-center hubcaps were installed. There was no change whatsoever to the models or body styles. Suburban production rose to 595, and the price rose from $1929 in 1946 to $2227—the first time a Nash model had listed at over $2000 since 1934. Despite such inflationary pressures, which affected all of Detroit, output rose to 101,000 units.

	Restorable	Good	Excellent
Nash 600	$1,000-2,500	$2,500-4,000	$4,000-6,000
Amb. Suburban	5,000-12,000	12,000-18,000	18,000-25,000
Ambassador, other	2,000-4,000	4,000-6,000	6,000-8,500

1942 Nash 600 trunkback four-door sedan

1942 Nash Ambassador Eight fastback four-door sedan

1946 Nash 600 fastback four-door sedan

1947 Nash Ambassador fastback four-door sedan

1947 Nash 600 Brougham two-door

1947 Nash Ambassador Suburban four-door

1948 Nash Ambassador Super four-door sedan

1949 Nash 600 fastback four-door sedan

1949 Nash Ambassador fastback four-door sedan

1950 Nash Rambler Custom Landau convertible coupe

1948

Nash responded to the vast buyer's market by expanding to three trim levels for the 600—DeLuxe, Super, Custom—and two for Ambassador—Super and Custom. A $2345 Ambassador Custom convertible was added, Nash's first ragtop since 1941. Nash had apparently saved the prewar tooling and thought the convertible an inexpensive way to add a little glamour to a carryover lineup. Output reached 1000 units. In addition, 130 wood-trimmed Suburbans, now priced at $2239, were built. There was little change to styling, the most obvious differentiation being the replacement of the full-length hood-to-rear-fender bright metal beltline molding with a short chrome strip on the rear side of the hood. Model year registrations this year were 110,000.

	Restorable	Good	Excellent
Nash 600	$1,000-2,500	$2,500-4,000	$4,000-6,000
Amb. Suburban	5,000-12,000	12,000-18,000	18,000-25,000
Ambassador cvt	5,000-12,000	12,000-18,000	18,000-25,000
Ambassador, other	2,000-4,000	4,000-6,000	6,000-8,500

1949

All-new styling by Bob Koto and Ted Pietsch, under the direction of Nash engineer Nils Wahlberg, culminated in the 1949 Airflyte, a bathtub-like design with genuine aerodynamic properties. It had, for example, only 113 pounds of drag at 60 mph, compared to 170 for the similar-looking '49 Packard. Airflytes were unique with their Unibody construction, enclosed front wheels, one-piece curved windshield, "Uniscope" gauge cluster under the steering wheel, fully reclining seatbacks, Weather-Eye heater, and pillowy ride. Two wheelbases, 112 and 121 inches, were offered for the two series. Both offered but three body styles—two- and four-door sedans and a Brougham (club coupe)—in Super or Custom trim. Unfortunately, there were no convertible or Suburban models this year. Power continued to be the small, 172.6-cid L-head six with 82 bhp for the 600, and the 235-cid overhead-valve six with 112 horses for the Ambassador. With overdrive, they were excellent over-the-road cars. Odd as the Airflytes look today, they were tremendously successful: Nash built 135,328 for '49, and shot into the Top 10 among the industry's automakers.

	Restorable	Good	Excellent
Nash 600	$500-2,500	$2,500-4,500	$4,500-6,000
Ambassador	1,000-2,500	2,500-5,000	5,000-6,000

1950

Nash's gregarious and forward-looking president George Mason spawned the first successful postwar compact in the Rambler, wisely avoiding a pinch-penny image by bringing out the little 100-inch-wheelbase Nash as a Custom Landau convertible and two-door Custom station wagon and equipping them with items that usually cost extra. Both were base-priced at only $1808, the ragtop's price being kept down by permanent window frames—the top peeled back from the windshield header. Styling carried a rounded, Nash-like look. In the virtually unchanged Airflyte line, the 600 was rechristened Statesman and given a slightly larger 184-cid engine, which developed three more horsepower than the old one, which was now assigned to Rambler. Nash model year registrations were 171,782, about 26,000 of them Ramblers.

	Restorable	Good	Excellent
Rambler Custom cvt	$1,000-3,000	$3,000-5,000	$5,000-7,000
Rambler Custom wgn	500-2,500	2,500-4,000	4,000-5,500
Statesman	500-2,500	2,500-4,500	4,500-6,000
Ambassador	1,000-2,500	2,500-5,000	5,000-6,000

1950 Rambler Custom two-door station wagon

1950 Nash Ambassador Super Brougham two-door

1951

The first Nash-Healey, designed and engineered by England's Donald Healey, was an aluminum-bodied two-seater sports car with a tuned Ambassador engine delivering 125 horsepower; 104 of the initial '51 models were built. Rambler introduced a second, slightly cheaper Super wagon and a new hardtop (Nash's first), the Custom Country Club. All Ramblers were again priced under $2000, and were reaping a growing harvest of customers. The Airflyte design, now in its final year, was easily recognized by its prominent squared-up rear fenders bearing upright taillights and its convex, vertical-bar grille. On Ambassadors, flanking chrome strips ran around the sides of the fenders. GM's Hydra-Matic was now available for both Statesman and Ambassador (about 65,000 were installed), but the limited body style selection remained the same. Spurred on by about 80,000 Ramblers, total model year registrations rose to 205,307 units.

1951 Nash-Healey 2-passenger roadster

	Restorable	Good	Excellent
Nash-Healey	$8,000-15,000	$15,000-25,000	$25,000-35,000
Rambler Custom cvt	1,000-3,000	3,000-5,000	5,000-7,000
Rambler wagons	500-2,500	2,500-4,000	4,000-5,500
Rambler 2d htp	750-2,500	2,500-4,500	4,500-6,000
Statesman	500-2,500	2,500-4,500	4,500-6,000
Ambassador	1,000-2,500	2,500-5,000	5,000-6,000

1951 Nash Rambler Custom Country Club hardtop

1952

For its big-car restyle, Nash called in Italy's Pininfarina, who made a few sketches and built a prototype. That didn't significantly influence the actual production styling, however, which was done by Nash's Ed Anderson. It was a clean design for the Fifties, marred only by the enclosed front wheel wells (which gave it a huge turning circle), a Nash styling trademark insisted on by president George Mason originally for the '49s. Both Statesman and Ambassador had a new Country Club two-door hardtop model and the Statesman's 114.3-inch wheelbase was 2.3 inches longer than before.

1952 Nash Ambassador Custom Country Club hardtop

1953 Nash Rambler Custom Country Club hardtop

1953 Nash Rambler Custom convertible coupe

1953 Nash Ambassador Custom Country Club hardtop

1952-53 Nash-Healey roadster by Pinin Farina

Ambassadors, on a 121.3-inch chassis, offered handsome two-tone combinations and a six bored-out to 252.6 cid, good for 120 bhp. Nash touted a variety of home-style comforts to go with its reclining seats, including mattresses, bug screens, and a full-width oddments net running across the headliner above the windshield. The Nash-Healey received a steel body with revised styling marked by a new, plainer grille with a single horizontal bar—and went on to take the checkered flag in its class at the famed Le Mans race. Only 150 were built. Ramblers were little changed, though prices now nudged just above $2000. Production cutbacks forced by the Korean War held model year registrations down to 154,291. About 55,000 of them were Ramblers, including 3108 convertibles and 25,785 Country Club hardtops. Big Nash hardtops were much scarcer: 869 Statesman Customs and 1228 Ambassador Customs.

	Restorable	Good	Excellent
Nash-Healey	$10,000-18,000	$18,000-27,500	$27,500-38,000
Rambler Custom cvt	1,000-3,000	3,000-5,000	5,000-7,000
Rambler wagons	500-2,500	2,500-4,000	4,000-5,500
Rambler Custom htp	750-2,500	2,500-4,500	4,500-6,000
Statesman htp	1,000-3,000	3,000-6,000	6,000-9,000
Ambassador htp	1,500-3,500	3,500-6,500	6,500-10,000
Full-size sedans	750-2,500	2,500-5,000	5,000-7,500

1953

A Nash-Healey coupe was announced, along with a horsepower increase to 140 for all Healeys. This same powerplant, featuring dual carburetors and a high compression head, was optional on the Ambassador as the "Le Mans" engine. Nash-Healey output rose to 162 units. The Rambler lineup was unchanged, though horsepower was up to 85, and those with Hydra-Matic got the Statesman's 195.6-cid six tuned to 90 bhp. Statesman models, meanwhile, were boosted to 100 bhp. Styling of the big Nashes was the same as 1952, except for small vertical chrome spacers on the cowl air-scoop. With the Korean War restrictions lifted, production should have risen, but instead it fell back to 121,793 units, this partly because of price/production battles between Ford and GM, which hurt all the independents and Chrysler as well. Some 3284 Rambler convertibles were produced, plus the following Country Club hardtops: 15,255 Ramblers, 6438 Ambassador Customs, and 7025 Statesman Customs.

	Restorable	Good	Excellent
Nash-Healey rdstr	$10,000-18,000	$18,000-27,500	$27,500-38,000
Nash-Healey coupe	5,000-12,000	12,000-17,500	17,500-25,000
Rambler Custom cvt	1,000-3,000	3,000-5,000	5,000-7,000
Rambler wagons	500-2,500	2,500-4,000	4,000-5,500
Rambler Custom htp	750-2,500	2,500-4,500	4,500-6,000
Statesman htp	1,000-3,000	3,000-6,000	6,000-9,000
Ambassador htp	1,500-3,500	3,500-6,500	6,500-10,000
Full-size sedans	750-2,500	2,500-5,000	5,000-7,500

1954

The Metropolitan, an 85-inch-wheelbase two-seat subcompact built in England with an Austin engine, was introduced at just under $1500, available as a coupe or convertible. An attractive new "floating bar" grille had been adopted for the '53 Rambler, so the Metro got a version of it too. The Rambler lineup expanded to include a two-door sedan and, more importantly, a four-door sedan and Cross Country wagon mounted on a longer 108-inch wheelbase. Now with DeLuxe, Super, and Custom trim, Rambler offered 10 models, up from just four in 1953. Prices ranged from $1550 to $2050. Only 221 ragtops were built, along with 4683 Country Club hardtops. Statesman and Ambassador also sported a floating grille, but theirs had a multitude of vertical bars instead of a single horizontal bar. The big car lineup was much the same, except that two-door sedans had been reduced in variety. A twin-carb option for the Statesman, called "Dual Powerflyte," raised that model's horsepower to 110, and the Ambassador's base rating moved up to 130. The Nash-Healey was offered only as a coupe this year; 90 were produced. The '54 Ambassador Country Club Le Mans was a smoothly styled, well appointed car with good performance. It's the obvious model to look for among full-size Nashes, but only 3581 were built. Hudson and Nash merged to form American Motors on May 1 this year. (Hudson models are listed separately.) Despite all this activity, model year registrations skidded to 91,121, not counting the 13,905 Metropolitans produced in late 1953 and '54 (including cars sent to Canada).

	Restorable	Good	Excellent
Nash-Healey coupe	$5,000-12,000	$12,000-17,500	$17,500-25,000
Metropolitan coupe	500-1,500	1,500-3,500	3,500-5,000
Metropolitan cvt	1,000-2,500	2,500-4,500	4,500-6,000
Rambler Cust cvt	1,000-3,000	3,000-5,000	5,000-7,000
Rambler wagons	500-2,500	2,500-4,000	4,000-5,500
Rambler htps	750-2,500	2,500-4,500	4,500-6,000
Statesman htp	1,000-3,000	3,000-6,000	6,000-9,000
Ambassador htp	1,500-3,500	3,500 6,500	6,500-10,000
Full-size sedans	750-2,500	2,500-5,000	5,000-7,500

1955

The big Nash appeared with a wraparound windshield, inboard headlights, bodyside two-toning, and a Packard-built 320-cid, 208-bhp V-8 for the Ambassador Eight, the first eight-cylinder Nash since before the war. The Ambassador Six continued with its Le Mans power option, the Statesman with a 100/110-bhp version of the small Rambler 195.6-cid six (the 184-cid unit was dropped this year). Rambler, now with front wheels exposed, accounted for the bulk of American Motors sales. It added three Fleet models, but deleted the convertible, thus expanding the lineup to 12. Hardtops numbered just 2993, but the attractive four-door Cross Country wagon found 25,617 homes. A handful of Nash-Healeys were registered as '55 models, but production of the sports cars had actually ended in

1953 Nash-Healey Le Mans coupe by Pinin Farina

1954 Nash Metropolitan convertible coupe

1955 ½ Nash Rambler Custom Cross Country wagon

1955 Nash Rambler Custom Country Club hardtop

1955 Nash Ambassador Custom Country Club hardtop

1956 Nash Rambler Super four-door sedan

1956 Nash Rambler Custom hardtop sedan

1956 Nash Rambler Custom Cross Country wagon

1956 Nash Ambassador Eight Custom four-door sedan

1956 Nash Ambassador Special Country Club hardtop

1954. The unchanged Metropolitan saw production plummet to 6096. At 121,261, model year registrations returned to the 1953 level, but this wasn't enough given the wide range of models offered. Though the big Nashes captured 40,133 customers, Country Club hardtops were scarce: 1492 Statesmans, 1395 Ambassador Sixes, and 1755 Ambassador Eights.

	Restorable	Good	Excellent
Nash-Healey cpe	$5,000-12,000	$12,000-17,500	$17,500-25,000
Metropolitan cpe	500-1,500	1,500-3,500	3,500-5,000
Metropolitan cvt	1,000-2,500	2,500-4,500	4,500-6,000
Rambler	1,000-3,000	3,000-5,000	5,000-6,500
Statesman htp	1,000-3,000	3,000-6,000	6,000-9,000
Ambassador 6 htp	1,500-3,500	3,500-7,500	7,500-11,000
Ambassador 8 htp	2,500-4,500	4,500-9,500	9,500-13,000
Full-size sedans	750-2,500	2,500-5,000	5,000-7,500

1956

The last Nash Statesman, a Super four-door sedan, appeared this year. Ambassador Eights used the Packard engine until mid-season, then switched to an anemic 190-bhp version of the new AMC 250-cid V-8 and became Ambassador Specials—if you have a choice, choose one with the Packard mill. Styling was busier, marked by flashy three-tone color combinations and "lollipop" combinations of vertical back-up and oval taillights. In the Rambler camp, the Custom Cross Country four-door hardtop wagon was an innovation—the first in the industry—and there was also a four-door hardtop sedan, both in the top-line Custom series. They'll be hard to find; only 2155 sedans and 402 wagons were built (Hudson added 1187 and 392, respectively). Ramblers were completely restyled, doing away with the rounded, pudgy look of yore. All models—four-doors only—were consolidated to the 108-inch wheelbase. Headlights were inboard, and bodyside two-toning emphasizing a "basket-handle" look at the C-pillars was available on Super and Custom models. Ramblers were still powered by sixes, but the 195.6-cid mill was now developing a commendable 120 horsepower with overhead valves. The Metropolitan received a mid-year facelift featuring a crosshatch grille and bodyside two-toning. It also got a larger engine with 52 bhp; such cars were designated 1500, for their metric displacement. Production increased to 9068 units. Full-size Nashes fell by nearly half to 22,283 units. Country Club hardtops were nearly non-existent: 796 Ambassadors Eights and 706 Ambassador Specials.

	Restorable	Good	Excellent
Metropolitan cpe	$500-1,500	$1,500-3,500	$3,500-5,000
Metropolitan cvt	1,000-2,500	2,500-4,500	4,500-6,000
Rambler	1,000-3,000	3,000-5,000	5,000-6,500
Ambassador 8 htp	2,500-4,500	4,500-9,500	9,500-13,000
Full-size sedans	750-2,500	2,500-5,000	5,000-7,500

1957

This was the final year for Nash; in 1958, the entire line would consist of Ramblers and Metropolitans. Nash offered Ambassador hardtops and sedans in two trim levels, Super and Custom, all powered by the AMC V-8, now up to 327 cid and 255 bhp. The headlamps, moved back out to the fenders, were vertically mounted quad units—tying with the Cadillac Eldorado Brougham for first time honors for a feature most everybody would have for '58. Styling was arguably overdone, with broad two-tone color sweep panels and fender-top parking lights, though the front wheels were finally exposed. Production for this last year was a mere 10,331 units, most of them four-door sedans. For the first time, Rambler offered a V-8, the 250-cid unit with 190 bhp—lively enough in the Rambler's relatively light body (3200-3400 pounds). Real performance arrived at mid-year with the limited-edition Rebel, a silver four-door hardtop with unique side trim enclosing gold anodized aluminum. It had the big Nash's 255-bhp 327 V-8, and though it could almost accelerate with a Corvette, the Rebel rebelled against Rambler's economy car image—only 1500 were built. Even rarer were the Rambler hardtop sedans and wagons: 485 Custom sedans (V-8), 182 Custom wagons (V-8), 612 Super sedans (six). The unchanged Metropolitan scored with a record 15,317 buyers.

	Restorable	Good	Excellent
Metropolitan cpe	$500-1,500	$1,500-3,500	$3,500-5,000
Metropolitan cvt	1,000-2,500	2,500-4,500	4,500-6,000
Rambler Rebel	2,500-5,000	5,000-7,000	7,000-10,000
Rambler, other	1,000-3,000	3,000-5,000	5,000-6,500
Ambassador 8 htp	2,500-4,500	4,500-9,500	9,500-13,000
Full-size sedans	750-2,500	2,500-5,000	5,000-7,500

1958

With perfect timing for what proved to be a recession year, AMC in mid-year revived its smaller, 100-inch-wheelbase Rambler, last seen in 1955. Called the American and fitted with a new mesh grille and larger rear wheel openings, the two-door business sedan and club coupe were priced low and sold 30,640 copies in short order. The larger Ramblers boasted 100 changes, including a more massive grille, quad headlamps, modest tailfins, and a pedal-type parking brake. The Rebel name was retained for the top-line 250 V-8 models. Of the 106,916 Sixes built, only 983 were Super four-door hardtops; among 10,056 Rebels, just 410 were Custom hardtop sedans. The 327 V-8, now with 270 bhp, went into the Ambassador, a new Rambler line on a stretched 117-inch wheelbase. This car was to have been a Nash or Hudson, but in a last-minute decision AMC President George Romney decided to place it under the popular Rambler marque. It, too, had Super and Custom trim levels, the latter accounting for 1340 hardtop sedans and 294 hardtop wagons. Even the pillared sedans and wagons weren't terribly common as total Ambassador production came to but 14,570 units. The Metropolitan went unchanged; output slipped a bit to 13,128.

1957 Rambler Rebel hardtop sedan

1957 Rambler V-8 Custom Cross Country wagon

1957 Nash Ambassador Custom Country Club hardtop

1957 Nash Ambassador Super four-door sedan

1958 Rambler American Super two-door sedan

1958 Rambler Ambassador Custom Country Club

1958 Rambler Rebel Custom Cross Country wagon

1959 Rambler American Super two-door station wagon

1959 Rambler Ambassador Custom Country Club

1960 Rambler Ambassador Custom Country Club

	Restorable	Good	Excellent
Metropolitan cpe	$500-1,500	$1,500-3,500	$3,500-5,000
Metropolitan cvt	1,000-2,500	2,500-4,500	4,500-6,000
Rambler American	500-1,500	1,500-3,500	3,500-5,000
Rambler Ambassador	1,500-3,000	3,000-5,500	5,500-7,500
Rambler, other	1,000-2,500	2,500-5,000	5,000-7,000

1959

The 1958 formula worked so well that AMC repeated it, earning $60 million in profit and building a record 374,420 cars in the process. The same models and powertrains were fielded and horsepower remained unchanged. For the American, the two-door wagon was revived, and total sales tripled to 91,491. The 108-inch wheelbase standard Ramblers were mildly facelifted with thin side moldings and simpler grilles. Production zoomed to 258,980 units, including 2683 Six Super hardtop sedans and just 691 Rebel V-8 Custom equivalents. The Ambassador continued on the 117-inch wheelbase with the 327 V-8 and more ornate trim, and watched output jump to 23,769 cars, among them 1447 Custom hardtop sedans and 578 Custom hardtop wagons. Metropolitans got an opening trunklid for the first time, plus more comfortable seats, vent windows, and tubeless tires. The 22,209 produced would be the Met's all-time high.

	Restorable	Good	Excellent
Metropolitan cpe	$500-1,500	$1,500-3,500	$3,500-5,000
Metropolitan cvt	1,000-2,500	2,500-4,500	4,500-6,000
Rambler American	500-1,500	1,500-3,500	3,500-5,000
Rambler Ambassador	1,500-3,000	3,000-5,500	5,500-7,500
Rambler, other	1,000-2,500	2,500-5,000	5,000-7,000

1960

With 458,841 cars built, Rambler beat Plymouth for third place in production this year, an incredible feat for an independent. George Romney's advertising onslaught against Detroit's dinosaurs, and a strong desire for compacts, fueled Rambler's success. The 108-inch-wheelbase Six and Rebel V-8 had less cluttered lines, modest canted tailfins, and a full-width grille. Some 314,440 were produced, making them the mainstay of AMC's drive forward. Models to look for are the Custom four-door hardtops: 3937 Sixes and 579 Rebels. Ambassador, also modestly facelifted, saw output hold steady at 23,798 units; Custom hardtops consisted of 1141 sedans and 435 wagons. The American was virtually unchanged except for the addition of a four-door sedan (in three trim levels), enough to spur total sales to 120,603. Metropolitan production ended this year with 13,874 built, though a few hundred would be registered during 1961 and 1962.

	Restorable	Good	Excellent
Metropolitan cpe	$500-1,500	$1,500-3,500	$3,500-5,000
Metropolitan cvt	1,000-2,500	2,500-4,500	4,500-6,000
Rambler American	500-1,500	1,500-3,500	3,500-5,000
Rambler Ambassador	1,500-3,000	3,000-5,500	5,500-7,500
Rambler, other	1,000-2,500	2,500-5,000	5,000-7,000

1961

This was another of Rambler's glory years. Even though total production fell to 377,902 units, AMC still outproduced Plymouth by 20,000+ vehicles to occupy third place behind Ford and Chevy. The completely reskinned American gained a squarer, more modern shape and a convertible, AMC's first since 1955. The American retained its 100-inch wheelbase and standard 90-bhp 196 six, though a 125-bhp overhead-valve version was now optional. Total output rose to 136,003 and—surprisingly perhaps—quite a few were top-line Custom convertibles (the only way they came): 10,855 regular, 2063 with bucket seats. Mid-range Rambler Sixes and V-8s, though only mildly facelifted, were now called Classics. As usual, they enjoyed the lion's share of sales, 223,057 this year (only 8880 of them V-8s). The Ambassador, with more controversial—and memorable—styling, continued on its special long wheelbase, but saw output fall to 18,842 units. As before, all Classics and Ambassadors were four-doors, sedans or wagons, the latter with six- or eight-passenger capacity. Unfortunately for collectors, both lost their slow-selling but more desirable four-door hardtop models this year. Sales of leftover Metropolitans numbered 969 this year.

	Restorable	Good	Excellent
Metropolitan cpe	$500-1,500	$1,500-3,500	$3,500-5,000
Metropolitan cvt	1,000-2,500	2,500-4,500	4,500-6,000
American cvt	1,500-3,000	3,000-5,500	5,500-7,000
American, other	500-1,500	1,500-3,500	3,500-5,000
Ambassador	1,500-3,000	3,000-5,500	5,500-7,000
Rambler	1,000-2,500	2,500-5,000	5,000-6,500

1961 Rambler Ambassador Custom four-door wagon

1961 Rambler American Custom convertible coupe

1962 Rambler American 400 convertible coupe

1962 Rambler Classic Custom two-door sedan

1962

AMC consolidated, dropping the 250 Rambler V-8 and the 117-inch Ambassador wheelbase. Standard Ramblers now comprised the Classic, with the 195.6-cid six (127 or 138 bhp), and the Ambassador, with the 327 V-8 (250 or 270 bhp). Both rode the old 108-inch wheelbase and were little different except for badging and trim, and both now offered two-door sedans and lost their little tailfins in a modest facelift. An ultra-luxury "400" model was offered in both lines as a two- or four-door sedan or four-door wagon. There was even an American 400 for all four of its body styles. AMC production increased to 442,346 cars: 125,678 Americans (including 13,497 "400" convertibles), 280,497 Classics, and 36,171 Ambassadors. Metropolitan registered 412 vehicles in its final model year.

	Restorable	Good	Excellent
Metropolitan cpe	$500-1,500	$1,500-3,500	$3,500-5,000
Metropolitan cvt	1,000-2,500	2,500-4,500	4,500-6,000
American 400 cvt	1,500-3,000	3,000-5,500	5,500-7,000
American, other	500-1,500	1,500-3,500	3,500-5,000
Classic	1,000-2,500	2,500-5,000	5,000-6,500
Ambassador	1,500-3,000	3,000-5,500	5,500-7,000

1963 Rambler Ambassador 990 four-door station wagon

1963 Rambler Classic 770 four-door sedan

1963 Rambler American 440-H hardtop coupe

1964 Rambler Classic Typhoon hardtop coupe

1964 Rambler American 440-H hardtop coupe

1963

Styled by Ed Anderson, the all-new Classic and Ambassador were smooth, clean-looking cars on a longer 112-inch wheelbase with a lower silhouette, concave grille, sculptured body panels, and curved side glass. There was still no convertible or hardtop, only two- and four-door sedans and four-door Cross Country wagons. Trim levels were designated 550/660/770 for the Classic, 800 (export)/880/990 for the Ambassador. *Motor Trend* was so impressed with these new, modern AMCs that it awarded them its "Car of the Year" honors. Americans were re-badged 220/330/440, the convertible continuing as a top-trim 440. Though priced at a remarkably low $2344 base, sales fell to 4750 units, perhaps because two hardtops were added: a 440 and a 440-H. They attracted 5101 and 9749 buyers. Attacked by Big Three compacts, Rambler lost its third place ranking in 1962, and even with output of 464,126 cars couldn't retain it for '63. Even so, AMC cranked out 105,296 Americans, 279,833 Classic Sixes, 41,186 Classic V-8s (287 cid, 198 bhp), and 37,811 Ambassadors.

	Restorable	Good	Excellent
American cvt	$1,500-3,000	$3,000-5,500	$5,500-7,000
American htps	1,000-2,000	2,000-4,000	4,000-5,500
American, other	500-1,500	1,500-3,500	3,500-5,000
Classic	1,000-2,500	2,500-5,000	5,000-6,500
Ambassador	1,500-3,000	3,000-5,500	5,500-7,000

1964

Though only slightly facelifted, Classics and Ambassadors received two-door hardtops for '64. In the Classic's case, it was a top-line 770, available with six or the 287 V-8. In addition, AMC brought out a new oversquare, lightweight-casting 232-cid Typhoon Six with 145 hp. To celebrate, 2520 specially trimmed, yellow-and-black Typhoon hardtops were built. The American was completely restyled by Dick Teague along Rambler Classic lines, and shared many of its parts. It looked much better on its longer, 106-inch wheelbase. Of interest were the two-door hardtops, 440 and 440-H, which found 19,495 and 14,527 buyers. The most collectible Rambler remained the American convertible, still the only soft top in the AMC line. Its pert new styling makes for a very good low-budget collectible; 8907 were built. Ambassador also gained two hardtops, 990 and a 990-H, and went on to sell 1464 and 2955 of them. The 990-H is the one to look for because of its luxurious interior and 270-bhp 327 V-8 (the 990 was less lush and got the 250-bhp 327). Though production of the American soared to 163,661 units, Classic fell back to 211,551, Ambassador to 18,647.

	Restorable	Good	Excellent
American cvt	$1,500-3,000	$3,000-5,500	$5,500-7,000
American, other	500-1,500	1,500-3,500	3,500-5,000
Classic	1,000-2,500	2,500-5,000	5,000-6,500
Ambassador	1,500-3,000	3,000-5,500	5,500-7,000
Typhoon 2d htp	2,500-3,500	3,500-6,000	6,000-8,000

1965

Under President Roy Abernethy, AMC had decided to depart from its econo-car image and do battle with the Big Three on all fronts. To face off rival fastbacks like the Barracuda, stylist Dick Teague developed the Tarpon show car based on the American. In reality, however, the Marlin ended up a glorified Rambler Classic with a fastback greenhouse, losing its trim lines in the process. With the 270-bhp 327 V-8 option, a Marlin could do 0-60 in less than 12 seconds and an 18-second quarter-mile. If this wasn't earthshaking, neither was it typical Rambler performance. To many, though, the '65 Marlin looked odd and ungainly, and only 10,327 were built. The Ambassador returned this year with its own 116-inch wheelbase and new, more elegant styling. Classic retained its 112-inch span, but was squarer and more important looking. There were now convertibles in both lines, and 3499 Ambassador 990s and 4953 Classic 770s were built. Ambassador hardtops numbered 11,416, Classics 20,484. Ambassador was the star this year as sales shot up to 63,881. The only slightly changed American saw a production run of 3882 ragtops and 21,948 hardtops. Total AMC production held steady at 391,366 units.

	Restorable	Good	Excellent
American cvt	$1,500-3,000	$3,000-5,500	$5,500-7,000
American, other	500-1,500	1,500-3,500	3,500-4,500
Classic cvt	1,500-3,000	3,000-5,500	5,500-7,000
Classic, other	1,000-2,500	2,500-5,000	5,000-6,000
Ambassador cvt	2,000-4,000	4,000-6,000	6,000-8,000
Ambassador, other	1,500-3,000	3,000-5,500	5,500-6,500
Marlin	1,500-2,500	2,500-4,500	4,500-6,500

1966

Marlin now went under the AMC marque instead of Rambler, but was little changed (a black vinyl roof became optional)—and saw sales tumble to just 4547 units. The lightly facelifted Ambassador also became an AMC and added the DPL, a luxury hardtop that found 10,458 buyers. It featured reclining bucket seats, fold-down center armrests, pile carpeting, and an extensive list of accessories. Though soft top output fell to 1814 units, total Ambassador output hit 71,692. The Classic, also much the same for '66, dropped the 660 series and added a top-line Rebel hardtop, of which 7512 were built. The 770 ragtop was down to 1806 units. The American ditched the mid-line 330 series, and added a Rogue hardtop; 8718 were called for. The 440 ragtop accounted for 2092 sales. Total AMC production took a big drop to 295,897.

	Restorable	Good	Excellent
American cvt	$1,500-3,000	$3,000-5,500	$5,500-7,000
American, other	500-1,500	1,500-3,500	3,500-4,500
Classic cvt	1,500-3,000	3,000-5,500	5,500-7,000
Classic, other	1,000-2,500	2,500-5,000	5,000-6,000
Ambassador cvt	2,000-4,000	4,000-6,000	6,000-8,000
Ambassador DPL	1,500-3,000	3,000-6,000	6,000-7,000

1965 Rambler Classic 770 convertible coupe

1965 Rambler Ambassador 990-H hardtop coupe

1965 Rambler Marlin fastback hardtop coupe

1966 Rambler Classic Rebel hardtop coupe

1966 Rambler American Rogue hardtop coupe

	Restorable	Good	Excellent
Ambassador, other	1,500-3,000	3,000-5,500	5,500-6,500
Marlin	1,500-2,500	2,500-4,500	4,500-6,500

1966 AMC Ambassador DPL hardtop coupe

1967 AMC Marlin fastback hardtop coupe

1967 AMC Ambassador DPL convertible coupe

1967 Rambler American Rogue hardtop coupe

1968 AMC AMX 2-passenger coupe

1967

The Ambassador's wheelbase was stretched two inches to 118 and curvier semi-fastback hardtop styling appeared, resulting in the most handsome AMC top-liners yet. DPL now consisted of a hardtop and ragtop (12,552 and 1260 built), and the 990 hardtop found 6140 buyers. The '67 Marlin was both the last and best of the breed, fully restyled on the longer Ambassador wheelbase and six inches longer than previous Marlins for better proportions. Options included four-speed gearbox, tachometer, bucket seats, and engines ranging up to 280 bhp. But Marlin lacked taut handling and was too big to pass as a sporting automobile. Only 2545 were sold. Mid-size Ramblers, previously called Classics, were now Rebels: 550, 770, and SST. Like the Ambassador, they sported curvier flanks and had a longer wheelbase, 114 inches. The SST hardtop attracted 16,663 buyers, the SST ragtop 1686, and the 770 hardtop 9721. The little changed American moved the convertible into the Rogue series, but only 921 were called for, and the hardtops were down, too: 4249 Rogues, 4994 440s. Despite the attractive new styling for the Ambassador and Rebel, total AMC output fell to 235,923.

	Restorable	Good	Excellent
American Rogue cvt	$1,500-3,000	$3,000-5,500	$5,500-7,000
American, other	500-1,500	1,500-3,500	3,500-4,500
Rebel SST cvt	1,500-3,000	3,000-5,500	5,500-7,000
Rebel, other	1,000-2,500	2,500-5,000	5,000-6,000
Ambassador DPL cvt	2,000-4,000	4,000-6,000	6,000-8,000
Ambassador, other	1,500-3,000	3,000-5,500	5,500-6,500
Marlin	1,500-2,500	2,500-4,500	4,500-6,500

1968

A more successful substitute for the vanished Marlin was the new AMC Javelin, a 109-inch-wheelbase ponycar in the Mustang image, beautifully styled and exciting. With its standard 145-bhp 232 six, Javelin cruised at 80; with its optional 225-bhp 290 V-8 it topped 100. Look for the "Go Package," including the 280-bhp 343 V-8 or 315-bhp 390, dual exhausts, power front disc brakes, handling suspension, and wide tires. First year sales were encouraging: 29,097 base and 27,347 SSTs. Even more desirable is the mid-year AMX, a short-wheelbase (97 inches), two-seater Javelin offering 290, 343, and 390 V-8s, tight suspension, full instrumentation, buckets, and optional four-speed gearbox. Especially desirable: the AMX Craig Breedlove Edition, named for a successful racing driver. AMX output was 6725 in the short model year. The mid-size Rebel shifted from Rambler to the AMC marque this year, retaining its convertible body style, which was available in base 550 or deluxe SST trim, though only 377 550s and 823 SSTs were built. All other AMC convertibles were dropped and "Rambler" per se now comprised only the American—base model, 440, and Rogue hardtop. Among the hardtops were 4765 Rogues, 7385 Rebel 550s, 4428 Rebel 770s, 11,516 Rebel SSTs, 3360 Ambassadors, 3696 Ambassador DPLs, and 7876 Ambassador SSTs. Javelin helped corporate output rise to 272,726 units.

	Restorable	Good	Excellent
American Rogue	$1,000-2,000	$2,000-4,000	$4,000-5,500
American, other	500-1,500	1,500-3,500	3,500-4,500
Rebel 550 cvt	1,000-2,500	2,500-4,500	4,500-5,500
Rebel SST cvt	1,500-3,000	3,000-5,500	5,500-6,500
Rebel, other	1,000-2,000	2,000-4,000	4,000-5,000
Ambassador	1,500-3,000	3,000-5,500	5,500-6,500
Javelin	1,500-2,500	2,500-4,000	4,000-5,000
Javelin SST	2,000-3,000	3,000-5,000	5,000-6,500
Javelin SST Go-pkg	2,500-4,000	4,000-6,000	6,000-8,500
AMX 290/343	3,000-5,000	5,000-8,000	8,000-11,000
AMX 390	4,000-6,500	6,500-10,000	10,000-13,500
AMX Breedlove	5,000-8,000	8,000-12,500	12,000-15,000

1969

Convertibles were dropped entirely and the Rebel was limited to two series: base and SST. A wider track, new grille, and restyled taillights were the changes of note. The only model of interest to collectors was the SST hardtop, but only 5405 were sold (plus 5396 base hardtops). As a marque, Rambler (no longer called American) was in its final year. It saw a repeat of the '68 lineup—plus a mini-muscle car, the SC/Rambler. It sported a 390 V-8 with 315 horsepower, Hurst shifter, bucket seats, and loud sporty styling. Though an impressive powerhouse, "Scramblers" attracted just 1512 buyers. Collectors today still say they're impressive performers—all that power and only 3100 pounds curb weight. In the regular Rambler line, 3543 Rogue hardtops were sold. Javelin was facelifted with a slightly different grille. Look for these option packages: the "Big Bad AMX" (284 orange, 195 blue, and 283 green cars, all with body-color bumpers and other special trim), and the "Mod Javelin" (the same colors and trim). Add 10-20 percent to the value of the car if it carries either package. Total Javelin production was 40,675. Hurst built about 50 Super Stock AMXs for drag racing; any extant examples may be in pretty rough shape, but they are highly desirable nevertheless. Some 8293 AMXs were built this year. The Ambassador wasn't much changed, but output increased to 76,194, 13,502 of them hardtops. Overall, AMC production perked up slightly to 282,809.

	Restorable	Good	Excellent
SC/Rambler	$3,000-6,000	$6,000-8,500	$8,500-11,000
Javelin	1,500-2,500	2,500-4,000	4,000-5,000
Javelin SST	2,000-3,000	3,000-5,000	5,000-6,500
Javelin SST Go-pkg	2,500-4,000	4,000-6,000	6,000-8,500
AMX 290/343	3,000-5,000	5,000-8,000	8,000-11,000
AMX 390	4,000-6,500	6,500-10,000	10,000-13,500

1968 AMC Rebel SST hardtop coupe

1968 Rambler American Rogue hardtop coupe

1968 AMC Javelin SST fastback hardtop coupe

1969 AMC Javelin SST fastback hardtop coupe

1969 SC/Rambler-Hurst hardtop coupe

1970 AMC AMX 2-passenger coupe

1970 AMC Rebel SST hardtop coupe

1971 AMC Hornet SC/360 two-door sedan

1971 AMC Javelin SST fastback hardtop coupe

1970

AMX's best styling came in its last year as a two-seater, when its body was smoothly integrated, appearing genuinely like the serious sports car it was. That didn't help, though, as only 4116 were built. Rebel sedans and hardtops were lengthened to accommodate a redesigned roof and rear fenders. An important addition to the line was the "Rebel Machine," packing the 390 V-8, four-speed with Hurst linkage, and a stump-puller 3.54:1 rear axle ratio. The hardtop body had a Ram-Air hood scoop, special red-white-blue paint job, 15-inch mag wheels with raised white letter tires, dual exhausts, low-back pressure mufflers, 8000 rpm tach, and a definite front end rake. Output came to 2326 units. Also highly collectible are the Javelin Trans Ams (front and rear spoilers, black interior, 390 Go-Package, mag wheels and wide tires, tachometer and 140 mph speedo, Hurst four-speed, 3.90:1 back axle). Only 100 were assembled to homologate special body parts for Trans Am competition. The other collectible '70 Javelin was the "Mark Donohue" with a thick-walled racing 360 V-8 and special duck-tail rear spoiler with Mark Donohue signature on the right side. Reportedly, 2501 Donohues were produced. Total Javelin sales fell to 28,210. AMC's new $40-million compact, the Hornet (on a 108-inch wheelbase), was announced—and its 96-inch-wheelbase derivation, the Gremlin, followed in the spring. Collectibility does not generally apply to these, nor to 1970 and later Ambassadors, though a few exceptions will be mentioned when appropriate. Corporate output settled in at about 276,000 cars this model year.

	Restorable	Good	Excellent
Rebel Machine	$2,500-5,000	$5,000-7,500	$7,500-10,000
Javelin	1,500-2,500	2,500-4,000	4,000-5,000
Javelin SST	2,000-3,000	3,000-5,000	5,000-6,500
Javelin SST Go-pkg	2,500-4,000	4,000-6,000	6,000-8,500
Javelin Trans Am	3,500-5,000	5,000-7,500	7,500-10,000
Javelin Donohue	3,000-4,500	4,500-6,500	6,500-9,000
AMX 360	3,000-5,000	5,000-8,000	8,000-11,000
AMX 390	4,000-6,500	6,500-10,000	10,000-13,500

1971

The Hornet SC/360 was an interesting performance two-door sedan, packing AMC's 360 small-block V-8 with 245 bhp (285 with four-barrel carb). Acceleration was vivid, held down by heavy duty suspension. SC/360s had styled steel wheels, fat tires, and modest tape striping; a four-speed gearbox with Hurst linkage was optional. But sales were few, so only 784 were built. The Matador appeared as a restyled successor to the intermediate Rebel—a plug ordinary car which has attracted little collector interest. The hot Rebel Machine and slow-selling AMX were dropped, so the AMX name was transferred to the top-end Javelin. The Javelin itself sported new styling—heavy sheetmetal surgery sporting humps over the wheels—and a one-inch-longer wheelbase, though the basic body was as before. Inside was a reworked dash. The ponycar heyday had passed, and Javelin never broke 30,000 units from this point through its demise in 1974. This year's tally was 29,130, including 2054 AMXs and 1306 Trans Am Specials. The last was basically a carryover of the Mark Donohue model sans spoiler or Donohue decals (a taller spoiler was optional). Instead, it bore red-white-blue Trans Am decals on the front fenders. Notable: the 330-horse 401, the ultimate development of AMC's small-block V-8, which became optional on Javelin (and Ambassador) during the year.

	Restorable	Good	Excellent
Hornet SC/360	$2,000-4,000	$4,000-6,500	$6,500-8,500
Javelin, incl. SST	2,000-3,000	3,000-4,500	4,500-6,000
Javelin 401 V-8	2,500-3,500	3,500-5,000	5,000-7,000
Javelin AMX	2,500-4,000	4,000-6,000	6,000-8,000
Javelin AMX Go-pkg	3,000-4,500	4,500-6,500	6,500-9,000

1971 AMC Javelin AMX fastback hardtop coupe

1972

This was a grim year for most American manufacturers, what with net horsepower ratings, crash standards, seatbelt interlocks, and another notch of the emission control crank either a reality or looming on the horizon. AMC was no exception, and its cars are mostly unattractive to today's collectors. About the only models with a pretense of collectibility are the Javelins, particularly the AMX with its standard V-8. The lineup was simplified to just SST and AMX (no more base models); output was 23,455 and 2729, respectively. The 401 V-8 was now rated at 255 net horsepower. Of peripheral interest was the Gucci Hornet Sportabout (semi-wagon), fashioned and colored by the Italian designer; 2584 were sold. There was also the Javelin Pierre Cardin, ditto by the Frenchman. It was offered in 1972 and '73, and 4152 were sold. The popularity of the Hornet and Gremlin helped push AMC output to 258,134 for the model run. Of the 94,808 Gremlins produced, 10,949 had the 150-bhp 304 V-8 that became available this year. When combined with the "X" package—stripes, slotted wheels and bigger tires, bucket seats, etc.—it made for a snappy little car.

1972 AMC Gremlin X hatchback coupe

	Restorable	Good	Excellent
Gremlin X (V-8)	$1,500-2,500	$2,500-3,500	$3,500-4,500
Hornet Gucci	1,000-2,000	2,000-3,000	3,000-4,000
Javelin, incl. SST	1,500-2,500	2,500-3,500	3,500-5,000
Javelin Cardin	2,000-3,000	3,000-4,000	4,000-6,000
Javelin AMX 360	2,000-3,500	3,500-5,000	5,000-7,000
Javelin AMX 401	2,500-4,000	4,000-6,000	6,000-8,000

1972 AMC Javelin SST fastback hardtop coupe

1972 AMC Javelin AMX fastback hardtop coupe

1973

The "Trans Am Victory Javelin" was a limited edition with a winner decal on the front fenders, rally wheels, white letter tires, and a space-saver spare tire. It celebrated AMC's Trans-Am race triumphs of 1971-72, though there wasn't much to party about as output was just 22,556 hardtops and 4980 AMXs. Go packages were still available with the 360 and 401 V-8s. A novel Gremlin, the "Levis" package, featured seats and door panels upholstered in spun

1972 AMC Hornet Sportabout wagon with Gucci trim

1973 AMC Hornet Hatchback coupe

1973 AMC Javelin SST fastback hardtop coupe

1973 AMC Javelin AMX fastback hardtop coupe

1974 AMC Matador X fastback coupe

1974 AMC Gremlin X Levis hatchback coupe

nylon fabric closely matching the famous blue jeans look, complete with copper rivets and Levi Strauss red labels. This option would continue for several years and could be combined with the sporty "X" package. A stylish Hornet hatchback coupe debuted, with vast (though shallow) load space; it too could be rendered sportier with the optional "X" and/or Levis packages. Of the 320,786 cars AMC built for the model run, 40,110 were Hornet hatchbacks, and 11,672 of the 122,844 Gremlins produced were V-8s.

	Restorable	Good	Excellent
Gremlin V-8	$1,500-2,500	$2,500-3,500	$3,500-4,500
Gremlin V-8 Levis	2,000-3,000	3,000-4,000	4,000-5,000
Hornet X hatchback	1,000-2,000	2,000-3,000	3,000-4,000
Javelin Victory edn	2,000-3,000	3,000-4,000	4,000-6,000
Javelin AMX 360	2,000-3,500	3,500-5,000	5,000-7,000
Javelin AMX 401	2,500-4,000	4,000-6,000	6,000-8,000
Javelin, other	1,500-2,500	2,500-3,500	3,500-5,000

1974

An attempt to inject pizzazz into the Matador's staid image was a new fastback two-door "X" model that AMC campaigned in stock car racing. It had a trim 114-inch wheelbase and smooth, curvy looks announced by an unusual front end in which the hood was shaped to form the upper portions of huge headlamp cavities. In the broad historical sense, this sleek Matador was one of stylist Dick Teague's purest efforts, and for that reason the more luxurious examples of it will definitely be collectible. Look for the Oleg Cassini designer edition, resplendent with copper accents inside and out; 6165 Cassinis were produced for '74. Also of interest was the Matador "X," the coupe with a sporty package including stripes, slotted wheels and bigger tires, etc. AMC built 10,074 of these. Much rarer, with just 3734 installations, was the 401 V-8, still rated at 255 net bhp and available for Matadors, Ambassadors, and Javelins. The last, still available with Go package, was now in its last year; 22,556 coupes and 4980 AMXs were built. In all, 431,798 AMC cars were produced for '74.

	Restorable	Good	Excellent
Gremlin V-8	$1,500-2,500	$2,500-3,500	$3,500-4,500
Gremlin V-8 Levis	2,000-3,000	3,000-4,000	4,000-5,000
Hornet X hatchback	1,000-2,000	2,000-3,000	3,000-4,000
Javelin AMX 360	2,000-3,500	3,500-5,000	5,000-7,000
Javelin AMX 401	2,500-4,000	4,000-6,000	6,000-8,000
Javelin, other	1,500-2,500	2,500-3,500	3,500-5,000
Matador X cpe	1,000-2,000	2,000-3,000	3,000-4,000

1975

Pacer, AMC's new "wide small car," was announced, with an egg-shaped hatchback body seemingly almost as wide as it was long. The passenger-side door was four inches wider than the driver's side door for easier rear seat entry. Pacer had been engineered to carry GM's Wankel rotary engine, but that project was canceled and AMC had to fall back on its old 232- and 258-cid inline sixes (100 and 110 bhp). The 100-inch-wheelbase Pacer was a disappointment—too heavy (2995 pounds base), too odd. The best ones to look for are the luxurious D/Ls equipped with snazzy interiors, or the sporty "X" models. Total output was 72,158 units. Pacers are just strange enough to acquire cult status among collectors, though they will never earn big bucks for investor types. On Matador coupes, the Cassini trim option remained available, but only 1817 of these were turned out. One source indicates that only four Matador coupes had the 401 V-8, likely since that engine wasn't officially available any longer. Also gone was the Ambassador. Hornet sported an attractive new grille, while the Gremlin was little changed. Both still offered V-8s—8075 were installed in Hornets, 3410 in Gremlins—and various trim packages. Total AMC production dropped to 241,501 units.

	Restorable	Good	Excellent
Pacer	$1,000-2,000	$2,000-3,000	$3,000-4,000
Gremlin V-8	1,500-2,500	2,500-3,500	3,500-4,500
Gremlin V-8 Levis	2,000-3,000	3,000-4,000	4,000-5,000
Hornet X hatchback	1,000-2,000	2,000-3,000	3,000-4,000
Matador X coupe	1,000-2,000	2,000-3,000	3,000-4,000

1976

Gremlin sported an attractive new grille, and output rose to 52,941. The sporty "X" tape-stripe package and the Levis interior continued to be available, as did the 304 V-8 (though only 826 were ordered). The Pacer "X" package was continued, with sporty color-keyed moldings, front-sway bar, bumper trim strips, and blackwall tires. Bucket seats were optional. The luxury Pacer D/L offered a basket-weave fabric interior, carpeted trunk, woodgrain dash appliqués, color-keyed scuff moldings, full wheel covers, and other trim. For added pep, a 120-bhp version of the 258 six was optional. Pacer production rose sharply to 117,244. The Matador coupe sported a revised grille and offered a new Barcelona trim package. It featured velvet-like upholstery, color-keyed pile carpets, Spanish tan interior and exterior accents, red and yellow side striping, and special identification. Gremlins and Hornets were little changed. AMC production rose this year to 283,577 units.

	Restorable	Good	Excellent
Pacer	$1,000-2,000	$2,000-3,000	$3,000-4,000
Gremlin V-8	1,500-2,500	2,500-3,500	3,500-4,500
Gremlin V-8 Levis	2,000-3,000	3,000-4,000	4,000-5,000
Hornet X hatchback	1,000-2,000	2,000-3,000	3,000-4,000
Matador X cpe	1,000-2,000	2,000-3,000	3,000-4,000

1977

The Gremlin was restyled with a laid-back finer mesh grille encompassing parking lights and flanked by square bezels for the headlamps. AMC's subcompact gained an 80-horse, 121-cid overhead-cam

1975 AMC Matador fastback coupe

1975 AMC Hornet Hatchback coupe

1976 AMC Pacer D/L hatchback coupe

1976 AMC Gremlin X hatchback coupe

1977 AMC Pacer D/L two-door station wagon

1977 AMC Gremlin X hatchback coupe

1977 AMC Matador Barcelona fastback coupe

1977 AMC Hornet AMX hatchback coupe

1978 AMC AMX fastback coupe

1978 AMC Gremlin X hatchback coupe

four and a new Borg-Warner four-speed stick with floor shift, but lost its V-8. Production fell to 46,171. The specially trimmed and equipped Hornet AMX hatchback, with 258 six or 304 V-8, was a nod in nostalgic directions, and one of the few Hornets that may someday be slightly collectible. AMC built 77,843 Hornets, 4091 with V-8s. Pacer unveiled a new station wagon body style, an interesting design and probably the sportiest American wagon since the mid-Fifties Chevy Nomad. Even with the wagon, production was way down: 20,265 hatchbacks, 37,999 wagons. Matador lost it high-performance 360 option, leaving it with just a 129-bhp 360, 126-bhp 304, or 98- or 114-bhp 258 sixes. Trim options were generally carried over for all AMC nameplates, which together accounted for 182,005 units—a dismal showing placing it last among all domestic makes.

	Restorable	Good	Excellent
Hornet AMX htchbk	$1,000-2,000	$2,000-3,250	$3,250-4,500
Pacer	1,000-2,000	2,000-3,000	3,000-4,000
Gremlin X/Levis	1,500-2,500	2,500-3,500	3,500-4,500
Matador X cpe	1,000-2,000	2,000-3,000	3,000-4,000

1978

The compact Hornet became the compact Concord. Reflecting AMC's dwindling resources, it wasn't all that different structurally or mechanically, but it was better finished, had a more "important" look, and benefitted from AMC's new stress on quality workmanship. It could be had with a four, six, or V-8 and with D/L or Sport packages. Output of all four body styles totaled 117,513. Derived from the Concord was the new AMX hatchback, with lots of black accents, a wild hood decal, needle instruments on a brushed aluminum panel, and an optional Levis interior. The problem was that this AMX was a toothless wonder: though it had disc brakes and radials, it came standard with a six, and if you opted for the small V-8 you had also to accept automatic transmission. Only 2540 AMXs were produced. Gremlin production plummeted to just 22,104 for '78. A GT package was new; it included a front air dam, front and rear fender flares, stripes, buckets, gauge package, and more. Pacer sported a raised hood and new grille and added the 304 V-8 as an option. Out of 21,231 Pacers built, 2514 had the V-8. After a run of only 10,576 cars, the Matador nameplate was retired. Barcelona Brougham trim was again available. AMC's position further eroded as only 137,860 cars were built for the model run.

	Restorable	Good	Excellent
AMX hatchback	$1,000-2,000	$2,000-3,250	$3,250-4,500
Pacer	1,000-2,000	2,000-3,000	3,000-4,000
Gremlin GT/Levis	1,500-2,500	2,500-3,500	3,500-4,500
Matador X coupe	1,000-2,000	2,000-3,000	3,000-4,000

1979

The Gremlin vanished, but lived on in Spirit, essentially the same car with smoother, more conventional styling. Joining the familiar chopped-tail two-door sedan was a slick new three-door Spirit coupe bearing a graceful superstructure for such a short wheelbase. Spirit output recovered to 52,478 units. The AMX now rode the Spirit platform, and was equipped with black bumpers, front air dam, rear spoiler, fender flares, black-out grille, aluminum wheels, white letter tires, and the usual extrovert graphics. This time, AMXs could be ordered with stick shift V-8s, and they all benefitted from a handling suspension—this is a good year to look for, though only 3657 were sold (six and V-8). It was now obvious that the Pacer had laid an enormous sales egg, so there were few changes. Of the 10,215 Pacers produced, only 184 had sunroofs. AMC output edged upward to 169,439 sales.

	Restorable	Good	Excellent
AMX hatchback	$1,000-2,000	$2,000-3,250	$3,250-4,500
Pacer	1,000-2,000	2,000-3,000	3,000-4,000

1979 AMC AMX fastback coupe

1980

Though it would continue to be used in Jeeps, the V-8 was no longer offered in AMC's passenger car line. Concord lost its hatchback body style, but evolved the four-wheel-drive Eagle, a novel offshoot reviving a name AMC owned through its Jeep subsidiary and the old Aero-Willys. Eagle used a transfer case that apportioned driving torque between front and rear wheels via slip-limiting silicone compound; it was neither car nor truck, but a specialty vehicle with some of the appeal of both. Available as a two- or four-door sedan or wagon, Eagle attracted 46,379 buyers. Concord sported a new grille and opera windows; 80,456 buyers liked the new look. The AMX tag was continued for a special "paint-on performance" Spirit hatchback. Power was supplied by a Pontiac-built four or AMC's own long-lived six. Heavy emphasis on quality meant the Spirit was better assembled than the Gremlin, but aging componentry was obvious. This was the Pacer's final year. Base D/L and luxury Limited models were offered, but only 1746 were called for. AMC model year production totaled 199,613.

1980 AMC Pacer D/L hatchback coupe

1980 AMC Eagle four-door sedan

	Restorable	Good	Excellent
Eagle	$500-1,000	$1,000-2,000	$2,000-3,000
AMX hatchback	1,000-2,000	2,000-3,250	3,250-4,500
Pacer	1,000-2,000	2,000-3,000	3,000-4,000

1980 AMC AMX fastback coupe

1981

AMC introduced a pair of short-wheelbase "Eaglets," the SX/4 and Kammback models, based on the Gremlin/Spirit platform. All Eagles featured automatic four-wheel drive with viscous coupling. Concord-based "senior" Eagles had rectangular grilles, shared with the junior editions. All carried a 2.5-liter four as standard, and a full line of power options was listed. Senior options included power seats, floor shift console, gauge package, and retractable cargo cover for the wagons—all desirable if you're shopping for one today. Production was

1981 AMC Eagle SX/4 hatchback coupe

1981 AMC Eagle Kammback coupe

1981 AMC Eagle four-door station wagon

1982 AMC Eagle Kammback coupe

1982 AMC Eagle wagon with Sport package

1983 AMC Spirit GT hatchback coupe

22,943 junior Eagles and 14,486 senior models. Spirit sported a new grille and continued to offer the GT package; Concord also got a new grille, plus revamped opera windows. Total AMC output was down to 137,145 units.

	Restorable	Good	Excellent
Eagle 30 (senior)	*	$1,000-2,000	$2,000-3,000
Eagle 50 (junior)	*	700-1,500	1,500-2,500
Spirit hatchback	*	1,500-2,500	2,500-3,500

* Purchase only in good or excellent condition

1982

A five-speed overdrive manual gearbox, numerically lower final drive ratios for all engine/transmission combinations, and wide-ratio gearing on sixes with automatic were featured on the '82 Eagles. Styling was a 1981 rerun, and the same models were listed. Ditto Spirit and Concord. Output this year was dismal: 20,182 Spirits, 43,810 Concords, 10,965 junior Eagles, and 26,958 senior Eagles.

	Restorable	Good	Excellent
Eagle 30 (senior)	*	$1,000-2,000	$2,000-3,250
Eagle 50 (junior)	*	1,000-2,000	2,000-2,750
Spirit hatchback 5-sp	*	1,500-2,500	2,500-3,500

* Purchase only in good or excellent condition

1983

American Motors cut the Eagle line, leaving only the short-wheelbase SX/4 three-door coupe and the senior Eagle four-door sedan and five-door wagon. The sedan was available only in DL trim, while the other models were offered in three trim levels. AMC Select-Drive, allowing changes from 2- and 4-wheel drive from inside, was standard on all models. A Pontiac-built four and four-speed gearbox were standard; the optional AMC 258 six had higher compression; five-speed was optional with either engine. AMC also fielded a new Spirit GT, tricked out with black exterior trim, handling package, steel belted radials, aluminum wheels, fog lamps, tachometer, gauge package, and other sporty items. Spirits, and Concords for that matter, came only with the AMC six. Production figures were abysmal: 3491 Spirits, 5300 Concords, 2259 Eagle SX/4s, and 15,471 senior Eagles. But not all was lost, for it was this year that AMC and Renault brought out the front-drive Alliance, a subcompact based on the Renault 9. Though assembled in Kenosha, engines (a 56-bhp 1.4-liter four), transmissions, and other parts came from France. It was offered as a two- or four-door sedan in several trim levels, and 142,205 were sold. *Motor Trend* chose it "Car of the Year," but quality problems would soon become apparent. In any case, there's nothing here of interest to collectors.

	Restorable	Good	Excellent
Eagle 30 (senior)	*	$1,250-2,500	$2,500-3,500
Eagle 50 (SX/4)	*	1,250-2,250	2,250-3,000
Spirit GT hatchback	*	$1,500-2,500	$2,500-3,000

* Purchase only in good or excellent condition

1984

American Motors, now in its last-ditch marriage with Renault and attempting to stay alive with home-built imports, dropped both Concord and Spirit, along with the short-wheelbase Eagle SX/4. This left only the 109-inch-wheelbase Eagle sedan and wagon. Both models were offered in base DL trim; an up-market Limited wagon was also available. Output totaled 4241 sedans and 21,294 wagons. Meanwhile, a hatchback edition of the Alliance, the Encore, debuted. It attracted 64,532 buyers, while Alliance found 121,015.

	Restorable	Good	Excellent
Eagle	*	$1,500-2,750	$2,750-3,500

* Purchase only in good or excellent condition

1985

"Shift on the fly" capability was added to the Eagle sedan and wagon. Previously, this was done by stopping to change drive systems; now it could be handled by the flick of a switch. The Pontiac four that had been standard in previous Eagles was dropped, replaced by an AMC 4.2-liter inline six with five-speed manual gearbox. Eagle output was 2655 sedans and 13,535 wagons. Marketed under the Renault badge but assembled by AMC in the United States was the new Alliance L convertible, at $10,295 the lowest priced ragtop in America ($11,295 for a DL). A 1.7-liter overhead-cam four with 77 bhp was standard. Out of the 91,664 Alliances produced, 7141 were ragtops. In addition, 58,525 Encores were built.

	Restorable	Good	Excellent
Alliance cvt	*	$2,000-3,000	$3,000-4,000
Eagle	*	2,000-3,000	3,000-3,750

* Purchase only in good or excellent condition

1986

The last car to carry the AMC nameplate, the '86 Eagle was a complete carryover from 1985, except for higher prices. The DL sedan and DL and Limited wagons continued unchanged, with AMC's six as the sole engine. Production was down by half to 1274 sedans and 6943 wagons. Alliance sales were falling off badly, owing to mechanical and quality problems. The Alliance convertible continued with a new instrument cluster, gas-charged shocks, larger diameter stabilizer bars, and an optional tilt steering wheel. Of the 68,110 Alliances built, 2015 were ragtops. Encore, meanwhile, stumbled to 19,109 units.

	Restorable	Good	Excellent
Alliance cvt	*	$2,000-3,000	$3,000-4,250
Eagle	*	2,000-3,000	3,000-4,000

* Purchase only in good or excellent condition

1987

AMC called the new 2.0-liter Renault Alliance GTA a "pocket rocket," pitting it against the likes of

1984 AMC Eagle four-door sedan

1985 Renault Alliance DL convertible coupe

1985 AMC Eagle Limited four-door station wagon

1986 AMC Eagle Limited four-door station wagon

1987 Renault Alliance L convertible coupe

1987 Renault Alliance GTA convertible coupe

VW's GTI and Ford's Escort GT—which were, alas, considerably more salesworthy. Convertibles were available in three forms: L and DL 1.7-liter (with standard five-speed and power top), and GTA, which had sport suspension and special aluminum wheels. Production of all three ragtop models totaled 1991. Encore was dropped, and only 36,336 Alliances were built. Carried over again, the Eagle was unchanged and nearing the end. It could trace its chassis back to the 1970 Hornet, its six-cylinder engine to earlier than that when Ramblers were still around. Output this year was 751 sedans and 4452 wagons.

	Restorable	Good	Excellent
Alliance DL cvt	*	$2,000-3,000	$3,000-4,250
Alliance GTA cvt	*	3,500-4,000	4,000-4,750
Eagle	*	2,500-3,500	3,500-4,500

* Purchase only in good or excellent condition

1988

In August 1987, American Motors was bought by Chrysler Corporation, which briefly brought out a 1988 Eagle, now sold at its new Jeep-Eagle dealers. The sole model was a DL station wagon, unchanged in specifications. What Chrysler didn't want was the unlamented Alliance—it had more and better small cars—so this final vestige of American Motors was sent packing. Thus ended the history of a firm that had once brought a car into third place, behind Chevy and Ford, in the American production race.

	Restorable	Good	Excellent
Eagle DL wagon	*	$2,750-4,000	$4,000-4,750

* Purchase only in good or excellent condition

Oakland

Pontiac was the only GM "companion make" to survive its original companion. The Oakland Motor Car Company was organized in 1907 in Pontiac, Michigan, and became a part of William C. Durant's fledgling General Motors empire two years later. Oakland prospered for a time, then experienced falling sales in the early Twenties. Pontiac was introduced as Oakland's companion make in 1926, and it was soon outselling its "parent" many times over. In 1930, it was 62,888 versus 21,943 and in 1931 Pontiac outsold Oakland 84,708 to 13,408. Thus, Oakland was finished in 1931, and there isn't much collector interest in its two model years of the 1930s. Club support is moderate (Pontiac-Oakland Club International), parts scarce, investment potential low.

1930 Oakland V-8 roadster

1931 Oakland V-8 rumble-seat coupe

1930-31

The final Oaklands rode a 117-inch wheelbase and were offered in a variety of open and closed bodies spanning $895-$1055. All were powered by an 85-bhp, 250-cid V-8 with uncommonly oversquare cylinder dimensions and a 180-degree crankshaft that made it a very rough runner. The most valuable versions are the 1930 Sport Roadster and phaeton; a convertible coupe was the only open body in 1931.

	Restorable	Good	Excellent
1930 rdstr/phtn	$3,500-8,000	$8,000-17,500	$17,500-25,000
1931 cvt cpe	2,500-7,000	7,000-12,500	12,500-20,000
1930-31 coupes	2,000-5,000	5,000-10,000	10,000-15,000
1930-31 sedans	1,000-3,000	3,000-5,500	5,500-8,000

Oldsmobile

Though for years Olds was regarded as the "experimental division" of General Motors, producing many technological breakthroughs such as Hydra-Matic, it has been a minor player among collector cars. High points include the stock car champion 1949-51 88, the exotic 1953 Fiesta, the early Toronado, and the muscle car 4-4-2s. Club support is good; parts supply sporadic, except for late models; investment potential generally low.

1930-39

Despite the Depression, this was a good decade for Oldsmobile. It produced synchromesh transmission in 1931, "Knee Action" independent front suspension in 1934, a semi-automatic Safety Automatic Transmission in 1937, Hydra-Matic Drive for 1940. The Viking, Oldsmobile's V-8 "companion make," expired after 1930. Oldsmobiles all carried sixes until 1932, when an eight was added—both were conventional L-heads. Oldsmobile had some of the most consistent designs during the 1930s, sticking to two series on two wheelbases from 1932 to 1938. Styling was classical upright in 1930-32, slightly streamlined in 1933, "potato shaped" for 1934. More massive front ends with cross-hatched or horizontal-bar grilles were seen in 1936-37; the 1938-39s had headlamp pods partly faired into the front fender aprons and designer Harley Earl's "twin catwalk" auxiliary grilles flanking the center grille. Introduced in 1939 alongside the Series 60 (six-cylinder) and 80 (eight-cylinder) was a mid-range Series 70, using the 80's wheelbase but running a six. In time, the 80 would develop into the famous 88. Open Oldsmobiles, the most collectible body styles, included a touring and convertible coupe during 1930, convertible coupes only from 1931. There were no soft top sixes in 1934.

Oldsmobile's engine in 1930-31 was a 197.5-cid six that developed 62/65 horsepower. From 1932-36 there were two engines: a 213.3-cid six (74-90 bhp) and a 240-cid straight eight (87-100 bhp). For the remainder of the decade the six displaced 229.7 cid

1930 Viking DeLuxe V-8 convertible coupe

1932 Oldsmobile Eight two-door sedan

1934 Oldsmobile Six Sport Coupe

1935 Oldsmobile Six station wagon

1937 Oldsmobile Eight convertible coupe

1938 Oldsmobile Eight trunkback Touring Sedan

1939 Oldsmobile Series 70 Club Coupe

1940 Oldsmobile Series 90 convertible coupe

1940 Oldsmobile Series 90 Convertible Phaeton

(90-95 bhp), the eight 257.1 cid (110 bhp). In 1939 only, a 90-bhp, 216-cid six powered the Series 60.

Oldsmobile opened the decade with a production run of 49,395 cars, but this deteriorated to 18,846 in 1932, after which output increased to a peak of 191,357 in 1936. Olds closed the decade by building 127,227 cars. Open models were often only in three figures, and even in 1936 convertible production was just 2136 Sixes and 931 Eights. The best selling open car of the decade was the 1931 DeLuxe Six convertible roadster; it found 3144 buyers.

	Restorable	Good	Excellent
1930 Viking cvt	$5,000-10,000	$10,000-17,500	$17,500-25,000
1930 Six, open	3,500-7,500	7,500-14,000	14,000-20,000
1930-32 coupes	2,500-6,000	6,000-10,000	10,000-13,500
1930-39, other clsd	1,500-5,000	5,000-7,500	7,500-10,000
1931-33 Six, open	4,000-9,000	9,000-18,000	18,000-23,500
1932 Eight, open	5,000-11,000	11,000-19,000	19,000-28,500
1933-34 Eight, open	4,500-10,000	10,000-17,500	17,500-25,000
1935-36, open	4,000-8,000	8,000-17,500	17,500-22,500
1937-39 Six, open	5,000-10,000	10,000-20,000	20,000-28,000
1937-39 Eight, open	5,000-12,500	12,500-22,500	22,500-32,500

1940

The line comprised three series, each having its own wheelbase: 116 inches for the Series 60, 120 for the 70, 124 for the 90. The Series 60 and 70 used a 95-bhp, 229.7-cid six; the Series 90 wrung 110 horses out of its 257.1-cid eight. Each line offered a group of body styles in keeping with its price category—with a range of $807 to $1570, Olds covered a good portion of the market. The big news this model year was Oldsmobile's introduction of Hydra-Matic fully automatic transmission, a four-speed unit that completely did away with the clutch. Notable collectibles are the 60 station wagon with its Hercules wood body (633 built); the 70 club coupe (8505 produced); the 90 convertible phaeton (a convertible sedan that saw a run of only 50); and the convertible coupe version of all three models: 1347 60s, 1070 70s, and 290 90s. Styling followed standard GM practice, with flush headlamps, freestanding fenders, and "Turret Top" roofs with closed rear quarters. In all, Olds built 192,692 cars for 1940.

	Restorable	Good	Excellent
60 convertible	$4,000-9,000	$9,000-18,000	$18,000-25,000
60 wagon	3,000-7,500	7,500-14,000	14,000-19,000
70 convertible	4,000-10,000	10,000-20,000	20,000-30,000
60/70, other	1,500-5,000	5,000-7,000	7,000-9,500
90 open models	8,000-15,000	15,000-28,000	28,000-38,000
90 sedan & coupe	3,000-7,000	7,000-10,000	10,000-14,000

1941

A step toward streamlining was taken this year: front fenders blended more smoothly into the bodysides, but the rear fenders remained separate. Up front, the grille was even fussier, while the rear end was graced with flush rectangular taillights. The design changes were accompanied by a model realignment: 119- and 125-inch wheelbases for six different series: 66/68 Special, 76/78 Dynamic Cruiser, and 96/98 Custom Cruiser—the second digit designating the number of cylinders. Specials used the shorter wheelbase and offered a convertible coupe body; 2822 were built as Sixes, 776 as Eights. Custom Cruiser ragtops numbered 325 Sixes and 1263 Eights. The Convertible Phaeton (sedan) remained available for the last time, but output was scant: 119, all 98 Custom Cruisers. Woody wagons were offered only on the short wheelbase; 604 66s and 96 68s were sold. Total Olds output was 270,040 cars, about half of them equipped with Hydra-Matic. Within the price spans listed below, Eights carry a 10 percent premium over Sixes, which were boosted to 100 bhp.

	Restorable	Good	Excellent
66/68 convertible	$4,000-9,000	$9,000-18,000	$18,000-25,000
66/68 wagon	3,000-7,500	7,500-14,000	14,000-19,000
66/68/76/78, closed	1,500-5,000	5,000-7,000	7,000-9,500
96/98, open bodies	8,000-15,000	15,000-28,000	28,000-38,000
96/98 sdns & cpes	3,000-7,000	7,000-10,000	10,000-14,000

1942

Oldsmobile built 67,999 examples of its "B-44" '42s before production stopped for the war in early February. A five-series line was offered, the Custom Cruiser Six (96) having been dropped. The Custom Cruiser Eight, meanwhile, moved up to a 127-inch wheelbase. A new Town Sedan with formal roofline was an interesting 60-series body. "Fuselage" fenders—elongated pontoon shapes faired into the front doors—were featured. Another fussy grille design boasted a strong horizontal bar that served as a "double duty bumper"; it was connected to the frame. To conserve resources, the government required that cars built after January 1 receive painted bumpers and trim—they're extremely rare. Some production figures: 66 convertible, 746; 68 convertible, 102; 98 convertible, 216; 66 woody wagon, 700, 68 wagon, 95.

	Restorable	Good	Excellent
66/68 convertible	$4,000-9,000	$9,000-18,000	$18,000-25,000
66/68 wagon	3,000-7,500	7,500-14,000	14,000-19,000
66/68/76/78, closed	1,500-5,000	5,000-7,000	7,000-9,500
98 convertible	8,000-15,000	15,000-28,000	28,000-38,000
98 sedans & coupes	3,000-7,000	7,000-10,000	10,000-14,000

1946

Running seventh in the production race, Oldsmobile got by with warmed-over '42s, the most notable difference being a four-bar, inverted "U" grille that was less fussy than the prewar designs. Series were trimmed to four, 68 being dropped. The base Special 66 rode the 119-inch wheelbase, the mid-range Dynamic Cruiser 76 and 78 the 125-inch

1941 Oldsmobile Dynamic Cruiser Club Sedan

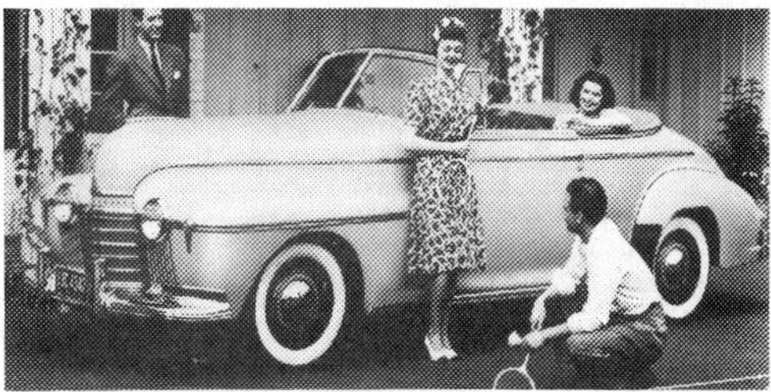

1941 Oldsmobile Special convertible coupe

1942 Oldsmobile Special Club Sedan

1942 Oldsmobile Custom Cruiser convertible

1946 Oldsmobile Special convertible coupe

1947 Oldsmobile Special Club Sedan

1946 Oldsmobile Custom Cruiser convertible

1948 Oldsmobile Futuramic 98 Club Sedan

1948 Oldsmobile Futuramic 98 four-door sedan

1948 Oldsmobile Futuramic 98 convertible coupe

span, and the Custom Cruiser 98 the 127-inch chassis. Engines remained at prewar specs: 100 and 110 horsepower. Convertibles were limited to the 66 and 98, and just 1409 and 874 were built. With the demise of the 68 series, the woody wagon now came only as a six-cylinder 66, and it was rare: 140 units for '46. Total model year production was 119,388 units despite materials shortages and a five-month strike by the United Auto Workers.

	Restorable	Good	Excellent
66 convertible	$3,500-8,000	$8,000-15,000	$15,000-22,500
66 wagon	3,000-7,500	7,500-14,000	14,000-19,000
98 convertible	5,000-10,000	10,000-18,000	18,000-25,000
Other models	1,000-3,000	3,000-5,500	5,500-8,000

1947

The Special 68 was brought back this year, and included a woody wagon. To identify the '47s, a V-shaped plastic hood ornament was adopted and the nameplate on the front fender moldings was larger. Olds continued to stress its popular Hydra-Matic, producing more automatic-equipped cars as a percentage of total volume than any other manufacturer, save Cadillac (which also used Oldsmobile's Hydra-Matic). Model year production increased to 194,388, including the following convertibles: 3949 66s, 2579 68s, and 3940 98s. Wagon output was 968 66s and 492 68s. With 24,733 built, the 98 four-door sedan was the most popular model.

	Restorable	Good	Excellent
66 convertible	$3,500-8,000	$8,000-15,000	$15,000-22,500
66/68 wagon	3,000-7,500	7,500-14,000	14,000-19,000
98 convertible	5,000-10,000	10,000-18,000	18,000-25,000
Other models	1,000-3,000	3,000-5,500	5,500-8,000

1948

Midway through the model year Oldsmobile brought out its first new postwar design, the Futuramic 98—long and low, styled with inspiration from the Lockheed P-38 wartime fighter aircraft. A marque identity was maintained via a two-bar, inverted "U" grille. Four-door and Club sedans were offered in standard and DeLuxe trim, while the convertible came as a DeLuxe only. Horsepower of the 257.1-cid straight eight was boosted to 115 for 98s. The 66, 68, 76, and 78, all now labeled "Dynamic," retained their prewar body styles. Model year identification consisted of a round hood medallion and the marque name spelled out in block letters on the hood, plus vertically positioned rectangular taillights. Other minor changes were the omission of fender nameplates and full-length chrome strips to cover the rocker panels. Sales of the 98 took off; of the 65,235 built, 12,914 were ragtops. In the other lines, Olds produced 1801 66 and 2091 68 ragtops and 1393 66 and 1314 68 wagons. This would be the last year for the "true" woody wagons. Olds model year production totaled 173,661 units.

	Restorable	Good	Excellent
66/68 convertible	$3,500-8,000	$8,000-15,000	$15,000-22,500
66/68 wagon	3,000-7,500	7,500-14,000	14,000-19,000
98 convertible	5,000-10,000	10,000-18,000	18,000-25,000
98 coupe & sedan	1,500-3,000	3,000-6,000	6,000-9,000
Other models	1,000-2,500	2,500-4,500	4,500-6,500

1949

The Rocket V-8 engine, designed by Gil Burrell, was one of the first two high-compression, overhead-valve V-8s, Cadillac's being the other. Oldsmobile's displaced 303 cubic inches, had five main bearings, oversquare bore and stroke, and developed 135 bhp at 3600 rpm. At the last minute, Olds decided to install it not only in the luxury 98, but in a new lightweight model 88, which shared bodies with the six-cylinder 76 (now at 257.1 cid and 105 bhp). The result was a made-to-order racer, and 88s dominated the stock car circuit from 1949 through 1951. Naturally, the race cars were fastback Club sedans and notchback coupes, not convertibles, so even the more plebeian body styles are of interest on this recognized Milestone car. Styling of the all-new Futuramic 76 and 88 was very similar to the larger 98, though on a shorter 119.5-inch wheelbase (compared to 125 inches). New to the 98 this year was the Holiday, Oldsmobile's first "hardtop convertible," a body style that would soon become the rage in Detroit. Due to a late introduction, output was limited to 3006 examples. Wood-trimmed wagons (with far less wood) were offered in both 76 and 88 lines. During the year they were replaced with all-steel wagons with a simulated woody look; the latter are worth much less today. Wagon output was 1545 76s and 1355 88s. Convertibles, all DeLuxes, numbered 5388 76s, 5434 88s, and 12,602 98s. Model year production shot up to 288,310.

	Restorable	Good	Excellent
76 convertible	$3,500-8,000	$8,000-14,000	$14,000-20,000
88/98 convertible	5,000-11,000	11,000-20,000	20,000-27,500
76/88 woody wagon	3,000-6,000	6,000-10,000	10,000-18,000
76/88 steel wagon	2,000-4,000	4,000-8,000	8,000-14,000
98 Holiday htp	3,500-8,000	8,000-15,000	15,000-20,000
Other models	1,000-3,000	3,000-6,000	6,000-9,000

1950

The Rocket V-8 proved so popular that Oldsmobile set a production record of 408,060 cars for the model year. Demand for the six-cylinder 76 was way down, however, so it was gone before the year was out. Look for the DeLuxe trim version of the 76 and 88 notchback sedans, club coupe, Holiday hardtop, and wagon, and the last examples of Oldsmobile's Club Sedan, an attractive two-door fastback. All wagons were all-steel this year—and the last Olds wagons until 1957. The 98, now on a shorter 122-inch wheelbase, also came in standard or DeLuxe trim in notchback and fastback sedans and Holidays. Styling was new, eliminating the separate rear fender look and incorporating squared-up rear fenders housing the first of Oldsmobile's

1949 Oldsmobile Futuramic 88 convertible

1949 Oldsmobile Futuramic 98 Holiday coupe

1950 Oldsmobile Futuramic 88 Holiday coupe

1950 Oldsmobile Futuramic 98 Holiday coupe

1951 Oldsmobile Super 88 convertible coupe

1951 Oldsmobile 98 Holiday four-door sedan

1952 Oldsmobile 88 DeLuxe two-door sedan

1952 Oldsmobile 98 Holiday hardtop coupe

"rocket" taillights. Convertibles in all three lines were sold only in one grade of trim. The 76 has remarkably low production figures for some models: 368 station wagons, 538 Holiday hardtops, 973 convertibles. But the 76 convertible doesn't begin to approach the 88 and 98 ragtops in value. Production in the 88 line included 9127 convertibles, 1366 Holidays, 11,316 DeLuxe Holidays, 1830 wagons, and 552 DeLuxe wagons. For 98s, the figures were 3925 ragtops, 317 Holidays, and 7946 DeLuxe Holidays. The 98 fastback Town Sedan was rare: 255 standards and 1523 DeLuxes.

	Restorable	Good	Excellent
76 convertible	$3,500-8,000	$8,000-14,000	$14,000-20,000
76/88 wagon	2,000-4,000	4,000-8,000	8,000-14,000
88/98 convertible	5,000-11,000	11,000-20,000	20,000-30,000
76/88/98 Holiday	3,000-7,000	7,000-13,000	13,000-17,500
Other models	1,000-3,000	3,000-6,000	6,000-9,000

1951

Oldsmobile dropped its six-cylinder series 76 and added a mid-range Super 88, while reducing the base 88 to sedans only. Styling of the Super 88 was more akin to the '50 98, but gaudier. The grille (shared with the 98) lost its inside inverted "U" bar in favor of a straight one, there was plenty of bodyside chrome, and rocket-style taillights forecast the future with tiny upright tailfins. Styling of the 88s was as in 1950, maintaining the separate rear fender look. The 135-bhp, 303 V-8 was now the sole engine, powering all three series. Super 88s saw production of 3854 convertibles and 14,180 Holiday hardtops; the figures for the 98 were 4468 and 14,012. Olds built 285,615 cars for '51.

	Restorable	Good	Excellent
Super 88 cvt	$5,000-10,000	$10,000-15,000	$15,000-20,000
Super 88 htp	2,000-5,000	5,000-9,000	9,000-13,000
98 convertible	5,000-12,000	12,000-18,000	18,000-23,000
98 Holiday htp	2,000-5,500	5,500-10,000	10,000-14,000
Other models	1,000-3,000	3,000-5,500	5,500-8,000

1952

The 88, now called DeLuxe 88, shared the Super 88's 120-inch wheelbase and its more slab-sided design, though with less brightwork—rubber rather than chrome gravel guards just ahead of the rear wheels, for example. As in 1951, only sedans were offered. Riding a two-inch-longer 124-inch wheelbase, the 98 sported revised bodyside styling similar to the Super 88. Through higher compression and carburetion changes, horsepower rose to 145 on the 88, 160 on the other models via a Quadri-Jet four-barrel carb. Front ends were similar to 1951, except for a center bumper guard, and silver medallions were seen front and rear. New options included power steering and Autronic Eye automatic headlight dimmer. Due to events in Korea, production was down to 213,490. This included 5162 Super 88 and 3544 98 convertibles and 15,777 Super 88 and 14,140 98 Holiday hardtops. Olds began spelling out Ninety Eight on its cars this year, but in press releases and the like often used "98" interchangeably, and would continue to do so.

	Restorable	Good	Excellent
Super 88 cvt	$5,000-10,000	$10,000-15,000	$15,000-22,000
Super 88 htp	2,000-5,000	5,000-9,000	9,000-13,000
98 convertible	5,000-12,000	12,000-18,000	18,000-24,000
98 hardtop	2,000-5,500	5,500-10,000	10,000-14,000
Other models	1,000-3,000	3,000-5,500	5,500-8,000

1953

Styling was more upright this year, with squarer rear fenders mounting the round taillights for the 88 and Super 88, bringing them more in line with the 98. All models sported a new grille with oval pods flanking the horizontal grille bar. One of the most sought after Oldsmobiles in history was the limited-edition 98 Fiesta convertible, a companion to the Cadillac Eldorado and Buick Skylark. Priced at $5717, the Fiesta featured a custom leather interior, wraparound windshield, bodyside two-toning, and a special 170-bhp Rocket V-8. Hydra-Matic, and power everything (brakes, steering, windows, seats) were standard, and Fiesta's "spinner" wheel covers became a favorite of the Kustom Kar set. Only 458 Fiestas were built. Horsepower on standard cars, which continued with no change in body styles, rose to 150 for the 88 and 165 for the rest. Power brakes and air conditioning joined the options list. Ragtop output was substantial for both Super 88 and 98—8310 and 7521—making these cars reasonably easy to find. Notice how the value of these convertibles builds up during the mid-Fifties—they are among the most desirable volume ragtops of the period. Olds enjoyed a good year by building 319,414 cars, and Holiday hardtops were twice as plentiful as in 1952: 36,881 Super 88s and 27,920 98s.

	Restorable	Good	Excellent
98 Fiesta cvt	$15,000-20,000	$20,000-38,000	$38,000-47,500
Super 88 cvt	5,000-10,000	10,000-15,000	15,000-23,000
Super 88 htp	2,000-5,000	5,000-11,000	11,000-15,000
98 convertible	5,000-12,000	12,000-18,000	18,000-26,000
98 hardtop	2,000-7,000	7,000 12,000	12,000 17,000
Other models	1,000-3,000	3,000-5,500	5,500-8,000

1954

New styling produced some of the most attractive Oldsmobiles of the decade—and, as a result, some of the highest prices on today's market. These lower, longer, wider cars rode a 122-inch wheelbase for both 88s, 126 for the 98. Styling front and rear continued established Olds themes, though with a flatter hood and rear deck; the Panoramic windshield, bodyside two-toning, and spinner hubcaps were borrowed from the '53 Fiesta. A bored out 324 V-8 with 3.9 x 3.4-inch bore and stroke delivered 170 bhp in the basic 88, 185 in the Super 88 and 98. Unlike Buick's Skylark and Cadillac's Eldorado, the Fiesta didn't return. Hardtops and ragtops in the 98 series sported unique bodyside two-toning; sedans shared theirs with the 88 and Super 88. Output rose to 354,001 units, enough to push Olds into fifth

1953 Oldsmobile 98 Holiday hardtop coupe

1953 Oldsmobile 88 DeLuxe two-door sedan

1954 Oldsmobile 88 four-door sedan

1954 Oldsmobile 98 Starfire convertible coupe

1954 Oldsmobile 98 DeLuxe Holiday hardtop coupe

1955 Oldsmobile 98 Starfire convertible coupe

1955 Oldsmobile Super 88 convertible coupe

1955 Oldsmobile 98 Holiday DeLuxe hardtop sedan

1955 Oldsmobile Super 88 four-door sedan

1956 Oldsmobile Super 88 Holiday hardtop sedan

place. This year, the 88 got a Holiday hardtop, and 25,820 were produced in addition to 42,155 Super 88s and 29,688 98s. Convertibles numbered 6452 Super 88s and 6800 98s. The big 98 soft top, named Starfire after the jet fighter, is particularly desirable.

	Restorable	Good	Excellent
88 hardtop	$2,000-6,000	$6,000-9,000	$9,000-13,000
Super 88 cvt	6,000-12,000	12,000-20,000	20,000-29,000
Super 88 htp	2,500-7,000	7,000-13,000	13,000-18,000
98 Starfire cvt	7,500-15,000	15,000-28,000	28,000-35,000
98 hardtop	3,000-10,000	10,000-15,000	15,000-21,000
Other models	1,000-3,000	3,000-5,500	5,500-8,000

1955

A record production year—583,179 units—saw Oldsmobile take over fourth place in the industry. New four-door hardtops were added to all three series. The '54 bodyshell was retained, though styling was updated with a new grille and more extroverted two-tone color combinations. Horsepower rose to 185 for the 88 and 202 for Super 88 and 98. The four-door Holiday hardtop proved hugely successful, causing Ford and Chrysler to hasten their own versions; it was available throughout the Olds line, including the base 88. Output was 41,310 88s, 47,385 Super 88s, and 31,267 98s. The most popular model, however, was the 88 two-door Holiday: 85,767 units. In addition, Olds built 62,534 Super 88 Holiday coupes and 38,363 98s. Soft tops this year numbered 9007 Super 88s and 9149 98 Starfires.

	Restorable	Good	Excellent
88 2d hardtop	$2,000-6,000	$6,000-9,000	$9,000-13,000
Super 88 cvt	6,000-12,000	12,000-20,000	20,000-29,000
Super 88 2d htp	2,500-7,000	7,000-13,000	13,000-18,000
98 Starfire cvt	7,500-15,000	15,000-28,000	28,000-35,000
98 2d hardtop	3,000-10,000	10,000-15,000	15,000-21,000
Holiday 4d htps	2,000-5,000	5,000-8,000	8,000-12,000
Other models	1,000-3,000	3,000-5,500	5,500-8,000

1956

Most of the changes this year were up front, where a large oval combination bumper-grille derived from the Starfire show car identified each Olds. Bodyside two-tones were altered into smoother patterns. Because of the horsepower race, the compression ratio of the 324.3-cid V-8 was raised to 9.25:1, bumping horsepower to 230 bhp for 88s and 240 for Super 88s and 98s. Model lineups remained as they were in 1955, though the DeLuxe tag applied to '55 Super 88 and 98 Holidays was removed. Production dipped to 485,458 for the model year, leaving Olds in fifth place. Olds built 9561 Super 88 and 8581 98 Starfire convertibles. Two-door Holiday hardtops were still popular: 74,739 88s, 43,054 Super 88s, and 19,433 98s. Four-door Holiday hardtops outsold the two-doors, except in the 88 series: 52,239 88s, 61,192 Super 88s, and 42,320 98s. There is virtually no difference in values between the '55 and '56 Olds in today's market.

	Restorable	Good	Excellent
88 2d hardtop	$2,000-6,000	$6,000-9,000	$9,000-13,000
Super 88 cvt	6,000-12,000	12,000-20,000	20,000-29,000
Super 88 2d htp	2,500-7,000	7,000-13,000	13,000-18,000
98 Starfire cvt	7,500-15,000	15,000-28,000	28,000-35,000
98 2d hardtop	3,000-10,000	10,000-15,000	15,000-21,000
Holiday 4d htps	2,000-5,000	5,000-8,000	8,000-12,000
Other models	1,000-3,000	3,000-5,500	5,500-8,000

1957

A vintage now renowned among Olds collectors, the all-new '57 was cleanly styled, with a broad stainless steel sweepspear dropping down from the mid-beltline and shooting backward along the rear fenders to delineate the two-tone area (similar to 1954). The oval bumper-grille was similar to 1956, but the general lines of the car were sleeker. The 88 and Super 88 acquired the name "Golden Rocket," after a recent Olds show car; all 98s were now Starfires. Back for the first time since 1950 were station wagons: a conventional four-door 88, and novel four-door hardtop wagons for both 88 and Super 88. All were called Fiesta. In addition, every series had a convertible this year. All models boasted a new 371.1-cid V-8 pumping out 277 horsepower—the most potent Olds Rocket V-8 to date. Most collectible: the mid-year J-2 engine with a special manifold mounting triple two-barrel carbs, 10.0:1 compression, and 300 horses. Much rarer is the 312-bhp competition J-2, which added a high-lift cam, racing pistons, and other beefed-up parts. Despite all the newness, production slid to 384,390. Convertibles: 6423 88s, 7128 Super 88s, 8278 98s. Holiday two-door hardtops: 49,187 88s, 31,155 Super 88s, 17,791 98s. Fiesta hardtop wagons were not too common, just 5767 88s and 8981 Super 88s.

	Restorable	Good	Excellent
88 convertible	$4,000-10,000	$10,000-18,000	$18,000-28,000
88 2d hardtop	2,000-6,000	6,000-9,000	9,000-14,000
Super 88 cvt	6,000-12,000	12,000-22,000	22,000-34,000
Super 88 2d htp	2,500-7,000	7,000-13,000	13,000-18,000
98 Starfire cvt	7,500-15,000	15,000-28,000	28,000-38,000
98 2d hardtop	3,000-10,000	10,000-15,000	15,000-21,000
88/Super 88 4d htps	2,000-5,000	5,000-8,000	8,000-12,000
98 4d hardtop	2,500-6,000	6,000-9,500	9,500-14,000
4d hardtop wagons	2,500-5,500	5,500-9,000	9,000-13,000
Other models	1,000-3,000	3,000-6,000	6,000-9,000

(add 50% for J-2 engine option)

1958

From sleek, understated styling in 1957, Oldsmobile spawned one of the most overdecorated lines in the industry, but still managed to sell well, aided by more powerful engines: 265 bhp for the 88, 305 for Super 88 and 98, and 312 for the J-2 option. The three-series lineup was continued as Dynamic 88, Super 88, and 98, with a virtually identical batch of body styles save for the lack of a Super 88 two-door sedan. Wheelbase was up a half-inch on all models, quad headlights were standard, and a New-Matic Ride air suspension was optional—and troublesome. Few were fitted. Another new option was a Transportable radio that slid in and out of the dash

1957 Oldsmobile 98 Starfire hardtop coupe

1957 Oldsmobile 98 Starfire four-door sedan

1957 Oldsmobile Super 88 Fiesta wagon prototype

1957 Olds Golden Rocket Super 88 convertible

1957 Oldsmobile Golden Rocket 88 Holiday coupe

1958 Oldsmobile Dynamic 88 Holiday coupe

1958 Oldsmobile Super 88 Fiesta hardtop wagon

1958 Oldsmobile 98 convertible coupe

1959 Oldsmobile Dynamic 88 hardtop coupe

1959 Oldsmobile Super 88 Fiesta station wagon

for use in or out of the car. Production was down to 294,374 units, including 4456 Dynamic 88 convertibles, plus 3799 Super 88 and 5605 98 ragtops. Two-door hardtops numbered 35,036 88s, 18,653 Super 88s, and 11,012 98s. Fiesta hardtop wagons became even rarer: 3323 88s and 5175 Super 88s. Note that the '58s have been mocked so often for their outlandish styling that their values are far off the high levels set by the 1954-57 models. Buy a '58 with these factors in mind, and don't count on rapid appreciation in the future.

	Restorable	Good	Excellent
88 convertible	$3,000-7,000	$7,000-15,000	$15,000-20,000
88/Super 88 2d htps	2,000-6,000	6,000-9,000	9,000-14,000
Super 88 cvt	5,000-10,000	10,000-20,000	20,000-27,500
98 convertible	6,000-13,000	13,000-25,000	25,000-33,000
98 2d hardtop	3,000-8,000	8,000-14,000	14,000-20,000
4d hardtops	2,000-5,000	5,000-8,000	8,000-11,000
4d hardtop wagons	2,500-5,500	5,500-9,000	9,000-12,000
Other models	1,000-3,000	3,000-6,000	6,000-9,000

1959

GM divisions began sharing bodyshells this year, but each make remained distinctly different on the outside. Olds was a big, roomy car offering high performance, with V-8s ranging from the 88's 371 with 270 or 300 horsepower to the new 394 with 315 bhp for the Super 88 and 98. Also, Oldsmobile's "Linear-Look" styling was relatively quiet, but with an Olds "look" front and rear. Four-door hardtops, called SportSedans, had a large, flat roof that overhung the rear window; two-door hardtops, called SceniCoupes, featured sloping C-pillars and huge backlights. Wagons were still called Fiesta, but were no longer hardtops. The usual vast array of colorful interiors in vinyl and jacquard was offered. Dynamic and Super 88s rode a 123-inch wheelbase, compared to the 98's 126.3-inch span. Production rose this year to 382,865. SceniCoupe output was 38,488 88s, 20,259 Super 88s, and 13,669 98s. Ragtops numbered 8491 88s, 4895 Super 88s, and 7514 98s. Values of convertibles exhibit incremental differences between the three series, but this doesn't apply as much to other body styles, whose price depends more on condition. Many collectors actually prefer the lighter Super 88 to the 98 when they have a choice, which isn't that often.

	Restorable	Good	Excellent
88 convertible	$3,000-7,000	$7,000-15,000	$15,000-20,000
Super 88 cvt	5,000-10,000	10,000-20,000	20,000-27,500
98 convertible	6,000-13,000	13,000-23,000	23,000-30,000
2d hardtops	2,000-5,000	5,000-8,000	8,000-12,000
4d hardtops	2,000-5,000	5,000-7,500	7,500-10,000
Other models	1,000-3,000	3,000-5,000	5,000-7,000

1960

This was the last year Oldsmobile would offer only "standard-size" behemoths. The lineup was traditional, and very good: Dynamic 88, the price leader; Super 88, the big-engined performance car; and 98, the luxury model. Engines were the same, though Dynamic 88s were detuned to 240 or 260 bhp; Super 88s and 98s still had 315 horses. Styling was understated, with a finless, flat deck and a modest full-width, rectangular-block grille. Convertibles were offered in all three series as usual, and a 98 paced the Indy 500. The supply of open models and Holiday two-door hardtops is fairly small, so these big Oldsmobiles should continue to appreciate at a good rate during the '90s. Ragtop output was 12,271 Dynamic 88s, 5830 Super 88s, and 7284 98s. Two-door hardtop production ended with 29,368 88s, 16,464 Super 88s, and 7635 98s. Total model year output was 347,141 units.

	Restorable	Good	Excellent
88 convertible	$3,000-7,000	$7,000-15,000	$15,000-20,000
Super 88 cvt	5,000-10,000	10,000-20,000	20,000-27,500
98 convertible	6,000-13,000	13,000-23,000	23,000-30,000
2d hardtops	2,000-5,000	5,000-8,000	8,000-12,000
4d hardtops	2,000-5,000	5,000-7,500	7,500-10,000
Other models	1,000-3,000	3,000-5,000	5,000-8,000

1961

Oldsmobile's F-85, part of the second wave of GM compacts, shared its bodyshell with the Pontiac Tempest, but its Buick 215-cid aluminum V-8 and drivetrain were more conventional. Styling was clean, less busy than the Buick Special, with sculptured bodysides, crisp roofline, and simple tucked-under grille similar to that on the full-size Olds. Body styles comprised a sedan, club coupe, and station wagon—nothing to write home about from a collector standpoint. More important to enthusiasts was the reborn Starfire convertible, a Super 88 often painted Garnet Red, with bucket seats, console, distinctive brushed aluminum bodyside trim, and a 330-bhp 394 V-8. Although it cost over $1000 more than a standard Super 88 ragtop, the Starfire sold 7600 copies against only 2624 standards—so the latter is considerably scarcer, yet not as pricey. Olds also built 9049 Dynamic 88 ragtops and 3804 98s. The Super 88 and 98 had a 325-bhp 394 V-8 this year, while the 88 got a 250-bhp version (325 optional). Styling of the big Oldsmobiles was new, though wheelbases remained the same. Model year production was 318,550 units, including 76,394 F-85s. Two-door hardtop output was 19,878 Dynamic 88s, 7009 Super 88s, and 4445 98s.

	Restorable	Good	Excellent
F-85, all	$500-2,000	$2,000-4,000	$4,000-6,000
88/Super 88 cvt	3,000-7,000	7,000-15,000	15,000-20,000
Starfire cvt	6,000-12,000	12,000-22,000	22,000-29,000
98 convertible	5,000-10,000	10,000-17,000	17,000-24,000
Other models	1,000-3,000	3,000-6,000	6,000-9,000

1962

The Cutlass, top model of the mildly facelifted F-85, came standard with a 185-bhp power-pack version of Buick's small V-8, and two ragtops were added this year. The Cutlass Sport Coupe attracted 32,461 buyers, while the Cutlass and F-85 ragtops found 9893 and 3660 buyers. A specialty Sport

1960 Oldsmobile Super 88 convertible coupe

1961 Oldsmobile Super 88 Starfire convertible

1961 Oldsmobile 98 Holiday hardtop sedan

1961 Oldsmobile F-85 Cutlass DeLuxe Sport Coupe

1962 Oldsmobile F-85 DeLuxe Jetfire hardtop coupe

1962 Oldsmobile Starfire hardtop coupe

1963 Oldsmobile Starfire convertible coupe

1963 Oldsmobile 98 convertible coupe

1963 Oldsmobile Starfire hardtop coupe

1963 Oldsmobile F-85 DeLuxe Jetfire hardtop

Coupe, the 215-bhp turbocharged Jetfire V-8, joined the line in mid-year. It had water injection (a water-alcohol mix) to prevent carbon build-up, but unfortunately the system proved unreliable. The Jetfire hasn't brought much of a premium on the collector car market. They're easily identified by their Starfire-like brushed aluminum bodyside moldings and special badges. Production was 3765 for '62. Starfires, in a separate series now, were far more common this year—output jumped to 41,988 due to the addition of a two-door hardtop; 7149 of them were ragtops. The regular Olds lineup continued much as before, but featuring new front and rear styling for a bulkier look. Two-door hardtops lost their airy "bubbleback" roofline in favor of wide C-pillars and a roof creased to give the look of a convertible with the top up. Though the Super 88 lost its ragtop, that body style generated 12,212 and 3693 orders in the Dynamic 88 and 98 series. Big Olds two-door Holiday hardtop output came to 39,676 Dynamic 88s, 9010 Super 88s, and 7546 98s.

	Restorable	Good	Excellent
F-85 Jetfire	$1,500-3,000	$3,000-6,500	$6,500-8,500
F-85 Cutlass cvt	2,000-4,000	4,000-6,000	6,000-8,500
F-85, other	500-2,000	2,000-4,000	4,000-6,000
88 convertible	3,000-6,000	6,000-10,000	10,000-18,000
Starfire cvt	6,000-12,000	12,000-22,000	22,000-27,500
Starfire 2d htp	3,000-6,000	6,000-9,000	9,000-13,000
98 convertible	5,000-10,000	10,000-17,000	17,000-22,000
88/98 2d htps	2,000-4,500	4,500-8,500	8,500-10,500
Other models	1,000-3,000	3,000-5,000	5,000-8,000

1963

The Starfire's identifying stainless steel bodyside panel became much narrower, the car itself more conventional. An identifying point was the concave rear window, unique in the Olds line but shared with Pontiac's Grand Prix. With 21,148 hardtops and 4401 ragtops built, it was the only Olds line to lose sales this year. Though it retained its 112-inch wheelbase, the F-85 received a longer, wider body—at the cost of its individuality, say some collectors. The Cutlass ragtop continued to be the most desirable body style, and indeed it registered 12,149 sales. Exactly 5842 turbocharged Cutlass Jetfire hardtops were produced in this its last year. The full-size line was reskinned with a more formal look, highlighted by massive grilles up front. Indicating Oldsmobile's intent, a Luxury Sedan (four-door hardtop) joined the line, and with 23,330 built it was the most popular 98. Convertible output came to 12,551 Dynamic 88s, and 4267 98s; Holiday two-door hardtops numbered 39,071 88s, 8930 Super 88s, 4984 98s, and (a new model) 7422 Custom 98s. Though the engine lineup remained the same, including horsepower ratings, a positive crankcase ventilation system was new. Total output was up to 476,753 units.

	Restorable	Good	Excellent
F-85 Jetfire	$1,500-3,000	$3,000-6,000	$6,000-8,000
F-85 Cutlass cvt	2,000-4,000	4,000-6,000	6,000-8,500
F-85, other	500-2,000	2,000-4,000	4,000-6,000
88 convertible	3,000-5,000	5,000-8,000	8,000-13,000

	Restorable	Good	Excellent
Starfire cvt	6,000-12,000	12,000-22,000	22,000-27,500
Starfire 2d htp	3,000-6,000	6,000-9,000	9,000-13,000
98 convertible	5,000-10,000	10,000-17,000	17,000-22,000
88/98 2d htps	2,000-4,500	4,500-8,500	8,500-10,500
Other models	1,000-3,000	3,000-5,000	5,000-8,000

1964

The F-85/Cutlass wheelbase grew to 115 inches and a 330-cid iron-block V-8 replaced the Turbo 215 as its performance engine. A major facelift gave it cleaner styling; it looked more like the big Olds than ever. The Cutlass Holiday hardtop and ragtop had a good year: 36,153 and 12,822 were built. Olds entered the muscle car age with the exciting 4-4-2 (four-speed gearbox, four-barrel carb, dual exhausts), its answer to the Pontiac GTO. The 4-4-2 competed with a 310-bhp 330 V-8, handling suspension, and optional bucket seats. Announced as a package for any F-85 or Cutlass (except wagons), 2999 were sold. The neatest wagon of the Sixties was Oldsmobile's new Vista Cruiser, with its raised, tinted-glass roof panels, inspired by the Vista-Dome streamlined rail passenger cars. Sales were modest due to a mid-year debut, making the Cruiser an interesting collectible. Just 3394 were built as F-85s, plus another 10,606 as Cutlasses. Starfires lost their stainless steel body panels, but gained simulated vents just behind the front wheels. Still, they had become very ordinary compared to earlier models. Production slipped to 13,753 hardtops and 2410 ragtops. Oldsmobile's modestly restyled full-size lineup was expanded with a four-model Jetstar series, basically a budget Dynamic 88 with a 245-bhp 330 V-8 instead of the 280-bhp 394 V-8. Another new model was the Jetstar I, a deluxe Dynamic 88 hardtop coupe with bucket seats and the Stafire's 345-bhp 394 V-8. In its role as a budget Starfire, it snagged 16,084 buyers. Full-size soft tops numbered 3903 Jetstars, 10,042 Dynamic 88s, and 4004 98s. As always, full-size Holiday hardtop coupes were plentiful, nearly 60,000 this year, though the 98s took only about one-sixth of the total. Model year sales of a very complicated Olds lineup increased to 546,112 units.

	Restorable	Good	Excellent
Cutlass cvt	$2,000-4,000	$4,000-6,000	$6,000-9,000
4-4-2 convertible	3,500-6,000	6,000-8,500	8,500-12,000
4-4-2 coupe/htp	2,500-4,500	4,500-6,500	6,500-8,500
Vista Cruiser wgn	500-2,500	2,500-4,000	4,000-6,000
F-85/Cutlass, other	500-2,000	2,000-4,000	4,000-6,000
Jetstar/88 cvts	3,000-6,000	6,000-10,000	10,000-15,000
Jetstar I 2d htp	2,000-5,000	5,000-8,000	8,000-10,500
Starfire cvt	4,000-8,000	8,000-14,000	14,000-20,000
Starfire 2d htp	3,000-6,000	6,000-9,000	9,000-13,000
98 convertible	5,000-10,000	10,000-15,000	15,000-20,000
Full-size 2d htps	2,000-4,500	4,500-8,500	8,500-10,500
Other models	1,000-3,000	3,000-5,000	5,000-8,000

1965

The 4-4-2 was hotter still, adopting a 345-horse 400 V-8 with 440 lbs/ft torque, an under-bored version of the big 425-cid engine used in full-size mod-

1964 Oldsmobile Starfire hardtop coupe

1964 Oldsmobile Jetstar I hardtop coupe

1964 Oldsmobile Cutlass Holiday hardtop coupe

1965 Oldsmobile Starfire hardtop coupe

1965 Oldsmobile Jetstar I hardtop coupe

1965 Oldsmobile Cutlass 4-4-2 convertible

1966 Oldsmobile Starfire hardtop coupe

1966 Oldsmobile Cutlass 4-4-2 Holiday hardtop

els. For $190, the 4-4-2 package included special wheels, shocks, springs, rear axle, driveshaft, engine mounts, steering, and frame; stabilizer bars front and rear; 11-inch clutch; wide tires; 70-amp battery; and special trim. A 0-60 sprint took about 7.5 seconds, good enough to entice 25,003 buyers to purchase the package. Other F-85s and Cutlasses received grille, taillight, and trim changes, and the line was expanded with an F-85 DeLuxe seven-model series. For 1965, Olds built 31,985 Vista Cruisers, top models of which were called Customs (Olds dropped the last of its full-size wagons this year). Cutlass saw production of 12,628 convertibles and 46,138 Holiday hardtop coupes. Though it got a 370-bhp, 425-cid V-8, the Starfire looked even more like the regular full-size cars; output was nearly the same as in 1964: 13,024 hardtops and 2236 ragtops. The Jetstar I, again with the Starfire engine, plummeted to 6552 sales. Olds renamed the long-running Super 88 series Delta 88 and added a two-door hardtop to the two four-door models. Base engine for the full-size Oldsmobiles was a 310-bhp 425, with 360 for the 98s, and 360- or 370-bhp optional for all the big ones. Ragtop output was 2879 Jetstars, 8832 Dynamic 88s, and 4903 98s. Model year production totaled 591,701.

	Restorable	Good	Excellent
Cutlass cvt	$2,000-4,000	$4,000-6,000	$6,000-9,000
4-4-2 convertible	3,500-6,000	6,000-8,500	8,500-12,000
4-4-2 cpe/htp	2,500-4,500	4,500-6,500	6,500-8,500
Vista Cruiser wgns	500-2,500	2,500-4,000	4,000-6,000
F-85/Cutlass, other	500-2,000	2,000-4,000	4,000-6,000
Jetstar/88 cvt	3,000-6,000	6,000-8,000	8,000-11,000
Jetstar I 2d htp	2,000-5,000	5,000-7,000	7,000-10,000
Starfire cvt	3,500-7,000	7,000-11,000	11,000-15,000
Starfire 2d htp	2,000-5,000	5,000-7,500	7,500-10,000
98 convertible	4,000-7,000	7,000-10,000	10,000-15,000
Other models	1,000-3,000	3,000-5,000	5,000-8,000

1966

A technical breakthrough, the Toronado was the first American front-wheel-drive production car since the prewar Cord 812, and took many of its styling cues from that great design of 1936-37 (grille and wheels/hubcaps, for example). Its 385-bhp 425 V-8 was teamed with a new "split transmission"—torque converter mounted behind the engine, gearbox under the left cylinder bank—connected by a chain drive and sprocket. This layout saved weight and space. The 119-inch-wheelbase "Toro" was and is a superb road car; it understeered, but not much, and it could do 125 mph off the showroom floor. It was probably the most outstanding single Olds of the decade. Prices today don't match its historical importance, probably because it didn't come as a convertible. Even so, 40,963 were built. The 4-4-2 had a black-out grille, fake fender scoops, bold wheel arches, and 350 horses (360 with a tri-carb option). A drag-racing W-30 option included fiberglass inner fenders, trunk-mounted battery, cold-air package, radical camshaft, and more. Still a package option itself, the 4-4-2 enticed 21,997 hot-blooded customers, 54 of whom were lucky enough to get the

W-30. The Vista Cruiser wagons were again offered in standard and Custom trim; 26,606 were built. The mid-size line welcomed two four-door hardtops: F-85 DeLuxe Holiday and Cutlass Supreme (a name still with us). They went on to record sales of 7913 and 30,871 units. The Cutlass convertible found 9410 buyers. In the full-size line, the Starfire was reduced to just a hardtop model, and after 13,019 were produced it was dropped. Jetstar I was gone; Jetstar 88 lost its ragtop, but the Delta 88 gained one. Soft top production was 5540 Dynamic 88s, 4303 Delta 88s, and 4568 98s. Total Olds output was 578,385.

	Restorable	Good	Excellent
Cutlass cvt	$2,000-4,000	$4,000-6,000	$6,000-10,000
4-4-2 convertible	3,500-6,000	6,000-8,500	8,500-12,000
4-4-2 coupe/htp	2,500-4,500	4,500-6,500	6,500-8,500
	(add 25% for 4-4-2 W-30 package)		
Vista Cruiser wgns	500-2,500	2,500-4,000	4,000-6,000
F-85/Cutlass, other	500-2,000	2,000-4,000	4,000-6,000
88/98 convertible	3,000-6,000	6,000-8,000	8,000-11,000
Starfire 2d htp	2,000-5,000	5,000-7,500	7,500-10,000
Toronado	3,000-5,000	5,000-7,500	7,500-10,000
Other models	1,000-3,000	3,000-5,000	5,000-8,000

1967

Happily, Toronado was little changed, distinguished by an eggcrate-style grille and flush-mounted headlamp covers. Not so happily, sales plummeted to 21,790. Vista Cruisers numbered 27,551—this body style would carry on for several more years, but later versions are worth no more than ordinary F-85s. Bodyside woodgraining could be seen on some models. Elsewhere in the mid-size line, Cutlass Supreme was made a five-model series, with the convertible attracting about 7800 buyers (another 4344 chose the regular Cutlass ragtop). The more smoothly styled 4-4-2 sported functional hood louvers, a revised black-out grille, and split taillamps. Though the tri-carb setup was gone, the W-30 option was still listed. Most of the 24,833 4-4-2s built were Holiday hardtops, leaving an estimated 3104 ragtops and 5215 coupes. In the big Olds line, a Delmont 88 series (with "330" or "425" engine) replaced the Jetstar 88, and the Delta 88 added a Delta 88 Custom series for the two hardtop models. Convertible sales were falling: 3525 Delmont 88 425s, 2447 Delta 88s, and 3769 98s. In all, Olds built 558,762 cars for 1967.

	Restorable	Good	Excellent
Cutlass convertible	$2,000-4,000	$4,000-6,000	$6,000-8,500
4-4-2 convertible	3,500-7,000	7,000-10,000	10,000-15,000
4-4-2 cpe/htp	2,500-4,500	4,500-6,500	6,500-10,000
	(add 25% for 4-4-2 W-30 package)		
Vista Cruiser wgns	500-2,500	2,500-4,000	4,000-6,000
F-85/Cutlass, other	500-2,000	2,000-4,000	4,000-6,000
88/98 convertible	3,000-6,000	6,000-8,000	8,000-12,000
Toronado htp cpe	3,000-5,000	5,000-7,500	7,500-10,000
Other models	1,000-3,000	3,000-5,000	5,000-8,000

1966 Oldsmobile Toronado hardtop coupe

1966 Oldsmobile Toronado hardtop coupe

1967 Oldsmobile Cutlass Vista Cruiser wagon

1967 Oldsmobile Cutlass 4-4-2 Holiday hardtop

1967 Oldsmobile Toronado hardtop coupe

1968 Cutlass S Hurst/Olds sport coupe

1968 Oldsmobile 4-4-2 Holiday hardtop coupe

1968 Oldsmobile Toronado hardtop coupe

1968 Oldsmobile 98 convertible coupe

1969 Oldsmobile Toronado hardtop coupe

1968

Redesigned along with all GM B-bodies, the Cutlass and 4-4-2 looked very fresh. A Hurst three-speed, the 350- or 360-bhp 400 V-8 (or even a two-barrel 260-bhp version), dual exhausts, and wide oval tires were 4-4-2 hallmarks, accompanied by Force-Air induction, power front disc brakes, transistorized ignition, limited-slip diff, needle gauges, and special striping and badging. The W-30 package was still around, too, and *Car Craft* recorded a 13.33-second quarter-mile pass at 103.56 mph. A series unto itself now, the 4-4-2 enjoyed a production run of 24,182 Holiday hardtops, 4282 Sport Coupes, and 5142 ragtops. The Hurst/Olds, a joint effort with the famous shifter company, was an extroverted car with flashy paint jobs and wild racing stripes. Under its hood was a 390-bhp 455 V-8 with hot cam, crankshaft, and high compression heads; transmission was Turbo Hydra-Matic with Hurst shifter. With these specs it was a genuine rocket, but a rare one. Only 459 hardtops and 56 coupes were built; 155 of them had air conditioning. Other mid-size two-door Oldsmobiles shared the 4-4-2's 112-inch wheelbase (116 for four-doors). Their styling was also new and sleeker, with semi-fastback rooflines for two-door Holiday hardtops, of which 85,517 were produced (Cutlass and Cutlass Supreme). Olds dropped the Supreme soft top, but went on to crank out 14,077 Cutlass versions, all with bucket seats. The Toronado received a heavy frontal lobotomy—a combination bumper grille that spoiled its original good looks. On the positive side, it also had a new, smooth, powerful 455 V-8 with 375 bhp, 400 optional—it was faster than ever, and just as tractable. Output recovered to 26,454. The full-size line featured split-grille styling and upped the 330 V-8s to 350 cid, the 425s to 455 cid. Convertibles numbered 2812 Delmont 88s and 3942 98s. In all, Olds built 562,459 cars for the model year.

	Restorable	Good	Excellent
Cutlass cvt	$2,000-4,000	$4,000-6,000	$6,000-8,500
4-4-2 convertible	3,500-7,000	7,000-10,000	10,000-15,000
4-4-2 cpe/htp	2,500-4,500	4,500-6,500	6,500-10,000
	(add 25% for 4-4-2 W-30 package)		
Hurst/Olds cpe/htp	4,000-8,000	8,000-11,000	11,000-15,000
F-85/Cutlass, other	500-2,000	2,000-4,000	4,000-6,000
88/98 convertible	3,000-6,000	6,000-8,000	8,000-12,000
Toronado	3,000-5,000	5,000-7,500	7,500-10,000
Other models	1,000-3,000	3,000-5,000	5,000-8,000

1969

The 4-4-2 had big numerals on its center grille divider, fenders, and deck; twin black horizontal grilles and a "two-plateau" hood with identifying stripes and special paint. An explosive option was the W-30 package: Force Air Induction 400 V-8, 360 bhp, and a choice of axle ratios all the way to 4.66:1. Regular models had 350 bhp, 325 with automatic. Production was down: 19,587 Holiday hardtops, 2475 Sport Coupes, 4295 ragtops. The Hurst variation was distinctive with a special gold-and-white paint job, twin-snorkel hood scoop, and big deck spoiler; production was 906, all Holiday hardtops. The F-85 was down to a single Sport Coupe. Two-door Cutlass models were now known as Cutlass S, and they recorded output of 13,734 ragtops, 67,061 Holiday hardtops, and 11,165 pillared Sport Coupes. Squared-off rear fenders and a more rounded decklid distinguished the '69 Toronado, which found 28,494 customers. The big Olds line was simplified to Delta 88 and 98; 5294 88 and 4288 98 convertibles were built. Total output came in at 655,241 units.

	Restorable	Good	Excellent
Cutlass S cvt	$2,000-4,000	$4,000-6,000	$6,000-10,000
4-4-2 convertible	3,500-7,000	7,000-10,000	10,000-15,000
4-4-2 cpe/htp	2,500-4,500	4,500-6,500	6,500-10,000
	(add 25% for 4-4-2 W-30 package)		
Hurst/Olds htp	4,000-8,000	8,000-11,000	11,000-15,000
F-85/Cutlass, other	500-2,000	2,000-4,000	4,000-6,000
88/98 convertible	3,000-6,000	6,000-8,000	8,000-12,000
Toronado htp cpe	3,000-5,000	5,000-7,000	7,000-9,000
Other models	1,000-3,000	3,000-5,000	5,000-8,000

1970

Toronado's ugly wrap-around bumper-grille was dropped in favor of nerf-like vertical bars inset in the front fenders. The quad headlamps, exposed for the first time, were mounted in a fine mesh grille flanked by slotted parking lights. Output this year was 25,433 units. The 4-4-2 was back and the W-30 package was again available—this time with a 365/370-bhp 455 V-8. A 4-4-2 convertible paced the Indy 500 and some Pace Car replicas were offered. Production fell to 14,709 Holidays, 1688 Sport Coupes, and 2933 ragtops. An interesting substitute for the Hurst/Olds was the Rallye 350, with a high-performance 350 V-8, hood air intake, sport steering wheel, decklid spoiler, rally suspension, and dual exhausts. Look for the W-45 appearance package: Sebring Yellow paint with black and orange decals, urethane Sebring Yellow bumpers, black-out grille, Super Stock II wheels, and "Rallye 350" decal. With just 3547 built, Rallye 350s are rare; the Holiday coupe was the most common version. On Cutlasses, look for the SX-455 option with the jumbo engine and accompanying special trim. The Cutlass S convertible moved up to become a Cutlass Supreme, and 11,354 were ordered. The mildly restyled full-size lineup was the same, with 3095 Delta 88 and 3161 98 convertibles rolling off the assembly line. Olds built a total of 633,981 cars for the model run.

	Restorable	Good	Excellent
Cutlass Supreme cvt	$2,000-4,000	$4,000-6,000	$6,000-10,000
Cutlass SX cvt	3,000-5,000	5,000-7,500	7,500-12,000
Cutlass SX coupe	2,000-4,000	4,000-5,500	5,500-8,500
4-4-2 convertible	3,500-7,000	7,000-10,000	10,000-16,000
4-4-2 cpe/htp	2,500-4,500	4,500-6,500	6,500-11,000
(add 25% for 4-4-2 W-30 package, 30% for Pace Car replica)			
Cutlass Rallye 350	2,000-5,000	5,000-8,000	8,000-12,000
88/98 convertible	3,000-6,000	6,000-8,000	8,000-12,000
Toronado htp cpe	3,000-5,000	5,000-7,000	7,000-9,000
Toronado GT	4,000-6,500	6,500-8,500	8,500-10,500

1969 Hurst/Olds 455 hardtop coupe

1969 Oldsmobile 4-4-2 Holiday hardtop

1970 Oldsmobile 4-4-2 Indy 500 Pace Car

1970 Oldsmobile 4-4-2 Holiday hardtop coupe

1970 Oldsmobile Toronado hardtop coupe

1971 Oldsmobile Toronado hardtop coupe

1971 Oldsmobile 4-4-2 convertible coupe

1971 Oldsmobile 4-4-2 Holiday hardtop coupe

1972 Oldsmobile Toronado hardtop coupe

1972 Hurst/Olds Indy 500 Pace Car convertible

1971

The 4-4-2, in its last year as a separate series, was somewhat slower. Horsepower was down to 340 or 350 due to a lower 8.5:1 compression ratio, so the car lost some of the excitement of its predecessors. It was also scarce: only 1304 ragtops and 6285 coupes were built. After this year, the 4-4-2 reverted to an option package for selected Cutlass models. The F-85 limped along as a four-door sedan, while the Cutlass and Cutlass Supreme lines received the usual freshening up. In the Supreme series, Olds built 10,255 convertibles, 60,599 Holiday hardtop coupes, plus 10,458 hardtop sedans. The big 98 convertible was dropped this year, leaving the Delta 88 Royale as the sole full-size ragtop—2883 were built, and you can still find good ones for well under $10,000. The Toronado was all-new this year: bigger, now riding a 123-inch wheelbase, and heavier (over 4500 pounds). It had a large prow-like hood and small bumper-mounted grilles beneath the headlights. Sales increased a bit to 28,980. Total Olds production dropped to 567,891.

	Restorable	Good	Excellent
Cutlass Supreme cvt	$2,000-4,000	$4,000-6,000	$6,000-10,000
Cutlass SX cvt	3,000-5,000	5,000-7,500	7,500-12,000
Cutlass SX coupe	2,000-4,000	4,000-5,500	5,500-8,500
4-4-2 convertible	3,500-7,000	7,000-10,000	10,000-16,000
4-4-2 cpe/htp	2,500-4,500	4,500-6,500	6,500-11,000
	(add 25% for 4-4-2 W-30 package)		
88 convertible	3,000-5,000	5,000-7,500	7,500-9,500
Toronado	2,500-4,000	4,000-6,000	6,000-8,000

1972

Marking Olds' 75th Anniversary was the 98 Regency four-door hardtop, a special edition with a black-and-gold velour interior, Tiffany clock, Anniversary Gold metallic paint job, and a special key with a sterling silver key ring. Several thousand were built, all powered by a 455 V-8 detuned to 225 net horsepower. Among Cutlass models, look for the Hurst/Olds convertible Indy Pace Car replica with 455 engine, power front disc brakes, tuned suspension, dual exhausts, cold-air induction, and Cameo White paint with gold striping. Hurst/Olds production included 629 hardtops and ragtops. The 4-4-2 package consisted mainly of appearance items and a suspension upgrade. To make it really go, one had to order the W-30 option: 455 V-8, dual exhausts, forced-air fiberglass hood, and non-spin rear end. Cutlass models sported a new grille, and the Supreme convertible appealed to 11,571 buyers. The only other Olds ragtop, the Delta 88 Royale, went to 3900 new homes. Toronado had vertical grille bars and saw output spurt to 48,900. It was a record year for Olds as it moved into third place based on a production run of 762,199 cars.

	Restorable	Good	Excellent
Cutlass Supreme cvt	$3,000-5,000	$5,000-7,500	$7,500-12,000
	(add 25% for 4-4-2 package)		

	Restorable	Good	Excellent
Hurst/Olds htp	5,000-8,000	8,000-13,000	13,000-18,000
Hurst/Olds cvt	7,000-12,000	12,000-18,000	18,000-23,000
	(add 35% for Pace Car replica)		
88 Royale cvt	3,000-5,000	5,000-7,000	7,000-8,500
Toronado htp cpe	2,000-3,000	3,000-4,500	4,500-6,000

1973

Omega, a new Oldsmobile compact riding a 111-inch wheelbase, arrived this year. Offered as a four-door sedan, coupe, or hatchback coupe, it has not joined the collector car ranks. Nor indeed have many other 1973 Oldsmobiles; though the Hurst variation was still desirable, and there was still an 88 Royale convertible that attracted 7088 buyers. Soft top versions of the popular Cutlass vanished as GM redesigned its intermediates, omitting the ragtops. Indeed, there weren't even any hardtops in the Cutlass line (the F-85 was gone now), this due to all-new "Colonnade" styling with fixed B-pillars. The 4-4-2 package was still available, but was simply a trim and handling option. The 455 V-8 was still offered, however, rated at 250 horsepower. Gone also was the Vista Cruiser's unique glass roof styling, replaced now by a hinged and tinted Vista Vent over the front seat. Olds built 219,857 examples of the stylish Cutlass Supreme coupe; it featured opera windows. Buyers could still opt for two- and four-door hardtops in the full-size line, and in fact those were the only body styles listed for the 98 series. Toronado had an excellent year: 55,921 were sold. For the second year in a row, Olds occupied third place, this year with 922,771 units.

	Restorable	Good	Excellent
Cutlass 2d 4-4-2	$2,000-3,000	$3,000-5,000	$5,000-7,000
88 convertible	3,000-5,000	5,000-7,000	7,000-8,500
Toronado htp cpe	2,000-3,000	3,000-4,500	4,500-6,000

1974

The Hurst/Olds returned as a peace-loving citizens pack, its 355 V-8 delivering 200 net horsepower and its body bearing GM's "Colonnade" coupe styling. A Hurst/Olds again paced the Indy 500, so an Indy Pace Car replica featuring white paint with gold striping was produced—an extremely rare model since only a fraction of the 380 Hurst/Olds's were so equipped. Toronado sported revised front styling and new taillights, but saw production falter to 27,582 units. Cutlass continued as the leading line, and the Supreme coupe racked up 172,360 sales. Delta 88 Royale convertible output was down to 3716. Big Oldsmobiles lost their two-door hardtops this year, but Olds did offer an Elegance package with padded vinyl roof and opera windows for the 98 Luxury or Regency coupe. Overall, output was way down this year to 581,195 due to the effects of the Arab oil embargo.

	Restorable	Good	Excellent
Cutlass 2d 4-4-2	$2,000-3,000	$3,000-5,000	$5,000-7,000
Hurst/Olds	2,000-3,000	3,000-5,500	5,500-7,500
	(add 20% for Pace Car replica)		

1973 Oldsmobile Toronado hardtop coupe

1973 Hurst/Olds "Colonnade" coupe

1974 Hurst/Olds W-30 Indy 500 Pace Car coupe

1974 Hurst/Olds W-30 Indy 500 Pace Car coupe

1974 Oldsmobile Toronado opera window coupe

1974 Oldsmobile Delta 88 Royale convertible

	Restorable	Good	Excellent
88 convertible	2,500-4,500	4,500-5,500	5,500-7,500
Toronado htp cpe	2,000-3,000	3,000-4,500	4,500-6,000

1975

Oldsmobile's Starfire, a rebadged version of the Vega-based hatchback Chevy Monza with a 110-bhp 231 V-6, was the smallest Olds in memory, but notably unsuccessful. Collectibility is in doubt, but its existence should be noted—look for the sporty "SX" model (starting in 1976). The Hurst/Olds was now a T-roof demi-convertible based on the '74 Indy Pace Car; paint was black or white with gold racing stripes and W-30 or W-31 lettering, designating the 350 or 455 V-8. The H/O was instantly recognizable, a hard-riding, indifferently built nostalgia piece, giving the appearance, if not the performance, of Sixties muscle cars; 2535 were built. A luxurious Brougham coupe was added to the Toronado line of front-drive grand tourers, which this year found 23,301 buyers. Hardtop styling was dropped in favor of opera windows. This was the last year for the 88 Royale convertible—21,038 were built, so there is no shortage and market prices have always been low. Both 88 and 98 four-door hardtops got a new roofline incorporating opera windows. With 150,874 produced, the Cutlass Supreme coupe was again the most popular Olds. Total output was 631,795 cars.

1975 Hurst/Olds W-30 coupe

1975 Oldsmobile Toronado coupe

	Restorable	Good	Excellent
Starfire	$1,000-2,000	$2,000-2,750	$2,750-4,000
Cutlass 2d 4-4-2	1,500-2,500	2,500-3,500	3,500-5,000
Hurst/Olds	2,000-3,000	3,000-5,000	5,000-6,500
88 convertible	2,500-4,500	4,500-5,500	5,500-7,500
Toronado htp cpe	2,000-3,000	3,000-4,500	4,500-6,000

1976 Oldsmobile Cutlass S 4-4-2

1976

A sporty Starfire GT package, introduced mid-year, included a special hood and stripe decor, Rallye wheels, white-letter tires, extra gauges, and GT decals applied on top of the SX model. The Toronado was facelifted, receiving a new face and stand-up hood ornament, the cleanest Toro in some years. All were comprehensively equipped, with disc front brakes, steel-belted radials, variable ratio power steering, "message center," and four-barrel 455 V-8. Brougham and Custom interiors were available. Output this year was 24,304. A 4-4-2 appearance/handling package was still offered on the Cutlass S, but there was no Hurst/Olds. The Cutlass Supreme added a luxury Brougham model; it found 91,312 buyers in addition to the 186,647 that chose the regular Supreme coupe. Quad rectangular headlights were standard this year for all series except Omega; they had been introduced for '75 on the Starfire, 98, and Toronado. Total Olds output for 1976 came to 891,368, more than enough to keep Olds in third place.

1976 Oldsmobile Toronado coupe

1976 Oldsmobile Starfire GT Sport Coupe

	Restorable	Good	Excellent
Starfire V-6	$1,000-2,000	$2,000-2,750	$2,750-4,000
Cutlass S 4-4-2	1,500-2,500	2,500-3,500	3,500-5,000
Toronado	2,000-3,000	3,000-4,500	4,500-6,000

1977

Extensive downsizing occurred on the big Oldsmobiles, resulting in a 116-inch wheelbase for 88s, 119 for 98s. Being much lighter, they were fitted with smaller, more economical engines. Among the larger cars, look for the Delta 88 Royale Pace Car replica, with black and silver color scheme, special identification, and Hurst shifter on the center console. The compact Omega sported new front and rear styling and offered a sporty SX package on the coupe. Starfire's standard engine was now a 140-cid four, with the V-6 optional—and far more desirable. Output this year was 19,091. Toronado's XS was notable for a curious wraparound rear window that reminded many of the first Studebaker Starliner 30 years earlier. It came with an electric sunroof, and 2714 were built. Also built was just one XS-R with an Astro Roof, glass panels that retracted into a center T-bar. Standard engine on all Toros was a 403 V-8 with an electronic monitoring system. Toro Broughams accounted for 31,471 sales. Cutlass continued its winning ways by building 242,874 Supreme coupes and 124,712 Supreme Brougham coupes. For the first time ever, Olds produced more than a million cars: 1,135,803 to be exact.

	Restorable	Good	Excellent
Starfire cpe	$1,000-2,000	$2,000-2,750	$2,750-4,000
Cutlass S 4-4-2	1,500-2,500	2,500-3,500	3,500-5,000
Delta 88 Pace Car	1,500-2,500	2,500-3,500	3,500-5,000
Toronado cpe	2,000-3,000	3,000-4,500	4,500-6,000
Toronado XS cpe	2,500-3,500	3,500-5,000	5,000-7,000

1977 Oldsmobile Cutlass S 4-4-2

1977 Oldsmobile Toronado SX coupe

1977 Oldsmobile Starfire SX Sport Coupe

1978

The intermediate Cutlass was downsized to a 108-inch wheelbase, losing up to 700 pounds in the process. The Supreme coupe was still Oldsmobile's best seller: 240,917 for '78. Also offered were Salon fastback coupes and sedans; though never very popular, they remained in the lineup for years and are an interesting alternative to the notchback Cutlasses, especially with the 4-4-2 appearance/handling package. Starfires listed a Firenza package, including front air dam, rear spoiler, Rallye suspension, and special paint and trim on a white, black, silver, or red body. The Starfire GT was a similar grouping of special paint, Rallye wheels, white-letter tires, and tachometer. Olds sold 17,321 Starfires for the model year. Toronado had a new grille but was otherwise little changed; 24,815 were built. Olds introduced a 350 V-8 diesel this year for the full-size models—it should be avoided (as well as the other diesels to follow). Olds topped the million mark again this year with 1,015,805 cars built.

	Restorable	Good	Excellent
Starfire cpe	$1,000-2,000	$2,000-2,750	$2,750-4,000
Cutlass Salon 4-4-2	1,500-2,500	2,500-3,500	3,500-5,000
Toronado cpe	2,000-3,000	3,000-4,500	4,500-6,000
Toronado XS cpe	2,500-3,500	3,500-5,000	5,000-7,000

1978 Oldsmobile Cutlass Salon 4-4-2

1978 Oldsmobile Starfire GT Sport Coupe

1979 Oldsmobile Cutlass Salon 4-4-2

1980 Oldsmobile Toronado coupe

1980 Oldsmobile Cutlass Calais 4-4-2 W-30

1980 Oldsmobile Starfire Firenza Sport Coupe

1981 Oldsmobile Toronado Custom Brougham coupe

1979

Starfires again offered GT and Firenza packages, which are worth having if you're buying a Starfire—but it's not something we'd want our daughters to marry. Output was just 20,299 units. A downsizing job to a 114-inch wheelbase did the Toronado considerable good, but an optional diesel engine didn't, and is not recommended—clogged injectors and inept service are perennial problems. Stick to the gasoline V-8. Buyers approved of the new Toro as they drove 50,056 of them home. Omega was in its last year as a rear-wheel-drive model. Cutlass added optional diesel power and still offered the 4-4-2 package. The Supreme coupe recorded 277,944 sales, the Supreme Brougham another 137,323. Total Olds production was 1,068,154 units.

	Restorable	Good	Excellent
Starfire cpe	$1,000-2,000	$2,000-2,750	$2,750-4,000
Cutlass Salon 4-4-2	1,500-2,500	2,500-3,500	3,500-5,000
Toronado cpe	2,000-3,000	3,000-4,500	4,500-6,000

1980

A new front-drive Omega heralded the 1980s, but this Olds has never been considered a collector car. Starfire, which ceased production in December 1979 after just 8237 cars, bowed out with its usual Firenza and GT options, though it was no longer available with a V-8. The Toronado wore a fresh face but was otherwise little changed. Optional was the XSC package, including heavy-duty suspension, bucket seats, console, leather-wrapped steering wheel, voltmeter, and oil pressure gauge—strongly recommended for its improved roadability. Toro output totaled 43,440. Cutlass continued to sell well: 169,517 Supreme coupes and 77,875 Supreme Brougham coupes. This year the 4-4-2 option was available only on the Calais coupe, which saw 26,269 sales. In addition to 4-4-2 and W-30 badging, the package provided a 350 V-8, Rallye suspension, special radial tires, and specific grille and stripes. Big Oldsmobiles received a facelift offering better aerodynamics, and the 98 Luxury Coupe was dropped. Total Olds output dropped to 910,306 cars this year.

	Restorable	Good	Excellent
Starfire cpe	$1,000-2,000	$2,000-2,750	$2,750-4,000
Cutlass Calais 4-4-2	1,500-2,500	2,500-3,500	3,500-5,000
Toronado cpe	2,000-3,000	3,000-4,500	4,500-6,000
Toronado XSC cpe	2,500-3,500	3,500-5,000	5,000-7,000

1981

A mild facelift gave the top-line Cutlass coupe crisp new looks: it had a more sloping hood and front fenders, restyled grille, flush-fitting rear quarter windows, and higher rear deck. Look for the small V-8 and the sporty Calais coupe, much scarcer than the luxury Supreme version. Only 4105 of the former were built compared to 187,875 of the latter (plus

93,855 Supreme Brougham coupes). Gone were the never popular Salon fastbacks (less than 5000 had been built for 1980). Toronado, continuing on a little-changed E-body shared with the Cadillac Eldorado and Buick Riviera, carried a V-6 as standard but a 5.0-liter V-8 was optional, and desirable. Output came to 42,604 Toros. In recessionary 1981, Olds production fell to 792,737 units.

	Restorable	Good	Excellent
Cutlass Calais V-8	*	$2,000-3,000	$3,000-4,000
Toronado coupe	*	$3,000-4,500	$4,500-6,000

* Purchase only in good or excellent condition

1981 Oldsmobile Cutlass Calais coupe

1982

Cutlasses were similar to the '81s except for new grilles and an optional 4.3 liter V-6. The small-block 307 V-8 was limited to Supremes. Sales this year were 89,617 Supremes, 34,717 Supreme Broughams, and 17,109 Calais models. Toronado, little changed again, enjoyed useful driveline improvements, including four-speed overdrive automatic for the optional 5.0-liter V-8 and diesel V-8. Output was 33,928 units. A reworked grille was the main styling change. The front-drive Firenza, an Oldsmobile version of the GM J-body, was introduced this year, but has not garnered collector enthusiasm despite an attractive fastback hatchback body style. Also new was the Cutlass Ciera, a 104.9-inch-wheelbase mid-sizer available in coupe and sedan form. It has not attracted collectors, either. For the year, Olds held steady with a production run of 789,452 cars.

	Restorable	Good	Excellent
Cutlass Calais	*	$2,000-3,000	$3,000-4,000
Toronado coupe	*	3,000-4,500	4,500-6,000

* Purchase only in good or excellent condition

1982 Oldsmobile Toronado Brougham coupe

1983 Oldsmobile Toronado Brougham coupe

1983

Back again for yet another round was the Hurst/Olds, a Cutlass Supreme Calais coupe with a 180-bhp version of the 307 four-barrel V-8, four-speed automatic with Hurst shifter, firm suspension, air shocks, and Eagle GT tires. Relatively low production of 3000 suggests future collectibility. While it was hardly a hot performer with its optional 140 horses, the Cutlass Supreme handled well and looked "right," and it appealed to 107,946 coupe buyers and another 28,451 who wanted to upgrade to the Brougham version. The Calais had black-painted headlamp doors and color-keyed paint stripes, and it too could have the 140-bhp 307. This model attracted 16,660 customers. Toronado was virtually a carryover, except for its exotic Delco-Bose electronically tuned sound system with four speakers and dual equalizer circuits. Toro fans bought 39,605 examples. Total Olds output rose to 939,157 in an improving economy.

	Restorable	Good	Excellent
Hurst/Olds coupe	*	$5,000-7,500	$7,500-10,000
Cutlass Calais	*	2,000-3,000	3,000-4,000
Toronado coupe	*	3,000-4,500	4,500-6,000

* Purchase only in good or excellent condition

1983 Hurst/Olds coupe

1984 Oldsmobile Toronado Caliente coupe

1984 Hurst/Olds coupe

1985 Oldsmobile Cutlass Supreme Brougham coupe

1985 Oldsmobile Toronado Caliente coupe

1986 Oldsmobile Toronado coupe

1984

The Hurst/Olds returned with a beefed up V-8, four-speed automatic with Hurst "Lightning Rod" shifter, firm suspension, air shocks, and Goodyear Eagle GT tires. Output rose to 3500 units. The sporty Calais was still part of the Cutlass array of coupes, and demand rose to 21,393. A Cutlass Calais 500 notchback coupe was available as a Pace Car replica. It featured metallic maroon paint and leather interior, special identification, and V-6 power. Toronado received another front-end facelift. A new luxury Toro Caliente package offered a padded Landau roof and stainless steel crown molding, full-length bodyside moldings, dual electric mirrors, locking wire wheel discs, leather interior, and electronic instrumentation. Total Toronado demand this year was 48,100. Olds came back into stride this year as 1,180,026 cars were called for.

	Restorable	Good	Excellent
Hurst/Olds coupe	*	$5,000-7,500	$7,500-10,000
Cutlass Calais V-8	*	2,500-3,500	3,500-4,500
Toronado coupe	*	3,500-5,000	5,000-7,000

* Purchase only in good or excellent condition

1985

The Calais name went on a front-drive people-hauler this year—coupe or sedan—but it hasn't excited collectors. Among the still-popular rear-wheel-drive Cutlass Supremes (more than 130,000 coupes built), the sportiest model was the Salon, with bucket seats, console, instruments, and handsome trim. It attracted 14,512 buyers. There was even a nostalgia piece, the 4-4-2 option package: special paint, tight suspension, 180-bhp V-8—actually the previous year's Hurst/Olds, without the Mickey Mouse Lightning Rod shifter. Because it lacks the Hurst name, this car is undiscovered and, we're sure, underpriced. It's also reasonably rare, as only 3500 were produced. All Toronados were again V-8s, but beware the diesel version, as usual. Toronado was hardly changed in appearance; the luxurious Caliente was still available. Toro production was 42,185. The big Oldsmobiles were again downsized this year, the 98 to a 110.8-inch wheelbase—barely more than an inch longer than the 1960 Ford Falcon! No matter, Olds enjoyed another good year: 1,135,527 cars for the model run.

	Restorable	Good	Excellent
Cutlass Salon 4-4-2	*	$4,000-5,000	$5,000-6,000
Cutlass Salon V-8	*	3,000-4,000	4,000-5,000
Toronado coupe	*	3,500-5,000	5,000-7,000

* Purchase only in good or excellent condition

1986

Toronado marked its 20th Anniversary with an all-new model, 18 inches shorter and 550 pounds lighter. The only engine was a 3.8-liter V-6, the first time Toronado was offered without a V-8. However, with sequential fuel injection, three-coil ignition, and roller valve lifters, the V-6 produced 150 bhp, 10 more than last year's V-8. One traditional Toro styling feature was the headlamps. In 1986, they were covered by doors that recessed beneath the lamps when turned on. Despite the fact that this new Toro was quicker and more maneuverable, output nosedived to 15,924 examples. The rear-drive Cutlass Salon coupe and its high-performance 4-4-2 variant swooped into '86 with modern aerodynamic composite headlamps—dual bulbs and reflectors covered by single, flush-mounted lens. Together they accounted for 9608 sales, compared to 134,929 Supreme and Supreme Brougham coupes. Olds was still on a roll, recording 1,157,990 sales this year.

	Restorable	Good	Excellent
Cutlass Salon 4-4-2	*	$4,000-6,000	$6,000-8,000
Cutlass Salon V-8	*	3,500-4,500	4,500-5,500
Toronado coupe	*	3,500-5,000	5,000-7,000

* Purchase only in good or excellent condition

1987

The road was finally narrowing for the much-liked rear-drive Cutlass that had catapulted Olds into third place and kept it there for so long. Its continued popularity was still impressive, but sales weren't what they had been in its heyday: 46,343 Supreme coupes, 28,607 Supreme Broughams two-doors, and just 8862 Salon coupes this year. The 4-4-2 package was again offered—thanks for the memories. It included a 5.0-liter V-8, dual exhausts, air conditioning, sporty trim, four-speed automatic, handling suspension, wide wheels/wide tires, and a 3.73 axle ratio. The Toronado was hardly changed, but it was clear that buyers didn't like this smaller version (Cadillac and Buick were having the same problem with the Eldorado and Riviera). Production fell to 15,040, and Olds as a whole skidded to 834,239 units. The newer front-drive models like the Calais and Cutlass Ciera were selling reasonably well, but they never captured the interest of buyers—or enthusiasts—like the Oldsmobiles of yore.

	Restorable	Good	Excellent
Cutlass Salon 4-4-2	*	$4,500-6,250	$6,250-8,500
Cutlass Salon V-8	*	4,250-5,250	5,250-6,250
Toronado coupe	*	4,500-5,500	5,500-6,500
Toronado Trofeo cpe	*	5,000-6,000	6,000-7,500

* Purchase only in good or excellent condition

1988

The old Cutlass Supreme, now properly dubbed "Classic" but bereft of its 4-4-2 option, hung around in standard and Brougham trim levels until its replacement was ready at mid-year—27,678 were built. The new Cutlass Supreme was a GM sports-clone, shared with the W-body Buick Regal and Pontiac Grand Prix. Smooth aero styling gave it a .32 drag coefficient; urge came from a 125-bhp V-6 and both automatic and manual transmissions were available on the sporty International Series—which

1986 Oldsmobile Cutlass Salon coupe

1987 Oldsmobile Toronado coupe

1987 Oldsmobile Toronado Trofeo coupe

1988 Olds Cutlass Ciera International Series

1988 Oldsmobile Toronado coupe

1988 Oldsmobile Cutlass Supreme coupe

1988 Olds Cutlass Supreme Classic Brougham

1988 Oldsmobile Toronado Trofeo coupe

1989 Olds Cutlass Supreme International Series

1990 Olds Cutlass Supreme International Series

is recommended if you think this car may become collectible. It was a pleasant enough road car (coupe only this year), and well put together, but the weak, noisy engine and sloppy transmission were handicaps. Even so, 94,723 were produced in three series. Toronado, with 15 extra horses, was hoping its Trofeo variation would perk up sales, but total demand came to only 16,496 units. Production was really down this year to 535,015.

	Restorable	Good	Excellent
Cutlass Supreme Classic	*	$5,000-6,250	$6,250-7,500
Cutlass Supreme (fwd)	*	4,500-,5,500	5,500-6,500
Cutlass Intn'l Series	*	5,500-6,500	6,500-7,500
Toronado coupe	*	4,500-5,500	5,500-6,500
Toronado Trofeo cpe	*	5,000-6,000	6,000-7,500

* Purchase only in good or excellent condition

1989

The front-drive Cutlass Supreme got a larger V-6 at mid-year and a head-up instrument display that projected images a few feet in front of the driver—vacuum fluorescent displays for a digital speedometer, turn signal indicators, low-fuel warning, and high-beam indicator. Anti-lock braking was optional. The International Series added a five-speed, quick steering, Information System, electronic tach and minor instruments, power door locks, power front bucket seats, rear bucket seats, intermittent wipers, tilt wheel, etc. Toronado/Trofeo had a "Visual Information Center" using a color cathode ray tube, with flashy color graphics, as a 1989 option. ABS was standard on the Trofeo. This generation Toronado didn't sell well—it just didn't look distinctive enough. That should be an indication of its limited viability as a future collector car. Despite calendar year sales of 600,037 cars, Toronado languished to 10,125, while Cutlass Supreme came in at 99,898.

	Restorable	Good	Excellent
Cutlass Supreme cpe	*	$5,000-6,000	$6,000-7,000
Cutlass Supreme SL cpe	*	5,500-7,000	7,000-8,000
Cutlass Intn'l Series	*	7,000-8,250	8,250-9,500
Toronado coupe	*	8,000-9,500	9,500-11,000
Toronado Trofeo cpe	*	10,000-11,000	11,000-12,000

* Purchase only in good or excellent condition

1990

The Supreme added two models, a four-door and a convertible, the first ragtop Cutlass since 1972. Only about 500 were built and they stand to be collectible, particularly since the Chevy sports-clone Beretta convertible was axed at the last minute. Opinions are mixed about the basket-handle midsection brace and the sedan-like feel created by the sharply sloped windshield. The standard Supreme engine was a 180-bhp HO Quad 4 and five-speed manual in the base and I-Series; SLs and convertibles had a V-6. All Supremes came with air conditioning and four-wheel disc brakes; ABS was optional. The head-up instrument display was now a regular option on the I-Series coupe. Every body panel except the hood was new on the '90 Toronado, which was 12 inches longer, helping recapture some of the big-car brashness lost in the '86 downsizing. A driver-side air bag was standard; suspension adjustments improved ride and handling. An interesting new Oldsmobile was the Silhouette, a space-age van and the first Oldsmobile "truck" anybody could remember. Based on Chevy's Lumina APV, it was very luxuriously trimmed with leather upholstery; the FE3 touring suspension was optional. Being the first of an entirely new breed of Oldsmobile and much scarcer than the Chevy APV, the Silhouette contains the possible elements of future collector interest.

	Restorable	Good	Excellent
Cutlass Supreme cvt	*	$12,000-14,000	$14,000-16,000
Cutlass Supreme cpe	*	6,500-7,250	7,250-9,000
Cutlass Supreme SL	*	7,500-8,750	8,750-10,000
Cutlass Intn'l Series	*	8,000-9,500	9,500-11,000
Toronado coupe	*	10,000-12,000	12,000-14,000
Toronado Trofeo cpe	*	12,000-14,000	14,000-16,000
Silhouette minivan	*	10,000-11,500	11,500-13,000

* Purchase only in good or excellent condition

1990 Oldsmobile Cutlass Supreme convertible

1990 Oldsmobile Toronado Trofeo coupe

1990 Oldsmobile Silhouette minivan

Packard

One of the blue chips of the collector car world, Packard is probably the most broadly recognized and defined American marque. Packards comprise almost half the cars in the Classic Car Club of America and three national Packard clubs are still growing 35 years since the last Packard was built. Club support is excellent, parts supplies very good, investment potential good to excellent.

1930-39

A huge array of different models and body styles was offered by Packard in the '30s, beginning with the classically beautiful 1930 Seventh Series and working through the Light Eight and Twelve (1932), the One Twenty (1935), the "new" Twelves and Packard Six (1937). Owing to the variety, consultation with Packard club authorities and careful review of price histories of individual models is strongly recommended.

The relatively light, fast Speedster Eight (Series 734) of 1930 is hotly sought after, but few in number—only 150 were built. The Custom and DeLuxe Eight with 385-cid engines represent the top of the line, but even the basic 320-cid Eight sold for the

1934 Packard Eight Coupe-Roadster

1935 Packard One Twenty Touring Sedan

1935 Packard One Twenty coupe

1936 Packard One Twenty four-door sedan

1938 Packard Twelve Limousine (7-pass)

1938 Packard Eight two-door Touring Sedan

price of a modest home. The 1931 Eighth Series comprised Eight, Custom Eight, and DeLuxe Eight with the same two engines; Eight individual customs included Dietrich convertible sedans and victorias and Packard's own cabriolets, landaulets, and town cars. These were the first cars with Bijur automatic chassis lubrication. Styling for 1932 was similar to 1930-31, but lower and more streamlined. Two important new '32s were the Light Eight and Twin Six, the latter called Twelve from 1933 on. The 1932-34 Twelves shared bodies and chassis with the top Eights, but cost considerably more—then and now. In 1935, when "senior" model production was consolidated, the Twelve and Super Eight adopted 139- and 144-inch wheelbases; custom bodies gradually declined as coachbuilders went out of business, so an increasing number of bodies were built by Packard as the '30s wore on.

The '32 Light Eight was a failed attempt to broaden Packard's sales during the Depression; far more successful was its down-market successor, the 1935 One Twenty, quickly followed in 1937 by the even cheaper Packard Six. These were not low-priced cars, but they were cheaper than any Packards before; today they comprise the majority of late Thirties Packards still in existence. By the time the Six arrived, Packard was building only a trickle of senior cars: the Eight disappeared completely after 1936 (One Twentys used the Eight name in 1938), and its 320 engine went into the Super Eight. From 1937, Super Eights and Twelves were far more modern, with independent front suspension and up-to-date styling—but they were found with fewer custom bodies, most of which were by then closed types such as town cars.

Packard entered the '30s by building 36,334 cars for 1930, but as the Depression deepened, this dropped to 4803 in 1933. The advent of the One Twenty and Six resulted in an all-time record of 122,593 cars for '37, but this had fallen back to 46,405 by 1939.

	Restorable	Good	Excellent
1930-31			
726 Eight sedan	$5,000-10,000	$10,000-20,000	$20,000-30,000
826 Eight sedan	7,500-15,000	15,000-30,000	30,000-45,000
733/833, open	20,000-50,000	50,000-80,000	80,000-125,000
733/833, closed	10,000-20,000	20,000-40,000	40,000-60,000
734 Spdstr, open	50,000-125,000	125,000-200,000	200,000-300,000
734 Spdstr, clsd	20,000-50,000	50,000-80,000	80,000-125,000
740 Custom, open	25,000-75,000	75,000-120,000	120,000-175,000
840 Custom, open	30,000-95,000	95,000-150,000	150,000-240,000
840, indiv. cstm	50,000-125,000	125,000-200,000	200,000-300,000
745 DeLuxe, open	50,000-100,000	100,000-200,000	200,000-300,000
Cust/DeL, clsd	15,000-30,000	30,000-50,000	50,000-75,000
1932 Eights			
Light Eight rdstr	10,000-25,000	25,000-40,000	40,000-55,000
Light Eight, clsd	5,000-12,500	12,500-20,000	20,000-30,000

	Restorable	Good	Excellent
Eight, open	20,000-50,000	50,000-80,000	80,000-125,000
Eight, closed	7,500-17,500	17,500-35,000	35,000-50,000
DeL Eight, open	25,000-60,000	60,000-100,000	100,000-150,000
DeL 8, indiv. cstm	50,000-100,000	100,000-200,000	200,000-300,000
DeL Eight, closed	10,000-22,500	22,500-50,000	50,000-70,000

1932-39 Twelves

1932-34, open	50,000-125,000	125,000-250,000	250,000-350,000
1932-34, indiv cstm	90,000-200,000	200,000-400,000	400,000-up
1932-34, closed	15,000-35,000	35,000-60,000	60,000-100,000
1932-34, indiv. cstm	25,000-50,000	50,000-100,000	100,000-up
1935-36, open	30,000-90,000	90,000-175,000	175,000-225,000
1935-36, closed	12,500-35,000	35,000-60,000	60,000-90,000
1937-39, open	30,000-75,000	75,000-140,000	140,000-200,000
1937-39, open lwb	40,000-100,000	100,000-175,000	175,000-250,000
1937-39, closed	15,000-35,000	35,000-50,000	50,000-65,000
1937-39, clsd lwb	20,000-40,000	40,000-60,000	60,000-80,000

1933-34 Eights

1001 Eight cvt	15,000-35,000	35,000-60,000	60,000-100,000
1002 Eight, open	25,000-75,000	75,000-125,000	125,000-175,000
1101 Eight, open	20,000-60,000	60,000-100,000	100,000-140,000
Eight, closed	7,500-18,000	18,000-30,000	30,000-45,000
Super Eight, open	35,000-80,000	80,000-150,000	150,000-200,000
Super Eight, clsd	10,000-20,000	20,000-40,000	40,000-75,000

1935-36 Eights

120, open	15,000-25,000	25,000-37,500	37,500-55,000
120, closed	4,000-12,000	12,000-22,500	22,500-30,000
Eight, open	10,000-25,000	25,000-50,000	50,000-75,000
Eight, lwb	20,000-40,000	40,000-70,000	70,000-100,000
Eight, closed	5,000-15,000	15,000-30,000	30,000-45,000
Super Eight, open	15,000-30,000	30,000-60,000	60,000-90,000
Super Eight, lwb	25,000-45,000	45,000-85,000	85,000-130,000
Super Eight, clsd	10,000-20,000	20,000-40,000	40,000-60,000

1937-39 Sixes

1937-39 cvt cpe	7,500-18,000	18,000-28,000	28,000-38,000
1937-39 wagon	7,500-18,000	18,000-28,000	28,000-38,000
1937-39 coupes	3,500-10,000	10,000-18,000	18,000-25,000
1937-39, other	2,000-7,000	7,000-14,000	14,000-20,000

1937 and 1939 120, 1938 Eight

Open bodies	10,000-25,000	25,000-35,000	35,000-50,000
Station wagons	7,500-20,000	20,000-32,500	32,500-42,500
Coupes/lwb models	4,000-13,000	13,000-22,500	22,500-32,500
Other models	2,000-9,000	9,000-18,000	18,000-25,000

1937-39 Super Eights

Open bodies	15,000-35,000	35,000-70,000	70,000-100,000
Open bodies, lwb	20,000-45,000	45,000-85,000	85,000-120,000
Closed bodies	10,000-20,000	20,000-40,000	40,000-60,000

1939 Packard One Twenty Touring Sedan

1940 Packard Darrin convertible sedan

1940 Packard Darrin Convertible Victoria

1940 Packard One Twenty Touring Sedan

1941 Packard One Twenty Touring Sedan

1940

These were among the most beautiful and most interesting Packards. The Six was now designated the One Ten; the convertible and woody wagon are equally desirable. A 100-bhp 245.3-cid L-head six provided the power. The One Twenty included standard and DeLuxe closed cars, convertible coupes and sedans, woody wagons, and the exotic Darrin Victoria. The last was an exquisite convertible with cut-down doors and a raked windshield—one of the few One Twentys afforded Classic status. This series of Packards was motivated by a 120-bhp, 282-cid L-head eight. Among senior Packards, the Twelve had been dropped, but an impressive line of Super and Custom Eights rode wheelbases from 127 to 148 inches. Custom coachwork included a Darrin convertible coupe and convertible sedan, Rollson cabriolet and Town Car. A 160-bhp 356 straight eight with nine main bearings powered the One Sixtys and One Eightys. But seniors numbered only 5662 One Sixtys and 1900 One Eightys out of 98,020 Packards built this model year. Sixes accounted for 62,300 cars, One Twentys for 28,138.

	Restorable	Good	Excellent
110 cvt/wagon	$7,500-18,000	$18,000-28,000	$28,000-38,000
110 coupes	3,000-7,500	7,500-12,500	12,500-20,000
110 sedans	2,500-5,000	5,000-10,000	10,000-15,000
120 Darrin cvt	20,000-50,000	50,000-80,000	80,000-130,000
120, open/wgn	10,000-25,000	25,000-37,500	37,500-50,000
120 coupes	5,000-12,500	12,500-17,500	17,500-25,000
120 sedans	3,000-7,500	7,500-12,500	12,500-20,000
160, open	10,000-25,000	25,000-55,000	55,000-80,000
160, closed	4,000-15,000	15,000-25,000	25,000-32,500
180 Darrin	25,000-60,000	60,000-90,000	90,000-145,000
180 Rollson	18,000-45,000	45,000-75,000	75,000-115,000
180, other models	7,500-20,000	20,000-35,000	35,000-50,000

1941

Perfecting its traditional four-square styling, Packard fielded an even lovelier line of cars for 1941, adding a LeBaron sport brougham, limousine, and touring sedan to its One Eighty customs. Electromatic Clutch, eliminating the need to use the pedal, was found on many models. A silky 356-cid straight eight with 160 bhp powered the One Sixty and One Eighty, a smaller eight and six the One Twenty and One Ten. This was the last appearance of the One Twenty convertible sedan. A new, fifth model was the mid-year Clipper, a handsome 127-inch-wheelbase four-door sedan with a new envelope body, priced midway between the One Twenty and One Sixty; it had a 125-bhp version of the 288 straight eight. Packard produced 72,855 cars for '41: 34,700 One Tens, 17,000 One Twentys, 16,600 Clippers, 3525 One Sixtys, and just 930 One Eightys.

	Restorable	Good	Excellent
110 cvt/wagon	$7,500-18,000	$18,000-28,000	$28,000-38,000
110 coupes	3,000-7,500	7,500-12,500	12,500-20,000
110 sedans	2,500-5,000	5,000-10,000	10,000-15,000
120, open/wgn	10,000-25,000	25,000-37,500	37,500-50,000
120 coupes	5,000-12,500	12,500-17,500	17,500-25,000

	Restorable	Good	Excellent
120 sedans	3,000-7,500	7,500-12,500	12,500-20,000
Clipper	2,500-7,500	7,500-11,000	11,000-15,000
160, open	10,000-25,000	25,000-55,000	55,000-80,000
160, closed	4,000-15,000	15,000-25,000	25,000-32,500
180 Darrin	25,000-60,000	60,000-90,000	90,000-145,000
180 Rollson	18,000-45,000	45,000-75,000	75,000-115,000
180 LeBaron Spt Br	10,000-25,000	25,000-50,000	50,000-75,000
180 LeBaron limo	7,500-20,000	20,000-40,000	40,000-57,500
180, other models	7,500-20,000	20,000-35,000	35,000-50,000

1942 Packard Clipper 120 Custom sedan

1946 Packard Clipper two-door Club Sedan

1942

Clipper styling permeated the line for the brief period when '42 models were built, starting now on a 120-inch wheelbase and embracing a two-door Club Sedan body style. The only traditional bodies left were convertibles and wagons, the latter built to order by wagon body suppliers—and very uncommon. Placing the Clipper body on the longer 138- and 148-inch chassis made for some dramatic cars, including the Rollson all-weather cabriolet and Town Car and the LeBaron limousine and long sedan. Darrin Victorias remained available on the normal wheelbase One Eighty chassis. Production was small: 11,325 One Tens, 19,199 One Twentys, 2580 One Sixtys, and 672 One Eightys.

	Restorable	Good	Excellent
110 convertible	$7,500-18,000	$18,000-28,000	$28,000-38,000
110, other models	3,000-7,500	7,500-12,500	12,500-17,500
120 convertible	10,000-25,000	25,000-37,500	37,500-50,000
120, other models	3,000-7,000	7,000-12,000	12,000-20,000
160 convertible	10,000-25,000	25,000-50,000	50,000-80,000
160 lwb models	4,000-15,000	15,000-25,000	25,000-32,500
160, other models	3,500-10,000	10,000-16,000	16,000-22,000
180 Darrin cvt	25,000-60,000	60,000-90,000	90,000-145,000
180 LeBaron	7,000-20,000	20,000-35,000	35,000-45,000
180 Rollson	18,000-45,000	45,000-75,000	75,000-115,000
180 lwb models	6,000-12,000	12,000-23,000	23,000-35,000
180, other models	4,500-12,500	12,500-20,000	20,000-26,500

1946

The first postwar models were revived Clippers, starting with a low-priced Six and Eight with identical bodies on a 120-inch wheelbase. Eight sedans came in two trim levels, standard and DeLuxe. Clipper Super and Custom sedans and Club Sedans rode a 127-inch chassis. The Custom included a seven-passenger sedan and limousine on a 148-inch wheelbase, and that was it—there was no time to develop a Clipper convertible. Packard's massive 356-cid straight eight with its 105-pound crankshaft continued in use on the Super and Custom. The latter were elaborately trimmed in beautiful broadcloth and leather combinations, with special carpeting and woodgrain paneling. Production came to 30,793 cars for 1946: 15,892 Sixes, 7214 Eights and DeLuxe Eights, 4924 Super Clippers, 1472 Custom Super Clippers (plus an additional 1291 on the 148-inch wheelbase).

1947 Packard Clipper Custom Super four-door

	Restorable	Good	Excellent
Six	$2,000-5,000	$5,000-7,500	$7,500-10,000
Eight	2,500-6,500	6,500-9,000	9,000-12,500
Super Eight	3,000-7,500	7,500-10,000	10,000-14,000
Custom Super Eight	3,500-8,500	8,500-11,500	11,500-16,000
Custom Super 8 lwb	5,000-10,000	10,000-17,500	17,500-25,000

1947

Save for elimination of the standard-trim Clipper Eight sedan, there was no change in the Packard lineup for 1947, and the cars can be told apart only by serial numbers. Prices were up, however, to $1912 for the Six Club Sedan, the cheapest model in the line, and $2149 for the DeLuxe Eight four-door sedan, the most popular model Packard offered. Production increased to 51,086 total units, including 14,949 Clipper Sixes, 23,855 DeLuxe Eights, 4802 Supers, and 7480 Custom Super Clippers (127- and 148-inch-wheelbase models).

	Restorable	Good	Excellent
Six	$2,000-5,000	$5,000-7,500	$7,500-10,000
Eight	2,500-6,500	6,500-9,000	9,000-12,500
Super Eight	3,000-7,500	7,500-10,000	10,000-14,000
Custom Super Eight	3,500-8,500	8,500-11,500	11,500-16,000
Custom Super 8 lwb	5,000-10,000	10,000-17,500	17,500-25,000

1948

A heavy facelift produced what enthusiasts call—affectionately and otherwise—the "pregnant elephants": big, heavy-looking, curvaceous Packards with flow-through fenderlines and up to 200 pounds more weight. Customs retained the big 356 engine, but Supers—now sharing a 120-inch chassis with Eights—had a new 327-cid straight eight with five main bearings. Eights used a 288-cid unit, while the six was relegated to export and taxi markets. The truncated-looking 1948 Super Eight was Packard's first postwar convertible, announced well before the official model year began. Topping the line was the $4295 Custom Eight convertible victoria, the most expensive standard-wheelbase car in America. Another novelty was the Eight Station Sedan, a mostly steel station wagon a with wood framed tailgate and door frames, and wood-trimmed doors. This semi-woody has become highly prized, though it's very scarce—exactly 3864 were built for 1948 and early '49. Long-wheelbase chassis existed for Super Eights and Custom Eights (141 and 148 inches, respectively). With 47,807 built, the DeLuxe Eights were the most popular, but 7763 Super Eight and 1105 Custom Eight convertibles were produced. Long-wheelbase models consisted of 1766 Super Eights and 230 Custom Eights.

	Restorable	Good	Excellent
Eight sedans	$2,500-5,000	$5,000-8,000	$8,000-12,500
Eight Station Sdn	6,000-15,000	15,000-25,000	25,000-35,000
Super Eight sdns	3,000-7,500	7,500-10,000	10,000-15,000
Super Eight cvt	6,000-12,000	12,000-20,000	20,000-27,500

	Restorable	Good	Excellent
Super Eight lwb	5,000-10,000	10,000-20,000	20,000-30,000
Custom Eight sdns	4,000-9,000	9,000-14,000	14,000-21,000
Custom Eight cvt	7,500-15,000	15,000-25,000	25,000-40,000
Custom Eight lwb	6,000-12,500	12,500-22,500	22,500-30,000

1949

The first part of the model year was a continuation of the 1948 line. In May 1949 the revised Twenty-Third Series models—honoring Packard's 50th Anniversary—were introduced, differing mainly through a chrome beltline spear. The Eight Station Sedan and long-wheelbase sedans and limousines were dropped from this second series '49 (though four 141-inch Super Eights were recorded). A new Super DeLuxe series, using the Custom's longer wheelbase and eggcrate grille, was added to the lineup. It included a convertible, so after May the short-wheelbase Super convertible was dropped. The big news was Ultramatic, the only automatic transmission developed by an independent, combining torque converter with multiple disc and direct-drive clutches and forward/reverse bands. Compared to GM's Hydra-Matic, it was much smoother, but provided only leisurely acceleration. Frequent use of Low for faster starts caused transmission wear, and Ultramatic cars should be carefully checked. Plenty of expertise and parts exist, however, and Ultramatic is a much better transmission than its detractors make it out to be. Early '49 (Twenty-Second Series) production was 53,158, including 1237 Super Eight and 213 Custom Eight ragtops. For the late '49s, 63,817 cars were built, among them 685 Super Eight and 68 Custom Eight convertibles.

	Restorable	Good	Excellent
Eight sedans	$2,500-5,000	$5,000-8,000	$8,000-12,500
Eight Station sdn	6,000-15,000	15,000-25,000	25,000-35,000
Super Eight sdns	3,000-7,500	7,500-10,000	10,000-15,000
Super Eight cvt	6,000-12,000	12,000-20,000	20,000-27,500
Super Eight lwb	5,000-10,000	10,000-20,000	20,000-30,000
Super Deluxe sdns	3,500-8,500	8,500-12,000	12,000-17,500
Super Deluxe cvt	7,000-13,000	13,000-22,500	22,500-35,000
Custom Eight sdns	4,000-9,000	9,000-14,000	14,000-21,000
Custom Eight cvt	7,500-15,000	15,000-25,000	25,000-40,000
Custom Eight lwb	6,000-12,500	12,500-22,500	22,500-30,000

1950

This year saw a repeat of the late 1949 Twenty-Third Series lineup. The only differentiation is through serial number prefixes, which add "-5" to distinguish them from the late 1949s. The long-wheelbase Super Eight chassis was eliminated and long Customs came only as bare chassis, usually to be fitted with commercial or hearse bodies by outside firms. Despite industry-wide booming sales,

1950 Packard Eight DeLuxe four-door sedan

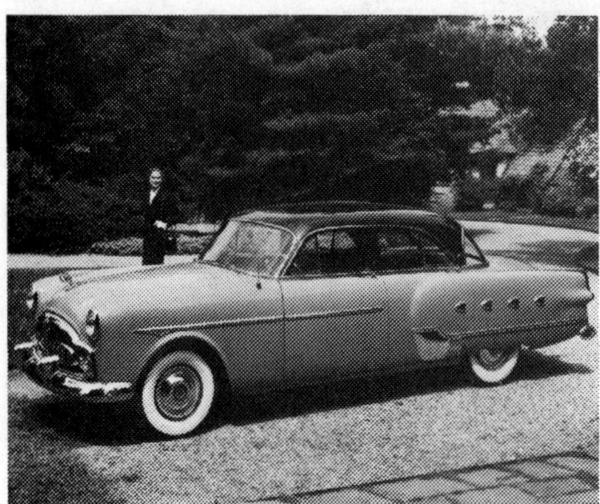

1952 Packard Patrician 400 four-door sedan

Packard was down to just 42,640 cars for the full model year, 36,471 of them being the base Eight/DeLuxe Eight models. Super Eights totaled just 4528, plus 600 convertibles; Custom Eights 707, plus 244 chassis and just 77 soft tops. Despite these dismal figures, the "pregnant elephant" Packards of 1948-50 had enjoyed a production run of 255,090, and they're still in relatively good supply.

	Restorable	Good	Excellent
Eight sedans	$2,500-5,000	$5,000-8,000	$8,000-12,500
Super Eight sdns	3,000-7,500	7,500-10,000	10,000-15,000
Super Deluxe sdns	3,500-8,500	8,500-12,000	12,000-17,500
Super Deluxe cvt	7,000-13,000	13,000-22,500	22,500-35,000
Custom Eight sdns	4,000-9,000	9,000-14,000	14,000-21,000
Custom Eight cvt	7,500-15,000	15,000-25,000	25,000-40,000
Custom Eight lwb	6,000-12,500	12,500-22,500	22,500-30,000

1951

Packard received a long-awaited restyle in 1951, mainly the work of John Reinhart, on 122- and 127-inch wheelbases. But whereas Cadillac had gone back after the war to a 100-percent luxury car lineup, Packard had made a decision to persist with lower-priced models. The base 200 series even included a business coupe, priced $500 below the cheapest Cadillac, plus two- and four-door sedans in standard and DeLuxe trim. The upper-level models were the 250 Mayfair hardtop and a convertible and the 300 and 400 Patrician sedans, all well-built, comfortable, luxury road cars. The 250s, however, rode the shorter wheelbase, and competed more with Olds and Buick than with Cadillac. There were no long-wheelbase cars in regular production. Engines were a 135-bhp 288 eight and a 150/155-bhp 327 for the upscale models. Collector interest today centers on the 250 and the Patrician, though the more numerous 300 isn't a bad bet. Production improved to 100,713, though the desirable models are scarce: 4640 Mayfairs and convertibles combined, 9001 Patricians, and 15,309 300 sedans.

	Restorable	Good	Excellent
200 2d/4d sdns	$1,000-4,500	$4,500-7,500	$7,500-10,000
250 Mayfair htp	2,500-7,000	7,000-11,000	11,000-16,500
250 convertible	4,000-10,000	10,000-15,000	15,000-22,000
300 sedan	1,500-5,500	5,500-8,500	8,500-11,500
400 Patrician sdn	2,000-6,500	6,500-10,000	10,000-15,000

1952

Basically unchanged from 1951, the '52 Packards suffered from Korean War raw materials cutbacks (a problem throughout Detroit), notably in the quality of chromium plate, which was thin and pitted easily. The 200 business coupe was dropped—and nobody much cared. Quick identification of the '52 is the pelican hood ornament (when equipped): wings were carried straight back instead of raised. Also, '52s didn't have the Packard name spelled out in block letters on the hood. More colorful interiors and better fabrics were found in the upper-end models. Power brakes were offered as an option. Partly because of the Korean situation, production was down to 62,921. This included 5201 Mayfairs and convertibles combined, 3975 Patricians, and 6705 300s.

	Restorable	Good	Excellent
200 2d/4d sdns	$1,000-4,500	$4,500-7,500	$7,500-10,000
250 Mayfair htp	2,500-7,000	7,000-11,000	11,000-16,500
250 convertible	4,000-10,000	10,000-15,000	15,000-22,000
300 sedan	1,500-5,500	5,500-8,500	8,500-11,500
400 Patrician sdn	2,000-6,500	6,500-10,000	10,000-15,000

1953

Under new Packard President James Nance the cheap 200 line was renamed Clipper and began evolving into a separate make. A less-known model that is very rare today was the Clipper Sportster, a two-door sedan with a colorful interior resembling that of the more expensive Mayfair hardtop—but just try to find one. Further upmarket, the 300 four-door sedan was rechristened the Cavalier, but, curiously, the name appeared nowhere on it. Determined to revive Packard's former gold-plated reputation, Nance revived a 149-inch long-wheelbase chassis for the Executive eight-passenger sedan and Corporation limousine; contracted with the Derham coachworks to provide a formal version of the Patrician; and had his young stylist, Dick Teague, design a sporty convertible called Caribbean. Taking its styling cues from Richard Arbib's 1952 Pan American show car, the Caribbean was a glamorous limited-edition car with a high $5210 price and bright two-tone interior color schemes. Just 750 were built. Packard fortunes improved to 90,252 units, including 3672 Clipper Sportsters, 5150 Mayfair hardtops, 1518 convertibles, 10,799 Cavaliers, 7456 Patricians, 25 Derham Formal Sedans, 50 Corporation limos, and 100 Executive sedans.

	Restorable	Good	Excellent
Clipper Sportster	$3,000-7,000	$7,000-12,000	$12,000-16,000
Clipper, other	1,000-4,500	4,500-7,500	7,500-10,000
250 Mayfair htp	2,500-7,000	7,000-11,000	11,000-16,500
250 convertible	4,000-10,000	10,000-15,000	15,000-22,000
Cavalier sdn	1,500-5,500	5,500-9,000	9,000-12,000
Patrician sdn	2,000-6,500	6,500-10,000	10,000-15,000
Caribbean cvt	6,000-12,500	12,500-25,000	25,000-35,000
Derham formal sdn	5,000-10,000	10,000-14,000	14,000-20,000
Executive sedan	4,000-8,000	8,000-12,000	12,000-15,000
Corporation limo	4,000-10,000	10,000-14,000	14,000-17,500

1954

Packard had hoped for all-new cars this year, but time and the purchase of Studebaker didn't permit it. Instead, a look-alike interim series was offered, distinguished on senior models by horn-rimmed headlamps and back-up lights built into the taillight assemblies. The old 250 series, now called the Pacific hardtop and Packard Convertible, were stuck with their 122-inch wheelbase, but were cleverly upgraded with senior-style trim and received the en-

1953 Packard Caribbean convertible coupe

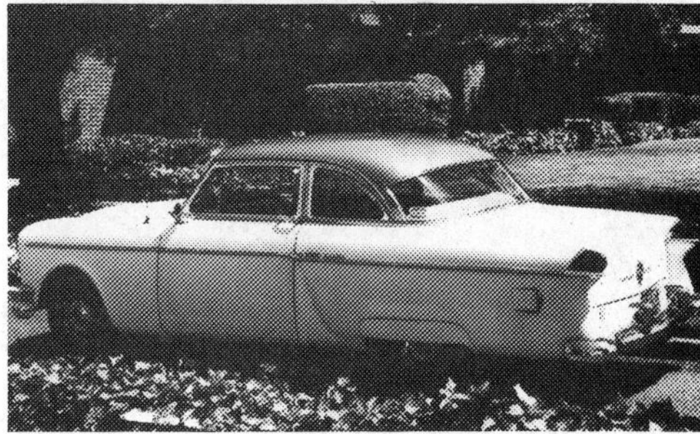

1954 Packard Clipper DeLuxe Sportster coupe

1955 Packard Clipper Custom Constellation

1955 Packard Patrician four-door sedan

1955 Packard Caribbean convertible coupe

1956 Packard Four Hundred hardtop coupe

1956 Packard Clipper Super hardtop coupe

larged, 212-horsepower, nine-main-bearing 359 straight eight—one of the finest evolutions of that type engine. Clippers sported new "sore-thumb" taillights. None of this prevented an enormous slide in sales to 31,291 units, resulting in numerous rarities: 35 limousines, 65 Executive sedans, 400 Caribbeans, 863 convertibles, 1180 Pacifics. In addition, there were 2580 Cavaliers, 2760 Patricians, and 3618 examples of the new Clipper Panama hardtop.

	Restorable	Good	Excellent
Clipper Panama htp	$3,000-7,000	$7,000-12,000	$12,000-16,000
Clipper, other	1,000-5,500	5,500-8,500	8,500-12,000
Pacific hardtop	3,500-9,000	9,000-13,000	13,000-18,500
Convertible	4,500-12,000	12,000-18,000	18,000-25,000
Cavalier sdn	2,000-6,000	6,000-10,000	10,000-14,000
Patrician sdn	2,000-6,500	6,500-10,000	10,000-16,000
Caribbean cvt	7,000-15,000	15,000-28,000	28,000-38,000
Derham formal sdn	5,000-10,000	10,000-14,000	14,000-20,000
Executive sedan	4,000-8,000	8,000-12,000	12,000-16,000
Corporation limo	4,000-10,000	10,000-14,000	14,000-18,500

1955

Going all out, Packard fielded one of its finest postwar lines, most models featuring Torsion-Level suspension, an interlinked torsion-bar system operating (unlike Chrysler's forthcoming '57s) on all four wheels. The straight eights were replaced by modern overhead-valve V-8s, 320 cid for Clippers, a whopping 352 for Packards. Caribbeans, with dual four-barrel 352s belting out 275 horses, were impressively fast road cars, Packards in the truest sense of the word. Styling was a clever heavy facelift of the old '51 body with many new hallmarks: panoramic windshield, "cathedral" taillights, peaked front fenders, an ornate grille. Hardtops proliferated: a new Packard Four Hundred riding the longer 127-inch wheelbase and two Clippers, Panama and Constellation. The Clipper had its own special grille and 1954-style taillights. These are among the most popular postwar Packards. Production increased to 55,247. Among the most desired models were 7016 Clipper Super Panama hardtops, 6672 Clipper Custom Constellation hardtops, 9127 Patricians, 7206 Four Hundred hardtops, and 500 Caribbean convertibles.

	Restorable	Good	Excellent
Clipper Panama htp	$2,500-6,000	$6,000-9,000	$9,000-12,500
Constellation htp	3,000-7,000	7,000-10,000	10,000-15,000
Clipper sedans	1,000-5,500	5,500-7,500	7,500-10,000
Four Hundred htp	3,500-8,000	8,000-12,000	12,000-18,000
Patrician sdn	2,000-6,500	6,500-10,000	10,000-16,000
Caribbean cvt	7,500-17,500	17,500-30,000	30,000-42,500

1956

Unfortunately, the '55 Packard was plagued by quality problems, most owing to a new body plant; this cut into sales of the much-better-built '56. Ultramatic had new electronic pushbutton controls and horsepower was up—310 for the Caribbean.

The Clipper, registered finally as a separate make, carried 352 V-8s; Packards had a larger 374. A hardtop Caribbean joined the convertible; both had unique reversible seat cushions, fabric on one side, leather on the other. In mid-year, the Packard Executive appeared on the shorter Clipper wheelbase, a sedan and hardtop bridging the Clipper-Packard gap. Executives wore the Clipper's pointed taillights but had Packard grilles. Caribbean production was minuscule: 263 hardtops, 276 convertibles. Clipper output was only 18,482, highlighted by 3999 Super Panama and 1466 Constellation hardtops. Packard fared even worse: 10,353, including 3775 Patricians and 3224 Four Hundreds, plus 1784 Executive sedans and 1031 hardtops. Alas, the '56s were to be the last of the real Packards—the Detroit plant was closed by summer.

	Restorable	Good	Excellent
Clipper Panama htp	$2,500-6,000	$6,000-9,000	$9,000-12,500
Constellation htp	3,000-7,000	7,000-10,000	10,000-15,000
Clipper sedans	1,000-5,500	5,500-7,500	7,500-10,000
Executive htp	3,000-7,000	7,000-10,000	10,000-16,500
Executive sedan	1,500-6,000	6,000-8,500	8,500-11,500
Four Hundred htp	3,500-8,000	8,000-12,000	12,000-18,000
Patrician sdn	2,000-6,500	6,500-10,000	10,000-16,000
Caribbean cvt	7,500-17,500	17,500-30,000	30,000-42,500
Caribbean htp	6,000-12,500	12,500-20,000	20,000-30,000

1957

An all-new line of Packards and Clippers based on the Predictor show car was slated for '57, but the finances couldn't be raised so a Studebaker-based 1957 Packard Clipper was fielded as a stopgap entry. It consisted of a 120.5-inch-wheelbase Town Sedan and 116.5-inch Country Sedan (station wagon), based on Studebaker's top-line President and trimmed to a very high level. Power was provided by Stude's excellent 289 V-8 with Paxton supercharger; it delivered 275 bhp, same as the '56 Packard Executive and Clipper Custom had. Styling evoked Packard themes, but of course these were not Packards. Only 4809 were built, 869 being wagons.

	Restorable	Good	Excellent
Town Sedan	$1,000-3,000	$3,000-5,000	$5,000-7,500
Country Sedan wgn	2,000-4,500	4,500-7,000	7,000-9,500

1958

The company still hoped to revive the big Packard, so another stopgap line of "Packardbakers" was designed for '58. Ultimately, no further Packards were ever produced, so these were the very last: a two-door hardtop and wagon on the shorter wheelbase, a four-door sedan and the unique Packard Hawk on the 120.5-inch chassis. The Hawk had a handsome full-leather interior and proper white-on-black instruments set into a turned metal dash, but the exterior was bizarre, with gold-mylar-covered tailfins, a grille that resembled a vacuum cleaner, and odd exterior armrests (said to

1957 Packard Clipper four-door Town Sedan

1958 Packard four-door station wagon

1958 Packard hardtop coupe

1958 Packard hardtop coupe

1958 Packard Hawk hardtop coupe

invoke the feel of classic open cockpit aircraft). On the sedan, wagon, and hardtop, quad headlamps were hastily grafted on to keep up with competition. Generally, collector interest here is settled on the Hawk; very few hardtops and only a handful of wagons exist. Production figures are low enough to be mentioned: 1,200 sedans, 675 hardtops, 588 Hawks, 159 wagons.

	Restorable	Good	Excellent
Hawk	$3,500-6,000	$6,000-10,000	$10,000-17,000
Hardtop	2,500-4,000	4,000-7,500	7,500-10,500
Station wagon	2,000-4,500	4,500-7,000	7,000-8,500
Sedan	1,000-3,000	3,000-5,000	5,000-7,500

1929 Pierce-Arrow Town Car by Willoughby ('30 similar)

Pierce-Arrow

Like Packard, Pierce-Arrow is a gilt-edged Classic, has a strong following and a very professional marque club—but an abbreviated history. Club support is excellent; parts supply fairly low; investment potential is excellent for major models and open bodies, moderate for others. All Pierce-Arrows built starting in 1925, the beginning of the Classic era as defined by the Classic Car Club of America, are recognized Classics.

1930-38

The distinctive 1930 Pierce-Arrows were good looking, fast, low-slung, and priced lower than their recent predecessors. Called Models A, B, and C, they were all straight eights (340, 366, and 385 cid), with 115, 125, and 132 bhp and increasingly long wheelbases, up to 144 inches. The lower-priced Model C included no open bodies. The '31s built upon this base offered a number of spectacular customs by LeBaron, including an elegant victoria coupe and lavish convertible sedan. In 1932, the Pierce V-12 appeared in two sizes: 429 and 398 cid, the latter soon dropped. The Twelve was enlarged to 462 cid for 1933, and a test model racked up a 112.91-mph average in a 24-hour endurance run by racing great Ab Jenkins. Unfortunately, these luxurious titans were exactly wrong for the times, because few could afford them, and those who could preferred not to advertise the fact. The '34s were restyled and became more streamlined; this basic look continued in 1935, the only external difference being rearranged hood louvers and a new dashboard. One of the most famous cars of its day was the elegantly streamlined Pierce Silver Arrow, appearing as both an Eight and a Twelve on the 144-inch wheelbase in 1934-35. The entire line was again redesigned for 1936, and body lines were fashionably rounded. A built-in trunk with top-hinged lid incorporated an interior light with a mercury switch—very exotic for its day. Pierce's long-wheelbase cars (usually 144 inches for Eights, 147 for Twelves) carried dignified luxury limousine, town car, and similar bodies. But production, which had started the decade at 9865 units, dropped to 1735 by 1934, then edged ever lower, so output was suspended in 1937 except for auto show models and spare parts. A 1938 line was announced, but only 30 cars had been registered by the end of the following year. The famous old Buffalo, New York, company had liquidated all its assets by the end of 1938.

	Restorable	Good	Excellent
Eights			
1930 C, closed	$8,500-18,000	$18,000-28,000	$28,000-40,000
1930 A/B, closed	15,000-35,000	35,000-55,000	55,000-80,000
1930-32, open	25,000-50,000	50,000-75,000	75,000-110,000
1931-32, closed	10,000-25,000	25,000-40,000	40,000-55,000
1933-38, closed	10,000-25,000	25,000-35,000	35,000-45,000
1934-37, open	20,000-37,500	37,500-50,000	50,000-75,000
1934-35 Slvr Arrow	25,000-50,000	50,000-75,000	75,000-110,000
1938, open	15,000-30,000	30,000-45,000	45,000-65,000
Twelves			
1932 53, open	30,000-50,000	50,000-80,000	80,000-120,000
1932 51, lwb	20,000-40,000	40,000-60,000	60,000-80,000
1932, other closed	12,500-30,000	30,000-45,000	45,000-60,000
1933 1242, open	20,000-40,000	40,000-70,000	70,000-95,000
1933 1247, open	30,000-50,000	50,000-80,000	80,000-120,000
1933 1247, closed	15,000-35,000	35,000-50,000	50,000-75,000
1934 1248/1250	15,000-35,000	35,000-50,000	50,000-75,000
1934-35 Slvr Arrow	30,000-50,000	50,000-80,000	80,000-120,000
1934-38, open	20,000-35,000	35,000-65,000	65,000-85,000
1935-38 lwb	15,000-35,000	35,000-50,000	50,000-75,000
1933-37, other	10,000-25,000	25,000-35,000	35,000-50,000

1933 Pierce-Arrow Silver Arrow show car

1934 Pierce-Arrow Silver Arrow Coupe

Plymouth

Plymouth

Usually a distant third to Chevy and Ford in the production race, Plymouth is in a similar position among car collectors. There are lots of notable models and good club support, but these are nothing compared to the enormous activity surrounding the "Big Two"—despite the fact that in many years Plymouth built a superior product. Club support is good; parts supply limited, except for recent models; investment potential moderate.

1930-39

The "New Finer Plymouth" of 1930 typically cost more than Ford and Chevy, but offered more as well, including all-steel bodies and four-wheel hydraulic brakes. Few changes were made for '31, but a new, lower body design arrived for 1932. Called the PA, it is best remembered for its innovative engine mounting system. "Floating Power" carried the engine in rubber mounts along its longitudinal axis, giving the Plymouth four "the smoothness of an

1932 Plymouth PB convertible coupe

1933 Plymouth PD DeLuxe Six four-door sedan

1935 Plymouth PJ DeLuxe Six convertible coupe

1936 Plymouth P2 DeLuxe Touring Sedan (lwb)

1937 Plymouth P4 DeLuxe coupe

1938 Plymouth DeLuxe Westchester Suburban wagon

1939 Plymouth P8 DeLuxe convertible coupe

Eight"—a factual exaggeration. In mid-1932, the longer PB was introduced, and sales picked up after bottoming in the early Depression. Plymouth switched to a 189.8-cid, 70-bhp L-head six and a shorter 107/108-inch wheelbase for the 1933 PC, which also sported a winged-female hood mascot and a chrome-plated radiator shell. But the "downsized" car didn't sell well, so a stretched PD version with a 112-inch chassis was a mid-year addition. The '34 PF and longer 114-inch-wheelbase PE debuted with independent coil-spring front suspension, one of the first applications of this design. They also looked more streamlined due to skirted front fenders. There was a complete restyle in 1935, when a tubular front axle replaced the more advanced independent suspension of the '34. A 201.3-cid six with 77 bhp debuted in 1934; it would get 81 horses in 1935 and continue in that form through 1939. Another restyle arrived in 1936, but despite being an inch lower than before, the new design looked very similar aside from a new "waterfall" grille. Plymouth was restyled again—not entirely successfully—in 1937. A new series for 1938 was the Roadking, a lower-priced line comprising sedan and coupe bodies, but lacking much of the decoration and comforts of the DeLuxe series. Styling was a carryover from 1937, though the headlights were moved down and rearward to differentiate the new model. For 1939, Chrysler's chief designer, former coachbuilder Ray Dietrich, brought out a completely new art deco look reminiscent of the Lincoln-Zephyr—rectangular flush headlamps and angled two-piece windshield. Also, independent front suspension made a comeback. The '39 is arguably the most intriguing style among '30s Plymouths, although some collectors dislike its switch from floor- to column-shift. By far the most desirable body style of this year is the convertible sedan, the last to be produced by Plymouth—and only 387 copies were built. It was also the first one to be offered since 1932, when 690 were built (along with 5680 roadsters and 528 phaetons, the last year for those body styles).

Plymouth's lowest production of the Depression decade came in 1930 when it built 76,950 cars. From there Plymouth gained every year except 1932, peaking at 551,994 in 1937. After falling back to 279,338 in recession-plagued 1938, Plymouth ended the decade with a production run of 417,529 cars in 1939. Open models were never that common, just 3110 convertible coupes in 1937, for example. Woody wagons were also rare, just 309 in 1936 and 1777 in 1939 (and none in 1937-38). Likewise the long-wheelbase sedans and limos, which managed less than 2000 per year most of the time.

	Restorable	Good	Excellent
Four-cylinder models			
1930-32, open	$3,000-9,000	$9,000-17,500	$17,500-25,000
1930-32, closed	1,000-4,000	4,000-6,000	6,000-10,000
Six-cylinder models			
1933-38, open	3,000-8,000	8,000-15,000	15,000-22,500
1933-35, closed	1,000-4,000	4,000-6,000	6,000-9,000

	Restorable	Good	Excellent
1936/1939 wagons	2,500-7,000	7,000-11,000	11,000-15,000
1937-39 sedan-limo	2,000-5,000	5,000-7,000	7,000-11,000
1937-39, other clsd	1,000-4,000	4,000-6,000	6,000-9,000
1939 cvt coupe	3,000-8,000	8,000-15,000	15,000-22,500
1939 cvt sedan	4,000-9,000	9,000-17,500	17,500-25,000

1940

Plymouth offered an improved body with "speedline" fenders and round sealed-beam headlamps in two series: Roadking and DeLuxe, both on a longer 117-inch wheelbase. The DeLuxe comprised two- and five-passenger coupes, sedans, convertible, and a wood-bodied eight-passenger wagon. In addition, there was a special 137-inch wheelbase for the DeLuxe seven-passenger sedan and limousine. The four-main-bearing six now developed 84 bhp, providing reliable cruising as well as economy. Production this year was 423,155, including 80 Roadking wagons plus the following DeLuxes: 6986 convertibles, 3126 wagons, 1179 long-wheelbase sedans, and 68 limos.

1940 Plymouth P10 DeLuxe convertible coupe

1940 Plymouth P10 DeLuxe station wagon

	Restorable	Good	Excellent
Convertible cpe	$3,000-7,500	$7,500-15,000	$15,000-22,500
Woody wagons 4d	2,500-7,000	7,000-11,000	11,000-15,000
Sedan-limo 4d	2,000-4,000	4,000-6,500	6,500-10,000
Other bodies	1,000-3,000	3,000-5,500	5,500-8,000

1941

The Plymouth engine was raised to 87 bhp and the bodies were facelifted, resulting in sales of 545,811 cars for the '41 model run. These good looking cars with their somewhat heart-shaped split grille, "speedline" fenders, and modest brightmetal side embellishments looked good for their time, but were hardly as memorable as the '39s. New for all models was Chrysler's first Safety Rim wheel, designed to prevent tire loss in the event of a blowout. Vacuum-aided Powermatic shift, which reduced the effort necessary to move the shift lever, was a new option. There were three series: standard, DeLuxe, and Special DeLuxe. The limousine was dropped after just 24 early '41s were built. Rarities to look for: the standard and DeLuxe club coupe, utility sedan, and station wagons. Their production numbers were 994, 204, and 468, plus 217 base and 5594 Special DeLuxe wagons. Convertibles numbered 10,545 Special DeLuxes, quite high for Plymouth; the seven-passenger Special DeLuxe sedan found 1127 buyers.

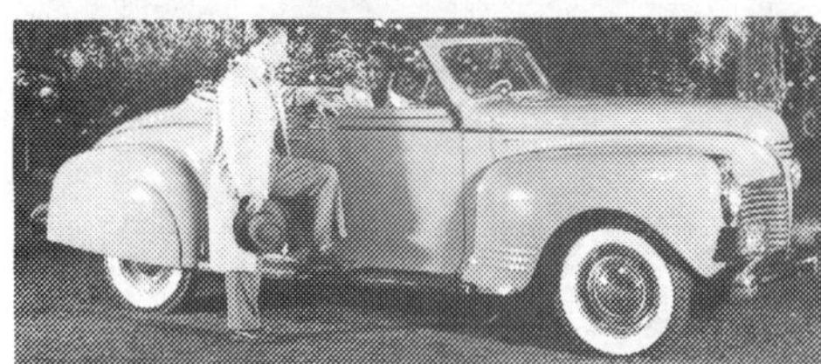

1941 Plymouth P12 Special DeLuxe convertible

1941 Plymouth P12 Special DeLuxe station wagon

	Restorable	Good	Excellent
Convertible cpe	$3,000-7,500	$7,500-15,000	$15,000-22,500
Woody wagon 4d	2,500-7,000	7,000-11,000	11,000-15,000
Sedan-limo	2,000-4,000	4,000-6,500	6,500-10,000
Other bodies	1,000-3,000	3,000-5,500	5,500-8,000

1942

Revised with doors extended to cover the running boards and a more massive horizontal grille, the '42

1941 Plymouth P11 DeLuxe business coupe

1942 Plymouth P14C Special DeLuxe convertible

1942 Plymouth P14C Special DeLuxe station wagon

1942 Plymouth Special DeLuxe four-door sedan

1946-48 Plymouth Special DeLuxe convertible

1946-48 Plymouth Special DeLuxe convertible

Plymouth retained its 117-inch wheelbase. Only two lines appeared, DeLuxe and Special DeLuxe, both with a more powerful 95-bhp engine. There were five DeLuxe models, all closed sedans and coupes, along with seven Special DeLuxes, including a convertible, wagon, and Town Sedan. The latter was a new Chrysler style, marked by closed rear roof quarters. Owing to early shutdown for the duration of World War II, Plymouth built only 152,427 of these models, and many are scarce: 80 utility sedans, 1136 wagons, and 2806 convertibles, for example.

	Restorable	Good	Excellent
Convertible cpe	$3,000-7,500	$7,500-15,000	$15,000-22,500
Woody wagon 4d	2,500-7,000	7,000-11,000	11,000-15,000
Other bodies	1,000-3,000	3,000-5,500	5,500-8,000

1946

For 1946, Plymouth brought out its '42s bearing a new grille composed of alternating thick and thin horizontal bars, rectangular parking lights, wide front fender moldings, a new illuminated hood ornament, and revised rear fenders. DeLuxe and Special DeLuxe returned, but body choices were fewer. Production was 264,660 units.

	Restorable	Good	Excellent
Convertible cpe	$3,000-7,500	$7,500-14,000	$14,000-20,000
Woody wagon 4d	2,500-7,000	7,000-11,000	11,000-15,000
Other bodies	1,000-3,000	3,000-5,500	5,500-8,000

1947

Like the '46s, '48s, and early '49s, these Plymouths are poor investments but very good collector cars. They fall into a period that has not produced many high rollers on the auction circuit; only the convertible and woody wagons have any pretenses as investments. But Plymouths of this era were well nigh indestructible, and they have good club support, plus a fair supply of parts. They also cost less, body style for body style, than a comparable Ford or Chevy. They are recommended for collectors who don't want to spend a fortune, or make one. There were no styling changes at all between 1946 and 1947. Output this year was 382,290.

	Restorable	Good	Excellent
Convertible cpe	$3,000-7,500	$7,500-14,000	$14,000-20,000
Woody wagon 4d	2,500-7,000	7,000-11,000	11,000-15,000
Other bodies	1,000-3,000	3,000-5,500	5,500-8,000

1948

Again Plymouth returned with the same models as the year before, but with higher prices—by up to $300. These '48s were continued as 1949 models starting in December 1948, while Plymouth readied its new postwar design for the spring. There were some engineering changes, including a switch in tire and wheel size from 6.00 x 16 to 6.70 x 15 in January 1948. The early '49s were reserialed, but otherwise identical; consult the following prices for these as well as true '48s. Combined production results of the 1946-early 1949 models reveals some interesting figures in the DeLuxe line: 16,177 business coupes and 10,400 club coupes. For Special DeLuxes, it was 31,399 business coupes, 156,629 club coupes, 15,295 convertibles, and 12,913 wagons. Two- and (especially) four-door sedans dominated the sales charts during these years.

	Restorable	Good	Excellent
Convertible cpe	$3,000-7,500	$7,500-14,000	$14,000-20,000
Woody wagon 4d	2,500-7,000	7,000-11,000	11,000-15,000
Other bodies	1,000-3,000	3,000-5,500	5,500-8,000

1946-48 Plymouth P15C Special DeLuxe sedan

1949

Plymouth's new "second series" or "true" '49 models were efficient, comfortable, roomy—and fairly dull. The chassis was slightly longer than before (now 118.5 inches) and there was a short 111-inch wheelbase for a two-door fastback sedan, coupe, and all-steel Suburban two-door station wagon. Plymouth often gets credit for the last as the first all-steel wagon, but Chevy, Olds, and Pontiac had similar models the same year and, if you count Willys-Overland's Jeep, the first steel wagons were on sale in 1946. Nevertheless, the Suburban cost only $1840 and sold 19,220 copies. The coupe found 15,715 buyers, the fastback 28,516. Among larger models, the Special DeLuxe again included the convertible and woody wagon, of which 15,240 and 3443 were built. A boxy grille extended under the headlamps, and taillamps were mounted high atop the rear fenders. Overall, Plymouth scored 520,385 sales.

1949 Plymouth P18 Special DeLuxe convertible

1949 Plymouth P18 Special DeLuxe woody wagon

	Restorable	Good	Excellent
Convertible cpe	$3,000-7,500	$7,500-14,000	$14,000-20,000
Wagon 4d (woody)	2,500-7,000	7,000-11,000	11,000-14,000
Suburban wgn (steel)	1,500-3,000	3,000-5,500	5,500-8,000
Other models	1,000-3,000	3,000-5,500	5,500-8,000

1949 Plymouth P19 DeLuxe Suburban steel wagon

1950

Through 1954, all Plymouths were powered by the same 217.8-cid L-head six that traced its origins to prewar years. There were two 1950 lines, DeLuxe and Special DeLuxe, the latter outselling the former by seven to five. Two innovations were an automatic electric choke and combination ignition and starter switch. Grilles were simplified, having just one horizontal bisecting bar, and new rear fenders had neatly integrated horizontal taillights. Plymouth built an astonishing 610,954 cars this year, including 34,457 Suburbans, 12,697 ragtops, and 2059 woody wagons. The woody disappeared after the model year.

	Restorable	Good	Excellent
Convertible cpe	$3,000-7,500	$7,500-14,000	$14,000-20,000
Wagon 4d (woody)	2,500-7,000	7,000-11,000	11,000-14,000

1950 Plymouth P20 Special DeLuxe sedan

1950 Plymouth P20 Special DeLuxe convertible

1951 Plymouth P23 Cranbrook four-door sedan

1952 Plymouth P23 Cranbrook Belvedere hardtop

1953 Plymouth P24-2 Cranbrook four-door sedan

1953 Plymouth P24-2 Cranbrook Club Coupe

	Restorable	Good	Excellent
Suburban wgn (steel)	1,500-3,000	3,000-5,500	5,500-8,000
Other models	1,000-3,000	3,000-5,500	5,500-8,000

1951

New model names and a slightly modified design with wider grille and swept-back hoodline highlighted the '51s. There were Concord two-doors, coupes, and wagons; Cambridge four-doors and coupes; and Cranbrook sedans, coupes, convertible, and a Belvedere hardtop. The last was Plymouth's first two-door hardtop, arriving a year behind Chevy's. It was distinguished from other models by a three-piece wraparound rear window. Since Plymouth combined production figures for 1951 and '52, it's hard to tell exactly how many '51 hardtops were built, but the two-year total came to 51,266—over three times the number of convertibles produced during the same period.

	Restorable	Good	Excellent
Cranbrook cvt cpe	$3,000-6,500	$6,500-12,000	$12,000-17,500
Belvedere 2d htp	2,000-5,000	5,000-7,500	7,500-10,000
Other models	1,000-3,000	3,000-5,500	5,500-7,500

1952

Plymouth, like other Chrysler products, was almost unchanged this year. The easiest identification was at the rear: the '52s had the Plymouth name integrated with the trunk handle assembly rather than on a separate piece of script. An important improvement was the Oriflow shock absorber, a hydraulic type designed to improve ride and handling. Korean War cutbacks caused Plymouth to build 200,000 fewer cars than usual, so these are relatively uncommon. Overdrive became an option for the first time this year. The Belvedere hardtop received attractive two-toning that started on the roof and flowed down over the C-pillar and on to the rear deck. Production figures for 1951-52 Plymouths were combined, yielding, in the Concord line, 14,255 business coupes, 49,139 fastback sedans, and 76,520 two-door wagons (Suburban and a slightly upmarket Savoy together). The Cranbrook ragtop found 15,650 buyers.

	Restorable	Good	Excellent
Cranbrook cvt cpe	$3,000-6,500	$6,500-12,000	$12,000-17,500
Belvedere 2d htp	2,000-5,000	5,000-7,500	7,500-10,000
Other models	1,000-3,000	3,000-5,500	5,500-7,500

1953

Flow-through fenders and a one-piece windshield arrived on a new, 114-inch chassis replacing the two chassis (111- and 118.5-inch) previously used. The Concord was dropped, while the Cambridge added a business coupe and wagon. Hy-Drive, a mid-year introduction, was a combination manual transmission and torque converter that reduced—but did not eliminate—the need to declutch. As such, it was considered a "semi-automatic" rather than a fully automatic transmission. It was mated to the old six that saw a small horsepower increase to an even 100. The Cranbrook four-door sedan was far and away the best seller, with nearly 300,000 built; convertible production numbered just 6301, the Belvedere hardtop 35,185. Total output was a very satisfying 650,451.

	Restorable	Good	Excellent
Cranbrook cvt cpe	$3,000-6,500	$6,500-12,000	$12,000-17,500
Belvedere 2d htp	2,000-5,000	5,000-7,500	7,500-10,000
Other models	1,000-3,000	3,000-5,500	5,500-7,500

1954 Plymouth P25-3 Belvedere four-door sedan

1954 Plymouth Belvedere Sport Coupe hardtop

1955 Plymouth P26-2 Belvedere Six Sport Coupe

1954

Aside from a revised grille and taillights and minor trim changes, the '54s looked very similar to the '53s. PowerFlite two-speed automatic was introduced as a mid-year option, bringing transmission choices to four: standard three-speed manual, overdrive, Hy-Drive, and PowerFlite. With the PowerFlite came a larger 230.2-cid engine (versus the standard 217.8) that was rated at 110 bhp—10 more than the base six. The three series bore new model names taken from famous hotels: Plaza, Savoy, and Belvedere. The Belvedere hardtop featured good looking, color-keyed interiors. Plymouth sales were dismal this year, owing to its staid styling and a sales war between Ford and Chevrolet. Production came in at 463,148; the Belvedere Sport Coupe (hardtop) found 25,592 buyers, the Belvedere ragtop 6900.

	Restorable	Good	Excellent
Belvedere cvt cpe	$3,500-7,000	$7,000-13,000	$13,000-18,500
Belvedere 2d htp	2,000-5,000	5,000-8,000	8,000-11,000
Other models	1,000-3,000	3,000-5,500	5,500-7,500

1955

Dramatic new "Forward Look" styling by Virgil Exner and a new, polyspherical-head V-8 marked the successful '55 Plymouths. The Hy-Fire V-8 was originally offered with 241 cid and 157 bhp, but grew at mid-year to 260 cubes and 167/177 bhp. Meanwhile, the base six was now rated at 117 horses. Also featured was a dashboard-mounted shift-control lever for the PowerFlite automatic, suspended foot pedals, tubeless tires, and optional air conditioning, power windows, and power seats. The Belvedere line included a sporty hardtop and convertible, the latter available with the V-8 only. During the '55 model year, Plymouth built 705,455 cars. Belvederes especially are good buys for collectors as there are few Fifties convertibles selling for under $20,000 in prime condition. Cheaper and almost as nice is the Belvedere hardtop, well fitted out and considerably tighter than a ragtop. Belvedere convertible and hardtop production numbered 8473 and 47,375, respectively.

1956 Plymouth P29-3 Belvedere convertible coupe

	Restorable	Good	Excellent
Belvedere cvt cpe	$3,500-7,000	$7,000-13,000	$13,000-18,500
Belvedere 2d htp	2,000-6,000	6,000-10,000	10,000-12,000
Other models	1,000-3,000	3,000-5,500	5,500-7,500

1956

Plymouth's Forward Look was mildly facelifted this year with minor front-end changes and modest new tailfins. Also arriving were many interesting new developments: pushbutton PowerFlite, Highway Hi-Fi record player, 12-volt electrics, a four-door hardtop, and a new Suburban line containing four different wagons. A budget collectible is the Savoy two-door hardtop, new for '56; 16,473 were built. But the most important '56 Plymouth was the limited-edition Fury (4485 sold), a white hardtop with gold anodized body appliqués. It packed a 303-cid V-8 with four-barrel carb and 9.25:1 compression delivering 240 horses. Lesser Plymouths had to make do with 270- or 277-cid V-8s of 180-200 bhp. Furys today are very desirable, and not so scarce that their prices have gone off the scales. Aside from the Savoy hardtop, always give preference to the Fury or Belvedere—more expensive but also far more collectible than the Savoy, Plaza, or wagons. Among Belvederes, output was 6735 soft tops, 24,723 Sport Coupes, and 17,515 Sport Sedan hardtops.

1956 Plymouth P29-3 Fury Sport Coupe hardtop

1957 Plymouth P31 Fury hardtop coupe

	Restorable	Good	Excellent
Fury 2d hardtop	$3,500-7,500	$7,500-10,000	$10,000-15,000
Belvedere cvt cpe	4,000-8,000	8,000-14,000	14,000-20,000
Belvedere 2d htp	2,000-6,000	6,000-10,000	10,000-12,000
Belvedere 4d htp	1,500-3,500	3,500-6,000	6,000-8,500
Other models	1,000-3,000	3,000-5,500	5,500-7,500

1957

These were the most interestingly styled Plymouths of the Fifties, with their dramatically low beltline, acres of glass, clean lines, simulated quad headlights, and the highest tailfins in their field. The hardtop roofline was so clean and elegant that it didn't appear to serve any structural purpose. The grille, usually an ornate chrome object in those days, was slim and graceful, its height reduced by a raised bumper that rode over a separate stone shield. Even sedans, though slightly ungainly looking compared to the sleek hardtops, had enormous glass area. A four-door hardtop Savoy was added during the year. Advertising proclaimed, "Suddenly, it's 1960." Mounted on a 118-inch wheelbase (122 for wagons), the '57s were the most powerful Plymouths ever: The Hy-Fire 277-cid V-8 delivered up to 235 bhp in the Plaza; a 301 gave up to 235 bhp in Savoy and Belvedere; and Fury's new 318 offered 290 bhp. Even the L-head six was boosted to 132 bhp. The '57 also introduced torsion-bar front suspension, a feature that would be used for some years to come. Fury production reached 7438, while Belvederes saw output of 9866 convertibles, 67,268 hardtop coupes, and 37,446 hardtop sedans. Savoy hardtops sold in far smaller numbers.

1957 Plymouth P31-3 Belvedere convertible coupe

1957 Plymouth P30-3 Belvedere Sport Coupe

	Restorable	Good	Excellent
Fury 2d hardtop	$3,500-8,500	$8,500-12,000	$12,000-17,500
Belvedere cvt cpe	4,000-8,000	8,000-14,000	14,000-20,000
Belvedere 2d htp	2,000-6,000	6,000-10,000	10,000-12,000
Bel./Savoy 4d htps	1,500-3,500	3,500-6,000	6,000-8,500
Savoy 2d htp	1,500-4,000	4,000-6,500	6,500-10,000
Other models	1,000-3,000	3,000-5,500	5,500-7,500

1958

The '58 was a facelifted '57, identifiable by its repeat of the grille pattern in the lower stone shield and "lollipop" taillights set into the big shark-like tailfins. Like other '58 models, however, it carried quad headlights—real this time. The standard V-8 was the 318-cid unit from the '57 Fury, with output of 225/250 bhp for all but the Fury, which got 290 horses. Optional on all models was a "Golden Commando" 350-cid V-8, rated at 305 bhp with dual four-barrel carbs, 315 with newly optional fuel injection (which would last only one year and be extremely rare). The 1958 recession resulted in fairly low production, the total down from 762,231 in 1957 to 443,799 in 1958. Fury output was 5303, but Plymouth did build 9941 Belvedere ragtops, about the same as in 1957, plus 36,043 Belvedere hardtop coupes and 19,500 equivalent Savoys.

	Restorable	Good	Excellent
Fury 2d hardtop	$3,500-8,500	$8,500-12,000	$12,000-17,500
Belvedere cvt cpe	4,000-8,000	8,000-14,000	14,000-20,000
Belvedere 2d htp	2,000-6,000	6,000-10,000	10,000-12,000
Bel./Savoy 4d htps	1,500-3,500	3,500-6,000	6,000-8,500
Savoy 2d htp	1,500-4,000	4,000-6,500	6,500-10,000
Other models	1,000-3,000	3,000-5,500	5,500-7,500

1959

Tailfins grew as big as they'd ever get in 1959, which resulted in a less elegant appearance, and taillights settled into horizontal pods just above the bumper. Front ends had a garish eggcrate grille and flatter hood, while the more expensive models used anodized silver panels for side decoration. The Plaza line vanished, and other model names moved down a notch in price. Fury became a separate series offering a convertible, four-door sedan, and four-door hardtop in addition to the traditional two-door hardtop. The new limited-edition performance model was the Sport Fury hardtop coupe and convertible, equipped as standard with a 260-bhp version of the 318 V-8. Sport Fury production amounted to 5990 convertibles and 17,867 hardtops. Fury added 21,494 hardtop coupes, while Belvedere accounted for 23,469 hardtop coupes and 5063 ragtops. Optional for all Plymouths but the Savoy business coupe was a new Golden Commando 395, a 361-cid engine with single four-barrel carb rated at 305 bhp. The "395" designation referred to its torque output of 395 lbs/ft.

	Restorable	Good	Excellent
Sport Fury cvt cpe	$4,000-8,500	$8,500-12,000	$12,000-16,000

1958 Plymouth LP2-H Belvedere Sport Coupe

1958 Plymouth Belvedere Sport Sedan hardtop

1958 Plymouth LP2-H Fury hardtop coupe

1959 Plymouth MP2-P Sport Fury convertible coupe

1959 Plymouth MP2-P Sport Fury hardtop coupe

1960 Plymouth Fury hardtop coupe

1960 Plymouth Valiant V-200 four-door sedan

1960 Plymouth Valiant V-100 four-door station wagon

1961 Plymouth Fury hardtop coupe

1961 Plymouth Valiant V-200 hardtop coupe

	Restorable	Good	Excellent
Sport Fury 2d htp	2,000-6,500	6,500-8,500	8,500-12,000
Fury 2d hardtop	2,000-5,000	5,000-8,000	8,000-11,000
Belvedere cvt cpe	3,500-7,000	7,000-10,000	10,000-15,000
Belvedere 2d htp	1,500-4,000	4,000-6,500	6,500-10,000
Other models	1,000-3,000	3,000-5,000	5,000-6,500

1960

A switch from body-on-frame to Unibody construction made for tighter bodies but greater susceptibility to rust. From the rear, the '60s looked like a reversion to 1957, when Plymouth had proclaimed, "Suddenly it's 1960." While tailfins were similar, however, the front end of the '60 Plymouth was considerably less elegant, and while there was even more glass, the dashboard was too garish and quality control had suffered. Even more disheartening was the fact that there was no separate Sport Fury this year. Output of the Fury convertible was 7080, while hardtop coupes amounted to 18,079 Furys and 14,085 Belvederes. Better news arrived in the form of the new Valiant, a straightforward compact on a 106.5-inch wheelbase. Unique styling boasted clean, square lines and fastback roof, and power was courtesy of a tough new 170-cid Slant Six overhead-valve engine. Though sold through Plymouth dealers, Valiant was a make unto itself—but only for this one year. The line consisted of sedans and wagons in two series, V-100 and V-200.

	Restorable	Good	Excellent
Fury cvt cpe	$3,000-6,000	$6,000-9,000	$9,000-13,500
Fury 2d hardtop	1,500-3,500	3,500-5,000	5,000-7,500
Belvedere 2d htp	1,500-3,000	3,000-4,000	4,000-6,500
Other full-size	1,000-2,500	2,500-4,000	4,000-5,500
Valiant	500-2,000	2,000-3,500	3,500-5,000

1961

Virgil Exner's drastically restyled, finless '61 Plymouth was described years later by one magazine as looking like a "Japanese sci-fi monster." One look at its strange, pinched grille and ponderous pod-like taillights, and one can see the connection. Underneath, however, was a well-engineered, roadworthy automobile, with V-8 options up to a 383 packing 330 bhp. But all that potential buyers saw was the ungainly styling, and the '61 has not fared well among latterday collectors, either. Valiant officially became a Plymouth this year and added a V-100 two-door sedan and V-200 two-door hardtop, which today is worth a bit more than the four-door sedans and wagons. At mid-year, Plymouth's 225 Slant Six became an option in addition to the 101- and 148-bhp 170 Slant Sixes.

	Restorable	Good	Excellent
Fury convertible	$3,000-6,000	$6,000-9,000	$9,000-13,500
Fury 2d hardtop	1,500-3,500	3,500-5,000	5,000-7,500
Other full-size	1,000-3,000	3,000-4,500	4,500-6,000
Valiant 2d htp	750-2,250	2,550-3,750	3,750-5,500
Valiant, other	500-2,000	2,000-3,500	3,500-5,000

1962

Plymouth's worst mistake of the decade was its truncated line of downsized standard cars, eight inches shorter and up to 550 pounds lighter than their forbearers. This sort of redesign would have been greeted like the Second Coming in the 1970s, but in 1962 it was pure looniness, and the result was a sales flop. The Sport Fury convertible and hardtop returned (1516 and 4039 built), and today they're worth somewhat more than the standard Furys, which saw production of 4349 ragtops and 9589 two-door hardtops. A few full-size Plymouths were equipped with a 413-cid V-8 with up to 410 bhp. As might be expected, these are both fast and very rare. Unlike Plymouth's big cars, the little Valiant was quite popular, and this year added a sporty, bucket-seat hardtop called Signet. Find one with the larger 225-cid six, and you have a fairly desirable Valiant—but even though 25,586 were built, Signets are not very common now. Total Plymouth production fell from an already dismal 350,285 in 1961 to 339,814 in 1962.

	Restorable	Good	Excellent
Sport Fury cvt	$4,000-6,000	$6,000-9,000	$9,000-11,500
Sport Fury 2d htp	2,000-4,000	4,000-6,000	6,000-8,500
Fury convertible	3,000-5,000	5,000-7,500	7,500-10,000
Fury 2d hardtop	1,500-3,500	3,500-5,000	5,000-7,500
Other full-size	1,000-3,000	3,000-4,500	4,500-6,000
Valiant Signet htp	1,000-2,500	2,500-4,000	4,000-6,000
Valiant, other	500-2,000	2,000-3,500	3,500-5,000

1962 Plymouth Sport Fury convertible coupe

1962 Plymouth Fury four-door station wagon

1963

With 488,448 cars produced, Plymouth rebounded from eighth to fourth in production in 1963, more through the success of the completely restyled Valiant than the still-shrunken standard models. The latter featured a more conventional grille, razor-edged fenders, and squared-off roof styling, but they remained too small for contemporary tastes. The top power option was a new 383-cid V-8 with up to 330 bhp. However, a few qualified racers were supplied with vehicles carrying a 426-cid wedgehead V-8—a rare find today. For Sixties American cars, these Plymouths are quite inexpensive, particularly the convertibles, of which 5865 were built, 1516 of them Sport Furys. In fact, at these prices, it's hard to think of more old car fun for the money. The Valiant, redesigned by new Chrysler styling head Elwood Engel, wore a conventional body, whose main interest to collectors is the presence of a convertible—both a V-200 and bucket-seat Signet (7122 and 9154 built). The Signet hardtop added 30,857 sales. As in 1962, try to find a Valiant with the 225 Slant Six, which gives remarkable performance for its size.

	Restorable	Good	Excellent
Sport Fury cvt	$4,000-6,000	$6,000-9,000	$9,000-11,500
Sport Fury 2d htp	2,000-4,000	4,000-6,000	6,000-8,500
Fury convertible	3,000-5,000	5,000-7,500	7,500-10,000
Fury 2d hardtop	1,500-3,500	3,500-5,000	5,000-7,500
	(add 50% for 426 V-8)		
Valiant cvts	2,000-4,000	4,000-5,500	5,500-9,000

1963 Plymouth Fury hardtop sedan

1963 Plymouth Valiant Signet 200 convertible coupe

1963 Plymouth Valiant Signet 200 hardtop coupe

1964 Plymouth Fury convertible coupe

1965 Plymouth Barracuda Formula S hardtop coupe

1965 Plymouth Fury III hardtop coupe

1965 Plymouth Fury I V-8 two-door sedan

1965 Plymouth Valiant Signet V-8 convertible coupe

	Restorable	Good	Excellent
Valiant Signet htp	1,000-2,500	2,500-4,000	4,000-7,000
All other models	500-2,000	2,000-3,500	3,500-5,000

1964

Barracuda, first of a famous breed, was the major news this year. Hastily tooled on the Valiant body as a reply to Corvair's sporty Monza, it had a "glassback" roofline with a huge backlight. Barracudas came standard with the 225 Slant Six, but a potent new 273-cid V-8 with 180 horsepower was optional. Both engines were also available on Valiants, as was a new four-on-the-floor gearbox. Like Mustang, the Barracuda was "built to be optioned"; 23,443 were built for its debut year. Valiants and big Plymouths were little changed, retaining about the same lineup of models and body styles. However, the 426-cid wedge V-8 was added as a regular production option for full-size cars, rated at 365 bhp for street use. Racers could get versions rated at 415/425 bhp. Plymouth showed a strong gain in production to 596,221 units. Output of some of the more desirable Valiants was: 5856 V-200 convertibles, 7636 Signet ragtops, and 37,736 Signet hardtops. In the Plymouth line there were 5173 Fury soft tops, 3858 Sport Fury ragtops, and 23,695 Sport Fury hardtops.

	Restorable	Good	Excellent
Sport Fury cvt	$4,000-6,000	$6,000-9,000	$9,000-11,500
Sport Fury 2d htp	2,000-4,000	4,000-6,000	6,000-8,500
Fury convertible	3,000-5,000	5,000-7,500	7,500-10,000
Fury 2d hardtop	1,500-3,500	3,500-5,000	5,000-7,500
	(add 50% for 426 V-8)		
Barracuda htp cpe	3,000-5,000	5,000-7,500	7,500-10,000
Valiant cvts	2,000-4,000	4,000-5,500	5,500-9,000
Valiant Signet htp	1,000-2,500	2,500-4,000	4,000-7,000
All other models	500-2,000	2,000-3,500	3,500-5,000

1965

Plymouth began planning a return to conventional full-size cars the moment the '62 laid an egg; they appeared this year on a 119-inch wheelbase (121 for wagons), designated Fury I, II, III, and Sport Fury. The most collectible big Plymouths are the Fury III and Sport Fury convertibles (5524 and 6272 built), but considering the prices asked for rival '65s like the Chevy Impala, they are bargains. Equipment plays a big role in determining value; air conditioning and big engines are important. The sedans and wagons bunch around $3000, and that's in top condition. Plymouth retained the 116-inch wheelbase for an intermediate line called Belvedere, nicely styled with clean lines and a stamped grille. Notable collector cars were the Belvedere I Super Stock hardtop and the Satellite V-8 hardtop and convertible. Super Stock production is unknown; Satellite hardtop and ragtop saw 23,341 and 1860 copies. Standard on the S/S (optional on other Belvederes and Furys) was a 426 wedgehead engine developing 365 bhp and 470 lbs/ft torque. Also available were 415/425 bhp versions. On its special 115-inch wheelbase, the Super Stock was a tremendous performer. Intended primarily for racing, it could also be ordered with the Hemi 426 as an option. On Barracudas, look for the sporty Formula S package: handling suspension, tach, Wide-Oval tires, special badging, and the new 235-bhp version of the 273 V-8. Barracuda output this year was 64,596 units, but part of that was at the expense of the Valiant, whose soft top sales fell to 2769 V-200s and 2578 Signets.

	Restorable	Good	Excellent
Fury III cvt	$2,500-5,000	$5,000-7,500	$7,500-10,000
Sport Fury cvt	3,000-6,000	6,000-8,500	8,500-12,000
Fury 2d hardtops	2,000-4,000	4,000-7,000	7,000-9,500
Belvedere I S/S 426	2,000-5,000	5,000-7,500	7,500-10,000
Belvedere II cvt	2,500-4,500	4,500-7,000	7,000-8,500
Belvedere Hemi	10,000-20,000	20,000-30,000	30,000-40,000
Belvedere Hemi cvt	15,000-25,000	25,000-35,000	35,000-50,000
Satellite cvt	3,500-6,500	6,500-9,500	9,500-12,500
Satellite 2d htp	2,000-4,000	4,000-6,500	6,500-8,000
(add 75% for Fury/Belvedere II with 426 wedge)			
Barracuda htp cpe	3,000-5,000	5,000-7,500	7,500-10,000
Formula S 235-bhp	4,000-6,000	6,000-8,500	8,500-12,000
Valiant cvts	2,000-4,000	4,000-5,500	5,500-9,000
Valiant Signet htp	1,000-2,500	2,500-4,000	4,000-7,000
All other models	500-2,000	2,000-3,500	3,500-5,000

1966 Plymouth Belvedere Satellite hardtop coupe

1966 Plymouth Barracuda Formula S hardtop coupe

1966 Plymouth Valiant Signet hardtop coupe

1966

The electrifying 425-bhp Street Hemi, with heavy-duty suspension and oversize brakes, was a regular option on Belvedere II and Satellite, at first offered with four-speed only, but later with TorqueFlite automatic. Equipped with proper tires and axle ratio, it could reach 120 mph in 12 seconds and was competitive in drag racing right off the showroom floor. Belvedere and its derivative Satellite were elegant-looking with or without the Hemi, with crisp, chiseled styling and a variety of V-8s: 273, 318, 361, and 383 cid. Barracuda was facelifted with an eggcrate grille, and watched output drop to 38,029. The Valiant convertible was restricted to the Signet series, but only 2507 were built. Mid-size ragtops numbered 2502 Belvedere IIs and 2759 Satellites. Among the big Plymouths, which added a ritzy VIP hardtop coupe and sedan, it was 4326 Fury IIIs and 3418 Sport Furys. Total Plymouth production was 683,879 units.

	Restorable	Good	Excellent
Fury III cvt	$2,500-5,000	$5,000-7,500	$7,500-10,000
Sport Fury cvt	3,000-6,000	6,000-8,500	8,500-12,000
Fury/VIP 2d htps	2,000-4,000	4,000-7,000	7,000-9,500
Belvedere II cvt	2,500-4,500	4,500-7,000	7,000-8,500
Belvedere Hemi	10,000-20,000	20,000-30,000	30,000-40,000
Belvedere Hemi cvt	15,000-25,000	25,000-35,000	35,000-50,000
Satellite cvt	3,500-6,500	6,500-9,500	9,500-12,500
Satellite 2d htp	2,000-4,000	4,000-6,500	6,500-8,000
Satellite Hemi	7,500-15,000	15,000-24,000	24,000-32,000
Satellite Hemi cvt	12,000-20,000	20,000-30,000	30,000-45,000
(add 75% for Fury/Belvedere II with 426 wedge)			
Barracuda htp cpe	3,000-5,000	5,000-7,500	7,500-10,000
Formula S 235-bhp	4,000-6,000	6,000-8,500	8,500-12,000
Valiant Signet cvt	2,000-4,000	4,000-5,500	5,500-9,000
Valiant Signet htp	1,000-2,500	2,500-4,000	4,000-7,000
All other models	500-2,000	2,000-3,500	3,500-5,000

1967 Plymouth Barracuda fastback hardtop coupe

1967 Plymouth Sport Fury "Fast Top" hardtop

1967 Plymouth Belvedere Satellite hardtop coupe

1968 Plymouth Fury III convertible coupe

1968 Plymouth Satellite convertible coupe

1967

Restyled to take on Ford's popular Mustang, the new Barracuda duplicated Mustang's body offerings of hardtop, fastback coupe, and convertible. Look for the optional 383 Barracuda V-8. Production was 28,196 hardtops, 30,110 fastbacks, and 4228 ragtops. Belvedere and Satellite continued with their crisp styling and high performance options, and the convertibles were as rare as ever (this applied to the full-size models, too). The Hemi was offered on the sporty new Belvedere GTX, in addition to a standard 375-bhp 440 wedge V-8. With silver-and-black grille and rear deck appliqué, simulated hood air intakes, striping, and dual exhausts, GTXs looked as fast as they ran. Both hardtop and convertible versions were offered, and 11,429 and 686 were sold. In the Valiant line, the convertible and hardtop were dropped, leaving nothing of interest to collectors.

	Restorable	Good	Excellent
Fury III cvt	$2,500-5,000	$5,000-7,500	$7,500-10,000
Sport Fury cvt	3,000-6,000	6,000-8,500	8,500-12,000
Fury/VIP 2d htps	2,000-4,000	4,000-7,000	7,000-9,500
Belvedere II cvt	2,500-4,500	4,500-7,000	7,000-8,500
Belvedere GTX cvt	5,000-8,000	8,000-14,000	14,000-22,500
Belv GTX cvt Hemi	15,000-25,000	25,000-35,000	35,000-50,000
Belvedere GTX htp	3,000-7,000	7,000-10,000	10,000-14,000
Satellite cvt	3,500-6,500	6,500-9,500	9,500-12,500
Satellite cvt Hemi	12,500-20,000	20,000-30,000	30,000-45,000
Satellite 2d htp	2,000-4,000	4,000-6,500	6,500-8,000
Sat./Belv. htp Hemi	10,000-20,000	20,000-30,000	30,000-40,000
	(add 50% for Fury/Belvedere 440)		
Barracuda cpe/htp	3,000-5,000	5,000-7,500	7,500-10,000
Barracuda cpe/htp 383	4,000-6,000	6,000-8,500	8,500-12,000
Barracuda cvt	3,000-6,000	6,000-9,000	9,000-12,500
Barracuda cvt 383	4,000-7,500	7,500-10,000	10,000-14,000
All other models	500-2,000	2,000-3,500	3,500-5,000

1968

Plymouth restyled its intermediates with more rounded, hippier lines and created the memorable Road Runner hardtop and coupe. Road Runner nameplates and cartoon birds decorated the sides and rear, but what mattered was under the hood: a 383 with 440 manifold and heads, or an optional 426 Hemi. The GTX suspension and four-speed gearbox were available as options. Plymouth sold far more than it expected: 29,240 pillared coupes and 15,359 hardtops. Road Runners were subjected to enormous hype during the boom days of the '80s, and prices soared far beyond their real value. They've stabilized now, but we wouldn't count even on today's prices to hold up during a real depression. The GTX continued as a hardtop or convertible, and probably due to the success of the cheaper Road Runner, production was limited to 17,914 coupes and 1026 ragtops. Barracudas received a vertical-bar grille to identify the '68s; output was down about a third, and only 2840 convertibles were called for.

Intermediate nameplates were revised as Belvedere, Satellite, and Sport Satellite. Hemis were not available in Satellites this year, and ragtops were rare: 1771 Satellites and 1523 Sport Satellites. Full-size soft tops fared a bit better: 4483 Fury IIIs and 2489 Sport Furys.

	Restorable	Good	Excellent
Fury III cvt	$2,500-5,000	$5,000-7,500	$7,500-10,000
Sport Fury cvt	3,000-6,000	6,000-8,500	8,500-12,000
Fury/VIP 2d htps	2,000-4,000	4,000-7,000	7,000-9,000
Road Runner 383	3,000-6,000	6,000-8,500	8,500-11,000
Road Runner 440	8,000-12,000	12,000-16,000	16,000-20,000
Road Runner Hemi	15,000-22,500	22,500-30,000	30,000-37,500
GTX convertible	5,000-8,000	8,000-14,000	14,00-22,500
GTX cvt Hemi	15,000-25,000	25,000-35,000	35,000-50,000
GTX 2d hardtop	3,000-7,000	7,000-10,000	10,000-14,000
GTX 2d htp Hemi	10,000-20,000	20,000-30,000	30,000-40,000
Satellite cvt	3,500-6,500	6,500-9,000	9,000-12,000
Satellite 2d htp	2,000-4,000	4,000-6,500	6,500-8,000
(add up to 125% for Hemi 426, 50% for Fury/Belvedere II 440)			
Barracuda cpe/htp	3,000-5,000	5,000-7,500	7,500-10,000
Barracuda cpe/htp 383	4,000-6,000	6,000-8,500	8,500-12,000
Barracuda cvt	3,000-6,000	6,000-9,000	9,000-12,500
All other models	500-2,000	2,000-3,500	3,500-5,000

1968 Plymouth Barracuda Formula S hardtop coupe

1968 Plymouth Sport Satellite hardtop coupe

1968 Plymouth Barracuda Formula S fastback hardtop

1969

A Road Runner convertible was added, but just 2128 were built—making it one of the most sought-after Plymouths of the Sixties. However, total Road Runner sales zoomed to 84,420. Aside from redesigned taillights, the Barracuda wasn't much changed. Output was down a bit again, and only 1442 ragtops were ordered. Full-size Plymouth Fury I, II, and III models were offered with sixes or V-8s as usual; optional were the 383 and 440 V-8s. The top model, as it had been since 1966, was the VIP. Convertibles were available in Fury III or Sport Fury trim; 4129 and 1579 were called for. Total Plymouth production was 720,209 cars.

	Restorable	Good	Excellent
Fury III cvt	$2,500-5,000	$5,000-7,500	$7,500-10,000
Sport Fury cvt	3,000-6,000	6,000-8,500	8,500-12,000
Fury/VIP 2d htps	2,000-4,000	4,000-7,000	7,000-9,000
Road Runner 383	3,000-6,000	6,000-8,500	8,500-11,000
Road Runner 440	8,000-12,000	12,000-16,000	16,000-20,000
Road Runner Hemi	15,000-22,500	22,500-30,000	30,000-37,500
(Road Runner convertibles: add 50% to above prices)			
GTX convertible	5,000-8,000	8,000-14,000	14,00-22,500
GTX cvt Hemi	15,000-25,000	25,000-35,000	35,000-50,000
GTX 2d hardtop	3,000-7,000	7,000-10,000	10,000-14,000
GTX 2d htp Hemi	10,000-20,000	20,000-30,000	30,000-40,000
Satellite cvt	3,500-6,500	6,500-9,000	9,000-12,000
Satellite 2d htp	2,000-4,000	4,000-6,500	6,500-8,000
(add up to 125% for Hemi 426, 50% for Fury/Belvedere II 440)			
Barracuda cpe/htp	3,000-5,000	5,000-7,500	7,500-10,000
'Cuda 383 coupe	4,000-6,000	6,000-8,500	8,500-12,000
Barracuda cvt	3,000-6,000	6,000-9,000	9,000-12,500
All other models	500-2,000	2,000-3,500	3,500-5,000

1969 Plymouth Barracuda 'Cuda 383 fastback hardtop

1969 Plymouth GTX 440 hardtop coupe

1970 Plymouth Road Runner SuperBird hardtop

1970 Plymouth Sport Fury S/23 hardtop coupe

1970 Plymouth Valiant Duster 340 coupe

1970 Plymouth Barracuda Hemi 'Cuda hardtop coupe

1970 Plymouth Barracuda AAR 'Cuda 340 hardtop

1970

The startling Superbird, a Road Runner with extended aero nose and huge tailfins carrying a stabilizer wing, packed a standard four-barrel 440 with TorqueFlite, while a six-barrel 440, Hemi, and four-speed gearbox were optional. Though similar to the Dodge Charger Daytona from 1969, the Superbird was built in greater numbers: 1920 versus about 505. Road Runner saw sales drop 50 percent to 43,404, and only 824 were ragtops. GTX was down to just the hardtop; 7748 were built. Barracuda was restyled: shorter, wider, and more conventional looking, with a notchback hardtop and convertible body style. The Hemi 'Cuda, one of the most impressive cars of the decade, was the prize of the Plymouth line that year. A less expensive but interesting mid-year variation was the AAR (All-American Racer) 'Cuda 340, identifiable by its "strobe" tape stripes. Standard were a 340 V-8 with three two-barrel carbs, Edelbrock manifold, special heads, and a modified valve train; H-D suspension; wide tires; matte-black hood with functional scoop; and rear spoiler. Only about 2800 were built. Other Barracuda production figures were: 25,651 hardtops, 1554 ragtops; 8183 luxury Gran Coupe hardtops, 596 ragtops; 18,880 'Cuda hardtops, 635 ragtops. On the likewise restyled Valiant, look for the Gold Duster, an option package using gold trim on the grille, body, and interior, and equipped with bucket seats and special wheel covers. For those wanting more performance, check out the Duster 340, with its four-barrel 275-bhp engine, front disc brakes, and three-speed floorshift. Even full-size Plymouths included rare performance models, such as the Sport Fury GT with standard 440 engine and tight suspension, and the S/23, with similar equipment and a 318 V-8. The luxury VIP was dropped, but Plymouth replaced it with the mid-year Gran Coupe, and the convertible was also gone after 1952 were built this year.

	Restorable	Good	Excellent
Fury III cvt	$2,500-5,000	$5,000-7,500	$7,500-10,000
Fury GT/S-23 htps	2,500-5,000	5,000-7,500	7,500-10,000
Superbird	10,000-20,000	20,000-33,000	33,000-45,000
Superbird Hemi	20,000-40,000	40,000-70,000	70,000-100,000
Road Runner 383	3,000-6,000	6,000-8,500	8,500-11,000
Road Runner 440	8,000-12,000	12,000-16,000	16,000-20,000
Road Runner Hemi	15,000-22,500	22,500-30,000	30,000-37,500
(Road Runner convertible: add 50% to above prices)			
Belvedere GTX 2d htp	3,000-7,000	7,000-10,000	10,000-14,000
GTX Hemi 2d htp	10,000-20,000	20,000-30,000	30,000-40,000
Satellite 2d htp	2,000-4,000	4,000-6,500	6,500-8,000
(add 75% for 440 Six-Pack)			
Barracuda coupe	3,000-5,000	5,000-7,500	7,500-10,000
Barracuda cvt	3,000-6,000	6,000-9,000	9,000-12,500
AAR 'Cuda 340 cpe	7,500-12,500	12,500-18,000	18,000-23,500
'Cuda 440	4,500-7,500	7,500-11,000	11,000-16,000
Hemi 'Cuda coupe	20,000-30,000	30,000-45,000	45,000-60,000
Hemi 'Cuda cvt			to $100,000
Duster 340	2,000-3,000	3,000-5,000	5,000-7,000
Gold Duster	1,500-2,500	2,500-4,000	4,000-6,000

1971

Plymouth met its competition head-on with 44 models and 70 basic trim and engine variations. Valiant's popular Duster coupe had a "Twister" option: flat-black hood and grille, tape stripes, Rallye wheels. The Gold Duster continued, and would be in the line through 1975. Also look for the "Space Duster," with wagon-style fold-down rear seatback and carpeted cargo area. Enthusiasts, meanwhile, snapped up 12,886 Duster 340s. The '71 Barracuda was a continuation of the restyled '70, but sales were meager, especially for convertibles: 1388, including just 374 'Cudas. Mid-size models were completely revamped, radically sculptured with large loop-style bumper-grilles. Convertibles were dropped, but the Road Runner and GTX were still around, and there was a smart new luxury hardtop called Sebring-Plus. Unfortunately, thanks ironically to federal mandates, these cars were heavier and thirstier than before, and not as quick. Road Runner was down to 14,218 units, and the GTX, now in its last year, fell to 2942. Total Plymouth sales were 702,115.

	Restorable	Good	Excellent
Fury GT 2d htp	$2,000-4,000	$4,000-6,500	$6,500-8,500
Road Runner 383	3,000-6,000	6,000-8,500	8,500-11,000
Road Runner 440	8,000-12,000	12,000-16,000	16,000-20,000
Road Runner Hemi	15,000-22,500	22,500-30,000	30,000-37,500
GTX 2d hardtop	3,000-6,000	6,000-9,000	9,000-11,000
GTX 2d htp Hemi	10,000-20,000	20,000-30,000	30,000-37,500
Satellite Sebring	2,000-4,000	4,000-6,500	6,500-9,000
	(add 75% for 440 Six-Pack)		
Barracuda coupe	2,500-5,000	5,000-7,000	7,000-9,000
Barracuda cvt	3,000-6,000	6,000-9,000	9,000-12,500
'Cuda 340 cpe	7,500-12,500	12,500-18,000	18,000-23,500
'Cuda 440 cpe	4,500-7,500	7,500-11,000	11,000-16,000
Hemi 'Cuda coupe	20,000-30,000	30,000-45,000	45,000-60,000
Hemi 'Cuda cvt			to $100,000
Duster 340	2,000-3,000	3,000-5,000	5,000-7,000
Gold Duster/ Scamp	1,500-2,500	2,500-4,000	4,000-6,000

1972

Barracuda was petering out, so the lineup was pared to standard and 'Cuda coupes; convertibles were scrubbed. 'Cudas came standard with the 318 V-8; Barracudas had a Slant Six or 318. The 340 V-8 with 240 *net* horsepower was optional for either. Sales were down to 10,622 hardtops and 7828 'Cudas. In the intermediate field, the Road Runner now came with a 255-bhp 400 V-8 standard, with the 240-bhp 340, 280-bhp 440, and 330-bhp triple-carb 440 optional. Also among the mid-size Plymouths were the Sebring and Sebring-Plus hardtops. Road Runner production was down to 7628, while the Sebring hardtop found 34,353 buyers, the Sebring-Plus 21,399. Big Plymouths still listed hardtops, available with 230- and 285-bhp 440 V-8s, but the move was clearly to luxury as the Sport Fury series was replaced by the Gran Fury.

1971 Plymouth Sport Fury hardtop coupe

1971 Plymouth Valiant Duster 340 coupe

1971 Plymouth Barracuda 'Cuda 340 hardtop coupe

1971 Plymouth Road Runner 440-6 hardtop coupe

1971 Plymouth Barracuda 'Cuda 340 hardtop coupe

1972 Plymouth Satellite Sebring Plus hardtop

	Restorable	Good	Excellent
Road Runner 340	$3,000-6,000	$6,000-8,500	$8,500-11,000
Satellite Sebring	2,000-4,000	4,000-6,500	6,500-9,000
	(add 75% for 440 Six-Pack)		
Barracuda htp cpe	2,500-4,000	4,000-6,000	6,000-8,000
'Cuda htp cpe	3,500-5,500	5,500-7,000	7,000-9,500
Duster 340 cpe	2,000-3,000	3,000-5,000	5,000-7,000
Gold Duster/ Scamp	1,500-2,500	2,500-4,000	4,000-6,000

1973 Plymouth Road Runner hardtop coupe

1973

Ironically, Plymouth now called Barracuda and 'Cuda "specialty compacts," but eliminated their six-cylinder versions; the 318 V-8 was standard, while a 340 was optional on 'Cuda. Production this year was 11,587 Barracudas and 10,626 'Cudas. The 318 was also standard on Road Runners, and there was no longer a "Six-Pack" induction system for the 440. Sales nonetheless increased to 19,056. Styling changes across the lineup were mostly minor, save for those required to accommodate new government-mandated five-mph bumpers up front. Sales-wise, 1973 was a banner year for Plymouth as it built 882,196 cars.

1973 Plymouth Barracuda hardtop coupe

	Restorable	Good	Excellent
Road Runner	$2,500-4,000	$4,000-7,000	$7,000-9,000
Satellite Sebring	1,500-3,000	3,000-5,500	5,500-8,000
Barracuda & 'Cuda	2,500-4,000	4,000-6,000	6,000-8,000
'Cuda 340	3,500-5,500	5,500-7,000	7,000-9,500
Duster 340	2,000-3,000	3,000-5,000	5,000-7,000
Gold Duster/ Scamp	1,500-2,500	2,500-4,000	4,000-5,500

1973 Plymouth Valiant Duster two-door coupe

1974

The Duster performance fastback got a shot in the arm this year when it gained a more emissions friendly 360 V-8 with 245 net bhp—but these cost less today than the previous Duster 340s. The Gold Duster trim package put in another appearance, and the Scamp remained Duster's V-8 hardtop. This was the Barracuda's last year—as before, the sole models were a standard and 'Cuda hardtop, and just 6745 and 4989 were built. As with Duster, the 'Cuda performance engine option was now the 360. A bulky new Fury arrived, sharing its body with the Chrysler Newport—incredibly ill-timed for the fuel crisis that came just as the cars were introduced. Road Runners ran with the 170-bhp 318 V-8 as standard, but a 275-bhp four-barrel 440 was optional. Production fell to 11,555 units. Though Plymouth regained third place in the sales race, production was down sharply to 739,894.

1974 Plymouth Road Runner hardtop coupe

	Restorable	Good	Excellent
Road Runner	$2,500-4,000	$4,000-7,000	$7,000-9,000
Satellite Sebring	1,500-3,000	3,000-5,500	5,500-8,000
Barracuda & 'Cuda	2,500-4,000	4,000-6,000	6,000-8,000
'Cuda 360	3,500-5,500	5,500-7,000	7,000-9,500
Duster 360	1,500-2,500	2,500-3,750	3,750-5,000
Gold Duster/ Scamp	1,000-1,500	1,500-3,000	3,000-4,000

1974 Plymouth Valiant Duster 360 coupe

1975

Plymouth dropped numerous long-running performance cars, including Barracuda, 'Cuda, and Satellite, and announced a new, intermediate Fury—the previous Belvedere design with heavily revised outer sheetmetal and a new name—but sales continued to be low. A Road Runner coupe was included, with stiff suspension, dual exhausts, and a choice of V-8s from 318 to 400 cid. Look for one with the bold rear deck graphics package, which was optional. To distinguish it from Fury, the full-size Plymouth was now called Gran Fury, but it didn't sell well either. An up-market Valiant Brougham, very handsomely trimmed, was offered in sedan and hardtop form—there was even a Scamp Brougham—a contradiction in terms. Total production skidded to 454,105 cars as the full effect of the Arab oil embargo took hold.

	Restorable	Good	Excellent
Road Runner	$1,500-2,500	$2,500-3,500	$3,500-5,000
Duster 360	1,000-1,500	1,500-3,000	3,000-4,000
Scamp htp./ Brougham	500-1,500	1,500-2,500	2,500-3,000
Valiant Brougham	500-1,500	1,500-2,500	2,500-3,000

1975 Plymouth Valiant Brougham four-door sedan

1975 Plymouth Valiant Duster Custom Coupe

1976

A Brougham was offered again in Valiant's last year. Also, look for the "Silver Duster" model in handsome combinations of silver, red, and black; and the "Feather Duster," featuring a 225 Slant Six tuned for economy, lots of aluminum parts, and special identification. The Duster 360 performance model had been dropped, although a 360 V-8 was available as an option (with automatic only) for all Dusters. At mid-year, Plymouth unveiled the Volaré, Valiant's ultimate replacement, but workmanship was a problem. The Road Runner name went to Volaré, in which form it appeared as a 318 V-8 coupe mounted on a performance suspension, with a three-speed floor shift and sporty interior.

	Restorable	Good	Excellent
Volaré Road Runner	$1,000-2,000	$2,000-3,000	$3,000-4,000
Silver Duster	500-1,000	1,000-2,000	2,000-3,000
Feather Duster	500-1,000	1,000-2,000	2,000-2,750
Scamp hardtop	500-1,500	1,500-2,500	2,500-3,000
Valiant Brougham	500-1,500	1,500-2,500	2,500-3,000

1975 Plymouth Fury Sport hardtop coupe

1976 Plymouth Valiant Feather Duster coupe

1977

With the retirement after this year of its full-size cars, Plymouth was giving itself over heavily to economy models. Valiant, Duster, and Scamp had departed, leaving the Volaré as the bread-and-butter model. The Plymouth name went onto a captive import, the Arrow. Close to 5000 Volarés had the Road Runner package, with louvered rear side windows and up to 175 bhp available via the optional four-barrel 360 V-8. In all honesty, this is the only 1977 Plymouth that is remotely collectible—how quickly the mighty had fallen!

1977 Plymouth Volaré Road Runner two-door coupe

1977 Plymouth Volaré Road Runner with "Hatch Roof"

1978 Plymouth Volaré Road Runner two-door coupe

1979 Plymouth Volaré Duster two-door coupe

1980 Plymouth Volaré four-door sedan

	Restorable	Good	Excellent
Volaré Road Runner	$1,000-2,000	$2,000-3,000	$3,000-4,000

1978

After this year, Plymouth would abandon all market segments above compact. Together with Dodge, the division introduced a five-door hatchback, front-wheel-drive subcompact, the Horizon. This was a twin to the Dodge Omni except for the grille, taillights, and badges, and shared the distinction of being the first domestic front-drive economy car. It offered good roadability and economy, and sold well, but it has not developed a collector following. From Mitsubishi came the Arrow and a new sport coupe called Sapporo. The rest of the line included workaday sedans and wagons on the old intermediate wheelbase—the last we'd see of the larger Plymouths. Production this year was 501,129 units.

	Restorable	Good	Excellent
Volaré Road Runner	$1,000-2,000	$2,000-3,000	$3,000-4,000

1979

A Horizon derivation, the TC3 hatchback coupe, made its first appearance this year; before long this popular package would be all over the roads. It had a shorter wheelbase than the Horizon (96.7 inches versus 99.2), but the same platform and chassis, plus a slotted grille, chiseled lines, and tape-stripe decorations. Look for the TC3 Sport or Rallye package, with special lettering, louvered quarter windows, and four-spoke steering wheel. Similar equipment was applied to the revived Duster, a kind of "full-race Volaré," if you know what we mean—it was strictly a styling package. The Volaré Road Runner 318 was still in the lineup, though just barely: only 1122 were built, so this is a rare model.

	Restorable	Good	Excellent
Volaré Road Runner	$1,000-2,000	$2,000-3,000	$3,000-4,000
Volaré Duster cpe	500-1,000	1,000-2,000	2,000-3,000
TC3 hatchback cpe	500-1,250	1,250-2,250	2,250-3,000

1980

Plymouth seemed to be fast disappearing by this year; the only domestic models left were the Horizon/TC3, a fast-fading Volaré, and an intermediate revival on a 118.5-inch wheelbase called Gran Fury—available only as a four-door sedan. Plymouth nameplates meanwhile decorated various captive imports including the Champ econobox from Mitsubishi. The Volaré Road Runner, production only 496, saw its last this year. If scarcity matters, find one of these—there really isn't much of a line for them. Chrysler's neglect of Plymouth was really showing now as only 290,174 domestic models were produced.

	Restorable	Good	Excellent
Volaré Road Runner	$1,000-2,000	$2,000-3,000	$3,000-4,500
Volaré Duster cpe	500-1,000	1,000-2,000	2,000-3,000
TC3 hatchback cpe	500-1,250	1,250-2,250	2,250-3,000

1981

Not dead yet, Plymouth replaced the unlamented Volaré with the Reliant, its version of the Chrysler K-car, saving its hide and its parent corporation's. No collectible Reliants are known to exist, however, so the sole point of interest was the older Horizon. This year it had a new 2.2-liter engine option, which is definitely the only one to have—the older 1.7 was pretty anemic. The TC3 hatchback continued with the optional Turismo package, which included the 2.2 engine. Also of some interest was the new Horizon Euro-Sedan, with upgraded interior, full instruments, stiffer suspension, cast aluminum road wheels, and black painted exterior; bolt this up with the 2.2 engine for some cheap fun.

	Restorable	Good	Excellent
Horizon Euro-Sedan	*	$1,000-1,500	$1,500-2,500
TC3 hatchback cpe	*	1,500-2,500	2,500-3,000

* Purchase only in good or excellent condition

1981 Plymouth Horizon 2.2 five-door hatchback

1981 Plymouth TC3 three-door hatchback

1982

Horizons and TC3s were reorganized into three price classes—the most collectible ones being the sporty TC3 Turismo and its Horizon equivalent, the E-Type. No Jaguar this, it had the 1.7 engine as standard—look for one with a 2.2. Avoid the cheaper versions of both these models, including the underwhelming Miser.

	Restorable	Good	Excellent
TC3 hatchback cpe	*	$1,500-2,500	$2,500-3,000
Horizon E-Type 5d	*	1,000-1,500	1,500-2,500

* Purchase only in good or excellent condition

1982 Plymouth Turismo TC3 three-door hatchback

1982 Plymouth Horizon five-door hatchback

1983

The TC3 name was abandoned and the hatchback was called simply Turismo. A Peugeot 1.6 replaced the older VW-based 1.7 during the year, and a new five-speed manual gearbox was optional with both this and the 2.2. Despite its long-throw cable shifter, the five-speed is recommended because of its far better spaced gears than the four-speed—with, of course, the 2.2 engine. Both goodies came standard on the Turismo 2.2, which also had a sport suspension and snorty exhaust. The Horizon E-Type was not offered, but it was possible to equip a Horizon Custom similarly.

	Restorable	Good	Excellent
Turismo 2.2 3d cpe	*	$1,500-2,500	$2,500-3,000
Horizon Custom 2.2	*	1,000-1,500	1,500-2,500

* Purchase only in good or excellent condition

1983 Plymouth Turismo 2.2 three-door hatchback

1984 Plymouth Horizon 2.2 five-door hatchback

1984 Plymouth Turismo 2.2 three-door hatchback

1985 Plymouth Turismo Duster hatchback coupe

1986 Plymouth Turismo Duster hatchback coupe

1987 Plymouth Turismo Duster hatchback coupe

1984

New instrument panels with lots of gauges were provided on the Turismo and Horizon, which were filled with good needle instruments on 2.2 models. The upscale Horizon Custom was now called the SE, for "Special Edition." The 2.2 was now a 110-bhp unit developed in 1983 for the Dodge Shelby Charger. Turismos had a new look with quad headlamps, and lost their clumsy fake hood scoop from 1983. Cloth-and-vinyl low-back bucket seats were standard on base models, but the better ones had full-vinyl high-back buckets with recline levers.

	Restorable	Good	Excellent
Turismo 2.2			
3d cpe	*	$1,500-2,500	$2,500-3,000
Horizon SE 2.2			
5d	*	1,000-1,500	1,500-2,500

* Purchase only in good or excellent condition

1985

The Plymouth Duster made one of its periodic reappearances this year, this time as a tape-stripe package for the Turismo hatchback; included were reclining bucket seats, rear spoiler, and rally wheels. The Turismo 2.2 included the larger engine and five-speed gearbox as standard, along with upgraded trim.

	Restorable	Good	Excellent
Turismo 2.2			
3d cpe	*	$1,500-2,500	$2,500-3,000
Horizon SE 2.2			
5d	*	1,000-1,500	1,500-2,500

* Purchase only in good or excellent condition

1986

The Horizon and Turismo were carried over unchanged except for a new center high-mounted stop lamp required by the government. Unfortunately, the Plymouth Turismo lacked the more sporting performance packages offered on the cousin Dodge Charger. As with earlier models, stick to the larger engine cars; despite its long throws and balky linkage, the five-speed is a more flexible gearbox than the four-speed.

	Restorable	Good	Excellent
Turismo 2.2 3d cpe	*	$1,500-2,500	$2,500-3,000
Horizon SE 5d sdn	*	1,000-1,500	1,500-2,500

* Purchase only in good or excellent condition

1987

This is a good year for Horizon and Turismo—not only recent enough to assure a good supply of cars in decent condition, but a year known for improvements to the breed. Reducing both models to a single series with limited option packages allowed Chrysler to eliminate 702 parts from production, increase standard equipment, and build in greater quality. The 2.2-liter engine and five-speed were standard; automatic was optional. The only other significant option was a basic package of automatic and power steering, and air conditioning. Also this year, Plymouth released a sporty compact called the Sundance, with generous standard equipment including tachometer, reclining buckets, and fold-down rear seatback. Most interesting of these was the turbocharged engine package out of Dodge's Shelby Charger, which gave the Sundance vivid performance.

	Restorable	Good	Excellent
Turismo 3d cpe	*	$1,500-2,500	$2,500-3,000
Horizon 5d sdn	*	1,000-1,500	1,500-2,500
Sundance Turbo	*	2,000-3,000	3,000-3,750

* Purchase only in good or excellent condition

1987 Plymouth Sundance three-door hatchback

1988

A sporty RS Sundance was available on both the three- and five-door bodies; it included a 2.5-liter four, unique front fascia with integral fog lamps, new front bucket seats with adjustable lumbar support for the driver, leather-wrapped steering wheel, rear defogger, and power door locks. The Turbo 2.2 was still available, and it was possible to combine the RS and Turbo packages; such Sundances stand a chance of eventually becoming collectible. The Turismo coupe, which could trace its line back to 1979, was dropped, but the Horizon, which went back to 1978, soldiered on with standard fuel injection. It was available in only one trim level, the America series launched in 1987, with three option packages and two individual options (air and AM/FM stereo cassette radio). Horsepower was down slightly.

1988 Plymouth Sundance RS Turbo Liftback coupe

1988 Plymouth Horizon America hatchback sedan

	Restorable	Good	Excellent
Horizon America 5d	*	$2,000-2,500	$2,500-3,000
Sundance RS Turbo	*	3,000-3,750	3,750-4,500

* Purchase only in good or excellent condition

1989

Horizon entered its 12th year with few changes, retaining its 93-bhp 2.2-liter four, with internal modifications made to provide quieter running. A five-speed manual gearbox was standard, and automatic optional as usual. On the Sundance, a Chrysler Turbo 2.5 replaced the Turbo 2.2 as the performance engine; it delivered 150 horsepower.

1989 Plymouth Sundance RS Turbo Liftback coupe

	Restorable	Good	Excellent
Horizon America 5d	*	$2,500-3,000	$3,000-3,750
Sundance RS Turbo	*	4,250-5,250	5,250-6,000

* Purchase only in good or excellent condition

1990

A brand new Plymouth, called Laser, was one of a trio of cars built in a Chrysler-Mitsubishi joint ven-

1989 Plymouth Horizon America hatchback sedan

1990 Plymouth Laser "Twin Cam 16 Valve" coupe

1990 Plymouth Sundance RS Turbo 2.5 coupe

1931 Pontiac Six two-door sedan

1933 Pontiac Eight two-door sedan

1935 Pontiac Eight two-door trunkback sedan

ture plant in Bloomington, Illinois, called Diamond-Star. The 2+2 sport coupe was called "the first Plymouth of the 90s." Riding a shortened 97-inch-wheelbase Mitsubishi Galant chassis, the Laser had a lively 1.8-liter four as standard, and a 2.0-liter, 16-valve four optional on the upper RS model. With intercooling and turbocharging for the RS Turbo model, this engine delivered an impressive 190 horsepower. A five-speed stick was standard, four-speed automatic optional with all but the turbo engine. The Horizon now came with driver-side air bag and without the "America" part of its name. Sundance continued with minor changes.

	Restorable	Good	Excellent
Laser, std. & RS	*	$6,000-7,500	$7,500-9,000
Laser RS Turbo 3d	*	7,500-9,000	9,000-10,500
Horizon 5d sdn	*	3,000-4,000	4,000-4,750
Sundance RS Turbo	*	5,000-5,750	5,750-6,750

* Purchase only in good or excellent condition

Pontiac

A long running favorite from the early Silver Streaks to the GTO, Pontiac has a good enthusiast following and a host of models broadly representing the history of the American automobile over the past 50 years. Club support is excellent; parts supplies variable, though fairly good from the '60s onward; investment potential varies with model—see individual year notes.

1930-39

Introduced in 1926 as a companion to the Oakland (see entry), Pontiac quickly eclipsed the older make in popularity and replaced it entirely during the 1932 model year. Up to that time, the line was all six-cylinder (60-65 bhp); in mid-1932, the Oakland 85-bhp, 251-cid V-8 became a Pontiac—but it didn't sell. A smooth 77-bhp, 223.4-cid straight eight was introduced in 1933—and was the only engine offered. It was enlarged to 232.3 cid in 1936 and to 248.9 cid and 100 bhp in 1937, and would then remain basically unchanged through 1949. "Knee-Action" independent front suspension debuted in 1934. Pontiac dropped its 200-cid inline six for 1933-34, but brought it back in 1935 upgraded slightly to 208 cid and 80 bhp. Despite being the "junior" model, the six managed to look distinctly upmarket compared to the Chevrolet (also a six-cylinder car), which was the whole GM idea. A broader model line was introduced that year, and the six was enlarged to 222.7 cid (and 85 bhp) for 1937.

Pontiac styling followed industry trends. The 1930-32s were boxy, upright, and undistinguished; the 1933-34s were among the prettiest medium-price cars of their day. For 1935, Pontiac built all-steel "Turret Top" closed bodies (shared with Chevrolet) and introduced its distinctive "Silver Streak" trim (not shared with Chevrolet), the work of Pontiac styling director Franklin Q. Hershey. In 1937, Pontiac shifted from Chevrolet's A-body to a B-body shared with Oldsmobile, LaSalle, and the smaller Buicks.

The restyled '39s had three attractive series, starting with the 115-inch-wheelbase, six-cylinder Quality DeLuxe. A hybrid was the DeLuxe 120—using the 85-bhp six on the 120-inch DeLuxe Eight wheelbase—which was priced about $50 below the Eight. Both series shared the same body styles. The Quality DeLuxe, priced about $50 less than the 120, had only coupes, sedans, and a wagon. There were no engine changes this year: the L-head six was reliable and economical; the 100-bhp eight smoother, thirstier, but adequately powerful.

Pontiac production started the decade at 62,888 units, and increased to 84,708 the next year, only to fall to 45,340 in 1932. Fortunes then improved to 236,189 in 1937, the decade's high point. Pontiac closed out the decade by building 144,340 cars for 1939, 34,774 of them Eights.

	Restorable	Good	Excellent
1930-32 Six, open	$4,000-9,000	$9,000-15,000	$15,000-20,000
1930-32 Six coupes	1,500-4,000	4,000-6,500	6,500-9,000
1930-32 Six sedans	750-3,000	3,000-4,500	4,500-6,000
1932-33 Eight, open	5,000-10,000	10,000-17,500	17,500-25,000
1932 Eight coupes	2,500-5,000	5,000-9,000	9,000-12,500
1932 Eight sedans	1,500-4,500	4,500-7,000	7,000-10,000
1933-34 Eight, open	4,000-9,000	9,000-15,000	15,000-20,000
1933-34 Eight, clsd	1,500-4,000	4,000-6,000	6,000-8,500
1935-36 cabriolets	3,500-6,000	6,000-10,000	10,000-15,000
1935-39 coupes	1,500-4,500	4,500-6,500	6,500-9,000
1935-39 sedans	1,000-3,000	3,000-5,000	5,000-8,000
1937-39 wagons	3,000-7,500	7,500-12,500	12,500-17,500
1937-39 cvt cpes	4,000-9,500	9,500-15,000	15,000-22,500

1940

There were two models for each engine: six-cylinder Special and DeLuxe (117- and 120-inch wheelbase); eight-cylinder DeLuxe and Torpedo (120- and 122-inch wheelbase). Each offered coupes and sedans; also included were a Special business coupe and wagon, DeLuxe Six "cabriolet" convertible, and DeLuxe Eight cabriolet and business coupe. Pontiac engines were sturdy, smooth runners delivering modest performance with economy. Horsepower ratings this year were 87 for the six, 100 for the eight. Prices ranged from $783 to $1072. Production came in at 106,892 Specials, 58,452 DeLuxe Sixes, 20,433 DeLuxe Eights, 31,224 Torpedos.

	Restorable	Good	Excellent
Cabriolet cvt	$5,000-10,000	$10,000-17,500	$17,500-25,000
Special wagon	2,500-8,000	8,000-14,000	14,000-20,000
Other models	1,500-5,000	5,000-7,500	7,500-9,500

1936 Pontiac DeLuxe Silver Streak Six Cabriolet

1938 Pontiac DeLuxe Six two-door Touring Sedan

1939 Pontiac DeLuxe Six four-door Touring Sedan

1940 Pontiac Torpedo Eight four-door sedan

1940 Pontiac DeLuxe Six Cabriolet

1941 Pontiac Custom Torpedo Eight DeLuxe wagon

1941 Pontiac Custom Torpedo Eight sedan

1942 Pontiac Torpedo Eight four-door sedan

1946 Pontiac Streamliner Eight Sedan Coupe

1946 Pontiac Streamliner Eight four-door sedan

1941

In keeping with GM's corporate-wide redesign, Pontiac adopted higher, crisper fenders, which were embellished with additional Silver Streaks. A new body style was the fastback sedan. Six separate series were offered: DeLuxe, Streamliner, and Custom Torpedos, each with either six- or eight-cylinder power (now 90 and 103 bhp). As before, bodies were shared with other GM divisions. DeLuxe models (119-inch wheelbase) were based on the Chevrolet A-body, Streamliners (122-inch wheelbase) on the Buick/Olds B-body, and Customs (also 122 inches) on the Cadillac C-body. The DeLuxe Torpedo comprised the widest range of bodies, including a sleek convertible and a Metropolitan sedan with blind rear roof quarters. Of the 330,061 cars built for the model run, Custom Torpedos were by far the rarest: 8257 Sixes and 17,191 Eights.

	Restorable	Good	Excellent
Cabriolet cvt	$5,000-11,000	$11,000-18,500	$18,500-27,500
Cstm Torpedo wgns	2,500-9,000	9,000-16,000	16,000-22,500
Other models	1,500-5,000	5,000-7,500	7,500-9,500

1942

In the abbreviated '42 model year Pontiac built 83,555 cars, most of them in the closing months of 1941. Pontiac styling followed GM practice with long front fenders blending into the front doors, rounded drop-off rear fenders, and a gaudy grille. Considerable model shuffling occurred. The '42s comprised only the Torpedo on the 119-inch wheelbase and the Streamliner on the 122-inch span, each available as a Six or Eight. Streamliners came in standard or Chieftain trim, which added about $50 to the tab. It cost only $25 to opt for an Eight instead of a Six, yet production was split about evenly between the two.

	Restorable	Good	Excellent
Cabriolet cvt	$5,000-11,000	$11,000-18,500	$18,500-27,500
Streamliner wgns	2,500-9,000	9,000-16,000	16,000-22,500
Other models	1,500-5,000	5,000-7,500	7,500-9,500

1946

Unlike most manufacturers, Pontiac produced annual styling changes for the first three postwar years, despite the use of prewar bodies. The '46s, which were put into production in September 1945, had triple chrome fender strips and a massive, full-width grille composed of vertical and horizontal bars. There were four series: the 119-inch wheelbase Torpedo and 122-inch Streamliner, Six or Eight. The Chieftain sub-series was eliminated, but body styles were the same as in 1942. All models came only with three-speed manual transmissions. Despite materials shortages and strikes, production this year was 137,640 units, 70,066 of them Sixes.

	Restorable	Good	Excellent
Torpedo cvts	$4,000-10,000	$10,000-15,000	$15,000-22,500
Streamliner wgns	2,000-7,500	7,500-12,500	12,500-19,000
Other models	1,500-4,000	4,000-6,000	6,000-8,000

1947

The Pontiac grille carried only horizontal bars this year, while all body styles were repeated. Added to the Torpedo line was a new DeLuxe convertible. Sales of Pontiac Eights began to surpass sales of Sixes—121,139 to 109,461 this year—a trend that would eventually cause Pontiac to abandon the Six.

	Restorable	Good	Excellent
Torpedo cvts	$4,000-10,000	$10,000-15,000	$15,000-22,500
Streamliner wgns	2,000-7,500	7,500-12,500	12,500-19,000
Other models	1,500-4,000	4,000-6,000	6,000-8,000

1948

Vertical grille bars returned, and a small upper grille bar carried the Pontiac name. This was also the first Pontiac to bear the Silver Streak nameplate, although the term had been used earlier in reference to styling. Despite name and appearance changes, however, these cars were still prewar in design and engineering. They used the same engines, the same conventional ladder chassis, the same suspension. Inexplicably, the Eight was listed as 104 bhp instead of the usual 103—the only specification change since 1941. Hydra-Matic automatic transmission was added as an option, and it proved a good selling tool as 80 percent of the Pontiac Eights had it. Output crept up to 235,419 cars for the model run, 158,415 of them Eights.

	Restorable	Good	Excellent
Torpedo cvts	$4,000-10,000	$10,000-15,000	$15,000-22,500
Streamliner wgns	2,000-7,500	7,500-12,500	12,500-19,000
Other models	1,500-4,000	4,000-6,000	6,000-8,000

1949

Pontiac restyled this year around a new, 120 inch-wheelbase chassis. The models were Silver Streak Six and Eight, offered as Streamliners and Chieftains, the first with fastback sedans (and for some strange reason, wagons), the second with notchback sedans, coupe, and the convertible. All came in regular or DeLuxe trim, though the ragtop was a DeLuxe only. DeLuxe added bodyside chrome trim, stainless steel rear fender gravel guards, and more bright trim around the windows. All of this resulted in a confusing 24-model lineup. Engines remained unchanged, but an optional high-compression head boosted output to 93 bhp for the Six and 106 for the Eight. Clean, attractive styling made the cars look lighter than the '48s, though they actually weighed more. Despite their historic importance as Pontiac's first true postwar cars, these models do not carry the values of 1946-48, and the woody wagons especially are very good buys (even though they didn't have nearly as much wood)—it's hard to find a top-condition woody wagon for less.

1947 Pontiac Streamliner Eight Sedan Coupe

1948 Pontiac Torpedo Eight Sedan Coupe

1949 Pontiac Streamliner Six DeLuxe sedan

1949 Pontiac Chieftain Eight DeLuxe sedan

1950 Pontiac Streamliner Eight DeLuxe sedan

1950 Pontiac Chieftain Eight Super Catalina

1951 Pontiac Chieftain Eight DeLuxe Catalina

1952 Pontiac Chieftain Eight DeLuxe convertible

Production increased to 304,819 units, 235,165 of them Eights. When shopping look for the DeLuxe versions—they're much richer looking.

	Restorable	Good	Excellent
Chieftain DeL cvt	$3,000-8,000	$8,000-13,500	$13,500-19,000
Streamliner wagon	2,000-6,500	6,500-10,000	10,000-15,000
Other models	1,500-3,000	3,000-5,000	5,000-7,000

1950

Pontiac's first "hardtop convertible," the Catalina, was introduced in four flavors: Chieftain Six and Eight in DeLuxe and Super guise. All told, about 42,000 hardtops were built this year. Sedans, coupes, all-steel wagons, convertibles, and two- and four-door fastbacks were still in the lineup, but the woody wagon had vanished during the 1949 model year. Styling was a mild facelift on 1949, notable for a toothier grille. Fastbacks were unpopular in their day and are not plentiful, but are definitely in demand among collectors—though they cost no more than notchback sedans. Output soared to 466,429 units, fueled by fears of a possible halt in auto production due to the military actions then current in Korea.

	Restorable	Good	Excellent
Chieftain DeL cvt	$3,000-8,000	$8,000-13,500	$13,500-19,000
Catalina hardtops	2,000-5,000	5,000-8,000	8,000-11,000
Streamliner wagons	2,000-3,500	3,500-6,000	6,000-9,000
Other models	1,500-3,000	3,000-5,000	5,000-7,000

1951

Only one fastback was left in the line—the Streamliner two-door—and it was dropped by spring 1951. Other models were little changed, save for a new "V" grille motif and revised chrome spears on the bodysides of DeLuxe models. Super DeLuxe Catalina hardtops featured Sapphire Blue and Malibu Ivory paint jobs (either color on top), and leather upholstery was optional, making these models particularly luxurious. Horsepower was up to 102 for the Six, 122 for the Eight. Pontiac had the second best production year in its history—370,159 units—but the success was largely due to the Eights, which now outsold the Sixes by about six to one.

	Restorable	Good	Excellent
Chieftain DeL cvts	$3,000-8,000	$8,000-13,500	$13,500-19,000
Catalina hardtops	2,000-5,000	5,000-8,000	8,000-11,000
Streamliner wagons	2,000-3,500	3,500-6,000	6,000-9,000
Other models	1,500-3,000	3,000-5,000	5,000-7,000

1952

The coupe body was dropped, reducing both Six and Eight to sedans, four-door wagons, convertibles, and Catalina hardtops. Within each line, now simply Chieftain Six and Chieftain Eight, remained three separate trim levels: standard, DeLuxe, and Super Deluxe, which are important only to Pontiac fans—condition is the key factor in determining values. This was the last year for the 1949 body, which was dolled up with a revised grille and more ornate side trim for DeLuxe models. Korean War restrictions and a nationwide steel strike slowed production to 271,272, so these cars are scarcer than the '51s. Again, Eights outsold Sixes by a wide margin—this time, about thirteen to one.

	Restorable	Good	Excellent
Chieftain DeL cvt	$3,000-8,000	$8,000-13,500	$13,500-19,000
Catalina hardtops	2,000-5,000	5,000-8,000	8,000-11,000
Chieftain wagons	2,000-3,500	3,500-6,000	6,000-9,000
Other models	1,500-3,000	3,000-5,000	5,000-7,000

1953

These models bore a distinct resemblance to the 1949-52s, but they now rode a 122-inch wheelbase and were a bit larger in most dimensions. New features were highlighted by a kicked-up rear fender line, a lower and more streamlined grille, upright-winged "chief" hood ornament, and one-piece windshield. Mechanical improvements included optional power steering and a lower axle ratio for Hydra-Matic models, giving them smooth top-end performance. About 18,500 Pontiacs were fitted with Chevy Powerglide automatics because of a major fire at the Hydra-Matic plant. Catalina hardtops, now with reverse-slant C-pillars, were growing in popularity; 1953 saw about 76,000 produced versus about 53,000 in '52. Total production increased to 418,619.

	Restorable	Good	Excellent
Chieftain DeL cvt	$3,500-9,000	$9,000-15,000	$15,000-22,500
Catalina hardtops	2,000-5,500	5,500-9,000	9,000-12,000
Chieftain wagons	2,000-3,500	3,500-6,000	6,000-9,000
Other models	1,500-3,000	3,000-5,000	5,000-7,000

1954

A smart facelift saw a narrow scoop-type grille bar (much beloved by customizers) and smoother side moldings. The new top series was the eight-cylinder Star Chief. Riding a 124-inch wheelbase, it was available in DeLuxe or Custom sedan trim, or as a DeLuxe convertible or Custom Catalina hardtop. In the final year of Pontiac's long-running straight eight, the 268.4-cid mill produced 127 bhp when fitted with Hydra-Matic, 122 with manual. Of the 287,744 '54s built, only about 23,000 were Sixes—the last of their breed. The convertible body was available only as a Star Chief, while Catalina hardtops were available in all three series.

	Restorable	Good	Excellent
Star Chief cvt	$4,000-10,000	$10,000-17,500	$17,500-25,000
Catalina hardtops	2,500-6,000	6,000-9,500	9,500-12,500
Station wagons	2,000-4,000	4,000-6,500	6,500-10,000
Other models	1,500-3,000	3,000-5,000	5,000-8,000

1952 Pontiac Chieftain Eight DeLuxe wagon

1953 Pontiac Chieftain Eight DeLuxe convertible

1954 Pontiac Star Chief Custom Catalina hardtop

1954 Pontiac Star Chief Custom four-door sedan

1955 Pontiac Star Chief convertible coupe

1955 Pontiac Star Chief Custom Safari wagon

1955 Pontiac Star Chief Custom Catalina hardtop

1956 Pontiac Star Chief DeLuxe convertible

1957 Pontiac Star Chief convertible coupe

1955

Strato-Streak, Pontiac's new oversquare 287.2-cid V-8, produced 173 bhp with manual transmission, 180 with Hydra-Matic, and 200 with optional four-barrel carburetor. The new V-8 was the standard—and only—engine for '55. Pontiac also claimed 109 other new features, including all-new styling and an improved chassis (on the same wheelbases), which nevertheless rode very hard compared to the competition. A wraparound windshield, cowl ventilation, new colors and bodyside two-toning, hydraulic lifters, tubeless tires, and a 12-volt electrical system were sales points. The Star Chief line included an exotic new hardtop-styled Safari two-door wagon based on the Chevy Nomad, but only 3760 were built. Still, it was a very good year, with record production of 553,808 cars that has left numerous survivors for modern-day enthusiasts. Star Chief convertibles numbered 19,762, and among Catalina hardtops there were 99,629 Star Chiefs and 72,608 Chieftain 870s.

	Restorable	Good	Excellent
Star Chief cvt	$5,000-12,000	$12,000-20,000	$20,000-29,000
Catalina hardtops	3,000-7,000	7,000-11,000	11,000-14,500
Safari wagon	4,000-8,000	8,000-12,000	12,000-16,500
Other models	1,500-3,000	3,000-5,000	5,000-8,000

1956

A mild facelift and the addition of four-door hardtops marked the '56 models. Four-door hardtops have never caught on with collectors; they are worth only about $1000 more than a sedan of the same model in comparable condition. Most notable styling changes were a new grille and front bumper that protruded further than that on the "flat-nosed" '55 and revised bodyside two-toning. The V-8 grew to 316.6 cid, and horsepower jumped to 205 with two-barrel carb (standard on Chieftains), 227 with four-barrel (standard on Star Chiefs, optional on Chieftains). The relatively hard ride continued to earn criticism. Production was down to 405,429, which included the following Star Chiefs: 13,510 ragtops, 43,392 Catalina two-doors, and just 4042 Safari wagons. The two Chieftain series added another 71,079 two-door hardtops, and 108,608 four-door hardtops were produced in all three series.

	Restorable	Good	Excellent
Star Chief cvt	$5,000-12,000	$12,000-20,000	$20,000-27,000
Catalina 2d htps	3,000-7,000	7,000-11,000	11,000-14,500
Catalina 4d htps	1,500-3,500	3,500-6,000	6,000-9,000
Safari wagon	4,000-8,000	8,000-12,000	12,000-16,500
Other models	1,500-3,000	3,000-5,000	5,000-8,000

1957

Bunky Knudsen took over as Pontiac general manager in July of 1956 and ushered in Pontiac's age of high performance with the specially trimmed '57 Bonneville convertible. With fuel injection, racing cam, and dual exhausts, it produced 310 horsepower. It was faster yet with optional Tri-Power (three two-barrel carbs). The Bonneville's $5782 price kept sales down to only 630, and it remains hotly sought after today. Another interesting model was the Custom Safari four-door wagon later known as the Transcontinental. It had unique side trim and deluxe fittings; 1894 were built. Though the '57 Pontiacs were essentially facelifted '56s, they looked quite different and boasted many new features: an enlarged 347-cid V-8 with 227-290 bhp; longer rear springs mounted on rubber shackles to improve the ride; smaller 14-inch tires; foot pedal parking brake; and an optional automatic antenna. Notably, the famed Silver Streaks disappeared. The model hierarchy was now Chieftain, Super Chief, Star Chief, and limited-production Bonneville. Output was down to 333,473, and most models of interest were too: 1292 Custom Safaris, 12,789 Star Chief soft tops, and 32,862 Custom Catalina hardtop coupes.

	Restorable	Good	Excellent
Bonneville cvt	$12,500-30,000	$30,000-45,000	$45,000-75,000
Star Chief cvt	5,000-12,000	12,000-20,000	20,000-27,000
Catalina 2d htps	3,000-7,000	7,000-11,000	11,000-15,000
Catalina 4d htps	1,500-3,500	3,500-6,000	6,000-9,000
Safari 2d wagon	4,000-8,000	8,000-12,000	12,000-16,500
Other models	1,500-3,000	3,000-5,000	5,000-8,000

1957 Pontiac Bonneville convertible coupe

1957 Pontiac Star Chief Custom Safari wagon

1958

An all-new body arrived, but so did a recession, holding production to 216,982. Yet this was a well-styled Pontiac, with a handsome, full-width grille, quad headlamps, and concave side spear. Bodies were lower, longer, and wider. The V-8 grew to 370 cid, offering 240-310 bhp, and fuel injection was still offered. At mid-year, two high-compression "Super-Tempest" 395-A mills were offered: a four-barrel version with 315 bhp, and a Tri-Power version with 330. Air suspension was a new (and troublesome) option. Seven Catalina hardtops were offered with two or four doors. Bonneville was still a limited-edition series, but not nearly as limited as before; 3069 ragtops were sold, as well as 9144 of the newly offered hardtop coupes. The other Pontiac convertible was moved to the Chieftain series to separate it adequately from the Bonneville; 7359 were sold. The Safari name was still used, now on run-of-the-mill four-door wagons.

	Restorable	Good	Excellent
Bonneville cvt	$8,000-15,000	$15,000-27,000	$27,000-38,000
Bonneville 2d htp	5,000-12,000	12,000-20,000	20,000-28,000
(add 25% for Bonnevilles with fuel injection)			
Chieftain cvt	3,000-9,000	9,000-15,000	15,000-22,500
Catalina 2d htps	2,000-5,000	5,000-8,000	8,000-11,000
Other models	1,500-3,000	3,000-5,000	5,000-8,000

1958 Pontiac Bonneville Custom convertible

1958 Pontiac Bonneville Custom hardtop coupe

1959

Pontiac now shared inner body panels with Chevy, Buick, and Olds, and built some of the best looking cars of the bunch. Pontiac was named "Car of the Year" by *Motor Trend* magazine for its engineering, high style, and performance. The first of the

1959 Pontiac Star Chief Vista hardtop sedan

1959 Pontiac Bonneville convertible coupe

1960 Pontiac Bonneville convertible coupe

1960 Pontiac Bonneville Custom Safari wagon

1961 Pontiac Bonneville convertible coupe

1961 Pontiac Ventura Sport Coupe hardtop

famous split grilles appeared, along with modest twin-fin rear fenders and minimal side trim, plus a new "Wide-Track" chassis. The V-8 went up to 389 cid and provided up to 315 bhp with Tri-Power (345 on the Tempest 420-A racing engine with Tri-Power). A new economy-tuned version of the 389 produced 215 bhp. The old Chieftain and Super Chief names were replaced by the Catalina, built on the 122-inch wheelbase, while the Star Chief and Bonneville shared a 124-inch wheelbase (save for Bonneville Custom Safari wagons, which rode the shorter chassis). Bonneville was no longer a limited-production model; in fact, it sold in greater numbers than the less-expensive Star Chief. With 382,940 cars built, Pontiac moved from sixth to fourth place. Ragtops numbered 11,426 Bonnevilles and 14,515 Catalinas.

	Restorable	Good	Excellent
Bonneville cvt	$7,000-14,000	$14,000-21,000	$21,000-28,000
Bonneville 2d htp	3,000-6,000	6,000-9,000	9,000-12,000
Bonneville 4d htp	1,500-3,000	3,000-6,000	6,000-9,000
Catalina cvt	4,000-9,000	9,000-17,500	17,500-22,500
Catalina 2d htp	1,500-3,000	3,000-6,000	6,000-9,000
Other models	1,500-3,000	3,000-5,000	5,000-8,000

(add 15% for Tri-Power V-8)

1960

Styling was altered for 1960, but dimensions remained about the same as in '59. The model line now consisted of Catalina, Ventura, Star Chief, and Bonneville—all smooth, airy-looking designs with broad expanses of glass and lots of body sculpturing. The split grille was dropped, but would return in 1961. Ratings for the 389 V-8 rose slightly, ranging from 215 to 348 bhp. Performance enthusiasts appreciated the newly optional four-speed manual transmission (available on special order only), though installations—whether three- or four-speed—were few. Production edged up to 396,179 units, including 17,062 Bonneville and 17,172 Catalina ragtops.

	Restorable	Good	Excellent
Bonneville cvt	$7,000-14,000	$14,000-21,000	$21,000-28,000
Catalina cvt	4,000-9,000	9,000-17,500	17,500-22,500
2d hardtops	1,500-3,500	3,500-8,000	8,000-11,000
4d hardtops	1,500-3,000	3,000-6,000	6,000-9,000
Other models	1,500-3,000	3,000-5,000	5,000-8,000

(add 15% for Tri-Power V-8)

1961

Pontiac's compact Tempest was an innovative car with a radical flexible driveshaft, rear-mounted transaxle, and independent link-type rear suspension. But it was a squirrely handler, so collectors should be as careful with 1961-63 Tempests in the rain today as their owners had to be back then. Sedans and wagons were introduced first; a pair of sport coupes (one boasting custom Le Mans trim) came later in the year. The standard 194.5-cid inline four was actually half of a 389-cid V-8, offered in power ratings from 110 to 155 bhp. Optional was a Buick-built 215 aluminum V-8 with 155 bhp. Sport coupe production totaled 14,887, about half of which had the custom trim. The full-size line was nicely redone, cleaner from the side, and comprised the same four series as 1960. Size and weight decreased somewhat; Catalina, Ventura, and Safari wagons rode a shorter 119-inch wheelbase, while Star Chief and Bonneville dropped an inch to 123. The new bodies were lower (by an inch), shorter (by four inches), and narrower (2½ inches). Track width decreased by 1½ inches, but the cars remained "Wide-Tracks." Curb weights dropped by nearly 200 pounds on some models. The 389 V-8 offered the same wide range of power ratings as the year before, though a "Super-Duty" 363-bhp version now topped the list. Late in the year, a small number of 421-cid "Super Duty" V-8s with 373 bhp were made available. Needless to say, a light Catalina (about 3700 pounds) motivated by 421 cubic inches of V-8 could be one mean machine.

	Restorable	Good	Excellent
Tempest	$1,000-2,500	$2,500-3,500	$3,500-5,000
Catalina cvt	3,000-6,000	6,000-9,000	9,000-13,500
Bonneville cvt	4,000-9,000	9,000-13,000	13,000-17,500
Other models	1,500-3,000	3,000-5,000	5,000-9,000

(add 15% for Super Duty V-8, 10% for Tri-Power)

1962

A Tempest convertible body style was added in deluxe and Le Mans versions, the top four-cylinder engine now produced 166 bhp, and the optional 215-cid aluminum V-8 added a 185-bhp version. With 20,635 ordered, 15,559 of them Le Mans, the ragtop was quite popular. For the Catalina coupe, Pontiac boosted the 421 to 405 bhp. Indications are that about 1500 cars were so equipped. For drag racing, Pontiac installed the 421 in special Super Duty Catalinas lightened with aluminum body panels, plastic side windows, and drilled-out frames—these dragsters are worth a fortune today. The Ventura's place was taken by the bucket-seated, limited-edition Grand Prix, an elegant hardtop coupe with crisp styling and svelte good looks; 30,195 were sold. Big convertibles this year numbered 16,877 Catalinas and 21,582 Bonnevilles. With 521,437 cars built, Pontiac found itself in third place.

	Restorable	Good	Excellent
Tempest cvt	$2,000-4,000	$4,000-7,000	$7,000-10,000
Tempest, other	1,000-3,000	3,000-4,000	4,000-6,000
Catalina cvt	3,000-6,000	6,000-9,000	9,000-12,500
Catalina Super Duty	12,500-27,500	27,500-45,000	45,000-75,000
Bonneville cvt	4,000-9,000	9,000-12,000	12,000-16,500
Grand Prix 2d htp	2,000-5,000	5,000-7,500	7,500-10,000
Other models	1,500-3,000	3,000-5,000	5,000-9,000

(add 15% for Super Duty V-8, 10% for Tri-Power)

1963

Full-size Pontiacs were redesigned this year with cleaner, squarer lines and narrow, split grilles framed by vertical headlights. A 421 HO (High Output) with up to 370 bhp was optional on Star Chief and Bonneville, while Catalinas could be or-

1961 Pontiac Tempest Sport Coupe

1962 Pontiac Tempest Le Mans convertible

1962 Pontiac Grand Prix hardtop coupe

1963 Pontiac Bonneville convertible coupe

1963 Pontiac Grand Prix hardtop coupe

1963 Pontiac Tempest Le Mans convertible coupe

1964 Pontiac Bonneville convertible coupe

1964 Pontiac Grand Prix hardtop coupe

1964 Pontiac Tempest GTO two-door coupe

1965 Pontiac Tempest Le Mans GTO convertible

dered with a 410-bhp Super Duty mill. The elegant Grand Prix hardtop, based on the smaller Catalina, wore a distinctive roofline with a concave backlight (shared only with the Olds Starfire)—a styling treatment that would be carried on through 1968. Sales took off, to 72,959. Tempest and its sporting Le Mans derivative gained more conventional, squared-off styling. A new 326 V-8 with 260 bhp was offered, and Le Mans became a separate series, with a bucket-seat coupe and convertible (45,701 and 15,957 built).

	Restorable	Good	Excellent
Tempest/ Le Mans cvt	$2,000-4,000	$4,000-7,000	$7,000-10,000
Tempest, other	1,000-3,000	3,000-4,000	4,000-6,000
Catalina cvt	3,000-6,000	6,000-9,000	9,000-12,500
Catalina Super Duty	12,500-27,500	27,500-45,000	45,000-75,000
Bonneville cvt	4,000-9,000	9,000-12,000	12,000-16,500
Grand Prix 2d htp	2,000-5,000	5,000-7,500	7,500-10,000
Other models	1,500-3,000	3,000-5,000	5,000-9,000

(add 25% for 421 High Output V-8, 10% for Tri-Power)

1964

For 1964, Pontiac lengthened the Tempest wheelbase to 115 inches and applied a new body with taut, geometric lines. This led to the GTO, the progenitor muscle car, a mid-year package boasting a 325-bhp 389 engine, three-speed floorshift, quick steering, stiff shocks, dual exhausts, and premium tires. Production for '64 reached a surprising 32,450 units, including 6644 convertibles. Any GTO is both quick and desirable; those with the optional 348-bhp Tri-Power engine even more so. Other optional equipment included four-speed gearbox, metallic brake linings, heavy-duty radiator, and limited-slip differential. Full-size Pontiacs were little changed, though Super Duty engines were no longer offered. Convertible sales this year were 22,016 Bonnevilles and 18,693 Catalinas. Total production was now up to 738,317 units.

	Restorable	Good	Excellent
Tempest/ Le Mans cvt	$2,000-5,000	$5,000-8,000	$8,000-11,000
GTO 2d coupe	2,000-6,000	6,000-9,000	9,000-13,000
GTO 2d hardtop	2,500-7,000	7,000-11,000	11,000-15,500
GTO convertible	3,500-8,000	8,000-13,500	13,500-20,000
Tempest, other	1,000-3,000	3,000-4,000	4,000-6,000
Catalina cvt	3,000-6,000	6,000-9,000	9,000-12,500
Bonneville cvt	4,000-9,000	9,000-12,000	12,000-16,500
Grand Prix 2d htp	2,000-5,000	5,000-7,500	7,500-10,000
Other models	1,500-3,000	3,000-5,000	5,000-9,000

(add 25% for 421 High Output V-8, 10% for Tri-Power)

1965

The Tempest, Le Mans, and GTO gained vertical headlights in 1965, but otherwise were little changed. GTO's 389 now came standard with 335 bhp; 360 with Tri-Power. Rumor has it that a few GTOs received 421-cid engines. Production jumped to 75,352, including 11,311 ragtops. Tempest convertibles numbered 8346 Customs and 13,897 Le Mans. Full-size cars were redesigned with bulging "Coke bottle" rear fenders and more rakish rooflines.

Catalina coupes and convertibles offered a sporty 2+2 option package that included a 338-bhp 421 V-8. All full-size models could be ordered with a 421 with up to 376 bhp.

	Restorable	Good	Excellent
Tempest/LeM cvt	$2,000-5,000	$5,000-8,000	$8,000-11,000
GTO 2d coupe	2,000-6,000	6,000-9,000	9,000-13,000
GTO 2d hardtop	2,500-7,000	7,000-11,000	11,000-15,500
GTO convertible	3,500-8,000	8,000-13,500	13,500-20,000
Tempest, other	1,000-3,000	3,000-4,000	4,000-6,000
Catalina cvt	3,000-5,000	5,000-7,000	7,000-11,000
Bonneville cvt	4,000-7,500	7,500-9,500	9,500-13,500
Grand Prix 2d htp	2,000-5,000	5,000-7,500	7,500-10,000
Other models	1,500-3,000	3,000-5,000	5,000-8,000

(add 25% for 421 High Output V-8, 10% for Tri-Power)

1965 Pontiac Grand Prix hardtop coupe

1965 Pontiac Catalina 2+2 421 hardtop coupe

1966

Pontiac's mid-size cars received curvier styling similar to what its big cars got the year before. The Pontiac Sprint, with a 230-cid overhead-cam six developing up to 207 bhp, was the first six-cylinder performance engine since the Hudson Hornet. Though not in league with the GTO, a Tempest/Le Mans with the Sprint engine was a satisfying car to drive, delivering 0-60 times in the 10-second range. But Tempest bodies grew bulky in 1968, so this model and the '67s, with their crisp styling and vertical headlights, are the ones to look for. Full-size styling was toned down a bit from '65, but there were few other changes. Sales of the sporty Catalina 2+2 hardtop and ragtop reached 6383. Pontiac built 830,778 cars for the model run, among them the following convertibles: 16,299 Bonnevilles, 14,837 Catalinas, 12,798 GTOs, 13,080 Tempest Le Mans, and 5557 Tempest Customs.

1966 Pontiac Tempest GTO convertible coupe

	Restorable	Good	Excellent
Tempest/LeM cvt	$2,000-5,000	$5,000-8,000	$8,000-11,000
GTO 2d coupe	2,000-6,000	6,000-9,000	9,000-13,000
GTO 2d hardtop	2,500-7,000	7,000-11,000	11,000-15,500
GTO convertible	3,500-8,000	8,000-13,500	13,500-18,500
Tempest, other	1,000-3,000	3,000-4,000	4,000-6,000
Catalina cvt	3,000-5,000	5,000-7,000	7,000-11,000
2 + 2 convertible	3,000-6,000	6,000-9,500	9,500-13,500
2 + 2 2d hardtop	2,000-4,000	4,000-6,000	6,000-8,000
Bonneville cvt	4,000-7,500	7,500-9,500	9,500-13,500
Grand Prix 2d htp	2,000-5,000	5,000-7,500	7,500-10,000
Other models	1,500-3,000	3,000-5,000	5,000-7,000

(add 25% for 421 High Output V-8, 10% for Tempest/Le Mans 326 V-8)

1966 Pontiac Grand Prix hardtop coupe

1967

Pontiac's Firebird, a ponycar based on the Chevy Camaro, had its own unique styling with the now-traditional divided grille, and an optional 400-cid V-8 could be ordered in place of a 326-cid V-8 or the Sprint Six. A convertible and coupe were offered; 67,032 and 15,528 were built. Tempest, Le Mans, and GTO carried on with few changes; the last sold 81,722 copies, of which 12,798 were convertibles. Rear fenders and bumpers were restyled in 1967 on the big Pontiacs, and vertical headlights were mounted so that the lower pair was contained in the split grille, the upper pair above it. The Grand Prix, whose sales were falling, got hidden headlights, and a convertible version was added. It would last but

1967 Pontiac Firebird hardtop coupe

1967 Pontiac Catalina 2+2 428 hardtop coupe

1967 Pontiac Grand Prix convertible coupe

1967 Pontiac Tempest GTO hardtop coupe

1968 Pontiac Tempest GTO hardtop coupe

1968 Pontiac Bonneville hardtop coupe

one year, and only 5856 built, making a '67 GP ragtop a rare collector's item today. The venerable 389 was bored to 400 cid, but power ratings remained about the same. The 421 was similarly enlarged to 428 cid, but again, there was little change in the horsepower ratings; the top offerings produced 360 and 376 horsepower, respectively.

	Restorable	Good	Excellent
Firebird htp cpe	$2,000-4,000	$4,000-5,500	$5,500-7,500
Firebird cvt	3,000-6,000	6,000-8,000	8,000-10,000
Tempest/LeM cvt	2,000-5,000	5,000-8,000	8,000-11,000
GTO 2d coupe	2,000-6,000	6,000-9,000	9,000-13,000
GTO 2d hardtop	2,500-7,000	7,000-11,000	11,000-15,500
GTO convertible	3,500-8,000	8,000-13,500	13,500-18,500
Tempest, other	1,000-3,000	3,000-4,000	4,000-6,000
Catalina cvt	3,000-5,000	5,000-7,000	7,000-11,000
Bonneville cvt	4,000-7,500	7,500-9,500	9,500-13,500
Grand Prix cvt	5,000-7,500	7,500-10,000	10,000-14,000
Grand Prix 2d htp	2,000-4,000	4,000-6,000	6,000-8,000
Other models	1,500-3,000	3,000-5,000	5,000-7,000

(V-8s: add 25% for 421 High Output, 20% for 400 Ram-Air, 10% for 400)

1968

Pontiac acquired the new GM intermediate body, which featured sloping rear roof pillars that flowed into the rear fenders. Front ends on Pontiac's versions had horizontal headlights surrounded by a split grille with protruding center snout. Wheelbases measured 112 for two-doors, 116 for four-doors. The Pontiac GTO, now sold only as a hardtop or convertible, came standard with a 400-cid V-8 developing 350 bhp; a Ram Air hood scoop added 10 more. GTO's appearance differed from the Tempest/Le Mans in that it carried a body-colored Endura rubber energy-absorbing front bumper. The successful redesign netted a total 87,684 GTO sales (9980 of them ragtops), the highest it had ever been—and the highest it would ever be. Conversely, Grand Prix sales were the lowest since debut '62—just 31,711. Big Pontiacs carried a frontal styling theme similar to the mid-size cars, but had horizontal taillights that drooped down into the bumper at the outer edges. Firebirds continued with few changes; convertibles numbered 16,960. Total Pontiac output moved up to 910,482, way ahead of fourth-place Plymouth.

	Restorable	Good	Excellent
Firebird htp cpe	$2,000-4,000	$4,000-5,500	$5,500-7,500
Firebird cvt	3,000-6,000	6,000-8,000	8,000-10,000
Tempest/LeM cvt	1,500-4,000	4,000-6,000	6,000-8,500
GTO 2d hardtop	2,500-6,000	6,000-9,000	9,000-12,500
GTO convertible	3,500-8,000	8,000-13,500	13,500-18,500
Tempest, other	1,000-3,000	3,000-4,000	4,000-6,000
Catalina cvt	2,000-4,000	4,000-6,000	6,000-8,000
Bonneville cvt	3,000-6,000	6,000-8,000	8,000-10,000
Grand Prix 2d htp	2,000-4,000	4,000-6,000	6,000-8,000
Other models	1,500-3,000	3,000-5,000	5,000-7,000

(V-8s: add 25% for 421 High Output, 20% for 400 Ram-Air, 10% for 400)

1969

Biggest news this year was the introduction of the redesigned "downsized" Grand Prix. With its long hood/short deck proportions and sleek styling, sales of the 118-inch-wheelbase Grand Prix were revitalized to the tune of 112,486—a phenomenal improvement. Intermediates wore a mild facelift, and GTO added "The Judge," with a 366-bhp Ram-Air V-8 and three-speed manual gearbox with Hurst shifter. Of the 64,851 GTO hardtops and 7436 ragtops, only a small number were Judges. The Judge's engine was standard in the new Pontiac Trans-Am high-performance coupe, a splendid American sporting car, but one that saw very limited production: only 689 coupes and a mere eight convertibles. Firebirds were reskinned with "eyebrow" creases above the wheelwells and a separate grille flanked by horizontal headlights. Large Pontiacs got a mild facelift. Convertibles sales were waning now: 5438 Bonnevilles, 5436 Catalinas, 5676 Tempest Le Mans, 2379 Tempest Customs, 11,649 Firebirds.

	Restorable	Good	Excellent
Firebird htp cpe	$2,000-4,000	$4,000-5,500	$5,500-7,500
Firebird cvt	3,000-6,000	6,000-8,000	8,000-10,000
Trans Am htp cpe	3,500-7,500	7,500-11,000	11,000-15,000
Trans Am cvt	8,000-15,000	15,000-20,000	20,000-30,000
Tempest/LeM cvt	1,500-4,000	4,000-6,000	6,000-8,000
GTO 2d hardtop	2,500-6,000	6,000-9,000	9,000-12,500
GTO convertible	3,500-8,000	8,000-13,500	13,500-18,500
GTO Judge 2d htp	3,000-7,500	7,500-11,000	11,000-16,500
GTO Judge cvt	10,000-17,500	17,500-27,500	27,500-35,000
Catalina cvt	2,000-3,500	3,500-5,500	5,500-7,500
Bonneville cvt	3,000-5,000	5,000-7,000	7,000-9,000
Grand Prix 2d htp	1,500-3,000	3,000-5,000	5,000-7,000
Other models	1,500-3,000	3,000-5,000	5,000-6,000

(V-8s: add 25% for Ram-Air IV, 15% for 400 Ram-Air III)

1970

Firebird's second generation model was a mid-year arrival: a sleek coupe designed under the direction of Bill Mitchell, offered in base, sporty Formula 400, luxury Esprit, and muscular Trans Am—the last with a standard a 345-horse 400 V-8. Production was 18,874 base coupes, 18,961 Esprits, 7708 Formula 400s, and 3196 Trans Ams. The '70 Tempest, GTO, Le Mans, and Le Mans Sport had revised styling that carried a similar profile, but featured new front and rear designs along with creased wheelwell "eyebrows" like the '69 Firebird. A new, emissions-control-designed 455 V-8 became the top engine option, producing up to 370 bhp in full-size cars and Grand Prix, 360 in the GTO. GTOs numbered 36,366 hardtops and 3783 ragtops (3629 and 168 Judges). Among Grand Prix models, look for the SJ—which came standard with the 455 engine and was sometimes called SSJ—with Hurst shifter, definitely worth a premium over run-of-the-mill GPs. GP sales were down dramatically in 1970, to 65,750. Full-size models received a facelift with a prominent vertical grille. Convertibles continued their downward spiral as just 3537 Bonnevilles and 3783 Catalinas were built. From this year onward, avoid Pontiacs not specifically listed in the price guide.

	Restorable	Good	Excellent
Firebird std/ Esprit	$1,000-2,500	$2,500-4,000	$4,000-6,000

1969 Pontiac Tempest GTO Ram Air IV hardtop

1969 Pontiac Grand Prix hardtop coupe

1969 Pontiac Firebird Trans Am hardtop coupe

1970 Pontiac Firebird Formula 400 hardtop coupe

1970 Pontiac Grand Prix SJ hardtop coupe

1970 Pontiac GTO "The Judge" hardtop coupe

	Restorable	Good	Excellent
Firebird Formula 400	2,000-4,000	4,000-6,000	6,000-9,000
Firebird Trans Am	3,000-6,000	6,000-9,000	9,000-12,500
Le Mans convertible	1,500-4,000	4,000-6,000	6,000-8,000
GTO 2d hardtop	2,500-6,000	6,000-9,000	9,000-12,500
GTO convertible	3,500-8,000	8,000-13,500	13,500-18,500
GTO Judge 2d htp	3,000-7,500	7,500-11,000	11,000-16,500
GTO Judge cvt	10,000-17,500	17,500-27,500	27,500-35,000
Catalina cvt	2,000-3,500	3,500-5,500	5,500-7,500
Bonneville cvt	3,000-5,000	5,000-7,000	7,000-9,000
Grand Prix SSJ	2,500-5,000	5,000-7,000	7,000-9,000
Grand Prix 2d htp	1,500-3,000	3,000-5,000	5,000-7,000

(V-8s: add 25% for Ram-Air IV, 15% for 400 Ram-Air III)

1970 Pontiac Le Mans GTO hardtop coupe

1971

Pontiac's last truly huge convertible, the Grand Ville, replaced the Bonneville this year. Riding the Bonney's 126-inch wheelbase, it was powered by the huge 455 V-8 with 325 bhp and sold for $4706 base. Production was low—only 1789 for 1971—so this is a car to look for through 1975 when the last were produced. Catalina convertibles were also offered, but they didn't fare much better: just 2036. The 455 V-8 with 335 bhp was standard equipment on the GTO Judge this year, and Judge values hold up even for this relatively late vintage, partly because only 357 hardtops and 17 ragtops were sold. Even the GTO was down to 9497 hardtops and 661 ragtops. The Judge's 455 engine was offered in the Firebird as well, and Trans Am models, of which 2116 were produced, remain in demand. Grand Prix got a facelift with single headlights, but little else changed except that output was down to 58,325. At the other end of the range, because Pontiac had nothing smaller than the intermediate Le Mans, it added a version of the compact Chevy Nova called Ventura II: a notably uncollectible model.

1971 Pontiac Le Mans GTO convertible coupe

	Restorable	Good	Excellent
Firebird std & Esprit	$1,000-2,500	$2,500-4,000	$4,000-6,000
Firebird Formula 400	2,000-4,000	4,000-6,000	6,000-9,000
Firebird Trans Am	3,000-6,000	6,000-9,000	9,000-12,500
Le Mans cvt	1,500-4,000	4,000-6,000	6,000-8,000
GTO 2d hardtop	2,500-6,000	6,000-9,000	9,000-12,500
GTO convertible	3,500-8,000	8,000-13,500	13,500-18,500
GTO Judge 2d htp	3,000-7,500	7,500-11,000	11,000-16,500
GTO Judge cvt	10,000-17,500	17,500-27,500	27,500-35,000
Catalina cvt	2,500-4,000	4,000-6,000	6,000-8,000
Grand Ville cvt	3,000-5,000	5,000-7,000	7,000-9,000
Grand Prix SSJ	2,500-5,000	5,000-7,000	7,000-9,000
Grand Prix 2d htp	1,500-3,000	3,000-5,000	5,000-7,000

(V-8s: add 25% for 455 V-8 except when standard)

1971 Pontiac Grand Prix hardtop coupe

1972

The last of the handsome 1969-72 generation Grand Prix was sold this year; fine examples are cheap, when you can find one. Production for this last edition was 91,961. The Catalina convertible put in its last appearance, leaving only the Grand Ville as Pontiac's surviving full-size convertible. Ragtop

1971 Pontiac Firebird Trans Am hardtop coupe

production for '72 was 2399 Catalinas and 2213 Grand Villes. Another convertible being seen for the last time this year was the Le Mans, which including its GT and Sport trim versions snared 3438 buyers. The GTO was now a Le Mans option package, comprising heavy-duty manual three-speed, front fender air extractors, firm shocks, stabilizer bars front and rear, and GTO badging; it cost $344 and saw just 5807 copies—how far the mighty had fallen! How many GTOs were convertibles is not known, but there couldn't have been many. A sporty Firebird Formula (without the "400") was offered for '72, and could be ordered with a 455 producing 300 bhp—the same engine standard in the Trans Am. But performance cars were on the wane, and Formula production stopped at 5249; Trans Am sold just 1286 copies. In 1970, Pontiac had still been in third place, then fell to fourth in 1971, and now found itself in fifth. Oldsmobile would now rule the roost as number three through most of the Seventies.

	Restorable	Good	Excellent
Firebird std & Esprit	$1,000-2,500	$2,500-4,000	$4,000-6,000
Firebird Trans Am	3,000-6,000	6,000-9,000	9,000-12,500
Le Mans convertible	1,500-4,000	4,000-6,000	6,000-8,000
GTO 2d hardtop	2,000-5,000	5,000-7,500	7,500-10,000
GTO convertible	3,000-6,000	6,000-10,000	10,000-15,000
	(add 15% for GTOs with 455 V-8)		
Catalina cvt	2,500-3,500	4,000-6,000	6,000-7,500
Grand Ville cvt	3,000-5,000	5,000-6,500	6,500-8,500
Grand Prix SSJ	2,000-4,000	4,000-5,500	5,500-7,000
Grand Prix 2d htp	1,000-2,500	2,500-4,000	4,000-5,500

1973

The GTO was disappearing as an option package, yet was still available on Pontiac's new-for-'73 intermediate line. A 400-cid V-8 was standard, a 455 optional. However, the GTO was overshadowed this year by the new Grand Am, which was also based on the new Le Mans body. Available in coupe and sedan body styles with "Colonnade" pillared styling (no more hardtops), it combined Grand Prix luxury with Trans Am performance. While some features were ungainly imitations of European sports sedans, a well-equipped Grand Am with its standard 230-bhp 400 V-8 was a fine road car. Like the GTO, a 455 was available, as was a four-speed manual transmission—a rare option. Grand Am coupes sold 34,443 copies, the sedans 8691. Look for the coupe, even though the GTO option package doesn't affect its value. The long-running Grand Prix went through a negative metamorphosis this year, adopting the Colonnade intermediate A-body. This was nothing more than a glorified two-door sedan, and—in our opinion—eminently non-desirable. A vertical grille and formal roofline set it off, but it was no longer a collectible Pontiac. Among Firebirds, the Formula version was back, and like the Trans Am was available with a 310-bhp 455 Super Duty V-8, which significantly increases the value of both models. This was a boom year with Pontiac building 919,870 cars, but even this wasn't enough to put it back in third place.

1972 Pontiac Grand Prix two-door hardtop

1973 Pontiac Firebird Trans Am coupe

1973 Pontiac Le Mans Sport with GTO option

1973 Pontiac Grand Ville convertible coupe

1973 Pontiac Firebird Esprit coupe

1973 Pontiac Grand Am two-door coupe

1974 Pontiac Ventura coupe with GTO option

1974 Pontiac Firebird Trans Am coupe

1975 Pontiac Grand Ville convertible coupe

1975 Pontiac Grand Am two-door coupe

	Restorable	Good	Excellent
Firebird std & Esprit	$1,000-2,500	$2,500-4,000	$4,000-6,000
Firebird Formula	2,000-4,000	4,000-6,000	6,000-9,000
Formula 455 SD V-8	3,000-6,000	6,000-9,000	9,000-14,000
Firebird Trans Am	3,000-6,000	6,000-9,000	9,000-12,500
Trans Am 455 SD V-8	5,000-9,000	9,000-14,000	14,000-20,000
Grand Am coupe	1,500-3,000	3,000-4,500	4,500-6,500
Grand Ville cvt	3,000-5,000	5,000-6,500	6,500-8,500
Grand Prix 2d cpe	2,000-3,500	3,500-4,500	4,500-6,000

1974

The hallowed GTO became a package for the compact Ventura platform instead of the Grand Am or Le Mans. This was a GTO in name only, basically a Ventura Sprint with a hood scoop, custom grille, and standard 350 V-8, priced $195 higher. Interestingly, Pontiac moved about 7000 of these pretenders before ringing down the curtain on the GTO—a year too late. Total Grand Am sales plummeted to only 13,961 coupes and 3122 sedans this year, so the Grand Am coupe is pretty scarce. The sedan is scarcer, but nobody cares. Among the big Pontiacs, the Grand Ville ragtop found 3000 buyers. The Firebird Trans Am was more successful, up from 4802 sales in 1973 to 10,225, and the Formula managed 14,519.

	Restorable	Good	Excellent
Firebird std & Esprit	$1,000-2,500	$2,500-4,000	$4,000-6,000
Firebird Formula	2,000-4,000	4,000-6,000	6,000-9,000
Formula 455 SD V-8	3,000-6,000	6,000-9,000	9,000-14,000
Firebird Trans Am	3,000-6,000	6,000-9,000	9,000-12,500
Trans Am 455 SD V-8	5,000-9,000	9,000-14,000	14,000-20,000
Grand Am coupe	1,500-3,000	3,000-4,500	4,500-6,500
Grand Ville cvt	3,000-5,000	5,000-6,500	6,500-8,500
Grand Prix 2d cpe	2,000-3,500	3,500-4,500	4,500-6,000

1975

Along with the Chevy Camaro, the Firebird carried on again this year as one of the few ponycars of the old school, available with stump pulling back axles, manual gearboxes, and jumbo engines—up to the 455 High Output in Formula or Trans Am guise. New for '75 was a wraparound rear window. The Trans Am had an excellent year: 27,274 deliveries, way ahead of the Formula's 13,670. The last of the original Grand Ams left the factory this year; production totaled only 8786 coupes and 1893 sedans. Another model being seen for the last time was the Grand Ville, Pontiac's last convertible—4519 were built for the model year.

	Restorable	Good	Excellent
Firebird std & Esprit	$1,000-2,000	$2,000-3,000	$3,000-5,000
Firebird Formula	1,500-3,000	3,000-4,000	4,000-7,000
Formula 455 SD V-8	2,500-4,000	4,000-5,000	5,000-10,000
Firebird Trans Am	2,000-4,000	4,000-6,000	6,000-9,000
Trans Am 455 SD V-8	3,000-5,000	5,000-7,000	7,000-12,500

	Restorable	Good	Excellent
Grand Am coupe	1,500-3,000	3,000-4,500	4,500-6,500
Grand Ville cvt	3,000-5,000	5,000-6,500	6,500-8,500
Grand Prix 2d cpe	2,000-3,500	3,500-4,500	4,500-6,000

1976

Firebird options now included a canopy top; only the Formula (350) and Trans Am (400) came standard with V-8s, but the Trans Am could still be ordered with an admittedly defanged 455 rated at 200 horsepower. Other T/A equipment included the usual console, air dam, rear spoiler, "shaker" hood, Rally wheels, full instrumentation, and GR70×15 tires. Look for the Trans Am Special Edition, with the canopy top and a big Firebird decal on the hood. Trans Am output continued upward, to 46,701 units, and the Formula increased, too, to 20,613. The Grand Prix was also doing great with 228,091 built, including SJ models. The Sunbird, Pontiac's H-body equivalent to the Chevy Monza, was introduced, but only as a notchback; the 2+2 fastback body, which is mildly collectible, didn't arrive at Pontiac until 1978.

	Restorable	Good	Excellent
Firebird std & Esprit	$500-1,500	$1,500-2,500	$2,500-4,500
Firebird Formula	1,500-2,500	2,500-3,000	3,000-6,500
Firebird Trans Am	2,000-4,000	4,000-6,000	6,000-8,000
(add 10% for SD 455 V-8, 10% for canopy top)			
Grand Prix 2d cpe	2,000-3,500	3,500-4,500	4,500-6,000

1977

Sharp new front-end styling kept the Firebird looking up to date. The usual four models were offered, but the base engine was now a 231 V-6, while the top performance mill was an Olds-built 403 V-8 (no more 455s). Notable was the Esprit Sky Bird trim package, with blue velour seating, blue aluminum wheels, and two-toned blue body. Trans Ams came with a 400 or 403 V-8 and carried the usual shaker hood scoop and T/A graphics. Sales were amazing: 68,745 Trans Ams, 21,801 Formulas, 34,548 Esprits, and 30,642 base coupes. Grand Prix was also doing just fine: 168,247 coupes, 66,741 LJs, and 53,442 SJs. Full-size Pontiacs were downsized this year, but that's of no consequence to collectors.

	Restorable	Good	Excellent
Firebird std & Esprit	$500-1,500	$1,500-2,500	$2,500-4,000
Firebird Formula	1,500-2,500	2,500-3,000	3,000-6,000
Firebird Trans Am	2,000-4,000	4,000-6,000	6,000-8,000
(add 10% for canopy top)			
Grand Prix 2d cpe	2,000-3,500	3,500-4,500	4,500-6,000

1978

The Grand Prix was downsized, and a much better car than it had been since 1972, but sales were down anyway. Some people save string, so there may be a place in future collector stables for the Sunbird 2+2 fastback—who knows? In its favor, a Chevy-built 145-bhp, 305-cid V-8 became optional

1976 Pontiac Firebird Formula coupe

1976 Pontiac Firebird Trans Am 400 HO coupe

1977 Pontiac Grand Prix SJ coupe

1977 Pontiac Le Mans with Can Am package

1978 Pontiac Firebird Trans Am "T/A 6.6" coupe

1979 Pontiac Firebird Trans Am coupe

1979 Pontiac Sunbird Formula hatchback coupe

1980 Pontiac Firebird Trans Am coupe

1981 Pontiac Grand Prix LJ two-door coupe

1981 Pontiac Firebird Formula coupe

on the Sunbird this year. Just over 25,000 of the 2+2s were built with fours, V-6s, and V-8s. The Grand Am name reappeared in the newly downsized Le Mans series, but this G/A was not nearly as special as the 1973-75 models, and production was low: 2841 four-doors and 7767 two-doors.

	Restorable	Good	Excellent
Sunbird 2+2 cpe	$500-1,000	$1,000-2,000	$2,000-3,000
Firebird Trans Am	2,000-3,000	3,000-4,000	4,000-5,000
Firebird, other	2,500-3,500	3,500-4,500	4,500-6,000
Grand Prix 2d cpe	1,000-2,500	2,500-3,500	3,500-4,500

1979

Sunbird was unchanged except for trim shifts, but 2+2 output was up to 40,560. A facelifted, grilleless Firebird debuted, still with base V-6 power and up to a 403 V-8 for the Trans Am, which came as usual with four-speed and T/A trim. Look for the limited-edition 10th Anniversary Trans Am, of which 7500 were built. Regular Trans Ams found 109,609 buyers, Formulas 24,851. The Grand Prix received a mild facelift; coming standard with Pontiac's smallest 301 V-8, it could be optioned with a 305, but horsepower was almost unchanged.

	Restorable	Good	Excellent
Sunbird 2+2 cpe	$500-1,000	$1,000-2,000	$2,000-3,000
Firebird Trans Am	2,000-3,000	3,000-4,000	4,000-5,000
Firebird, other	2,500-3,500	3,500-4,500	4,500-6,000
Grand Prix 2d cpe	1,000-2,500	2,500-3,500	3,500-4,500

1980

An optional turbocharged 301 Firebird V-8 was issued rated at 210 bhp, and offered only a bit less go than the big-blocks of old—yet was much easier on gas. Standard engine for Trans Ams was a normally aspirated version of that engine, rated at 170 bhp. Production fell back to 50,896 Trans Ams, 9356 Formulas. The Phoenix name went on Pontiac's version of the GM X-body front-drive compact, in retrospect an unfortunate series of cars. The Phoenix was a nicer workout than the Chevy Citation, but if any have been salted away against a future replete with rich Phoenix enthusiasts, we don't know of them. Sunbird lost its V-8 option, a mark against it from a collector's standpoint even though 52,952 2+2s were sold. Pontiac produced 770,100 cars this year, good enough only for fifth place.

	Restorable	Good	Excellent
Sunbird 2+2 cpe	$500-1,000	$1,000-2,000	$2,000-3,500
Firebird Trans Am	2,000-3,000	3,000-4,000	4,000-5,000
Firebird, other	2,500-3,500	3,500-4,500	4,500-6,000
Grand Prix 2d cpe	1,000-2,500	2,500-3,500	3,500-4,500

1981

Grand Prix was facelifted, with a lower, more sloping nose, smoother bumpers, flush side windows, and a higher rear deck. A V-6 was standard, a small 120-bhp V-8 optional, along with an Olds-built diesel (definitely not recommended). Sales remained good: 74,786 coupes, 46,842 LJs, and 26,083 Broughams. The Sunbird was phased out after the 1980 model run. The Firebird, in its twelfth and final year for the second styling generation, was scheduled for major revision in 1982 and was little changed. The Formula was downgraded to a standard 265-cid V-8, but still available with four-speed, while the Trans Am got a 305 V-8; automatic was standard on the six-cylinder Esprit. A Trans Am Special Edition was available again. Last year's Turbo engine remained optional on the Formula and Trans Am. Styling was carried over from 1980. Trans Ams totaled 33,493 this year, Formulas 5927.

	Restorable	Good	Excellent
Firebird Trans Am	*	$4,000-5,000	$5,000-6,000
Firebird, other	*	3,000-4,000	4,000-5,000
Grand Prix 2d cpe	*	3,000-4,000	4,000-5,000

* Purchase only in good or excellent condition

1981 Pontiac Firebird Trans Am coupe

1982

A new, smaller Firebird riding a 101-inch wheelbase paralleled the new Camaro, but with distinct differences. Base engine was a 2.5-liter fuel-injected four. Replacing the Esprit was the luxurious S/E, powered by Chevy's 2.8-liter V-6. The Formula was dropped, but the Trans Am carried over, a punchy car with Chevy's 305-cid V-8—the only Firebird with dual-throttle-body fuel injection—but it came only as an automatic. If you like to shift, look for a four-speed S/E. Output was encouraging: 41,683 coupes, 21,719 S/Es, and 52,960 Trans Ams. Grand Prix carried on with little change, and sales were down significantly.

1982 Pontic Grand Prix Brougham coupe

	Restorable	Good	Excellent
Firebird Trans Am	*	$3,000-4,000	$4,000-5,000
Firebird, other	*	2,000-3,000	3,000-4,000
Grand Prix 2d cpe	*	3,000-4,000	4,000-5,000

* Purchase only in good or excellent condition

1982 Pontiac Firebird S/E coupe

1983

Firebird was better yet, with a new integral-rail shift mechanism replacing 1982's cable linkage on the wide-ratio four-speed manual gearbox, which was standard with the four-cylinder base Firebird. But what you want is the close-ratio five-speed overdrive manual, standard on the V-6 S/E and baseline Trans Am. Among Firebirds this year, look for the limited-edition Daytona 500 25th Anniversary model, and well-optioned 'Birds with zowee Lear/Sieglar or Recaro bucket seats. Trans Am was down this year to 31,930 units, S/E to 10,934. Grand Prix was carried over with little change. The front-drive 6000 had debuted for '82 in coupe and sedan guise, but this year added an STE "Special Touring Edition" Euro-style sport sedan. Its 135-bhp V-6 wasn't the liveliest, but the handling was excellent and the appointments first class; 6719 were built. It may have some potential collector interest.

1983 Pontiac Firebird S/E coupe

1984 Pontiac Grand Prix two-door coupe

1984 Pontiac Fiero Indianapolis 500 Pace Car

1984 Pontiac Fiero 2-passenger coupe

1985 Pontiac Firebird Trans Am coupe

1985 Pontiac Fiero GT coupe

	Restorable	Good	Excellent
Firebird Trans Am	*	$3,500-4,500	$4,500-5,500
Firebird, other	*	2,000-3,000	3,000-4,000
Grand Prix 2d cpe	*	3,000-4,000	4,000-5,000
6000 STE 4d sdn	*	1,000-2,000	2,000-3,000

* Purchase only in good or excellent condition

1984

Pontiac struck out into fresh territory with the mid-engine Fiero two-seater, featuring full-independent suspension and disc brakes at both ends, and corrosion-free plastic body panels attached to a space frame that was similar to the roll cage of a racing car. The initial engine was Pontiac's 2.5-liter overhead-valve four, with four-speed or automatic—a V-6 was not added until 1985. This is certainly a car with collector potential, but it has a reputation for squirrely handling in the wet, and the stuff underneath those plastic panels is steel, and does rust. Fiero jumped off to a great start—136,840 were built the first year. All Firebirds were available with four-speed overdrive automatic. Trans Am's previous injected V-8 was replaced by a 190-bhp carbureted version of Chevy's 305, introduced late in the 1983 model run. The base four had higher 9.0:1 compression and standard four-speed. Look for the Trans Am aero package, featuring a larger air dam, new front and rear fascia, body-color rear wing, and other functional and appearance changes. Even more important to the collector is the Trans Am 15th Anniversary model, presently worth at least double the price of a comparable condition standard T/A. Trans Ams numbered 55,374. This year, Pontiac built 19,236 6000 STEs.

	Restorable	Good	Excellent
Fiero 2P coupe	*	$2,500-3,500	$3,500-4,500
Firebird Trans Am	*	3,500-4,500	4,500-6,000
Trans Am 15th Ann.	*	7,000-10,000	10,000-12,500
Firebird, other	*	2,000-3,000	3,000-4,500
Grand Prix 2d cpe	*	3,000-4,000	4,000-5,000
6000 STE 4d sdn	*	1,200-2,300	2,300-3,300

* Purchase only in good or excellent condition

1985

During the 1985 model year, Pontiac added a 140-bhp V-6 Fiero GT wearing a distinctive rounded nose, giving the little sportster more flair and fire at the same time. The GT found 22,534 buyers. Trans Am got some styling refinements, but the biggest news was a return to fuel injection with the "Tuned Port Injection" 305 V-8 producing a healthy 205 bhp. Even so, sales dropped to 44,028. The 6000 STE, meanwhile, edged upward to 22,728 units, while the Grand Prix was maintaining a 60,000-unit pace.

	Restorable	Good	Excellent
Fiero 2P cpe	*	$2,500-4,000	$4,000-5,500
Firebird Trans Am	*	3,500-4,500	4,500-6,000
Firebird, other	*	2,000-3,000	3,000-4,500
Grand Prix 2d cpe	*	3,000-4,000	4,000-5,000
6000 STE 4d sdn	*	1,500-3,000	3,000-4,000

* Purchase only in good or excellent condition

1986

Fiero had larger standard tires and wheels, a new sound system, and a handsome gold color, alternated with white during the model year—carried over were red, silver, and black. Base, Sport Coupe, and SE trim levels were offered at the start of the year; a GT with fastback roofline appeared later. From this point on, V-6 Fieros are clearly the ones to look for, especially since there are plenty of cars to go around. Production this year was 9143 base coupes, 24,866 Sport Coupes, 32,305 SEs, and 17,660 GTs. Firebirds all rode 15-inch tires and all V-6 and V-8 models had a "Rally Tuned" suspension. Look for the V-8s, which accounted for well over half the production. They sound and feel like Sixties muscle cars, but have better tires and brakes to handle the ample power. Trans Ams this year numbered 48,870. The 6000 STE came in at 26,299 units. Of particular interest was the 2+2, a Grand Prix with a "bubbleback" rear window built to homologate it for NASCAR racing. It came with a 165-bhp 305 V-8, laid-back twin-nostril grille, four-inch-high rear deck spoiler, sport suspension, fast-ratio power steering, and a dandy interior. Only 200 were built. New to the Pontiac stable was the Sunbird Turbo GT convertible. Sunbird had had a ragtop since 1984, but the new 150/165-bhp Turbo four made it go. This model ran through 1989, and about 7000 were built. Grab a nice one now for about $7000 to $10,000—likely it will be collectible somewhere down the road.

	Restorable	Good	Excellent
Fiero V-6	*	$3,000-4,750	$4,750-6,500
Fiero 4-cyl	*	2,500-3,500	3,500-4,500
Firebird Trans Am	*	3,500-4,500	4,500-6,000
Firebird, other	*	2,000-3,000	3,000-4,500
Grand Prix 2d cpe	*	3,000-4,000	4,000-5,000
2+2 "aero" coupe	*	4,000-5,250	5,250-6,000
6000 STE 4d sdn	*	1,800-3,300	3,300-4,500

* Purchase only in good or excellent condition

1987

Fiero styling was handsomely revised, and V-6s received an excellent new five-speed manual gearbox. But sales were falling, this year to 15,968 GTs and 3875 SEs. Firebirds lost their gaudy hood decals this year and gained a potent 5.7-liter Corvette V-8, available for both the Formula and Trans Am, but only with automatic. Option packages were the "Formula" for the base Firebird and the GTA for the Trans Am. The Formula included a 5.0-liter four-barrel V-8, with optional fuel injection and five-speed or automatic; the GTA included the 5.7 engine, automatic, limited-slip differential, performance handling package, special tires and wheels, and four-wheel disc brakes. It was possible to order GTAs with the more peace-loving 5.0-liter V-8, so don't be surprised if you find such a combination—but don't pay as much for it. Trans Ams numbered 32,890, Formulas 13,264. The Grand Prix still survived, sharing its GM "G" body with the Buick Regal, Olds Cutlass Supreme, and Chevy Monte Carlo. Production was down to just 16,542 total units. The 6000 STE came in at 8802.

1986 Pontiac Grand Prix coupe

1986 Pontiac 2+2 "aero" coupe

1986 Pontiac Firebird Trans Am coupe

1987 Pontiac Grand Prix 2+2 coupe

1987 Pontiac Fiero GT coupe

1987 Pontiac Firebird Trans Am GTA coupe

1988 Pontiac Firebird Trans Am GTZ coupe

1988 Pontiac Grand Prix LE coupe

1989 Pontiac Firebird Formula coupe

1989 Pontiac Grand Prix Turbo coupe

	Restorable	Good	Excellent
Fiero V-6	*	$4,500-5,500	$5,500-7,000
Fiero 4 cyl	*	3,500-4,500	4,500-5,500
Firebird T/A GTA	*	6,500-8,000	8,000-9,500
Firebird Trans Am	*	4,500-5,500	5,500-7,000
Firebird, other	*	2,500-3,500	3,500-5,000
6000 STE 4d sdn	*	3,000-4,500	4,500-6,000

* Purchase only in good or excellent condition

1988

A new front-drive Grand Prix coupe was Pontiac's version of GM's new W-body, shared with Buick's Regal and Oldsmobile's Cutlass Supreme. The GP was truly aerodynamic, with a Cd rating of .299, making it one of the slipperiest production cars in the world. The performance model was the SE, with standard five-speed, but all GPs carried only one engine, a 2.8 V-6 with 130 net bhp. Production was 86,357. At mid-year a Grand Prix McLaren Turbo debuted (see the 1989 listing). Firebird continued with the base and Trans Am models, along with their Formula and GTA trim packages. Unlike Chevrolet, no convertible body style was offered. A reworked suspension greatly improved Fiero handling; the sportiest, albeit hardest, ride was from the WS6 suspension package, standard on the Fiero GT. This was the last Fiero—and the best. But only 26,402 were built, so get one while you can still find mint originals, as this is no car to restore. Late in 1988, a 6000 STE AWD sedan was introduced, basically the familiar STE with all-wheel drive.

	Restorable	Good	Excellent
Fiero V-6	*	$5,500-6,500	$6,500-9,000
Fiero 4-cyl	*	3,500-5,500	5,500-7,000
Firebird T/A GTA	*	8,000-10,000	10,000-12,000
Firebird Trans Am	*	6,000-7,500	7,500-9,000
Firebird, other	*	4,000-5,500	5,500-7,000
Grand Prix 2d cpe	*	4,000-6,000	6,000-7,500
6000 STE 4d sdn	*	4,500-6,500	6,500-7,500

* Purchase only in good or excellent condition

1989

A turbocharged Firebird went on sale to mark the 20th Anniversary of the Trans Am. Until then, changes were a new theft-deterrent system and standard rear disc brakes on all four models: base, Formula, Trans Am, and GTA. Only about 1500 of the Anniversary Trans Ams were built, using a V-6 last seen in the Buick Regal Grand National. It was rated at 245 bhp and was capable of a 13-second quarter mile. All Anniversary T/As were painted white with tan interiors. The Grand Prix added optional anti-lock brakes and continued with the turbocharged model. This was the McLaren Turbo Grand Prix, with an intercooled 3.1 V-6 developing about 200 bhp, more than any other front-drive GM car. ABS and automatic were standard on this special, as were specific exterior treatment and a bells-and-whistles interior. About 2000 were built for 1988-89.

	Restorable	Good	Excellent
Firebird 20th Ann.	*	$17,000-20,000	$20,000-23,500
Firebird T/A GTA	*	10,000-11,500	11,500-13,000

	Restorable	Good	Excellent
Firebird Trans Am	*	7,500-8,750	8,750-10,000
Firebird, other	*	5,000-6,500	6,500-8,000
Grand Prix	*	5,500-7,500	7,500-9,000
Turbo Grand Prix	*	7,000-9,000	9,000-12,500
6000 STE AWD sdn	*	7,000-8,500	8,500-10,000

* Purchase only in good or excellent condition

1990 Pontiac Firebird GTA coupe

1990

Firebird, Pontiac's perennial ponycar, offered more power and some new interior appointments this year. The 5.7 V-8, for example, increased from 225 to 235 bhp. Base models had a 140 bhp V-6. The first four-door to wear the Grand Prix name debuted this year; ignore it, and stick to the traditional coupe, particularly the hot Turbo Grand Prix.

	Restorable	Good	Excellent
Firebird T/A GTA	*	$11,500-13,500	$13,500-15,500
Firebird Trans Am	*	9,500-11,000	11,000-12,000
Firebird, other	*	6,500-8,000	8,000-10,000
Grand Prix 2d cpe	*	7,000-9,500	9,500-11,500
Turbo Grand Prix	*	10,000-12,500	12,500-15,000

* Purchase only in good or excellent condition

Reo

The car named for Ransom Eli Olds expired in 1936, but not before issuing some of the prettiest designs of the Thirties. Not common in any form, Reos are among the more interesting middle-price examples of '30s production. Club support is low, parts scarce, investment potential modest. Note that some of the '30s Reos are recognized Classics.

1931/32 Reo Royale four-door sedan

1930-36

Reo didn't build many cars during the Depression, but many of them were classically beautiful. The '30s were closed body styles, powered by 60- and 80-bhp sixes and styled by Amos Northup. Through mid-1931, all bore the name Flying Cloud, and displayed a fine sense of proportion along with quality workmanship and interior furnishings. For 1931, the sixes were joined by a pair of straight eights developing 90 and 125 bhp, the larger 358-cid unit on three different wheelbases: 130, 131, and 135 inches. The big eight powered the magnificent Royale, with Northup's new streamlined bodywork including fashionable skirted fenders. Trying to cut costs during the Depression, Reo reduced model offerings in 1932-33. A new 80-bhp six appeared for the small 6-S Flying Cloud, available in many body styles and two trim levels. Completing the line were the Royale in standard and Custom trim, powered by the nine-main-bearing 358-cid eight and riding wheelbases of 131, 135, and an impressive 152 inches for limousines and long sedans.

The first 1934 Reos were carryovers, but in April came the beautiful S-4 Flying Cloud with a handsome new hood and grille, more deeply skirted fenders, hood side louvers, and optional built-in trunk. Despite its performance and good looks, it didn't help faltering sales. The Royale and its eight-cylinder engines were scrubbed after 1934, in which no open models had been offered. After a management skirmish and a new president, Reo offered an ambitious "1935½" Flying Cloud, the A-6 fastback two- and four-door sedans on a 115-inch wheelbase, powered by a 90-bhp six. Up front, the A-6 resembled Auburn, with flared fenders and a V-shaped bumper. A more substantial restyling came in 1936: fuller fenders, another new hood and grille, vertical grille bands extending up into the radiator shell, rubber tipped bumper guards, and optional "Zeppelin" fender lamps. By this time, however, automaking had become a sideline and Reo was concentrating mainly on trucks. The firm officially left the car business in September, but would continue as a truck manufacturer for over 40 years.

Reo production opened the decade with 11,450 cars built, then slipped to 6762 for 1931. Business improved to 15,716 units for 1932, amazing in that deep Depression year. Output skidded to 4112 in 1933, then held steady at 4460 in 1934 and 4692 in 1935. But after building only 3206 cars for 1936, Reo had little choice but to retrench into trucks.

	Restorable	Good	Excellent
Flying Cloud			
1930-31 Six, clsd	$2,500-7,500	$7,500-10,000	$10,000-15,000
1931 Six phaeton	4,000-10,000	$10,000-17,500	17,500-25,000
1931 Eight, clsd	3,500-9,000	9,000-13,000	13,000-20,000
1932 Six, closed	3,500-8,000	8,000-13,000	13,000-20,000
1932-34 Eight, clsd	4,000-9,000	9,000-17,500	17,500-25,000
1935-36 Six, clsd	3,000-8,000	8,000-12,500	12,500-19,500
1935 Six cvt cpe	6,000-12,500	12,500-22,500	22,500-30,000
Royale			
1932-34, closed	4,000-11,000	11,000-18,000	18,000-27,500
1932-33, open	7,500-15,000	15,000-27,500	27,500-40,000

Shelby

Built by the famous racing driver under his own name, Shelbys were the ultimate form of Ford's Mustang and remain among the most desirable American cars of the late Sixties. Club support is excellent, parts supply good, investment potential excellent. Dodges formed the basis of the Shelby-built cars of the Eighties.

1965 Shelby GT-350 fastback coupe

1965

The first Shelby was by many standards the best. Called GT-350, it was a blue-striped white Mustang fastback powered by a 306-horsepower version of Ford's 289 small-block V-8, with high-rise manifold, big four-barrel carburetor, and free-flow exhaust headers. Further changes produced 350-horse racing versions. All GT-350s came with a Borg-Warner T-10 four-speed gearbox, a regular Mustang option. Instead of the stock Mustang's Falcon-based rear axle, however, GT-350s had a beefier axle from the Fairlane. Other special Shelby components were metallic-lined rear brakes, Koni shock absorbers, heavy-duty front disc brakes with metallic pads, quick steering, and special 15-inch cast aluminum wheels shod with high-performance Goodyear tires. Shelbys had a different look, with the galloping pony emblem removed from the grille and a special fiberglass hood containing a prominent scoop and hold-down pins. The Mustang's simulated bodyside scoops were opened to make them functional. Exactly 562 of these cars were built. Because the '65 is the first Shelby and the purest, it is considered by many to be the most desirable of the breed.

	Restorable	Good	Excellent
GT-350 cpe	$10,000-20,000	$20,000-40,000	$40,000-60,000

(Note: Asking prices vary over a wide range, and are recorded up to $79,000)

1966

The Mustang fastback's stock rear quarter air extractor vents were replaced by plastic windows. Internally, the only changes were competition three-inch seatbelts and a mahogany-rimmed steering wheel. GT-350s also came without the stock Mustang's rear seat, with the spare tire lashed down in the vacated space. Shelby offered a kit so the buyer could put the spare in the trunk and install a rear seat. The front seats were stock Mustang. Also this year, Hertz Rent-A-Car ordered 936 Shelbys painted black with gold stripes. Called the GT-350H, they rented for $17 a day and 17 cents a mile, a lot of money back then. Aside from the paint job and automatic transmission, they were stock Shelbys. Inevitably, a few were rented by weekend racers and some actually performed with success in sports car road racing. But they cost Hertz more to run than they earned, and were dropped in 1967. Total 1966 production was 2380.

	Restorable	Good	Excellent
GT-350 cpe	$8,000-15,000	$15,000-35,000	$35,000-48,000
GT-350H cpe	8,000-15,000	15,000-37,500	37,500-50,000

1967

When Mustang offered a 390-cid V-8 this year, Shelby went them one better and tossed in the huge 428. The result, called GT-500, was advertised at 335 horsepower, but its real output was probably closer to 400. Conversely, while the GT-350 continued to advertise 306 bhp, its output was likely somewhat below 300 because it didn't have steel-tube exhaust headers like previous models. The '67 Shelby had its own fiberglass front end to distinguish it from production Mustangs, plus other minor styling and chassis refinements. It also bore the patented Cobra emblem in anodized gold. Interiors featured a huge, black-painted roll bar, to which were affixed inertial-

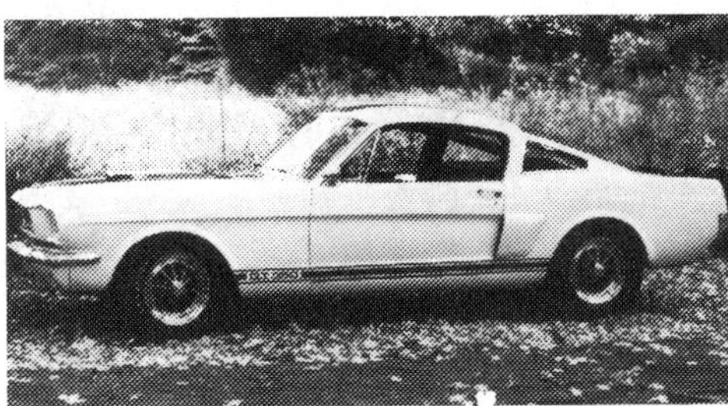

1966 Shelby GT-350 fastback coupe

1967 Shelby GT-350 fastback coupe

1968 Shelby GT-500 convertible coupe

1968 Shelby GT-500 fastback coupe

1968 Shelby GT-500KR (King of the Road) coupe

1969 Shelby GT-500 convertible coupe

reel seatbelts instead of the three-way harness. Production was 1175 GT-350s and 2050 GT-500s.

	Restorable	Good	Excellent
GT-350 cpe	$6,500-12,500	$12,500-27,500	$27,500-37,500
GT-500 cpe	8,000-18,000	18,000-32,500	32,500-45,000

1968

This year saw Shelby's broadest line of cars ever. In addition to a new convertible selling for only $120 more than the fastback coupe, there was a new model, the GT-500KR (King of the Road), with Ford's Cobra Jet 428 block, oversize heads and intake manifold, and a Holley 735-cfm four-barrel carburetor. The KR sold for about $4500, or, say $20,000 in today's money—quite a bargain. (Unfortunately, it takes a bit more than that to buy one today.) Styling of the '68 edition was only slightly altered—a wider hood scoop was the main exterior change. Interiors were lifted from the stock Mustang, but a Stewart Warner oil pressure gauge and ammeter were mounted on the central console. Output of the fastback coupes and convertibles was: GT-350, 1253 and 404; GT-500, 1140 and 402; GT-500KR, 933 and 318.

	Restorable	Good	Excellent
GT-350 coupe	$6,500-12,500	$12,500-27,500	$27,500-37,500
GT-350 cvt	10,000-20,000	20,000-35,000	35,000-50,000
GT-500 coupe	8,000-18,000	18,000-32,500	32,500-42,500
GT-500 cvt	12,500-25,000	25,000-42,500	42,500-62,000
GT-500KR coupe	9,000-20,000	20,000-35,000	35,000-47,500
GT-500KR cvt	15,000-30,000	30,000-47,500	47,500-67,500

1969

Federal emission and safety regulations were now beginning to interfere with the total-performance approach of Carroll Shelby to his cars. Mechanically, the '69s were more closely related to the production Mustang than any of their predecessors, sharing much of the Mustang's new '69 styling. Air scoops were cut into the fiberglass front fenders, and side stripes were relocated midway up the bodysides. The GT-500KR models were discontinued. Production this year was 1085 GT-350 fastbacks and 194 convertibles; GT-500s numbered 1536 coupes and 335 ragtops.

	Restorable	Good	Excellent
GT-350 coupe	$6,500-10,000	$10,000-20,000	$20,000-30,000
GT-350 cvt	8,000-17,500	17,500-30,000	30,000-45,000
GT-500 coupe	7,500-15,000	15,000-27,500	27,500-35,000
GT-500 cvt	10,000-25,000	25,000-35,000	35,000-50,000

1970

All Shelbys sold this year were reserialed 1969 models, because production had ended before 1969 was out. A combination of government regulations and spiraling insurance rates—the cars' accident record was staggering—prompted Carroll Shelby to ask then-president of Ford, Lee Iacocca, to cancel the cooperative program that produced the cars.

There were of course no changes in models or specifications for the 350 GT-350s and 286 GT-500s sold as 1970 models.

	Restorable	Good	Excellent
GT-350 coupe	$6,500-10,000	$10,000-20,000	$20,000-30,000
GT-350 cvt	8,000-17,500	17,500-30,000	30,000-45,000
GT-500 coupe	7,500-15,000	15,000-27,500	27,500-35,000
GT-500 cvt	10,000-25,000	25,000-35,000	35,000-50,000

1986

After Lee Iacocca moved to Chrysler Corporation and oversaw the firm's return to profitability, he soon reestablished ties with Carroll Shelby in the hopes of putting some pizzazz into a line of mundane (though profitable) K/L-cars. The result was the 1983 Dodge Shelby Charger and the Omni GLH—cars tweaked with Carroll's input, but built by Dodge and badged and sold as Dodges. But in 1986, the first of the limited-edition, front-drive Dodges produced by a reborn Shelby Automobile, Inc., in Whittier, California, were offered. Known as the Shelby GLH-S, it was essentially a more specialized rendition of the 1983-86 Omni GLH ("Goes Like Hell"), its main distinction being a 175-bhp version of the normal GLH's optional 146-bhp turbo 2.2 "Trans-4" engine. Modified plenum chamber, added air-to-air intercooler, and equal-length intake runners accounted for the extra power. Also standard were a manual five-speed transaxle (no automatic available), heavy-duty suspension, wide tires on multi-hole alloy wheels, tachometer, console, and snazzier cabin trim. Gloriously unrefined, almost crude in engine and chassis behavior, it was fast, noisy fun (0-60 in less than eight seconds). High performance plus low production (only 500 built) and Shelby mystique suggest this as at least a minor collector's item in the not-too-distant future. For prices, see 1989.

1987 Shelby Charger GLH-S hatchback coupe

1987 Shelby Lancer hatchback sedan

1987

The run of Shelby GLH-S four-doors was completed in 1987, but also appearing this year was the Shelby Charger GLH-S fastback coupe. It had the same 175-bhp turbocharged and intercooled engine as the sedan, and it was also similar in chassis specs and equipment. Do not confuse it with the 1983-87 Shelby Charger, which was a Dodge. Production of this model was about 1000 units. Another Shelby appearing in 1987 was the Shelby Lancer, a more luxurious latterday Shelby based on Dodge's H-body Lancer five-door sedan, the division's mid-'80s mid-sizer and erstwhile "Eurosedan" competitor. This one came with power everything, offered a remote-control CD audio system and leather interior as options, and featured a Shelby signature dashboard plaque, sport steering wheel, and lacy-spoke road wheels. Also unique was a no-cost exterior "aero" package that added a front air-dam, side and rear skirts, and a rear spoiler to the already smooth Lancer shape. Suspension was stiffened per Shelby practice, which meant a very hard ride but superb front-drive handling (0.85g)—pro-

1987 Shelby CSX hatchback coupe

1989 Shelby CSX hatchback coupe

vided you kept a rein on the 175-bhp turbo-four engine. Carroll liked to portray this as an American answer to the Mercedes 190E 2.3-16, only far more affordable. The production schedule called for 800 cars, 400 with automatic (and a less potent 146-bhp Turbo four). Note: In 1988, Dodge came out with a Lancer Shelby (catch the name difference), virtually identical to the Shelby Lancer save for slightly quieter looks. Only 279 of these were produced, so likely they will have some collector interest, too. For prices, see 1989.

1988

The Shelby CSX appeared late in 1987. The basis this time was the new-for-'87 P-body Dodge Shadow, the once-and-future replacement for the L-body Omni, thus bringing the late-'80s series of special Shelbys more or less full circle. The CSX was a three-door hatchback, much smoother and more modern-looking, and followed the same basic technical formula as the Shelby Lancer, but was slightly faster owing to its smaller size and lower curb weight. It could do 0-60 in around 7.1 seconds (versus 7.7) and the standing quarter-mile in 15.1 seconds at 90 mph (versus 15.7 at 89). Top speed for both was 135 mph. CSXs built from 1988 on benefitted from Chrysler's VNT—Variable Nozzle Technology—turbocharging system that all but eliminated throttle lag for more responsive low- and mid-range acceleration. This was the most numerous Dodge-based Shelby: 750 in 1987 and 1000 in 1988. The '88s were interesting in that they were sold to Thrifty Car Rental, and they came with the standard Chrysler-built 146-bhp turbocharged engine. For prices see 1989.

1989

For 1989, Shelby produced its last 500 CSXs. These were the 175-bhp models. Though not in the scope of this book, Shelby also produced 1500 Shelby Dakota pickup trucks with a 175-bhp 318 V-8 and other Shelby mods. Chrysler, it might be noted, later added a V-8 option to the Dakota. Prices for the limited-edition 1986-89 Shelbys are problematical because not that many have changed hands and because they are really considered used cars at this point. Certainly they are worth a premium over the Dodges on which they are based, but how much? Our guess would be about 25 percent above the top-ranked equivalent Dodge, and likely more for mint specimens. Buy one of these cars more because you want one than as an investment—and buy one only in top-notch shape.

Studebaker

More appreciated among the knowledgeable than the general public, Studebaker has become synonymous with Edsel in the dialogue of comedians, but in fact it built some of the finest cars in its class repeatedly from the 1930s through its demise in the 1960s. Club support is excellent, body parts supply good, mechanical parts supply excellent. Investment potential is moderate.

1939 Studebaker Champion business coupe

1939 Studebaker President Cruising Sedan

1941 Studebaker President DeLux-Tone sedan

1930-39

Studebaker's top-of-the-line President was impressive throughout the '30s. Designed by famed engineer Barney Roos, its 337-cid straight eight with integral block and crankcase turned only 2800 rpm at 60 mph. In 1931 it acquired nine (instead of five) main bearings and 122 bhp, rising to 132 for 1933. Economic misfortune ended the big-inch Presidents that year, but they compiled a great racing and endurance record. So fine, in fact, were these cars that the Classic Car Club of America has designated all 1929-33 Presidents (except for the 1933 Model 82) as bona fide Classics. Studebaker also produced the Dictator and Commander in the early 1930s, ranging in output from 68-101 bhp and riding 114-125-inch wheelbases. After entering receivership in 1933, the firm was rescued by Harold Vance and Paul Hoffman, who turned a profit in 1934. Styling was consistently good despite business woes. By mid-decade, Studebaker had adopted pontoon fenders and rounded grilles, but retained a crisp, individual appearance. Technical developments included Warner overdrive and "planar" independent front suspension (1935), "Hill Holder" clutch/brake coupling to prevent rolling backward on hills with the clutch engaged (1936), automatic choke, vacuum-powered brakes, rotary door latches, and all-steel bodies. The '38 Studebakers were styled by Raymond Loewy; their lines imitated the streamlined locomotives he had designed for the Pennsylvania Railroad. The '39s were similar, somewhat like the Lincoln-Zephyr, but nevertheless distinctive. Production faltered in 1938, but bounced back with the new 1939 Champion, a light 110-inch-wheelbase "compact" car powered by an economical six that delivered up to 25 miles per gallon. Champions came in Custom and DeLuxe trim levels and three body styles: coupe, club sedan, and four-door sedan. Open Studebakers were few in the late 1930s: there were none at all in 1936-37, and only one in 1938-39. That one is highly collectible: a convertible sedan, available as either a Commander or President in both years. Some woody wagons were also built on Commander chassis by Hercules in 1939, but they are very scarce.

Studebaker opened the '30s with a production run of 123,126 cars, but fell to just 12,531 in 1933, topped out at about 98,000 in 1937, and ended the decade in 1939 with 85,834. In addition, Studebaker

1939 Studebaker Champion business coupe

1939 Studebaker President Cruising Sedan

1941 Studebaker President DeLux-Tone sedan

built the lower-priced Rockne in 1932-33: 22,715 the first year, 13,326 the second.

	Restorable	Good	Excellent
1930-32 Pres, open	$7,500-20,000	$20,000-35,000	$35,000-50,000
1930 Com/Dic, open	5,000-15,000	15,000-25,000	25,000-35,000
1930-31 Six, open	5,000-15,000	15,000-25,000	25,000-32,500
1932 Com/Dic, open	6,000-17,500	17,500-28,000	28,000-40,000
1932 Six/Rockne, open	4,000-15,000	15,000-25,000	25,00-32,500
1930-32 Pres, clsd	3,000-8,500	8,500-15,000	15,000-25,000
1930-32, other clsd	2,000-5,000	5,000-7,500	7,500-10,000
1933 Pres, open	5,000-15,000	15,000-22,500	22,500-35,000
1933, other open	4,000-10,000	10,000-20,000	20,000-30,000
1933, closed	2,000-5,000	5,000-10,000	10,000-15,000
1934, open	4,000-10,000	10,000-20,000	20,000-30,000
1935, open	3,000-8,000	8,000-17,500	17,500-25,000
1939 Champion	1,000-3,500	3,500-5,000	5,000-7,000
1934-39, other clsd	2,000-4,000	4,000-7,000	7,000-10,000
1938-39 cvt sdns	5,000-12,500	12,500-20,000	20,000-30,000

1940

A five-passenger coupe body style gave Champion four closed bodies and base and DeLuxe trim for eight models. Still riding a 110-inch wheelbase, the Champion was powered by a little 164.3-cid L-head six. Upmarket was the 116.5-inch-wheelbase Commander, offering only a Custom three-passenger coupe, Club Sedan (two-door), and a four-door Cruising Sedan. Powered by a 90-bhp, 226.2-cid six, Commanders featured more elaborate styling, including a sharply creased nose and a latticework grille rather like the '40 Ford. Presidents continued with the 250.4-cid nine-main-bearing eight delivering 110 bhp, and rode the longest wheelbase: 122 inches. Body styles and styling duplicated those of the Commander. Open models were again discontinued. Production totaled 107,185: 66,264 Champions, 34,477 Commanders, and just 6444 Presidents.

	Restorable	Good	Excellent
Champion	$1,000-3,000	$3,000-5,000	$5,000-7,500
Commander	1,500-4,000	4,000-6,500	6,500-10,000
President	2,000-5,000	5,000-7,500	7,500-12,000

1941

The Raymond Loewy Studios reworked the Studebaker line with more formal, elegant styling. Land Cruiser, a sedan with closed rear roof quarters, was new to the Commander and President lines. Loewy pioneered bodyside two-toning called DeLux-Tone: a below-the-beltline color sweep starting at the hood and gradually narrowing to a point at the back of the body. The Champion engine was stroked out to 169.6 cid and 80 bhp, while the Commander was tweaked to 94 bhp, the President's eight to 117. Top trim level for Commander and

President was Skyway, with rich trim and standard fender skirts. Generally speaking, '41s hold more value than comparable '40s. Production was up to 133,900, but this included only 41,996 Commanders and 6994 Presidents.

	Restorable	Good	Excellent
Champion	$1,000-3,500	$3,500-6,000	$6,000-8,000
Commander	1,500-4,500	4,500-7,500	7,500-11,000
President	2,500-5,000	5,000-9,500	9,500-15,000

1942

Before the war put an end to car production, Studebaker built 50,678 units. Using the same body as 1941, they had more massive grilles, with parking lights removed from the fendertops and integrated with the grillework. Aside from a simplified Champion line, the model hierarchy was unchanged.

	Restorable	Good	Excellent
Champion	$1,000-3,500	$3,500-6,000	$6,000-8,000
Commander	1,500-4,500	4,500-7,500	7,500-11,000
President	2,500-5,000	5,000-9,500	9,500-15,000

1946

The Skyway Champion, using the prewar body with its 110-inch wheelbase and slightly revised styling, was Studebaker's only '46 model. Styling revisions were modest: the upper grille molding extended under the headlights, side hood moldings were eliminated, and optional parking lamps appeared atop the fenders. The usual four body styles, two coupes and two sedans, were offered. Only 19,275 of these cars were built, making them quite uncommon today.

	Restorable	Good	Excellent
Skyway Champion	$1,000-3,000	$3,000-5,000	$5,000-7,000

1947

The first all-new design from a prewar manufacturer, the '47 Studebaker was mainly designed by Virgil Exner, who had joined the Loewy Studios but later split with Loewy and carried on as a free-lancer before going to Chrysler. Aside from the convertibles, a very desirable body style is the Starlight coupe, with its radical four-piece wraparound backlight and trim lines (and one piece curved windshield)—happily, Starlights cost little more than sedans, though they are honored as Milestones by the Milestone Car Society. The Commander joined the Champion, but the Skyway designation, and the President, were absent. Commanders were offered in DeLuxe and Regal DeLuxe trim, along with a Regal convertible. The Champion followed the same pattern on a 112-inch wheelbase, compared to the Commander's 119, and there was even a special 123-inch-wheelbase Commander Land Cruiser. The Commander six now displaced 226.2 cid and deliv-

1947 Studebaker Champion Starlight coupe

1947 Studebaker Champion Regal DeLuxe convertible

1948 Studebaker Commander Regal DeLuxe convertible

1949 Studebaker Commander Regal DeLuxe convertible

1950 Studebaker Commander Starlight coupe

ered 94 bhp; no eight was offered. The public was wowed by the new Studes, and snapped up 161,496 of them, including 2251 Champion and 1503 Commander Regal DeLuxe convertibles. Coupes, both three- and five-passenger, numbered 25,331 Champions and 14,646 Commanders.

	Restorable	Good	Excellent
Champion cvt	$3,000-7,000	$7,000-12,000	$12,000-17,500
Commander cvt	3,500-8,500	8,500-14,000	14,000-20,000
Strlght & Land Crsr	1,500-3,500	3,500-6,000	6,000-8,000
All other models	1,000-3,000	3,000-5,000	5,000-7,000

1948

The '48 Studebakers looked the same as the '47s, but instant recognition was provided by their winged hood medallions. Model offerings remained the same, and the big selling point continued to be styling, which was like nothing else in the industry. The new body incidentally allowed for an increase of six inches in front seat width and 10 in the rear, despite the trim exterior proportions. Among the 184,993 cars built this year were 9996 Champion and 7982 Commander ragtops.

	Restorable	Good	Excellent
Champion cvt	$3,000-7,000	$7,000-12,000	$12,000-17,500
Commander cvt	3,500-8,500	8,500-14,000	14,000-20,000
Strlght & Land Crsr	1,500-3,500	3,500-6,000	6,000-8,000
All other models	1,000-3,000	3,000-5,000	5,000-7,000

1949

Save for a vertical chrome center strip on the grille, the Commander was a continuation of the '48, while the Champion sported a new grille composed of horizontal and vertical louvers forming three rows of rectangular openings. Mechanically, the Commander's L-head six was boosted to 245.6 cubic inches and 100 horsepower. Probably because of intense competition from all-new Big Three cars, production sank to 129,298. Ragtops were down, too, to 7035 Champions and 1702 Commanders, both still available only in Regal DeLuxe trim. Starlights numbered 18,106 Champions, 8990 Commanders.

	Restorable	Good	Excellent
Champion cvt	$3,000-7,000	$7,000-12,000	$12,000-17,500
Commander cvt	3,500-8,500	8,500-14,000	14,000-20,000
Strlght & Land Crsr	1,500-3,500	3,500-6,000	6,000-8,000
All other models	1,000-3,000	3,000-5,000	5,000-7,000

1950

A radical "bullet-nose" front end was adopted for 1950, this innovation being contributed entirely by the Loewy Studios. Although controversial, the '50 demonstrated the strong central grille theme that would appear on many Big Three models a few years later. Also new were squarer rear fenders sporting vertical taillights. Studebaker's excellent automatic transmission, introduced later in the model year, was designed in cooperation with Borg-Warner. Horsepower was boosted to 85 and 102, the latter for the Commander. Production skyrocketed to 320,884, including 9362 Champion and 2867 Commander convertibles.

	Restorable	Good	Excellent
Champion cvt	$3,000-7,000	$7,000-12,000	$12,000-18,500
Commander cvt	3,500-8,500	8,500-14,000	14,000-21,000
Strlght & Land Crsr	1,500-3,500	3,500-6,000	6,000-8,000
All other models	1,000-3,000	3,000-5,000	5,000-7,000

1951 Studebaker Commander four-door sedan

1951

Commanders now boasted a new overhead-valve V-8, an important development which would help keep Studebaker's performance even with much of its competition—indeed, Chevy and Plymouth wouldn't get V-8s until four years later. Displacing 232.6 cubic inches, it developed 120 horsepower and was very reliable. The cars were much the same as in 1950. The main difference was body size—Commanders now shared a 115-inch wheelbase with Champions, while the Land Cruiser shrank from 124 to 119 inches and became less distinctive as a result. The bullet nose was de-emphasized via the use of less chrome, the air vents alongside the grille were deleted, and model names were spelled out on the front edges of the hood. Output was still excellent at 246,195 units; ragtops numbered 4742 Champions, 3770 Commanders.

	Restorable	Good	Excellent
Champion cvt	$3,000-7,000	$7,000-12,000	$12,000-18,500
Commander cvt	3,500-8,500	8,500-14,000	14,000-21,000
Strlght & Land Crsr	1,500-3,500	3,500-6,000	6,000-8,000
All other models	1,000-3,000	3,000-5,000	5,000-7,000

1952 Studebaker Commander Land Cruiser sedan

1952 Studebaker Champion Regal Starliner hardtop

1952

Studebaker, which had begun as a wagonmaker, celebrated its 100th Anniversary this year, but the cars were mere facelifts. The bullet nose was dropped in favor of a low, toothy grille that some detractors called the "clam digger" or "shovel nose." It was certainly less distinctive, though not unattractive, but the '52s don't sell these days for quite the money of the 1950-51 models. Still, there was an interesting new model, Studebaker's first hardtop, the Starliner, available in the top trim level for each model: Champion Regal and Commander State. With the livelier V-8, Commanders were taking a bigger percentage of sales. This year they accounted for 84,849 units, including 14,548 Starliners and 1715 convertibles, both in top State trim. Champions, which sold to the tune of 101,390 units, saw 12,119 Starliners and 1575 ragtops, both in Regal trim.

	Restorable	Good	Excellent
Champion cvt	$3,000-7,000	$7,000-12,000	$12,000-17,500
Commander cvt	3,500-8,500	8,500-14,000	14,000-19,000

1953 Studebaker Commander Land Cruiser sedan

	Restorable	Good	Excellent
Champion Starliner	2,000-4,000	4,000-6,500	6,500-8,500
Commander Starliner	2,500-4,500	4,500-7,500	7,500-9,500
Strlght & Land Crsr	1,500-3,500	3,500-6,000	6,000-8,000
All other models	1,000-3,000	3,000-5,000	5,000-6,500

1953

The legendary "Loewy" coupe, one of the finest industrial designs of all time, made its debut both in pillared Starlight and pillarless Starliner body styles, as a Champion Six or Commander V-8. The coupe bodies are tighter, but the hardtops are prettier, and far more popular. Some collectors prefer the Champion, which has a conventional dash—the Commander buried its gauges in low-mounted pods resembling miniature traffic lights—and better weight distribution than the V-8. Many quality and some brake problems affected the '53s, and they were late to market, which hurt sales. The coupes and hardtops rode a new, 120.5-inch wheelbase, giving them much nicer proportions than the 116.5-inch sedans, which many thought looked dumpy. The Land Cruiser sedan—Commander only—also used the long wheelbase, setting a pattern that would be followed for years. Due to the factors mentioned, production slipped to 151,576. Starlights numbered 9422 DeLuxe and 16,066 Regal Champions, plus 6106 DeLuxe and 14,752 Regal Commanders. The more desirable Starliners came only in Regal trim, and 13,058 Champions and 19,236 Commanders were produced. Buyers also purchased 15,981 Land Cruisers.

	Restorable	Good	Excellent
Champion coupe	$1,000-3,000	$3,000-6,000	$6,000-9,000
Champion hardtop	1,500-4,000	4,000-7,000	7,000-10,000
Commander coupe	1,500-4,000	4,000-7,500	7,500-11,500
Commander hardtop	2,000-5,000	5,000-8,500	8,500-12,500
Land Cruiser	1,000-3,000	3,000-5,500	5,500-8,000
Other models	500-2,500	2,500-4,000	4,000-6,000

1954

A two-door station wagon, named "Conestoga" after Studebaker's original 1852 product, was added to the lineup, along with a distinguishing egg-crate grille. The cars had better build quality, but production plummeted to just 68,708. The problem confronting collectors is whether to go for a '54 with its improved quality and better brakes, or a '53 with its purer design, especially the grille. The choice usually depends on what you can find when you shop. Those who like wagons might find the Conestoga of interest, but they're hard to come by given the low production: 3910 DeLuxe and 3074 Regal Champions; 1912 DeLuxe and 2878 Regal Commanders. Starlight coupes were a bit more numerous: 7042 DeLuxe and 5125 Regal Champions; 2868 DeLuxe and 3151 Regal Commanders. Starliner hardtops, again only in Regal trim, were also rare: 4302 Champions and 5040 Commanders. Likewise Land Cruisers, of which only 6383 were built.

	Restorable	Good	Excellent
Champion coupe	$1,000-3,000	$3,000-6,000	$6,000-9,000
Champion hardtop	1,500-4,000	4,000-7,000	7,000-10,000
Commander coupe	1,500-4,000	4,000-7,500	7,500-11,500
Commander hardtop	2,000-5,000	5,000-8,500	8,500-12,500
Land Cruiser	1,000-3,000	3,000-5,500	5,500-8,000
Other models	500-2,500	2,500-4,000	4,000-6,000

1955

"A chrome happy kid had a holiday," said *Consumer Reports* about the facelifted 1955 Studebaker, particularly its "fish-mouth" grille. But stung by its 1953-54 experience, management had decided that glitz sold better than elegant European lines. A wraparound windshield was adopted in mid-model year, so '55s come with two different greenhouse patterns. The Land Cruiser was dropped, while the President name was resurrected for a top-end series of sedans, coupes, and hardtops on the 120.5-inch coupe wheelbase. The Commander V-8 was shrunk to 224.3 cid, though horsepower was up to 140, while Presidents used a larger, 259.2-cid V-8 with 175 horses. Even the hoary six was bumped to 101 bhp. A very special President was the $3253 Speedster, wildly two-toned with special "quilted" leather seats, tooled metal dash filled with white-on-black instruments, and gold anodized script. Speedster production was a mere 2215. This was the progenitor to the Studebaker Hawks, and is clearly the most desirable '55 model. Despite a bitter strike (the first against Studebaker), production rebounded to 116,333. Output for the revived President was 1021 DeLuxe sedans, 14,634 State sedans, 3327 State coupes, and 3468 State hardtops.

	Restorable	Good	Excellent
Champion coupe	$1,000-3,000	$3,000-6,000	$6,000-9,000
Champion hardtop	1,500-4,000	4,000-7,000	7,000-10,000
Commander coupe	1,500-4,000	4,000-7,500	7,500-11,500
Commander hardtop	2,000-5,000	5,000-8,500	8,500-12,500
President coupe	1,500-4,000	4,000-8,000	8,000-12,000
President hardtop	2,000-5,000	5,000-9,000	9,000-13,000
President Speedster	3,000-7,500	7,500-11,000	11,000-15,000
Other models	500-2,500	2,500-4,000	4,000-6,000

1956

Gamely, Studebaker restyled, with new, squarer bodies designed by Vince Gardner and a handsome line of sporty Hawks, using the old coupe/hardtop bodies with classic-style square grilles. There were four of the latter: the six-cylinder Flight and V-8 Power Hawk coupes (101 and 170 bhp), descended from the old Starlight; the Sky Hawk and tailfinned Golden Hawk based on the Starliner hardtop. The Golden Hawk was powered by a 322-cid, 275-bhp V-8 provided by Packard, which had purchased

1955 Studebaker President Speedster hardtop

1956 Studebaker Golden Hawk hardtop coupe

1956 Studebaker Sky Hawk hardtop coupe

1956 Studebaker Champion Sedanet two-door

1956 Studebaker Champion two-door sedan

1956 Studebaker President Classic sedan

1957 Studebaker Commander two-door sedan

1957 Studebaker Golden Hawk hardtop coupe

1957 Studebaker Silver Hawk two-door coupe

1958 Studebaker Commander four-door sedan

Studebaker and merged the two corporations in 1954. The Sky Hawk had Studebaker's 289, rated at 225 bhp. Though total Studebaker output dropped to 69,593, Hawk production was encouraging: Flight, 4949; Power, 7095; Sky, 3050; Golden, 4071. The President Classic sedan, with its attractive bodyside two-toning, also rode the longer Hawk wheelbase. It attracted 8507 buyers.

	Restorable	Good	Excellent
Flight/Power Hawk	$1,500-4,000	$4,000-7,000	$7,000-10,000
Sky Hawk	2,500-7,000	7,000-10,000	10,000-13,500
Golden Hawk	3,500-9,000	9,000-12,500	12,500-17,500
Other models	500-2,500	2,500-4,000	4,000-6,000

1957

Although Studebaker styling had changed drastically in 1956, and was further updated with a wraparound grille and larger taillights in 1957, the basic bodyshell still dated to 1953. On the shorter wheelbase, the Champion and Pelham wagon were joined by the Scotsman. Available in two- and four-door sedan and two-door wagon models, this ultra-stripped model (painted hubcaps and grille) sold for as little as $1776—but only 9348 were sold. The same wheelbase carried the 259 V-8 Commander, Provincial, and Parkview wagons, as well as the 289 V-8 President sedans and Broadmoor wagon. The Provincial and Broadmoor wagons were four-doors. As before, the President Classic rode the longer Hawk wheelbase. Hawk models were down to two: the Silver Hawk coupe with the 101-bhp six or 210/225 bhp 289 and the Golden Hawk hardtop with a Paxton-supercharged 289 developing 275 horses. Both sported large, concave tailfins, the Golden Hawk's covered in gold mylar. Output was 15,318 Silver Hawks (including 368 hardtops for export) and 4356 Golden Hawks. A special model was the Golden Hawk 400 with full leather interior—10 prototypes and 41 production 400s were built, making this a very rare and desirable Studebaker. The firm's fortunes continued to decline, this year to 63,101 cars, including 6063 President Classics. Wagons were rare, just 1530 top-line Broadmoors, for example.

	Restorable	Good	Excellent
Silver Hawk	$2,000-4,500	$4,500-7,000	$7,000-10,000
Golden Hawk	3,500-9,000	9,000-12,000	12,000-16,000
Golden Hawk 400	4,500-10,000	10,000-15,000	15,000-20,000
President	1,000-2,500	2,500-4,000	4,000-6,000
Commander wagons	1,000-2,500	2,500-3,500	3,500-5,500
Other models	500-2,000	2,000-3,500	3,500-4,500

1958

The grille became a bit more massive-looking and quad headlamps were grafted onto all models except the Scotsman—they looked exactly like what they were, a hasty effort to remain stylish on a shoestring budget. A new and attractive body style was the Starlight two-door hardtop, offered in both

Commander and President form on the shorter wheelbase. The Hawk line remained unchanged. Studebaker sales slid in this recession year, and only 44,759 were built (53,830 including Canada and export). Many models were downright rare: 7350 Silver Hawks, 878 Golden Hawks, 2555 Commander Starlights, 1171 President Starlights, 3570 President sedans. However, 20,960 Scotsmans were produced, convincing Studebaker to pursue the economy end of the market.

	Restorable	Good	Excellent
Silver Hawk	$2,000-4,500	$4,500-7,000	$7,000-10,000
Golden Hawk	3,500-9,000	9,000-12,000	12,000-16,000
President	1,000-2,500	2,500-4,000	4,000-6,000
Commander Starlight	1,000-2,500	2,500-4,000	4,000-6,000
Commander wagons	1,000-2,500	2,500-3,500	3,500-5,500
Other models	500-2,000	2,000-3,500	3,500-4,500

1958 Studebaker President Classic sedan

1960 Studebaker Lark VIII convertible coupe

1959

Studebaker's new Lark, with fresh styling that hid a body still based largely on the '53s, temporarily saved the company. Stylists like Duncan McRae and Randy Faurot had given it boxy, practical styling that appealed to Americans taken with Volkswagens and "compacts," and the Big Three didn't have anything to compete with it—yet. Sedans, two-door wagons, and two-door hardtops were offered on a 108.5-inch wheelbase (113 for wagons). Look for the V-8s—"Lark VIII"—whose 259.2-cid mill was rated at 180 bhp, 195 with the desirable four-barrel carb. The 289 V-8 wasn't offered this year. Alas, the Golden Hawk was eliminated, leaving only the Silver Hawk coupe, of which 2417 were built as sixes, 5371 as V-8s. Total production shot up to 125,156, including 7075 Regal VI and 7996 Regal VIII hardtops.

	Restorable	Good	Excellent
Silver Hawk	$2,000-4,500	$4,500-7,000	$7,000-10,000
Lark VI Regal htp	1,000-2,000	2,000-4,000	4,000-5,000
Lark VIII Regal htp	1,250-2,250	2,250-4,500	4,500-6,000
Lark, other	500-2,000	2,000-3,500	3,500-4,500

1960

Lark added a pretty convertible and adopted a new grille composed of thick and thin horizontal bars, but was otherwise the same car as in 1959. Also new was a four-door wagon. With Big Three compacts in the sales race, fewer were sold (120,465) and Studebaker barely turned a profit. The Hawk—now minus its "Silver" designation—was carried over virtually unchanged, but now had the 289 V-8 as standard equipment; look for the four-barrel carb version, with 225 horses instead of the standard 210. Production this year included 4507 Hawks, 3107 six-cylinder and 5464 V-8 Regal convertibles, and 2829 six-cylinder and 4565 V-8 Regal hardtops.

1961 Studebaker Hawk two-door coupe

1962 Studebaker Gran Turismo Hawk hardtop coupe

	Restorable	Good	Excellent
Hawk	$2,000-4,500	$4,500-7,000	$7,000-10,000
Lark VI Regal cvt	2,000-4,500	4,500-6,500	6,500-9,500
Lark VI Regal htp	1,000-2,000	2,000-4,000	4,000-5,000
Lark VIII Regal cvt	2,500-5,000	5,000-7,500	7,500-10,000
Lark VIII Regal htp	1,250-2,250	2,250-4,500	4,500-6,000
Lark, other	500-2,000	2,000-3,500	3,500-4,500

1961

An important new option was a four-speed all-synchromesh manual gearbox, which added to the fun of the Hawk—look for this, and add 10 percent to the car's value if you find it. Except for a color flash on the rear fenders, the Hawk was again virtually unchanged in styling. Output was just 3929 units. The Lark was modestly facelifted, and its ancient six-cylinder engine was converted to overhead valves, yielding 112 bhp. A new model in the old Land Cruiser tradition was the Lark Cruiser sedan, fitted with rich upholstery and riding the 113-inch Lark wagon wheelbase. An interesting option was the Skytop fold-back fabric sunroof. But this was another disappointing sales year—only 59,713 units—and the company lurched back into red ink. Some production figures for the Lark VI: 1870 Regal hardtops, 979 Regal ragtops, 24 Regal Cruisers (for export). For the Lark VIII: 1666 Regal hardtops, 1002 Regal ragtops, 5232 Regal Cruisers.

	Restorable	Good	Excellent
Hawk	$2,000-4,500	$4,500-7,000	$7,000-10,000
Lark VI Regal cvt	2,000-4,500	4,500-6,500	6,500-9,500
Lark VI Regal htp	1,000-2,000	2,000-4,000	4,000-5,000
Lark VIII Regal cvt	2,500-5,000	5,000-7,500	7,500-10,000
Lark VIII Regal htp	1,250-2,250	2,250-4,500	4,500-6,000
Lark, other	500-2,000	2,000-3,500	3,500-4,500

1962

The old Hawk was brilliantly restyled by Brooks Stevens, who used the hardtop body, sheered off the dated tailfins, designed a crisp "formal" Thunderbird roofline, filled a metal and woodgrained dash with purposeful gauges, and called the result the Gran Turismo Hawk. The GT's optional 225-bhp 289 (210 standard) provided 0-60 in less then 10 seconds. This handsome car is one of the most collectible of the late Studebakers—beware the vinyl seat inserts, which are prone to splitting but can be replicated by clever upholsterers. It's a shame that only 9335 were built. Stevens also tinkered with the Lark, adding a Mercedes-like grille, high-mounted round taillights, and a smoother roofline for sedans and hardtops. A sporty Daytona Six and V-8 hardtop and convertible featured faddish bucket seats and Studebaker's optional four-speed gearbox. Daytonas and Lark Cruisers could be ordered with the 289 V-8, so look for this, and the four-speed. A Daytona convertible served as the Indy 500 Official Pace Car this year. Production increased to 89,318, including 8480 hardtops and 2681 ragtops (Regal and Daytona).

	Restorable	Good	Excellent
GT Hawk	$2,500-5,000	$5,000-8,500	$8,500-12,500
Lark VI Regal cvt	2,000-4,500	4,500-6,500	6,500-9,500
Lark VI Regal htp	1,000-2,000	2,000-4,000	4,000-5,000
Lark VIII Regal cvt	2,500-5,000	5,000-7,500	7,500-10,000
Lark VIII Regal htp	1,250-2,250	2,250-4,500	4,500-6,000
Lark Daytona cvt	2,500-5,000	5,000-8,000	8,000-11,000
Lark Daytona htp	1,500-2,500	2,500-5,000	5,000-7,000
Lark, other	500-2,000	2,000-3,500	3,500-4,500

1963 Studebaker Lark Daytona hardtop coupe

1963 Studebaker Lark Daytona Wagonaire four-door

1963

Studebaker's last serious attempt at automotive survival included a revamped Lark line, a GT Hawk with optional performance engines, and the exciting new Avanti, a sports coupe designed by the Loewy Studios, which management hoped would spark a new generation of family cars. With its coke-bottle fiberglass body, enormous rear window, built-in rollbar, grilleless front end, and asymmetrical hood hump, the Avanti certainly looked different, though it rode a conventional Lark convertible frame. Inside were red lighted instruments, an aircraft-inspired control panel above the windshield, slim-bucket seats (designed after Alfa Romeo's), lots of crash padding, and a novel trapdoor giving access to the trunk from the package shelf. Disc front brakes and a supercharged "R1" 289 engine delivering 240 horsepower were standard. Also available was the supercharged R2 with 290 horses, and a bored-out 304.5-cid R3. (Yet more exotic R4 and R5 engines were designed, but not regular production options; indeed, only a handful of R3s were built.) Due mainly to early production problems, only 3834 Avantis were produced. The Lark received a restyled grille with a finer cross-mesh, but still looked very Mercedes-like. Its dashboard, as in 1962, had needle instruments, rocker control switches, even a pop-up "vanity" glovebox. Convertibles were restricted to the Daytona model, but only 1015 were built. Even hardtops numbered only 3763. An innovative "Wagonaire" station wagon, with a sliding rear roof panel, was another idea of Brooks Stevens. Look for the Daytona wagon, which was new this year; 11,915 wagons of all models were produced. The GT Hawk, of which 4634 were sold, continued with a fully woodgrained dash, a new grille, and amber parking lights. Only a very few Hawks were optioned with the R1 and R2 Avanti engines. Total Studebaker output sagged to 69,555 units.

	Restorable	Good	Excellent
Avanti	$3,000-7,500	$7,500-14,000	$14,000-20,000
Avanti R2	6,000-12,000	12,000-20,000	20,000-30,000
Avanti R3:	No price information but probably up to $50,000		
GT Hawk	2,500-5,000	5,000-8,500	8,500-13,500
	(add 10% for R1 "Super Hawk," 25% for R2)		
Lark Daytona cvt	2,500-5,000	5,000-8,000	8,000-11,000
Lark Daytona htp	1,500-2,500	2,500-5,000	5,000-7,000
Lark, other	500-2,000	2,000-3,500	3,500-5,000

1964

The Lark—a name Studebaker was now playing down—was neatly facelifted with a clean stamped grille forming an inverted trapezoid and comple-

1964 Studebaker Daytona convertible coupe

1964 Studebaker Commander four-door sedan

1965 Studebaker Daytona Sport Sedan two-door

1966 Studebaker Eight Cruiser four-door sedan

mented with a stand-up hood ornament. Its six-inch-longer body looked less stubby. A stripped Challenger line was added and an R3 engine option was announced for the Lark and Hawk. The Gran Turismo Hawk was mildly facelifted, acquiring a smoothed-off deck and matte black dash. Detail changes were made to the Avanti during production, the most obvious being grillework for the under-bumper scoop. But sales remained dismal, and in December 1963 Studebaker shut down its South Bend, Indiana, factory, concentrating a rump operation at its plant in Hamilton, Ontario. Low production created some interesting figures: 809 Avantis, 1767 GT Hawks, 2414 hardtops, 703 ragtops. Total output was just 36,697.

	Restorable	Good	Excellent
Avanti	$3,000-7,500	$7,500-14,000	$14,000-20,000
Avanti R2	6,000-12,000	12,000-20,000	20,000-30,000
Avanti R3:	No price information, but probably up to $50,000		
GT Hawk	2,500-5,000	5,000-8,500	8,500-13,500
	(add 10% for R1 "Super Hawk," add 25% for R2)		
Lark Daytona cvt	2,500-5,000	5,000-8,000	8,000-11,000
Lark Daytona htp	1,500-2,500	2,500-5,000	5,000-7,000
Lark, other	500-2,000	2,000-3,500	3,500-5,000

1965

Technically these are imports, but it hardly seems appropriate to leave out the last products of a great American company. The Avanti and Hawk were dropped as the Hamilton plant concentrated on Larks, although that name had now vanished in favor of Commander and Cruiser Six and Eight, and Daytona (V-8 only). The engines were provided by Chevrolet: a 194-cid six and a 283 V-8 with 120 and 195 horsepower, respectively. Hardtops and convertibles were scrubbed, although there was a Daytona two-door Sport Sedan and a continuation of the Daytona wagon that had been around since 1963. Production was down to 19,435: 10,239 four-doors, 7372 two-doors, and 1824 wagons.

	Restorable	Good	Excellent
All models	$1,000-2,500	$2,500-4,000	$4,000-6,000

1966

The last Studebakers ever had new front-end styling with twin headlamps instead of quads, a new grille with rectangular panels, new bodyside moldings, and air-extraction ports in the rear panel. But production had hit only 8947 units when the Canadian plant ceased operations. A six-cylinder Daytona two-door was added, while the Daytona wagons were dropped. Despite their rarity and status as the last of the marque, these '66s are worth no more than earlier Larks.

	Restorable	Good	Excellent
All models	$1,000-2,500	$2,500-4,000	$4,000-6,000

Stutz

One of America's grand marques, Stutz is among the most cherished Classic cars—and they are Classics "all" according to the Classic Car Club of America—but they are a rare sight, even at Classic Car Club meetings. Club support is fair, parts supply low, investment potential high.

1930 Stutz Model M Convertible Victoria by Rollston

1932 Stutz DV-32 Sport Coupe by Waterhouse

1933 Stutz DV-32 convertible coupe

1930-36

The basis for most of the few Stutz cars built in the 1930s was the Vertical Eight, except for the 1930 Blackhawk, which had a Continental engine. Vertical Eight Stutz speedsters could outrun any American car of their day save for the Model J Duesenberg, but sedans were buzz boxes below 50 mph, thanks to low rear axle ratios. The 1930 Model M, with wheelbases of 134.5 and 145 inches, had high horsepower for the day (113), but middling performance because of its great weight (4595-5210 pounds). Unable to afford a V-12 or V-16, Stutz tried a supercharger, which raised the Eight to 143 bhp, but it was noisy and carburetion was a problem. For 1931, Stutz designed a new 32-valve head with twin overhead camshafts, which delivered 161 horsepower and was a gem of an engine. Three groups of DV-32s toured the nation after introduction, led by a new model with an old name: Bearcat. The first of these rode the stock 134.5-inch wheelbase, but later appeared as a Super Bearcat with lighter bodywork on a short 116-inch wheelbase. The latter could easily do 100 mph, but even standard DV-32s were capable of at least 90 mph—incredible at that time. Bodies were provided by LeBaron, Fleetwood, Rollston, Weymann, Brunn, Waterhouse, Derham, and others. Stutz also offered an aluminum body for the Monte Carlo sedan. A cheaper model, the 1931 Model L (officially LA, then LAA for 1932-33) was a six-cylinder Stutz powered by what was really a Vertical Eight less two cylinders, which dropped horsepower to 85. For 1932, the previous four-speed gearbox was replaced by a rugged Muncie three-speed, freewheeling became optional, the hot air manifold was replaced with a hot water heating system, and an oil cooler was added. A new trunk rack and dust valance were installed, the body dropped in a curving line to cover the straight frame, and single-bar bumpers replaced double-bar units. Stutz ceased car production in early 1935, tried to survive on a contract for small trucks, but filed for bankruptcy in April 1937. It was inevitable—during the Twenties Stutz produced 2000-3000 cars per year, but for its entire life during the Thirties, less than 1500 were built.

	Restorable	Good	Excellent
1930 M speedsters	$35,000-60,000	$60,000-100,000	$100,000-150,000
1930 M cabriolets	15,000-35,000	35,000-65,000	65,000-95,000

	Restorable	Good	Excellent
1930 M Longchamps, Versailles, and Torpedo	10,000-30,000	30,000-50,000	50,000-70,000
1930, other models	7,500-20,000	20,000-35,000	35,000-55,000
1931-33 L spdstr	25,000-50,000	50,000-90,000	90,000-125,000
1931-33 L cabrio	20,000-40,000	40,000-60,000	60,000-80,000
1931-33 L, other	7,500-17,500	17,500-30,000	30,000-45,000

1932-36 SV16

Speedster	40,000-75,000	75,000-110,000	110,000-145,000
Other open	30,000-60,000	60,000-90,000	90,000-125,000
Torpedo	15,000-35,000	35,000-55,000	55,000-85,000
Closed, 134.5 wb	10,000-25,000	25,000-40,000	40,000-60,000
Closed, 145 wb	12,500-30,000	30,000-70,000	70,000-95,000

1932-36 DV32

1932-33 Bearcat	50,000-90,000	90,000-140,000	140,000-180,000
1932-33 Super Brct	55,000-95,000	95,000-150,000	150,000-200,000

(Other models priced fractionally higher than SV16)

1937 Terraplane panel delivery

1937 Terraplane four-door station wagon

Terraplane

Terraplane was registered as a separate make from Hudson for four years. Club support is excellent, parts supply small, investment potential modest.

1934-37

Replacing Hudson's Essex after being known as an Essex Terraplane in 1932-33, the '34 Terraplane used an 80/85-bhp six and was available in a wide variety of bodies. Since the days of the first Essex Terraplanes, the name had been associated with speed; a 1936 road test of a sedan recorded 0-60 in 26.6 seconds and a top speed of 82 mph, highly creditable for a car of that era weighing nearly 2800 pounds. During its four years as a separate make, Terraplane accounted for more than 300,000 sales, taking most of Hudson's production each year and built up to a peak of 90,253 in 1937. The model line expanded, too, ultimately comprising 16 separate offerings in DeLuxe and Super trim. No roadsters or phaetons were listed, but there were convertible coupes and broughams in regular and "touring" (trunkback) form, and even a woody wagon in 1936. Though sales were good in 1937, Hudson became convinced that separate-make status was no longer necessary. Terraplane was incorporated into the Hudson line for 1938, but vanished a year later—its place taken by the low-end '39 Hudsons.

	Restorable	Good	Excellent
1934, open	$3,000-7,500	$7,500-14,000	$14,000-19,000
1934, closed	1,500-4,000	4,000-6,500	6,500-9,500
1935-37, open	2,500-6,000	6,000-10,000	10,000-15,000
1935-37, closed	1,000-3,000	3,000-5,500	5,500-8,000

Willys

Once number two in the industry, Willys-Overland had become a peripheral manufacturer of low-priced cars by the end of the 1930s. Revived for a few years in the Fifties, it remained peripheral. Today, it has the same standing among collectors despite some interesting models. Club support is fair, parts supply low, investment potential small.

1930-39

The Willys-Overland badge was dropped in 1930 in favor of just Willys. Besides a group of conventional models, including the low-priced Willys-built Whippet that was dropped in early 1931, the sleeve-valve Willys-Knight continued through 1933. Replacing the usual cam-and-spring actuated poppet valves was a double sliding sleeve that let the fuel-air mixture directly into the cylinders. Many makes used sleeve-valve engines, but Willys continued them longer than anyone else. The Willys-Knights of this period were sixes in two sizes of engine and wheelbase. The rest of the line comprised conventional L-head sixes and eights with attractive styling and competitive prices. Though the firm had sold more than 315,000 cars as recently as 1928, the Depression forced Willys into bankruptcy in 1933. But it was reorganized by Toledo financier Ward Canaday, under whose management all resources were put into a new 100-inch-wheelbase econo-car called the Willys 77, which continued through 1936, powered by a small 134.2-cid, 48-bhp four. The radiator was hidden under the hood, and the vertical grille was rounded at the top, giving rise to the nickname, "potato digger." In 1937, the car was restyled and renamed the Model 37, gaining a round body with pontoon fenders and a front end reminiscent of the sharknose Graham. Redesignated Model 38 the following year, and 38 and 48 in 1939, it was successful in its first year, but the 1938 recession cut sales again. A similar line returned in 1939, abetted by a revived Overland nameplate on the new Model 39.

	Restorable	Good	Excellent
1930-33 Willys-Knight			
Open, 120 wb	$5,000-12,500	$12,500-20,000	$20,000-30,000
Open, 110 wb	3,500-8,000	8,000-15,000	15,000-22,500
Closed	2,000-6,000	6,000-9,000	9,000-12,500
Willys			
1930-33, open	4,000-8,000	8,000-14,000	14,000-20,000
1930-33 coupes	2,000-4,000	4,000-7,000	7,000-12,000
1930-33 sedans	1,000-2,000	2,000-5,000	5,000-8,000
1933-36 Model 77	1,500-2,500	2,500-6,000	6,000-9,000
1937-39 Model 38/48	1,000-2,000	2,000-5,000	5,000-8,000

1931 Willys Six (Series 97) two-door Coach

1931 Willys Eight DeLuxe Victoria coupe

1932 Willys Eight two-door coupe

1932 Willys Overland Eight roadster

1939 Willys Overland two-door sedan

1940 Willys DeLuxe two-door sedan

1941 Willys Americar DeLuxe two-door coupe

1941 Willys Americar DeLuxe station wagon

1940

Ward Canaday hired Joe Frazer from Chrysler Corporation, who brought in much more conventional styling for 1940. The new model was designated the 440 (four cylinders for the model year) and was powered by Willys' 61-bhp L-head four, which displaced 134.2 cubic inches and delivered an easy 25 miles per gallon. The chassis was a conventional ladder design with an X-braced center and 102-inch wheelbase. There were three body styles—coupe, four-door sedan, woody wagon—in two trim levels: Speedway and DeLuxe. The most desirable body is the woody wagon. Production was recorded as 26,698 units.

	Restorable	Good	Excellent
Woody wagon	$3,000-7,500	$7,500-10,000	$10,000-15,000
Coupe & sedan	1,500-2,500	2,500-5,500	5,500-8,000

1941

For the 1941 series 441, Frazer and his team made further improvements and named the result Americar. Together with the patriotic appeal came more horsepower (63), a longer wheelbase (104 inches), and three trim levels: Speedway, Deluxe, and Plainsman. All were coupes and sedans except for a DeLuxe wagon. Styling resembled that of Ford, with faired-in headlamps on the front fenders and a sharply pointed nose over a small vertical-bar grille. Output was an estimated 22,100 units.

	Restorable	Good	Excellent
Station wagon	$3,000-7,500	$7,500-10,000	$10,000-15,000
Coupe & sedan	1,500-2,500	2,500-5,500	5,500-8,000

1942

Willys production for 1942 was cut short earlier than most manufacturers because Willys had begun building Jeeps for the Army. Only 11,910 cars were built. The '42 Americars were the same as in 1941—three body styles, seven models. Prices rose slightly, ranging from $695 to $978.

	Restorable	Good	Excellent
Woody wagon	$3,000-7,500	$7,500-10,000	$10,000-15,000
Coupe & sedan	1,500-2,500	2,500-5,500	5,500-8,000

1946-47

A Jeep-like all-steel station wagon—arguably the first of its type—was Willys' sole product designed specifically for the civilian market in the first two postwar years. Advertised as "America's greatest all-purpose car!" it used the prewar L-head four rated at 63 horsepower and rode a 104-inch wheelbase, dead giveaways to its Americar heritage. Rugged and individual looking, it was a great favorite, and several have been restored. It certainly makes for a practical collector car, or truck. . . . Only 6533 were built in 1946, but that climbed to 33,214 for 1947—a record for station wagons up to that point.

	Restorable	Good	Excellent
Station wagon	$1,500-3,000	$3,000-5,000	$5,000-7,000

1948

Willys continued the wagon while adding two new vehicles: the four-cylinder Jeepster "phaeton" priced at $1765, and the six-cylinder Station Sedan, which sold for $1890. The Jeepster, a pleasant little touring car designed by Brooks Stevens, borrowed the Jeep's winning lines with a big open compartment behind the cowl and a mechanical soft top; 10,326 buyers found it irresistible. The Station Sedan was a luxury version of the four-cylinder wagon, with a larger body and wider seats—a progenitor, in a way, of the later Wagoneer and Cherokee.

	Restorable	Good	Excellent
Station wgn/sdn	$1,500-3,000	$3,000-5,000	$5,000-7,000
Jeepster	2,000-4,000	4,000-7,000	7,000-10,000

1949

Willys continued with the wagon and two Jeepsters in its four-cylinder lineup. The second series Jeepster appeared in January, powered by Willys' first F-head engine, which upped horsepower to 72. Continued were the six-cylinder Station Sedan and wagon. A Jeepster Six debuted at $1530. A total of 2307 Jeepsters were sold, 653 of them Sixes. Wagon sales were 29,290 and four-wheel-drive was now offered.

	Restorable	Good	Excellent
Station wgn/sdn	$1,500-3,000	$3,000-5,000	$5,000-7,000
Jeepster	2,000-4,000	4,000-7,000	7,000-10,000

1950

Conversion to the more robust F-head valve configuration was complete on all models by 1950, but business was becoming slack. Against the 10,000 Jeepsters sold in 1948, only 4066 Fours and 1778 Sixes were purchased in 1950-51 combined. So Jeepster's are pretty scarce in this model year. The Station Sedan was dropped, but the basic Jeep wagon could still be ordered with four or six cylinders. It did well this year: 32,218 units.

	Restorable	Good	Excellent
Station wagon	$1,500-3,000	$3,000-5,000	$5,000-7,000
Jeepster	2,000-4,000	4,000-7,000	7,000-10,000

1951

This was a repeat of 1950; indeed, all of the '51 Jeepsters were leftover '50 models registered in the following model year. The Jeep wagon lineup was also the same as in 1950, and 25,316 were built during the calendar year.

	Restorable	Good	Excellent
Station wagon	$1,500-3,000	$3,000-5,000	$5,000-7,000
Jeepster	2,000-4,000	4,000-7,000	7,000-10,000

1946-48 Willys two-door Station Wagon

1948 Willys Jeepster phaeton-convertible

1948 Willys Jeepster phaeton-convertible

1952 Willys 4-Wheel Drive Station Wagon

1953 Willys Aero-Eagle hardtop coupe

1954 Willys Aero-Eagle hardtop coupe

1954 Willys Aero-Ace DeLuxe four-door sedan

1954 Willys Aero-Ace DeLuxe four-door sedan

1952

The company re-entered the passenger car market with the pretty Aero-Willys, an ultra-clean, unitbody design engineered by Clyde Paton and styled by Phil Wright. Four models were offered: Aero-Lark two-door sedan with the older L-head six; Aero-Wing and Aero-Ace two-doors and Aero-Eagle hardtop with F-head engines. The 90-bhp,161-cid six was a good performer for its size, and provided 25 miles to the gallon. The big problem with the Aero-Willys was its price, which was not competitive with Chevy-Ford-Plymouth. The most desirable model is clearly the Aero-Eagle hardtop, which listed at $2155. First year production was a modest 31,363 units, including 2364 Eagles. Though the Jeepster was now out of production, the Jeep wagon would continue to be built into the mid-Sixties.

	Restorable	Good	Excellent
Aero-Lark/ Wing/Ace	$1,000-2,500	$2,500-3,500	$3,500-5,000
Aero-Eagle	1,500-3,000	3,000-4,500	4,500-6,000
Jeep wagon	1,500-3,000	3,000-5,000	5,000-7,000

1953

Willys celebrated its Golden Anniversary with an expanded line of Aeros. Red-painted wheel cover emblems and a gold-plated "W" on the grille bar signify the '53s. The Aero-Wing was replaced by the Aero-Falcon and a new four-door sedan was developed for the Lark, Falcon, and Ace. The hardtop Eagle again topped the line. Output this year increased to 42,057, highlighted by 7018 Eagle hardtops.

	Restorable	Good	Excellent
Aero-Lark/ Falcon/Ace	$1,000-2,500	$2,500-3,500	$3,500-5,000
Aero-Eagle	1,500-3,000	3,000-4,500	4,500-6,000
Jeep wagons	1,500-3,000	3,000-5,000	5,000-7,000

1954

Willys-Overland was purchased by Kaiser Motors, which then formed the Toledo-based Kaiser-Willys Sales Corporation. The first '54 Aeros appeared to be just '53s with larger two-lens taillights and revised interiors. But in March 1954, the company made the Kaiser 226-cid L-head six available as an option for the Ace and Eagle. To further complicate matters, there were Ace and Eagle "Customs," the designation indicating the presence of a "continental" outside spare tire. With the 115-bhp Kaiser engine, the Aero was pretty quick, running the 0-60 sprint in 14 seconds. A few cars were fitted experimentally with the supercharged Kaiser Manhattan six, which gave V-8-style performance—but alas, this was not a production option and is rarely encountered. The '54s also handled better, thanks to adjustable threaded trunions, stronger A-arms, and longer idler arm, kingpins, and springs. A crossmember connected the left and right front suspension assemblies to eliminate lateral torque and reduce toe-in variations. Thus the '54 Aero-Willys had one of the best ride/handling combinations in the American industry. The Eagle Custom with the 226 engine is quite a prize for Aero enthusiasts. Unfortunately, production skidded to just 11,856, and only 1556 of them were Eagle hardtops.

	Restorable	Good	Excellent
Aero-Lark/ Falcon/Ace	$1,000-2,500	$2,500-3,500	$3,500-5,000
Aero-Ace 226	1,500-3,000	3,000-4,000	4,000-5,500
Aero-Eagle	1,500-3,000	3,000-4,500	4,500-6,000
Aero-Eagle 226	2,000-3,500	3,500-5,000	5,000-6,500
Jeep wagons	1,500-3,000	3,000-5,000	5,000-7,000

1955 Willys Custom four-door sedan

1955

Only 6565 copies of the last Willys passenger car were built before Kaiser-Willys left the car business and transferred the Willys dies to its Brazilian factory. No longer called Aeros, the line comprised a Willys Custom two- and four-door sedan and a Willys Bermuda hardtop. (There were also a few Ace sedans, although this model name appears to have been abandoned early.) Engine options included the usual 161 F-head and 226 L-head. A styling facelift resulted in a concave, vertical-bar grille and bodyside two-tone patterns, along with new taillights mounted in chrome housings with quirky little pointed back-up lights underneath. In South America, Willys do Brazil continued to produce a cleaned up version of the '55 model through 1962. Interestingly enough, 90,889 Aeros were built in Toledo, Ohio, before production ceased, but the Brazilian operation produced 99,621 plus 17,216 Itamaratys (an off-shoot model), for a total of 116,837.

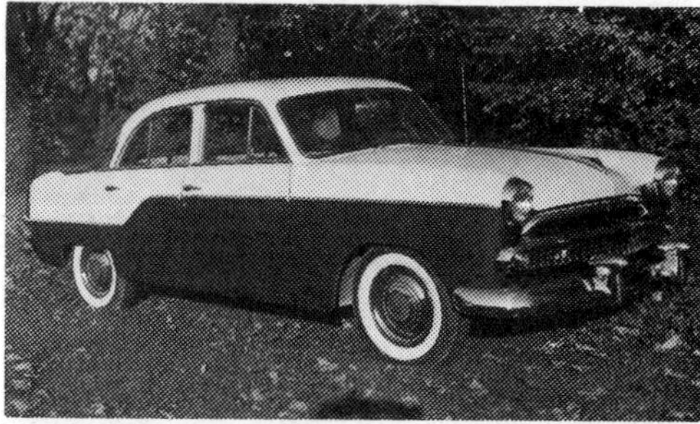

1954 Willys Ace DeLuxe four-door sedan

	Restorable	Good	Excellent
Ace/Custom 4d	$1,000-2,500	$2,500-3,500	$3,500-5,000
Custom 2d	1,500-3,000	3,000-4,500	4,500-6,000
Bermuda htp	2,000-3,500	3,500-5,000	5,000-6,500
Bermuda 226 htp	2,500-4,000	4,000-6,000	6,000-7,500
Jeep wagons	1,500-3,000	3,000-5,000	5,000-7,000

1959 Willys Maverick two-door Station Wagon